EXPLORING TORT LAW

Tort law provides individuals or groups redress for wrongful harm to every dimension of life from physical injury to property damage to personal insult. Over past decades no body of law within the civil justice system has experienced greater ferment than the law of torts. This edited collection comprises new scholarship from many of today's most influential contributors to the evolving law of torts. Topics include provocative analyses of original tort-type norms; punitive damages, proportional liability; the political-legal dynamics of the Restatement process; landmark modern torts decisions; the future of collateral source rules relative to various types of insurance; the role of risk information in assignment of seller liability; privity and freedom of contract; the vitality of negligence and duty rules, and optimal rules for vicarious liability. The collection closes with chapters from civil code nation authorities on the European view of causation in toxic harm suits and on collective rights and actions in South America and in Europe.

M. Stuart Madden is Distinguished Professor of Law at Pace University School of Law. His primary teaching and scholarly interests are in the areas of torts, environmental torts, and products liability. He is an elected member of the American Law Institute and serves on various policy advisory groups and scholarly advisory boards. He has lectured internationally on tort and accident prevention subjects and has given testimony before both Houses of Congress on tort reform issues.

EXPLORING TORT LAW

Edited by

M. Stuart Madden

Distinguished Professor of Law
Pace University School of Law

CAMBRIDGE
UNIVERSITY PRESS

CAMBRIDGE UNIVERSITY PRESS
Cambridge, New York, Melbourne, Madrid, Cape Town, Singapore, São Paulo

Cambridge University Press
40 West 20th Street, New York, NY 10011-4211, USA

www.cambridge.org
Information on this title: www.cambridge.org/9780521851367

First published 2005

Printed in the United States of America

A catalog record for this publication is available from the British Library.

Library of Congress Cataloging in Publication Data

Exploring tort law / edited by M. Stuart Madden.
p. cm.
ISBN 0-521-85136-x (hardcover) – ISBN 0-521-61680-8 (pbk.)
1. Torts – United States. 2. Torts. I. Madden, M. Stuart, 1948– II. Title.
KF1250.A2.E97 2005
346.7303 – dc22 2005004259

ISBN-13 978-0-521-85136-7 hardback
ISBN-10 0-521-85136-x hardback

ISBN-13 978-0-521-61680-5 paperback
ISBN-10 0-521-61680-8 paperback

For my precious wife, Maria, with all of my love.

CONTENTS

CONTRIBUTORS

Kenneth S. Abraham
Robert E. Scott Distinguished Professor of Law, University of Virginia
School of Law

Jennifer Arlen
Norma Z. Paige Professor of Law, NYU School of Law

Guido Calabresi
Judge, United States Court of Appeals for the Second Circuit; Sterling
Professor of Law Emeritus and Professorial Lecturer, Yale Law School

Richard A. Epstein
James Parkar Hall Distinguished Service Professor of Law, University of
Chicago, The Law School

Michael D. Green
Bess and Walter Williams Distinguished Chair in Law, Wake Forest
University School of Law

Juan Carlos Henao
Permanent Professor, Universidad Externado de Colombia; Guest Professor,
Universities of Paris 3 (Iheal), Cergy-Pontoise and Montpellier; Lecturer,
Institut d'Etudes Politiques of Paris

James A. Henderson, Jr.
Frank B. Ingersoll Professor, Cornell Law School

W. Bentley MacLeod
Professor of Economics and Law, University of Southern California

M. Stuart Madden
Distinguished Professor of Law, Pace University School of Law

David G. Owen
Carolina Distinguished Professor of Law, University of South Carolina

Robert L. Rabin
A. Calder Mackay Professor, Stanford Law School

Jane Stapleton
Ernest E. Smith Professor, University of Texas School of Law; Professor of
  Law, Research School of Social Sciences and the Australian National
  University, Canberra

Federico Stella
Professor of Criminal Law, Universita' Cattolica del Sacro Cuore, Milan

Ernest J. Weinrib
University Professor and Cecil A. Wright Professor of Law, University of
  Toronto

PREFACE

This collection originated in a colloquium held at Pace University School of Law in November 2003. The title of the colloquium and the title originally envisioned for this collection was THE FUTURE OF TORTS. The scholars invited to give papers at this gathering include many of the leading torts scholars in the United States, with contributions also from scholars from Australia, Canada, Colombia, and Italy. Each was asked to prepare a paper responding in some way to the question of what will be the future directions of tort law. All, with the exception of the University of Milan's Federico Stella, were able to present their papers at the School of Law, and the eleven invited papers, together with that of Prof. Stella, were each of the highest quality, innovative, and provocative.

However, by the time the participants completed their final papers some months later, two things had become clear. First, and a point mentioned by some early on, it is unlikely that any volume today could fulfill the promise entailed in a title THE FUTURE OF TORTS. Moreover, even if such an ambitious title could be validated by the work of some individual author or authors, no one could reasonably expect that a group of such highly individualistic scholars as convened here would cleave harmoniously to any single objective, even one so deceptively simple as that of viewing torts prospectively.

The inevitable and desirable result is that this collection of some of the finest torts scholarship that has found recent publication was renamed EXPLORING TORTS, a title that more accurately represents the work product. The chapters, derived from the colloquium papers, emphasize a large proportion of the themes that engage the attention of persons pursuing the study and evaluation of modern tort themes.

EXPLORING TORTS is published with the expectation that it will find interested audiences among jurists, scholars, attorneys, and students, including students studying law, political science, and philosophy. With specific reference to law students, the editor and the publisher believe that this volume might well suit upper-level torts, jurisprudence, or law and philosophy offerings.

Principally, however, we hope that you will find it stimulating and enjoyable to read the scholarship of many of the finest torts thinkers and writers of this era.

Appreciation is due several persons the help of whom has been instrumental to this project: Faculty Assistant Mary Stagliano, Kay Longworth and Carol DelBalzo of the School of Law staff, Marie Newman, Professor of Law and Librarian, and also Vickie Gannon, Circulation Librarian, Marilyn Belo, Maryam Afif and Michael Stalzer, my Research Assistants, and my wife, Maria Madden.

M. Stuart Madden
White Plains, New York
2005

INTRODUCTION

For the last forty years, no body of law within the civil justice system has experienced greater ferment than has the law of torts. This dynamism withal, the most prominent identified objectives of tort law continue to be the creation of an optimally uniform body of law that gives notice to all that certain behaviors that cause injury or loss to others will trigger obligations, usually including (1) the cessation of the conduct; and (2) compensation of the injured party for harm caused in a measure that will place him, to the extent money damages can do so, in the *status quo ante*. More recently, these corrective justice motivations have been reevaluated and enlarged to include tort law justifications with an economic basis. These economic models have been assigned modifiers such as "law and economics" or "efficiency-deterrence" or "cheapest cost avoider." As a general proposition, the economic paradigms suggest that the informed and rational individual will make decisions that tend to ensure that the benefits he enjoys by his activities are not outweighed by the sum total of the internalized potential liability costs, including secondary and social costs.

The uneasy heterogeneity existing between the "corrective justice" and the "efficiency" models for tort norms is but one of the modern fault lines in the field. The movement, once seemingly inexorable, from fault-based liability to strict liability is now seen to have produced tort rules of responsibility that are either only nominally "strict," are limited to the most select of circumstances, or both. Whether the tort relates to personal physical injury or to other noncontractual harm, collective, group, joint, alternative, and market share liability have all been tested, and found effective in effectuation of these objectives in some instances, and of limited or no utility in others.

During the same time, state court and state legislators have added actively to the development of tort policy. State courts have initiated changes in the treatment of duty, proximate cause, compensable damages, aggregative actions,

1

and cases involving indeterminate defendants. Legislatures in virtually every state have passed laws affecting such subjects as statutes of limitation, statutes of repose, recovery for noneconomic harm, and the availability of punitive damages. The Supreme Court has established new standards for (1) the introduction of expert causation evidence, applicable both to complex medical and scientific matters and also to other more prosaic but nonetheless expert-reliant causation evidence; (2) the appropriate application of fundamental class action fairness safeguards to settlement class actions; and (3) punitive damages.

In this milieu, the American Law Institute commenced the broad-gauge Restatement (Third) of Torts. In terms of international attention to liability rules, following the European Economic Community's publication of its strict products liability Directive, there continues nation by nation code adaptation of liability provisions to respond to new types of injuries, together with new means, including collective actions, necessary to respond thereto. In Europe and elsewhere, more than one private law entity labors in an American Law Institute fashion to publish tort rules that might offer a coherence to tort law and its ever-broadening international application.

This collection is divided into four sections. The first, titled TORT LAW IN THE NEW MILLENNIUM: PAST AS PROLOGUE, includes two chapters that, each in their own way, provide a springboard for the volume. Chapter 1, titled *Tort Law through Time and Culture: Themes of Economic Efficiency*, is an investigation of the original stimuli for tort-type norms. My inquiry takes me from ancient Mesopotamia forward, with what I think to be several illuminating patterns that show a continuum of efficiency and deterrence motivations behind old and new tort norms alike. In Chapter 2, *Past as Prelude: The Legacy of Five Landmarks of Twentieth-Century Injury Law for the Future of Torts*, Robert L. Rabin selects for analysis five tort landmarks: (1) *MacPherson v. Buick Motor Co.*; (2) workmen's compensation legislation; (3) the concurring opinion of Justice Roger Traynor in *Escola v. Coca Cola Bottling Co.*; (4) the primarily legislative movement from contributory to comparative fault; and (5) *United States v. Carroll Towing Co.* As to *Carroll Towing*, Rabin maintains that its noteworthiness was reinvigorated when Judge Learned Hand's opinion came to be recognized as a cornerstone of the law and economics movement. The focal points of his chapter are the "rich thematic influence[s]" each decision or legislature movement had on torts among Western nations, and the respective effects, sometimes substantial, sometimes less so, that each is likely to have on the future of tort law.

Section II of the collection is titled COMPENSATION AND DETERRENCE IN THE MODERN WORLD. Together Chapters 3 and 4 provide an enriching treatment of two central tort themes. Regarding compensation first, in Chapter 3, *Twenty-First-Century Insurance and Loss Distribution in Tort Law* Professor Kenneth S. Abraham first surveys the different sources of compensation for personal injury, illness, and death, and shows that there is a vast system of loss distribution, of which tort is only a small part. As to the gaps in the larger system, Abraham suggests, the question remains as to whether these gaps should be filled by tort law or by the other sources. Examining the relationship between tort and the rest of the loss distribution system, and exploring the impacts of four possible variants of the collateral source rule, the chapter looks at the rarely considered, distinct treatment accorded to life insurance and savings under existing rules. He then recommends an alternative approach that would afford first-party insurance policyholders the option of transferring all their tort rights of recovery to their insurers.

In Chapter 4, *Beyond Master-Servant: A Critique of Vicarious Liability*, Professors Jennifer H. Arlen and W. Bentley MacLeod examine important issues in the second element of the compensation/deterrence diad: the effectiveness of rules of vicarious liability in deterring *corporate* torts. To Arlen and MacLeod, for tort liability rules to regulate risk-taking efficiently, such rules must make it beneficial for corporations to take cost-effective precautions to regulate agent conduct. The authors proceed to show the ways in which current tort law falls short of this objective, and specifically how, by holding organizations liable for employee torts but not for the torts of independent contractors, vicarious liability discourages organizations from asserting direct control over agents, even when such control would be efficient.

Section III is titled DUTY RULES, COURTS, AND TORTS, and comprises chapters on themes including the vitality of duty rules; the practical limitations on litigation of design defect claims (be they programmatic or product-related); the contemporary role of the privity rule; the proper objectives for the Restatement (Third) of Torts; the viability of a legal regimen in which persons who are fully apprised of a risk or a hazard should be precluded from recovery in tort; the perils of the path the Supreme Court has chosen as regards standards for imposition of punitive damages; and the extraordinary effects, applications, and complexities of proportional liability, with particular attention to toxic substances causation.

In Chapter 5, *The Disintegration of Duty*, Professor Ernest J. Weinrib sounds a clarion warning that the relational underpinnings of common law duty have been in noticeable erosion. In answer to the question: "When does an actor owe a duty?," Weinrib begins with the defining 1932 decision of English negligence law, *Donoghue v. Stevenson*, in which Lord Atkin asserted that "there must be, and is, a general conception of relations giving rise to a duty of care."

Unfortunately, Weinrib writes, courts in more and more modern decisions have seemingly abandoned an effort to identify and apply this unitary conception of duty, and have opted instead to identify a multiplicity of particular duties that Lord Atkin would have deplored. Weinrib sets about the task of analyzing the landmark cases of the twentieth century to show how duty fits with other negligence concepts to connect the defendant's act to the plaintiff's injury in a normatively coherent way. He describes the internal structure of the duty of care, and what its constituents must be if it is to reflect a coherent conception of wrongdoing.

In Chapter 6, *Managing the Negligence Concept: Respect for the Rule of Law*, James A. Henderson Jr. evaluates the risks of open-ended judicial review of complex tort issues, and specifically "design" issues. "Design" issues are defined more broadly than they are in their familiar context of products liability law, and Henderson includes in this subject grouping medical malpractice and governmental "design" claims. Examining such issues as institutional competency, enterprise liability, the prima facie case, and evidentiary requisites, he concludes that courts have taken an appropriately "humble" approach, avoiding open-ended review in contexts in which the pressures to engage in such review are the greatest. After first reviewing products liability themes, the author turns to medical malpractice litigation, in which courts rely on professional custom to supply specific standards that render negligence claims adjudicable. In negligence claims against the government, courts and legislatures have built on the traditional principle of sovereign immunity to allow courts to impose tort liability on governmental actors while avoiding open-ended review of complex institutional programs of policies. In each setting, Handerson writes, courts have adopted approaches that successfully contain the negligence concept and keep it with in its proper bounds.

In Chapter 7, *Rebuilding the Citadel: Privity, Causation, and Freedom of Contract*, Richard A. Epstein identifies this watershed issue affecting compensation for physical and financial harm: whether to deal with these through tort law or through contract. The modern direction of cases, Epstein writes, seems to favor tort remedies over contractual arrangements, with the latter's frequent restrictions on the damages recoverable. Financial loss claims, in turn, find favor in contract. Epstein poses this question: Is there something about the structure of a physical harm claim versus that of a financial harm claim that is sufficiently similar to undercut the argument that only one, rather than both, should be subject to contract rules? A second part of Epstein's analysis is the examination of the decline of privity rules, and involves a new look at the venerable origins of privity. He notes a contrapuntal distinction between the original justification of privity and its actual history, and concludes that, nevertheless, the privity limitation continues to play a role in a number of important contexts, including environmental and financial losses, in which potentially ruinous unlimited liability is thought to be of the greatest significance. Ultimately, Epstein defends both those limitations and the contractual efforts to restrict recovery for consequential losses.

Jane Stapleton begins Chapter 8, *Controlling the Future of the Common Law by Restatement*, by noting how daunting it is to restate a common law for the United States, a nation of such a state-by-state diversity in liability rules and remedies. She analyzes the architecture of the current Restatement (Third) of Torts, and considers the extent to which tort standards can be crystallized in bright-line rules, as well as how the underlying institutional competition between the trial judge and the jury imposes a unique dynamic to the restatement process. For example, Stapleton argues, in "traditional" duty contexts, that is where the defendant's own affirmative careless action directly caused physical injury, and also in special prior relationship settings, the Reporters can find sufficiently objective and determinate criteria on which a rule of law might clearly be based, thereby facilitating directed verdicts. Outside these areas, however, the rationale for denial of liability rests on the absence of the sort of contextual facts that are usually seen as relevant to the breach or scope of duty issues, matters traditionally decided by the jury. If, therefore, the Restatement proposes to allocate to the trial judge institutional power to enter a directed verdict in the defendant's favor in such cases, Stapleton suggests, it will need to formulate the criteria on which he or she might do so in terms of what have hitherto been seen as no-breach or outside-scope factors in the particular case.

Chapter 9, *Information Shields in Tort Law*, by David G. Owen, begins with that proposition that a person possessed of correct information about the nature of a dangerous thing or situation is more likely to make informed, safe, and efficient choices about how or whether to confront such risks, and the more likely such choices are to be cost-effective and rational. The chapter inquires into the extent to which tort law should impose responsibility on actors for harm to persons who possess full and complete risk information. Owen presents a model Liability Shield statute that would preclude failure to warn liability for manufacturers who provide consumers with full information of product hazards. For the attractions of such an approach, he proceeds to note, such a rule may place unrealistic reliance on multiple assumptions about human rationality, and about the nature and abilities of the central institutions in a program of this type: manufacturers, safety agencies, and insurers. The chapter thus concludes that today's tort law has correctly moved beyond the wooden construct of no-duty rulings to the flexible assessments of victim responsibility permitted by comparative fault.

Guido Calabresi, in Chapter 10, *The Complexity of Torts: The Case of Punitive Damages*, addresses the tension between those, be they courts, legislatures or scholars, who view tort law as serving numerous (or multidimensional) goals, and those who may be quick to identify a single, simple goal – whether it be economic efficiency, furthering loss spreading, or anything else – and, having examined tort doctrines and cases on that basis, are properly attacked for being reductionists. His thesis is that pursuit of one-dimensional goals in tort law is fraught with risk. Calabresi is troubled by the ever-increasing incursions by federal courts into the tort process, a problem that is worsened when the incursion is by the Supreme Court. Concentrating on punitive damages, Calabresi states that exemplary awards in tort law can further at least five very different objectives, including: (1) a desire to enforce societal norms, through the use of private attorneys general; (2) a desire to employ "the multiplier," in the sense that the proper measurement of the deterrent assessed is not the harm to any one victim but, rather, that harm multiplied by all those victims whose harms, although real, are not otherwise likely to be charged to the injurer; (3) the "Tragic Choice" Function, such as is represented in the Pinto case; (4) Recovery of Generally Non-Recoverable Compensatory Damages; and (5) Righting of Private Wrongs. Calabresi suggests that the Supreme Court's modern decisions regarding punitive damages fail to take into account the multiple functions a state or states may have intended that these awards perform, and that it is rare that such single mindedness as the Court has demonstrated can fully appreciate a slowly developed field of law such as torts.

Proportional liability is identified by many as one of the most important developments in modern tort law. In Chapter 11, *The Future of Proportional Liability: The Lessons of Toxic Substances Causation*, Michael D. Green analyzes the reform of contributory negligence into a scheme of comparative fault through the lens of environmental and toxic tort litigation, the most notable of which have included case aggregations involving asbestos, Agent Orange, DES, silicone gel breast implants, and tobacco. Litigation of such cases relies on probabilistic evidence, the most probative of which is epidemiology. Green writes that the confluence of comparative fault principles and probabilistic evidence of causation in toxic substances cases raises the question of whether liability should be imposed proportionally based on the probability of causation. He critically assesses the potential for such an approach by examining the precision and fallibility of epidemiological evidence, and concludes that proportional liability would not provide the deterrence benefits many have claimed for it.

Section IV (the final section of this collection) is titled Torts in a Shrinking World. As the section's title suggests, and as the two chapters presented show, modern scholars and policy makers should take into proper account that civil code nations, among others, are responding to domestic and international tort-type challenges with sophisticated decisional, legislative and constitutional approaches. Federico Stella of the University of Milan contributed Chapter 12, *Causation in Products Liability and Exposure to Toxic Substances: A European View*. Stella examines the multitextured similarities and contrasts between the United States treatment of causation in toxic substances cases and that followed in Italy and also in a representative selection of other European nations. Explaining how many European nations have yet to elaborate a developed body of decisional law, individually or collectively, in the subject matters of toxic torts and products liability, Stella describes how many such claims have been brought as criminal matters. In the final decades of the preceding century, he continues, European nations, and Italy particularly, were confronted with a surge of such hybrid toxic tort-criminal liability suits that placed in issue the obstacles to proving individual causation. On a case-by-case basis, problems in proving causation might be overcome by the expedient of replacing the notion of *condicio sine qua non* with the standard of risk elevation and, beginning in 2000, in Italy and elsewhere, nations took this different tack. There followed, however, an influential decision of the Italian Supreme Court that held that simple risk elevation would not suffice to prove individual causation in criminal prosecutions. Rather, the prosecution would be required to prove not only "but for" cause but also sustain that burden beyond a reasonable doubt. Stella notes, however, that in an increasing number of Italian universities, professors of civil liability systems have begun to teach the evidentiary and doctrinal approaches to causation used by the American civil courts.

Suits to vindicate collective or popular rights are recognized in numerous nations. They represent means that are at once similar to and dissimilar from the aggregative suits (class actions and consolidations) that may be brought in the United States. At this date, such claims are not recognized in the form often taken in the United States, such as when numerous claims arise from the same tortious conduct. Instead, collective or popular actions are more likely to arise to challenge governmental action, or failure to act, that has deprived citizens of rights guaranteed by legislation or by the country's constitution. In the concluding selection to this collection, Chapter 13, *Collective Rights and Collective Actions: Examples of European and Latin American Contributions*, Colombian and French scholar Juan Carlos Henao takes on the ambitious task of a comparative analysis of how such claims are provided for, and how they have been prosecuted, in France and in Colombia. Describing how achieving remediation for violation of collective rights is a well developed constitutional, legislative and decisional principle in many civil law countries, Henao explains how an increasing number of constitutions in civil law countries include, to name only two: (1) the right to a safe and healthy environment; and (2) the right to the preservation of open space. He explains the similarities between such claims and public or private nuisance actions in common law nations. Juxtaposing the law of France with that of Colombia, the chapter includes a critical assessment of how such approaches preserve separation of powers, democratic participation in the protection and preservation of public property, and the respective powers of the judge and the citizen.

M. Stuart Madden
White Plains, New York
May, 2005

TORT LAW IN THE NEW MILLENNIUM: PAST AS PROLOGUE

CHAPTER ONE

TORT LAW THROUGH TIME AND CULTURE: THEMES OF ECONOMIC EFFICIENCY

M. Stuart Madden

ABSTRACT. As human societies developed, a bedrock necessity was the development of expectations and norms that protected individuals and families from wrongful injury, property damage, and taking. Written law, dating to the Babylonian codes and early Hebrew law, emphasized congruent themes. Such law protected groups and individuals from wrongful injury, depredation of the just deserts of labor, interference with the means of individual livelihood, and distortion of the fair distribution of wealth.

Hellenic philosophers identified the goals of society as the protection of persons and property from wrongful harm, protection of the individual's means of survival, discouragement of self-aggrandizement, and the elevation of individual knowledge that would carry forward and perfect such principles. Roman law was replete with proscriptions against forced taking and unjust enrichment, and included rules for *ex ante* contract-based resolution of potential disagreement. Customary law perpetuated these efficient economic tenets within the Western world and beyond. The common law has pursued many of the same ends. From the translation of the negligence formula of Judge Learned Hand into a basic efficiency model to the increasing number of judicial opinions that rely explicitly upon economic analysis, efficiency themes can be predicted to enjoy a continued and increasingly conspicuous place in modern tort analysis.

I. INTRODUCTION

Tort law represents a society's revealed truth as to the behaviors it wishes to encourage and the behaviors it wishes to discourage.[1] From causes of action for the simple tort of battery to the more elegant tortuous interference with prospective advantage, the manner in which individuals or groups can injure

---

[1] There will be some rarified instances of behavior that tort law would not discourage, such as abnormally dangerous activities, but instead may wish to modify or limit, and in any event, assign strict liability.

M. Stuart Madden, Distinguished Professor of Law, Pace University School of Law. The author notes with appreciation the research assistance of Maryam Afif, Michael Stalzer, Natara Feller, and Lynn Belo in the preparation of this chapter.

a protected interest of others seems almost limitless. Despite the amplitude of interests protected by tort law, from its earliest exercise in prehistoric groups up to its modern implementation, there have existed a finite number of goals of tort law, whether the "law" referred to be an unwritten norm, a judicial decision, or a modern statute. There is general agreement that these objectives, however imperfectly accomplished, include: (1) returning the party who has suffered a loss to the position he enjoyed before the wrongful activity; (2) requiring the wrongdoer to disgorge the monetary or imputed benefit derived from his actions; and (3) by the remedy meted out, or by its example, deterring the wrongdoer and others in a similar situation from engaging in the same wrongful and injurious pursuit. Another manner of describing tort goals has been to order them as serving either goals of (4) "corrective justice and "morality"; or (5) "efficiency and deterrence."

Aligning tort rules to be consistent exclusively with any one of these five goals requires some ungainly packaging, as each of the five themes described actually also serves the other four. This is to say, for example, a remedy that focuses on corrective justice will serve simultaneously the goals of disgorgement of unjust enrichment, morality, efficiency, deterrence, and so on. More specifically, the goal of returning the injured party to the *status quo ante*, the objective most closely associated with corrective justice, is ordinarily reached by a decree ordering the wrongdoer to return to the plaintiff in money the equivalent to what the plaintiff lost. But damages calculated in this way also may be seen as an inexact surrogate for what the wrongdoer gained, actually or by imputation, by perpetrating the wrong. Further, whereas the wrongdoer's disgorgement of his gain often provides corrective justice for the claimant, it also, importantly, punishes the wrongdoer for failing to achieve the plaintiff's *ex ante* approval of the transaction – an omission deemed to be inefficient by exponents of efficiency theory.[2] So it is not surprising that although many suggest that tort rules and remedies aligned with economic and efficiency models provide the most deterrence for civil wrongs, most agree that the tort rules recognized by the corrective justice-morality school also deter in measurable ways. Indeed, in the inexact taxonomy employed by

---

[2] When the loss is personal injury or property damage, a rough estimation of this inefficiency (or waste) may often be the combined amount of the claimant's economic and noneconomic damages. Of course the theme of punishment deterrence is but the flip side of a theme of creating an incentive for efficient behavior. As suggested by Professors David W. Barnes and Lynn A. Stout, "Tort law may be viewed as a system of rules designed to maximize wealth by allocating risks so as to minimize the costs associated with engaging in daily activities." DAVID W. BARNES & LYNN A. STOUT, CASES AND MATERIALS ON LAW AND ECONOMICS 85 (1992).

tort scholars, there are so many instances of overlap between what tort goals are claimed to serve corrective justice-morality, but that serve simultaneously goals of efficiency and deterrence, that the legal pragmatist would be tempted to characterize them as functionally equivalent.[3] Even conceding the absence of neatness in any attempt at categorization, the division of tort goals along these or similar lines is nevertheless illuminating and predictive.

Accident law is a model of social expectations, and these social expectations are at once moral and economically efficient. Emphasizing for present purposes the economic aspect, it can be shown that in broad terms, written or unwritten rules pertaining to civil wrongs cleave to an ethos of efficiency. This efficiency norm has, in turn, an organizing principle of waste avoidance, the protection of persons and their property from injury and wrongful appropriation, the preservation of the integrity of individual or collective possessions or prerogatives from wrongful interference, and the prudent marshaling of limited resources. Although the corrective justice-morality objectives of many tort norms will often, for what appears initially, eclipse any apparent underpinnings of efficiency, still and all, subtle economic themes of efficiency and deterrence can be recognized in almost all tort-type customs, expectations, and rules. Indeed, as this chapter will demonstrate, the parallel and harmonious impetus for almost all of what today we call tort law today can be found in principles of economic efficiency.

This chapter examines preliminarily a selection of past and contemporary societal choices regarding identification, assignment, and implementation of remedies for civil wrongs. Rather than exploring each of the five principal themes of tort analysis noted earlier, I devote this examination solely to tort rules revealing economic themes. Although there are only a limited number of such rules that reveal an economic analysis on the surface, in the examples this chapter summons the economic goals can be teased readily to the surface.

Evaluation of accident law as it has evolved during the period of written history is by any assessment a prodigious task. Even with modern translation, there are numerous gaps in the historical record. The potential for analytical error in bridging these gaps is compounded by the difficulties legal scholars and legal historians confront in reading the legal-historical record within the only context that may reveal it reliably: the cultural and political circumstances of its origins. As to prehistoric man, no more than a small part of the history of

---

[3] Put another way, both corrective justice and efficiency principles must be regarded as "true" in that they hold significant, albeit nonexclusive, predictive value in anticipating the development of tort law. *See* M. Stuart Madden, *Selected Federal Tort Reform and Restatement Initiatives Through the Lenses of Corrective Justice and Efficiency*, 32 GA. L. REV. 1017 (1998) at nn. 297–98 and accompanying text.

the earliest human societies may ever be scientifically reconstructed, because of natural loss, or frequently deliberate or inadvertent later human meddling. Forever lost are countless ancient remnants that might suggest the societal norms employed to make group decisions based on what behaviors would bring collective benefit and what would not.

The adoption of durable writing or imagery accelerated our modern understanding of ancient legal norms. The discovery and translation of the first integrated legal codes from the sites that were within ancient Babylonia, a codification of what was surely the customary law that preceded it, provided the first written evidence of regularized norms for civil behavior, identification of civil wrongs, and the remedies for such wrongs. However, even anticipating the development of permanent written records, much regarding human norms and customs may be deduced logically. Taking into account the difficulties in identifying the customs of early humans, experts are of one view that the success and survival of early social groupings bore a more or less exact correlation to their adoption of norms that furthered advancement of knowledge, material comfort, and economic stability. For all human groups, achievement of these attributes would, from prehistory onward, be characterized as "good."[4] It follows that early family clans, and the tribes and ever larger social aggregations that would follow, have shared one sentiment: to pursue such "good" for their members.[5]

Philosophers have disagreed as to whether man in his natural state was innately "good," but any original impulse for good stood no meaningful chance for survival as human concentrations grew and evolved. Group order and expectations in the form of norms, and the subscription to such norms by individuals and families, became necessary for communal survival. It will be seen that at its core, tort law, together with its unwritten normative antecedents, bears witness to the fundamental social need for self-limitation. To the sociologist Emile Durkheim, the peaceful process of society has always depended on the individual's submission to inhibitions of or restrictions on personal "inclinations and instincts." Whether the "venerable respect" tendered to a collective "moral authority" is faith-dependent or not, Durkheim

---

[4] Robert Redfield, *Maine's Ancient Law in the Light of Primitive Societies*, THE WESTERN POLITICAL QUARTERLY 3, 586–89 (1950), in which Redfield writes of primitive societies: "[E]conomic systems are imbedded in social relations. Men work and manufacture not for motives of gain. They tend to work because working is part of the good life ... "

[5] By "members" is meant the collective, for, as Maine observed: "Ancient Law ... knows next to nothing of Individuals. It is concerned not with Individuals, but with Families, not with single human beings but groups." HENRY SUMNER MAINE, ANCIENT LAW 229 (1861).

continues, "social life would be impossible"[6] without general subscription to such limitations. And so by necessity, social groups developed expectations, norms, customs, and, eventually, laws that (1) encouraged behaviors that contributed to the common good and economic success of the community; and (2) discouraged individualistic pursuit of personal aggrandizement to the extent that the same involved disavowal of community responsibility.

Accordingly, human experience of the ages has demonstrated that man as a social animal has turned almost invariably to structures and norms consistent with defined and enforced standards of "good" as would further the innate and overarching instinct for individual and group survival. By virtue of this ascendant sentiment of most societies of all historical epochs to attain both group and individual "good," the collective conclusions as to what constitutes "good" evolved gradually to this: what is "good" has always been, as it is today, that which is just, moral and equitable.[7] Encouragement of "good" conduct has been logically accompanied by discouragement of "bad" conduct, which is to say, behavior considered to be unjust, immoral, or inequitable. And all such systems, save the brashest of totalitarian societies, have included standards by which a person might seek the correction of or compensation for harm caused by the wrongful acts of another. Initially established as practices, then as norms and customs, and eventually as law, evolving social strictures would operate to either cabin or punish the behaviors of those succumbing to the seemingly irresistible human appetite for bad, wrongful, and harmful behavior.

In a sense, tort law, past and present, has operated as the societal superego, a generally subscribed-to social compact in which most persons rein in such impulses as might lead them to trammel the protected rights of others, inasmuch as the norms of tort law require rectification operating *post hoc* to restore the wronged person to the position previously enjoyed.[8] This restoration may be perfect, such as when it is in the form of returning goods where there has

---

[6] EMILE DURKHEIM, THE ELEMENTARY FORMS OF RELIGIOUS LIFE 237 (1915) (1965 ed.).

[7] Conceding that Socrates wrote from beyond the spheres of governing power, it is telling that Socrates' ethics are suffused with the goal of avoiding doing harm, and with the argument that a principal marker of "justice" is the simple "returning what was owed." ANTHONY GOTTLIEB, THE DREAM OF REASON: A HISTORY OF PHILOSOPHY FROM THE GREEKS TO THE RENAISSANCE 164 (2000).

[8] The true explanation of the reference of liability to a moral standard . . . is not that it is for the purpose of improving men's hearts, but that it is to give a man a fair chance to avoid doing the harm before he is held responsible for it. It is intended to reconcile the policy of letting accidents lie where they fall, and the reasonable freedom of others with the protection of the individual from injury.
OLIVER WENDELL HOLMES, THE COMMON LAW 115 (Mark DeWolfe Howe, ed.) (1963).

been a trespass to chattels and there has been no diminution in value, or when there has been a misappropriation. Or it may be imperfect, such as in settings involving a wrongful physical injury, as to which rectification in the form of money can never truly restore the injured party to the *status quo ante*. As suggested initially, whatever the corrective justice limitations of money damages, they do serve other objectives identified with tort law, which include deterrence of the same or similar conduct by the actor or others similarly situated. Money damages also, in an economic sense, command a transfer of wealth that achieves a figurative rectification of the wrongdoer's "forced taking" of the injured party's bodily integrity. The money damages also, at least conceptually, deprive the wrongdoer of the "unjust enrichment" achieved by creating a tear in the fabric of consensual or contract-based social interaction.

My objective in this chapter is to examine this question: In the norms, rules, and philosophical bases for early tort law through and including its modern representations, can there be found a continuous vein of the goals of (1) efficiency and (2) deterrence? It will not surprise students of tort law that numerous social, philosophical, and legal systems, from past to present, are redolent of the economic norms of waste avoidance and the discouragement of unconsented-to taking. In this chapter, I will discuss a spare, but illustrative, selection of groups and societies the organization of which followed written and unwritten norms so showing. I also will touch on modern philosophical and legal tenets that inform us regarding the tenacity of economic efficiency themes in tort law and theory. The chapter will conclude with observations as to how this abundant history of human recognition of these economic considerations augurs for the future of tort law.

II. ECONOMIC IMPERATIVES IN EARLY SOCIAL GROUPINGS

A. Generally

The raw and primal imperative of simple human survival has required of each successful community the ordered pursuit of "good" for its members, including necessarily standards to discourage or interdict activity that interrupted or compromised pursuit of a "good" social order. In the shadow of such overarching needs, the norms or apparatus of "justice" and "morality" would necessarily be subordinate to the collective pursuit of economic stability, growth, and the elevation of human knowledge. Retaining a focus on the three goals of elevation of human knowledge, material comfort, and economic stability, it follows that within the context of prehistory, of particular pertinence to the furtherance of each goal was the creation and preservation of group circumstances in which persons could expect to live peaceably without physical injury at the hands of others. It also was expected that the community would provide congruent protection against wrongful taking or damage of the property justly acquired by its members. It was collectively thought necessary that man would gradually impose on his groups, and eventually civilizations and states, norms and rules that served to protect the personal physical autonomy and security of group members, and also protect their belongings, against wrongful interference. The group visualization of these norms, and their progressive imposition, would assume the aura of inevitability, and the *gravitas* of a cultural imperative. For successful social groupings, principal among such norms was the expectation there would be some form of remediation for an impermissible intrusion on physical or property interests, including common property rights.[9] And, finally, along this line of civilizing thought, the ideation of society was that this remediation ought properly come from the malefactor.

B. A Presymbolic Scenario

At some distant time in the African veldt, the birthplace of modern man, *homo sapiens* formed family-based social groups or clans. From the time of early family groupings to the development of ever-more complex communities, all successful human gatherings developed work specializations *inter se*.[10] For example, a group depending on fishing for its sustenance would need individuals to prepare nets or baskets for the catch. Others in the group would dedicate themselves to the actual fishing, and travel to the water source with, let us say, spherical fishing baskets that contained a hole on one side that lured fish seeking shade. Swift retrieval of the basket would catch the fish and provide food for the community. Naturally, the entire community would not survive if the actual fishing specialists arrogated to themselves the catch, and so there developed norms of allocative efficiency, a so-called "generosity" norm, that would ensure that all in the community, including infants and the aged, would be provided for adequately.[11] This allocation of goods

---

[9] DENNIS LLOYD, THE IDEA OF LAW 49 (1976) (referencing, *inter alia*, Mosaic law).

[10] As Darwin pointed out for flora and fauna and as Durkheim noted in the case of human societies, an increase in numbers when area is held constant (i.e, an increase in density) tends to produce differentiation and specialization, as only in this way can the area support increased numbers.

[11] "[F]or example, the [primitive] Australian hunter who kills a wild animal is expected to give one certain part of it to his elder brother, other parts to his younger brother and still other parts of the animal to defined relatives. He does this knowing that [the other brothers] will

constituted a micro prototype of efficiency-based exchange of goods that recognized duties owed by the community to its individuals, duties owed by community members to others, and the common interest in nonwasteful behavior that would characterize all societies to follow.

This economic cooperation characteristic of primitive communities was the antithesis of economic self-interest, and understandably, Karl Polanyi writes that in tribal society, "[the individual's economic interest is rarely paramount, for the community keeps all its members from starving unless it is itself borne down by catastrophe."[12] Moreover, in the circumstances of tribal society, past and present alike, exclusive pursuit of economic self-interest was itself contrary to the economic survival of the group. Early task assignment and economic differentiation within a clan or a small social group required, by "code of honor" or "generosity," recognition that each member of the community served the whole. From the earliest hunting and gathering communities to the later agricultural groupings, task allocation was accompanied by mutual expectancies that the bounty in food or materials gathered by one group would be shared with the others. The others would include, nonexclusively, the homemakers, children, and the elderly. For the vital hunting population to forsake its obligation to return from the hunt with food to share with the family, clan, or tribe would sabotage the very existence of the social group. Failure to share with the homemaker and the children would bring about the speedy end of the bloodline. As to elders, with some exceptions, tribal groups recognized that the aged acted as secondary caregivers and essential repositories of the group's oral history and traditions.

In time, with the increase in population and in the course of the proved northward migration of many human groups,[13] early man found that the working norms for family, clan and single community survival would be taxed by contact with other families or groups. For an untold time, the response of the principal family was simply that of preserving territorial integrity, familial safety, or both. An intruder would be frightened away, or if necessary, beaten

---

make a corresponding distribution of meat to him." Robert Redfield, *Maine's Ancient Law in the Light of Primitive Societies,* in J. C. SMITH AND DAVID N. WEISSTUB, THE WESTERN IDEA OF LAW 81 (1983).

[12] PRIMITIVE, ARCHAIC AND MODERN ECONOMIES: ESSAYS OF KARL POLANYI 7 (George Dalton, ed., 1968).

[13] Such extraordinary migrations as would take man out of Africa and eventually permit his species' dispersal throughout all but one continent was facilitated by his evolved ability to walk on two feet, to travel long distances, and to carry objects and infants. J. M. ROBERTS, THE NEW HISTORY OF THE WORLD 5 (2003).

or killed. If the intruder or his group prevailed in any contest, the principal family, with its injured or killed, would abdicate its territory.

In a succession of discrete and unidentifiable moments, this motif would change. Increased populations, changes in climate that made one area more hospitable than another, or migratory patterns of available prey, made contact with other groups more frequent. A group's choices were essentially two. They might preserve their reflexive and potentially mortal repulsion of competition. However losses suffered in noncooperative contact with other groups might have stimulated a group's conclusion that preservation of pristine territorial integrity was perhaps a pearl of too great a price. And so, alternatively, their response to other communities might begin to partake of peaceable aspects. Noncombative resolution of intrafamilial allocative tensions might have served as a model for introduction of cooperative behavior in interfamilial matters. As to the latter, cooperation would lessen or eliminate the enormous waste and cost of violent response to intrusion.

Perhaps at the instigation a group elder, families and tribes eventually developed behaviors and expectations that could coexist within the context of available resources in such ways as to achieve a tenable resource-based economic stasis.[14] Should, for example, our hypothesized fishing community come into contact with a hunting community, the sharing of territory, and perhaps even barter, might well become recognized for its very significant benefit in reducing the group's loss of its ablest members to combat, and thus become a common ideal or norm.

Historians have recognized the similar options presented to later agricultural communities, with the permissible inference of the peaceable and efficient resolution of such options. In the description of J. M. Roberts, "As the population rose, more land was taken to grow food. Sooner or later men of different villages would have to come face to face with others intent on reclaiming marsh which had previously separated them from one another. . . . There was a choice: to fight or to cooperate. . . . Somewhere along the line it made sense for men to band together in bigger units than hitherto for self-protection and management of the environment."[15] Of necessity the norms developed within such larger social groups reflected the wisdom of not only *ex ante* resource

---

[14] Of course the genetic significance of intergroup coexistence is inestimable, but would, in any event be unknown to early man until the development of the incest taboos.

[15] J. M. Roberts, *supra* note 13 at 49–50. These early incentives toward political and economic cooperation weigh in against the more pessimistic vision of Garrett Hardin. Garrett Hardin, *The Tragedy of the Commons*, 62 Sci. 1243, 1244 (Dec. 13, 1968) (arguing that "ruin is the destination toward which all men rush, each pursuing his own best interest.").

allocation but also of strictures intended to discourage disruption of such allocation by forced takings or otherwise.

The above hypothetical yet historically realistic example gives to us our first chance to measure highly plausible human behavior, and attendant norms, by a yardstick of human economic efficiency. Although multiple economic models are available, one that seems well suited is that propounded by Vilfredo Pareto in the early 1900s. The Pareto analysis imagines a setting in which all goods have been previously allocated, and permits an evaluation of different approaches to reallocation of such goods. A reallocation that left one or more individuals better off, but no one worse off, would be considered a Pareto Superior change.[16] Even better, from a wealth-maximization perspective, is a result in which with the reallocation of goods or resources all affected parties are better off – a result described as Pareto Optimal or Pareto Efficient.[17]

Applying the Pareto approach to early man's described movement away from territorial combat to gradually more peaceable allocations of land and other resources presents this question: Is such rational cooperation efficient? A syllogism posed in a coarse correlation between competition and efficiency may be, on these facts, misleading. That syllogism would go: competition is, generally speaking, efficient. The antithesis of competition is cooperation. Therefore, cooperation is inefficient. However in the example given earlier, rational cooperation between early human social groups regarding the sharing of limited land resources was not only efficient, it also can be seen to be the only means by which early societies could flourish. The alternative was either the continuation of wasteful combat, or the relegation of some groups to a continued nomadic life, or both. Thus, cooperation, and its concomitant benefits to participants in agricultural communities, was Pareto Optimal.

Furthermore, as to the theme of surplus, and surplus accumulation, it is widely proposed that the development of agriculture and animal husbandry created the first human experience of surplus.[18] This surplus, in turn, accelerated the development of specialization of labor.[19] Specialization of labor affected the reciprocal entitlements and obligations of three principal groupings: (1) those engaged in agriculture; (2) artisans; and (3) those to whom

---

[16] The Pareto criteria for wealth maximization analysis are summarized in DAVID W. BARNES & LYNN A. STOUT, THE ECONOMIC ANALYSIS OF TORT LAW 11 (1992).

[17] MARK SEIDENFIELD, MICROECONOMIC PREDICATES TO LAW AND ECONOMICS 49 (1996). For a general description of Pareto optimality principles, see ROBIN PAUL MALLOY, LAW AND ECONOMICS: A COMPARATIVE APPROACH TO THEORY AND PRACTICE (1990).

[18] Agriculture and animal husbandry will be referred to collectively as "agriculture."

[19] J. M. ROBERTS, supra note 13 at 51.

fell domestic and child-rearing obligations. Those engaged in agriculture had, of course, the duty to efficiently and productively produce and to husband the resources and the comestible rewards entrusted to them. Unlike the expectations typical of the hunting and gathering communities, the development of agriculture both permitted and required that what was produced not be consumed immediately, and that when it was consumed, that it not be consumed exclusively by those who produced it. Rather, the expectation for and the duty of those tilling the fields or tending the animals was to harvest the crops and to preserve the harvest, or to slaughter the livestock and to preserve the meat through salting or otherwise, for distribution among the entire community. The artisans were expected to perform such tasks as the creation of the specialized tools that might be associated with chopping, sewing, tilling, the making of clothing, the building of shelter, and more. The artisans' expectation was that, in exchange for their labor, they would partake of the agricultural production of the fields.

The homemakers also might not participate directly in agricultural production, or if they did, they might do so to a lesser extent than those to whom that task would fall principally. The homemakers' primary tasks would include the bearing, raising, and nurturance of children, and the maintenance of a habitable home site, thus freeing both the laborers in the field and the artisans to pursue their work unimpeded of at least the most time consuming obligations of home and child. In return for these responsibilities, the homemakers would rely on the sowers and the reapers, and also the artisans, to share on an equivalence what they had produced.

The significance of these simple group structures, duties, and expectations lay in their promise of and similarity to the more complex duties and expectations that would develop as agriculture permitted the development of larger and more concentrated communities. These larger social or societal groupings would, with the advent of writing and symbolic communication, become the earliest instance of what is now called civilization. And it is in the writings of the earliest civilizations that are found the first organized principals of what we now describe as civil responsibility for wrongdoing, or tort law.

III. DEVELOPING HISTORICAL EXAMPLES OF EFFICIENT FORM AND FUNCTION

A. Mesopotamian Law

The watershed discovery and translation of approximately three thousand years of law from the cradle of civilization, framed by the Tigris and the

Euphrates Rivers, permitted research, evaluation, and legal synthesis of myriad legal matters. Mesopotamian ancients were, many claim, the first to
write their laws in an organized and lasting manner.[20] As discovered by
later archaeologists, these laws were collected in the Laws of Hammurabi,
the Laws of Ur-Nammu, and the Laws of Lipit-Ishtar.[21] The epoch contemplated by these principal bodies of law is approximately 4600 B.C. to 1600 B.C.,
or three millennia. Although these legal codes were promulgated, published,
and republished under the aegises of different rulers and over such a long
period of time, scholars suggest that the "similarities"[22] in the form of
the "academic tradition," and the provisions themselves, "suggest enduring commonalities in the customary law of Babylonia."[23] For present purposes, the legal themes and systems to be discussed will be those of such
form and substance as the ancients devoted to systems of customary, normative, and eventually statutory law governing the rights of individuals to be
free from wrongful injury, property damage, or coerced takings initiated by
others.

For all that is apparent, Hammurabi himself intended that his law reconcile wrongs and bring justice to those aggrieved. His unmistakable goal was
the economic stability and enhancement of his people.[24] Before the laws of
Hammurabi there were published the laws of King Ur-Nami (2112–2095 B.C.).
In the Mesopotamian law collections, the provisions characteristically begin
with an "if" clause (the prostasis), and end with a "then" clause (the apodasis).
Thus, the prostasis identifies a circumstance or activity that the lawmakers
concluded needed a legal rule, whereas the apodasis describes the legal consequences for the creation of such a circumstance or the engagement in
such activity.[25] This approach bears significant markings of code-based law
throughout the ages and is widely followed today.

Review by scholars has revealed examples of remedies for civil wrongs in
which Mesopotamian law responded to the delict by penalizing, by money
judgment, the wrongful disposition (or eradication) of another's right or

---

[20] RUSS VERSTEEG, EARLY MESOPOTAMIAN LAW 3 (2000). Several of the references to the
principal Mesopotamian codes derive from this work.
[21] Id.
[22] Id. at 5, quoting Raymond Westbrook, Slave and Master in Near Eastern Law, 70 CHICAGO-
KENT L. REV. 1631, 1634 (1995).
[23] Id. at 5, quoting Robert C. Elllickson, Charles D. A. Thorland, Ancient Land Use Law:
Mesopotamia, Egypt, Israel, 70 CHIGAGO KENT L. REV. 321, 331 (1995) (internal citations
omitted).
[24] Id.
[25] Id. at 11.

vested expectancy. This approach was of particular and felt economic significance in instances when the wronged individual was in a weaker social or economic position than the wrongdoer. Thus, the laws of Ur-Nami provided that a father whose daughter is promised to a man, but who gave the daughter in marriage to another, must compensate the disappointed man twice the property value of what the promisee of marriage had brought into the household.[26]

As was true particularly of early legal formulations, the law of Mesopotamia emphasized the protection of person, property, and commerce from forced divestiture of a right or a prerogative. Regarding navigation, a collision between two boats on a body of water having a perceptible upstream and downstream would trigger a presumption of fault on the part of the upstream captain, on the logic – faulty or not – that the upstream captain had a greater opportunity to reduce avoidable accidents than did his counterpart, as the former would be traveling at a slower speed.[27]

A subtle interplay between norms of duty, nuisance and causation is evident in the following rule: Neighbors were bound by a rule that served to deter letting one's unoccupied land elevate a risk of trespass or burglary to the neighboring property. The Law of Lipit-Ishtar provided that upon notice from one neighbor that a second neighbor's unattended property provided access to the complainant's property by potential robbers, that should a robbery occur, the inattentive neighbor would be liable for any harm to the complainant's home or property.[28] Particularly harsh legal consequences might be visited on the landowner who failed to contain his irrigation canals, as flooding of the water might "result not only in leaving crops and cattle dry and parched in one point, but also widespread floods in another part of the district."[29] In the simple case involving only damage to grain, replacement of a like amount might give sufficient remedy. But an unmistakable diterrence of more severe consequences would be clear to those knowing that should the careless farmer be unable to replace the grain, the neighbors might be permitted to sell his property and to sell him into slavery to achieve justice.[30]

---

[26] Ur-Nami § 9.
[27] Driver and Mills, Babylonian Law § 431–32, referenced in Versteeg at 130.
[28] Lipit-Ishtar § 11.
[29] Driver and Mills, Babylonian Law 50, *from* Versteeg at 136.
[30] Hammurabi § 54. *See also* Raymond Westbrook, *Slave and Master*, 70 Chicago-Kent L. Rev. 1631, 1644 (1995).

B. Early Religion – The Law of the Torah

It is accepted that much of modern society was suckled at the breast of faith, and that much of mankind's law and morality "were born of religion."[31] Often this faith partook of earlier myth, and transformed it to suit the extant needs of the time and the place. And, invariably, the adopted faith adopted strictures against conduct that was inconsistent with the bountiful sustenance of the whole.

The Law of the Torah, with its accompanying interpretation in the Talmud, cannot be described as either ancient or modern, as it is both.[32] It represents the longest continuum of international private law that exists. The domain of the Law of the Torah is, strictly speaking, the population of observing Jews. It is, though, of a piece with the same Mosaic law that is the foundation of Christianity,[33] and thus its influence has always reached and continues to reach populations and cultures greatly exceeding in number its Jewish adherents.

Israel, and its law, did not differentiate "between the secular and religious realms." Rather, all of Jewish life "was to be lived under Yahweh's command, within his covenant."[34] Included among the contributions of Hebraic law to western legal development was the recognition that man-made law must give way to God-given, moral law should the two be in conflict.[35] The Torah and its interpretations guide Jews in a very broad spectrum of individual and common pursuits. Naturally, this chapter is devoted only to such strictures as pertain to the identification of (1) civil wrongs to others; (2) the remedies for such wrongs; and (3) the sensitivity of such written or traditional law to norms of economic efficiency, and deterrence.

---

[31] ELEMENTARY FORMS *supra* note 6 at 87.

[32] Fittingly, religious law – including but not limited to the Law of the Torah – continues to this day to be a part of the weave of both customary law and of national legislation. For example, HON H. W. TAMBIAH QC, PRINCIPLES OF CEYLON LAW 111 (1972) ("Religion is a source of law through custom or legislation. Difficult questions arise as to the relations between general law and special customary law.").

[33] The gravitational interplay between Hebrew scripture and Greek philosophy is well treated in other works. For example, BERTRAND RUSSELL, A HISTORY OF WESTERN PHILOSOPHY 326–27 (1945).

[34] BERNARD W. ANDERSON, UNDERSTANDING THE OLD TESTAMENT 96 (2d ed.) (1966). *See also* DENNIS LLOYD, *supra* note 9 at 49–50 (explaining that Hebrew law, revealed law of the Almighty God and embodied in the Law of Moses and later prophets, "showed that merely man-made laws could not stand or possess any validity whatever in the face of divine laws which the rulers themselves were not competent to reveal or interpret."

[35] LLOYD, *id.* at 50.

The Torah includes the word of God as revealed in the books of Genesis, Exodus, Leviticus, Numbers, and Deuteronomy.[36] These writings, the sociolegal bedrock of Judaism, contain copious treatments, sometimes systematized, of how society ought respond to civil wrongs, and the reasons therefore. Whereas much Western law, particularly modern Western law, is phrased in prohibitory terms, Halakhic law is more apt to treat its society of believers in terms of duty, or put otherwise, "The observant Jew should..."[37]

Many of these duties are remarkably fuller and more demanding than those recognized in other systematized bodies of law. For example, within the Torah, Leviticus states that a person who stands by while another is put at risk commits a "crime of omission."[38] In the United States and the majority of other legal systems, there is no *ab initio* duty to come to another's aid; rather, such a duty arises only in particular circumstances. The approach stated in Leviticus doubtless describes the higher and more moral road. But might its rationale also resonate in some other social premium important to Jewish society? Apart from obedience to God, another central and seemingly perpetual goal of Jews has been mere survival. It requires no particular boldness to recognize that violence to the persons or the property of members of the Jewish community has always been a closely-held awareness of Jewish communities.[39]

A predicate to the advancement of the welfare, progress, and justice of a social group or a state is of course that the group survive as a human community. As the chosen people with no property of their own, it is proven that the historical Jews were set on by army after army, and it is quite certain that what behavior, from simply cruel to savage, that was not visited on them collectively was surely inflicted on them in discrete, individual and unrecorded incidents. An interpretation that the Law of God required spontaneous protection of other Jews from danger might be seen as a simple and justifiable requirement of the survival of Judaism and its believers.

The Code of the Covenant, set out at EXODUS 24: 3–8, describes rights and restrictions regarding "slaves, cattle, fields, vineyards and houses."[40] The civil code-like provisions therein are replete with strictures that provide guidance

---

[36] This corresponds to what Christians would later recognizes as the first five and similarly named Books of their First Covenant.

[37] J. DAVID BLEICH, CONTEMPORARY HALAKHIC PROBLEMS 204 n. 15, *referenced in* CONTRASTS IN AMERICAN AND JEWISH LAW 226 (Daniel Pollack, ed.) (2001).

[38] CONTRASTS, *id.* at 226 (Ch. 6, Daniel Pollack, Naphtali Harcztark, Erin McGrath, Karen R. Cavanaugh, *The Capacity of a Mentally Retarded Person to Consent: An American and a Jewish Legal Perspective*).

[39] *Compare* Ernest J. Weinrib, *The Case for a Duty to Rescue*, 90 Yale L. J. 247 (1980).

[40] ROLAND DE VAUX, ANCIENT ISRAEL 143 (1961), *from* SMITH AND WEISSTUB, *supra* note 11 at 197.

to the community regarding permissible and impermissible community conduct as it affects land, material, and economic transactions. One borrowing
another's cloak must return it by nightfall.[41] Should one's bull gore a man,
the bull is to be stoned.[42] Even an unworthy thought process that might lead
to wasteful bickering or more is enjoined in the admonition "Thou shalt not
covet thy neighbor's house, . . . nor his ass[.]"[43]

The Talmud and harmonious rabbinical writings are explicit in the condemnation of waste. The "waste of the resources of this universe [are]
prohibited because of *bal tashit*."[44] Such prohibitions include the wasting
of food or fuel, the burning of furniture, and the unnecessary killing of
animals.[45]

IV. EARLY PHILOSOPHICAL TENETS FOR IDEAL INDIVIDUAL
AND COLLECTIVE PURSUITS

A. Hellenic

For a philosophical epoch of greater significance than any other, the Hellenists
defined virtue, morality, and ethics in terms that remain the foundation
of Western philosophy. Putting aside only a few proponents of distracting
philosophic anomalies, the Greek philosophers first identified an ideal of
individual behaviors that accented study, modesty in thought and deed, and
respect of law. Second, the Hellenist thinkers envisioned a society (at that
point a city state) of harmony, accepted strata of skill and task, and, naturally
again, respect of law.

However unrealistic may have been the imagination of such a city state
as being led by a politically detached, supremely wise Philosopher-King, the
more important instruction is that the Hellenist image of a society and its
individual participants was one of social harmony, rewards in the measure
of neither more nor less than one's just deserts, and subordination to law.
Although undemocratic in many respects, and indeed slave-holding, for a
predemocratic, progressive and just ideal evaluated in recognition of its time,
the Greece of this era measures up respectably.

---

[41] EXODUS 22: 25.

[42] EXODUS 18: 28.

[43] EXODUS 20: 17.

[44] CONTRASTS, *supra* note 38 at 110 (Ch. 4, Daniel Pollack, Jonathan Reis, Ruth Sonshine,
Karen R. Cavanaugh, *Liability for Environmental Damage: An American and a Jewish Legal
Pespective*).

[45] Shabbat 67b; 129a; Chullin 7b; Sanhedrin 100b at *id.*

Hints of the political circumstances in which Stoics found themselves can be found in the graphics handed down to us from antiquity that portray the various philosophers either speaking to small groups or, from all that appears, to no one at all. There are no representations of them speaking in political groups, or advising political representatives. The reason for this seeming isolation of the philosophers from the political process is that by the time of much of the enduring work of the most influential Greek philosophers, political power in the Greek mainland had passed over to the Macedonians. This political powerlessness necessarily affected the focus of many of the philosophers from the politically tinted "How can men create a good state?" to such generally moral issues such as "individual virtue and salvation" and the attendant question "How can men be virtuous in a wicked world, or happy in a world of suffering."[46]

The end sought by Socrates was happiness. How can a philosophy grounded in the pursuit of "happiness" influence its adherents, much less any larger population, in the ways of efficient civil justice, the ostensible theme of this chapter? The answer is that to Socrates and other mainstream Hellenic thinkers, happiness could only be achieved through pursuit of the virtuous life, and both the vision and the reality of the virtuous life are suffused with themes of justice, waste avoidance, and deterrence of unjust enrichment. The entire structure of Socrates' ethics is permeated by the principle of avoidance of doing harm;[47] and (2) in parts of his lectures Socrates hypothesizes that perhaps the identifying marker of all acts of "justice" were simply "returning what was owed."[48] For the individual, justice pertained not to the "outward man" but, rather, to the "inward man." The just man "sets in order his own inner life, and is his own master and his own law, and [is] at peace with himself." For the just man, reason governs "spirit" and "desire."[49]

To Socrates, self-knowledge was the very essence of virtue. Without such self-knowledge, any man's accumulation of wealth or power would leave one "baffled[,] ... disappointed[,] ... and unable to profit ... " from any success. Rejecting the Sophists' lax attitudes toward generalizable moral or ethical standards, Socrates thought that to be effective self-knowledge must become so familiar to the adherent that it, and its attendant guidance in virtuous and ethical matters, would be worn like one's very skin.[50] To Socrates, wisdom,

---

[46] BERTRAND RUSSELL, A HISTORY OF WESTERN PHILOSOPHY 230 (1945).

[47] Id. at 164.

[48] Id. at 159–60.

[49] PLATO'S REPUBLIC, BOOK IV, in PLATO 448–49 (Buchanan, ed.) (2003) (hereinafter PLATO).

[50] NORMAN P. STALLKNECHT, ROBERT S. BRUMBAUGH, THE SPIRIT OF WESTERN PHILOSO-PHY 53, 54 (1950).

or self-knowledge, was to be found, at least in one's early years, through the teaching of wise men. And according to Socrates' account there was a broad-based societal subscription to this goal. As all men "have a mutual interest in the justice and virtue of one another," Plato records, "this is the reason why every one is so ready to teach justice and the laws[.]"[51]

To Socrates, temperance conveyed a meaning different than the modern implication of simple forbearance, be it avoidance of alcohol or any other ine-briant. Instead, temperance meant the avoidance of "folly" or acting "fool-ishly." He nevertheless wonders whether virtue was the sum of the parts "justice," "temperance," and "holiness" when he spoke in these words to Protagoras: "[W]hether virtue is one whole, of which justice and temperance and holiness are parts; or whether all these are only names of one and the same thing: that is the doubt which still lingers in my mind."[52]

Further to the question of *why* a man should choose the path of justice over injustice, Socrates termed the tension as one of "comparative advantage." He posed the issue as this: "Which is the more profitable, to be just and to act justly and practice virtue whether seen or unseen by gods and men, or to be unjust and act unjustly, if only unpunished and unreformed?"[53] Socrates hypothesized the "tyrannical" man, one in whom "the reasoning... power is asleep[,]" and asked "[H]ow does he live, in happiness or in misery?" Here Socrates imagines a man of pure impulsivity, a man capable of any "folly or crime[.]" He follows the sad and desperate path of this man, and states that his "drunken, lustful, [and] passionate" habits will require "feasts and carousals and revelings" to satisfy him. Soon such revenues as he may have are spent. In order to continue to feed his uncontrolled desires, the tyrannical man seeks to "discover whom he can defraud of his money, in order that he may gratify [his desires]."[54] If his parents do not voluntarily submit to his demands, he will try "to cheat and deceive them[,]" and if this fails, he will "use force and plunder them."[55]

The intemperate and unjust man is doomed to a spiral of ever-worsening degradation, Socrates warns. This tyrannical man, Socrates and Adeimantus conclude, is "ill governed in his own person"[56] knows no true friends, as when they have "gained their point" from another "they know them no more"; and

---

[51] PLATO, PROTAGORAS, in PLATO 69, *supra* note 50.
[52] *Id.* at 72, 75–76.
[53] PLATO'S REPUBLIC, BOOK IV, in PLATO, *supra* note 50 at 451.
[54] PLATO'S REPUBLIC, BOOK IX, *id.* at 625, 628.
[55] PLATO'S REPUBLIC, BOOK X, *id.* at 680.
[56] PLATO'S REPUBLIC, BOOK IX, *id.* at 637.

never knows "true freedom," as he is a simple instrument of his desires, and is "the most miserable" of men.[57]

Socrates' encomium of temperance in all pursuits is of course quite analogous to the recognition in later tort theory of the central role of self-restraint. Socrates characterizes as "invalids" those who "hav[e] no self-restraint, [and] will not leave of their habits of intemperance." In essence, Socrates thought temperance could be achieved by "a man being his own master," which is to say, "the ordering or controlling of certain pleasures or desires," and the avoidance of "the meaner desires."

Socrates compares evil to bodily illness. As a bodily illness can corrupt and destroy bodily health, so, too, can evil destroy a man's soul: "Does the injustice or other evil which exists in the soul waste and consume her?,"[58] and do they not "by attaching to the soul and inhering in her at last bring her to her death, and so separate her from the body?"[59]

Socrates subscribes fully to the existence of a heaven and a hell, as is illustrated by the story he tells Glaucon of Er, the son of Armenius, whose body, after he has fallen in battle, is seemingly uncorrupted by death. On the twelfth day, and prior to his burial, he awakens and tells a tale of men being summoned to justice in a mysterious place in which men's deeds are "fastened on their backs." The good and the just are led to a "meadow, where they encamped as at a festival[,]" whereas those found unjust or evil are thrown into a hell in which their punishments are tenfold the average of a man's years, or ten times one thousand in the mythical account.[60]

Plato's Socrates "argued for the identity of law *and* morality."[61] Reverence for the law followed from recognition of an implied agreement, to Dennis Lloyd, "an early form of social contract," for adhering to the law irrespective of the consequences.[62] Morality, by contrast, would never override the articulated law of the State. While morality might persuade the individual to conclude that the existing law was immoral or unjust, when the two were in conflict, the disputant's "duty" is "confined to trying to persuade the state of its moral error."[63]

In the Hellenic dialogues of Socrates, it is evident that justice entails calling into "account" the transgressor, or a pre-Aristotelian expression of corrective

---

[57] *Id.* at 631, 632.
[58] PLATO'S REPUBLIC, BOOK X, *id.* at 680.
[59] *Id.*
[60] PLATO'S REPUBLIC, BOOK X, in PLATO, *supra* note 50 at 687, 688.
[61] DENNIS LLOYD, *supra* note 9 (emphasis added).
[62] *Id.*
[63] *Id.*

justice. As the Sophist Protagoras suggests in PLATO's PROTAGORAS, the City stands in the shoes of the schoolmaster in giving to "young men" the laws to be followed. "[T]he laws," states Protagoras, "which were the invention of good lawgivers living in the olden time; these were given to the young man in order to guide him in his conduct whether he is commanding or obeying[.]" "[H]e who transgresses them[,]" Protagoras continues, "is to be corrected, or in other words, called into account."[64]

Socrates himself speaks even more forcefully of the corrective importance of the defect of misbehavior, and of the deterrent value of punishment. In Book XI of PLATO's REPUBLIC, Socrates tells Glaucon, no man "profits" from "undetected and unpunished" wrongdoing, as such a man "only gets worse[.]" To Socrates, it is better that the man be detected and punished in order that "the brutal part of his nature [be] silenced and humanized[,]" and that "the gentler element in him is liberated[.]" The man's "whole soul is perfected and ennobled by the acquirement of justice and temperance and wisdom[.]"[65] Socrates discouraged in the most direct terms individual miserliness, hoarding, and a spirit of contention and ungoverned ambition. To him, these unworthy characteristics in men were "due to the prevalence of the passionate or spirited element," uncontained by temperance and reason.[66]

To Socrates, the ideal "State" was largely an extrapolation of the ideal man. The State should, Socrates states, have "political virtues" of "wisdom, temperance, [and] courage" that could stand on a parity with Socrates' ideal for the individual.[67] For Socrates, however, identification and description of the fourth virtue, "justice," was more rarified and elusive, and Socrates comments tellingly: "The last of those qualities which make a state virtuous must be justice, if only we knew what that was."[68] A life of virtue and ethics could only be sustained in "a law abiding and orderly society."[69] Whatever such state sanctioned justice might be, Socrates commended abidance with existing law, a commitment that ultimately led to his rejection of opportunities to flee his death sentence.

Hellenist thinking cannot be reduced to the aphorism "virtue is its own reward." Rather, there were specific rewards associated with a life of virtue, as well as real or imagined disincentives to the adoption of a baser life and the collateral degrading pursuits associated therewith. Time and time again

---

[64] PLATO's REPUBLIC, BOOK IV, in PLATO, *supra* note 50 at 432.
[65] PLATO's REPUBLIC, BOOK IX, *id.* at 655.
[66] PLATO's REPUBLIC, BOOK VIII, *id.* at 592.
[67] PLATO's REPUBLIC, BOOK IV, in PLATO, *supra* note 50 at 422, 425, 430–31, 434.
[68] *Id.* at 434.
[69] *Id.* at 59.

the philosophers stated that a life of excess, be it eating, drinking, or both, incapacitated the actor from realization of the contributions available to and expected of citizens of virtue.[70] To both Plato and Socrates, the just man would be content, if not happy, and the unjust man miserable.[71] In addition, and more specifically, such excesses invited physical illness and impairment, a certain departure from God's, or a god's, charge to mankind.

For those who might be tempted to depart from a good life, Hellenic writing portrayed strong deterrents, a Sword of Damocles writ large. At an individual level, the writings repeatedly allude to the dissipating results of a life of excess, to wit, personal physical deterioration, coupled with personal and communal moral degradation. At such time as man should shed his mortal coil, Socrates and other believers in reincarnation wrote of another reason why a man should choose the path of good. Incapable of disproof and widely believed, Socrates and others propounded the belief that they had lived before in other forms, and that after their demise they would be reincarnated in some animal form.[72] If a person had led a virtuous life, he would be reincarnated in the form of an animal respected by man, such as a horse. If in his life a man had strayed from the life of virtue, his just desserts might well be reincarnation as an insect, perhaps even a dung beetle.

In Plato's version of Socrates' words, even if the definition of "justice" might be elusive, that "justice" is efficient is quite clear. Even more specifically, the lasting philosophy of this age stated that individual good and justice were, in fact, more than efficient – they were *profitable*. Socrates states just this: "On what ground, then, can we say that it is profitable for a man to be unjust or self indulgent or to do any disgraceful act which will make him a worse man, though he can gain money and power?" Happiness and profit inure to the man who, alternatively, "tame[s] the brute" within, and is "not be carried away by the vulgar notion of happiness being heeping up an unbounded store[,]" but instead follows the rule of wisdom and law encouraging "support to every member of the community, and also of the government of children[.]"[73]

---

[70] To Protagoras Socrates spoke of the physical dangers of excess, stating that "pleasure for the moment . . . lay[s] up for your future life diseases and poverty, and many other similar evils[.]" PLATO'S LYSIS, in SOCRATIC DISCOURSE BY PLATO AND XENOPHON 288 (J. Wright transl.) (A.D. Lindsay, ed.) (1925).

[71] ANTHONY GOTTLEIB, *supra* note 7 at 174.

[72] *See* discussion of the choices for their future reincarnation by a panoply of demigods by Socrates in his recitation of the story of Er. BOOK X, PLATO'S REPUBLIC, in PLATO, *supra* note 50 at 694–95.

[73] THE REPUBLIC OF PLATO 318–320 (Francis McDonald Cornford, transl.) (1969).

A principal means to the end of justice, to Plato, was education to such a level of legal sophistication that the individual would learn understanding of and respect for the legal process, including such legal process as might pertain to the redress of injury. This is revealed in Socrates' dialogue with Adeimantus in Book IV of THE REPUBLIC. Here Socrates states plainly that it is through education that the individual learns "about the business of the agora, and the ordinary dealings between man and man, or again about dealings with artisans; about insult and injury, or the commencement of actions, and the appointment of juries[.]"[74]

Returning what was owed, in effect giving up the actual or conceptual unjust enrichment associated with a wrongful taking, is of course a core model for the appropriate remediation of unconsented-to harm, a concept that is the darling of corrective justice and efficiency advocates alike. It is also part and parcel to the analysis of Aristotle, in NICHOMACHEAN ETHICS Book V, Ch. 2, in which "The Thinker" is credited with laying the cornerstone of the corrective justice principles of today's common law,[75] although as suggested the logic has equivalent bearing on economic considerations. Aristotle's understanding was that corrective justice would enable restoration to the victim of the *status quo ante major*, insofar as a monetary award or an injunction can do so.[76] Under the Aristotelian principle of *diorthotikos*, or "making straight," "at the remedy phase the court will attempt to equalize things by means of the penalty, taking away from the gain of the wrongdoer." Whether the wrongdoer's gain is monetary, or measured in property, or the community's valuation of a personal physical injury consequent to the defendant's wrongful act, by imposing a remedy approximating the actor's wrongful appropriation and "loss" to the sufferer, "the judge restores equality.... "[77]

Aristotle classified among the diverse "involuntary" transactions that would invite rectification of "clandestine" wrongs "theft, adultery, poisoning,... false witness[;]" and "violent" wrongs, including "assault,

---

[74] PLATO'S REPUBLIC, BOOK IV, *in* PLATO, *supra* note 50 at 421–422.

[75] "[T]he law . . . treats the parties as equal, and asks only if one is the author and the other the victim of injustice or if the one inflicted and the other has sustained an injury. Injustice in this sense is unfair or unequal, and the endeavor of the judge is to equalize it." ARISTOTLE, NICOMACHEAN ETHICS 154 (J. Welldon trans., 1987), discussed in David G. Owen, *The Moral Foundations of Punitive Damages*, 40 ALA. L. REV. 705, 707–08 & n.6 (1989).

[76] "Therefore the just is intermediate between a sort of gain and a sort of loss, viz, those which are involuntary; it consists in having an equal amount before and after the transaction." *Id.* at Ch. 4, p. 407.

[77] 2 THE COMPLETE WORKS OF ARISTOTLE 786 (Jonathan Barnes ed.) (1984).

imprisonment, . . . robbery with violence, . . . abuse, [and] insult."[78] He proceeds to distinguish between excusable harm and harm for which rectification may appropriately be sought. For an involuntary harm, such as when "A takes B's hand and therewith strikes C[,]" or for acts pursuant to "ignorance," a more nuanced legal response is indicated. Even for such involuntary acts as "violat[e] proportion or equality," Aristotle suggests opaquely, some should be excused, whereas others should not be excused. As to voluntary and harmful acts attributable to ignorance, Aristotle distinguishes between acts in which the ignorance is excusable and acts in which the ignorance is not.[79] The former, which we might today characterize as innocent, would not prompt remediation, whereas the latter would. Thus, Aristotle describes an act from which injury results "contrary to reasonable expectation" as a "misadventure," and forgivable at law.[80] To Aristotle, an unintentional act[81] that causes harm, but in which such harm "is not contrary to reasonable expectation[,]" constitutes not a misadventure but a "mistake." To Aristotle, "mistake" is a fault-based designation. The example used is redolent of the sensibility of what would be termed "negligence" in today's nomenclature e.g., a man throwing an object "not with intent to wound but only to prick[.]" This man, although not acting with an intent to wound another in any significant way, would nonetheless be subject to an obligation in indemnity, for to Aristotle, when "a man makes a mistake[;] . . . the fault originates in him[.]"[82]

Aristotle's famous "Golden Mean" hypothesizes that virtue analyzed linearly is the mean between two extremes. Either extreme is a vice. So, for example, if appropriate self-sustenance is a virtue, then it follows that, at one extreme, self-denial to the point of ill health is a vice. At the other extreme, gluttony is a vice. Importantly, Aristotle does not propose distributive justice, in the sense that a man may remedy his antecedent unequal position vis-a-vis another.[83] Rather, only the prospect of corrective justice is a fool that is

---

[78] ARISTOTLE, NICOMACHEAN ETHICS Bk. 5, Ch. 2 *in* INTRODUCTION TO ARISTOTLE 402 (Richard McKeon, ed.) (1947).

[79] *Id.* at Ch. 8, p. 414.

[80] *Id.* at 415.

[81] An act that "does not imply vice[.]" *Id.*

[82] *Id.*

[83] To Aristotle:

Justice (contrary to our own view) implies that members of the community possess unequal standing. That which ensures justice, whether it is with regard to the distribution of the prizes of life or the adjudication of conflicts, or the regulation of mutual services is good since it is required . . . for the continuance of the group. Normativity, then, is inseparable from actuality.

ESSAYS OF KARL POLANYI, *supra* note 12, at 83.

so confined as to provide that the only remedies available to the judge are those that work to rectify the marginal inequality that the wrongdoing has imposed.[84]

B. Roman Law

It is recognized generally that the Romans added little to the metaphysics of law. Nevertheless, Roman law represents the watershed between the law of ancient society and that of modern society. As suggested by Sir Henry Sumner Maine, the rights and the duties under law of ancient society derived from status, or "a man's position in the family," whereas under Roman law and thereafter, "rights and duties derived from bilateral arrangements."[85] Regarding delicts, or harms that were neither crimes nor grounded in contract, it became the special province of Roman lawyers and lawmakers to record and categorize a sprawling array of specific wrongs and consequent remedies. This approach of Roman law would become the origin of code-based law that governs European lawmaking to this day.

Cicero, the Roman orator, wrote of the truth of an ethic that sounded simultaneously in terms of corrective justice and efficiency-deterrence. In ON MORAL DUTIES he wrote that even after "retribution and punishment" have been dealt to the transgressor, the person who has been dealt the wrong owes a duty to bring a close to any such misadventure by permitting a gesture such as repentance or apology. From the extension to the wrongdoer of the opportunity to apologize or to repent could be reaped the immediate good of reducing the likelihood that he would "repea[t] the offense," as well as the broader and eventual good of "deter[ing] others from injustice."[86]

Cicero further propounded a cluster of maxims that if followed could conduce to Pareto Superior changes, in the sense that the actor would be no worse off and the affected party or parties would be better off. As to persons beyond a benefactor's core family or kinship group, to Cicero there existed a duty to the entire world as to such things "we receive with profit and give without loss." Thus, in order that we may receive such blessings as are identified in the maxims such as "Keep no one from a running stream[;]" or "Let anyone who pleases take a light from your fire[;]" or "Give honest advice

---

[84] NICOMACHEAN ETHICS, *supra* note 79, Ch. 3 at 403: "[A]wards should be made "according to merit"; for all men agree that what is just in distribution must be according to merit in some sense, though they do not all specify the same sort of merit[.]"

[85] ESSAYS OF POLANYI, *supra* note 12 at 82–83.

[86] ON MORAL DUTIES 16, *in* BASIC WORKS OF CICERO 16 (Moses Hadas, ed.) (1951).

to a man in doubt[;]" Cicero writes, it follows that we must be willing to give likewise of the same in order to "contribute to the common weal."[87]

Two of the delicts of greatest importance were damage to property, real and personal, and personal physical harm to others, giving rise to the *action injuriarum*. The victim could bring an action for "profitable amends," or money damages, or "honorable amends," which is to say, a formal and public apology. The latter remedy would most likely arise in a setting of a dignitary tort, such as defamation. Roman jurists and the Roman legal community were committed to the identification of the delineation between what is "just and what unjust," and therefore the Institutes of Justinian and other sources of Roman law reflected an endeavor to "give each man his due right," and comprise "precepts" to all Romans "to live justly, not to injure another and to render to each his own."[88]

The Institutes included rules that reveal numerous strictures against the imposition of one's will over the rights of a neighbor, and strong deterrents for the disregard thereof. Specifically as to urban estates, in Book III, Title II Para. 2 there was a prohibition on the obstruction of a neighbor's view,[89] a rule bearing a resemblance to one recognized today that limits a neighbor's liberty to interfere with "ancient lights." In another notable example, pertaining to what would today be called the law of private nuisance or trespass, a provision of Roman law goes so far as to detail a preference that adjoining landowners bargain in advance for agreement as to contemporaneous uses of land that might trigger dispute. In Book III Para. 4, the Institutes provide that one "wishing to create" such a right of usage "should do so by pacts and stipulations." A testator of land may impose such agreements reached on his heirs, including limitations on building height, obstruction of light, or introduction of a beam into a common wall, or the construction of a catch for a cistern, an easement of passage, or a right of way to water.[90] These last two examples reflect a clear preference for *ex ante* bargaining over economically wasteful *ex post* dispute resolution. The provision permitting the testator to bind his heirs to any such agreement is additionally efficient in a manner akin to the approach that was taken later and famously by Justice Bergen in the cement plant nuisance case of *Boomer v. Atlantic Cement Co., Inc.*,[91] in

---

[87] *Id.* at 23.

[88] THE INSTITUTES OF JUSTINIAN BOOK I, Preamble; para. 1; para. 3, in THE INSTITUTES OF JUSTINIAN 84, 85 (J. A. C. Thomas trans) (1975).

[89] THE DIGEST (or PANDECTS) BOOK III TITLE II para. 2., para. 3 *supra* note 89, at *id.*

[90] THE INSTITUTES OF JUSTINIAN BOOK III para. 4, *supra* note 89 at 84, 85.

[91] 257 N.E.2d 870 (N.Y. 1970).

which the court's award of damages ensured that its disposition of the matter would be indeed a one-time resolution of the dispute by requiring that the disposition of the claim be entered and recorded as a permanent servitude on the land.

V. MODERN ASSIGNMENT OF ECONOMIC NORMS

A. Customary Law

The organized law of the modern state is a fairly recent phenomenon when compared to the existence of effective and nuanced customary law around which premodern societies organized. For both ancient and modern societies, and irrespective of whether that society developed a written law, written or unwritten law is affected by "underlying social norms which determine much of its functioning." This customary law has been described as "living law."[92]

In the historical development of tort law, customary law has regularly followed social norms in giving form, context and content to sociolegal principles.[93] That such law must for the most part conform to societal custom was urged by writers as early as Thomas Aquinas. At such later time as a culture or a nation-state has begun to render its law in the form of written adjudicatory rulings, or legal codes, customary law characteristically diminishes in its significance as an engine for resolution of disputes. For example, in England during the period of the conquest of Scotland, approximately 1290–1305, there arose a "lawyer class" that was a moving force in "hardening customary [law] into legal rights[.]" With notable French influence, the theories of Roman law became ascendant,[94] and the recitation of and reliance upon customary norms receded proportionately. And yet it will be seen that in many cultures customary law continued to, it does today, inform legal development. In some settings, customary law sets parameters for later legal development, or even precludes later law that would contradict earlier custom.

The influence of Roman law on the development of European, Latin American, and Anglo-American law is commonly acknowledged. A concise tour of the lasting effects of customary law, Roman law, and its hybrid, Roman-Dutch law, on a particular national community – Ceylon – well illustrates the systemic commitment to wealth maximization, avoidance of waste, and deterrence of behaviors inconsistent therewith.

---

[92] DENNIS LLOYD, *supra* note 9 at 227 (citation omitted).
[93] *Id.* (discussion of the sources and growth of custom).
[94] J. R. GREEN, A SHORT HISTORY OF THE ENGLISH PEOPLE 204 (1878).

For Celanese customary law to be considered valid for the purposes of modern adjudication, it must be (1) reasonable; (2) consistent with common law; (3) universal in application; and (4) grounded in antiquity.[95] Although the first and second standards might at first glance seem to subordinate customary law into insignificance, an additional look makes this approach appear more sensible. This is so because (1) as with common-law adjudication, as no court is required to apply common law that is unreasonable, it would be illogical to require application of customary law that was not reasonable; and (2) as both common law and customary law claim lineage in a society's reasoned conclusions as to legal standards best suited to societal well-being, customary law that was at war with common law on the same or similar subject would be presumptively defective in either its rationality or in its claimed representational authenticity.

In some legal systems, legal scholars remain oracles of greater or lesser significance. This was true of the Roman-Dutch tradition, in which schools of legal scholarship, or the scholars themselves were influential. There existed two schools of writers: (1) Grotius, van Leeuwen and Voet, who emphasized the Roman law antecedents of the developing hybrid law; and (2) an "historical school" that emphasized custom as the appropriate principal source of the law."[96] Although the Napoleonic Code superseded the Roman-Dutch law in Holland itself in the early nineteenth century, the great Dutch East and West Indian Trading Companies carried Roman-Dutch law into their settlements. So strong was the influence of custom in the Roman-Dutch tradition that in principle at least, a statute could be rendered nugatory or obsolete by sufficient proof of a conflicting custom.[97]

Under the so-called *Lex Aquilia* of Roman-Dutch law, the Aquilian action required the claimant's showing of a wrongful act, patrimonial loss, and the defendant's fault, because of either the intentional nature of the act or negligence. Borrowing from British law applicable to nonintentional injuries, the law courts of Ceylon adopted the British concept that the plaintiff's claim in negligence must include proof that the defendant owed to plaintiff a duty.[98]

---

[95] H. W. Tambiah, Principles of Ceylon Law 87–89 (1972). *See generally*, T. Nadaraja, The Legal System of Ceylon in its Historical Setting (1972).

[96] H. W. Tambiah, *at id*; J. R. Green, *supra* note 95 at 148. The opinions most often referenced could be found in Johannes Voet, Commendtarius Ad Pandectas (1698, 1704); Hugo Grotius, Inleiding tot de Hallanesche Rechtsgeleertheyd (2d ed.) (R. W. Lee ed.) (1953); and Simon Van Leeuwen's Commentaries on Roman-Dutch Law (J. G. Kotze trans.) (1886).

[97] *Id.*

[98] *Id.* at 399.

In Aquilian actions, no compensation would be awarded in the absence of physical injury, with physical injury classically defined as excluding emotional distress or dignitary harm.

Regarding redressable injuries caused by the positive act of the defendant, should a person be in possession of a thing, including a chattel or an instrumentality, that had the potential for causing harm if not stewarded with care, the actor, owner, or manager would have a positive duty to exercise such care. Should another be injured because of the failure to take such care, liability could be imposed. Even a mere omission to act might be a stimulus to liability if the actor's omission was "connected with some prior positive act." Accordingly, a remedy might be available under the *Lex Aquilia* if the defendant had earlier "created a potentially dangerous state of things," and the failure to correct that caused the claimant's harm.

Various dimensions in the Roman-Dutch tradition recognized the society's commitment to the integrity of persons and property from forced takings. Assault was an *injuria*, and therefore redressable, on a showing of *contumelia*. For grazing animals that damaged another's property, if the animal's transgression involved the "animal acting contrary to nature of its class," the owner might be required to pay damages, or even be confronted with the potentially stronger deterrent of giving up the animal. Surely, too, a strong message of deterrence is found in the rule that a person finding another's animals on that person's property could impound them.[99]

For "intentional" wrongs, the intentional torts of today, the requisite intent, or *dolus*, was provided by the defendant's desire to accomplish the act, irrespective of whether he was aware that the act constituted an invasion of the plaintiff's rights. "*Culpa*" was interpreted as a "violation of a duty that [is] imposed by law[,]"[100] an approach revealing the influence of the British common law requirement that the tort plaintiff prove duty. The respondent could avoid liability by showing that the injury could not have been avoided even by the exercise of reasonable care. Furthermore, in order to avoid unjust enrichment, persons could not recover for claims arising from acts or activities to which they consented voluntarily.

---

[99] *Id.* at 392–95, 399, 418, 420. For damage caused by trespassing dogs, the claimant would be required to show scienter.

[100] Within this approach there could be seen a strong overlay of moral blameworthiness: "It is doubtful whether Roman and Roman-Dutch writers regarded negligence objectively or subjectively, but partly under the influence of canon law, and its offspring natural law, the modern systems based on Roman law took *culpa* to imply moral blameworthiness." *Id.* at 397.

For intentional torts such as false imprisonment, the third requirement of the *Lex Aquila*, that of foreseeability, would be satisfied by a showing that the defendant intended the act. Then, as it is today, a reflection of the rigorous economic guardianship of customary law, Roman law, and Dutch law attached primacy to protection of property and economic rights, and imposed an almost automatic requirement of disgorgement of any unjust enrichment associated with the wrongful interference therewith. Trespass, or the willful and forcible entry into another's property, constituted *injuria*. As has been true for any successful socio-economic unit, the Roman-Dutch tradition recognized the rights of a person to protect his property from any form of unjust interference.[101]

At the same time, it was recognized that a landlord owed a duty to his tenants to take reasonable steps to protect them from injury caused by unsafe conditions on the land.[102] In what could be loosely styled as a public nuisance proscription, the Roman-Dutch customary law removed earlier Praetorian edicts prohibiting certain animals from sharing public places, and put in place of such strict prohibitions rules requiring the payment of damages.[103] Private nuisance, in turn, was seemingly remediable in an action for damages or for equitable relief.[104]

Roman-Dutch customary law includes at least one example of the law and its official apparatus not being required to stand idly by to await the social costs of an accident that will occur or that will continue to occur in circumstances in which the parties had not reached a prior agreement as to risks and rewards. Should a neighbor come to fear that a dangerous condition existed in his neighbor's house that, left unabated, might cause damage to the property of the complainant, the complainant could bring an action demanding the neighbor's payment of security against such prospective and potential harm.[105]

B. Modern United States Assignment of Efficiency-Based Norms

The analysis of tort law has long emphasized its original and lasting tenets in the logic of corrective justice and morality. Another model, more recent but

---

[101] *Id.* at 142, 397, 399, 418.
[102] *Id.* at 399.
[103] *Id.* at 422.
[104] *Id.* at 396.
[105] *Id.* at 422.

already essential to legal analysis, is that of economic efficiency. Economists, political scientists and legal scholars resort with increasing frequency and interest to the examination of economic truths within the function of injury law. This examination has included evaluation of evolving decisional law against the measure of whether such decisions adhere, explicitly or silently, to goals of economic efficiency.

Chronologically, the Anglo-American development of the doctrine of liability for negligent acts causing harm to others or to their property followed a lengthy legal devotion to liability without fault, or strict liability.[106] Some scholars associated the perfection of fault-based liability, or negligence, with the Industrial Revolution in England.[107] However, observers seem not to have established satisfactorily whether the availability of negligence liability was a gesture of socio-legal benevolence to persons and chattels or quite the contrary: a legal prophylaxis that reduced the potential liability of businesses by requiring the putative plaintiff to prove not only injury and causation but also that the actor had proceeded with an absence of due care under the circumstances.[108]

It is established that (1) tort law is devoted to the protection of persons and property from unreasonable risk of harm; and (2) the actor's liability in tort is limited by concepts of reasonable forseeability. Putting aside the cabined domain of truly strict liability, modern accident law is concerned primarily with the provision of reparations to persons suffering personal injury or property loss because of fault, with fault conventionally defined as a failure of others to act with due care under the circumstances.

Numerous analysts have identified a common-law tropism towards efficiency.[109] Importantly, scholars have also concluded that efficient rules of law actually predict efficient litigation strategies, including settlement

---

[106] See generally DAN B. DOBBS, THE LAW OF TORTS 259–63 (2000).

[107] The development of negligence law "was probably stimulated a good deal by the enormous increase of industrial machinery and by the invention of railways in particular." PERCY H. WINFIELD, THE PROVINCE OF THE LAW OF TORTS 404 (5th ed. 1950).

[108] Compare WINFIELD, id. ("At that time railway trains were notable for neither speed nor for safety. They killed any object from a Minister of State to a wandering cow, and this naturally reacted upon the law.") with Robert J. Kazorowski, The Common-Law Basis of Nineteenth-Century Tort Law, 51 OHIO S. L. J. 1 (1990) (referencing scholarly proponents of theory that negligence liability arose in a court-stimulated effort to moderate the liability of businesses and to permit devotion of industrial capital to production rather than to satisfaction of legal liability).

[109] For example, George L. Priest, The Common Law Process and the Selection of Efficient Rules, 6 J. LEG. STUD. 65 (1977); Ramona L. Paetzold & Steven L. Willborn, The Efficiency of the Common Law Reconsidered, 14 GEO. MASON. L. REV. 157 (1991).

strategies.[110] Wes Parsons, even while disputing these premises, collected scholarship revealing in fact the broad range of cost internalization achievements of evolving common-law doctrine.[111] Included in Parson's review was scholarly attribution to the common law of accidents as "promot[ing] efficient resource allocation";[112] the efficiencies of the common law of rescue, salvage and Good Samaritan assistance;[113] and the efficiency of the economic loss rule in tort.[114]

A leading exponent of the efficiency role of the common law of tort has been Dean, and now Judge, Guido Calabresi. Calabresi has argue persuasively that in matters of compensation for accidents, civil liability should ordinarily be laid at the door of the "cheapest cost avoider," the actor who could most easily discover and inexpensively remediate the hazard. Together with A. Douglas Melamed, Calabresi has written that considerations of economic efficiency dictate placing the cost of accidents "on the party or activity which can most cheaply avoid them [.]"[115]

Ordinary economic rationales also have described the role of compensatory damages as an effective means of discouraging a potential torfeasor from bypassing the market, and by their substandard or risk-creating conduct injuring an unconsenting third party. Such conduct is wasteful, it is both posited and can be proved, in terms of identifiable accident costs. Better, theoretically at least, to pressure the actor into bargaining with any willing and knowing other for the right to expose him or her to risk.[116]

A lucid adoption of Calabresi and Melamed's approach is found in the Ninth Circuit decision of *Union Oil Co. v. Oppen*,[117] a California coastal oil spill case in which the court allowed commercial fishermen to recover from the defendant their business losses caused by lost fishing opportunity during a period of pollution. Noting some difficulties in applying the "best or cheapest cost avoider" approach in concrete circumstances, the court followed

[110] As stated by Ramona L. Paetzold and Steven L. Willborn, "[w]here both parties to a dispute have a continuing interest in precedent, the parties will settle if the existing precedent is efficient, but litigate if the precedent is inefficient." Paetzold & Willborn, *id.*

[111] Wes Parsons, Note, *The Inefficient Common Law*, 92 YALE L. J. 862 (1983).

[112] William M. Landes & Richard A. Posner, *The Positive Economic Theory of Tort Law*, 15 GA. L. REV. 851, 852 (1981).

[113] William A. Landes & Richard A. Posner, *Savors, Finders, Good Samaritans and Other Rescuers: An Economic Study of Law and Altruism*, 7 J. LEG. STUD. 83, 128 (1977).

[114] William Bishop, *Economic Loss in Tort*, 2 OXFORD J. LEG. STUD. 1, 2–3 (1982).

[115] Guido Calabresi & A. Douglas Melamed, *Property Rules, Liability Rules, and Inalienability*, 85 HARV. L. REV. 1089, 1096–97 (1972). *See also* MARK C. RUDERT, COVERING ACCIDENT COSTS: INSURANCE, LIABILITY AND TORT 29, 32–33 (1995).

[116] Today, one cannot help but think of the newest "trash" TV shows and derivitives thereof.

[117] 501 F.2d 558 (9th Cir. 1974).

Calabresi and Melamed's requirement that it "exclude as potential cost avoiders those group activities which could avoid accident costs only at extremely high expense."[118] This approach, to the mind of the appeals court, militated against the conclusion that the cost of preventing or repositioning the loss should be borne directly by consumers (fishermen or seafood purchasers) in the form of precautionary measures (whatever they might hypothetically be), or by first party insurance. Rather, the court found, justice and efficiency were served by placing responsibility for the loss on the "best cost avoider," in this setting the defendant oil company. The court explained its reasoning:

> [T]he loss should be borne by the party who can best correct any error in allocation, if such there be, by acquiring the activity to which the party has been made liable. The capacity to "buy out" the plaintiffs if the burden is too great is, in essence, the real focus of Calabresi's approach. On this basis, there is no contest – the defendant's capacity is superior.[119]

Referencing a 1991 American Law Institute Reporters' Study, Steven D. Sugarman noted tartly "one of the last places to find lucid thinking about the desirable direction of tort law is in the published opinions of state and federal judges."[120] Although his complaint surely represents hyperbole for effect, Sugarman is correct in observing that discussion of tort principles in the decisional law is frequently colloquial, with courts often doing no more than lumping together as coextensive such objectives as expeditious claims resolution, reduced transaction costs, and efficiency. In congressional endeavors to normalize diverse segments of tort law, too, the discussion and fact-finding, in turn, frequently have been more polemic than informative.

Explicit judicial adoption of the tenets of either corrective justice or law and economics has been sporadic, and even when mentioned in decisions, either the expression or the application of the two theories is often inexact. Nevertheless, some courts have consciously elevated their jurisdiction's awareness of economic concepts in fashioning tort law. Illustrative is the Third Circuit's decision in *Whitehead v. St. Joe Lead Co.*,[121] a lead poisoning case in which the defendants included the suppliers of lead to plaintiff's industrial employer. Reversing summary judgment for defendants, the court observed:

> [I]t may well be that suppliers, acting individually or through their trade associations, are the most efficient cost avoiders. Certainly it could be found to be

---

[118] *Id.* at 569.
[119] *Id.* at 569–570.
[120] Stephen D. Sugarman, *A Restatement of Torts*, 44 STAN. L. REV. 1163, 1165 (1992) (review essay).
[121] 729 F.2d 238 (3d Cir. 1984).

inefficient for many thousands of lead processors to individually duplicate the industrial hygiene research, design, and printing costs of a smaller number of lead suppliers.

To like effect is the decision of the Wyoming Supreme Court in *Schneider National, Inc. v. Holland Hitch Co.*[122] There the court explicitly relied upon Richard Posner's "alternative care joint tortfeasor" evaluation to reach the conclusion that indemnity should not be available "where both actors have a 'joint care' obligation to avoid the injury." The court noted, however, that when the actors' culpability varied, that is, they were not *in pari delicto*, the higher relative fault of one defendant, the "lower cost avoider," would vest indemnity rights in the other tortfeasor.[123]

In the insurance declaratory judgment context, the dissenting opinion in *Insurance Co. of North America v. Forty-Eight Insulations, Inc.*,[124] proposed a "discoverability" rule for triggering insurance carrier coverage of asbestos claims, asserting that this approach would, relying on a least cost avoider rationale, provide incentives within the insured-insurer relationship that could hold the promise of reducing accident costs. Specifically, the dissent reasoned that:

> The more "early" insurers that are liable upon a victim's exposure, the more likely it is that the potential harm will be discovered and the public warned. If an insurer sees that the product poses some risks, he may raise premiums accordingly. This may ultimately cause the manufacturer to remove the product from the market or to give better warnings in order to lower insurance premiums. This in turn reduces accident costs.

Whichever gloss is placed on economic analysis – its deterrent effect, or its ability to reduce accident costs – its concepts can be understood "even at the rudimentary level of jurists," at least according to Judge Patrick

---

[122] 843 P.2d 561 (Wyo. 1992).

[123] *Id.* at 575. *See also Ogle v. Caterpillar Tractor Co.*, 716 P.2d 334, 342 (Wyo. 1986). There the court stated:

> When a defective article enters the stream of commerce and an innocent person is hurt, it is better that the loss fall on the manufacturer, distributor or seller than on the innocent victim.... They are simply in the best position to either insure against the loss or spread the loss among all consumers of the product.

Ogle was later described by the Wyoming Supreme Court as an indication of how strict liability "introduced economic analysis to tort law." *Schneider Nat'l, supra* note 123 at 580. The *Schneider Nat'l* court proceeded to analogize *Ogle's* "risk allocation" theory to a "cheapest cost avoider" approach. *Id. See also Wilson v. Good Humor Corp.*, 757 F.2d 1293, 1306 n.13 (D.C. Cir. 1985) (identifying but not pursuing cheapest cost avoider analysis in action brought by parents of child fatally injured while crossing street to meet ice cream vending truck).

[124] 633 F.2d 1212 (6th Cir. 1980).

Higgenbotham. In *Louisiana ex rel. Guste v. M. V. Testbank*,[125] the renowned vessel collision case involving claims for economic loss not accompanied by physical damage to a proprietary interest, the Fifth Circuit Court of Appeals justified its refusal to permit such recovery and continued its adherence to the economic loss doctrine of *Robins Dry Dock & Repair Co. v. Flint*.[126] The court relied on reasoning that permitting liability for the "unknowable" amounts that might be posed as economic loss claims arising from any substantial mishap would erode the efficient deterrent effect of such a tort rule, as a rational, wealth-maximizing actor would be unable to gauge the optimal pre-cautionary measures for avoidance of a predictable accident cost. In Judge Higgenbotham's words:

> That the [economic loss] rule is identifiable and will predict outcomes in advance of the ultimate decision about recovery enables it to play additional roles. Here we agree with plaintiffs that economic analysis, even at the rudimentary level of jurists, is helpful both in the identification of such roles and the essaying of how the roles play. Thus it is suggested that placing all the consequence of its error on the maritime industry will enhance its incentive for safety. While correct, as far as such analysis goes, such *in terrorem* benefits have an optimal level. Presumably, when the cost of an unsafe condition exceeds its utility there is an incentive to change. As the costs of an accident become increasing multiples of its utility, however, there is a point at which greater accident costs lose meaning, and the incentive curve flattens. When the accident costs are added in large but unknowable amounts the value of the exercise is diminished.[127]

Even without explicit recognition of economic, utilitarian, or corrective justice concerns, other influential decisions have adopted and promoted such precepts, sometimes distending these established tort principles into ungainly hybrids. In the setting of environmental harm, notions of corrective justice and utilitarianism (or efficiency and equity[128]) have coexisted uneasily for decades. Originally, even the most economically powerless landholder could seek and secure an injunction against a neighboring activity that interfered substantially with the plaintiff's use of property. Numerous early decisions evidenced a judicial unwillingness to "balance" injuries, that is, to weigh the defendant's cost and the community hardship in losing the industry against the often modest provable harm to plaintiff's ordinarily small and noncommercial property. As the New York Court of Appeals stated in *Whalen v.*

---

[125] 752 F.2d 109 (5th Cir. 1985).
[126] 275 U.S. 303 (1927).
[127] *Testbank*, 752 F.2d at 1029.
[128] *See* A. MITCHELL POLINSKY, AN INTRODUCTION TO LAW AND ECONOMICS Chap. 3 (1989).

Union Bag & Paper Co.,[129] to fail to grant the small landowner an injunction solely because the loss to him, in absolute terms, was less than would be the investment-backed loss to the nuisance-creating business and lost employment within the community, would "deprive the poor litigant of his little property by giving it to those already rich."

In contrast, the modern rule governing injunctions, including environmental injunctions, might seem coldly utilitarian. The Restatement (Second) of Torts § 936 lists factors for injunction issuance, which expressly include weighing of "the nature of the interest to be protected," thus presumably inviting an elevation of plaintiff's bona fides in cases in which the court considers the activity meritorious (perhaps a Camp Fire Girls campground) and a devaluation in which the court deems it less valuable (perhaps an automobile scrapyard). Along similar lines, hardship to the defendant of ceasing or changing its activity, and "the interests of third persons and of the public" are proper considerations.[130] The reference to third persons and the public represent a clear invitation to introduce concepts of social costs into environmental damage litigation.

Representative of such an approach is the result reached in *Boomer v. Atlantic Cement Co.*,[131] a litigation that involved a large-scale industrial nuisance in the form of airborne cement dust emanating from an upstate New York cement plant. In the lower court, a nuisance was found, and temporary damages awarded, but plaintiffs' application for an injunction was denied. Recognizing that to deny the injunction would depart from *Whalen*'s corrective justice–no balancing approach discussed earlier, the court nevertheless adopted a utilitarian approach that weighed the hardships imposed on plaintiffs against the economic consequences of the requested injunction. In what might be described as a split decision, the court denied the injunction and awarded permanent, one-time damages that would be recorded as a continuing servitude on the land. The court explained: "The ground for denial of injunction, notwithstanding the finding both that there is a nuisance and that plaintiffs have been damaged substantially, is the large disparity in economic consequences of the nuisance and of the injunction."

Boomer permits examination of modern nuisance law in terms of a cost-benefit or utilitarian rationale, and the decision stands as a vindication of what the New York court concluded were the overall best economic interests of the community. However, other important elements to an economic

---

[129] 101 N.E.2d 870 (N.Y. 1913).
[130] RESTATEMENT (SECOND) OF TORTS § 936(1)(e)–(g).
[131] 257 N.E.2d 870 (N.Y. 1970).

analysis of nuisance law are at play, to wit, the elements of social cost. In the introductory paragraph to *The Problem of Social Cost*,[132] Ronald H. Coase illustrates the operation of social cost analysis by employing the example of a factory emitting demonstrably harmful pollutants – in this sense an important distinction with *Boomer*. Coase suggests that application of pure economic principles might prompt economists to conclude that it might be desirable to have the factory pay damages, proportionate or otherwise, or even to shut down. Such results, he proposes, may be "inappropriate, in that they lead to results which are not necessarily, or even usually, desirable."[133]

In a pollution scenario, the most efficient course of conduct will be where the polluter and the complainant reach an *ex ante* agreement regarding the level of harm the complainant is willing to sustain in return for the payment of money. This result, reached through cooperation and which avoids litigation, offers the lowest possible transaction costs, and the optimal, or most efficient resolution. It is received wisdom that any tort rule associated with a redressable phenomenon, in this case nuisance, to be efficient, should encourage a resolution that keeps the matter out of litigation. Thus, the question arises: What is the tort rule in nuisance that elevates to the highest like-lihood the parties' disposition of the dilemma by negotiation, rather than by litigation?

A. Mitchell Polinsky advances Coase's analysis in its nuisance law context.[134] He first employs the methodology of Calabresi and Melamed in which the authors identify two steps in conceptualizing a nuisance claim: first, an *entitlement* must be established; and, second, a conclusion must be reached as to how to vindicate that entitlement.[135] One approach, Polinsky writes, is that of the injunction. Injunctive relief was rejected in its pure form in *Boomer*, as the court permitted the low-level polluter to continue to cause damage, and to "buy off" the property owners holding the entitlement. Using the example of one polluter and one resident, Polinsky describes the pollution in units, the factory's profits, and the resident's damages. For one unit of pollution, the factory's profits are $10,000, and the resident's damages $1,000. If the factory pays $1,000 in damages, its net profit is $9,000. If the factory doubles its pro-duction, and it pollution, to two units, Polinsky assigns a net additional profit to the factory of $4,000. Yet, at the same time the resident's damages actually

---

[132] Ronald H. Coase, *The Problem of Social Cost*, 3 J. L. & Econ. 1 (1960), *reprinted in* Founda-tions of Tort Law 3 *et seq.*, (Saul Levmore, ed.) (1994).

[133] *Id.*

[134] Polinsky, *supra* note 129 at 11, 15.

[135] *See* Guido Calabresi & A. Douglas Melamed, *Property Rules, Liability Rules, and Inalienability: One View of the Cathedral*, 85 Harv. L. Rev. 1089 (1972); Polinsky, *supra* note 129 at 15.

may not rise arithmetically, but rather in multiples, to, say, $15,000. Two conclusions are evident. First, under a "payment of damages–avoid an injunction" approach the factory is best served by maintaining and not increasing either its level of pollution or its level of production. Second, the *Boomer* requirement that the factory pay one-time damages in order to secure the right to continue its operation at current levels is the efficient solution.

Key to the efficient operation of a nuisance remedy is the assignment of nuisance damages that equal the complainant's actual loss. An impediment to this goal may arise when one or both parties engage in "strategic" behavior in which either the polluter or the complainant adopts a litigation or settlement strategy that is inconsistent with the optimal payment of actual loss, that is, the polluter seeks to pay less than the proved damages, or the complainant seeks to recover more than his actual damages.

Moreover, a tort rule that did *not* limit the complainant to one-time damages, and preclude future recovery by subsequent owners, would be inefficient. Subjecting the polluter to serial recoveries into the indefinite future would constitute overdeterrence on the model of *Boomer*. Indeterminate liability would potentially fail to cap Atlantic Cement's potential financial responsibility at a level that would permit it to continue to conduct business, and would thereby be inconsistent with the rule expressed in Restatement (Second) of Torts § 826(b), which permits the finding of nuisance even when the utility of the actor's conduct outweighs the damage suffered by the complainant, so long as the damages are not set at a level that would prevent the defendant from continuation of its business. Additionally, an absence of the "one-time damages" provision of *Boomer* would unjustly enrich the property owners, as they would recover first from Atlantic Cement, and then recover again by the sale of overvalued property, which is to say, property priced at a level that failed to take into account the chronic low-level future pollution.

VI. CONCLUSION

An optimal tort rule – and coincidentally one that is both just and moral – is efficient. It advises those behaving under its regimen of what is expected, of what is discouraged, and of the consequences of departure from the desirable. It does not compensate excessively but, rather, in proportion to the harm. Neither does it undercompensate, as only through justifiable compensation is the rule's deterrent value most effective. It stands in the stead of *ex ante* agreements as to condoned or expected behavior in situations where contract would be impossible. As Jules Coleman put it: "The rules of tort liability allocate risk, but they do not do so on the model of private contract. Tort law is not simply a necessary response to the impossibility of contract, but a genuine alternative to contract as a device for allocating risk."[136] And, at the same time, and by the same means as tort law discourages extracontractual elevation of risk, tort rules encourage safer behavior.

Tort law has always been apiece with human optimism, and confidence in the capacity of man to improve himself and by so doing, improve society. No other legal, ethical, or moral schema has so consistently hewn to the magisterial human experiment of moderation, fairness, efficiency, equality, and justice in social groupings. Any recitation of the path of tort law identifies objectives consonant with those described in a contemporary self-identification of a major liberal philanthropy, the pursuit of "a just, equitable, and sustainable society."

This history of tort law is the history of the tension between self-aggrandizement and self-abnegation.[137] In this chapter are found multiple examples, from disparate groups, of both prophylaxes against and responses to wrongful infliction of harm to individuals or to the social collective. In historical contexts, such groupings, and such examples, have ranged from the Babylonian response to the flooding of another's land; to Socrates' and Aristotle's injunctions against unconsented-to taking; to Roman development of the law of nuisance; to Talmudic rules regarding waste. With conspicuous reference to the law of nuisance, modern U.S. decisional law demonstrates the continued fidelity to the goal of mediating between these two extremes.

Moreover, the inexorable and permeating nature of these precepts of economic efficiency, avoidance of waste, and cultivation of circumstances in when persons may preserve and protect their physical autonomy and their property, is by now evident in almost all cultures. These goals have been effected by rules reflecting societal expectations of personal liberty as leavened by personal responsibility. And as is seen, such rules, be they norms or written strictures, have been in greater or lesser harmony. This direction of tort law has been and will continue to be its elevation in comprehensiveness, its shedding of error, and its ongoing self-instruction guiding, it to what is denominated sometimes as a "right fit" in its time and culture. This ageless improvement of tort law over time would be predicted by Socrates, in his constant references to the imperative of man's path of enhancing the life of

---

[136] JULES L. COLEMAN, RISKS AND WRONGS 203 (1992).

[137] As to the former, see BERTRAND RUSSELL, A HISTORY OF WESTERN PHILOSOPHY 624 (1945), in which is found a 1656 quotation attributed to one Joseph Lee, and which is representative of a *laissez-faire* social construct: "It is an undeniable maxim that every one by the light of nature and reason will do that which makes for him his greatest advantage.... The advancement of private persons will be the advantage of the public."

the individual and the polity through education, even if simply experiential, self-knowledge, and the inevitable influence of these attributes to the task of political or judicial development of tort law.

To Immanuel Kant, only a norm respecting personal physical integrity and nonwasteful behaviors would be suited to a rule that if applied to all mankind would bring evenhanded good. Tort law's supple receptivity to change in response to ever-perfectible societal norms is fully harmonious with the norm Kant identified as "acting from duty," as distinct from "acting according to duty." The concept of acting *from* duty is captured in the example of the merchant conducting an honest business because of his "purely moral interest in obeying the [duty] of objectively correct behavior[,]" irrespective of what the state may or may not ordain.[138] It is noteworthy that philosophers reaching back to the Greeks proposed similarly that an individual achieved "good" when leading a life in harmony with nature, and that "virtue" was demonstrated by a man's "will" that was "in agreement with nature."[139] Indeed, Bertrand Russell noted the striking comparisons between the philosophical structures of Kant and those of the Stoics.[140]

If it is true that the development of efficient norms and laws for the treatment of civil wrongs characterizes human development to this date, does this alone demonstrate that employment of such methods will continue, through trial and error, into the future? Of course, such a historical showing, available in this chapter only in selected sketches, does not so prove, in the same way that coincidence does not demonstrate causation. The evidence here falls far short of a philosophical proof that admits of no contrary conclusion. Yet, there exists a strong basis for a prediction that tort law's development along these lines will, in fact, continue.

Historians attending to broader topics have reached agreement that the path of history is one of steady improvement. The so-called "law of progress," affecting all disciplines from biology to history, is discussed by the influential R. G. Collingswood,[141] who proposes further that progress in history means simply that man builds his knowledge on the incidents of his history and that of others. Man does not and will not know that he participates in this progress, nor is any assumption of this progress predicated on the identification of

---

[138] Paul Dietrichson, *What Does Kant Mean by Acting From Duty*, in KANT: A COLLECTION OF CRITICAL ESSAYS 317 (Robert Paul Wolff, ed., 1967).

[139] BERTRAND RUSSELL, A HISTORY OF WESTERN PHILOSPHY 254 (1945), referencing, among others, Seneca and Democritus.

[140] *Id.* at 268.

[141] R. G. COLLINGSWOOD, THE IDEA OF HISTORY 322–323 (Jan Van Der Dussen ed.) (Rev. ed. 1992).

man as a "child of nature," thus binding the prediction of societal progress to the laws of evolution.[142] Importantly, progress does not necessarily mean improvement, as the former can be gauged objectively, whereas the latter is in the eye of the beholder.[143] Concerning progress *qua* progress, as distinct from progress as improvement, the law of historical progress has been foundational to the development of man's economic life. Success historical development is achieved when man's construction of societal change is made actual as fully as possible, by knowledge of the past in such measure as will permit him to avoid its errors. It does not necessarily involve replacement of the bad with the good. As often it will be the replacement of the good with the better. This much is true irrespective of whether history is regarded as a transcendental concept, an empirical pursuit, or a mixture of both. And if a seemingly uncontradicted string of proofs of this progress is shown to be applicable to man's economic development,[144] it would be incongruous to fail to recognize the rightful place of economic efficiency in society's development of rules governing the economic stability of individuals, including tort rules.

Applying these concepts to tort-type law, we can see that principles of economic efficiency have always been part and parcel of civil remediation of wrongful harm. And yet the strong philosophical and theistic ties to early tort rules retarded a sensible and explicit recognition of the equivalent and largely harmonious efficiency rationales for such rules. In the past, as now, the legal approaches to tort-type remedies is maturing rather than matured. To use only one example, for their philosophical advances in a philosophy of corrective justice and in ethics, the slave-holding Greek culture did not recognize that inequality is inefficient, but, then, neither did other nations for another millennium.

Nevertheless, it can be predicted with confidence that principles of economic efficiency, waste avoidance, repulsion of unjust enrichment, and deterrence will continue to affect tort theory, policy and law. That to date economic analysis plays only an episodic and subordinate role in decisional law should not vitiate this prediction. Moreover, the presence of proto-efficiency arguments, however crude and polemic, in state and federal tort reform initiatives, should presage that more matured efficiency interpretations will hold increasing sway in the proliferation of statutes governing injury law.

---

[142] *Id.*

[143] *Id.* at 325, giving the example of a primitive group's development of a more efficient way to catch fish, resulting in the availability of not one, but instead five fish a day. Although this might be considered progress, those in the community content with the availability of one fish per day might not call it an improvement.

[144] *Id.* at 331.

The entirety of history's philosophical development has been devoted to the identification and description of a scientific model of human and societal behavior. In injury law today, principles of economic efficiency and correlative deterrence represent the only applied scientific model. It would be anomalous to suppose that injury law, by reason of its ancient articulation in moral terms, ought be immune from scientific deconstruction and reanalysis in the scientific terms of economic efficiency, and it verges on impossibility to propose that it will fail to find greater and greater employment in tort theory, adjudication, and statutory adoption.

CHAPTER TWO

PAST AS PRELUDE: THE LEGACY OF FIVE LANDMARKS OF TWENTIETH-CENTURY INJURY LAW FOR THE FUTURE OF TORTS

Robert L. Rabin

ABSTRACT. This chapter offers some thoughts on prospective developments in injury reparation through the prism of what are, in my view, the principal landmarks of twentieth-century American tort and compensation law. I discuss, in roughly chronological order, the four developments that seem to me most critical in restructuring the very foundations of tort law in the twentieth century: First, Judge Benjamin Cardozo's opinion in the landmark case of *MacPherson v. Buick Motor Co.*; second, the Progressive Era adoption of workmen's compensation legislation; third, the concurring opinion of Justice Roger Traynor in *Escola v. Coca Cola Bottling Co.*; and fourth, the primarily legislative movement from contributory to comparative fault.

The chapter then turns to a fifth landmark, *United States v. Carroll Towing Co.*, which attained its status by serving as a catalyst for intellectual ferment, rather than through its direct impact on the tort system. In this last instance, I depart from chronological presentation because the noteworthiness of *Carroll Towing* came not in its immediate aftermath, but some twenty-five years later when Judge Learned Hand's opinion came to be recognized as a cornerstone of the law and economics movement. My focal point will be the themes that emerge from each of these developments, for it is the rich thematic influence in every instance that forced reexamination of the basic goals, as well as the appropriate domain, of tort law. Similarly, that rich thematic material creates continuing resonance for my corresponding discussion of future developments in the torts area.

I. INTRODUCTION

In this chapter, I want to offer some thoughts on prospective developments in injury reparation through the prism of what are, in my view, the principal landmarks of twentieth-century American tort and compensation law. In particular, I will discuss, in roughly chronological order, the four developments that seem to me most critical in restructuring the very foundations of tort law in the Twentieth Century: First, Judge Benjamin Cardozo's opinion in

Robert L. Rabin, A. Calder Mackay Professor of Law, Stanford Law School.

the landmark case of *MacPherson v. Buick Motor Co.*;[1] second, the Progressive Era adoption of workmen's compensation legislation;[2] third, the concurring opinion of Justice Roger Traynor in *Escola v. Coca Cola Bottling Co.*;[3] and fourth, the primarily legislative movement from contributory to comparative fault.[4] I will then discuss a fifth landmark, *United States v. Carroll Towing Co.*,[5] which attained its status by serving as a catalyst for intellectual ferment, rather than through its direct impact on the tort system. In this last instance, I depart from chronological presentation because the noteworthiness of *Carroll Towing* came not in its immediate aftermath, but beginning some twenty-five years later when it was recognized as a cornerstone of the economic analysis of tort law.

My focal point will be the themes that emerge from each of these developments, for it is the rich thematic influence in every instance that forced reexamination of the basic goals, as well as the appropriate domain, of tort law. Similarly, that rich thematic material creates continuing resonance for future developments in the torts area.

What are those themes? In the discussion that follows, I will begin by noting the role of *MacPherson* in establishing the dominance of a tort perspective over an earlier contract-driven approach to claims for redress of personal injury. Scope of duty issues – the modern way of framing these relational considerations – continue to be a lively topic of debate, as a look at some current developments will suggest.

At about the same time that *MacPherson* was decided, a major wave of legislative reform arose that replaced tort law with workmen's compensation schemes – eventually in every state – as the means of redress for job-related injuries. Here, too, the erosion of a nineteenth-century contract-grounded perspective was evident. But the principal theme in this instance, as I see it, is even more far-reaching; it is the dominance of a social welfare over a tort perspective. As the present century unfolds, the appropriate role of no-fault remains an open question – a point that I develop through

---

[1] 111 N.E. 1050 (N.Y. 1916).

[2] *See generally* MORTON KELLER, REGULATING A NEW SOCIETY: PUBLIC POLICY AND SOCIAL CHANGE IN AMERICA, 1900–1933, 197–202 (1994). Because my discussion of this legislation is primarily historical in character, I will refer to the legislation as it was known at the time, "workmen's compensation." If I were discussing the model outside of its historical context, I would use the modern, gender-neutral "workers' compensation" terminology.

[3] 150 P.2d 436, 461 (Cal. 1944).

[4] For comprehensive treatment of the subject, *see* VICTOR E. SCHWARTZ, COMPARATIVE NEGLIGENCE (4th ed. 2002).

[5] 159 F.2d 169 (2d Cir. 1947).

discussion of the experience with the September 11 Victim Compensation Fund.[6]

In an important sense, a direct connection can be traced from the pioneering legislative reform embodied in workmen's compensation to the prominent concurrence of Justice Traynor in *Escola*, advocating what can be regarded as an enterprise liability framework within the judicial domain.[7] In like fashion, workmen's compensation had embraced the notion that industry was better positioned than victims of enterprise risk of injury to spread the losses and take measures to reduce the prospects of accidental harm. Just as early observers of the workmen's compensation movement, such as Jeremiah Smith, recognized the direct challenge posed to the common law of negligence,[8] Traynor's position eventually led to what many observers took to be a revolution in the area of products liability.[9] The accuracy of this perception is another matter, but revolution or not, the challenge of enterprise liability thinking remains an intellectual force that has spilled beyond the boundaries of products liability law, as I will indicate.

Notwithstanding Traynor's opinion in *Escola* – at the time a stand-alone concurrence to a routine application of *res ipsa loquitur* in a negligence case – nearly a half-century of relative quiescence stood between the foundational changes in the common law of tort during the Progressive Era and a new impulse to engage in fundamental reform. The second coming was encapsulated in the enactment of comparative negligence legislation, replacing nearly two centuries of adherence to the judicially-fashioned doctrine of contributory negligence.[10] At the most basic level – the thematic level, as I have called it – this replacement movement represented a rejection of a fundamental tenet of the common law: the adherence to an all-or-nothing approach. Once again, the spillover effects into the twenty-first century are intriguing, perhaps most dramatically represented by continuing efforts in the political arena, under the banner of tort reform, to enact ceilings and limitations on individualized damages.[11]

---

[6] I discuss this question in greater detail in Robert L. Rabin, *The September 11 Victim Compensation Plan: A Circumscribed Response or an Auspicious Model?*, 53 DePaul L. Rev. 783 (2004).

[7] 150 P.2d 436, 461 (Cal. 1944).

[8] Jeremiah Smith, *Sequel to Workmen's Compensation Acts*, 27 Harv. L. Rev. 235, 363 (1914).

[9] *See*, for example, Robert G. Berger, *The Impact of Tort Law Development on Insurance: The Availability/Affordability Crisis and Its Potential Solutions*, 37 Am. U. L. Rev. 285, 290 (1988).

[10] The leading case was *Butterfield v. Forrester*, 103 Eng. Rep. 926 (K.B. 1809).

[11] *See*, for example, Ralph Blumenthal, *Malpractice Suits Capped at $750,000 in Texas Vote*, The New York Times, Sept. 15, 2003, at A12; Perry H. Apelbaum & Samara T. Ryder, *The*

The fifth landmark, *Carroll Towing*, was decided roughly contemporaneously with *Escola*. By contrast to Justice Traynor's concurrence, however, which on its face constituted an effort to recast the standard of liability in product injury cases, Judge Learned Hand's "formula" appeared to have the far more modest purpose of offering a somewhat systematic way of thinking about the traditionally unstructured due care inquiry in negligence cases. As such, *Carroll Towing* was assured a low profile until law-and-economics advocates posed it as a social welfare calculus that stimulated debate on the normative superiority of a cost-benefit approach to a more open-textured way of addressing the negligence question – a debate that also came to question the administrative feasibility of the Hand formula.[12] I will suggest that these questions have not yet been put to rest.

A final note on the landmark themes that I am about to discuss in greater detail. I have limited my scope to personal injury law. If I had defined my field more broadly to include injuries to interests in personality, I would without hesitation have included *New York Times v. Sullivan*.[13] The case dramatically reconstituted the common law of defamation, and in a singular fashion addressed the tension between recognizing the continuing salience of personality-based tort protection and delineating a zone of protection for free speech. In doing so, unlike the other injury law landmarks of the twentieth century, *New York Times v. Sullivan* highlighted the intersection of two well-traveled doctrinal thoroughfares: torts and constitutional law. But it did so outside the realm of accident law.

Nor have I included a mainstay in the lore of tort law, *Palsgraf v. Long Island Railroad Co.*,[14] despite its continuing popular appeal. Here, I must simply confess a long-standing failure to appreciate the celebrity status of the case among torts precedents, apart from its stylistic flourish. With only mild apology, then, I turn to discussion of my set of landmarks of the recent past – with corresponding attention to where they may point for the tort law of the foreseeable future.

Third Wave of Federal Tort Reform: Protecting the Public or Pushing the Constitutional Envelope?, 8 CORNELL J. L. & PUB. POL'Y 591 (1999). As I indicate *infra* in text, the "spillover" is with respect to incremental erosion of the all-or-nothing approach. I am not suggesting a more specific causal connection between comparative negligence reform and current tort reform efforts.

12 The main stimulus to regarding *Carroll Towing* as the centerpiece of an economic approach to negligence in the judicial forum was Richard A. Posner, *A Theory of Negligence*, 1 J. LEGAL STUD. 29 (1972).

13 376 U.S. 254 (1964).

14 162 N.E. 99 (N.Y. 1928).

II. FIVE LANDMARKS

A. *MacPherson* and the Reconceptualization of Duty

MacPherson has long been regarded as a prototypical illustration of the common law process in action. This perspective on the case is well taken. Judge Cardozo was very arguably in a class by himself in weaving a seamless web that made new law appear as the natural outgrowth of precedents that could have as easily led to reaffirmation of the status quo as to a departure that moved the law along a path not yet taken. And surely this was true in *MacPherson*. The relevant exception to the privity bar in product injury suits against manufacturers – that the product was "imminently dangerous" if negligently made – left plenty of room for Cardozo to decide that a duty was owed to the plaintiff (that is, that automobiles posed hazards at least as great as coffee urns and building scaffolds when improperly assembled), or for that matter to reach the contrary result, within the confines of preexisting law. But instead, of course, he chose to characterize the automobile as "a thing of danger" when unreasonably made,[15] and in doing so relegated the privity bar in products cases to the scrap heap of outworn doctrine; the exception had swallowed up the old rule. To put a fine finish on the common-law template of *MacPherson*, Cardozo gives not a hint of the policy considerations, reflecting a new era of socioeconomic development, which might have motivated the decision: the dramatic growth in enterprise scale; the significant rise in highway accidents; and the steady proliferation of intermediaries in commercial sales chains.

The process dimension of *MacPherson*, then, makes it a wonderful historical artifact and a prime teaching device in the classroom. But it cannot in itself elevate the case to landmark status in the annals of tort law, because there are so many other lines of tort cases to which one could similarly turn to illustrate the common-law methodology. Consider in this regard, the evolution of land occupier's liability from rigid and limited status-based duty categories, through the accretion of special categories, to a general obligation of due care to all land entrants in those states that follow the *Rowland v. Christian* approach.[16] Or, the evolution of the law in the area of bystander recovery for emotional distress, where many states have moved from a blanket rule of no recovery to a limited-in-scope duty of due care based on a set of factors

---

[15]   111 N.E. 1050, 1053 (N.Y. 1916).
[16]   443 P. 2d 561 (Cal. 1968). The evolution of the law is discussed in DAN B. DOBBS, THE LAW OF TORTS 615–20 (2000).

assuring genuineness of the claim.[17] Of course, many other examples could be given. The point is that *MacPherson* is a particularly useful illustration of the common-law process of change and expansion in the torts area, but it is by no means singular in that regard.

To understand the foundational importance of *MacPherson*, an apt starting point is the profile of accidental injuries at the dawn of the twentieth century in which causal responsibility might have been assigned to a third party. Apart from industrial injuries, road accidents (of the horse-and-buggy variety, of course, until shortly before *MacPherson*), and grade-crossing collisions, it seems doubtful that any *category* of personal injuries generated a substantial number of claims on an annual basis.[18] Still, there was a recognized area of doctrine for accident-related harms. By 1900, the negligence tort was well defined in doctrinal terms, torts casebooks and treatises gave it extensive coverage, and there was a significant body of leading precedents.[19]

What is most striking, nonetheless, is the constrained nature of the law of tort in that era. Industrial injury law is probably the most frequently-cited example. Defenses of assumed risk and fellow servant responsibility remained a substantial bar to recovery in the early years of the twentieth century, although somewhat less insurmountable than in the latter part of the nineteenth century.[20] Land occupier responsibility was similarly narrowly confined; in this case through duties limited by reference to the purposes for which the entrant came on the land.[21] As *MacPherson* makes evident, the privity requirement remained a major obstacle to recovery for product-related injuries, unless the injured consumer was claiming against the immediate supplier. And a host of immunities existed, protecting municipalities, charitable entities, and family members from suit.[22] The tie that binds all of these variegated injury scenarios together – and that distinguishes them from highway accidents, and grade-crossing fatalities where negligence liability was less doctrinally constrained – was

---

[17] The leading case is *Dillon v. Legg*, 441 P. 2d 912 (Cal. 1968).

[18] It is critical to distinguish between claims and harms. Under today's tort law, of course, many areas of personal harm can be identified where claims simply would not have been brought with any notable frequency a century ago; for example, medical mishaps for which a responsible defendant might have been identified.

[19] *See*, for example, JAMES BARR AMES & JEREMIAH SMITH, 2 A SELECTION OF CASES ON THE LAW OF TORTS (2d ed. 1893).

[20] For discussion, *see* Lawrence M. Friedman & Jack Ladinsky, *Social Change and the Law of Industrial Accidents*, 67 COLUM. L. REV. 50 (1967).

[21] *See* DOBBS, *supra* note 16, at 591–608.

[22] *Id.* at 693–95, 751–66.

the importance attached to the status relationships between plaintiff and defendant.[23]

This is where *MacPherson* enters the picture and makes its claim for recognition as a landmark. Although the case did not demolish the just-mentioned status limitations on recovery for negligence in one fell swoop, it did set the stage for expansionary developments in the scope of duty, particularly later in the twentieth century, "purifying" the negligence concept.[24] Essentially, *MacPherson* turned preexisting conceptual thinking about the realm of tort inside-out. Where status relationships had previously served as a screening-out device that confined the field of tort liability for accidental harm, *MacPherson* anchored the notion of obligation (duty, that is) in foreseeability – and if anything, status considerations, or "special relationships," later came to be a *source* of duty rather than a constraint.[25]

In the new century, a principal issue will be whether tort law has reached the outer limit of these expansionary tendencies. A quick and cursory examination suggests that a foreseeability-driven notion of duty may in fact have reached its high-water mark in the late twentieth century. Certainly, outside the area of physical injury this seems to be the case. Thus, in the realm of claims for negligent infliction of emotional distress, even the more plaintiff-friendly jurisdictions such as New Jersey and California have resisted efforts to move beyond "zone of danger" limits in direct claims and circumscribed relational tests in bystander claims.[26] The more recent types of emotional distress claims that especially characterize the late twentieth/early twenty-first century – in particular, toxic tort and HIV exposures – have only marginally expanded the limiting conception of duty; more specifically, through the recognition of

---

[23] *See generally* Robert L. Rabin, *The Historical Development of the Fault Principle: A Reinterpretation*, 15 Ga. L. Rev. 925 (1981). There was, of course, a contributory negligence defense available in highway and grade-crossing cases, but this defense was part of the tort/fault paradigm, rather than an extraneous policy basis for nonrecovery.

[24] For discussion of the expansive tendencies, *see* Gary T. Schwartz, *The Vitality of Negligence and the Ethics of Strict Liability*, 15 GA. L. REV. 963, 964–77 (1981).

[25] *See*, for example, Wagner v. Int'l Ry. Co., 133 N.E. 437 (N.Y. 1921) (duty to rescuers); *Tarasoff v. Regents of the Univ. of Cal.*, 551 P. 2d 334 (Cal. 1976) (duty of therapist to third party endangered by patient). Consider also the use of special relationships to create inroads into the traditional reluctance to recognize duties to those witnessing emotional distress, and to those relying on a traditional distinction between the obligations of those charged with nonfeasance rather than misfeasance.

[26] *See*, for example, *Burgess v. Superior Court*, 831 P. 2d 1197 (Cal. 1992) limiting an earlier, expansive foreseeability-based approach to "direct" negligent infliction of emotional distress claims to its facts; *see also Thing v. La Chusa*, 771 P. 2d 814 (Cal. 1989), reading narrowly the *Dillon v. Legg* factors, *supra* note 17, in bystander emotional distress cases.

HIV claims as tantamount to a special-category exception to a zone of danger requirement (along the lines of long-standing special-category recovery for emotional distress from negligently-sent death telegrams and mishandling of corpses).[27]

In the area of negligently-inflicted economic loss, where parallel concerns exist about the "ripple effects" of recognizing an expansive conception of duty, the courts have tread with even greater caution. In the late 1980s, New Jersey offered the invitation to a more expansive test of duty, "particular foreseeability," in *People Express Airlines, Inc. v. Consolidated Rail Corp.*,[28] a case involving a chemical spill on adjoining property that closed down the plaintiff's operations at Newark Airport. But this invitation has been ignored elsewhere. In a particularly revealing instance, immediately preceding September 11, the New York Court of Appeals decided related cases involving widespread neighboring commercial loss from the collapse of large office buildings.[29] The court appears to express the dominant sentiment in the new century in reaffirming the "economic loss rule" and relegating the claims for loss of business expectation to the domain of contract.[30]

It is far more hazardous to prognosticate across-the-board about the likely scope of duty in the highly diverse field of personal injury claims – the more immediate legacy of *MacPherson*. Suffice to say that in a number of areas where pathbreaking new frontiers of duty were recognized to third parties in the latter part of the twentieth century, a new mood of caution seems to have settled in.[31] Thus, *Tarasoff* liability, which remains a salient consideration for therapists nationwide in counseling homicidal patients, has not spilled substantially beyond its boundaries to establish widespread physician liability to third parties for diagnostic and prescriptive negligence.[32] Liability for physical

---

[27] On the reluctance to recognize "pure" emotional distress claims for toxic exposure in the absence of "impact" with the plaintiff, *see Metro-North Commuter R.R. Co. v. Buckley*, 521 U.S. 424 (1997) (surveying state law holdings as well); on the treatment of HIV as a special category, while adhering more generally to a zone of danger limitation in direct emotional distress claims, *see Williamson v. Waldman*, 696 A.2d 14 (N.J. 1997).

[28] 495 A.2d 107 (1985).

[29] 532 *Madison Ave. Gourmet Foods, Inc. v. Finlandia Center, Inc.*, 750 N.E.2d 1097 (N.Y. 2001).

[30] *Id.* at 1103.

[31] *See generally* Gary T. Schwartz, *The Beginning and the Possible End of the Rise of Modern American Tort Law*, 26 GA. L. REV. 601, 647–83 (1992).

[32] *See*, for example, *Schmidt v. Mahoney*, 659 N.W.2d 552 (Iowa 2003) (refusing to extend duty to general public to warn of danger of driving by epileptic patient even though physician had reason for concern); *McNulty v. City of New York*, 792 N.E.2d 162 (N.Y. 2003) (refusing to extend duty to close friend, despite query about risk from physician's patient who had meningitis).

assaults on tenants or patrons on or near a land occupier's premises has been
constrained by cost considerations tempering foreseeability.[33] Social host liability for injuries to third persons from the subsequent errant driving of an
intoxicated guest has been largely denied, as has gun manufacturer liability
to third-party victims.[34]

These illustrative cases, of course, fall far short of a comprehensive overview
of the field. But they are, in my view, indicative of a now-prevailing way of
thinking about the scope of obligation. In addressing the problem of redress
for accidental harm, the dominance of tort law over competing common-law
regimes – the singular contribution of *MacPherson* – remains firmly established. At the same time, however, tort law appears to have moved into what
might be called a mature phase, in which conservative tendencies notably rein
in the potentially boundless conception of foreseeability-based scope of duty.

B. Workmen's Compensation and the Emergence
of a Social Welfare Perspective

In the early years of the twentieth century, the common law of tort remained
strongly grounded in norms of individual responsibility. Oliver Wendell
Holmes's classic treatment of the subject in THE COMMON LAW, authored
only twenty years earlier, reflected this thinking.[35] To Holmes, the overriding argument for the common-law regime of negligence, as distinguished
from strict liability, was maximizing individual autonomy by anchoring tortious responsibility in foreseeability and freedom of choice.[36] In fact, Holmes
was arguably not entirely consistent in his commitment to this position. At
another point, he argues for an external standard of liability, which "the hasty
and awkward" would be hard put to meet, on the grounds that "when men
live in society, a certain average of conduct, a sacrifice of individual pecu-
liarities going beyond a certain point, is necessary to the general welfare."[37]
But this norm as well, despite the reference to "the general welfare," remains

---

[33] *See*, for example, *Posecai v. Wal-Mart Stores, Inc.*, 752 So.2d 762 (La. 1999); *Sharon P. v. Arman,
Ltd.*, 989 P. 2d 121 (Cal. 1999), *cert denied* 530 U.S. 1243 (2000); *Williams v. Cunningham Drug
Stores, Inc.*, 418 N.W.2d 381 (Mich. 1988).

[34] *See*, for example, *Reynolds v. Hicks*, 951 P. 2d 761 (Wash. 1998) (rejecting social host liability for
provision of liquor); *Hamilton v. Beretta U.S.A. Corp.*, 750 N.E.2d 1055 (N.Y. 2001) (rejecting
manufacturer liability to victim harmed by acts of third-party handgun users); *Merrill v.
Navegar, Inc.*, 28 P. 3d 116 (Cal. 2001) (rejecting products liability claim of shooting victims, in
part based on state statutory exemption for manufacturers of legal, nondefective firearms).

[35] OLIVER WENDELL HOLMES, THE COMMON LAW (1881).

[36] *Id.* at 94–96.

[37] *Id.* at 108–110.

firmly grounded in individual responsibility and a conception of *fault*, based on adherence to customary standards of conduct as the linchpin for liability. Indeed, in a passage of enduring fame, Holmes explicitly rejects a social welfare norm as the foundation for compensating injury victims:

> The state might conceivably make itself a mutual insurance company against accidents, and distribute the burden of its citizens' mishaps among all its members. There might be a pension for paralytics, and state aid for those who suffered in person or estate from tempest or wild beasts. As between individuals it might adopt the mutual insurance principle *pro tanto*, and divide damages when both were at fault . . . or it might throw all loss upon the actor irrespective of fault. The state does none of these things, however, and the prevailing view is that its cumbrous and expensive machinery ought not to be set in motion unless some clear benefit is to be derived from disturbing the *status quo*. State interference is an evil, where it cannot be shown to be a good. . . . The undertaking to redistribute losses simply on the ground that they resulted from the defendant's act would not only be open to these objections, but . . . to the still graver one of offending the sense of justice.[38]

Interestingly, at the time Holmes wrote – and in fact until relatively late in the twentieth century – strict liability itself reflected a conception of individual responsibility, if not "blameworthiness." Thus, the blasting cases, the principle of *Rylands v. Fletcher*,[39] and, later, the emerging concept of liability for abnormally dangerous activities, rested on moralistic notions of responsibility in interpersonal situations in which one party imposed a particularly high (and irreducible) risk of injury on another entirely innocent party.[40] In this context, then, it comes as no surprise that a prominent student of the tort system, Jeremiah Smith, would have reacted with dismay to the advent of workmen's compensation:

> If the fundamental general principle of the modern law of torts (that fault is requisite to liability) is intrinsically right or expedient, is there sufficient reason why the legislature should make the workmen's case an exception to this general principle? On the other hand, if this statutory rule as to workmen is intrinsically just or expedient, is there sufficient reason for refusing to make this statutory rule the test of the right of recovery on the part of persons other than workmen when they suffer hurt without the fault of either party?[41]

---

[38] *Id.* at 94–96.
[39] L.R. 3 H.L. 330 (1868).
[40] For discussion, *see* Robert L. Rabin, *The Ideology of Enterprise Liability*, 55 MD. L. REV. 1190 (1996).
[41] Smith, *supra* note 8, at 251.

For Smith, the answer was clear, so the advent of workmen's compensation was a forewarning of doom. But as history has taught, consistency has never been the dominant characteristic of responsibility for accidental harm; on the contrary, the American system is a patchwork of fault, strict liability, and, beginning with workmen's compensation, no-fault recovery. Nonetheless, workmen's compensation constituted a striking departure from the long-standing conception of liability based on personal responsibility. Drawing on Progressive Era ideology of preventing and redressing harm from a social welfare perspective, the states enacted workmen's compensation legislation side-by-side with maximum hour and child protection initiatives targeting workplace health and safety concerns.[42] From the new perspective, industrial injuries were to be viewed as mishaps "arising out of the workplace" – an ordinary cost of doing business – without reference to fault.

This paradigm shift in assigning responsibility provided a ready model for thinking about another emerging social phenomenon generating a high volume of accidental harm, the automobile. And indeed, in the early 1930s, a major study out of Columbia University suggested that an auto compensation scheme based on the workmen's compensation model, should be adopted:

> In many respects there is a close analogy between the industrial situation where workmen's compensation has been developed and the motor vehicle situation where the application of a like principle is now being discussed. Accidents are inevitable, whether in industry or in the operation of motor vehicles. It has been accepted as sound policy that the major part of the cost of accidents to employees should be borne by the industry, and it is proposed that the major part of the cost of those caused by the operation of motor vehicles should be cast upon the persons for whose benefit the motor vehicles are being operated. The conditions calling for the application of the compensation plan are similar: The failure of the common law system to measure up to a fair estimate of social necessity.[43]

For a moment, then, Jeremiah Smith appeared to be a prophet in his own time. But the enthusiasm for expansive application of the workmen's compensation model failed to take hold in the political arena. It was not until the latter half of the twentieth century that the foundation laid by workmen's compensation began to exhibit generative force; in particular, the notion that designated categories of injuries might be compensated on an enterprise (or activity) liability theory, characterized by broad risk-spreading and relatively

---

[42] *See generally* Keller, *supra* note 2, at 197–215.

[43] Report by the Committee to Study Compensation for Automobile Accidents to the Columbia University Council for Research in the Social Sciences 134–36 (1932).

even-handed treatment of injury victims. In truth, interest group politics, even more than social welfare ideology, fueled the adoption of no-fault systems in areas as disparate as motor vehicle accidents, coal miner's black lung disease, and childhood vaccine injuries. But then political unrest had been a major ingredient in the recipe for enactment of workmen's compensation legislation, as well. Even so, *realpolitik* considerations do not diminish the importance of the workmen's compensation model as a sharp departure from preexisting liability for personal harm based on tort – a departure appropriately regarded, in my view, as a second landmark of twentieth-century accident law.

What of the new century? The tragic events of September 11, 2001, will loom large, of course, in every future account of historic moments in the twenty-first century. The impact on the American system of reparation for personal harm is no exception. Within ten days of the catastrophe, reacting with unprecedented speed to a mass disaster, Congress enacted the September 11 Victim Compensation Fund ("the Fund"), a no-fault scheme for the personal injury victims and surviving families of the terrorist acts.[44]

There is no reason to think that the Fund will be the last word in no-fault benefits for identifiable categories of personal harm in the coming years. But in its sharply contrasting features from the classic workmen's compensation model, it does raise provocative questions about the future direction of no-fault compensation. To begin with, the Fund rejected the trade-off central to the conception of the workmen's compensation model: that in return for benefits available without reference to fault, those eligible under the scheme should be limited to recovery of economic loss – with the wage loss component of any such recovery further subject to scheduled limitations based on type of harm and ceilings reflecting notions of horizontal equity. Instead, the Fund would allow recovery of economic loss, defined to include not just medical expenses and loss of present earnings, but "loss of business or employment opportunities" – presumably future lost income – "to the extent recovery for such loss is allowed under applicable state law."[45] Along with this strikingly open-ended, individualized approach to economic loss, the Fund provided for noneconomic loss recovery, not in the lump sum, limited terms found in some no-fault schemes (assuming *any* noneconomic loss is recognized), but with allowance of "losses for physical and emotional pain, suffering, inconvenience, physical impairment, mental anguish, disfigurement, loss of enjoyment of life, loss of society and companionship, loss of consortium

---

[44] Air Transportation Safety and System Stabilization Act, Pub. L. No. 107–42, § 405 (b)(2), 115 Stat. 230, 239–40 (2001).

[45] *Id.* at § 402(5).

(other than domestic service), hedonic damages, injury to reputation, and all other nonpecuniary loss of any kind or nature."[46]

This sweeping provision for noneconomic loss – exceeding even the bounds of traditional tort recovery for pain and suffering – was subsequently redefined in lump sum terms in the regulations adopted by the Special Master appointed to administer the Fund.[47] And the Special Master also established a schedule of "presumed economic loss" that gave sharper definition to recovery for lost income, as well as establishing a presumptive ceiling on recovery – albeit an extraordinarily high one, the ninety-eight percentile of projected loss under the Table.[48] But the question remains whether the Fund, with its distinctly tortcentric perspective on recovery, as contrasted to the workmen's compensation model, grounded in social welfare notions of horizontal equity, represents the direction for the future.

There is good reason to think that the Fund model will have a very limited shelf life, and that any future resort to no-fault replacement of tort is likely to reflect the principles first established nearly a century ago in the workmen's compensation model. On this score, the Special Master's regulations are particularly revealing. As indicated earlier, the statutory language adopting an individualized, case-by-case approach to lost income and noneconomic loss in claims of survivors – tantamount to the most liberal version of wrongful death recovery schemes in tort – was simply overridden by the Special Master in an effort to reshape the structure of benefits under the Fund in more traditional, categorical terms through reliance on presumptions, scheduling, and capping of damage awards.[49]

Moreover, the hybrid tort/compensation model adopted by Congress for September 11 redress can well be regarded as *sui generis*. In its rush to judgment, Congress was particularly concerned about solvency of the airlines – and, in fact, capped the aggregate liability in tort for those who chose to opt out of the Fund at the insurance limits of the airlines and other potential defendants.[50] Because there was a general sense that these aggregate claims – including property damage tort claims outside the Fund – might far exceed insurance limits, the tort option could well have been viewed as creating a

---

[46] *Id.* at § 402(7). In contrast to these tort-type provisions, the Act had a strong preclusive provision regarding collateral sources. For discussion, *see* Robert L. Rabin, *The Quest for Fairness in Compensating Victims of September 11*, 49 CLEVE. STATE L. REV. 573, 575–81 (2001).

[47] September 11th Victim Compensation Fund of 2001, 28 C.F.R. § 104.44 (2002).

[48] *Id.* § 104.43.

[49] The Special Master's regulations were upheld against a challenge that he had exceeded the authority in the enabling statute. *See Schneider v. Feinberg*, 345 F. 3d 135 (2d Cir. 2003).

[50] *Supra* note 44, § 408.

limited fund for victims that would fall far short of traditional tort recovery; hence, the impulse to build tort-type compensation into the Fund option. In addition, in the immediate aftermath of the tragedy, there clearly was a sense that the victims were stand-ins for all Americans – that they should be viewed as heroes, martyrs, or both, and afforded whatever special recognition could be attached to the extinguishment of their lives.

Note, too, that this special sense of generosity was very quickly exhausted. Efforts to extend Fund-type recoveries retroactively to the surviving families of earlier acts of terrorism that might well have been regarded as similar in character – the Oklahoma City bombing and the earlier bombing at the World Trade Center – were to no avail. A related no-fault fund established with little fanfare after September 11 for smallpox vaccination victims was designed along traditional lines.[51] And more generally, the state crime victim compensation statutes, which might be regarded as broadly analogous in purpose to any future provision for victims of terrorist-related activity, are far more modestly designed to meet the immediate out-of-pocket needs of eligible claimants.[52]

Looking beyond victims of terrorism and criminal activities, however, the broader question is whether the workmen's compensation no-fault model is likely to seem an inviting pathway for departing from tort and adopting a legislative compensation scheme in other areas of high-incidence harm from personal injury. In the latter part of the Twentieth Century, these efforts failed, and there is no reason to be more sanguine about broad-based no-fault reform in the coming years. Apart from the vagaries of legislative politics, the central conceptual difficulty remains the inability to define a satisfying "designated compensable event," to use the term initially coined in medical malpractice reform efforts. In the medical area, the reservations have centered on the complexity of identifying eligible medical mishaps without cycling back to a determination that negligent treatment has occurred. In the products area, the difficulty has turned on designating compensable injuries in the use of

---

[51] Smallpox Emergency Personnel Protection Act of 2003, Pub. L. No. 108-20, 117 Stat. 638 (2003). The Act provides no-fault benefits to health care workers and other emergency personnel who suffer injury or death after receiving the vaccine. Eligible individuals who are permanently and totally disabled are provided a benefit comparable to that received by police officers and firefighters under the Public Safety Officers' Benefits Program, currently $262,100. Survivors of those who die as a result of vaccination receive a similar award. Lesser injuries trigger lost income reimbursement of 66 2/3 percent (75 percent when there are dependents) up to an annual ceiling of $50,000 and a lifetime ceiling set at the PSOB death benefit, earlier. Reasonable medical expenses are also covered. All benefits are secondary to other public benefit programs. There is no provision for noneconomic loss.

[52] *See* discussion in Rabin, *supra* note 6, at 796–798.

everyday consumer products like ladders and bicycles, where victim responsibility for injuries often plays a central role. In the toxic injury area, the dilemma results from the background risks of life-style and genetic makeup that frequently cast doubt on the causal responsibility for exposure to a designated source.

At bottom, there is a more fundamental issue here that takes us back full circle to Jeremiah Smith. Whether the prospective category for no-fault recovery is victims of terrorism or toxic exposure, fairness considerations require addressing the question of why *any* particular category should be designated for special treatment, and not *all* innocent persons who happen to suffer the unexpected misfortune of accidental personal harm. At times, our political system has answered this question in pragmatic terms: workmen's compensation arose because industrial accidents imposed a high injury toll that was seriously undercompensated in tort and seriously undermining peace in the workplace – reasons considered sufficient to address this problem and worry about others later. Political exigencies have driven the adoption of other, focused no-fault schemes such as childhood vaccine injury compensation. But these remain the occasional exception. As dramatic a departure as workmen's compensation turned out to represent, the tort system appears likely to remain the principal avenue of recourse for most personal injury claimants in the foreseeable future.

C. *Escola v. Coca Cola Bottling Co.* and the Judicial Embrace of Enterprise Liability

Gladys Escola's claim against the Coca Cola Bottling Co. appeared no different, on the surface, from others that fell into what had come to be regarded as the "exploding bottle" cases. Escola, a waitress at Tiny's Waffle Shop in Merced, California, was injured by just such an occurrence as she restocked coke bottles from a case into a refrigerator. These claims were routinely handled under negligence theory by recourse to the doctrine of *res ipsa loquitur*. And the majority of the California Supreme Court found no reason to depart from this approach in *Escola v. Coca Cola Bottling Co.*[53]

But one judge saw the matter differently: Justice Roger Traynor, who twenty years later would come to be recognized as the leading jurist in setting out a new approach to defective products cases – strict liability in tort. In his concurring opinion in *Escola*, Traynor suggested that it was time to move beyond negligence doctrine in products cases. In a striking display of advocacy,

---

[53]   150 P. 2d 436 (Cal. 1944).

he offered an impressive array of arguments, blending policy, process, and pragmatic considerations. But the essence of his position is captured in a single paragraph:

> Even if there is no negligence, however, public policy demands that responsibility be fixed wherever it will most effectively reduce the hazards to life and health inherent in defective products that reach the market. It is evident that the manufacturer can anticipate some hazards and guard against the recurrence of others, as the public cannot. Those who suffer injury from defective products are unprepared to meet its consequences. The cost of an injury and the loss of time or health may be an overwhelming misfortune to the person injured, and a needless one, for the risk of injury can be insured by the manufacturer and distributed among the public as a cost of doing business.[54]

In this concise, straightforward rendering, Traynor set out the two-pronged enterprise liability conception that would animate the adoption of strict liability for defective products twenty years later. As Traynor saw it, strict liability promoted two dominant goals of tort law: creating optimal incentives to safety through internalization of the costs of accidents, and enhancing risk-spreading of injury costs through the pricing mechanism. Today, of course, these goals are viewed as part of the received wisdom of tort theorizing – albeit not without qualification and critical reservations. But in 1944, systematic thinking about torts from what might be regarded as an economic perspective, especially in the domain of the judiciary, was far from commonplace.

And indeed it did take two decades for the doctrinal aspect of Traynor's thinking to take hold in any systematic way. Not until 1963, in *Greenman v. Yuba Power Products, Inc.*,[55] was he able to muster a majority of the California Supreme Court for the proposition that strict liability in tort should be the governing liability principle in product injury cases. *Greenman*, in turn, was decided contemporaneously with the adoption by the American Law Institute of the highly influential section 402A of the Restatement (Second) of Torts, similarly enunciating a strict liability principle for products cases.[56] On this score, it is particularly interesting to note comment *c* to the new provision, which revealed on its face indebtedness to *Escola*:

> On whatever theory, the justification for the strict liability has been said to be that the seller, by marketing his product for use and consumption, has undertaken and assumed a special responsibility toward any member of the consuming public who may be injured by it; that the public has the right to and does expect,

[54] *Id.* at 440–41.
[55] 337 P. 2d 897 (Cal. 1963).
[56] RESTATEMENT (SECOND) OF TORTS § 402A (1965).

in the case of products which it needs and for which it is forced to rely upon the seller, that reputable sellers will stand behind their goods; that public policy demands that the burden of accidental injuries caused by products intended for consumption be placed upon those who market them, and be treated as a cost of production against which liability insurance can be obtained; and that the consumer of such products is entitled to the maximum of protection at the hands of someone, and the proper persons to afford it are those who market the products.[57]

With the benefit of hindsight, Traynor's forceful embrace of strict liability for product-related injuries clearly cannot withstand an indictment of over-breadth. By the 1970s, courts had begun to differentiate more sharply among manufacturing, design, and warning defects, and to apply principles in the latter two categories that distinctly suggested a negligence-type approach.[58]

But the importance of *Escola* nonetheless can hardly be overstated. Work-men's compensation, as a model for *judicial* adoption of enterprise liability thinking, was a nonstarter from the outset. From a tort perspective, the work-men's compensation model, through its trade-off on the benefits side (caps on recovery of economic loss, nonrecognition of intangible loss), promoted cost internalization only in a limited sense – and failed the test of administrative feasibility through judicial edict; in particular, category-based scheduling of injury awards. From a risk-spreading perspective, courts were reluctant, in the *Escola* era, to conceive of tort as an insurance mechanism. It fell to Traynor to plant the seed that would prove fertile in more congenial soil – the consumer-oriented 1960s – and in fact would germinate in neighboring areas, including the domain of traditional strict liability, as well.

On the latter score, traditional strict liability had long been dominated by corrective justice notions of *sic utere tuo* and nonreciprocal imposition of risk. But by the early 1970s, consider how a court responded to defendant railroad's argument that it would be "unjust" to charge a carrier with strict liability for an explosion, where the railroad had been required to accept dangerous cargo:

> If California predicated liability solely upon the "fairness" rationale appearing in [*Green v. General Petroleum Corp.*, 270 P. 952 (Cal. 1928)], it might well find that strict liability was inappropriate. Under the *Green* rationale strict liability is imposed because the ultrahazardous actor intentionally exposes others to a serious danger – an anti-social act is being redressed. Where the carrier has no choice but to accept dangerous cargo and engage in an ultrahazardous activity, it is the public which is requiring the carrier to engage in the anti-social activity. The carrier is innocent.

---

[57] *Id.* cmt. c.
[58] This more refined approach is reflected in the Restatement (Third) of Torts: Products Liability, § 2(a)–(c) (1998).

But, there is no logical reason for creating a "public duty" exception when the rationale for subjecting the carrier to absolute liability is the carrier's ability to distribute the loss to the public. Whether the carrier is free to reject or bound to take the explosive cargo, plaintiffs are equally defenseless. Bound or not, Southern Pacific is in a position to pass along the loss to the public. Bound or not, the social and economic benefits which are ordinarily derived from strict liability are achieved.... A more efficient allocation of resources results. Thus, the reasonable inference to be drawn from the adoption of the risk distribution rationale in *Smith v. Lockheed Propulsion Co.*, [56 Cal.Rptr. 128 (App. 1967)] is that California would ... find that carriers engaged in ultrahazardous activity are subject to strict liability.[59]

Moreover, in my view, the dual notion of tort liability as an engine for distributing risk and creating incentives for safety – captured in the enterprise liability conception – manifested a growth potential extending considerably beyond strict liability.[60] The erosion of the immunities for example, particularly municipal immunity,[61] and extensions of affirmative obligations of due care to third parties in certain circumstances – *Tarasoff v. Regents of Univ. of California*[62] is a prime example – are grounded in a broader conception of the enterprise liability themes. Although a wide variety of socioeconomic factors contributed to these developments, it is nonetheless notable that the California Supreme Court played such a dominant role in influencing the judicial reception of these liability-enhancing tendencies. And the lineage, indeed the stewardship, of these developments is directly traceable to Justice Traynor and his *Escola* concurrence.

Have the pathways opened by *Escola* and successor developments now reached their outer limits? How much vitality does Traynor's concurrence retain? Many observers have called into question the comparative efficiency of tort as an insurance mechanism.[63] Surely the daunting administrative cost of shifting dollars through tort poses a challenge that went unrecognized at the time of *Escola*; and to be fair, it was undoubtedly far less significant then. At the same time, there are serious questions about the extent to which tort achieves a close approximation to optimal deterrence.[64] Undoubtedly, these reservations are not lost on the judiciary – and, as a consequence, leading

---

[59] *Chavez v. S. Pac. Transp. Co.*, 413 F. Supp. 1203, 1213–14 (E.D. Cal. 1976).

[60] *See* Rabin, *supra* note 40, at 1199–1203.

[61] *See*, for example, *Muskopf v. Corning Hospital District*, 359 P. 2d 457 (1961).

[62] 551 F.2d 334 (Cal. 1976) (in effect, treating "activity liability" – engaging in therapeutic practice – as tantamount to enterprise liability).

[63] *See*, for example, Stephen D. Sugarman, *Doing Away with Tort Law*, 73 Cal. L. Rev. 555, 559–590 (1985).

[64] *See*, for example, Gary T. Schwartz, *Reality in the Economic Analysis of Tort Law: Does Tort Law Really Deter?*, 42 U.C.L.A.L. Rev. 377 (1994–95).

observers of the tort scene in recent years have proclaimed an end to the expansionary era of tort.[65]

More centrally to *Escola*, there is an evident tension between the two prongs of enterprise liability thinking that is elided in Traynor's concurrence. I refer to the strikingly different goals of enterprise risk-spreading and enterprise safety optimization. Pharmaceutical manufacturers and the suppliers of safety devices for factory machinery undoubtedly are better placed than injury victims, from a category-wide perspective, to spread the losses associated with use of their products. But it does not follow that they are best placed, from an optimal incentives standpoint, to reduce the residual risks associated with their products once a clear warning has been provided. Prominent tort scholarship identified this tension in the heyday of *Escola* influence.[66]

These various reservations in no way undercut the significance of Traynor's *Escola* concurrence in illuminating the foundations of manufacturer liability, or more broadly, the foundations of obligations in tort for accidental harm. If tort law is now in a more mature phase of development, the *Escola* concurrence, through articulation of fundamental aspirations of tort, played a major role in getting the system there.

D. Comparative Fault and the Erosion of an All-or-Nothing Approach

A central characteristic of the common law of tort was its staunch adherence to all-or-nothing rules. This feature of the system was driven principally by its highly individualistic approach. Thus, the plaintiff who was entitled to recover – a "deserving victim" – was entitled to establish personal projections of lost earning power and future pain and suffering, as well as out-of-pocket costs for full medical expenses and lost income already realized. No ceilings of any sort were recognized; indeed, under the thin-skulled plaintiff rule even idiosyncratic consequences were compensable. Similarly, the defendant who was identified as a malefactor was responsible for the full damage award. Moreover, this was true, under the rules of joint-and-several liability, even if another codefendant was also found to be a responsible party. Similarly, causal uncertainty was put to rest, once the threshold of more-probable-than-not was exceeded, by awarding full damages rather than probabilistic awards that would have discounted for uncertainty. And, intervening negligent parties typically either broke the causal chain of responsibility for negligent acts and

---

[65] *See* G. Schwartz, *supra* note 31 at 647–83.
[66] *See* GUIDO CALABRESI, THE COSTS OF ACCIDENTS 26–29 (1970).

were exclusively responsible, or bore no responsibility at all under the sorting mechanism of proximate cause.

At the core of this uncompromising system was the doctrine of contributory negligence, which held that a plaintiff who was at fault was entirely barred from recovery no matter how minimal the victim's contribution to the harm might be. Even the rules that somewhat mitigated this sternly moralistic position served to reinforce the all-or-nothing character of this part of the system. Thus, a plaintiff who could establish that the defendant had "the last clear chance" was no longer barred from recovery – but the pendulum then swung entirely in the other direction and the defendant was responsible for the full damages arising from his conduct. Similarly, the defendant whose conduct was viewed not merely as unreasonable, but rose to the level of reckless misconduct, was held to account for full damages even though the plaintiff may have been partially at fault.

Comparative fault was not the initial thrust into this uncompromising terrain, but it certainly was the deepest.[67] The movement gathered momentum in the period around 1970, principally through state legislative reform, largely as a reaction to the perceived destabilization of the tort system by proposals for no-fault auto compensation schemes, and to related empirical data indicating a highly skewed pattern of reparations in auto cases.[68]

But interestingly, unlike other roughly contemporaneous "tort reform" efforts, such as dollar limitations on medical malpractice recoveries and statutes of repose for product claims, comparative fault legislation was never limited in focus to motor vehicle claims.[69] This was an initiative aimed at systemwide reform.

Moreover, the comparative negligence movement swept broadly in two other highly significant ways. First, like workmen's compensation, comparative negligence eventually was adopted in virtually all the states – in contrast to every other state-based tort reform initiative to this very day. Second, the movement had an internal dynamic that transformed an array of related basic tenets of the tort system. Thus, assumed risk, which had previously been regarded as an absolute defense, was now parsed in many states into "primary"

---

[67] For example, apportioned liability for damage awards among multiple responsible defendants had already been universally adopted.

[68] See *The Department of Transportation's Auto Insurance Study and Auto Accident Compensation Reform*, 71 COLUM. L. REV. 207, 214, Table 3 (1971) (small nuisance claims were considerably overcompensated and large, serious injury claims were strikingly undercompensated, in the aggregate).

[69] In a handful of states, comparative fault was adopted through judicial overruling. *See*, for example, *Li v. Yellow Cab Co.*, 532 P. 2d 1226 (Cal. 1975).

and "secondary" assumed risk, with comparative principles applicable only to the latter. Absolute doctrinal bars like last clear chance were synthesized into the comparative framework and no longer treated as having independent meaning. Contribution among codefendants – unrecognized at early common law, under the all-or-nothing approach – was transformed from equal responsibility to comparative responsibility. Strict products liability defenses that had been narrowly limited to instances of subjective appreciation of the risk were reformulated, in many states, in broader terms to include inadvertent plaintiff misconduct. These and like reconstructive efforts continued to take shape throughout the remaining years of the twentieth century.[70]

And what of the legacy, the spillover, into the new century? Whatever the direct influence of the advent of comparative fault, the erosion of the all-or-nothing character of the common law tort system has maintained its momentum. Limitations on punitive damages, noneconomic loss, and joint-and-several liability are perhaps the most notable hallmarks of a tort reform era that has yet to reach its outer bounds.[71]

From one perspective, these later initiatives in the political arena can be seen as at cross-purposes with the thrust of comparative fault. Virtually all of the more recent reforms cut back on the conception of particularized entitlements to "deserving victims" embodied in the common law. By contrast, comparative negligence alleviated the harshness of the common law moralistic, subjective focus on "deservingness."

The commonality remains, however. Whatever the political sentiments of the day, comparative negligence stands as a landmark in calling into question the traditional legislative deference to a common law tort regime that defined entitlements in all-or-nothing terms. It was the first significant wave of *incremental*, systemwide reform of tort, as distinguished from the replacement philosophy of no-fault. And as such, it was a gateway to the limiting initiatives that remain in vogue today.

E. *Carroll Towing* and the Delineation of Due Care

In *United States v. Carroll Towing Co.*,[72] Judge Learned Hand and his colleagues addressed a relatively garden-variety question of due care: whether the absence of a bargee from his post for an extended period of time without explanation

---

[70] *See generally* VICTOR E. SCHWARTZ, *supra* note 4.
[71] For discussion, see MARC A. FRANKLIN & ROBERT L. RABIN, TORT LAW AND ALTERNATIVES: CASES AND MATERIALS 787–92 (7th ed. 2001).
[72] 159 F.2d 169 (2d Cir. 1947).

constituted contributory fault, where his presence might have prevented the sinking of the barge and consequent loss of cargo. Unlike *MacPherson*, no longstanding tension between negligence and no-liability thinking was before the court. In contrast to *Escola* (as Traynor conceived it), no question of competing systems of liability – fault and strict liability – shaped the agenda. Rather, Hand saw an opportunity to clarify the due care standard:

> Since there are occasions when every vessel will break from her moorings, and since, if she does, she becomes a menace to those about her; the owner's duty, as in other similar situations, to provide against resulting injuries is a function of three variables: (1) The probability that she will break away; (2) the gravity of the resulting injury, if she does; (3) the burden of adequate precautions. Possibly it serves to bring this notion into relief to state it in algebraic terms: if the probability be called P; the injury, L; and the burden, B; liability depends upon whether B is less than L multiplied by P: i.e., whether $B < PL$.[73]

Carroll Towing failed to attract notable attention until the early 1970s, when law-and-economics scholars, steadily growing in influence, afforded the Hand formula pride of position in expressing the social utility norm that they regarded as the foundation for liability in accidental harm cases.[74] This scholarship, in turn, sparked a lively debate with corrective justice adherents over both the normative and descriptive underpinnings of tort liability rules.

Although it would far exceed the scope of this essay to explore these opposing themes – which pitted economically oriented thinkers against viewpoints ranging from corrective justice to natural rights proponents[75] – what is perhaps most striking about this debate, in hindsight, is its "distance" from the routine functioning of the tort system. With particular reference to *Carroll Towing*, consider the breach of duty issue in negligence cases; juries are never instructed along lines that even hint at the Hand formula. Rather, juries are charged, in highly general terms, to determine how a reasonable person would have acted under the circumstances. In this regard, California's model jury instruction is fairly typical:

> Negligence is the doing of something which a reasonably prudent person would not do, or the failure to do something which a reasonably prudent person would do, under circumstances similar to those shown by the evidence.
>
> It is the failure to use ordinary or reasonable care.

---

73 *Id.* at 173.
74 *See especially*, Richard A. Posner, *supra* note 12.
75 *See* the survey of scholarship in Gary T. Schwartz, *supra* note 24 at 977–1005; Izhak Englard, *The System Builders: A Critical Appraisal of Modern American Tort Theory*, 9 J. Legal Stud. 27 (1980).

Ordinary or reasonable care is that care which persons of ordinary prudence would use in order to avoid injury to themselves or others under circumstances similar to those shown by the evidence.[76]

Although I am unaware of any empirical studies of the question, it seems very likely that the Hand formula – that is, equating due care with cost-benefit considerations – is far more congenial to appellate court thinking. But even if this is closer to the mark, it nonetheless raises serious issues of administrative feasibility. The difficulty is perhaps most clear in negligence cases arising in the context of alleged *personal* failure to exercise due care. Is it intelligible to monetize a burden of adequate protection – the "B" term in the Hand formula – in assessing the conduct of a defendant who suddenly changes lanes when driving, or who fails to remove a banana peel from her front driveway?

Moreover, even in *business conduct* cases, as Judge Posner, the leading champion of Hand-formula breach analysis, pointed out in *McCarty v. Pheasant Run, Inc.,*[77] *Carroll Towing* eludes particularized application. In *McCarty*, a case involving allegedly inadequate safety precautions to avoid an assault by an intruder at defendant's resort, Posner cautioned:

> Conceptual as well as practical difficulties in monetizing personal injuries may continue to frustrate efforts to measure expected accident costs with the precision that is possible, in principle at least, in measuring the other side of the equation – the cost or burden of precaution. For many years to come juries may be forced to make rough judgments of reasonableness, intuiting rather than measuring the factors in the Hand Formula; and so long as their judgment is reasonable the trial judge has no right to set it aside, let alone substitute his own judgment.[78]

"For many years to come," Posner tells us, such analytical clarity in applying the Hand formula may be impossible. Have tort jurists now reached that point in time, or are they at least on the brink of doing so in the early years of the twenty-first century? It is hard to see what has changed, or is likely to change through either new technology or advances in statistical analysis, which would usher in greater proficiency in Hand-formula quantification.

In fact, throughout the twentieth century it was possible to identify competing approaches to the cost-benefit dictates of *Carroll Towing* within the

---

[76] California Jury Instructions Civil [BAJI] (8th ed.) § 3.10 (1994).

[77] 826 F.2d 1554 (7th Cir. 1987).

[78] *Id.* at 1557 (internal citation omitted). Judge Hand himself had earlier expressed similar skepticism about the operational capacity of the formula. *See Moisan v. Loftus*, 178 F.2d 148 (2d Cir. 1949).

very same domain of promoting the social good. Revered common-law judges such as Cardozo and Hand himself appeared to be recognizing a "soft" version of *Carroll Towing*-type analysis in leading cases without expressly saying so.[79] And there is no reason to think that a nonrigorous version of *Carroll Towing*, stressing the importance of assessing the ability to reduce the risk of harm in light of the cost of doing so, is likely to seem less appealing to tort jurists in the coming years.[80]

More generally, as we look to the future, and claims are inevitably made for expanding strict liability in tort or adopting new no-fault schemes, these proposals will invariably need to be evaluated against some baseline – the "as compared to what" question. Whatever its imprecision, *Carroll Towing*, and the academic thinking it animated, are likely to continue serving that benchmark function of providing intellectual respectability to the negligence formulation against which other ideologies can be assessed.

III. CONCLUDING THOUGHTS

The Twentieth Century witnessed a remarkable expansion in the domain of compensation for accidental harm. The landmarks I have discussed pointed the way. The scope of duty was highly constrained prior to *MacPherson*. Although privity-type thinking still retains some vitality today, it functions now essentially as a check against crushing liability rather than as a paradigmatic viewpoint that contract dominates tort in characterizing recovery for personal injury. No-fault compensation was not even a glimmer in the eye of tort reformers at the onset of the twentieth century, before the rise of the workmen's compensation movement. Today, no-fault is almost invariably regarded as a serious option in the case of mass tort incidents, albeit one that is infrequently adopted. Strict liability was a relatively obscure corner of the tort system, reserved largely for unusually dangerous activities, particularly handling explosives, at the time of Traynor's concurrence in *Escola*. By

---

[79] *See*, for example, Judge Cardozo's opinion in *Adams v. Bullock*, 125 N.E. 93, 93 (N.Y. 1919) (adverting to the costs of eliminating the dangers of an electrified trolley that injured the plaintiff); Judge Hand's opinion in *Carroll Towing* itself (raised the possibility that the bargee might not have been at fault if his absence had been limited to overnight and was in conformance with custom; a consideration that seems irrelevant to the cost of hiring a second-shift bargee). By contrast, in *The T. J. Hooper*, 60 F.2d 737, 740 (2d Cir. 1932), Hand had taken a more provisional view of the importance of custom.

[80] For general discussion of the Hand formula, as well as competing perspectives on assessing reasonable care, *see* Stephen G. Gilles, *United States v. Carroll Towing Co.: The Hand Formula's Home Port*, in ROBERT L. RABIN & STEPHEN D. SUGARMAN, TORT STORIES (2003).

century's end, the question was how much of the products liability area had come within the domain of strict liability, rather than whether the theory would remain confined to uncommon activities on land. Injury victims – even those only slightly at fault – were, at least in theory, entirely barred from recovery for negligent acts under the all-or-nothing perspective of the common law prior to comparative fault. Now, legislative reassembling of the basic framework of common-law liability and damage rules is commonplace. None of these landmark developments worked in isolation to recast the contemporary landscape of accident law, but each made a significant contribution.

All of these landmarks worked in the direction of expanding compensation for personal injury. Interestingly, only *Carroll Towing*, among the five landmarks, was "neutral" in its impact on tort contestants, neither overtly pro-plaintiff nor pro-defendant in a categorical sense. This is so not simply because the major impact of *Carroll Towing* was on academic thinking, but would be true even if it had been feasible to incorporate the Learned Hand formula into the workday life of the tort system.

It is also striking that the first four landmarks share the common characteristic of establishing a new baseline of sociolegal expectations about loss allocation. There is no turning back from these developments. No one argues for rolling back products liability to the pre-*MacPherson* mindset of limiting personal injury recovery to those in privity of contract, or for rethinking the adoption of comparative negligence. Similarly, despite all the justified criticism of costly inefficiencies in the administration of workers' compensation, reform efforts are incremental in character, and take it as a given that the system is here to stay. The legacy of Traynor's *Escola* opinion is more complex. As is generally accepted now, both design defect and warning defect law have substantially, if not entirely, taken on the features of negligence-type liability. Even here, however, the failure to bring strict liability to full realization does not undercut the judicial acknowledgement of Traynor's enterprise liability impulse to recognize broad spreading of accident costs and the creation of effective incentives to safety as two principal goals in allocating losses from dangerous products.

It is one thing to conclude that these landmarks have become enduring characteristics of the American accident reparation system. Whether they contain the seeds of further growth is quite another matter. On this score, it is hazardous to look too far into the future. From the vantage point of the present cost-conscious legal system, expansive notions of risk-spreading – either through extension of common-law strict liability to, say, professional services or premises occupiers, or through adoption of broad-based no-fault schemes – seem out of favor. At the same time, the core concept of linking accident prevention to cost-benefit type thinking appears to maintain its persuasive power. That is to say, the substantive conception of negligence, within a framework loosely reflecting the *Carroll Towing* formula, retains its dominant position in accident law. However, the remedial/damages side of tort law – its all-or-nothing approach – seems increasingly vulnerable to incremental erosion. "Tort reform," in its modern guise, shows distinct signs of continuing political appeal.

Clearly, there is an inherent tension between remaining committed to a social utility calculus for allocating the costs of accidents and politically redefining the input terms of the Hand formula in the legislative arena. Perhaps the larger, and unsurprising, lesson from the landmarks of twentieth-century tort law is that they were grounded in the socioeconomic and political developments of the times – and their continuing vitality in the foreseeable future will be no less so. Holmes had it right: the life of the law is not logic; it has been experience.

COMPENSATION AND DETERRENCE IN THE MODERN WORLD

CHAPTER THREE

TWENTY-FIRST-CENTURY INSURANCE AND LOSS DISTRIBUTION IN TORT LAW

Kenneth S. Abraham

ABSTRACT. This chapter begins by surveying and quantifying the magnitude of the different sources of compensation for personal injury, illness, and death. The survey places tort law in perspective, both by locating it within our larger "system" of compensation and by comparing its functioning and scope with the other methods of loss distribution that are employed by the system. The examination reveals the extent to which there is in fact a vast system of loss distribution, of which tort is only a small part. By contrast, that system is by no means comprehensive; it contains important gaps.

The central issue is whether these gaps should be filled by tort law or by the other sources, and how that might be accomplished. To begin to address this issue the chapter then turns to the relationship between tort and the rest of the loss-distribution system. It analyzes the different possible relationships by identifying and exploring the loss-distributional and other impacts of four possible variants of the collateral source rule. Finally, the chapter looks at the rarely-considered, distinct treatment accorded to life insurance and savings under existing rules, and then recommends an alternative approach to tort law's treatment of all collateral sources, including life insurance, that would help to fill the compensation gap. This approach would afford first-party insurance policyholders the option of transferring all their tort rights of recovery to their insurers, in return for lower premiums or more generous first-party insurance coverage.

I. INTRODUCTION

As recently as the middle of the twentieth century, loss distribution was at the center of debate about the proper functions of tort law. Tort theorists such as Fleming James, Justice Roger Traynor, and Charles Gregory argued that greater liability should be imposed on enterprises whose activities cause

Kenneth S. Abraham, Robert E. Scott Distinguished Professor of Law, University of Virginia School of Law. Thanks are due to Vincent Blasi and David Rosenberg for their comments on an earlier draft of this chapter.

physical injury and damage.[1] One of the principal bases for this argument was
that business and professional enterprises were in the best position to spread
the cost of losses associated with their activities, either directly, by increasing
the price of their products and services, or indirectly, by purchasing liability
insurance.[2]

Looking at the subject fifty years later, it is clear that viewing loss distribution as a principal goal of tort law has long been out of academic fashion.
This has occurred for two reasons. First, the second half of the twentieth
century witnessed an explosion of other methods of distributing losses, predominantly in the form of private first-party and social insurance. To many
tort theorists, it is not now necessary for tort law to promote loss distribution,
whatever the argument for doing so may once have been, because first-party
insurance is now performing that task.

Second, because of the rise of first-party and social insurance, because
it is now less obvious than it once seemed to be that enterprises can easily
insure against the risk of civil liability,[3] and for reasons of academic taste, tort
theorists have become preoccupied with issues other than loss distribution.
Whether and how tort law should promote optimal deterrence occupied the
lion's share of tort theorists' attention for the last several decades of the
twentieth century. Recently, corrective justice and related views have experienced something of a renaissance in academic circles.[4] The attention paid to

---

[1] James's campaign for the adoption of enterprise liability is reflected both in his torts treatise and in a series of articles he authored both before and after publication of the treatise.
   See generally FOWLER W. HARPER AND FLEMING JAMES JR., THE LAW OF TORTS (1956).
   Traynor's most famous statement of his position favoring enterprise liability was his concurring opinon in *Escola v. Coca Cola Bottling Co.*, 150 P.2d 436 (Cal. 1944). Gregory's position
   is expressed in Charles W. Gregory, *Trespass, to Negligence, to Absolute Liability*, 37 VA. L.
   REV. 359 (1951). For an account of the overall movement, *see* George L. Priest, *The Invention of Enterprise Liability: A Critical History of the Intellectual Foundations of Modern Tort
   Law*, 14 J. LEGAL STUD. 461 (1985). A fairly recent effort to revive the movement can be
   found in VIRGINIA E. NOLAN & EDMUND URSIN, UNDERSTANDING ENTERPRISE LIABILITY
   (1995).
[2] Dean William Prosser, the leading tort scholar of the time, also acknowledged loss distribution as a legitimate function of tort law. *See* WILLIAM L. PROSSER, HANDBOOK OF THE LAW
   OF TORTS 22 (4th ed. 1971). The classic exposition of the relation between loss distribution
   and other goals, of course, is to be found in GUIDO CALABRESI, THE COSTS OF ACCIDENTS
   39–54 (1970).
[3] See Kenneth S. Abraham, *The Rise and Fall of Commercial Liability Insurance*, 87 VA. L. REV.
   85 (2001).
[4] *See*, for example, JULES L. COLEMAN, RISKS AND WRONGS (2002); ERNEST J. WEINRIB,
   THE IDEA OF PRIVATE LAW (1995); John C. P. Goldberg & Benjamin Zipursky, *Unrealized
   Torts*, 88 VA. L. REV. 1625 (2002).

deterrence and corrective justice, and to the proper role of each within tort law, has largely crowded out concern with loss distribution.

Regardless of whether academicians consider loss distribution to be an important goal of tort liability, however, loss distribution issues cannot be avoided in thinking about tort. In practice, the tort system has been anything but indifferent to loss distribution. The major expansions in the incidence and scope of liability that occurred in the 1970s and 1980s can be ascribed at least in part to loss-distributional aims. The same can be said of the consistent increases in real tort costs from that period to the present,[5] as well as the continued willingness of contemporary courts to maintain the legal precedents that helped to generate the expansion of products and mass tort liability during the past few decades.[6] Achieving loss distribution through tort may have largely vanished from academic radar screens, but it is still alive in the actual operation of tort law.

Moreover, even we were able to rule out purposely shaping the scope of liability rules to achieve greater loss distribution, tort must have a method of addressing the relationship between its own liability and damages rules and the vast range of sources of compensation for personal injury and illness which operate outside of tort. These "collateral" sources, comprised largely of private first-party and social insurance, have almost always already provided tort claimants with some compensation, and often with very substantial compensation, by the time a tort case finally comes to be tried or settled. The payment of additional benefits to claimants by these sources is also often held in prospect for those with continuing or permanent injuries. Whatever rule governs the relationship between tort damages and these other sources, such compensation inevitably will have a loss-distributional (or antidistributional) impact. Tort must therefore confront the question of how it will deal with these sources, as well as the loss-distributional effects of the options that are available.

Naturally enough, tort law's traditional approach to its relation to collateral sources has been termed the "collateral source rule." But in fact there are at least four possible collateral source rules, each with its own approach to the treatment of benefits paid or payable by collateral sources, and each with corresponding loss-distributional effects and implications. In this chapter, I

---

[5] *See* Tillinghast-Towers Perrin, U.S. Tort Costs (2003 Update) 12 (hereinafter "U.S. Tort Costs").

[6] *See* Gary L. Schwartz, *The Beginning and Possible End of the Rise of Modern American Tort Law*, 26 Ga. L. Rev. 601 (1992).

examine these effects and implications, in an effort to make sense out of the relation between tort liability and the disparate world of first-party and social insurance. I argue that, because tort liability is a comparatively poor method of distributing losses, we should reshape the relationship between tort liability and collateral source payments. First-party insurance policy-holders and social-insurance beneficiaries, who are all of course potential plaintiffs in personal injury litigation, should be permitted to transfer all their tort rights to their first-party insurers, in return for lower premiums or more generous coverage. This "full-subrogation" approach would pre-serve the deterrent effect of the threat of tort liability, but at the same time enhance the possibilities for loss distribution through forms of insurance that are superior to tort because they pay a higher percentage of their expendi-tures to victims and provide more certain recovery. Because the approach would be optional rather than mandatory, it would not put the state in the business of deciding the proper mix of tort rights and insurance for all indi-viduals. Rather, individuals would be permitted to make this decision for themselves.

In order to place tort law in an insurance perspective, Part II of this chapter reviews and quantifies the magnitude of the different sources of compen-sation for personal injury, illness, and death. This survey locates tort liabil-ity within our larger system of compensation and compares its functioning and scope with the other methods of loss distribution that are employed by the system. This review reveals the extent to which there is in fact a vast system of loss distribution, of which tort is only a small part. By con-trast, that system is by no means comprehensive, as it contains important gaps.

The central issue addressed by this chapter is whether these gaps should be filled by tort or by the other sources, and how that might be accomplished. Accordingly, Part III of this chapter then turns to the relationship between tort and the rest of the loss-distribution system. It analyzes the different possible relationships by identifying and exploring the loss-distributional and other impacts of four possible variants of the collateral source rule. My conclusion in this part is that none of these variants satisfactorily reconciles the tension between tort law's deterrence goal and its comparative ineffectiveness at loss distribution. Finally, Part IV examines the rarely considered, distinct treatment accorded to life insurance and savings under existing rules, and then recommends the full-subrogation approach to tort law's treatment of collateral sources, in order to retain tort law's deterrence potential but enhance overall loss distribution.

II. THE TORT SYSTEM IN AN INSURANCE PERSPECTIVE

A. Generally

Lawyers and academics are tortcentric.[7] We tend to think of the tort system as the center of the personal injury and illness universe, whereas – as is shown later – in quantitative terms tort is only a minor player in this universe. As lawyers we are inclined to think naturally in terms of lawsuits, not insurance or compensation programs. We read decisions, we litigate cases, we derive the rules on which we base legal advice from cases. Private and social insurance generally lie at the periphery of this world of litigation and judicial decisions. The primary domain of insurance is instead a set of abstruse contracts that typically are not read by policyholders, or obscure and bureaucratic regimes such as social security, whose contours are vague until the time comes to apply for the benefits they provide. Ask the average lawyer what her rights would be if she were injured by a negligent driver, and she will have a pretty good idea of the correct answer. Ask her what she would receive from social security and under what circumstances she would receive it if she became disabled, and the chances are she would draw a blank. One consequence of this differential awareness, I think, is that as lawyers we tend to overrate the importance of tort, both as a method of deterring unsafe conduct and as a source of compensation, and to underrate the other methods of promoting safety and compensating the victims of illness and injury.[8]

---

[7] *See* Richard B. Stewart, *Crisis in Tort Law? The Institutional Perspective*, 54 U. CHI. L. REV. 184 (1987).

[8] There are other reasons for this tortcentricity as well. The central place that the course in torts has played in the law school curriculum for over a century, and continues to play today, has a profound influence on the legal consciousness. Torts occupies its honored place in the first year of law school partly because it is as good a subject as any to provide the basis for teaching about the common law and the legal process, and partly because it provides a template for thinking about the noncontractual (and nontort) civil liabilities that are the subject of more advanced courses in the curriculum. Many of these subjects – securities law, employment discrimination, even copyright – depend on the notions of duty, breach, damage, and causation, track a tort-type conceptual framework. Thus, tort concepts, perhaps more than tort law itself, are the necessary building blocks in a legal education.

Areas other than torts in which the law also does the work of compensating injury or promoting safety do not receive nearly the same curricular prominence. Courses in safety regulation are divided by medium, for example, environmental law or food and drug law. Courses in product safety regulation are infrequent, although there are often courses on products liability law. On the compensation side, such courses on insurance as exist are virtually always about private insurance alone. Public or social insurance receives little attention in the typical curriculum, and when a course does address the subject it is often from the

In a sense this is because tort is unique in its features. Tort liability is the only significant device we employ specifically to compensate the victims of third-party wrongdoing. In another sense, however, tort is just one component of a larger system of compensation for personal injury and illness. Viewing tort not in isolation from this larger system, but as a part of it, helps to reveal tort's comparatively modest scope. The sheer amount of money spent each year to compensate the victims of injury and illness tell a story that words alone do not adequately capture.[9]

B. The Tort System

The total direct cost of the tort system is roughly \$233 billion per year. This is a more than one-hundred-fold increase since 1950, when tort costs were about \$2 billion. The increase in tort costs during this period has outstripped economic growth by a factor of three.[10] Not all of this sum, however, is paid on account of losses associated with personal injury and illness. Some portion of the total is paid in connection with claims for property damage, for pure economic loss, and for losses associated with dignitary torts such as defamation and invasion of privacy. For the sake of simplicity I will assume conservatively that 75 percent of the \$233 billion annual cost of tort is the result of claims for personal injury and illness. Consequently, the proper figure to keep in mind for purposes of comparison with other sources is a direct tort cost of \$175 billion.

The percentage of this sum that is paid to personal injury and illness victims cannot be pinpointed exactly. One recent estimate is that only 46 percent of all expenditures, which based on the above calculation amounts to about \$80 billion per year, is paid to victims.[11] There is also somewhat less recent data on particular subfields within tort. Only a bit more than half of all money

---

perspective of welfare or poverty policy. Workers' compensation receives even less attention. Only twenty-two individuals were reported to be teaching a course on Workers' Compensation in an American law school during the year 2003–04. *See* THE AALS DIRECTORY OF LAW TEACHERS 1442–43 (2003).

[9] Unfortunately, the most recent year for which cost and benefits-paid data is available varies, depending on the compensation source or program in question. I have chosen to use data from the latest year available for each source or program, in order to provide the most accurate picture of each separate source or program as is possible. As a consequence, my survey adds together or compares data from different years for different sources. Given the hundreds of billions of dollars involved and the relatively modest changes that occur from year to year, however, the inaccuracy that results is probably minimal.

[10] All this data can be found in U.S. TORT COSTS, *supra* note 5, at 1.

[11] *See id.* at 17.

expended on automobile liability goes to victims.[12] In contrast, products liability and medical malpractice pay a considerably smaller portion of their expenditures to victims – perhaps as little as one third.[13]

Only half or even less of what we spend on tort is paid to victims, of course, because the system spends a great deal for the individualized fact-finding regarding negligence, causation, and damages that are so characteristic of tort. The theory of corrective justice requires monetary awards that are carefully tailored to the evidence of each particular plaintiff's past and probable future losses, both economic and emotional. And the search for optimal deterrence dovetails with this individualized tailoring of awards. To achieve deterrence the system must strive to threaten and to impose liability on defendants for all, but no more than all, of the costs that their negligence causes. Making this determination can be costly. In this respect, the two approaches that compete for the dominance of tort theory converge, both requiring that a considerable portion of the tort dollar be spent on the cost of administration rather than on compensation itself.

C. Workers' Compensation

Workers' compensation pays benefits for injuries "arising out of or in the course of employment." Benefits paid by this nonfault system of compensation for job-related injuries are lower than those paid by tort, $46 billion as compared to tort's $80 billion.[14] Because workers' compensation is essentially a system of absolute liability on the part of the employer, however, fact-finding as to liability is usually unnecessary. As a consequence, the cost of administration related to that issue is generally low. Therefore, workers' compensation pays a much higher percentage of the total dollars it expends in benefits than does tort – over 82 percent.[15] Although benefit levels vary from state to state, typically injured workers are paid all their medical costs. However, wage protection is limited. Most states limit payment to about two thirds of the employee's weekly wage, and then up to a maximum of $15,000 to $20,000 per year. Lump-sum payments for specified permanent disabilities are also paid.

---

[12] *See* JAMES S. KAKALIK & NICHOLAS M. PACE, COSTS AND COMPENSATION PAID IN TORT LITIGATION 72 (1986).

[13] *See* COMMITTEE FOR ECONOMIC DEVELOPMENT, WHO SHOULD BE LIABLE? 53 (1989) (estimates of 35–45 percent); STEPHEN D. SUGARMAN, DOING AWAY WITH TORT LAW 23–24 (1989) (citing estimates of 37–40 percent).

[14] *See* UNITED STATES BUREAU OF THE CENSUS, STATISTICAL ABSTRACT OF THE UNITED STATES 352, Table 532 (2002) (hereinafter "STATISTICAL ABSTRACT").

[15] *Id.* (calculated by comparing benefits paid to total expenditures).

D. Health Insurance

By far the largest nontort source of compensation for personal injury and illness is health insurance. Health care costs in the United States exceed $1.1 trillion per year.[16] Third-party payments made for direct health care costs (as distinguished from medical research, etc.) total about $846 billion per year, of which payments by public sources such as Medicare, Medicaid, and other smaller programs account for $423 billion,[17] and private insurance for roughly the same amount.[18] Together these sources pay about 79 percent of all personal health care expenditures,[19] leaving individuals to pay $194 billion per year themselves.[20] A significant portion of these personal expenditures is incurred by persons with no health insurance or inadequate insurance. About 15 percent of the population has no health insurance at all.[21]

E. Life Insurance

Life insurance is also a significant method of loss distribution. The average insured household is covered by nearly $200,000 of life insurance.[22] Fixing the proper of amount of life insurance benefits to figure into the calculus requires some estimation, however, because life insurance represents both insurance

---

[16] *Id.* at 92, Table 113.

[17] *Id.* at 340, Table 510.

[18] *Id.* at 92, Table 113. The remaining third-party-paid funds are paid by nonpatient revenues and other sources. *Id.*, n. 1.

[19] *Id.*

[20] *Id.* All but a very small proportion of the cost of hospital care is insured, whereas nearly one fifth of the cost of ambulatory care is paid by individuals. U.S. Census Bureau, Report No. P60-215: Health Insurance Coverage 2000, Tables 3–5 (in 1997, 2.6 percent of the cost of hospital care and 17.3 percent of the cost of ambulatory care was paid for out-of-pocket). Private insurers pay about 95 percent of the premium dollar in benefits. *See* Statistical Abstract, *supra* note 14, at 93, Table 113 and 93, Table 117 (calculated by comparing total benefits paid of $423 billion to total premiums of $444 billion). Payout ratios for all the public sources cannot easily be calculated because of their methods of accounting, but the ratio for the largest – Medicare – is similar at 96 percent. *Id.* at 92, Table 113, and 340, Table 511 (calculated by comparing total benefits paid of 215 billion to total expenditures 224 billion). These comparatively high payout ratios are not achieved because health insurers and government bureaucrats necessarily do their jobs efficiently, but because of the nature of these compensation systems. Because a right to health insurance benefits is triggered by the mere occurrence of a health care expense, the determination of eligibility and the proper amount of payment is largely a clerical rather than a fact-finding function.

[21] *Id.* at 102, Table 137.

[22] American Council of Life Insurers, Life Insurers Fact Book 117, Table 7.14 (2001) (hereinafter "Life Insurers Fact Book 2001").

and savings. Each year over $44 billion is paid to the beneficiaries of life insurance policyholders as death benefits.[23] But an additional $31 billion is paid as living benefits, in the form of cash surrender or investment return.[24] An indeterminate portion of this sum is undoubtedly used by recipients to cover injury and illness costs.

Life insurance has sometimes been considered to be payment to assuage grief. But it is more accurate and useful to conceive of life insurance as compensation for loss of earning power or human capital. A household that purchases insurance on the life of its principal income earner is not buying protection against grief; rather, it is insuring against the possibility that it will be deprived of support by the premature death of the insured. Life insurance is therefore best understood mainly as a method of compensating for income lost because of death resulting from illness or injury.[25] On this view, although $200,000 may seem like a significant amount of insurance, it is in fact inadequate protection against lost income for virtually all families – at current interest rates this sum would yield an annual income of less than $10,000.

F. Disability Insurance

The majority of payments for disability – income lost because of the inability to work – are made by the Social Security Disability program. This program pays about $55 billion per year for total, long-term disability.[26] But the average monthly benefit is only $814 to each disabled beneficiary and $238 to children of disabled beneficiaries.[27] Statistics on benefits paid by privately purchased long-term disability insurance are difficult to obtain, because these payouts are comparatively small – they may be on the order of $10 billion per year.[28] Roughly 25 percent of private sector employees have long-term disability insurance – although the discrepancy in the percentage of individuals in

---

[23] AMERICAN COUNCIL OF LIFE INSURERS, LIFE INSURERS FACT BOOK 75–77 (2002).

[24] Id.

[25] See Kenneth S. Abraham and Kyle D. Logue, The Genie and the Bottle: Collateral Sources under the 9/11 Victims Compensation Fund, 54 DE PAUL L. REV. 591 (2004).

[26] See UNITED STATES BUREAU OF THE CENSUS, STATISTICAL ABSTRACT OF THE UNITED STATES 345, Table 526 (2001).

[27] Id. at 346, Table 519.

[28] See LIFE INSURERS FACT BOOK 2001, supra note 22, at 137, Table 9.1 ($13 billion in private disability insurance in force in 2000); Kenneth S. Abraham and Lance L. Liebman, Private Insurance, Social Insurance, and Tort Reform: Toward a New Vision of Compensation for Illness and Injury, 93 COLUM. L. REV. 75, 82 (1993) (estimating payments of $6 billion in 1988).

TABLE 3.1. *Annual personal injury and illness compensation costs (in $ billions)*

	Expenditures	Benefits paid
Tort	175	80
Workers Compensation	56	46
Health Insurance	1100	846
Health Care Out-of-Pocket	194	–
Life Insurance	48	44
Disability Insurance	96	88
TOTAL	1669	1104

different wage groups who are covered is striking. Whereas 47 percent of white-collar employees are covered, only 13 percent of blue collar employees are.[29] In addition, benefits paid for short-term disability, in the form of paid sick leave, are available to about one half of the workforce.[30] Based on the data available, my very rough estimate is that the magnitude of these payments is $23 billion per year.[31] Thus, payouts from all these forms of disability coverage total about $88 billion annually.[32]

Putting these figures together, as reflected in Table 3.1, yields a rough idea of the quantitative importance of tort liability within our broader system of compensation for illness and injury. In very rough terms, that broader system

[29] National Academy of Social Insurance, 1996 Disability Panel Interim Report 33–34. Part of the explanation for this discrepancy is that because the disability protection afforded by workers' compensation and social security covers a much higher proportion of the typical blue collar worker's potential loss of income, such workers have less need for additional, private coverage.

[30] *See* THE ENVIRONMENT OF DISABILITY INCOME POLICY: PROGRAMS, PEOPLE, HISTORY AND CONTEXT 34 (Jerry L. Mashaw and Virginia P. Reno, eds.) (1996).

[31] Sick pay costs are about $.17 for every $15.80 in wages and salaries paid, or about 1.1 percent of pay. STATISTICAL ABSTRACT, *supra* note 14, at 406, Table 618. The mean hourly wage of U.S. workers is $16.35. Bureau of Labor Statistics, Occupational Employment Statistics 2001, available at <http://www.bls.gov/oes/2001/oes_ooal.htm>. If we assume an average of forty hours per week of work for fifty-two weeks each year, worked by the 50 percent of the 127 million workers for whom sick pay is available, *see id.*, then sick leave costs to employers are roughly $.18 per hour, or $374 per year for each of about 64 million workers – say, $24 billion annually. Assuming about $1 billion in administrative costs yields an estimate of benefits paid per year of $23 billion.

[32] There are a number of other programs, public and private, that pay benefits to the victims of injury and illness. These include the federal childhood vaccine compensation plan; the Florida and Virginia birth-related neurological injury compensation funds; and auto no-fault plans in force in over a dozen number of states. These programs are important conceptually, because – along with workers' compensation – they reflect an activity-based alternative to the largely fault-based approach of tort. But quantitatively they pay only a few billion dollars per year to victims and therefore have a barely perceptible importance.

costs about $1.7 trillion annually, of which $175 billion, or about 10 percent, is for personal injury and illness tort costs.[33] Looking at percentages of benefits paid rather than percentages of costs, $1.1 trillion in benefits is paid each year, of which about $80 billion, or just over 7 percent, is paid to the relevant subset of tort victims.

Thus, as suggested at the outset of this chapter, tort law plays only a small role in our system of public and private loss distribution. Moreover, tort is also a comparatively inefficient compensation mechanism, in that it pays a much smaller percentage of its expenditures to victims than the other approaches. And because the other approaches compensate on a broader basis, they are superior not only at loss distribution but also at risk distribution. By contrast, payments made by the overall system are far from sufficient to compensate all the victims of illness and injury for all their losses. Although there is therefore at least a potential a role to be played by tort in filling the gaps in our overall loss distribution system, the question is whether expanding tort or the features of our broader system of compensation is the better method of addressing this problem.

III. THE RELATION BETWEEN TORT AND FIRST-PARTY AND SOCIAL INSURANCE

There can be little question that, whatever might be said about the treatment of collateral sources in tort for loss-distribution purposes, optimal deterrence is best served by a rule that ignores these sources in determining the amount of damages for which a defendant is liable. Otherwise, defendants are not threatened with liability for the full social cost of their actions. Of the four possible rules explored later, the first three – each a different version of the "nonoffset" approach – serves the deterrence goal. The last, or "offset" approach, is less concerned with deterrence, and instead threatens defendants only with liability for the losses that plaintiffs have actually suffered, net of insurance.

Each of the approaches has different loss-distributional consequences. Thus, even if one takes the extremely plausible position that because tort is an inefficient approach to affording compensation its rules should emphasize deterrence, the different loss-distributional consequences of the three nonoffset approaches that reflect this emphasis still are worth considering. Similarly, given the criticism that the traditional, nonoffset collateral source

---

[33] To make this calculation I have assumed that the programs for which I have data only on payouts, but no meaningful or usable data on premiums or receipts, pay about 90 percent of their receipts as benefits.

rule continually receives at the hands of the proponents of certain versions of tort reform, the distributional consequences of the offset approach should also be considered. Thus, even if loss distribution is ruled out as a major goal of tort, it is not possible to escape thinking about loss distribution in establishing and evaluating tort law's treatment of collateral sources. Perhaps more important, examination of each of the existing approaches to the treatment of collateral sources reveals that none of them satisfactorily reconciles the tension between tort law's goal of promoting deterrence and achieving effective loss distribution.

A. The Collateral Source Rule and Insurance Reality

A recurring theme in the tort law literature and in debates about tort reform has been the proper role of payment by collateral sources in determining the successful plaintiff's damages.[34] Should there always be a full award of damages to tort claimants, notwithstanding past or anticipated future payment of benefits to the claimant by these sources, or should the amount of benefits paid to the claimant by collateral sources such as insurance be offset against the award, in order to avoid duplicate recovery?

For almost as long as this theme has existed, however, it has been understood that posing the question in this way is simplistic. When the traditional collateral source rule applies and there is no offset against the award, the plaintiff does not necessarily secure duplicate recovery. Even setting aside the fact that the damages awarded may be incomplete and that contingent counsel fees ordinarily must be paid out of the award, another device is designed to preclude double recovery: subrogation.[35]

Subrogation is the process by which one party is substituted for another party relative to the latter's rights against a third party. By operation of law or by contract, virtually all forms of private insurance and many forms of social insurance have rights of subrogation, transferring to insurers the policyholder's or beneficiary's right of recovery against third parties, to the extent of payment by the collateral source. For example, a health or workers' compensation insurer that has paid a policyholder's medical expenses is typically subrogated to the policyholder's rights of recovery against a tortfeasor responsible for the injury that generated these expenses.

[34] *See*, for example, FOWLER W. HARPER & FLEMING JAMES, JR., 2 THE LAW OF TORTS § 25.22 at 1343–54 (1956); John G. Fleming, *The Collateral Source Rule and Loss Allocation in Tort Law*, 54 CALIF. L. REV. 1478 (1966).

[35] *See* KENNETH S. ABRAHAM, DISTRIBUTING RISK: INSURANCE, LEGAL THEORY, AND PUBLIC POLICY 153–56 (1986).

Although this right of subrogation can in theory be vindicated in a direct action brought by the insurer against the tortfeasor, the more conventional method of vindication is through reimbursement of the insurer of the policyholder out the policyholder's tort recovery. In short, through what I will call "subrogation reimbursement," duplicate recovery by the tort claimant can be avoided. Indeed, in a sense the traditional collateral source rule exists precisely in order to make such reimbursement possible without depriving the policyholder of the potential for obtaining full compensation.

In practice, however, three factors impede this seemingly ordered approach. First, insurers do not always monitor tort suits brought by their policyholders so as to be in a position to vindicate their subrogation reimbursement rights when there is a tort recovery subsequent to the payment of insurance benefits. Doing so over a period of years is costly, and in the case of comparatively small potential reimbursement, not necessarily cost effective. Second, as most cases are settled, an administratively simple method of dividing a settlement that isolates the insurer's proper share of an incomplete pie is necessary, to make it possible for reimbursement to take place automatically. But none of the alternatives is entirely satisfactory, and not all states have clearly specified one.[36]

Third, to function ideally, the system also should permit future subrogation reimbursement. That is, after any claimant has recovered in tort not only for past but also for future losses, the claimant will begin to incur additional out-of-pocket losses as a result of the harm for which she has already received damages from the defendant. A collateral source that then pays insurance benefits to such a claimant should in theory receive subrogation reimbursement from that same claimant, because the claimant has already recovered in tort for some or all of these losses. But whether these future payments are made on account of losses resulting from the prior tort or from an independent illness or injury becomes, as time progresses, increasingly difficult and correspondingly more expensive to determine. Accounting for the benefits paid and the subrogation reimbursement due also would be bizarre. It is difficult to imagine a health insurer paying for a policyholder's medical care and then billing the policyholder for reimbursement to the extent that the care had been provided on account of an injury for which the policyholder had already received a tort recovery.

For these reasons among others, it is common for health and disability insurers who are about to receive subrogation reimbursement at the time

---

[36] For an illustration of the problems that arise in fashioning such a method, *see Associated Hospital Service of Philadelphia v. Pustilnik*, 396 A.2d 1332 (Pa. Super. 1979).

of a tort recovery to waive any right they have to future reimbursement, in return for present reimbursement. But of course these particular insurers will not necessarily be the insurers of the claimant at all times in the future, and the claimant's future insurers are not bound by such a waiver. Especially in cases involving severe, permanent injury, in which a substantial portion of the recovery awarded to the plaintiff may be for future out of pocket losses, the potential for subrogation reimbursement to fail in this major way is significant.

Thus, for a variety of reasons, although we must take the possibility of subrogation reimbursement into account in considering the distributional consequences of different approaches to the treatment of collateral sources in tort, we also should recognize that subrogation theory and subrogation reality may differ, and sometimes substantially.

B. The Loss-Distributional Choices

Modern tort law has developed two different general arrangements for dealing with collateral sources. The traditional, or *nonoffset*, approach is known as the "collateral source rule," and denies the tortfeasor any credit for benefits paid or payable to the plaintiff by collateral sources. Subrogation reimbursement by collateral sources is then permitted to ensure that the plaintiff does not secure any duplicate recovery. The alternative *offset* approach enacted in a minority of states provides the tortfeasor with a credit that reduces the plaintiff's tort recovery by amounts paid (and sometimes payable) by collateral sources.

Under these two approaches the issue is not whether to avoid duplicate compensation – both nonoffsets linked with subrogation reimbursement and offsets have the potential to achieve that goal. Rather, the issue is which party should be the primary cost bearer – the tortfeasor and its liability insurer, or loss-based sources of insurance. If tort damages are offset by payments from loss-based sources, then these latter sources are primary insurers. If there are no offsets, then the tortfeasor and its liability insurer are primary insurers, because they pay in full and the plaintiff's collateral sources receive reimbursement for their payments out of the tort award.

But it turns out that these are merely general categories. There are in fact potential variations that yield four different possible treatments of the relation between tort recoveries and the benefits that are paid or payable by collateral sources. The different approaches that are available have quite different impacts on the distribution of loss. The following examination of these approaches begins with the nonoffset approaches, and within this category moves from the variation that is most generous to tort claimants and least advantageous to nontortiously harmed victims, to the variation that is least generous to tort victims and most advantageous to nontortiously harmed victims. It then explores the alternative, offset approach.

1. *Nonoffsets without Collateral Reimbursement*

The broadest existing approach for using tort law's treatment of collateral sources for loss distribution purposes is to preclude offsets through the traditional collateral source rule but also to preclude subrogation reimbursement of first-party and social insurance sources. This is the approach that has always applied to life insurance, and largely to life insurance alone.[37] Applied more broadly, this approach would maintain the traditional rule's focus on ensuring that the cost of tortiously caused loss is channeled through the tortfeasor or its liability insurer. At the same time, however, this approach would recognize that because most tort recoveries are partial, even the plaintiff's tort recovery plus her first-party insurance and benefits may not provide full compensation. Tort recoveries are often incompletely compensatory in part because the contingent-fee system almost automatically produces undercompensation for any claimant who recovers less than her full losses by judgment or settlement. In the aggregate, the sums paid by plaintiffs as counsel fees are equal to 79 percent of the awards for noneconomic loss net of counsel fees.[38] When a contingency-based counsel fee is subtracted from full, or much more often, from partial recovery, the claimant is therefore likely to be undercompensated. Thus, the majority of victims, who settle for less than their full losses, probably are left less than fully compensated for their out-of-pocket losses even before paying any subrogation reimbursement they owe to their health or disability insurers.

In addition, a high percentage of all tort claims – certainly over 90 percent – are settled. Virtually by definition the claimants in these cases receive less than full compensation. There may well be a certain amount of "excess" compensation that claimants who settle have been paid by collateral sources that is not ultimately returned to insurers because of the shortfalls in enforcement of

---

[37] Although rare in connection with other forms of insurance, this approach is occasionally prescribed by statute applicable in other limited contexts. *See*, for example, Ann. Code of Md. § 19–109 (2002) (prohibiting subrogation by insurers providing medical payments coverage under auto insurance policies).

[38] *See* U.S. Tort Costs, *supra* note 5, at 17 (claimants' attorneys fees constitute 19 percent of total tort costs, whereas awards for noneconomic loss constitute 24 percent).

subrogation reimbursement to which I referred earlier. But in the aggregate this excess is likely to be more than offset by the payment of counsel fees.[39] In short, many claimants probably do not recover even their full economic losses, and those that do recover these losses in full probably succeed in doing so only if they are not forced to reimburse their health and disability insurers out of their recoveries.

There are three distributional objections, however, to institutionalizing a no-subrogation reimbursement rule to go along with the nonoffset approach. First, this approach would favor tort victims at the expense of victims of non-tortiously caused injury and illness. Subrogation reimbursement is a means by which premium levels or costs for first-party and social insurance are contained. Denying these sources reimbursement would provide a benefit to the minority of policyholders or beneficiaries who suffered tortiously-caused injury, but only by disadvantaging the majority whose losses are not tortiously-caused, by increasing their premiums or reducing the amount of coverage that would otherwise be available to them.

Moreover, as seen in part I of this chapter, tort is a comparatively expensive way to provide insurance against loss, paying at most only 50 percent of all of its expenditures to victims. Those who pay tort "premiums" as part of the price of products or health care would rationally prefer to use those premiums to buy more first-party insurance rather than tort insurance. That would provide more actual insurance for the money. In addition, first-party insurance provides more of the kind of insurance that individuals rationally would prefer. First-party insurance provides a more certain payoff than tort and it provides a payoff of out-pocket-expenses only. Ordinarily, suffering a nonpecuniary loss does not alter an individual's need for money. From an insurance standpoint, therefore, more than a modicum of tort insurance against nonpecuniary loss, or pain and suffering, is not a sensible purchase for most people.

Second, denying insurers subrogation reimbursement would accord a priority to compensating for intangible loss rather than first ensuring compensation for out-of-pocket loss resulting from illness or injury. That is, the compensation shortfall experienced by some claimants means at least in part that reimbursing their insurers for already paid out-of-pocket loss deprives the claimants of some or all of their pain and suffering damages. Denying

---

[39] As total payments for economic loss net of counsel fees are only slightly greater than amounts paid for counsel fees, *see id.* (awards for economic loss constitute 22 percent of total tort costs; awards for claimants' counsel fees constitute 19 percent), counsel fees are likely to exceed the amount of the claimant's prior collateral source payments that are not reimbursed to the insurer.

insurers reimbursement would result in an increase in the cost of first-party insurance, in order to permit claimants to retain these pain and suffering damages. In effect, potential tort victims would be paying their first-party insurers a premium for the right to retain all the pain and suffering damages they recovered. For the reasons specified earlier, this is probably not a purchase most policyholders rationally would or should want to make.[40]

Third, a no-reimbursement rule would in effect charge first-party policyholders an additional premium for the chance of recovering more than their net losses in the event that they were tortiously injured and were fully compensated in tort. A claimant fully compensated in tort but without any subrogation reimbursement obligation would double-recover at least some out-of-pocket losses. First-party insurance premiums would rise, because the absence of subrogation reimbursement would decrease insurer revenues. This would amount to the mandatory purchase by policyholders of a lottery ticket that would pay off if they were tortiously injured and brought completely successful tort suits. This would not constitute insurance, however, which distributes the risk of suffering loss, but a gamble that would provide the chance of obtaining a net financial gain as a result of being tortiously harmed. A rational purchaser of insurance would not want to spend money on this kind of gamble.

2. Nonoffsets with Collateral Reimbursement Subject to a Make-Whole Constraint

This is a version of the traditional collateral source rule precluding offsets, but with a qualification that is added in some jurisdictions. Under this variation, collateral sources have no right of reimbursement until the plaintiff has been made whole.[41]

The crucial feature of this "make-whole" requirement is its treatment of pain and suffering damages. Typically, a prerequisite to the insurer's right to subrogation reimbursement under the make-whole rule is that the plaintiff has been fully compensated for both out-of-pocket and intangible loss.[42]

---

[40] For an argument to the contrary, *see* Steven D. Croley & Jon D. Hanson, *The Non-Pecuniary Costs of Accidents: Pain and Suffering Damages in Tort Law*, 108 HARV. L. REV. 1785, 1812–34 (1995) (arguing that under certain conditions consumers might desire to insure against pain and suffering).

[41] *See*, for example, *Duncan v. Integon General Ins. Corp.*, 482 S.E.2d 325 (Ga. 1997). *See also* Elaine M. Rinaldi, *Apportionment of Recovery Between Insured and Insurer in a Subrogation Case*, 34 TORT & INS. PRAC. J. 803 (1994).

[42] *See*, for example, *Rimes v. State Farm Automobile Ins. Co.*, 316 N.W. 2d 348 (Wis. 1992).

In such cases, the make-whole constraint precludes reimbursement virtually every time a case has settled, as well as in cases tried to judgment in which the defendant had a partial defense such as comparative negligence. For practical purposes, therefore, this approach tends to preclude subrogation reimbursement in most cases, and is subject in these cases to the objections detailed in the preceding section.

By contrast, if – as tends not to be the case – compensation for pain and suffering were excluded from the make-whole calculation, then the make-whole constraint would establish tort as a gap filler, providing compensation for out-of-pocket loss in precisely those cases in which a plaintiff's first-party insurance was insufficient to cover all such loss. Because in the aggregate the amount of pain and suffering damages retained by plaintiffs after paying counsel fees is roughly equal to counsel fees themselves, the make-whole constraint would generally enable plaintiffs to retain the amount of any recovery of uninsured damages for out-of-pocket loss that was still left after paying counsel fees, plus perhaps some pain and suffering damages as well.

This approach would meet some but not all of the objections to nonreimbursement analyzed earlier. It would not risk overcompensating for out-of-pocket loss. And any first-party insurance premium increases occurring on account of the make-whole constraint on subrogation reimbursement would be paid so as to ensure full recovery of out-of-pocket loss rather than to enable the policyholder to retain pain and suffering damages. However, like the blanket prohibition on subrogation reimbursement, the make-whole constraint privileges tort claimants at the expense of victims of nontortiously caused injury and illness, whose first-party insurance premiums are higher than they would be in the absence of the make-whole constraint on subrogation reimbursement. The effect is therefore to give priority to expensive loss distribution through tort, rather than less expensive and therefore more loss-distributive first-party and social insurance.

Moreover, the administrative complications associated with a make-whole constraint on subrogation reimbursement can be substantial. The problem is how to determine whether the plaintiff was or was not made whole, regardless of the conception of being "made whole" that is employed. Note first that this problem would not arise in cases in which there had been no reduction in damages because of comparative negligence or a similar defense and the case was tried to a verdict. By definition these are cases in which the plaintiff has been or at least could be treated as having been fully compensated for her losses. But no such presumption could be made in cases involving reduced verdicts; only if all cases were required to employ special verdict procedures could the verdict reveal whether and to what extent the make-whole constraint had been satisfied.

More important, the vast majority of tort claims are compromised through settlement. One of the main advantages of a settlement is that it avoids the need to adjudicate the amount of the plaintiff's losses. But only by knowing each category as well as the total amount of the plaintiff's losses can the amount that has as yet been uncompensated be determined. So the consequence of a make-whole rule is that, after every tort case that is settled, the damages portion of the case may have to be litigated anyway, in order to determine whether the plaintiff has been made whole. This can be done in something less than a full-scale damages trial. But an adjudicative proceeding of some sort, with all the expense entailed in fact-finding and possibly substantial discovery, would be necessary.[43] Thus, any appealing features of even the modified make-whole rule described earlier would require further complicating and thereby rendering more expensive the resolution of most tort claims.[44]

3. Nonoffsets with Off-the-Top Collateral Reimbursement

Under this approach the plaintiff is entitled to full recovery in tort regardless of payments made by collateral sources,[45] but those sources are entitled to subrogation reimbursement off-the-top of tort judgments or settlements, regardless of whether this will deprive the claimant of full compensation – that is, keep the claimant from being made whole.

By returning more money to first-party insurers than would the make-whole approach, in the aggregate this approach either permits the purchase of more first-party insurance than would otherwise be available, or reduces the cost of premiums. It would therefore give to all policyholders, rather than merely tort claimants, these potential advantages. As a matter of loss distribution this benefits more people and at lower cost than the preceding two nonoffset approaches. There is admittedly still some administrative cost

[43] For somewhat anecdotal but nonetheless suggestive evidence that, in order to avoid this problem, in practice the insured, the insurer, and plaintiff's counsel often agree on an even, three-way split of settlements, *see* Tom Baker, *Blood Money, New Money, and the Moral Economy of Tort Law in Action*, 35 LAW & SOC'Y Rev. 275, 304–08 (2001).

[44] A variation on this approach that is occasionally applied, though to settlements only, apportions the settlement between the insurer and insured in the proportion that the amount the insurer has paid to the policyholder bears to the policyholder's total loss. *See* ALAN I. WIDISS AND ROBERT E. KEETON, INSURANCE LAW § 310 (b)(1) at 234 (1988). The fact finding difficulties entailed in this approach parallel those posed by the make-whole approach.

[45] *See* RESTATEMENT (SECOND) OF TORTS § 920A(2) (1979).

entailed in accomplishing subrogation reimbursement, as it involves the cost of collection by first-party and social insurers. But this cost is lower than under the make-whole rule, which requires fact finding as to the proper amount of reimbursement in addition to the cost of collection. In contrast, under the off-the-top approach the proper amount of reimbursement is always a specified sum – the full amount the insurer has paid to or on behalf of the claimant.

In short, the rule embodied in this variation preserves the deterrence-promoting potential of any nonoffset rule, but also channels more loss-distribution resources through first-party and social insurance than the other nonoffset variations. It does this with a comparative sacrifice in the net compensation of tort victims, in effect tolerating potential undercompensation in tort in return for enhancing loss distribution through these other, more cost-effective methods of distributing loss.

4. Offsets with No Collateral Reimbursement

I now turn to the offset approach, which reduces the amount of the plaintiff's tort recovery by benefits paid or payable from first-party and social insurance sources. This approach sacrifices potential deterrence in return for eliminating the risk that the plaintiff will be overcompensated through the combined receipt of first-party insurance and tort damages. It also avoids the cost of collecting subrogation reimbursement.

This approach has been enacted by statute in a minority of states, thus reversing the traditional collateral source rule.[46] Under this approach any sum that has been paid or, as is often the case, that will be payable in the future by collateral sources is offset against the plaintiff's tort recovery. The plaintiff therefore recovers in tort only the difference between the amount paid or payable by collateral sources and her total losses. To the extent that the plaintiff is fully insured for out-of-pocket losses, then, her tort recovery consists exclusively of pain and suffering damages. Only to the extent that the plaintiff is underinsured does she recover out-of-pocket losses in tort. In effect, tort is a gap filler under this approach, "topping up" the plaintiff's total recovery to ensure full compensation. To make tort a true gap filler only, first-party and social insurers therefore have no subrogation reimbursement

---

[46] See, for example, N.J. STAT. § 2A:15-97 (2003); Mont Code Ann § 27-1-308 (2004) (applicable to actions for injury or death where total award exceeds $50,000). Some states apply this approach only where a collateral source has no subrogation rights, thus adopting the traditional rule for sources with subrogation rights and the offset rule for sources without such rights. See, for example, CONN. GEN. STAT. § 52-225 (a) (2003).

rights under this approach. This approach is thus a rough mirror image of the nonoffset variation that is subject to a make-whole constraint, under which first-party and social insurance "top up" tort recoveries.

From a loss-distribution standpoint alone, this approach more sensibly uses tort as a secondary source of compensation rather than as a primary source as is done under the nonoffset approach. But of course this is just a complicated way of saying that tort is a comparatively inefficient insurance mechanism, and of underscoring that it is mainly the nondistributional purposes of deterrence and corrective justice that lie behind the nonoffset approaches.

Perhaps more importantly, once it is recognized that the sums paid as counsel fees tend to be roughly equal to the amount pain and suffering damages that plaintiffs retain,[47] the underlying political motive behind the enactment of this approach comes into view. The plaintiff is likely to bring a tort action under this approach only if she has substantial uninsured out-of-pocket expenses or the potential for recovering substantial pain and suffering damages. Otherwise she will be unable to find counsel willing to take the case on a contingent-fee basis, as potential recovery will be prohibitively small. So whatever its loss-distributional effects, the actual motive behind the "offsets with no collateral reimbursement" approach is to obtain tort relief for potential defendants.

Interestingly, however, by making tort merely a gap filler in this way, the offset approach also reduces the income regressive effect of certain forms of tort liability. In contract settings that may give rise to tort liability, the *de facto* tort "premium" paid as a component of product or health care prices, for example, is not calibrated to the probable amount of income loss that the purchaser will incur if she is injured by a defective product or by medical malpractice.[48] The result is that both comparatively poor and comparatively wealthy purchasers pay the same "tort insurance premium" as part of the price of products or of health care, but the wealthier claimants get more tort insurance for that same premium because they are more likely to have higher income loss than the poor when they are injured. The effect is therefore that compensating for lost income through tort has an income-regressive impact. The lesser role that is left for tort by the offset approach reduces this effect, as the effect is mitigated or eliminated by first paying for income loss out of first-party and social insurance, whose premiums are more proportional to

---

47 *See* U.S. TORT COSTS, *supra* note 5, at 17.
48 *See* George L. Priest, *The Current Insurance Crisis and Modern Tort Law*, 96 YALE L. J. 1521, 1558–59 (1987); David Rosenberg, *The Causal Connection in Mass Exposure Cases: A "Public Law" Vision of the Tort System*, 97 HARV. L. REV. 851, 918–19 (1984).

the amount of income loss insured and therefore much less (or note at all) income-regressive than tort.

Finally, although the effect of this approach is to employ a make-whole norm with tort as only a secondary source of payment, the approach does not create the same fact finding difficulties or corresponding expense that the make-whole constraint creates under the nonoffset approach, which makes tort the primary source of payment. Because first-party insurers are not entitled to any subrogation reimbursement under this approach, there is no need for any adjudicatory proceeding in cases involving verdicts reduced because of defenses such as comparative negligence, or in settled cases, in order to determine the share to be recovered by first-party insurers. Rather, juries are instructed to apply offsets, or to find the facts necessary for the court to apply them. Settlement then would presumably occur in the shadow of the rule that offsets will be applied in any case that goes to judgment. The make-whole norm under an offset approach is in this sense self-applying.

IV. TOWARD A NEW TREATMENT OF COLLATERAL SOURCES

We now have several aspects of the loss distribution issue on the table: (1) the scope of our tort and first-party and social insurance systems; (2) the gaps in first-party insurance that sometimes appear to make employing tort for loss distribution purposes appealing; (3) the different ways in which these two parts of the system may relate to each other; and (4) the loss distribution implications of these different possible relations. Still missing, however, is a sense of how one important form of coverage, life insurance, figures in the picture.

In fact, life insurance is wholly exempt from the treatment that other sources receive. As noted earlier, the nonoffset-without-collateral-reimbursement approach applies almost exclusively to life insurance. Once we consider treating life insurance in the same manner as all other collateral sources, however, then none of the four possible collateral source rules seems satisfactory. An alternative approach, which would transfer not only a right of reimbursement, but all the tort claimant's rights to first-party insurers, then begins to be attractive.

A. Life Insurance: No Longer a Special Case?

Life insurance has always fallen outside the scope of both the majority and minority approaches to collateral sources. For tort law, it is as if life insurance simply did not exist.

The majority approach to the treatment of all other collateral sources involves nonoffsets in tort, with subsequent collateral reimbursement for most sources. Life insurers have no equitable rights of subrogation,[49] and never provide for subrogation rights by contract. Consequently, tort claimants have no obligation to reimburse their life insurers out of tort recoveries or settlements. True duplicate recovery – rather than the only apparent duplicate recovery that occurs prior to the subrogation reimbursement of health and disability insurers out of tort recoveries – may actually occur as a result of this arrangement. Correspondingly, in the minority of jurisdictions that take the offset approach to other collateral sources, life insurance benefits are always exempted from the required offset.

This seemingly anomalous treatment of life insurance is, I think, the legacy of two factors. First, the courts long treated life insurance as though its purpose was to assuage grief rather than to indemnify future economic loss. But few families can afford or find it rational to spend current dollars protecting against the risk of suffering future grief. So in fact life insurance is purchased primarily to provide income replacement on the death of a family's income earner. Nonetheless, because traditionally the courts made equitable subrogation available only to indemnity insurers – that is, only to insurers who insured against out-of-pocket losses – life insurers were never permitted this form of subrogation reimbursement out of tort recoveries in the absence of policy provisions granting them this right.[50]

Second, although the courts might well have permitted life insurers to provide for such subrogation reimbursement by contract – as health and disability insurers have long provided – this practice never developed either. The explanation probably is that market forces prevented contractual subrogation in life insurance from arising. Any life insurer seeking to vindicate its subrogation rights would likely have had to do so against a widow or orphan who had obtained a tort recovery for the death of an insured husband or father. These circumstances would not have been propitious ones for companies in an industry competing largely on the basis of reputation and reliability rather than product differentiation. So subrogation rights stayed out of life insurance policies.

---

[49] *See*, for example, Spencer L. Kimball and Don A. Davis, *The Extension of Insurance Subrogation*, 60 MICH. L. REV. 841, 845 (1962) ("In life insurance, there seems little doubt that, absent contractual stipulation, subrogation would be denied uniformly. Dicta are plentiful, but no cases actually decide the matter.").

[50] *See*, for example, *Michigan Hospital Service v. Sharpe*, 63 N.W.2d 638, 644 (Reid, J. dissenting), (quoting 29 AM. JUR. 1003–04) (Mich. 1955) ("There seems to be little doubt that a life insurance company cannot recover of one who has caused the death of an insured the amount which it has thereby been compelled to pay.")

Until relatively recently, this state of affairs was almost certainly reinforced by the limitations on recovery for wrongful death that obtained. Unlike recovery for nonfatal injury or illness, recovery for wrongful death is a creature of statute. And originally the statutes creating a cause of action for wrongful death contained two important limitations: a right to recover for economic loss only, and comparatively modest monetary ceilings on recovery even for economic loss.[51] In view of these limitations on recovery of the amount of loss resulting from tortiously-caused death, the absence of life insurers' subrogation reimbursement rights may well have been seen as a sensible counterweight to the risk of undercompensation. Life insurance helped to top up partial recoveries in tort for wrongful death and thereby to promote full compensation overall. Exempting life insurance from the treatment accorded all other collateral sources, that is, was a way to promote loss distribution.

In the second half of the twentieth century, however, the last vestiges of the two limitations on the damages that may be recovered for wrongful death largely disappeared. Both the prohibition on awarding damages for intangible loss resulting from wrongful death, and monetary ceilings on total recoveries, were eliminated. The rationale for exempting life insurance payments from the treatment accorded the other forms of insurance that also are available to tort claimants and their families has therefore also disappeared.

Any altered treatment of life insurance under the collateral source rule, however, would have implications for more fundamental questions about the relationship between tort recoveries and need. Life insurance is merely one form of savings. Why should those who have chosen this form of savings have it deducted from their tort recoveries, whether directly or indirectly, whereas those who have chosen a different form of savings do not incur a deduction?[52] That is, would it be inconsistent to subject life insurance benefits to the same treatment as other collateral source payments but to ignore other sources of wealth available to the victim's survivors?

The argument that there would be no inconsistency is that life insurance is a very particular form of savings. Unlike any other form, life insurance (and the devices allied with it, such as lifetime annuities) is stochastic. That is, setting aside any investment feature that is added to it, life insurance is never

---

[51] See DAN B. DOBBS, THE LAW OF TORTS § 296, at 807–11 (2000).

[52] This is essentially the problem that has created the most controversy over the SEPTEMBER 11 VICTIMS' COMPENSATION FUND, which, unlike tort, does reduce the benefits recoverable from the Fund by life insurance payments. See Kenneth S. Abraham & Kyle Logue, The Genie and the Bottle: Collateral Sources under the 9/11 Victims Compensation Fund, 54 DEPAUL L. REV. 591 (2003).

available until death is certain, or virtually so.[53] Life insurance is designed to protect against future loss of income, whereas other forms of savings are or could immediately be converted into present income. Thus, life insurance is a current asset, but not current income. Indeed, conceived as savings, perhaps the asset value of life insurance is only the premium that is paid for it.

The distinction between assets and income does not resolve the issue, however, but merely shifts the focus of the question. Why not offset against recoveries in tort for wrongful death both all current income and all assets that can be converted into income, rather than offsetting only insurance benefits? The answer depends on how this would fit with the goal of promoting loss distribution. One view is that loss distribution is desirable in general, because of the diminishing marginal utility of money. The very fact that people tend to be risk-averse and therefore purchase various forms of insurance is some confirmation of this view. It follows from this view that imposing a comparatively small loss on a large number of people will reduce overall utility less than imposing a large loss on one person, regardless of these individuals' wealth. To the extent that this is true, then it may make sense to ignore assets and savings in determining how tort law should treat collateral sources.

An alternative view, however, is that we value loss distribution not only because of the diminishing marginal utility of money generally. From a moral standpoint, we also may value loss distribution because it has the potential to satisfy the needs of those who have no other means of obtaining compensation for their losses. In this sense, loss distribution is a good because of its potential for improving the condition of those who need to have their losses mitigated. To the extent that this is the case, the savings or wealth of a claimant should be treated in the same way as her first-party and social insurance "wealth," because the wealthier the claimant, the less need there is to mitigate her losses.

Of course, putting this line of reasoning into practice would bring us a long way from the traditional collateral source rule, and would ask tort law to take more factors into account in calculating damage recoveries than would be realistic. We are not about to means-test tort recoveries, precisely because loss distribution is not tort law's main goal. Concerns about deterrence and corrective justice so dominate tort that, even if we thought it otherwise desirable

---

[53] Accelerated, or "viatical" settlements in connection with life insurance are the exception to the notion that life insurance policies pay only on the death of the party whose life is insured. These settlements are paid when death is virtually certain and imminent. *See* KENNETH S. ABRAHAM, INSURANCE LAW & REGULATION: CASE AND MATERIALS 293–94 (2000).

to do so, there would be no way to means-test recoveries across the board and still maintain the levels of liability necessary to achieve deterrence and corrective justice. Potential defendants' levels of care would significantly decline, because of the decreased magnitude of liability they would face, and everyone would be significantly worse off because of the substantial increase in tortiously-caused loss that would result. Any loss-distributional aims that tort law pursues must therefore be interstitial, deferring where necessary to tort law's more dominant purposes.

B. Transforming the Treatment of Collateral Sources

With the interstitial loss distribution effects of different approaches to collateral source payments and the issue of how to treat life insurance both on the table, it is time to take a step back and look at the big picture. We have seen that the central challenge for tort law's treatment of collateral sources is how to preserve deterrence, while at the same time taking advantage of the much greater efficiency of first-party and social insurance as methods of compensation. Offsets sacrifice deterrence in order to accord these forms of insurance loss-distributional priority. Nonoffsets preserve deterrence, but at the cost of some combination of possible overcompensation, significant administrative expense, and making tort – an inefficient loss distributor – the primary source of compensation. We are thus faced with a choice between unsatisfactory alternatives.

Two principles can help lead away from this dilemma. The first principle, already noted, is that first-party and social insurance are superior to tort as methods of affording compensation, because the compensable event under these systems is simple and easily applied. The result is that a much higher proportion of the money invested in loss distribution finds its way into the pockets of victims under first-party and social insurance than in tort. The second principle is that, from a loss-distributional standpoint, out-of-pocket expenses should have a higher compensation priority than intangible loss. It may be arguable that awarding pain and suffering damages serves corrective justice; and in my view awards of at least some damages for pain and suffering are necessary to promote optimal deterrence. But although pain and suffering is a real social cost, the loss that pain and suffering damages reflect cannot be "distributed" by awarding victims monetary compensation. The victims of pain and suffering do not need their losses distributed; they need their pain and suffering relieved. Paying damages for pain and suffering does not relieve pain and suffering. It is instead an economic substitute for relief, as well as a means of attempting to ensure that the plaintiff's counsel fees can be paid without depriving her of compensation for out-of-pocket loss.[54]

Combining these two principles with the desirability of preserving deterrence suggests an alternative approach. We should permit potential tort victims to invest their available insurance dollars more heavily in first-party insurance protecting them against the risk of suffering out-of-pocket loss, rather than on tort "insurance." But we should continue to threaten defendants with liability for the full social cost of harm they cause, including intangible loss.

A number of scholars have proposed full-subrogation approaches that would allow this ideal to be approached. In one way or another they propose authorizing plaintiffs to sell their tort causes of action in return for additional protection against out-of-pocket loss.[55] What these approaches amount to, using the kind of terminology I employed in part II, is "nonoffsets with total collateral recovery." The plaintiff would continue to have formal tort rights, but her first-party insurance contract would provide that her total tort recovery – not merely the benefits already paid or payable by the insurer – would be returned to her insurer as subrogation reimbursement. The plaintiff would then be a plaintiff in name only, as the real party in interest would be her first-party insurer.

This general approach would preserve the deterrence that is a central feature of the nonoffset approaches but would enable potential tort claimants to transform their right to recover pain and suffering damages into less expensive, or more broadly protective, first-party insurance. Of course, the

---

[54] It may be that ceilings on pain and suffering damages, otherwise deeply objectionable on equitable grounds, are also a crude reflection of the idea that only secondary priority should be accorded to pain and suffering awards. Ceilings, however, extract the entire burden of reform from two groups. The first group is composed of those who are awarded damages for pain and suffering that exceed the pain and suffering they have actually experienced. This group has no legitimate complaint about ceilings. The second group, however, is composed of those whose pain and suffering would otherwise warrant an award in excess of the ceiling. Because life expectancy is a prime ingredient in the determination of a pain and suffering award where pain and suffering is permanent, this group will be disproportionately composed of young, seriously injured victims – especially children. Therefore, it is seriously-injured children who are likely to be most disadvantaged by the enactment of ceilings.

[55] See, for example, CHARLES FRIED & DAVID ROSENBERG, MAKING TORT LAW 91–92 (2003) (tort rights to be transferred to first-party insurers); Robert Cooter & Steven D. Sugarman, *A Regulated Market in Unmatured Tort Claims: Tort Reform by Contract*, in NEW DIRECTIONS IN LIABILITY LAW 174 (Walter Olson, ed.) (1988) (tort rights to be transferred to employers); Jeffrey O'Connell & Janet Beck, *Overcoming Legal Barriers to the Transfer of Third-Party Tort Claims as a Means of Financing First-Party No-Fault Insurance*, 58 Wash. Univ. L. Quart. 55 (1979) (tort rights to be transferred to first-party insurers).

details of this approach need to be worked out in more detail. It ought to be provided as an option for policyholders to accept or reject, and even then only after significant efforts have been made to ensure that the policyholder has given informed consent to the arrangement. That way, the state would not decide the proper mix of tort rights and insurance for all individuals; that decision would be made individually rather than collectively, as is now done.

Because the vast majority of private first-party insurance is employment-related group health insurance, a method of returning premiums saved or providing additional coverage to the individual policyholders electing the option would have to be developed as well. A method of designating the insurer that would hold the newly-enhanced right of subrogation reimbursement would also be required. It is easy enough to picture a bifurcation, however, under which health insurers, for example, received the right to payment of all damages for out-of-pocket expenses and conscious pain and suffering, whereas the right to recover damages for wrongful death was transferred to life insurers, with corresponding reductions in premiums or increases in the amounts of coverage provided by these sources.

The victims of torts might also have to be provided with an incentive to participate actively in the insurer's conduct of tort suits, as victims would effectively become mere witnesses without any economic stake in the outcome. Some sharing of pain and suffering damages by the victim and the insurer above a specified level might prove to be an optimal method of obtaining this participation. Because certain insurance companies might come to specialize in this form of recovery, and as a secondary market involving tort lawyers representing these insurers probably would develop, competition among insurers would likely generate a variety of options. Finally, the subrogation reimbursement rights of other collateral sources would have to be preserved, so that, for example, disability insurers were reimbursed by health insurers out of the tort recoveries that health insurers obtained.

But these are operational features, some of which the proponents of this approach already have addressed. Although the devil is sometimes in the details, the principle of the matter must be the first item on the agenda. No doubt the most seriously-injured victims who had previously opted into the new approach would experience *ex post facto* regret at the choice they had made. However, this would be no different from the other tort-waiver choices that we permit individuals to make, and indeed no different than some choices we make for them – including the universal enactment of workers' compensation as a substitute for tort and the enactment of mandatory auto no-fault in a number of states.[56] In any event, at present we make the opposite decision mandatory, by holding in most instances that the waiver of tort rights prior to injury is invalid.[57]

This approach might well help to fill part of the gap in the fabric of protection against out-of-pocket loss that still remains and so troubles both the tort and social-welfare systems. As noted earlier, there are still substantial gaps in the fabric of protection provided by first-party insurance. Fifteen percent or more of the population has no health insurance; nearly one fifth of the cost of out-patient medical care is uninsured; few income-earners have private or public disability insurance that provides more than slightly above subsistence level wage-loss protection, many having only social security protection against long-term, total disability; and most families have insufficient life insurance to protect them against the income loss they would suffer on the death of the principal wage-earner in the family.[58]

Tort has not filled these gaps, nor has political action on the health and disability insurance fronts for several decades now. Perhaps by creating a market for potential tort claims, revision of the collateral source rule can do what we have thus far failed to do – contribute to the provision of sufficient health care and income-loss protection for everyone in the United States. If the uninsured cannot now afford to pay for health and disability insurance with currently available funds, some of them may be willing to pay part of the necessary premium for such coverage by transferring their right to recover for personal injury in tort to these insurers, in return for insurance coverage that they can afford. We would then have achieved greater loss distribution, not by expanding the scope of tort liability but by modifying the relationship between tort recoveries and collateral sources and creating a means by which

---

[56] Admittedly, however, these systems usually eliminate the tort rights of the least-seriously injured, not those with the greatest prospects of recovering pain and suffering damages. For what may be the earliest proposal to make the choice between tort and auto no-fault optional, *see* Guido Calabresi, *The New York Plan: A Free Choice Modification*, 71 Colum. L. Rev. 267 (1971).

[57] *See*, for example, *Tunkl v. Regents of the University of California*, 383 P.2d 441 (Ca. 1963).

[58] B. Douglas Bernheim, Lorenzo Forni, Jagadeesh Gokhale, & Laurence J. Kotlikoff, *The Adequacy of Life Insurance: Evidence from the Health and Retirement Survey* (NBER Working Paper #7372) (October 1999). In the authors' sample, almost one third of wives and more than 10 percent of husbands would have suffered living standard reductions of 20 percent or more had their spouses died in 1992. The authors also found that underinsurance tends to be more common among low-income households, couples with asymmetric earnings, younger households, couples with dependent children, and nonwhites. Among some groups, the frequency of underinsurance exceeds two thirds. This paper can be found at <http://www.nber.org/papers/w7372>.

tort rights can be transformed into superior forms of insurance. I do not want to argue that this change alone would be sufficient to provide health or disability insurance to all the uninsured. But it might make a start.[59]

At the same time, the effects on the market for legal services might be salutary. At present, the contingent-fee system is necessary at least in part because plaintiffs have no other way to manage the huge payment that would otherwise be due their attorneys. Once the purchasers of the services of plaintiffs' personal injury attorneys are more often also first-party insurers, they may be able to take advantage of the greater clout that the reform would put in their hands.[60] A more competitive and perhaps very different market for the services of personal injury attorneys might be the result.

V. CONCLUSION

The world of insurance has changed enormously since the collateral source rule was first developed. At that time the payment of insurance benefits to tort plaintiffs by collateral sources was a rarity. Now this is routine. Similarly, the reasons for the exemption of life insurance from standard subrogation rules and practices no longer apply. But gaps in the fabric of first-party and social insurance protection still exist. By looking at tort and this fabric of protection as one system, we can see that neither the collateral source rule as we know it nor legislative reversals of the rule optimize the deterrence and insurance functions of this system. To achieve this goal, individuals should be given the right to transfer full subrogation rights to first-party insurers, in return for lower premiums or expanded insurance.

[59] A rough but conservative calculation would run as follows. Of the $80 billion in tort payments made each year, slightly more than half, or about $40 billion, is paid for noneconomic loss. *See* U.S. Tort Costs, note 5 *supra*, at 17. Approximately 15 percent of the population is uninsured for health care. Therefore, about 15 percent of $40 billion, or $6 billion, is available for recovery by first-party insurers on behalf of previously uninsured or underinsured individuals. Total health insurance benefits paid each year are $846 billion. *See* text at note 5, *supra*. Providing corresponding benefits to the 15 percent of the population that is uninsured would cost an additional 15 percent of this sum, or about $125 billion. Thus, transferring full rights of tort recovery by the uninsured to first-party insurers would pay for about 5 percent of the cost of providing health insurance to these individuals.

[60] For discussion of the flaws in this market, *see* LESTER BRICKMAN, MICHAEL J. HOROWITZ, AND JEFFREY O'CONNELL, RETHINKING CONTINGENCY FEES: A PROPOSAL TO ALIGN THE CONTINGENCY FEE SYSTEM WITH ITS POLICY ROOTS AND ETHICAL MANDATES (1994).

CHAPTER FOUR

BEYOND MASTER–SERVANT: A CRITIQUE OF VICARIOUS LIABILITY

Jennifer H. Arlen[†] and W. Bentley MacLeod[‡]

ABSTRACT. In order to regulate risk-taking efficiently, tort liability rules governing organizations' liability for torts by their agents must ensure that organizations both want their agents to take cost-effective precautions and benefit from using all cost-effective mechanisms to regulate agents. This chapter shows that vicarious liability, the current the rule governing organizations' liability for their agents' torts, does not satisfy these objectives. By holding organizations liable for torts committed by employees, but not by independent contractors, vicarious liability discourages organizations from asserting direct control over agents, even when control is the efficient way to induce optimal care. Organizations governed by vicarious liability also do not employ all cost-efficient tools available to them to induce efficient care-taking by independent contractors because organizations do not maximize profits by inducing efficient care. Indeed, vicarious liability encourages organizations to undermine the effect of individual tort liability by hiring judgment-proof independent contractors.

I. INTRODUCTION

Tort liability is essential to the effective functioning of a free market economy because it encourages people who impose risks on others to take cost-justified

---

[†]Norma Z. Paige Professor of Law, New York University School of Law.
[‡]Professor of Economics and Law, University of Southern California.
    This article was prepared for a conference held at Pace Law School, November 21, 2003. We would like to thank participants at the Pace University School of Law Conference on the Future of Tort Law and at the 2004 annual meeting of the American Law and Economics Association, as well as Richard Brooks, Robert Lee Hotz, Mark Ramseyer, Catherine Sharkey, and J. H. Verkerke for helpful comments. We also thank our excellent research assistants Adam Goldberg and William Bunting. We benefited from the financial support of Pace University School of Law. The first author also thanks the NYU School of Law and the second author thanks the Industrial Relations Section of Princeton University for support for this research.

precautions to reduce the expected costs of their activities.[1] In order for tort liability to fulfill its promise, it must provide efficient incentives to organizations, as well as individuals. Torts often are caused by individuals working for, and under the influence of, organizations (generally corporations).[2] These organizations are not passive bystanders, but instead ultimately determine whether agents strive to take cost-effective precautions against harm.

Organizations regulate agents' precautions through a variety of mechanisms that supplement individual tort liability. These tools include the assertion of direct control over precaution, monitoring agents, selection of agents, and the use of financial sanctions to either enhance or mute agents' potential tort liability.[3] Accordingly, in order to deter inefficient risk-taking, tort liability must ensure that organizations want their agents to take optimal care and benefit from using all cost-effective means available to them to get their agents to do so.

This chapter examines vicarious liability, the prevailing rule governing organizations' liability for torts committed by their agents, to determine whether it is efficient. Vicarious liability (or *respondeat superior*) holds organizations (and other principals) liable for their agents' torts, committed within the scope of the agency relationship, but only if the organization and the agent are in a master-servant relationship, such as an employer-employee relationship. Organizations generally are not liable for torts by independent contractors, even if committed within the scope of the agent's authority. The central distinction between a master-servant agency relationship and a non-master-servant (e.g., independent contractor) agency relationship turns on whether the principal had the capacity to control the physical conduct of the job.[4]

This chapter examines whether it is efficient to restrict organizations' liability for their agents' torts to situations where the principal has the capacity to control its agent's performance (as in an employer-employee relationship).

---

[1] *See*, for example, Guido Calabresi & A. Douglas Melamed, *Property Rules, Liability Rules and Inalienability: One View of the Cathedral*, 85 HARV. L. REV. 1089 (1972); John P. Brown, *Toward an Economic Theory of Liability*, 2 J. LEGAL STUD. 323 (1973); Steven Shavell, *Strict Liability Versus Negligence*, 9 J. LEGAL STUD. 1 (1980).

[2] Indeed, such torts dominate the standard torts course: the bargee in *U.S. v. Carroll Towing Co.*, 159 F.2d 169 (2d Cir. 1947), the tug boat captain in *The T. J. Hooper*, 60 F.2d 737 (2d Cir. 1932) (L. Hand, J.), *cert. denied*, 287 U.S. 662 (1932), the railway conductor in *Palsgraf v. Long Island R. Co.*, 248 N.Y. 339, 162 N.E. 99 (1928), the doctors and nurses in *Ybarra v. Spangard*, 25 Cal.2d 486, 154 P. 2d 687 (1944), and the cab driver in *Li v. Yellow Cab Co. of Calif.*, 532 P. 2d 1226 (Cal. 1975), all were operating within organizations or other principal-agent relationships.

[3] *See infra* section II.

[4] RESTATEMENT (SECOND) OF AGENCY § 2 (1958); *see infra* section IV & note 31 (discussing vicarious liability in more detail).

We examine the effect on organizations of having a different entity-level liability rule for torts by employees and torts by independent contractors. We also examine the effect of insulating entities from liability for independent contractors. We show that both aspects of vicarious liability can be inefficient.[5]

Accordingly, when it is optimal for organizations to influence their agents' care-taking, tort liability must ensure that organizations want their agents to take efficient precautions and profit from using all cost-effective measures available to them to induce agents to take optimal care. Tort liability can do this by ensuring that organizations bear the costs of their agents' torts. Thus, organizations able to optimally regulate their agents' care-taking should be held directly liable for their agents' torts whenever individual tort liability alone cannot ensure that agents and principals bear the full cost of agents' torts, such as when agents do not have enough wealth to pay optimal damage awards.[6] In addition, tort liability must ensure that organizations obtain the full benefit of any measures they use to deter excessive risk-taking. Vicarious liability fails to achieve either objective. Moreover, vicarious liability is least likely to be effective when it is most needed: when agents are likely to be judgment-proof.

---

[5] *Compare* William M. Landes & Richard A. Posner, THE ECONOMIC STRUCTURE OF TORT LAW (1987) (vicarious liability should be imposed only on principals who exert direct control because principals are not in a good position to supervise inputs used by independent contractors and thus should not be liable for the latter's torts).

 The present analysis focuses on the "capacity to control" requirement of vicarious liability, including the rule exempting principals from liability for torts by independent contractors. It does not examine the impact of vicarious liability on those principals who use master-servant relationships. For a discussion of the problems arising from the application of strict or absolute entity-level liability to govern master-servant relationships see Jennifer Arlen, *The Potentially Perverse Effects of Corporate Criminal Liability*, 23 J. LEGAL STUD. 833 (1994) (showing that absolute entity-level liability for agents' torts may deter organizations from monitoring for, or reporting, agents' wrongdoing); Jennifer Arlen & Reinier Kraakman, *Controlling Corporate Misconduct: An Analysis of Corporate Liability Regimes*, 72 NYU L. REV. 687 (1997) (showing that duty-based mitigation regimes are superior to absolute entity-level liability for employee wrongdoing); *see also* Jennifer Arlen & William Carney, *Vicarious Liability for Fraud on Securities Markets: Theory and Evidence*, 1992 ILL. L. REV. 691 (discussing special problems arising from entity-level liability for securities fraud).

[6] *See infra* note 10. For example, Lewis Kornhauser, *An Economic Analysis of the Choice Between Enterprise and Personal Liability for Accidents*, 70 CALIF. L. REV. 1345 (1982) (the rule governing entity-level liability matters when agents cannot pay expected damages equal to the harms they cause); Alan O. Sykes, *An Efficiency Analysis of Vicarious Liability Under the Law of Agency*, 91 YALE L. J. 168 (1981) (same); *see* Jennifer Arlen & W. Bentley MacLeod, *Torts, Expertise and Authority: Liability of Physicians and Managed Care Organizations*, RAND J. ECON. (forthcoming 2005) (extending this result to the situation where principals regulate agents with both incentive contracts and by limiting the scope of the agent's authority). Entity liability also may matter when plaintiffs can establish that an agent of the entity committed a tort but cannot establish which agent is responsible.

When organizations hire wealth-constrained agents, individual tort liability cannot provide adequate incentives for agents to invest in care because agents know they will not pay for all the harms they cause. Indeed, agents with sufficiently low wealth expect that they will not even be sued. These agents may not take efficient precautions unless tort liability induces organizations to assert more direct control over their agents' care-taking, for example by providing equipment or directly monitoring and controlling agents' behavior, as in employee-employer relationships.

Yet far from encouraging organizations to assert control, vicarious liability often discourages organizations from controlling their agents, even when it would be efficient for them to do so. Vicarious liability discourages the efficient exercise of control because organizations that exert control over agents are likely to be deemed "masters," and thus face liability for their agents' torts. Those that eschew control can avoid such liability. Organizations with insolvent agents thus increase their own liability for any accidents that occur should they hire agents as employees. If they do so they must pay the full cost of their agents' torts. Otherwise their costs are limited to compensating agents for their expected individual liability (which is low when agents are judgment-proof). Consequently, vicarious liability discourages entities from asserting control in the very circumstance where control is most needed: where agents cannot be adequately regulated by individual liability alone because they are judgment-proof. Indeed, the present chapter shows that, from the standpoint of encouraging firms to exert control over agents, vicarious liability can be worse than pure individual liability in some circumstances, because it discourages the use of control even by firms that benefit from using control to protect themselves from agents' risks.

Vicarious liability also is inefficient because it distorts independent contractor relationships by providing organizations which hire independent contractors with excessive incentives to employ thinly capitalized independent contractors. Under vicarious liability, competitive market forces favor thinly capitalized agents because they can charge less for tasks that create risk because they face lower expected tort liability. Thus, organizations seeking to minimize costs will face strong economic pressures to hire thinly capitalized independent contractors, notwithstanding that thinly capitalized independent contractors are more likely to take excessive risks because they face little risk of tort liability for any harms caused. This results in people bearing excessive risks as a result of organizations' activities.

Finally, vicarious liability fails to provide organizations with efficient incentives to use the other tools available to them, such as financial incentives, to induce wealth-constrained independent contractors to take efficient care to prevent harm to others. Organizations bear the full cost of care, but they do not obtain the full benefit of preventing accidents, when their independent contractors cannot pay for the harms they cause. Exempting organizations from liability for their agents' torts, thus, leaves them free to provide inefficient incentives to agents to favor speed over quality, or cost reduction over precaution, because they can externalize the cost of accidents caused by their judgment-proof independent contractors onto tort victims.[7]

This chapter thus shows that organizations operating in unregulated free markets may use independent contractors to impose excessive risks on society so long as organizational liability for agents' torts is governed by a regime of vicarious liability instead of a broader entity-level liability regime.[8] The chapter thus potentially lends support to those jurisdictions that are expanding the reach of entity-level liability to certain organizations which hire independent contractors.[9] It also reveals the importance of further scholarship seeking to define the optimal limits of entity liability for agents' torts.[10]

This chapter proceeds as follows. Section II discusses optimal tort law. Section III examines optimal liability in a principal–agent context. Section IV discusses when the rule of principal-level liability matters. Section V demonstrates the perverse effect of vicarious liability on organizations' use of control to regulate agents' behavior. Section VI shows that vicarious liability also leads organizations to encourage excessive risk-taking by independent contractors.

---

[7] For example, most courts employing traditional vicarious liability analysis conclude that Managed Care Organizations (MCOs) are not liable for their affiliated physicians' negligence provided they do not directly control physicians' performance, even when they use financial incentives and utilization review to influence physicians' treatment decisions. *See* Jennifer Arlen & W. Bentley MacLeod, *Malpractice Liability for Physicians and Managed Care Organizations*, 78 NYU L. REV. 1929, 1975–79 (2003) (discussing evidence on the impact of MCOs on quality of care).

[8] Vicarious liability is not the only rule that encourages excessive risk-taking by organizations. Limited liability also encourages excessive risk-taking by corporations, especially when it insulates parent corporations from torts by their wholly-controlled subsidiaries. For example, Henry Hansmann & Reinier Kraakman, *Towards Unlimited Shareholder Liability for Corporate Torts*, 100 YALE L. J. 1879 (1991) (arguing for pro-rata shareholder liability for corporate torts); David W. Leebron, *Limited Liability, Tort Victims, and Creditors*, 91 COLUM. L. REV. 1565 (1991) (arguing against limited liability for corporate torts); *see also* Lynn M. LoPucki, *The Death of Liability*, 106 YALE L. J. 1 (1996).

[9] For example, some jurisdictions now hold hospitals liable for torts by physicians who practice primarily within the hospital (such as radiologists and anesthesiologists), even when they are hired as independent contractors.

[10] This chapter explores reasons why the existing regime is not efficient in many situations, but does not seek to define the scope of an optimal entity-level liability regime. We leave that issue for future work.

II. ROLE OF TORT LIABILITY

Although popular debate often paints tort liability as the enemy of the free market, in fact many markets are not efficient absent tort liability for harms caused. Free markets serve their promise when people in the pursuit of profit take actions that increase society's total welfare. Yet free markets can be destructive when individuals seek personal gain by wasting valuable resources that could be better used elsewhere.

People pursuing their own aims within free markets will pursue socially profitable projects, and avoid wasteful ones, if they not only obtain the benefit, but also bear costs, of their actions. In this situation, individuals seeking to maximize their own net gain also will maximize society's net gain, avoiding any activity which produces greater social costs than benefits. By contrast, if people are permitted to retain the benefits of their activities, without having to pay for all the costs, then people's efforts to maximize profits may reduce society's wealth because people may profit from activities that produce more costs than benefits. People also will not spend enough on preventing harm to others. Achieving the promise of a free market economy thus generally requires that people bear the costs of the risks they create.

One of the resources that businesses use in pursuit of profits is people's lives. Many businesses profit by taking actions that put others in peril. Businesses cannot manufacture, deliver, or sell most goods without creating a risk that someone will be hurt. This risk of injury is a cost of doing business similar to other more direct costs, such as labor or capital. Accordingly, a central problem for a free market economy is how to get those who profit from risk to refrain from creating risks that generate more harm than benefit.[11] Businesses also must be induced to take cost-justified precautions to reduce risk – to invest in care whenever doing so reduces total expected accident costs (defined as the costs of care plus expected accident costs).

Businesses can be relied on to regulate risk efficiently if the cost of the harm falls on the business itself. Businesses that both obtain the benefit, and bear the cost of, risk profit from adopting cost-effective measures to regulate their agents' risk-taking. Yet, left to their own, businesses will not regulate risk efficiently if the cost of harm falls on others. Businesses that bear the cost of precautions, but do not bear the cost of harms caused by their agents' risk-taking, have little reason to invest in reducing risk. Thus, they will not take cost-effective precautions to reduce risk. Accordingly, a central problem

---

[11] This chapter assumes that business should not impose inefficient risks without taking a position on whether businesses should be entitled to impose all efficient risks.

for a market economy is to induce those who create risk to treat costs that fall on others as equivalent to those that fall on them directly.

A primary purpose of tort liability is to promote the free market by giving people who benefit from, and can influence, risk a reason to treat as their own the cost of risk that falls on others, by making risk-imposers pay victims for injuries they cause. Tort liability can do this by requiring those who regulate risk-taking to pay for the injuries their activities cause.[12]

III. LIABILITY AND PRINCIPAL-AGENT RELATIONSHIPS

Tort liability provides efficient incentives to those who regulate risk-taking in different ways, depending on whether risk is created by a purely autonomous individual or instead by someone working on behalf of, and under the influence of, an organization. In the former situation, tort liability can induce efficient care-taking by using liability imposed on the individual risk-taker to provide direct financial incentives to those in charge of precautions. In the latter case, tort liability can induce efficient care-taking only if it ensures that the organizations who regulate risk-taking by their agents want their agents to take efficient precautions.[13]

In the case of injuries arising from the actions of autonomous individuals, tort liability often is the primary outside force operating to influence care. Thus, to regulate care, tort liability must be targeted directly at the individuals in charge of care, that is, individual injurers. Tort liability imposed directly on individual risk-imposers provides risk-takers with a direct financial incentive to take cost-justified precautions (assuming that liability rules are optimal and that expected damages equal the harm caused by the injurer's activities).[14]

Tort liability performs a different function when regulating risk-taking by people operating on behalf of, and within a contractual relationship with,

---

[12] *See,* for example, Guido Calabresi, THE COSTS OF ACCIDENTS (1970); Shavell, *supra* note 1. Tort liability may serve an important deterrent function even when injurers and victims are in a market relationship if victims either under-estimate the risks imposed on them, *see* Michael Spence, *Consumer Misperceptions, Product Failure, and Product Liability,* 64 REV. ECON. STUD. 561 (1977), or face collective action problems because care is a collective good. *See* Arlen & MacLeod, *supra* note 7, 2003–04.

[13] *See* Arlen & MacLeod, *supra* note 7, at 1988–89.

[14] *See,* for example, Steven Shavell, ECONOMIC ANALYSIS OF ACCIDENT LAW, Ch. 2 (1987). The present chapter focuses only on how vicarious liability undermines the promise of tort liability as a tool for regulating risk. It thus assumes that tort liability rules otherwise are optimal (with the due care standard set at optimal care and damages set efficiently) and then examines distortions caused by vicarious liability. This chapter also focuses on care and does not examine the impact of liability on activity levels.

an organization. In this situation, tort liability is no longer the primary force regulating individuals' care-taking. Organizations also influence care-taking. Moreover, it is organizations, not the tort system, that ultimately determine the extent to which – indeed whether – tort liability influences agents. Organizations can support the goals of tort liability through incentives designed to induce due care. Alternatively, they can work against tort liability by either indemnifying sanctioned agents or hiring agents who are beyond the reach of the tort system (e.g., agents who are judgment-proof). Accordingly, in order for tort liability to induce individual agents to take optimal care, it must ensure that organizations want their agents to take efficient precautions.

Beyond this, tort liability must ensure that organizations want to induce efficient precautions by using the most cost-effective means at their disposal. One potential benefit of risk-taking that occurs within an organizational framework is that organizations have more tools available for regulating agents than does the tort system. The tort system influences care-taking using crude financial incentives tied to outcomes (e.g., accidents). By contrast, organizations often can regulate care-taking through a variety of mechanisms, including more finely-tuned financial incentives (e.g., based on precaution taken, and not just outcomes), monitoring, direct control over care-taking, and control over the scope of the agency relationship. Efficient regulation of risk-taking requires that the tort system provide organizations with optimal incentives to induce their agents to take efficient precautions, using the most cost-effective tools available to them for doing so.

A. Financial Incentives and Selection of Agents

Like the tort system, organizations can regulate their agents' care-taking by providing financial incentives designed to induce the care they desire. Organizations can use these incentives either to support or to erase the incentive effects of the tort system. Organizations can erase the incentives provided by tort liability by agreeing to indemnify agents for any liability they incur. Alternatively, organizations can enhance the financial incentives provided by the tort system. Organizations can impose additional sanctions on agents (including dismissal). They also often can use more finely-honed sanctions than are available to the tort system, sanctioning agents who are negligent even if no suit is brought.

Of particular importance, organizations can alter the power of the financial incentives provided by tort liability through their choice of agents. The expected cost to an agent of tort liability depends not on the damages she expects the court to impose, but instead on the damages she expects to pay. An agent's expected liability will be less than the damage award whenever she does not have enough wealth to satisfy the judgment. Judgment-proof agents are a problem for the tort system because agents who do not expect to pay for the harms they cause do not invest in efficient precautions.[15] The problem of agent insolvency is particularly great when agents' wealth available to a tort judgment is sufficiently low that plaintiffs cannot profitably pursue a tort suit, even if negligence is clear.

Organizations can influence the expected sanction its agents bear through their decisions of whether to hire more or less wealthy agents.[16] Moreover, this control over agents' wealth levels extends not only to the individuals that organizations hire, but also to organizations' decisions to use corporate independent contractors. The owner-managers of closely-held corporate independent contractors often can determine the amount of wealth available to tort claimants through their choice of whether to keep the company thinly capitalized.[17]

Organizations thus can support or undermine the incentives provided by the tort system both through their influence over whether agents are judgment-proof and through their ability to alter the financial incentives provided by the tort system. Thus, the tort system can provide efficient incentives only if it ensures that organizations want to use their power to induce efficient precautions. Tort liability can do this by ensuring that organizations bear the cost of their agents' risk-taking.

B. Other Intervention

Providing organizations with proper incentives also is important because organizations can improve the efficiency of the tort system by using other mechanisms, beyond financial incentives, to induce agents to take efficient precautions.

Organizations can often regulate agents' care-taking at lower cost than can the tort system if they can be provided efficient incentives to do so. The tort system only has one instrument available to it to regulate care – financial

---

[15] *See, generally*, Steven Shavell, *The Judgment Proof Problem*, 6 INT'L REV. LAW & ECON. 45 (1986) (injurers will not take optimal care if they do not have sufficient wealth to pay optimal damages).

[16] *See* Kornhauser, *supra* note 6; Sykes, *supra* note 6.

[17] *Cf. infra* section V.B.3 (discussing agent insolvency when accidents also hurt the principal).

sanctions. Moreover, the tort system can use only a crude form of financial incentives – sanctions imposed for negligent conduct that produces a lawsuit. Financial sanctions can be an expensive way to regulate risk-taking when agents are risk averse because agents must obtain additional compensation, beyond the expected liability, to compensate them for the risk of financial loss. This imposes an additional cost on organizations.[18]

Organizations can regulate risk at lower cost than can individual tort liability if they can induce agents to take efficient precautions using lower sanctions or no sanctions at all.[19] Organizations may be able to regulate agents with lower sanctions by monitoring agents' care-taking and imposing a sanction whenever an agent takes inadequate precautions, even when this does not result in an actionable tort.[20] In addition, organizations often can directly control the level of care. They may be able to control care directly by providing the means of production, such as when care depends on the quality of some durable technology used by the agent (e.g., equipment). Alternatively, organizations can control care by refusing to let the agent perform the task unless she employs the requisite equipment. In other cases, organizations can control precaution by monitoring its agents' conduct and terminating agents who take less than appropriate care.[21]

Finally, principals can affect care through their choice of whether to allocate a task to an agent (and if so, which agent) instead of performing the task themselves. Tort liability can enhance economic efficiency if it induces principals to perform activities themselves whenever this affords higher net benefits (net of total accident costs) than does delegating to agents (whose care-taking may be inefficient).[22]

---

[18]   See Paul Milgrom & John Roberts, ECONOMICS, ORGANIZATION & MANAGEMENT, at Chap. 7 (discussing sanctions when agents are risk averse).

    Perfectly informed agents should not bear any risk should principals use a "duty based" sanction that imposes a sanction only on agents who fail to take moderate care because agents could avoid the sanction by taking moderate care. Often, however, agents do not possess costless information about optimal care: they can determine optimal care only by expenditures on expertise, and even then, they may err. See Arlen & MacLeod, *supra* note 6 (discussing expertise in the context of medical care). In such circumstances, agents face potential liability even if they invest in optimal expertise and attempt to take optimal care. *Id.*

[19]   See Milgrom & Roberts, *supra* note 18, Chs. 6, 7, 8 (1992) (discussing methods available to principals who want to alter agents' behavior).

[20]   See Arlen & MacLeod, *supra* note 7, at 1993–1995.

[21]   For example, Kornhauser, *supra* note 6; Sykes, *supra* note 6 (same).

[22]   For a discussion of principals' decisions to retain control over tasks or delegate them to agents *see* Phillippe Aghion & Jean Tirole, *Formal and Real Authority in Organizations*, 105 J. POL. ECON. 1 (1997); *see also* Arlen & MacLeod, *supra* note 6 (discussing authority in the context of MCOs).

C. Efficient Tort Liability

Thus, when risks are created by people operating within agency relationships, the central role of tort liability is not to regulate risk-takers directly; rather, it is to ensure that those who do regulate agents – organizations – have the right incentives to use the tools available to them to regulate agents. This implies that tort liability must ensure that organizations want their agents to invest in efficient precautions.[23] It also must ensure that organizations benefit from employing all cost-justified measures to induce agents to take optimal care.

Organizations should want to make cost-justified expenditures to prevent accidents if they ultimately bear the full cost of the harms their agents commit, because in this case they maximize their own profits by expenditures that produce an equal or greater reduction in expected accident costs. Accordingly, to regulate organizations efficiently, tort liability must ensure that organizations treat the harms that flow from risks their agents create as their own.[24]

IV. WHEN DOES ENTITY-LEVEL LIABILITY MATTER?

Accordingly, in order to induce organizations to regulate risk efficiently, tort liability must ensure that organizations capable of influencing risk bear the full cost of any accidents that result from their agents' carelessness. The question is, must liability be imposed directly on organizations or does liability imposed only on agents suffice.

Both agent-only (or individual) liability and entity-level liability can induce efficient behavior by organizations if they each cause organizations to bear the full cost of their agents' risk-taking. Thus, if agents' risk-taking imposes the same costs on organizations when only agents are liable as when the organization also can be found liable, then the decision of whether to use agent or entity-level liability will not affect organizations' incentives to regulate risk. Accordingly, both entity-level and individual liability are efficient if agents pay expected damages equal to the harms they cause. Entity-level liability is needed, however, if agents do not have enough wealth to pay optimal damages.[25]

---

[23] See Arlen & MacLeod, *supra* note 7, at 1988–89.

[24] Kornhauser, *supra* note 6, at 1358–59; *see* Arlen & MacLeod, *supra* note 6 (discussing optimal liability for torts where either the agent or the principal can directly determine the level of care).

[25] This result was originally established by Lewis Kornhauser and Alan Sykes. *See* Kornhauser, *supra* note 6; Sykes, *supra* note 6.

A. Solvent Agents

Individual and entity-level liability provide principals with equivalent incentives to reduce risk when agents have sufficient assets to pay expected damages equal to the harms they cause, because each rule results in the principal bearing the full expected cost of its agents' torts. Under entity-level liability the principal pays the costs directly; under individual agent liability the principal bears liability through the wages it pays its agents. Thus, each rule provides the same incentives to the parties.

Principals bear the costs of their solvent agents' risk-taking even when only agents are liable because principals must pay their agents additional wages equal to the expected costs of agents' liability. Agents view tort liability as a cost of agreeing to work for the principal and thus will not work for an organization unless it compensates them for the expected costs associated with employment, including agents' expected liability. Thus, principals do not escape the burden of tort liability that falls on agents, They bear the burden in the form of higher wages.

This implies that when agents are solvent, the impact of liability on organizations does not depend on whether the tort system imposes liability directly on the organization or directly on the agent, because in either case the organizations bears the cost of any liability imposed. Thus, the tort system can induce principals to regulate their agents efficiently, provided that expected damages equal the harm caused. Accordingly, when there is no risk of agent insolvency, the precise nature of the entity-level liability rule does not matter.[26]

B. Judgment-Proof Agents

The choice between entity and individual liability does not matter when agents are solvent because it does not affect the cost to the principal of its agents' negligence. The choice of rule does matter, however, when it affects the expected costs to the principal of its agents' negligence. This is the case when agents do not to have enough wealth to pay efficient damage awards.

When agents do not have enough wealth to pay optimal damages, pure individual liability does not ensure that either agents or principals bear the full expected cost of agents' actions. When agents' wealth is less than the

---

[26] This is the case whenever agents cannot avoid all risk of tort liability by simply taking due care. Tort liability is a cost of working for the organization if the task is complicated and agents may fail to take care by accident. See Arlen & MacLeod, supra *note 7* (discussing negligence liability for unintentional negligence).

optimal damage award, expected liability imposed on agents is less than victims' expected losses. Thus, tort liability imposed on individual agents does not provide agents with efficient incentives to take care.

Beyond this, individual agent liability also does not provide principals with efficient incentives to regulate risk-taking by judgment-proof agents. Principals only need to compensate agents for the liability agents actually expect to pay. Thus, under individual liability, the cost to principals of their agents' risk-taking also is limited by their agents' wealth. Accordingly, under pure individual liability, principals who hire judgment-proof agents do not have optimal incentives to deter agents' risk-taking.

By contrast, organizations held jointly and severally liable for their agents' torts do have efficient incentives to regulate care because they bear the full amount of damages even if agents are judgment-proof. Accordingly, under entity-level liability principals should make efficient use of the tools available to them to induce agents to take optimal care.

Thus, when agents are judgment-proof, tort liability is no longer neutral with respect to whether liability is imposed only on agents or also on organizations. Organizations held directly liable for their agents' torts will regulate risk efficiently if damage awards and liability rules are efficient. When only agents are liable, organizations with judgment-proof agents are insulated from the full costs of their agents' torts and thus will not regulate risk efficiently.[27]

C. Risk of Agent Insolvency

Before turning to the question of whether vicarious liability is efficient in situations where agents may be insolvent, it is important to briefly discuss the degree to which agent insolvency is a serious issue. In many important situations – such as torts involving personal injury, death or serious environmental damage – agent insolvency is likely to be the rule, not the exception. Agent insolvency must be measured not with respect to existing damage rules but, rather, with respect to optimal damage awards. Optimal deterrence requires that expected damages equal the cost to the victim of the harm imposed. For accidents involving serious permanent injury or death, this implies that

---

[27] Kornhauser, *supra* note 6; Sykes, *supra* note 6. These analyses of entity-level liability assume that individual liability for the underlying activity is governed by a strict liability rule. For an analysis of entity-level liability under a negligence regime, *see* Arlen & MacLeod, *supra* note 6 (providing a formal proof of the neutrality proposition under a negligence regime when principals regulate agents through both incentive contracts and limitations on agents' authority).

optimal damages usually are many millions of dollars.[28] This exceeds the wealth of all but a handful of individual agents.

Moreover, this may understate the magnitude of the optimal award. In order to provide efficient incentives, damages must exceed victims' expected losses.[29] Whenever negligent agents often are not sued, damage awards must equal a multiple of victims' expected losses, where the multiplier is based on the probability that a wrongdoer avoids liability.[30] The need for extraordinary sanctions heightens the likelihood that individual agents will be unable to pay optimal damage awards.

Accordingly, in considering optimal tort rules for accidents involving serious permanent injury, death, or serious environmental harm it is appropriate to assume that individual agents cannot pay optimal damages. Pure agent liability, therefore, will not provide organizations with efficient incentives to regulate these important risks. In order to provide organizations with efficient incentives to regulate risk-taking, the tort system must employ an efficient rule governing entity-level liability.

V. IMPACT OF VICARIOUS LIABILITY ON ORGANIZATIONAL STRUCTURE

This section examines vicarious liability, the rule that usually determines the scope of organizational liability. Vicarious liability is a hybrid between pure agent liability and entity-level liability. It holds principals liable for torts

---

[28] *See* Jennifer Arlen, *Tort Damages: A Survey*, in ENCYCLOPEDIA OF LAW & ECONOMICS (Boudewijn Bouckaert & Gerrit De Geest, eds.) (2000) (discussing empirical evidence that optimal deterrence damages for death and serious permanent injury exceed average existing awards); Jennifer Arlen, *An Economic Analysis of Tort Damages for Wrongful Death*, 60 NYU L. REV. 1113 (1985).

[29] Medical malpractice is probably the best documented area in which negligent injurers often are not sued. For example, Lori Andrews, et al., *An Alternative Strategy for Studying Adverse Events in Medical Care*, 349 LANCET 309 (1997) (on-site observation of hospital error found that whereas 480 of the 1047 patients treated were injured by their medical treatment, with 17.7 percent of these patients suffering serious injury; only thirteen of these patients filed claims); Paul Weiler, MEDICAL MALPRACTICE ON TRIAL, 12–13 (1991) (*Harvard Medical Practice Study* found that only one in eight potentially valid medical malpractice claims was actually filed; in the case of serious injuries, approximately one claim was filed for every three serious injuries.).

[30] Gary Becker, *Crime and Punishment: An Economic Approach*, 76 J. POL. ECON. 169 (1968) (where wrongdoers may avoid liability, the optimal sanctions equals H/p, where H is the harm caused and p is the probability that a wrongdoer will be held liable). Thus, for example, if only one in eight victims of negligence recover, the damage award must equal eight times the victim's expected harm, in order to ensure that each potential injurer bears expected costs equal to the victim's harm for each injury he causes.

committed by some agents within the scope of their agency relationship, but only those agents who are "servants," having granted their principals the right to control the physical conduct of their performance. Principals who hire independent contractors usually are not liable for their torts, even when they know that an independent contractor cannot pay its foreseeable tort liability.[31]

Some law and economics scholars have defended the "control" requirement for vicarious liability as being either benign or potentially beneficial. The basic intuition behind this support for vicarious liability appears to be as follows: Organizational liability is important only when agents are insolvent, and then only when organizations can affect their agents' risk-taking. When agents are insolvent, however, organizations cannot easily regulate them through financial sanctions. Organizations often can affect risk-taking only if they can directly control or monitor agents' behavior. Consequently, a rule that holds organizations liable only when they can directly control or monitor agents' behavior focuses liability on those circumstances where organizations can affect care, and avoids imposing liability when organizations cannot affect care.[32]

This analysis has numerous limitations. One is that it fails to recognize that organizations also should bear liability in order to optimally regulate their activity levels. Beyond this, however, this chapter shows that there are additional problems with this argument.

The preceding analysis focuses on the effect of vicarious liability only after an organization has hired the agent but does not consider the effect of vicarious liability on organizations' choice of both how to hire an agent (as an employee or not) and which agent to hire. Independent contractor relationships are not

---

[31] RESTATEMENT (SECOND) OF AGENCY § 2 (1958). Principals may be liable for torts of independent contractors in special circumstances, such as where the principal was subject to a nondelegable duty to take care to protect the plaintiff. Nevertheless, these exceptions to the general rule do not undermine the central argument of this chapter, because many areas in which principals use independent contractors fall outside these exceptions. In addition, principals can be held liable for independent contractors if there is an apparent master-servant relationship. We do not consider this rule, as well-advised principals usually can avoid liability based on ostensible or implied authority by taking actions to ensure that third parties know that the agent is an independent contractor.

[32] Landes & Posner, *supra* note 5 (vicarious liability should apply only to principals who exert direct control because principals are not well positioned to supervise independent contractors' care taking); Richard Epstein & Alan O. Sykes, *The Assault on Managed Care: Vicarious Liability, ERISA Preemption, and Class Actions*, 30 J. LEGAL STUD. 625, 638–41 (2001) (defending the rule exempting MCOs from liability for independent contractor physicians, even though MCOs influence care directly through utilization review and indirectly through financial incentives, because the ultimate care decisions rests with physicians).

set in stone. They are a product of choice. Thus, to be efficient, vicarious liability must not only be efficient as applied to existing independent contractor relationships, it also must provide efficient incentives for principals to establish efficient principal-agent relationships. Principals must be induced to use independent contractor relationships only when these are efficient. They also must have efficient incentives when determining which agents to hire – in particular, when determining whether to hire judgment-proof agents.

Vicarious liability fails on both of these scores. Vicarious liability distorts organizations' decisions on how to structure their agency relationships, providing them with excessive incentives to hire agents as independent contractors even when this is not efficient. Indeed, in its impact on organizational form, vicarious liability can be worse than an agent-only liability regime, because vicarious liability actively discourages principals from asserting control over agents even when it otherwise would be in their interests to do so.

Vicarious liability also is inefficient because it encourages firms to hire thinly capitalized independent contractors, because they can reduce their expected liability through the use of judgment-proof nonemployee agents.

Finally, defenders of vicarious liability do not adequately address the negative impact of agent-only liability for independent contractors on organizations' incentives to regulate their independent contractors. Insulating organizations from liability for their independent contractors' torts provides organizations with insufficient incentives to reduce their agents' risk-taking. Organizations may even encourage their agents to take excessive risks whenever they benefit from their agents' risk-taking but the costs fall on third parties.

A. Nature of Vicarious Liability

Vicarious liability holds principals liable for agents' torts – jointly and severally with agents – in those cases, but only in those cases, where the principal and the agent were in a "master-servant" relationship. The determination of whether a principal-agent relationship is a master-servant relationship generally turns on whether the principal "controls or has the right to control the physical conduct of the [agent] in the performance of the service."[33]

Courts have struggled with what it means for a principal to "control" an agent. Generally, courts have not determined control based on whether the principal can influence the agent's conduct – such as through financial

---

[33] RESTATEMENT (SECOND) OF AGENCY, § 2 (Master; Servant; Independent Contractor) (1958). See supra note 31 (discussing situations in which principals may be liable for torts of independent contractors).

incentives – but instead have focused on whether the principal can exert direct physical control over the agent. Accordingly, the master-servant test permits principals to exert some form of influence without being deemed "masters," and only predicates entity-level liability on particular forms of influence, those associated with more direct control. Thus, for example, a court is very likely to hold that a principal is a master if it supplies the instrumentalities or place of the work or directly supervises the agent on-site. By contrast, a principal who hires an agent to work off-site, using instrumentalities supplied by the agent is unlikely to be deemed a master, even if the principal uses financial incentives to influence the agents' behavior.[34] Accordingly, vicarious liability in effect imposes entity-level liability only on principals who attempt to control agents directly (or monitor them), and agent-only liability when principals regulate agents only through financial incentives.

B. Principals' Incentives to Assert Control

This part examines the effect of vicarious liability on principals' incentives to assert control over agents. To do so, it compares the incentives vicarious liability provides principals with the incentives principals would have if they bear the costs of their agents' torts directly (where the latter are efficient). Because the rule governing entity-level liability matters most when agents cannot pay for the harms they cause, this part assumes that agents are judgment-proof. We compare the decisions a principal would make regarding how to hire judgment-proof agents under vicarious liability with those of a principal who bears the cost of the harms its agents cause.

To compare the two situations, we use a simple example. Assume that a principal hires a risk-neutral agent[35] (with wealth of 60) to do a project that could cause 160 in harm. Assume that the probability of harm depends on how much the agent invests in care, as shown in Table 4.1. The principal

---

[34] RESTATEMENT (SECOND) OF AGENCY § 2, cmt. c. *See supra* note 31 (discussing situations in which principals may be liable for torts of independent contractors).

[35] In the examples, we focus on risk-neutral agents (who care only about the expected cost of their actions and not the variance in their wealth) both to simplify the discussion and because the concerns raised by vicarious liability are particularly great when principals hire corporate agents as independent contractors to perform tasks that are an essential part of the principals' business. These corporate independent contractors are likely to be effectively risk-neutral if their owners have diversified shareholdings. Allowing for agent risk aversion would not change our fundamental conclusions about the distorting effects of vicarious liability. Indeed, the penalty vicarious liability imposes on the use of control is more costly when agents are risk-averse because agent risk aversion increases the costs of using financial incentives instead of control to regulate agents. *See* Milgrom & Roberts, *supra* note 18, Ch. 7 (discussing the costs of financial sanctions when agents are risk-averse).

TABLE 4.1. *Social costs of risk-taking*

Level of care	Cost of care	Prob. of accident	Cost of accident	Expected accident costs	Total expected costs
None	0	1/10	160	16	16
Low	.8	1/12	160	13.33	14.13
Moderate	3	1/16	160	10	13
High	6	1/20	160	8	14

determines how much care it wants its agents to take based on the cost to it of its agent's risk-taking.

Table 4.1 shows the relationship between the agent's expenditures on care and the total expected cost to society of the agent's activities, as given by the cost of care plus the resulting expected cost of accidents. Social welfare is maximized when agents take the level of care that minimizes total accident costs (as given by column 6). This implies that total costs are minimized when the agent takes moderate care of 3. Although the agent could further reduce expected accident costs by increasing care to 6, it would be wasteful for him to do so, because increasing care by 3 would only yield an expected gain of 2 (i.e., 10 − 8) in reduced expected accident costs.

Observe that Table 4.1 shows that it would be efficient for the agent to take moderate care even if the only way to get the agent to spend anything on care is to invest $1 in directly controlling his behavior. Moderate care is still efficient because the cost of moderate care (with control) is 14, which is less than the cost of having no control, 16 (or control with low or high care, which is 15.13 and 15, respectively).

1. *Principal Bears Costs of the Agents' Risks*

Consider a principal who expects to bear the costs of its agent's risk-taking directly. Assume, for example, that the accident would cause environmental damage to land the principal needs to use. Alternatively, assume that the harm falls on third parties, but the principal is liable for its agent's torts. This principal has efficient incentives.

In this situation, the principal bears all the costs associated with its agent's activities. It bears accident costs directly; it bears the costs of care through its wage obligations to its agents. Thus, the principal's expected costs equal the social costs of its agent's activities, as given by column 6 in Table 4.1. The principal thus can minimize its costs by inducing the agent to take efficient (i.e., moderate) care.

TABLE 4.2. *Expected costs of agent with wealth of 60*

Level of care	Cost care	Prob. of accident	Max. sanction	Expected sanction	Total expected costs
None	0	1/10	60	6	6
Low	.8	1/12	60	5	5.8
Moderate	3	1/16	60	3.75	6.75
High	6	1/20	60	3	9

The principal will use its available tools to attempt to induce the agent to take moderate care. In some cases, the principal can induce its agent to select moderate care by imposing financial penalties for agent negligence. Yet financial incentives alone are not always sufficient, particularly when agents have limited assets. Financial sanctions do not provide judgment-proof agents with sufficient incentives to invest in care, because insolvent agents bear little of the expected sanction (because their wealth is so low). In this case, principals can regulate agents more effectively by supplementing sanctions with other methods, including direct control over care (or monitoring supplemented by sanctions).[36] Accordingly, when principals bear the costs of their agents' harms, a principal hiring a judgment-proof agent often is better off asserting more direct control over care by hiring the agent as an employee and directly dictating the level of care.

This can be illustrated by considering a principal who plans to hire an agent with wealth of 60.[37] If the principal hires the agent and relies only on financial incentives, the agent would face the following costs as given in Table 4.2. Because the agent's expected sanction is so low (see column five), he will only take low care, even though the principal wants him to take moderate care, because the agent's expected liability is not large enough to justify additional expenditures on care.

When the principal bears the full costs of the agent's torts, the agent's low care hurts the principal by subjecting it to expected costs of $14.13 instead of

[36] Financial incentives also are not optimal when principals are risk-neutral, and agents are risk-averse and cannot take actions to avoid the sanction. All else equal, in this case it would be optimal to impose ex post costs on principals, not agents, because risk is costly to agents but not principals. Thus, joint welfare is higher when the principal bears the risk. *See generally* Milgrom & Roberts, *supra* note 18, at 216–218.

[37] In fact, principals can reduce the problem of agent insolvency by paying large upfront wages designed to increase the sanction available to the principal should the agent fail to take optimal care. *See* Milgrom & Roberts, *supra* note 18, at 363 (discussing efficiency wages). This is an expensive way to regulate agents, however, because this wage must be paid to all agents, and hence principals often find it more cost-effective to monitor agents.

$13 (see Table 4.1). The principal, thus, may seek additional ways to regulate the agent. The principal may decide to exert direct control over care-taking by hiring the agent as an employee if it can assert control for less than $1.13. A principal who bears the cost of its agent's harms will use employment relationships whenever the resulting net benefit of the reduced risk exceeds the costs of exerting control.

2. Principals' Behavior Under Vicarious Liability

Whereas a principal with efficient incentives will assert control when it is efficient to do so, a principal governed by vicarious liability may not. Moreover, vicarious liability is particularly likely to deter organizations from asserting control when control is most likely to be efficient: when financial incentives are ineffective because agents do not have enough wealth to pay for the harms they cause.

Under vicarious liability, a principal that asserts control is liable for the full costs of any its agents' torts, whereas a principal that eschews the right to control its agents pays only for its agents' expected liability as limited by their wealth. Accordingly, when agents are judgment-proof, vicarious liability penalizes principals which assert control by enhancing their expected liability for any torts that occur by the amount of their agents' unfunded liability (by the amount that agents' expected liability exceeds their expected capacity to pay). This liability enhancement effect deters the efficient use of control if it exceeds the benefit a principal derives from using control to reduce the expected number of torts.[38] As the liability enhancement effect is greater the lower agents' wealth, vicarious liability is particularly likely to deter principals from asserting control when control is most valuable – when agents have very little wealth (and thus financial incentives are least effective).[39]

---

[38] *Cf.* Arlen & Kraakman, *supra* note 5, at 706–12 (showing that strict entity-level liability can deter corporations from using monitoring and reporting to regulate agent wrongdoing if the liability enhancement effect from the greater expected liability occasioned by monitoring and reporting exceeds the deterrent effect from the impact of monitoring and reporting on the expected amount of agent wrongdoing).

[39] *Compare with* Richard Brooks, *Liability and Organizational Choice*, 45 J. LAW, ECON. & ORGAN. 91 (2002). Professor Brooks found that oil companies reduced their use of independent contractor shippers after sanctions for spills increased. This could happen under vicarious liability if the deterrent effect exceeds the liability enhancement effect, even when principals can control agents' solvency. Nevertheless, it should be noted that the legal regime that Brooks studied is not a vicarious liability regime as defined in this chapter. According to Brooks, in many states oil companies face liability for torts of their shippers even when they employ independent contractors. Specifically, ten states (including California and Alaska) impose liability on the cargo owner regardless of whether the shipper is an

TABLE 4.3. *Principal's expected costs with insolvent agents*

Level of care	Cost care	Prob. of accident	Expected costs for employee (including control)	Expected costs for independent contractor
None	0	1/10	16	6
Low	.8	1/12	15.13	5.8
Moderate	3	1/16	14	n/a
High	6	1/20	15	n/a

To see this, consider our example, only now assume that risks fall on third parties and that the principal's liability is governed by vicarious liability. For simplicity assume that liability for the underlying activity is governed by strict liability.[40] The expected costs and benefits to the principal of hiring the agent under vicarious liability are presented in Table 4.3. As shown in column 4, if the principal hires the agent as an employee it assumes full liability for the agent's torts. Although the principal can use control to induce the agent to take moderate care (thereby reducing the probability of an accident), asserting control is costly. The principal now must pay for care, control, and the full costs of any torts that do occur. The principal, in other words, must assume the full costs of its activities (as in Table 4.1), including the costs of control.

By contrast, if the principal hires an independent contractor it does not have to assume the full cost of his activities. Instead, it bears only that independent contractor's costs (as given in Table 4.2). This ability to avoid its independent contractor's unfunded expected liability may reduce the principal's per-accident costs to such a degree that the principal is better off using the independent contractor relationship, even though this means facing a higher risk of tort liability because it cannot induce more than low care using financial incentives alone (as is shown in Table 4.3).

independent contractor. Moreover, courts in other jurisdictions have concluded that oil companies retain sufficient control to be liable for their shippers' torts. *Id.* at 104. Finally, many states regulate the financial well-being of the shipper, thereby limiting the magnitude of the unfunded liability. *Id.* at 100. Thus, as oil companies are unable to use independent contractors to externalize risk to the degree permitted by vicarious liability, they can be expected to respond to increased sanctions by exerting control in order to reduce the risk of an accident.

[40] Our analysis would apply as well to negligence liability when agents who endeavor to take optimal care nevertheless may be negligent, for example because they do not always know whether they are taking optimal care. For a discussion of optimal negligence liability when risk-imposers may be negligent accidentally *see* Arlen & MacLeod, *supra* note 6; Arlen & MacLeod, *supra* note 7.

Thus, vicarious liability creates perverse incentives for principals to prefer independent contractors over employees when the risks fall primarily on third parties in the very situation in which control may be most socially beneficial, when agents are judgment-proof. Accordingly, as a result of vicarious liability, principals which could induce efficient care-taking by agents may fail to do so, allowing agents to take excessive risks to the detriment of society. Thus, the principal in Table 4.3 hires its judgment-proof agents as independent contractors, even though this means that it must accept a greater probability of accident, because any effort to attempt to control care through the use of control subjects the principal to full liability for any torts its agents cause.[41]

Beyond this, vicarious liability distorts principals' incentives to regulate their independent contractors (as is discussed below). From Table 4.3, we see that whereas the principal wants its agents to take optimal care when it is liable for its agents' torts, it does not want agents to take optimal care when only the agent is liable (as can be seen from column 6 of Table 4.2). The principal, thus, no longer wants the independent contractor to take optimal care because it now faces the same net expected costs of care as the judgment-proof agent. Thus, if the agent does not face sufficient liability to warrant taking efficient precautions, the principal does not bear sufficient costs to want the agent to take efficient precautions.

3. *Disincentive to Assert Control*

Vicarious liability not only is inefficient when compared with a regime that ensures that principals bear the costs of harms they cause, in some cases it may be worse than a regime in which entities are never liable. Vicarious liability may be worse than pure agent liability in those situations in which principals

---

[41] Consistent with this, evidence suggests that firms often alter their internal structures to shift certain dangerous activities onto temporary contract workers whom they hire through independent contractors. Principals may leave these corporate independent contractors in charge of training and supervision even when independent contractors are less effective at training people to work for the firm than is the firm itself. Organizations employ this inefficient structure to enable them to treat these on-site contract workers as independent contractors in order to reduce their expected liability. *See*, for example, James B. Rebitzer, *Job Safety and Contract Workers in the Petrochemical Industry*, 34 INDUS. RELATIONS 40 (1995) (showing how the petrochemical industry sought to insulate itself from liability for workplace accidents by hiring contract workers and assigning all training and supervision of these workers to off-site independent contractors less capable of regulating safety). Principals' excessive incentives to employ independent contractors are exacerbated by employee benefit laws and tax laws that impose significant financial burdens on principals who hire employees often can be avoided by hiring independent contractors.

TABLE 4.4. *Pure agent liability*

Level of care	Cost care (control)	Expected accident costs	Expected social costs	Expected cost for employee	Expected costs for independent contractor
None	0	16	16	11	11
Low	.8 (+1)	13.33	15.13	10.96	n/a
Moderate	3 (+1)	10	14	10.87	n/a
High	6 (+1)	8	15	12.5	n/a

governed by pure agent liability might nevertheless have incentives to exert direct control over agents' care-taking, even when agents are judgment-proof.

Principals often will want to deter agents' risk-taking because they also may be injured by agents' negligence. For example, careless agents may destroy the principals' property as well as harming a third party; principals also may suffer reputational penalties when their agents are negligent and injure third parties. In such situations, principals can reduce their expected costs by reducing the risk of harm, even if they are not liable for their agents' torts.

A principal often can best reduce risk by hiring agents as employees, particularly when it must hire agents who cannot pay for the harms they may cause. In this case, a principal who wants to induce care may be best off bringing the agent within the firm, so that it can use direct control or monitoring to supplement any financial incentives.

Yet vicarious liability penalizes principals that hire agents as employees by causing them to be liable for harms to third parties in addition to harms to themselves. This may result in a principal paying more when it asserts control than when it does not, even though total social costs are minimized when it asserts control. As a result, a principal that might assert control to regulate care-taking under pure agent liability may eschew control under vicarious liability if the cost of their agents' unfunded liability dwarfs the benefits of control.

To see this, return to our example where accidents result in a cost of 160, but assume that the principal bears 110 and the third party bears 50 of any accident costs. For simplicity, assume that the agent has no wealth and thus would not take care if hired as an independent contractor. Assume, however, that the principal could induce care (low, moderate or high care) by hiring the agent as an employee and spending $1 to assert direct control over care.

The situation facing the principal under pure agent liability is presented in Table 4.4. Although the principal does not bear the full cost of its agent's

TABLE 4.5. *Vicarious liability*

Level of care	Cost care (control)	Expected accident costs	Expected social costs	Expected costs: hire employee	Expected costs: independent contractor
None	0	16	16	11	11
Low	.8 (+1)	13.33	15.13	15.13	n/a
Moderate	3 (+1)	10	14	14	n/a
High	6 (+1)	8	15	15	n/a

harms, it nevertheless will use control to reduce risk because this enables the principal to reduce its expected costs (including the costs to it of its agent's negligence). Indeed, in the present example, the principal will use control to induce agents to take efficient care (moderate care), although it may not in other circumstances.

By contrast, as shown in Table 4.5, under vicarious liability the principal will not hire the agent as an employee because vicarious liability forces the principal to pay for the third parties' costs if he asserts control but not otherwise. Because in the present example the cost to the principal of paying for the agents' unfunded liability exceeds the benefit of reducing accidents, the principal will hire the agent as an independent contractor (paying expected costs of 11 for an agent who takes no care) rather than hiring the agent as an employee (paying expected costs of 14 for an agent who takes efficient care). In this situation, a switch from pure agent liability to vicarious liability thus reduces social welfare by deterring principals from taking cost-effective measures to reduce risk.

Indeed, the inefficient effect of vicarious liability may be even greater than this analysis suggests because a principal that hires an independent contractor may be able to use financial incentives to increase the care its agents take to avoid harm to itself, while leaving third parties vulnerable to its agents' carelessness. In these circumstances, principals may be able to use independent contractor relationships at little cost to themselves, but potentially great cost to society.[42]

---

[42] MCO contracts with physicians are examples of these types of contracts. Physicians can impose costs on both patients (through error) and MCOs (through providing excessively costly treatment). MCOs, which usually are not liable for the medical negligence of their independent contractor physicians, currently use financial incentives to induce physicians to avoid excessively costly treatment, but generally do not employ sanctions to punish physicians who provide suboptimal care.

C. Incentives to Hire Judgment-Proof Agents

The perverse effects of vicarious liability on principals' incentives to regulate agents through the use of control are even greater than the preceding analysis suggests because vicarious liability encourages principals to avoid liability for their agents' torts both by hiring agents as independent contractors and selecting agents who are less vulnerable to tort suit.

Principals can affect their agents' care-taking both through how they structure their relationships (as independent contractors or employees) and through their choice of which agents to hire (more or less judgment-proof). An important test of a liability rule is whether it provides principals with efficient incentives in their choice of agents.

Vicarious liability discourages principals from hiring insolvent agents as employees because principals bear the full cost of their employees' torts (unaffected by agents' wealth). Moreover, a principal that hires an independent contractor may reduce its expected costs by hiring one with very little wealth because this reduces the expected burden to the principal of tort liability. The principal's ability to reduce its expected cost by hiring thinly capitalized independent contractors enhances the benefit to principals of independent contractor relationships, increasing principals' incentives to make inefficient use of independent contractors. Vicarious liability thus provides principals with perverse incentives to make inefficient use of independent contractors, and to hire those who are less financially solvent (and thus particularly difficult to regulate).

To see this, return to our example, and assume that the costs of the agent's torts are borne by third parties. A principal trying to decide whether to use an employee or independent contractor will compare the expected costs of an employee with those of an independent contractor, bearing in mind that it can use its choice of which independent contractor to hire to further reduce its tort liability. Indeed, the principal may be able to reduce its expected costs dramatically by hiring an independent contractor who is completely judgment-proof, thereby eliminating all costs resulting from its agent's torts. This increases the principal's profits relative to hiring either an employee or hiring an independent contractor with wealth 60, as can be seen by comparing column 6 of Table 4.6 with column 5 of Table 4.3. This comes at the expense to the third parties who bear the greater risks associated with the insolvent independent contractors' expected failure to take care.

Accordingly, rather than inducing principals to adopt efficient mechanisms to regulate agents' risk-taking, vicarious liability distorts principals' behavior. First, principals may gain from hiring insolvent agents, provided they hire them as independent contractors instead of as employees. Second, principals

TABLE 4.6. *Vicarious liability when agent has zero wealth*

Level of care	Cost care (control)	Expected accident costs	Expected social costs	Expected costs for employee	Expected costs for independent contractor
None	0	16	16	11	0
Low	.8 (+1)	13.33	15.13	15.13	n/a
Moderate	3 (+1)	10	14	14	n/a
High	6 (+1)	8	15	15	n/a

that hire independent contractors may benefit from hiring agents who are particularly difficult for the tort system to regulate – those that have little wealth.

D. Vicarious Liability Predicated on Capacity to Control

The perverse effects of vicarious liability could be reduced if courts abandoned their focus on whether the organization in fact has the capacity to directly control the agent, and instead predicate entity-level liability on whether an organization could have structured its relationship with the agent to allow it to influence the agent's behavior, regardless of whether it actually did so. This approach would remove the disincentive to exert control, because entity-level liability would depend (in theory) on factors beyond a principal's control, and not on a principal's actual decision of whether to exert control. In other words, the nature of the potential relationship would determine liability, not the nature of the actual relationship. Principals held liable whenever they could have hired the agent as an employee, even if they do not, would no longer have an incentive to hire agents as independent contractors when it is not efficient for them to do so. This could induce principals to make an efficient choice of whether to hire an agent as an independent contractor or not.[43]

Although this approach is superior to the existing rule, it does not remedy all the problems caused by vicarious liability. First, courts are not well equipped to determine capacity to control, independent of the actual exercise of control, since this depends on whether it would have been efficient for the principal to structure its relationships with its agents in some way other than the way it did. It is often hard to determine whether the principal chose not to exert control because it was seeking to hide behind the protections afforded by pure agent liability, or whether it did so because it could not assert control in a cost-effective way.

[43] Alan O. Sykes, *The Economics of Vicarious Liability*, 93 YALE L. J. 1231, 1262 n. 78 (1984).

In addition, even if courts could determine capacity to control accurately, this rule would not be efficient because it still enables principals that hire independent contractors to avoid the costs of third party torts, even when principals can influence care-taking through their choice of agent and through financial incentives. This rule would still provide incentives for principals which hire independent contractors to hire thinly capitalized independent contractors and would not induce them to invest in inducing agents to take efficient care.

VI. REGULATING INDEPENDENT CONTRACTORS

The preceding analysis shows that the current regime of vicarious liability provides principals with inefficient incentives to externalize risk by hiring agents as independent contractors and selecting thinly capitalized independent contractors, even when this reduces the ability of both principals and the tort system to deter agents from taking excessive risks. Beyond this, vicarious liability also affects how principals structure their independent contractor relationships.

To be efficient, an entity-level liability regime must not only provide principals with efficient incentives to choose between hiring agents as employees and as independent contractors, it also must ensure that principals structure their independent contractor relationships efficiently. This implies that entity-level liability must ensure that principals capable of influencing agents' risk-taking bear the full costs of their agents' torts. Vicarious liability fails to satisfy this goal because it exempts principals from entity-level liability for their independent contractors' torts even when agents are judgment-proof.

It might appear that this rule of agent-only liability for independent contractors is benign as applied to situations in which the principal would have hired an independent contractor even under a pure entity-level liability regime. After all, in this situation, the principal can only regulate agents through financial incentives and would appear to be no better able to do this than the courts. This is incorrect. First, principals usually have more tools available to them than courts, because they can affect risk-taking through their selection of independent contractors, and their choice of whether to use an independent contractor or do the job themselves. Second, principals that use financial sanctions often can use them more effectively than can courts. Thus, for both reasons, efficient regulation of independent contractors requires that tort liability provide efficient incentives to the organizations that hire them.

As previously discussed, principals can determine the effectiveness of financial sanctions through their choice of agent. Thus, even if principals could not increase care-taking, the rule exempting principals from liability for independent contractors may be inefficient because under this rule principals benefit from selecting judgment-proof independent contractors (because agents who cannot pay for tort judgments will charge less than those who can). Thus, this rule encourages principals to hire less wealthy independent contractors who are less susceptible to the incentive the tort system provides to take care.[44]

Moreover, even when principals cannot alter their choice of agent, agent-only liability for independent contractors is inefficient because it does not provide principals with efficient incentives to use financial incentives to regulate agents in those circumstances where principals are better able than courts to carry out this task. Principals have a larger portfolio of sanctions, including dismissal and control over promotion, that in some cases can provide more powerful motivation than monetary sanctions alone.[45]

In addition, principals can make more effective use of financial sanctions than can courts if they have better information on agents' care-taking. Principals often can sanction agents who take insufficient care even if no harm results. This greater probability of sanction allows the principal to provide efficient incentives using a lower sanction, which the agent is more likely to be able to pay. Thus, in our example, a principal able to sanction an agent whenever she takes low care could induce an agent with wealth of 60 to take moderate care with a sanction as low as 2.3, because the cost of moving from low care to moderate care is 2.2. Thus, principals which can observe agents' conduct better than can courts may be able to induce optimal care even when agents cannot pay optimal tort damages.[46]

Yet principals will only use this power to provide efficient financial incentives if they bear the cost of their agents' risk-taking.[47] As principals governed

---

[44] *See supra* section IV.C.

[45] Sykes, *supra* note 43, at 1253–54. Beyond this, principals may be able to use efficiency wages to reduce the problem of agent's insolvency, paying agents above market wages in order to increase agents' incentives to take the care necessary to save their jobs. *Id.* at 1248. For a general discussion of efficiency wages, *see* Milgrom & Roberts, *supra* note 18, at 250–59.

[46] *See* Milgrom & Roberts, *supra* note 18, at 226–28 (discussing monitoring and the informativeness principle).

   Principals also may be better able to regulate agents than courts, even if principals cannot observe agents' care but can observe when accidents occur. Principals may be able to use sanctions to provide agents with optimal incentives if they can detect accidents resulting from negligence even when victims do not sue. *See* Arlen & MacLeod, *supra* note 7, at 1939 (discussing data showing that the majority of patients injured by medical negligence do not sue). In such cases, organizations can use financial incentives more effectively than can courts by increasing the threat of sanction, thereby imposing greater expected liability for negligence. *See* Arlen & MacLeod, *supra* note 7.

[47] *Cf.* Arlen, *supra* note 5 (a central purpose of entity-level liability is to induce principals to take measures to increase the probability wrongful agents are sanctioned).

by vicarious liability do not bear the full costs of independent contractors' risks, this rule fails to provide them with efficient incentives to use their greater ability to regulate their independent contractors.

Finally, when agents are insolvent with respect to optimal damages, vicarious liability leads principals to make inefficient decisions with respect to whether to perform the task directly or allocate it to the agent, in those circumstances in which principals subject to vicarious liability hire agents as independent contractors. The principal should use agents when this maximizes social welfare and should do the task himself when this affords the highest net welfare. Thus, it often may be optimal for a principal to perform the task himself if he would be forced to hire judgment-proof independent contractors, who are difficult to regulate. Vicarious liability, however, encourages principals to delegate tasks to independent contractors in those circumstances where the risks of doing so are greatest – when the independent contractor is judgment-proof – because principals can externalize the costs of the risk by hiring an insolvent independent contractor. Accordingly, vicarious liability is least effective at inducing principals to avoid delegating tasks to agents when it is particularly important that they not do so: when the social benefits of agents' activities is likely to be lowest because agents' care-taking is not effectively regulated by either the threat of tort liability or by principals.

VII. CONCLUSION

Organizations profit from hiring people to perform tasks that impose risks on all of us. Although organizations can reduce the amount of this risk, they will not do so efficiently unless they profit from inducing their agents to take cost-effective care. A properly designed tort system can provide organizations with the necessary incentive to employ the tools at their disposal to reduce their agents' risk-taking. Tort liability can induce organizations to care about harms to others by ensuring that they bear the costs of these harms. Because agents often are judgment-proof, tort liability can guarantee that organizations bear the full cost of their agents' harms only if it imposes liability directly on organizations for injuries resulting from their agents' negligence.

Vicarious liability does not hold organizations liable whenever they can influence care, either through their choice of agent, control, monitoring, or financial incentives. Instead, it predicates the imposition of liability on a showing that an organization could exert direct control over the agent. This control-based test is inefficient. By imposing entity-level liability on principals that assert control, but not on those who do not, vicarious liability deters principals from using employee relationships in the very situation in which they are most needed – when agents are hard to control efficiently through financial incentives alone. Vicarious liability, thus, can cause principals to avoid any actions that might be viewed as control, even if control is the most cost-effective means to deter excessive risk-taking. This may result in organizations making excessive use of independent contractor relationships.

Beyond this, vicarious liability distorts independent contractor relationships by insulating principals from liability for their independent contractors' torts even when principals are better able to regulate independent contractors' care-taking than are courts. This rule encourages principals to favor thinly capitalized independent contractors because thinly capitalized independent contractors can charge less to assume risk. The rule also does not provide principals with adequate incentives to use financial sanctions to induce their independent contractors to take efficient care because it insulates them from full liability for judgment-proof independent contractors' torts. Principals insulated from tort liability have the same incentives as the judgment-proof agents to take care to avoid harms to third parties. Thus, when agents' wealth is sufficiently low that tort liability is of little consequence, principals have little reason to encourage agents to take precautions to protect third parties, even when they are capable of doing so. Indeed, under this rule, principals may use incentives in ways that increase risk-taking (e.g., by encouraging extra speed or reduce costs), without fear of paying for the consequences to victims of their actions.

Accordingly, a society that wants to use market forces to regulate organizations' risk-taking cannot rely on a rule of vicarious liability to govern organizations' liability for their agents' torts. This rule fails to induce organizations to regulate risk efficiently, and can even be worse than no entity-level liability at all. A central focus on torts scholarship should be on determining the proper scope of organizational liability for agents' torts.

DUTY RULES, COURTS, AND TORTS

CHAPTER FIVE

THE DISINTEGRATION OF DUTY

Ernest J. Weinrib

ABSTRACT. Throughout the common-law world, there is no liability for negligence unless the defendant breached a duty of care owed to the plaintiff. But when is such a duty owed? In the foundational judgment of English negligence law in 1932, *Donoghue v. Stevenson*, Lord Atkin asserted that "there must be, and is, a general conception of relations giving rise to a duty of care." Lord Atkin thereby gave expression to the view that the law cannot treat the collection of duties as a chaotic miscellany of disparate norms. Rather, the systematic nature of legal norms requires both that all duties of care be thematically unified through the same underlying principle and that each particular duty be internally coherent. More recently, however, courts seem to have given up on the attempt to formulate or appeal to a general conception of duty and have returned to the multiplicity of particular duties that Lord Atkin deplored. This has caused a "disintegration of duty."

The general conception of the duty of care – its theoretical basis, its structural constituents, its more recent disintegration back into particular duties, and the need to recapture what a general conception of duty implies – is the subject of the present chapter. It first shows through an analysis of the landmark cases of the Twentieth Century how duty fits with other negligence concepts (failure to exercise reasonable care, factual causation, and proximate cause) to connect the defendant's act to the plaintiff's injury in a normatively coherent way. It then sets out the internal structure of the duty of care, that is, what its constituents must be if it is to reflect a coherent conception of wrongdoing. The chapter then examines the two-stage test for negligence that is used in Canada and other jurisdictions, arguing that this internally-fractured test is inadequate for the development of a coherent jurisprudence of negligence. Finally, the chapter discusses the meaning and relevance of the much-invoked "policy" for the determination of the duty of care, concluding that the coherence of its underlying justifications is itself the supreme policy of the law of obligations.

Ernest J. Weinrib, University Professor and Cecil A. Wright Professor of Law, University of Toronto. I am greatful to Sophia Reibetanz Moreau, Ariel Porat and Martin Stone for their comments on earlier versions.

I. THE GENERAL CONCEPTION OF DUTY

In his great judgment in *Donoghue v. Stevenson*[1] Lord Atkin, before articulating the neighbor principle, noted a deficiency in the judicial treatment of duties of care in negligence. Only rarely had the common law formulated "statements of general application defining the relations between the parties giving rise to a duty of care."[2] Instead, proceeding on a case-by-case basis, the courts had concerned themselves with the particular kind of relationship before them on any occasion and had therefore focused on the specific status of one or other of the parties, "whether manufacturer, salesman or landlord, customer, tenant, stranger, and so on."[3] Thus, the only way to determine whether a duty of care existed was to see whether the case could be referred to some "particular species"[4] that the law had already recognized. He continued:

> And yet the duty which is common to all cases where liability is established must logically be based upon some element common to all the cases in which it is found to exist.... [T]here must be, and is, some general conception of relations giving rise to a duty of care, of which the particular cases found in the books are but instances.[5]

The neighbor principle[6] was Lord Atkin's attempt set out this general conception.

The general conception of the duty of care – its theoretical basis, its structural constituents, its more recent disintegration back into particular duties, and the need to recapture what a general conception of duty implies – is the subject of the present chapter.

Lord Atkin regarded the existence of a general conception as a necessity ("there must be, and is, some general conception"). Although he said little about the nature of this necessity, he presumably had in mind something like this: the common law, by its own internal logic and dynamism, cannot treat the particular instances of duty as a chaotic miscellany of disparate and

---

[1] [1932] A.C. 562 (appeal taken from Scot).
[2] *Id.* at 579.
[3] *Id.*
[4] *Id.* at 580.
[5] *Id.*
[6] "The rule that you are to love your neighbour becomes in law, you must not injure your neighbour; and the lawyer's question, 'Who is my neighbour?' receives a restricted reply. You must take reasonable care to avoid acts or omissions that you can reasonably foresee are likely to injure your neighbour. Who, then, in law is my neighbour? The answer seems to be persons who are so closely and directly affected by my act that I ought to have them in contemplation as being so affected when I am directing my mind to the acts or omissions which are called into question." *Id.*

independent norms.[7] Duties of care are constituents of a normative system. The coherence of such a system requires that that all duties of care should be thematically unified through the same underlying principle. The general conception of duty reflects the common aspect that each particular duty must have if it is to be systematically related to every other particular duty. The necessity to which Lord Atkin refers is a juridical one: the general conception of duty is an implication of the internal coherence required by the law's systematic nature.

In recent years the sense of juridical necessity apparent in Lord Atkin's judgment has waned. Lord Atkin's own formulation of the general conception in terms of a duty to avoid foreseeable harm to a neighbor, path-breaking as it was, has been recognized not to provide a practical test. Moreover, the very idea of a general conception is sometimes thought to be superfluous given the casuistic nature of common-law reasoning.[8] Even in courts that accept the need for an overarching framework for the duty of care, the general conception takes the form of multistaged formulae that are verbally comprehensive without necessarily being juridically coherent.[9] The widely-accepted idea that duty is a matter of "policy" (whatever that might mean) has led to a distaste for the abstract practical reasoning that undergirds a general conception of duty.

The result has been a disintegration of duty in two related senses. First, because each kind of duty reflects the particular set of policies deemed appropriate to it or the particular constellation of casuistic considerations from which it emerges, the preoccupation with particular species of duties, which Lord Atkin decried, has returned. Duties are differentiated, usually according to the kinds of harms with which they deal (physical injury, economic loss, psychiatric injury and so on), without attention to (in Lord Atkin's words) "the element common to all cases in which [a duty] is found to exist" and therefore without awareness of the strands that weave all duties of care into a coherent system in which each duty illuminates, and is illuminated by, all the others. Second, not only has the whole ensemble of duties disintegrated into a collection of particular kinds of duties, but the very idea of a duty has disintegrated. Instead of the duty of care being an internally-coherent normative category, it has been fragmented into the separate factors that determine the duty's ground and limits. Hence, the reasoning in support of a duty is marked by *ad hoc* compromises among these separate factors rather than by

---

[7] This point was made by Deane, J. in *Stevens v. Brodribb Sawmilling*, 160 CLR 16, 51 (1986).

[8] For an example, *see* Dawson, J. in *Hill v. Van Erp*, 188 CLR 159, 177 (1997).

[9] Below at Section IV.

an elucidation, in the context of a particular case, of the conception under which the defendant's act and the plaintiff's injury form a unified normative sequence. These two senses of disintegration go together, because the absence of coherence within the notion of duty renders otiose the necessity for coherence that Lord Atkin postulated between particular duties.

This disintegration of duty has undermined the most notable achievement of negligence law in the Twentieth Century. However indeterminate Lord Atkin's own formulation of the general conception of duty, the leading negligence cases of the subsequent decades carried forward the striving for coherence to which he gave voice. In contrast, the more recent disintegration of duty manifests a failure to develop tort law in a normatively-coherent way. If I am right about this, a principal task for negligence law in this new millennium is to grope its way back to the conception of coherence that was implicit in Lord Atkin's celebrated judgment.

In this chapter, I want to discuss these developments from the standpoint of corrective justice.[10] This standpoint is especially germane, because corrective justice is the theoretical notion that accounts for whatever coherence private law might have. Corrective justice ties coherence to the justifications that inform private law's characteristic concepts. Legal doctrine is viewed as coherent only to the extent that its underlying justifications are coherent. These justifications, in turn, are coherent only if their force as reasons is congruent with – rather than artificially truncated by – the structure of the relationship between the parties. Because liability relates the defendant as doer of the injustice to the plaintiff as sufferer of the same injustice, the justifications that support liability are coherent when they simultaneously treat the parties as correlatively situated. Coherence thus requires that the reasons for considering the defendant to have done an injustice be the same as the reasons for considering the plaintiff to have suffered that injustice.

This conception of coherence reflects the correlative structure of liability, that is, the fact that the liability of the defendant is always a liability to the plaintiff. In holding the defendant liable to the plaintiff, the court is making not two separate judgments (one that awards something to the plaintiff and the other that coincidentally takes the same thing from the defendant), but a single judgment that embraces both parties in their interrelationship. Each party's position is intelligible only in the light of the position of the other. The defendant cannot be thought of as liable without reference to a plaintiff

---

[10] On corrective justice, *see* ERNEST J. WEINRIB, THE IDEA OF PRIVATE LAW (1995); Ernest J. Weinrib, *Corrective Justice in a Nutshell*, 52 U. TORONTO L.J. 349 (2002).

in whose favor such liability runs. Similarly, the plaintiff's entitlement exists only in and through the defendant's correlative obligation.

For corrective justice, the correlative structure of liability matches the structure of the injustice that liability corrects. Liability is an appropriate response to the injustice only because that injustice also is correlatively structured. As is evidenced by the judgment's simultaneous correction of both sides of the injustice, the injustice done by the defendant and the injustice suffered by the plaintiff are not independent items. Rather, they are the active and passive poles of the same injustice, so that what the defendant has done is the basis of liability only because of what the defendant has suffered, and vice versa.

Because liability treats the parties as doer and sufferer of the same injustice, tort law (and the law of obligations more generally) elaborates legal categories that reflect the identical nature of the injustice on both sides. The determination of injustice is not a matter of mere assertion but is a normative ascription that must be justified by an appropriate set of reasons. Accordingly, the correlativity of the injustice means that the reasons for concluding that something is an injustice also have a correlative structure. Because the defendant, if liable, has committed the same injustice that the plaintiff has suffered, the only considerations that matter for elucidating the wrong are those that apply correlatively to both parties. By exhibiting the parties as the doer and sufferer of the same injustice, such considerations reflect the unity of the parties' relationship. Tort reasoning then functions as a coherent enterprise in justification rather than as the enumeration of a hodgepodge of factors separately relevant only to one or the other of the parties.

With justificatory coherence comes fairness as between the parties. A justification that is inconsistent with corrective justice fails to match the correlative structure of the parties' relationship. Such a justification necessarily favors one of the parties at the expense of the other, thereby failing to be fair from the standpoint of both. In contrast, by insisting that the normative considerations applicable to liability reflect the parties' correlative situation, corrective justice construes tort law as setting terms for the parties' interaction that take account of their mutual relationship and are thus fair to both of them.

Seen in the light of corrective justice, Lord Atkin's comments can be understood as follows. The notion that the law of negligence is a coherent system of justification precludes particular duties of care from being regarded as isolated norms. Rather, the particular duties are systemically related to one another because they participate in a shared general conception of duty. To play its role as a necessary determinant of coherence across particular duties, the general conception of duty must itself be an expression of the very coherence that it imparts. For "the relation between the parties" (as Lord Atkin calls it)[11] to be coherent, that relation has to be regarded as correlatively structured through the defendant's doing and the plaintiff's suffering of the same wrong. This is turn has two complementary aspects. On the one hand, the general conception of duty must be part of an integrated ensemble of concepts that allows the sequence from the defendant's doing of the negligent act to the plaintiff's suffering of the injury to be understood as a normatively coherent unit in which the injustice done and the injustice suffered are the same. On the other, the general conception of duty considered in itself must be formed from normative elements that reflect the correlative structure of the parties' relationship. The general conception of duty, then, embodies the correlative structure of justification that renders any particular duty coherent both with the other members of the ensemble of negligence concepts and with other particular duties. There "must be" such a general conception (as Lord Atkin insists) because otherwise the law of negligence would be incoherent – a possibility that he assumes the law cannot acknowledge.

Taking corrective justice as the theoretical notion underlying Lord Atkin's insistence on a general conception of duty, this chapter discusses the disintegration of duty in the following steps. Section II is concerned with the first aspect of coherence mentioned above, that is, with how duty fits with other negligence concepts (failure to exercise reasonable care, factual causation, and proximate cause) to connect the defendant's act to the plaintiff's injury in a normatively coherent way. Accordingly, the section outlines the role of the landmark cases of the twentieth century in treating the injustice done by the defendant as identical to the injustice suffered by the plaintiff.

Section III deals with the second aspect of coherence; it sets out the internal structure of the duty of care, that is, what its constituents must be if it is to reflect a coherent conception of the doing and suffering of a wrong. In so doing, the section sets out the general conception of the duty of care that juridical coherence requires. The duty of care will thereby be exhibited as having a definite structure toward which the legal reasoning of any particular case ought to be oriented. The presence of such a structure suggests that it is mere dogmatism to maintain, as tort scholars often do, that duty is nothing but "a shorthand statement of a conclusion, rather than an aid to analysis."[12]

Applying this notion of coherence to a contemporary formulation of duty, Section IV examines the two-stage test for negligence that is used in Canada

---

[11] *Donoghue v. Stevenson*, [1932] A.C. 562 (appeal taken from Scot).
[12] W. PAGE KEETON, DAN B. DOBBS, ROBERT E. KEETON, AND DAVID G. OWEN, PROSSER AND KEETON ON THE LAW OF TORTS (5th ed.) 358 (1984).

and elsewhere. My argument is that this internally-fractured test, as applied by the Supreme Court of Canada, provides a conspicuous example of the disintegration of duty and, accordingly, is inadequate for the development of a coherent jurisprudence of negligence.

Finally, Section V discusses the meaning and relevance of the much-invoked "policy" for the determination of the duty of care. The disintegration of duty is the consequence of thinking that duty is a matter of policy, and that policy, in turn, refers to the various independent goals that liability might serve. On this view, each particular kind of duty represents the balance of goals, in themselves diverse and competing, that is peculiar to it. However, another notion of policy refers to the exercise of practical judgment in elucidating what the general conception of duty might mean in particular circumstances. The general conception provides not (as has often been assumed) a test of duty, but a structure of thinking that is actualized in legal reasoning through the casuistic assessment of facts or comparison of cases or through the eluci-dation of its particular normative features in the overall context of a legal system that values coherence. This second notion of policy is, I suggest, not only compatible with but indeed required by the general conception of duty.

II. THE PLACE OF DUTY AMONG THE NEGLIGENCE CONCEPTS

How, then, does negligence doctrine treat the plaintiff and the defendant as the correlatively-situated doer and sufferer of the same wrong? Negligence concerns the plaintiff's being wrongfully injured through the defendant's creation of an unreasonable risk. If negligence liability is to be a coherent normative phenomenon, the injury and the risk creation have to be under-stood as the constituents of a single wrong that is elucidated through an integrated ensemble of legal concepts. In this way, the differing experiences of the parties as doer and sufferer and the temporal gap between the doing and the suffering are subsumed under a unified set of normative categories that render the wrong done identical to the wrong suffered.

Coherence requires that the injustice relate act to injury and vice versa. Precluded are definitions of the injustice between the parties in terms that pertain to one of them alone. As negligence law recognizes, the injustice does not consist merely in the unreasonably-created risk considered in itself; that would one-sidedly focus on the defendant's wrongful action and entail liability for unreasonable risk creation even without damage. Nor does it consist in the harmful effect considered in itself; that would one-sidedly focus on the plaintiff's injury and entail strict liability, rather than negligence.[13] Nor, again, does the injustice consist in the combination of wrongful action and injury each considered one-sidedly; that would mean that, although the defendant has committed a wrong and the plaintiff has suffered one, these are two different wrongs, each resting on its own foundation. Rather, the injustice embraces the entire span from the act to injury: the defendant's act is viewed as a wrong because of its potential to cause this kind of injury, and the plaintiff's injury is viewed as a wrong because its potential occurrence is a reason for considering the defendant's act wrongful. Then the sequence from act to injury forms the single wrong that the defendant can be said to have done and the plaintiff to have suffered.

To be coherent, tort doctrine elaborates legal concepts that treat the defendant's act and its effect on the plaintiff as an integrated sequence in which there is a single injustice that is the same for both parties. In legal terms this sequence begins with defendant's breach of the standard of reasonable care and ends in the factual causation of injury. However, the sequence can be regarded as integrated only if its two termini operate not as atomistic elements that the law simply adds together, but as constituents of liability that, for purposes of tort law, each derive their significance from the other. Hence, the unreasonableness of the risk created by the defendant must lie in the possible occurrence of the kind of injury that the plaintiff suffered. This way of relating the negligent act to the injury makes the injustice of unreasonable-risk creation the same for both parties.

The signal achievement of negligence law in the Twentieth Century was to develop the concepts of negligence analysis in a way that coherently links the unreasonable risk to the harm suffered. Duty and proximate cause are crucial components in this linkage. These concepts connect wrongdoing and injury by describing the wrongful risk in terms of the range of the potential victims and consequences through which the risk is to be understood as wrongful. Duty connects the defendant as a wrongdoer to the plaintiff as a member of the class of persons wrongfully put at risk. Similarly, proximate cause connects the defendant's negligence to the plaintiff's suffering of the kind of injury or accident the risk of which rendered the defendant's act wrongful. Because both duty and proximate cause are requirements of liability, the defendant is not held legally responsible for the materialization of a harm that is not within the set of possibilities that supply a reason for exercising due care. When, however, the injury suffered by the plaintiff is to a member of the class

---

[13] For a recent analysis of negligence either in terms of risk caused or harm suffered without attending to the possible unity of the sequence as a whole, *see* Heidi M. Hurd & Michael S. Moore, *Negligence in the Air*, 3 Theoretical Inquiries in Law 333, 348 (2002).

of persons that the defendant wrongfully put at risk and is the kind of injury or accident that that due care is supposed to avoid, then the wrongfulness of both the defendant's action and the plaintiff's injury is referable to the same sort of risk. Under those circumstances, the sequence from the defendant's creation of an unreasonable risk to the materialization of that risk in injury to the plaintiff constitutes the same injustice for both parties.

The leading twentieth-century cases on duty and proximate cause gave legal expression to this conception of negligence liability. Three developments were particularly noteworthy. The first, of course, was *Donoghue v. Stevenson*[14] (and its United States predecessor *MacPherson v. Buick Motor Co.*).[15] In place of a fragmented collection of duties that varied according to the particular social and contractual relationships between the parties, *Donoghue* established that the duty of care flowed from the defendant's risk-creating action as such and from its reasonably foreseeable effect on those who ought to have been within the defendant's contemplation. The general conception of the duty of care formulated in this case thereby connected the defendant, as the creator of an unreasonable risk, to the plaintiff, as a person whose endangerment made the risk unreasonable.

A more explicit and complete development of the same idea appeared in Cardozo's opinion in *Palsgraf v. Long Island Railroad Co.*[16] Cardozo there wrote that there could be no liability unless the defendant's breach of duty was a wrong in relation to the plaintiff. Because in that case the defendant's conduct was not wrongful toward the plaintiff (although it was arguably wrongful toward someone else), the defendant was held not to be under a duty with respect to the plaintiff's loss.

Cardozo's explicit purpose was to construe the wrongfulness of negligence in a way that was specifically appropriate to tort law. He noted "the shifting meanings of such words as 'wrong' and 'wrongful.'"[17] What the plaintiff had to show was a wrong that was "a violation of her own right, and not merely a wrong to some one else, nor conduct 'wrongful' because unsocial but not 'a wrong' to any one."[18] To detach the notion of wrong from a beach of duty owing to the plaintiff "is to ignore the fundamental difference between tort and crime."[19] For Cardozo, tort liability – in contrast to other kinds of societal judgments about culpability – featured a wrong done by the defendant

---

[14] *Donoghue v. Stevenson*, [1932] A.C. 562 (appeal taken from Scot).
[15] 111 N.E. 1050 (N.Y. 1916); *see* John C. P. Goldberg and Benjamin C. Zipursky, *The Moral Of MacPherson*, 146 U. Pa. L. Rev. 1733 (1998).
[16] 162 N.E. 99 (N.Y. 1928).
[17] *Id.* at 100.
[18] *Id.*
[19] *Id.* at 101.

in relation to the plaintiff. Accordingly, the very reason for thinking that the defendant acted wrongfully also had to be the reason for thinking that the injury suffered by the plaintiff was wrongful. The duty of care in negligence law was to be understood as rendering the normative significance of the wrong identical for both parties. "Negligence . . . is thus a term of relation."[20]

Cardozo's outstanding contribution was to align the relational nature of tortious wrongdoing with the relational significance of unreasonable risk. In the words of the opinion, "The risk reasonably to be perceived defines the duty to be obeyed, and risk imports relation."[21] As a way of referring to the harmful potentialities inherent in a given act, risk is not intelligible in abstraction from a set of perils and a set of persons imperiled. A negligent act releases a set of harmful possibilities that due care should have avoided. The plaintiff cannot recover unless the injury she suffered actualizes a possibility within this set. The imperiling of the foreseeably-affected class of persons is the reason for considering the defendant's act negligent; it also must be the reason for thinking that the plaintiff has been wronged. Only if the plaintiff is among that class does the reason for thinking of the defendant's action as wrongful pertain to the plaintiff. Because in *Palsgraf* the prospect of the plaintiff's injury was not a reason for considering the defendant's action negligent, the defendant was not under a duty toward her.

Cardozo's treatment of duty forges a normative connection between the defendant's action and the plaintiff's injury. The connection is normative, because it is based on the reason for considering an act to be wrongful. Given that the structure of the relationship between the parties is one of correlativity, that reason must simultaneously provide a ground both for holding the defendant liable and for holding the plaintiff entitled to recover. Under Cardozo's analysis of the relational quality of unreasonable risk, the duty of care makes the same reason pertain to both parties.

In contrast, Andrews's dissenting judgment in *Palsgraf* connects the parties in a historical but not a normative way. The connection is merely historical, because the element of fault required for the defendant's liability to the plaintiff is satisfied by the fact that the defendant's negligence is the historical antecedent of the plaintiff's injury. In Andrews's view, the injury suffered can be the basis of the plaintiff's recovery even though the wrong was relative to a third party rather than the defendant. Unanswered is the question of why the merely historical connection between the defendant's negligent act and the plaintiff's injury should justify liability on the basis of fault. It is no answer

---

[20] *Id.*
[21] *Id.* at 101.

to say that this negligence caused the injury; that answer, by transforming cause into the determinant of the plaintiff's recovery, should also apply to causally effective action that is innocent (and thus as nonculpable relative to the victim as the defendant's conduct in *Palsgraf*). Negligence liability would then collapse into strict liability.

Another difficulty flows from Andrews's position. Ever since the devastating critique of strict liability by Oliver Wendell Holmes, no one has been able to sustain the position that liability should be based on causation.[22] The particular problem that Holmes identified is that causation is unable to generate its own limits, so as to preclude a regression to causes, however distant. Andrews is not insensitive to this problem. He insists that for the defendant to be liable, the negligence must be not merely a cause, but the proximate cause of the damage. However, having rejected the notion that the parties are normatively connected (and thus liability is limited) through the idea of unreasonable risk, he has no coherent conceptual framework within which judgments about the proximateness of causation can be situated. In Andrews's own account the determination of proximate cause turns out to be an arbitrary exercise in practical politics, intelligible more through rhetoric and metaphor than through legal analysis.[23]

A more coherent conception of proximate cause than the one Andrews put forward emerged from yet another major development of tort jurisprudence in the twentieth century, the Privy Council's decision in *Wagon Mound (No. 1)*.[24] There the Privy Council held the requirement of proximate cause to be unsatisfied when the defendant negligently exposed the plaintiff to the risk of one kind of injury, but the plaintiff suffered an injury of a different kind. This decision made proximate cause run parallel to Cardozo's conception of duty.[25] Just as *Palsgraf* required that the plaintiff be within the class of persons unreasonably imperiled, *Wagon Mound* required that the injury or accident be of the sort that renders the defendant's risk creation

---

22   OLIVER WENDELL HOLMES, THE COMMON LAW, Lecture III (1881). For a criticism of Richard Epstein's more recent attempt to vindicate strict liability, *see* ERNEST J. WEINRIB, THE IDEA OF PRIVATE LAW 172–177 (1995).

23   *Palsgraf*, 162 N.E. at 103.

24   *Overseas Tankship (UK) v. Morts Dock and Engineering (Wagon Mound No. 1)*, [1961] A.C. 388 (P.C., 1961).

25   The connection of *Wagon Mound* and *Palsgraf* is sharply put in a leading text on tort law in the United States: "The decision is the logical aftermath of Cardozo's decision in the *Palsgraf* case, since there is an obvious absurdity in holding that one who can foresee some harm to A is liable to consequences to A which he cannot foresee, but is not liable for similar consequences to B." PROSSER & KEATON, *supra* note 12 at 296. A similar point was made in the *Wagon Mound*, [1961] A.C. at 425.

unreasonable. Thus, with respect both to the person injured and to the injury or accident, the harm that occurred actualized the possibilities for danger that it was negligent for the defendant to have created. Duty and proximate cause both functioned to make the wrongfulness of what the defendant did the same as the wrongfulness of what the plaintiff suffered.

When this complex of leading cases is considered as a whole, the main categories of negligence liability – duty, breach of duty, proximate cause, and factual cause – form a coherent set that traces the sequence from the defendant's negligent act to the plaintiff's injury. Breach of duty and factual causation are the termini of this sequence, with the former referring to the defendant's creation of unreasonable risk and the latter to the materialization of risk in injury to the plaintiff. Duty and proximate cause integrate these termini into a normatively-coherent unit by characterizing in terms of the same unreasonable risk the wrongfulness of what the defendant did and of what the plaintiff suffered. The result is that the duty of care is a member of an interconnected ensemble of concepts through which the parties to a finding of negligence can be understood as doer and sufferer of the same injustice.

III. RIGHT AND CORRELATIVE DUTY

Having situated the duty of care within the ensemble of concepts that allows negligence liability to be understood as a normatively-coherent phenomenon, this section will focus more specifically on the duty itself. What are its constituents and how do they give expression to the correlative notion of liability? The answer to this question indicates the internal structure of the duty of care, thus revealing (in Lord Atkin's words) "the general conception of relations giving rise to a duty of care, of which the particular cases found in the books are but instances."[26]

For tort law (as well as for the law of obligations more generally), the overarching categories expressive of correlativity are the plaintiff's right and the defendant's corresponding duty. A right is an inherently-correlative concept whose existence immediately creates in others a duty not to wrongfully infringe it. Right and duty are correlated when the plaintiff's right is the basis of the defendant's duty and, conversely, when the scope of the duty includes the kind of right-infringement that the plaintiff suffered. Then the reasons

---

[26] *Donoghue v. Stevenson*, [1932] A.C. 562 (appeal taken from Scot).

that justify the law's protection of the plaintiff's right are the same as the reasons that justify the existence of the defendant's duty.

Cardozo's judgment denying liability in *Palsgraf* provides the most explicit judicial elucidation of this notion of right and correlative duty. Cardozo observes that liability requires that "the plaintiff sues in her own right for a wrong personal to her, and not as the vicarious beneficiary of a breach of duty to another. A different conclusion would involve us, and swiftly too, in a maze of contradictions."[27] In *Palsgraf* the defendant arguably created an unreasonable risk to the third-party's package but was being sued for a wrongful infringement of the plaintiff's right to bodily integrity. The right that the defendant unreasonably put at risk was therefore different from the right whose wrongful infringement was the basis of the plaintiff's complaint. The duty to the person carrying the package was thus not correlative to the plaintiff's right in her bodily integrity. Liability to the plaintiff would mean that the defendant was being held liable for the infringement of a right that its employee did not wrongfully imperil, so that the award of damages would then not represent the wrong that the defendant did. The contradiction is that under these circumstances liability to the plaintiff would be inconsistent with the nature of tort law as a mechanism for obligating defendants to make reparation for the rights that they have wrongfully injured.

As Cardozo points out, *Palsgraf* featured a particularly striking example of "the maze of contradictions." *Palsgraf* was a case in which the defendant's breach of duty and the plaintiff's complaint involved a diversity both in the nature of the rights (property and personal integrity) and in the holders of the rights (the passenger carrying the package and the injured plaintiff). Cardozo correctly observes that the same contradiction would obtain even if the rights were of the same order but the person foreseeably endangered was different from the person actually injured.[28] He also suggests, as *Wagon Mound (No. 1)* later decided, that the contradiction would also be present if the discrepancy between the defendant's breach and the plaintiff's injury were to rights of different orders.[29] In all these instances there would be no liability because the plaintiff would have been injured with respect to a right that was not the basis of the duty that defendant breached.

When negligence law is conceived in terms of the correlativity of right and duty, the issue of the duty of care is composed of two constituents. First,

[27] *Palsgraf,* 162 N.E. at 100.
[28] *Id.*
[29] *Id.* at 101.

the interest of the plaintiff that is protected against the defendant's conduct must have the status of a right as against the defendant. Second, the duty breached must be correlative to that right. These two constituents are the complementary aspects of a unified conception of the duty of care, because a right both implies and is required by the correlative structure of liability. A right implies correlativity because a right always entails the existence of a corresponding duty. A right is required by correlativity, because (along with its corresponding duty) it is the only normative concept that has the correlative structure inherent in a regime of liability. Thus, the notions of right and correlative duty together form a unified general conception of the duty of care.

Cardozo's treatment of duty in the *Palsgraf* case gives paradigmatic legal expression to this conception of the duty of care. For Cardozo, the principal issue presented by the case was that of correlativity. Because in that case the defendant's conduct was not wrongful toward the plaintiff (although it was arguably wrongful toward someone else), the defendant was held not to be under a duty with respect to the plaintiff's loss. Although Cardozo's focus was on the absence of correlativity between the duty breached and the injury, Cardozo also insists that the duty breached has to be correlative to a right: "Negligence is not actionable unless it involves the invasion of a legally protected interest, the violation of a right."[30] Because "the commission of a wrong imports the violation of a right,"[31] the plaintiff is precluded from recovering unless the defendant's conduct is a wrong in relation to that right. Hence, "[w]hat the plaintiff must show is a wrong to herself, *i.e.*, a violation of her own right."[32] That the plaintiff had a right to her bodily security was not disputed in the case, but the defendant's action was not wrongful relative to that right. Thus, Cardozo affirms that the existence of a right held by the plaintiff is presupposed in the requirement that the duty breached by the defendant be a wrong relative to her.

Accordingly, Cardozo's opinion presents the two interrelated functions of the inquiry into the defendant's duty. The first function is to establish whether the plaintiff's damaged interest has the status of a right, because it is only to a right that the defendant's duty can be correlative. The second function is to establish whether correlativity obtains in the case at hand, that is, whether the defendant breached a duty correlative to that right by creating an unreasonable risk to persons such as the plaintiff. When these two

[30] *Id.* at 99.
[31] *Id.* at 101.
[32] *Id.* at 100.

functions are brought together, the question of duty produces a structure of inquiry geared to ascertaining whether the parties can plausibly be regarded as the doer and sufferer of the same injustice. Action by the defendant that is incompatible with the plaintiff's right marks the injustice of the defendant's conduct, and that injustice is the same for both parties.

In this understanding of the duty of care, correlativity restricts the kinds of justification available to support the right. The normative valence of a right does not derive from considerations that, however morally compelling they might be in some context other than that of liability, are not themselves correlatively structured. For purposes of liability, therefore, a right is not the conclusion of a calculation that maximizes wealth, welfare, or utility; however desirable these might be, their normative significance is not immediately tied to a correlative implication for anyone else. That a person has or might have a certain level of wealth, welfare, or utility is merely a fact about that person, rather than an element that operates correlatively between that person and any other particular person. Nor is there any room within the duty of care for policy, regarded as discreet considerations of social expediency that do not pertain to the immediate relationship between plaintiff and defendant.[33] Rather, a right signifies a normative consideration with regard to which the same injustice can be done and suffered. It is the irreducibly correlative marker of the normative connection between the prospective or actual doer and sufferer of a wrong.[34]

Similarly, one must distinguish between injury to a right and the suffering of harm or loss. A right immediately signifies the existence of a correlative duty; harm or loss does not. Neither the harm as something suffered by the plaintiff nor the process of suffering it at the defendant's hand establishes a link between

---

[33] I return to the treatment of policy below at Section V.

[34] That the law recognizes rights that function in this way (for example, rights to bodily integrity or to property) is sufficient for present purposes. In the corrective justice approach a "right" is not the label for a conclusion, any more than a duty is. A right is a distinctive normative ingredient of legal argument, and is systemically treated as such by the law. One aspect of this systemic treatment is the pervasive specification of those under a corresponding obligation through the distinction between rights *in rem* and rights *in personam*. Another is the elaboration of a jurisprudence of acquisition in connection with rights to external things. For an example of the impact of such considerations, see below, note 38. A further question of course can be raised about the basis or nature of rights so conceived. From the standpoint of corrective justice, rights are the juridical manifestations of personality, that is, of the capacity for purposive agency as it achieves an external existence in social interactions through its exercise by or embodiment in an agent. *See* Ernest J. Weinrib, *Correlativity, Personality, and the Emerging Consensus on Corrective Justice*, 2 THEORETICAL INQUIRIES IN LAW 107, 119–126 (2001). This conception of rights does not involve recourse to moves that maximize wealth, welfare or utility.

the parties that is at once correlative and normative. Being harmed is merely a fact – that the normal person is now less advantageously situated than before – that in itself has no correlative normative significance. And the plaintiff's suffering of harm at the defendant's hand links the parties historically through the link between cause and consequence or grammatically as subject and object of the same verb, rather than normatively as the doer and sufferer of an injustice. Because one can be harmed without being wronged, harm considered in itself is not a notion from which one can, within the correlative structure of negligence law, impute a wrong. Harm matters only inasmuch as it stands under a right, for only when the duty breached by the defendant is correlative to the plaintiff's right do the parties occupy correlative normative positions. Accordingly, if the loss of which the plaintiff is complaining is not the subject matter of a right or if the defendant's conduct is not wrongful with respect to that right, then the defendant is not under a duty of care to the plaintiff. In the old language of the law, harm is then mere *damnum absque injuria*.

The supposed absence of a right accounts for some of the situations where the common law does not recognize (or earlier had been reluctant to recognize) the existence of a duty. In situations of nonfeasance, for example, the entitlement claimed is not merely to one's own physical integrity – which *ex hypothesi* the defendant has not endangered – but to the defendant's positive assistance. Under the common law, however, one has no general right to be benefited by another. Similarly, the perceived absence of a right in the plaintiff also may explain, at least in part, the law's slowness to recognize negligence liability for psychiatric and prenatal injury. In the case of psychiatric injury, the psychological interest was perhaps regarded as too speculative or insubstantial to count as part of one's right to physical integrity. Over the past century a stronger appreciation of the psychological aspect of physical integrity has rightly led to a steady broadening of liability and to a growing dissatisfaction with arbitrary restrictions.[35] In the case of prenatal injuries, the common-law position that legal personality begins at birth allowed them not to be viewed as violations of the child's rights. This fallacious view has now been repudiated: even if the plaintiff was not in existence at the time of the negligent act, that act can subsequently materialize in a wrongful infringement of the plaintiff's right to physical integrity.

---

[35] The treatment of psychiatric injury in Great Britain, where "control mechanisms" function "as more or less arbitrary conditions" to restrict liability has been particularly unfortunate. *White v. Chief Constable of South Yorkshire Police*, [1999] 2 A.C. 455, 502. *See* criticism of the English approach in *Tame v. New South Wales; Annetts v. Australian Stations Pty*, 191 A.L.R. 449 (2002).

The role of rights has also been crucial for the traditional approach to liability for economic loss.[36] Traditionally, the common law restricted liability to situations in which the economic loss represented the quantified value of a right belonging to the plaintiff and negligently injured by the defendant. On this basis the plaintiff could recover for "financial damage ... consequential on foreseeable physical injury or damage to property,"[37] that is, for lost earnings because of physical injury or for the lost economic value of property negligently damaged by the defendant. In such cases the basis of liability was the plaintiff's right to physical integrity or to the exclusive use of the property. Concomitant to these rights – indeed, part of their meaning – was a correlative obligation on others (including the defendant) not to wrongfully interfere. The economic loss was merely the monetary measure of the right's infringement. Conversely, if the economic loss was independent of a right that ran between the parties, the plaintiff could not recover for it. The law thereby recognized that a set of economic advantages enjoyed or anticipated by the plaintiff was not in itself the subject matter of a right. Although such economic advantages make the plaintiff better off than he or she would be without them, they have no inherently correlative significance for anyone else; the defendant, therefore, was not liable for them. Negligence law expressed this conclusion about these free-standing economic losses by saying either that no duty of care existed toward someone whose proprietary right was not injured or that such losses, being the result of an injury to someone else's rights, were too remote.[38]

---

[36] On economic loss, see the important article by Peter Benson, *The Basis for Excluding Liability for Economic Loss in Tort*, in PHILOSOPHICAL FOUNDATIONS OF TORT LAW 427 (David G. Owen, ed. 1995).

[37] *Spartan Steel & Alloys v. Martin*, [1972] 3 All E.R. 557, 571.

[38] The former formulation is exemplified by *Weller v. Foot and Mouth Disease Research Institute*, [1966] 1 Q.B. 569, the latter by *Conn. Mu. Life Insur. v. N.Y. & New Haven R. Co.*, 25 Conn. 265 (1856). The paradigmatic situation, of which these cases are examples, is that of the plaintiff who operates a business that depends on some facility (*e.g.*, a bridge, pipeline, electrical cable) that the plaintiff does not own but that is negligently damaged by the defendant, causing the plaintiff economic loss because business operations cannot proceed as normal. One cannot plausibly argue that, within the systemic logic of the law, the plaintiff has a right to the free-standing economic gain that he or she was prevented from realizing. Because the parties are strangers, there is no possibility of an *in personam* right. Nor can the plaintiff have an *in rem* right to the prospective economic gain. First, the intentional diversion of the gain by a competitor is permissible; but it would be a very odd *in rem* right if someone could rightfully interfere with it intentionally but not negligently. Second, the plaintiff can have a right to an external thing only if the plaintiff has acquired that thing; but there is no mode of acquisition for the prospective economic gain from the existence of another's facility. Indeed, the classic case of acquisition, *Pierson v. Post*, 3 Cai. R. 175 (N.Y. 1805) repudiates the notion that the prospect of a gain in itself creates a right. (I am indebted to Abraham

The traditionally restrictive approach to economic loss, then, excludes liability except as compensation for wrongful injury to the plaintiff's right. In the standard instances of lost income or diminished value, the right in question is, respectively, a right to bodily integrity and a right to property or possession, where the entitlement against the defendant is merely an aspect of the plaintiff's exclusive entitlement against the whole world. These rights precede the plaintiff's interaction with any specific defendant. With respect to them the defendant is under a duty to act with reasonable care because the whole world is.[39]

During the Twentieth Century another kind of right gained recognition in the context of economic losses resulting from negligent misrepresentation.[40] This was a right based on justified detrimental reliance, created through the interaction of the parties and giving the plaintiff an entitlement as against the defendant specifically, to recover the economic loss flowing from the defendant's reliance-inviting conduct. Although the plaintiff has no right against the world for economic loss as such, in situations of justified detrimental reliance the plaintiff recovers for economic loss because of the special relationship that arose between the parties. The relationship is special in that, given the circumstances in which the misrepresentation took place, the defendant can reasonably be regarded as having invited the plaintiff to rely on it for a particular transaction or kind of transaction, and thus as having voluntarily assumed responsibility for the loss that results from that transaction.[41] After leading the plaintiff reasonably to rely on the representation or on other reliance-inviting conduct for the kind of transaction in question, the defendant cannot fairly disclaim responsibility for the consequences. What places

Drassinower for discussion of these points.) And so the plaintiff's argument must be based on the suffering of the economic loss even though the plaintiff had no right to what was lost. This is the argument that the common law traditionally rejected using the language of duty or remoteness.

[39] The question of whether in any particular case the plaintiff had a right as against the defendant is of course subject to legal argument, even in the case of the proprietary and possessory rights that are paradigmatic in this context; see, for example, *Courtenay v. Knutson*, 26 DLR 2d 768 (1961) (liability to the bailee of a barge). An interesting variant is *Perre v. Apand*, 164 A.L.R. 606 (1999), where the defendant, by supplying diseased seed to one potato grower, caused potatoes of the plaintiff, a neighboring potato grower, to be embargoed even though the plaintiff's crops were not infected. The defendant was held liable for the plaintiff's economic loss; although the defendant's land was not contaminated, the defendant's negligence caused it to be treated as if it were.

[40] *Glanzer v. Shepard*, 135 N.E. 275 (N.Y. 1921); *Hedley Byrne v. Heller*, (1964) A.C. 465. *See* the exemplary treatment by Benson, *supra* note 36, at 450–454.

[41] The fact that the entitlement is created through the interaction of the parties and is thus personal to them rather than good against the whole world puts the parties into what Lord Devlin called "a relationship equivalent to contract;" *Hedley Byrne*, [1964] A.C. at 530.

the loss within the scope of the defendant's duty is the imputation to the defendant, based on his or her knowledge of the purpose to be served by the representation, of an express or implied invitation to the plaintiff (or to the class of persons that includes the plaintiff) to rely on the representation for that kind of purpose.[42] This purpose, known by the defendant and detrimentally acted on by the plaintiff, links the defendant's act to the plaintiff's loss by making the prospect of the loss the reason for considering the act to have been negligent. Using the analogy to contract,[43] one might say that by making the representation the defendant has offered the plaintiff information that purports to be reliable for the purpose of a particular kind of transaction, and that the plaintiff, by detrimentally acting on this information, has accepted it as reliable for the purpose for which it was offered. Therefore, to the extent of the plaintiff's detrimental reliance, tort law views the plaintiff's preexisting economic situation as an entitlement that runs against the defendant. The basis of the entitlement – the invitation to rely for a particular (kind of) purpose – also defines the scope of the duty correlative to it. Accordingly, detrimental reliance that falls outside the purpose for which the representation was made does not lead to liability even if the reliance that the representation in fact occasions is reasonably foreseeable.[44] Because it is created by justified detrimental reliance, the entitlement in question applies only as between the parties; it does not count as a right held by the plaintiff against the world as a whole. Recognition of such an entitlement thereby leaves intact the traditional restrictions on recovery for economic loss, which reflect the idea that economic advantage (and the prospect of impairing it) does not as such generate duties in everyone else to avoid causing loss.[45]

In the traditional treatment of liability for economic loss, no difficulty arises about what some of the more recent cases regard as crucial, the avoidance (in Cardozo's famous words) of "liability in an indeterminate amount for an

---

[42] For example, in *Haig v. Bamford*, 72 DLR 3d 68 (1976), the defendant knew the purpose for which it was asked to prepare an audited financial statement. Similarly, in *Hedley Byrne*, [1964] A.C. 465 *supra* note 40, the defendant knew the purpose of the plaintiff's inquiry about its client's credit-worthiness.

[43] *Hedley Byrne*, [1964] A.C. at 530.

[44] *Caparo Industries v. Dickman*, [1990] 1 All E.R. 568.

[45] It may be that such interactional rights arise also in situations that do not involve reliance. An example may be the issue presented when an intended beneficiary sues the solicitor for negligence in drawing up, or failing to draw up, a will; *See White v. Jones*, [1995] 1 All E.R. 691; *Hill v. Van Erp*, 188 CLR 159 (1997). The solicitor retained to draw up the will is the technical channel for bringing into being a proprietary right held by the plaintiff that is created by the death of the testator; the question of whether in these circumstances the plaintiff has or needs what Gaudron J. contends is a right to have the testator's estate properly administered is canvassed in *Hill v. Van Erp*.

indeterminate time to an indeterminate class."[46] It is of course true that, given
the interdependence of economic activity within society, economic losses to
some will foreseeably lead to further economic losses to others, which in
turn will foreseeably lead to still further economic losses, and so on. But the
indeterminacy of losses is problematic only if liability is a response to the
suffering of a loss. Implicit within the traditional treatment of economic loss,
however, is the notion that tort law concerns itself not with losses as such but
with injuries to rights, so that economic losses matter only as quantifications
of those injuries. The plaintiff's right, therefore, both grounds and limits the
defendant's liability.

One should, therefore, appreciate the significance of references, such as
Cardozo's, to indeterminate liability in the traditional treatment of economic
loss. The point is not that liability for economic loss as such exists but has to
be cut off to avoid indeterminacy. Rather, the prospect of indeterminacy is
adduced to indicate the implausibility of supposing that such liability exists to
begin with. As Cardozo himself said, the indeterminate nature of the supposed
liability "enkindle[s] doubt whether a flaw may not exist in the implication
of a duty that exposes to these consequences."[47]

In recent years some jurisdictions, Australia and Canada among them,[48]
have abandoned the traditional framework of liability for economic loss.
The basis of the defendant's liability has shifted from injuring a right to
inflicting a loss. Loss differs from right in that it lacks both the distinct legal
content and the correlative significance that together impose coherent limits
on liability. Yet, as is universally acknowledged, some limit must be formulated
because the interdependence of economic interests makes it intolerable for
liability to follow merely from the foreseeability of creating an economic loss.
Accordingly, the duty of care imposed on the defendant by the foreseeability
of the plaintiff's loss is made subject to the limitation of a policy-based notion
of "proximity."

This development has been accompanied by a transformation of the role
of Cardozo's famous phrase about indeterminate liability. Almost invariably

---

[46] *Ultramares v. Touche*, 174 N.E. 441,444 (N.Y. 1931).
[47] *Id.; see also Weller v. Foot and Mouth Disease Research Institute*, [1966] 1 Q.B. 569.
[48] *Caltex Oil v. The Dredge "Willemstad,"* 11 A.L.R. 227 (1976); *Canadian National Railway v. North Pacific Steamship*, 91 D.L.R.4th 289 (1992). Over the last decade or so, Jane Stapleton has
provided an illuminating and sympathetic elucidation of these and related developments.
See Jane Stapleton, *Pure Economic Loss: A Judicial Exemplar*, in GERARD V. LAFOREST AT THE
SUPREME COURT OF CANADA (1985–1997) 449 (The Supreme Court of Canada Historical
Society 2000); Jane Stapleton, *Comparative Economic Loss: Lessons from Case-Law-Focused
"Middle Theory,"* 50 U.C.L.A. L.Rev. 531 (2002).

invoked in the judgments on economic loss, it is no longer taken as an indication that the basis of negligence liability must be sought elsewhere than in the foreseeable loss. Instead, it has become the prelude to attempts to mark the border to which liability based on foreseeable loss is to expand. The prospect of indeterminate liability prompts the court to assess whether, in the circumstances of the particular case, the plaintiff's loss was (despite its foreseeability) insufficiently proximate to the defendant's negligence. That foreseeability of loss is the basis of liability is taken for granted; the focus is on the criterion for limiting liability.[49]

However, formulating the limiting conditions that satisfy the requirement of proximity in a principled way has turned out to be troublesome. This is hardly surprising. Unlike the notions of right and correlative duty, loss and proximity do not form a unified juridical conception. Proximity limits foreseeability by considerations that are not intrinsic to it. On the one hand, foreseeable losses are initially regarded as possibly worthy of attracting liability simply by reason of their being foreseeable losses. On the other hand, such losses are not ultimately regarded as worthy of attracting liability except through the additional presence of proximity factors that artificially limit the reach of liability. Because the same normative considerations do not both ground and limit liability, a constant tension arises between the unrelated normative impulses that respectively support and confine the defendant's duty. Having abandoned the inner coherence of having restrictions on liability that are conceptually indigenous to the correlativity of right and duty, the courts struggle to formulate new and artificial restrictions on the excessively broad liability that would be engendered by the mere foreseeability of loss.[50]

---

[49] Bruce Feldthusen, *Liability for Pure Economic Loss: Yes, But Why?*, 28 WEST. AUSTL. L.REV. 84 (1999).

[50] Among the markers of proximity that have been suggested are: knowledge that the defendant has or ought to have of the specific individual(s) likely to suffer economic loss (Stevenson, J. in *Canadian National Railway*, *supra* note 48; Mason, J. *in Caltex Oil*, *supra* note 48); knowledge that the defendant has or ought to have of the class of first line victims (McHugh J. in *Perre*, *supra* note 39); salient features about the defendant's actual or constructive knowledge of the prospective injury, about the nature of the detriment and about the nature of the damages claimed (Stephen J. in *Caltex Oil*, *supra* note 48); the relationship between the parties, physical propinquity, assumed or imposed obligations and close causal connection (McLachlin J in Canadian National Railway, *supra* note 48); and the preexistence of contractual; arrangements between the parties. (*Martel Building v. Canada*, [2002] S.C.R. 860). Acknowledging that their treatments of the problem of indeterminate recovery are themselves quite indeterminate, Stephen J. and McLachlin J. expect that over time the judicial decisions will crystallize the characteristic features of various situations for future guidance. One can be skeptical, however, that the positive law will provide legal certainty if it lacks conceptual coherence.

In this respect, the new approach to liability for economic loss represents a jurisprudential decline.

How, finally, does correlativity illuminate Lord Atkin's general conception of the duty of care? Adapting the biblical precept that one is to love one's neighbor, Lord Atkin famously characterized the "neighbour" to whom the duty of care is owed as "persons so closely and directly affected by my act that I ought to have them in mind as being so affected."[51] In the correlative conception of liability, the obligation on the defendant to have these persons in mind arises from their possession of a right that runs against the defendant and thus places the defendant under an obligation to not injure it. An act "closely and directly" affects this right when the act's tendency to endanger the right is a reason for considering the act negligent. The duty that results is one that draws its justification from its correlativity with the plaintiff's right. Such a duty defines the "relationship between the parties" in terms that are at once legal and general. The legal dimension lies in demanding not the beneficence of neighborly love, which Lord Atkin considered excessively broad for a legal system, but the more restricted avoidance of injury. The general dimension lies in construing this legal notion of injury as expressing the most general normative categories applicable to the relationship between the parties in private law, that of right and correlative duty. Because correlativity requires that the content of the right be the same as the object of the duty, the plaintiff's suffering is unjust for the same reason that the defendant's action is. This conception of the duty of care thus captures the coherence presupposed in Lord Atkin's insistence that that, aside from particular duties, there must be a general conception of duty that all particular duties instantiate.

IV. THE TWO-STAGE TEST FOR THE DUTY OF CARE

As the previous sections indicate, one can discern two broad strategies for elucidating the duty of care. One strategy, represented preeminently by the landmark cases of the twentieth century, coherently integrates the duty of care both into the entire ensemble of negligence concepts and into the correlativity of right and duty. Under this strategy the plaintiff's right both grounds and limits the defendant's liability. An alternative strategy, evident in Andrews' dissenting opinion in *Palsgraf* and in the more recent economic loss cases, allows the foreseeability of loss initially to expand the scope of liability, which is then limited by some other mechanism. In Andrews's opinion the danger

---

[51] *Donoghue v. Stevenson*, [1932] A.C. 562 (appeal taken from Scot).

to anyone creates a duty to whoever is in fact injured, but proximate cause excludes certain consequences from the expanded liability that would otherwise ensue. In the more recent economic loss cases, the foreseeability of loss triggers a duty subject to considerations of proximity that address the problem of indeterminacy. Under this strategy the limit emerges from a factor independent of the one that creates the initial possibility of liability.

In the last decades of the twentieth century several common-law jurisdictions developed a comprehensive version of this latter strategy. Starting from the idea that Lord Atkin's neighbor principle "ought to apply unless there is some justification or valid explanation for its exclusion,"[52] the House of Lords worked out a two-stage test for the duty of care.[53] This test was adopted elsewhere and, although subsequently abandoned in England and Australia, continues to be used in a number of jurisdictions.[54] The two-stage test required the courts to consider, first, whether the parties had a relationship as neighbors that was sufficient to give rise to a prima facie duty and, then, whether there were any considerations that ought to negative or limit the duty. Foreseeability of loss was a significant component of the first stage, opening the road to a broad liability that the second stage could narrow.

Perhaps the most steadfast champion of the two-stage test has been the Supreme Court of Canada, which has continued to apply it even after its repudiation by the House of Lords. In its current Canadian formulation the two-stage test goes as follows:

> In order to decide whether or not a private law duty of care existed, two questions must be asked:
>
> 1. is there a sufficiently close relationship between the parties . . . so that in the reasonable contemplation of the [defendant], carelessness on its part might cause damage to [the plaintiff]? If so,
> 2. are there any considerations that ought to negative or limit (a) the scope of the duty (b) the class of persons to whom it is owed or (c) the damages to which the breach of it may give rise?[55]

The first stage of this formulation incorporates the traditional notion of reasonable foreseeability to establish a prima facie duty. At this stage the judge attempts to discern "whether, as a matter of simple justice, the defendant may

---

[52] *Home Office v. Dorset Yacht*, [1970] A.C. 1004, 1027.

[53] *Anns v. Merton London Borough Council*, [1978] A.C. 728.

[54] Daniel More, *The Boundaries of Negligence*, 4 THEORETICAL INQUIRIES IN LAW 339, 343–345 (2003).

[55] *Kamloops v. Nielsen*, 10 DLR (4th) 641, 662 (1984).

be said to have had an obligation to be mindful of the plaintiff's interests."[56] The second stage allows that prima facie duty to be circumscribed or canceled because of the presence of "policy concerns that are extrinsic to simple justice but that are nevertheless fundamentally important."[57]

The two-stage test of the duty of care has radically altered negligence law in Canada. Negligence analysis no longer consists in scrutinizing the parties' relationship in the light of a coherent series of concepts. The mode of argument that underpinned the great doctrinal achievements of the twentieth century has been abandoned. Instead of examining whether the materialization of the risk created by the defendant is an injustice to the plaintiff, the test directs the Court to a melange of justice and policy considerations. This momentous change has had several questionable features. This section will outline these features, then illustrate the operation of some of them by comparing a Canadian case with its English counterpart, and finally discuss a recent Canadian case that, although reaffirming and supposedly clarifying the two-stage test, may mark the Court's initial step back to a more coherent jurisprudence.

Application of the two-stage test has the following characteristics. First, a decisive factor in liability is the importance of the policy considerations relevant to the second stage, in that they have the power to override the conclusions about justice reached in the first stage. These considerations are uncontrolled by the relationship between the parties and indeed may be beyond the court's institutional competence to judge. A plaintiff can therefore be denied compensation on the basis of policy considerations that, although one-sidedly pertinent to the defendant or to persons carrying on a similar activity, have no normative bearing on the position of the plaintiff as the sufferer of an injustice. From the plaintiff's point of view, the denial of recovery, operating (as the Court says) extrinsically to simple justice, amounts to the judicial confiscation of what was rightly due to the plaintiff, in order to subsidize policy objectives unilaterally favorable to the defendant and those similarly situated.

Second, even as policy analysis the second stage is one-sided. It refers only to policy considerations that negate liability, not to those that might confirm liability. Under the Court's formulation, the plaintiff's claim for compensation is entirely constituted by the first stage; the second stage is devoted to factors favorable to defendants. Although the Court occasionally gestures in the direction of a policy adverse to the defendant, it rarely engages either in an extended examination of that policy or in a rigorous comparison of the

---

[56] *Hercules Managements v. Ernst & Young,* 146 DLR (4th) 577, 591 (1997).
[57] *Id.*

competing policy considerations.[58] Indeed, to do so would expose a further difficulty, that, given the heterogeneity of possible policy considerations, a rigorous comparison would require the elaboration and application of some metric of social gains and losses – a task beyond judicial competence. How, for instance, is a court to know whether, in a case of negligent misrepresentation by auditors, the benefits of deterring carelessness are outweighed by the disadvantages of indeterminate liability?[59] It is therefore hardly surprising that the policy considerations that interest the Court are those that, as the wording of the test indicates, "ought to negative or limit" the duty.[60]

Third, the relationship between plaintiff and defendant is fragmented not only by the very presence at the second stage of policy concerns extrinsic to that relationship, but also by the disjunction between the justice and policy considerations of the two stages. This disjunction, in turn, requires judges to balance categorically different considerations, in order to determine whether in a given

---

[58] In defense of the Court on this point, Justice Major said that:

> [T]his criticism is too narrow in view of what was said in *Hercules* [*supra* note 56]. In that case LaForest J. considered not only indeterminate liability, which is a policy consideration that negates liability, but also deterrence, which is a policy consideration that favours liability. Although the concern for indeterminate liability won the day, it is clear that the policy analysis was not completely one-sided.

John Major, *Anns and the Law of Negligence, in* THE CONTINUING LEGAL EDUCATION SOCIETY OF BRITISH COLUMBIA, TORTS – 2001, posted April 12, 2001 *at* <http://www.cle. bc.ca/CLE/Analysis/Collection/01-5123601-anns>. In *Hercules* the Court's entire treatment of deterrence was as follows:

> Certain authors have argued that imposing broad duties of care on auditors would give rise to significant social and economic benefits so far as the spectre of tort liability would act as an incentive to auditors to produce accurate (*i.e.*, non-negligent) reports. I would agree that deterrence of negligent conduct is an important policy consideration with respect to auditors' liability. Nonetheless I am of the view that, in the final analysis, it is outweighed by the socially undesirable consequences to which the imposition of indeterminate liability on auditors might lead. (citations omitted).

Hercules Managements v. Ernst & Young, 146 DLR (4th) at 593 (1997) (internal citations omitted). It seems extravagant to characterize this desultory mention of deterrence as showing that deterrence was "considered" in the "policy analysis."

[59] *Id.*

[60] For example, in *Dobson v. Dobson*, 174 DLR 1, 31 (1999) the Court held decided that a mother was not liable for the prenatal injuries that she caused her own child by her negligent driving. Although injury was foreseeable under the first stage, the Court negatived liability on policy grounds in order to safeguard the pregnant woman's autonomy and privacy. However, the Court also rejected the suggestion that the existence of a mandatory automobile insurance regime justified liability on policy grounds. Thus, a judicially-enunciated policy prevented the victim of negligent driving from gaining access to insurance proceeds whose availability had been legislated. Elsewhere, in *Can. Nat'l Ry v. Norsk Pac. SS*, 91 DLR 4th 289 (1992) *supra* note 48, the Court had given extensive attention to insurance factors in determining whether to deny liability, but insurance is apparently not available as a policy factor that can support liability at the second stage of the two-stage test.

case the policy considerations are more important than the justice considerations that they can displace. How is this balancing of incommensurables
to be done? In effect, the two-stage test puts into circulation two different
normative currencies between which no rate of exchange exists.

Fourth, the two-stage test for duty of care transfigures the notion of foreseeability itself. When considered within the framework of injustice done and
suffered, foreseeability is an intrinsically correlative notion through which the
law constructs the identical nature of the injustice on both sides by linking
the plaintiff's injury to the reason for characterizing the defendant's action as
wrongful. Accordingly, foreseeability is internally limited by the scope of the
wrongfulness to which it refers. In contrast, under the two-stage test, foreseeability constitutes a "relatively low threshold"[61] for recognizing a prima
facie duty, which is then extrinsically limited by policy considerations. Any
reasonably prospective damage counts as being foreseeable under the first
stage of the test, without inquiry into why the defendant's action should be
characterized as a wrongful infringement of the plaintiff's right.[62]

Fifth, even taken on its own the first stage is internally fractured. Although
the formulation of the first stage refers to the existence of "a sufficiently close
connection between the parties," that connection is analyzed not (as coherence would require) in terms of a reason for characterizing the defendant's
action as a wrong relative to the plaintiff's right, but as a combination of two
factors, foreseeability (with its low threshold) and proximity. Thus, in its first

---

[61] *Ingles v. City of Toronto*, 183 DLR (4th) 193, 202 (2002); *Ryan v. City of Victoria*, 168 DLR (4th)
     513, 525 (1999). In these cases the Court treats proximity as yielding a low threshold that is
     synonymous with reasonable foreseeability, not as imposing an additional restriction. *Ryan*
     formulates the first stage as follows:

     > In order to establish a *prima facie* duty of care, it must be shown that a relationship of
     > proximity existed between the parties such that it was reasonably foreseeable that a careless
     > act by the [defendant] could result in injury to the [plaintiff]

     In *Ingles* the formulation is substantially the same, except that "would" replaces "could."

[62] As Robert Keeton observed:

     > [P]utting the crucial question in terms of whether the injuries were foreseeable ... carries the
     > misleading implication that the scope of legal responsibility extends to every consequence
     > that is foreseeable as a possibility in any degree.... The crucial standard is better expressed
     > as the question whether all her injuries were within those risks by reason of which the
     > defendants' conduct was characterized as negligence.

     ROBERT KEETON, LEGAL CAUSE IN THE LAW OF TORTS 55 (1963). A graphic expression of
     how low the threshold of foreseeability can be appears in *Modbury Trangle Shopping Centre v.
     Anzil*, 176 ALR 411 at 436 (2000):

     > In almost every case in which a plaintiff suffers damage it is foreseeable that, if reasonable
     > care is not taken, harm may follow. As Dixon CJ said in argument in Chapman v. Hearse,
     > "I cannot understand why any event that does happen is not foreseeable by a person of
     > sufficient imagination and intelligence." Foresight of harm is not sufficient to show that a
     > duty of care exists.

stage the two-stage test takes over the tensions, noted in the discussion of eco-nomic loss in the previous section of this chapter, that result from ascribing to proximity a policy-based limiting function; the second stage then piles on top of proximity yet another layer of policy considerations that also have a limiting function. Within this complex structure, "proximity" is merely a conclusory label that, as the Court frankly observed, states a result without itself providing a principled basis for liability.[63] It stands for a variety of case-specific factors that go to the determination of whether it is fair and just, having regard to the relationship between the parties, to impose a prima facie duty of care.[64] Where the duty of care has already been recognized by law, proximity is the term under which one subsumes the various factors that differentiate the different categories of liability, such as physical and propri-etary harms, negligent misrepresentation, certain cases of economic loss, the municipality's obligation to prospective purchasers to inspect new housing developments, the duty of public authorities who have undertaken a pol-icy of road maintenance to execute the maintenance with due care, and so on.[65] In this way proximity thematizes not the unifying principle underlying the general conception of duty, but the disparateness of particular kinds of duty.

In short, the introduction of the two-stage test has transformed Cana-dian negligence law into an enquiry into one-sided policy considerations at the ultimate stage that are extrinsic to justice between the parties and that are mysteriously balanced against a first stage that combines an excessively expan-sive notion of foreseeability with the invocation, under the term "proximity," of a miscellany of limiting case-specific factors. This ramshackle enquiry, composed of mutually alien parts that labour to contain the specter of unlim-ited liability that it itself lets loose, is hardly conducive to the elaboration of coherent and principled justifications for liability.[66] The test represents a

---

[63] *Hercules Managements v. Ernst & Young*, 146 DLR (4th) at 588 (1997).

[64] *Cooper v. Hobart*, 206 DLR (4th) 193, 204 (2001).

[65] *Id.* at 205.

[66] A practical difficulty about the two-stage test is that, given the test's complexity, even judges at the highest level can lose track of the connection between the reasons they offer and the specific aspect of the test that is at issue. Two examples illustrate this.

In *Hall v. Hebert*, 101 DLR (4th) 129 (1993), the Court, having restricted the defense of illegality, had to determine whether the remaining scope for the defendant's invocation of the plaintiff's illegal conduct should be situated within a separate defence or within the second stage of the duty enquiry. The majority of the Court favored the former on the following grounds, *Id.* at 169:

Policy concerns unrelated to the legal rules which govern the relationship between the parties to an action have not generally been considered in determining whether a duty of care lies. This follows from the fact that the justice which tort law seeks to accomplish is justice

high point for the disintegration of duty. It conceives of the notion of duty as internally fragmented between and within its stages. It also conceives of the duties themselves as particular species each of which represents its own specific considerations of policy and proximity. All that remains of Lord Atkin's notion of a general conception is the comprehensive verbal umbrella that applies to, but does not coherently unify, these different duties.

A contrasting pair of recent cases illustrates some of these themes. In the past few years the highest courts in England and then in Canada have dealt with the liability of auditors for negligently preparing the annual report of a corporation's accounts. As is well known, investors in the stock market buy and sell on the basis of the information in these reports. Previously, accountants had been held liable for the reliance losses caused by negligence in a report they knew was prepared for the guidance of a specific class of investors with respect to a specific class of transactions.[67] The question that now arose was whether investors generally could recover for their admittedly

> between the parties to the particular action; the court acts at the instance of the wronged party to rectify the damage caused by a particular defendant. *See* Ernest J. Weinrib, *The Special Morality of Tort Law*, 34 McGILL L. J. 408 (1989).
>
> The relationship between plaintiff and defendant which gives rise to their respective entitlement and liability arises from a duty predicated on foreseeable consequences of harm. This being the concern, the legality or morality of the plaintiff's conduct is an extrinsic consideration. In the rare cases where concerns for the administration of justice require that the extrinsic consideration of the character of the plaintiff's conduct be considered, it seems to me that this is better done by way of defence than by distorting the notion of the duty of care owed by the defendant to the plaintiff.

These observations, however, support not only the exclusion of plaintiff's illegal conduct from the second stage of the two-stage test of duty. They also support not having a two-stage test at all, because that test explicitly puts extrinsic policy considerations into the second stage. Conversely, given the existence of the test, these observations cannot count as reasons for not treating illegality as a matter of duty under the second stage of the two-stage test.

In *Dobson v. Dobson*, 174 DLR (4th) 1 (1991), Major J. argued in dissent that there is no reason of policy under the second stage of the two-stage test for not holding a pregnant woman liable for prenatal damage done to her child by her own negligent driving. He disagreed with the majority's view that the woman's autonomy provided a policy ground negativing liability under the second stage: the woman was already under a duty of care to third parties with respect to her driving so that liability to the child would entail no diminution of the woman's freedom. In reply, McLachlin J., concurring with the majority, maintained, *Id.* at 35, that Major J.'s approach:

> violates the principle that the duty of care in tort must be founded on the relationship between the actual parties to the dispute before the court, and makes recovery conditional on the serendipitous coincidence that another person stood to be injured by the pregnant woman's act or omission. I am not persuaded that the common law can be narrowed to achieve the result here sought while staying true to its principles.

McLachlin J.'s argument, correct though it is on its own, is not appropriate to the second stage of the two-stage test, because that stage is explicitly concerned with policy considerations extrinsic to the relationship.

[67]   *Haig v. Bamford*, 72 DLR (3rd) 68 (1976).

foreseeable reliance on statements in a report prepared for the corporation's annual meeting. Both the English and the Canadian courts answered in the negative, but they used different modes of reasoning.

For the House of Lords,[68] the crucial issue was whether the requisite normative link existed between the defendant's negligence and the plaintiff's loss. Foreseeability of the loss could not ground liability, because the duty of care could not be considered in abstraction from the kind of damage that the defendant must avoid causing. In this case the audit was presented to fulfill a statutory obligation aimed at the informed exercise by the corporation's stakeholders of their powers of corporate governance. Because the plaintiff's loss was not connected to the purpose of the audit, the defendant owed no duty of care with respect to that loss.

The Canadian case[69] followed the English decision in result but transformed the structure of its thought. Applying the two-stage test, the Supreme Court of Canada determined that a prima facie duty of care arose because investor reliance on the audit was both reasonable and foreseeable. This duty, however, was negatived by the undesirable social consequences of the indeterminate liability generated by so broad a conception of foreseeability. Among these consequences were the increased insurance premiums, the higher costs faced by accountants, the opportunity costs in time spent on litigation rather than on generating accounting revenue, reduction in the availability in accounting services as marginal firms are driven to the wall, and increased costs for consumers. Looking to the purpose of the auditor's report, as was done in the English case, was, "in reality, nothing more that a means by which to circumscribe – for reasons of policy – the scope of the representor's potentially unlimited liability."[70]

The contrast between these two cases is stark. The English judgment straightforwardly applied the mode of reasoning that had been set out in the classic twentieth-century cases adapted to negligent representation. The House of Lords examined whether the investor suffered the kind of loss that lies within the scope of the auditor's duty, which, in turn, was defined and limited by the purpose for which the audit was required. Given that such audits are not prepared for the guidance of decisions to buy or sell shares, the defendant could not be viewed as having assumed responsibility for the plaintiff's losses. Because these investment transactions fell outside the range

---

[68] *Caparo Industries v. Dickman*, 1 All ER 568 (1990). For an illuminating discussion of this case, *see* Chapman, *Limited Auditors' Liability: Economic Analysis and the Theory of Tort Law*, 20 Can. Bus. L. J. 180 (1992).

[69] *Hercules Managements v. Ernst & Young*, 146 DLR (4th) 577 (1997).

[70] *Id.* at 590.

of the defendant's duty, the plaintiff's loss, despite being the foreseeable outcome of a negligently-prepared report, did not count as the suffering of a
wrong at the defendant's hands. In this judgment the purpose of the audit
functions as the normative idea through which the court considers the connection between parties. The reasoning is relational throughout, and liability
is denied because the plaintiff's loss is not normatively correlated to the defendant's negligence.[71]

The Canadian case transforms this relational reasoning into a policy-based
restriction on liability. The two-stage test, so the Court claims, allows us to
recognize the relational criteria "for what they really are – policy-based means
by which to curtail liability."[72] Reliance that is reasonable and foreseeable,
now no longer situated within the framework of doing and suffering the
same injustice, creates a prima facie duty that is "potentially infinite."[73] To
solve this problem of its own creation, the Court curtails the scope of the duty
by reference to policy factors. Hence, what the Court calls the simple justice of
the plaintiff's claim yields to the need to preserve the availability of accounting
services in Canada. The Court does not explain why justice is to be sacrificed
to the need for accounting services, or why the policy to maintain accounting
services outweighs the policy of deterrence, or how the Court knows that
the current level and pricing of accounting services in Canada is optimal.
Instead of offering reasons for thinking that the defendant did not wrong the
plaintiff, the Court indulges in speculations beyond its competence about
the undesirable consequences of liability for the providers and consumers of
accounting services.[74]

These particular differences in the two judgments reflect a wider contrast
between the nature of the justifications that they employ. The English judgment assumes that the justifications relevant to liability embrace both parties

---

[71] The following passage from the English case is a striking judicial formulation of the notion
that the sequence from negligence to injury forms a single normative unit:

> [A] postulated duty of care must be stated with reference to the kind of damage that the
> plaintiff has suffered and in reference to the plaintiff or the class of which the plaintiff is a
> member. . . . His duty of care is a thing written on the wind unless damage is caused by the
> breach of that duty; there is no actionable negligence unless duty, breach and consequential
> damage coincide . . . ; for the purpose of determining liability in a given case, each element
> can be defined only in terms of the others.

Caparo Industries, 1 All E.R. at 599 per Lord Oliver, quoting Brennan J. in Council of the Shire
of Sutherland v. Heyman, 60 A.L.R. 1, 48 (1985).

[72] Hercules Managements, 146 DLR (4th) at 592.

[73] Id. at 591.

[74] For similar speculations as to whether auditor liability for foreseeable loss is in the public
interest, see Esanda Finance Corporation v. Peat Marwick Hungerfords (Reg), 142 A.L.R. 750,
782 (1997).

as the doer and the sufferer of the same injustice. Because of liability's correlative significance for both parties, such justifications are required if a judgment is to provide coherent reasons for considering whether one party is liable to the other. Conversely, a court that decided issues of liability without reference to such justifications would fail to treat the parties fairly in relation to each other. The reasoning in the Canadian judgment provides an example of this failure. Its expansive conception of foreseeability at the first stage focuses on the prospective damage that might result from the defendant's action without articulating the reason for regarding that damage as a wrongful injury to the plaintiff's right. Similarly, its restrictive elucidation of policy at the second stage deals only with the effect of liability on accountants and is thus unrelated to the plaintiff's claim to have suffered a wrong. As a result the judgment contains a series of unintegrated considerations that are divorced from the articulation of the wrong that that might link the parties to the action. Such considerations are inherently incapable of fairly and coherently determining whether the defendant should be held liable to the plaintiff.

More recently the Supreme Court of Canada has reaffirmed the two-stage test for duty of care, but in terms that might open a path back to a more coherent approach to the duty issue. In *Cooper v. Hobart*[75] the plaintiff was an investor who was suing for money lost by advancing funds to a registered mortgage broker who had used the funds for unauthorized purposes. The investor sued the statutory regulator, the Registrar of Mortgage Brokers, claiming that her losses would have been avoided or diminished had the Registrar acted more promptly in suspending the broker or notifying investors that the broker was under investigation. The Court held that under the two-stage test the Registrar did not owe the investor a duty of care even though the investor might well have been able to show that her losses were the reasonably foreseeable consequence of the defendant's alleged negligence.

The crucial determination in *Cooper* was that the proximity required by the first stage was lacking. The Registrar's powers and duties were entirely the creation of statute, and an analysis of the statute showed that the Registrar's duties were owed to the public rather than to individual investors. The point of the regulatory scheme was to ensure efficiency in the mortgage marketplace. This required the Registrar to consider not only the private interests of individual investors but also the public interests in access to capital through mortgage financing and in public confidence in the system as a whole. Consequently, the statute could not be construed to impose on the Registrar

---

[75] *Cooper v. Hobart,* 206 DLR (4th) 193 (2001); *see also* the companion case *Edwards v. The Law Society of Upper Canada,* 206 DLR (4th) 211 (2001).

a tort duty of care that is specific to individual investors. Such a duty would be inconsistent with the overall regulatory purposes evident in the powers granted under the statute. The statutory purpose thus defined the notion of proximity applicable to the relationship of the parties. The Court concluded that even if foreseeability was present, proximity was not. Therefore, the search for a duty of care did not survive the first stage. However, for the sake of completeness, the Court proceeded to the second stage, where it found that even if a prima facie duty had been established, it would have been negated for overriding policy reasons.

Even as the Court reaffirms the two-stage test, a significant feature of the *Cooper* decision is the comparative effacement of the second stage. The second stage remains as the point at which one examines "residual policy considerations" that concern not the relationship between the parties but the effect of postulating a duty on the legal system and society more generally.[76] However, in contrast to the Court's previous jurisprudence, which had often treated the second stage as decisive, the second stage has now become less prominent.

There are three indications of this. First, the Court explicitly says that the second stage will never arise if the duty of care falls within a recognized category of liability. Moreover, in its decision (where the Court indicated that overriding policy reasons would have negated a prima facie duty, even had one been found at the first stage) the considerations mentioned as relevant did little independent work. Most of the "residual policy considerations" centered on the Registrar's exercise of a public function entailing discretionary decisions that balance public and private interest. The policy considerations of the second stage were therefore not different in kind from the considerations that went to proximity at the first stage. Third, the Court treated the purpose of the statutory provisions as relevant to the elucidation of proximity in the first stage, in striking contrast to its earlier treatment of the statutory requirement of an audit in the negligent misrepresentation case mentioned earlier. The effect of using the statute to inform proximity is to bring the analysis close to the parallel English case, in which the duty was defined and limited by the purpose for which the statute mandated an audit. The Court's application of the two-stage test in *Cooper v. Hobart* can, accordingly, perhaps be regarded as implicitly repudiating its earlier reduction of relational criteria to policy factors that are extrinsic to the parties' relationship.

Accordingly, the following picture emerges from *Cooper v. Hobart* about the second stage. The second stage is now to have only a restricted application; considerations that appear at the second stage largely replicate the contents

[76] *Cooper*, 206 DLR (4th) at 206.

of proximity at the first stage; and factors previously considered at the second stage as extrinsic to the relationship are now to be analysed as relational at the first stage. Perhaps, as its previous content is poured out of the second stage into the first and what remains is seen as redundant, Canadian courts will pay less and less attention to the second stage. If so, the new case will be seen as the first step in the atrophy of the two-stage test.

What about the first stage? *Cooper v. Hobart* contains a welcome emphasis on the relational nature of the considerations that govern the first stage.[77] Perhaps this attention to the relational aspect of the duty issue will be further strengthened if the second stage does indeed atrophy, and the reasoning about duty is effectively confined to the examination of what is foreseeable and proximate. For the moment, however, the Court has not yet developed a fully adequate view of what it means for considerations to be relational. Instead of being understood as a coherent and integrated whole, the first stage is seen as an amalgam of foreseeability plus proximity, with proximity itself embodying a collection of specific indicia that vary with the particular relationship in question.[78] Perhaps its newly announced sensitivity to the relational quality

---

[77] "The proximity analysis involved in the first stage of the Anns test focuses on factors arising from the relationship between the plaintiff and the defendant." *Id.* at 203.

[78] An example of the determination of duty in the aftermath of *Cooper v. Hobart*, is *Odhavji Estate v. Woodhouse*, [2003] 3 S.C.R. 263. In *Odhavji*, the estate and family of the victim of a police shooting sued the chief of police for negligence (as well as for malfeasance in a public office) for the emotional damage caused by his failure to have the police officers cooperate in a statutorily-mandated investigation by an independent civilian board. The chief of police was unsuccessful in his motion to strike the statement of claim for disclosing no reasonable cause of action. The Court held that the chief of police was under a duty of care to the plantiffs.

The prima facie stage of the duty was based on the foreseeability of injury combined with the finding of a relationship of proximity. After stating the "essential purpose" of the proximity requirement in the broadest possible terms (para. 50: "whether it is fair and just to impose a duty of care"), the Court enumerated three factors that "strengthened the nexus" (para. 56–58): the relatively direct causal link between the alleged misconduct and the supposed harm, the public's reasonable expectation that the chief would be mindful of the injuries arising from police misconduct, and the general statutory obligation of the chief to ensure that police officers carry out their duties. Between the most general reference to what is "fair and just" and the specific factors marking proximity in this particular situation, there is no intermediate consideration of how these three factors particularize a conception of 'justice and fairness" that normatively relates the parties as the obligor and obligee of a private law duty. Accordingly, the Court supplies no clue as to how these three specific factors coalesce into a coherent conception of proximity. One might have expected, following *Cooper v. Hobart*, an assessment of whether the purposes of the statutorily-mandated investigation included not only the need to maintain proper police procedures and to discipline police misconduct but also attention to the emotional state of family members of the victims of police shootings. Only thus could one have determined whether the prospect of emotional harm by the deceased's family is a reason for considering as negligent the chief's failure to ensure that his officers cooperated in the investigation of the shooting.

of the first stage will eventually lead the Court to two salutary realizations. The first is that proximity cannot capture what is normatively significant about the relationship between the parties so long as it is regarded simply as something that is added to an expansive notion of foreseeability from the outside in order to restrict it. Rather (if these terms are to be used) proximity should be understood to reveal the restricted meaning that forseeability itself has in the negligence context, that is, that foreseeability is a way of inquiring into the risks by reference to which the defendant's action is characterized as negligent. The second is that the relational quality that the Court now highlights has to be expressed in normative categories that are themselves relational. Accordingly, behind the particular duties must stand a general conception of duty governed by the correlativity of right and duty, that is, by a normative framework whose elements are intrinsically related to each other. Then the duty issue will again take its place in the coherent ensemble of concepts that treats the defendant's creation of the unreasonable risk and the plaintiff's suffering from the risk's materialization as falling under the same correlatively structured wrong.

V. TWO NOTIONS OF POLICY

This final section will focus on the connection between duty and policy. Throughout the common-law world, the notion that the formulation of the duty of care involves a determination of policy is accepted almost as a truism. In his tort judgments Lord Denning often gave voice to this supposed truism. For instance, whether corrections officers owe a duty to persons whose property might be damaged by the escape of borstal trainees is, he said, "at bottom a matter of public policy that we as judges must resolve."[79] Similarly, in dealing with liability for economic loss he observed that "whenever the courts draw a line to mark out the bounds of duty, they do so as a matter of policy."[80] The argument in this section is that the link with policy, at least as it is commonly understood, has played a major role in the disintegration of duty and yet rests on a misconception.[81] The misconception involves running together two distinct notions of what policy means.

---

[79] *Dorset Yacht v. Home Office*, [1969] 2 All ER 564, 567.
[80] *Spartan Steel & Alloys Ltd. v. Martin*, [1972] 3 All ER 557, 561; *see also Lamb v. London Borough of Camden*, [1981] QB 625, 636.
[81] The difficulties in the invocation of policy have been illuminatingly discussed in essays by Martin Stone *See* Martin Stone, *Focusing the Law: What Legal Interpretation is Not*, in LAW AND INTERPRETATION: ESSAYS IN LEGAL PHILOSOPHY 31, 72–84 (Andrei Marmor ed, 1995); Martin Stone, *Formalism*, in THE OXFORD HANDBOOK OF JURISPRUDENCE AND PHILOSOPHY OF LAW 166, 187–204 (Jules Coleman & Scott Shapiro eds., 2002).

The first notion is the common view that policy involves articulating some independently desirable goal(s) and then dealing with a particular tort case in a way that forwards these goals or, if they are in tension, balances some against others to produce a result that is desirable overall. The goals are independent both in the sense that they rest on justifications that are independent of tort law, to which they are then applied, and that they are independent of one another, so that they may represent incompatible normative impulses that need to be balanced. For instance, a favorite policy of Lord Denning was that losses should be widely distributed, because it is easier for many to bear comparatively small losses than for a single person to bear a comparatively heavy one.[82] The justification for this policy is independent of tort law, in that the policy states a normatively appealing way to deal with any sort of loss, not with a loss merely caused by tortious wrongdoing. Indeed, tort law imposes an artificial limit on its operation by restricting the distribution of losses to the insurance pool brought into play by tort law's initial allocation of the loss.[83] Moreover, when this policy favors the defendant, it may come into conflict with other policies, such as deterrence, that would be forwarded by liability. Hence, a determination that takes account of all the heterogeneous policies can be regarded as involving a process of balancing those that favour the plaintiff against those that favor the defendant.

The invocation of such independent policies entails the disintegration of duty as a systematic and coherent concept. Given the heterogeneity of the available policies and their different weightings in the balancing process, a systematically unified conception of duty based on (in Lord Atkin's words) "the element common to all cases in which [a duty] is found to exist"[84] is out of the question. The variety of policies and the shifting balance among them leaves no place for a common element on which the various duties (again in Lord Atkin's words) "must logically be based."[85] In these circumstances there can only be different specific kinds of duty, with each kind representing the particular policies or the particular balance among policies that are recognized as decisive in situations of that sort. Moreover, the conception of duty is inwardly fragmented into the various policies that favor one party or the other. The duty issue is therefore seen as the locus not for defining the wrong identically from the standpoint of both parties, but for forwarding or

---

[82] *Spartan Steel & Alloys,* [1972] 3 All ER at 564; *Lamb v. London Borough of Camden,* [1981] QB 625, 637 (CA).

[83] ERNEST J. WEINRIB, THE IDEA OF PRIVATE LAW 36–38 (1995).

[84] *Donoghue v. Stevenson,* [1932] A.C. 562 (appeal taken from Scot).

[85] *Id.*

balancing policies that rest on considerations that apply differently to each of them.

Were the duty issue necessarily to involve policies of this sort, the general conception of duty as coherently linking the parties as doer and sufferer of the same wrong would be a chimaera. That such policies are crucial to determining the duty of care is often taken for granted. In *Cooper v. Hobart*, for instance, the Supreme Court of Canada approved the proposition that a decision about duty "is in fact a conclusion embracing within it, and yet concealing the identity of, the several considerations of policy, and the balancing of interests which have led the court to decide that a duty is owed."[86] Thus, the Court regards it as self-evident that the duty issue requires the consideration of a multiplicity of policies that represent interests to be balanced.

But is this really self-evident? It is notable that in *Cooper v. Hobart* the Court, after proclaiming the necessity of balancing, seemed at the first stage to resolve the proximity issue (which it declares to be an issue of policy) without doing any balancing whatsoever. The judgment did not compare the interests of the investors with the interests of the Registrar of Mortgage Brokers, putting each set of interests into notional pans whose contents were calibrated to some notional measurement of weight, and seeing which pan notionally sank.[87] Rather, it analyzed the statute under which the Registrar of Mortgage Brokers operated to show that the Registrar's duty was of a public nature and thus not owed to specific individuals. The Court merely drew out what it thought, rightly or wrongly, was implicit in the statutory scheme within which the Registrar functioned. The exercise in question was not one of balancing policies or interests but of specifying the nature of the Registrar's duty through analysis of the institutional framework created by the statute.

Perhaps, one might respond, the Court was doing what it said it was doing after all: the Court's conclusion "embrac[ed] within it and yet conceal[ed]"[88] the policies and the balancing that led it to its decision. On this view, by not presenting its disposition of the case as an exercise in balancing, the Court's own judgment would provide an example of the concealment to which it referred. It is not clear how one could substantiate this interpretation or why any plausibility should be attributed to it. One might in a pinch be tempted to describe the result as establishing the legally recognized balance between the

---

[86] *Cooper*, 206 DLR (4th) at 202.
[87] The procedure envisaged would perhaps be reminiscent of the timeless spoof on balancing in Aristophanes' *Frogs*, where Dionysus in the underworld judges between Aeschylus and Euripides by employing a set of scales that balances the ponderous verse of the former against the fluffy verse of the latter.
[88] *Id.*

investor's interests and the Registrar's. But describing the result as a balance does not mean that one reached the result through the activity of balancing, let alone that such activity was necessary for the result. Moreover, the putative response would imply that in its judgment the Court clarified the process of its reasoning by pointing to what it concealed – and then continued to conceal it. The point of the Court's announcing and then performing this feat of mystification is not immediately apparent.

The comment about policy in *Cooper v. Hobart* exemplifies a peculiar inversion. The comment posits the existence of a familiar practice about which unsophisticated observers might make certain assumptions, and then treats those assumptions as an illusion that can be dispelled by pointing to what is "in fact" the case. The practice in question is the giving of reasons for holding that a duty of care exists, and the illusory assumption is that this practice does not involve attention to "the several considerations of policy and the balancing of interests." The comment then purports to dispel this illusion by insisting that determinations of duty "in fact" do require the embracing of multiple policies and the balancing of interests. But at the point of application this effort at enlightenment is immediately undermined by reasoning that exemplifies the very illusion that was supposed to have been dispelled. The Court's consideration of the actual duty at stake suggests that the comment about policy has gotten it backward. It turns out that the illusory assumption, rendered familiar over the years by constant scholarly and judicial repetition in the aftermath of legal realism, is that the duty issue necessarily involves the balancing of the interests represented by different policies. The illusion can be dispelled by attention to what "in fact" happens in cases that ignore this supposed necessity.

There is, however, a second notion of policy that is both required by and consistent with the conception of tort liability as a response to the doing and suffering of a wrong. Consider Lord Diplock's judgment in *Home Office v. Dorset Yacht*,[89] where the issue was whether corrections officers were under a duty of care to a yacht owner whose vessel was damaged when borstal boys under their supervision were negligently given an opportunity to escape from an island on which they were working. In terms of the framework for duty suggested above in Section III, this called for a determination of whether the officers' negligent behavior breached a duty that was correlative to the plaintiff's undisputed right in the boat. Lord Diplock began by signaling his agreement with Lord Denning's view that issue was "at bottom a matter of

---

[89] [1970] A.C. 1004, 1057.

public policy that we, as judges, must resolve."[90] However, the significance
that Lord Diplock attached to public policy was different from the one that
appears in many of Lord Denning's judgments. Whereas Lord Denning often
equated policy with independent goals such as loss spreading, Lord Diplock
understood the reference to the judges' role in resolving matters of policy to
be an invitation to explore the specifically judicial function of casuistically
developing the law. The task for Lord Diplock was not to identify and balance
independent goals, but to elucidate the meaning of Lord Atkin's general conception of duty in the circumstances of the present case. This required a number of steps: (1) an identification of the relevant characteristics, as informed
by the general conception, of the kinds of conduct and relationships that have
been held to give rise to a duty; (2) a comparison, again influenced by the
general conception, of the characteristics of the situation he was considering
with the characteristics of other situations where a duty had been found; and
(3) in a novel case in which these sets of characteristics from different situations
were not congruent, an evaluation, still under the guidance of the general conception, of the significance of the differences and of the substitutability of a
present characteristic for a missing one. The general conception of the duty
of care thereby constituted the standpoint from which the characteristics of
various situations were selected, compared, and evaluated.

In *Dorset Yacht*, this reference to policy, that is, to the process of casuistic
judgment under the general conception of duty, worked as follows. Previous
cases had held the corrections authority liable for negligence that resulted
in one detainee's injuring another.[91] Lord Diplock considered it a "rational
extension"[92] of the principle in those cases to substitute for the custodian's
right to control the physical proximity between detainees the knowledge that
the custodian had or ought to have had of the particular risk to which, because
of the physical proximity of its property, the plaintiff would be exposed by
the defendant's negligence. The general conception of the duty of care, which
Lord Atkin formulated as owed to persons so closely and directly affected by
the act that the actor ought to have them in contemplation, led Lord Diplock
to differentiate between the particular risk of damage consequent on escape,
which affected only those in the vicinity, and the general risk of suffering
from criminal activity, to which all members of the public are exposed. It was
the former that constituted the unreasonable risk created by the defendant's

---

[90] *Id.* at 1658.

[91] *Ellis v. Home Office*, [1953] 2 All ER 149; *D'Arcy v. Prison Commissioners*, THE TIMES,
November 17, 1955.

[92] *Home Office*, [1970] A.C. at 1071.

conduct, and that therefore rendered the plaintiff a person so closely and directly affected that the prospect of this damage ought to have been in the defendant's contemplation. Because the escape was from an island and could not be attempted without watercraft, the owners of boats moored in the vicinity were within the class to whom a duty of care was owed. The damage to the plaintiff's yacht was, therefore, the materialization of a risk that was unreasonable because of the prospect of this kind of damage. Thus, the parties were the doer and sufferer of the same wrong.

This second notion of policy reflects the existence of scope for judgment in the determination of a duty of care. The duty of care does not operate in a mechanistic or syllogistic fashion. This is especially the case when particular kinds of duties or duties in particular cases are regarded as instantiations of a general conception of duty. The general conception is, after all, a conception and not a recipe or even a "test." The general conception does not state a specific formula from which one can immediately discern whether a duty is present in any and every particular case; rather, it brings out what duty must be if the law of negligence is coherently to link the defendant's negligent act and the plaintiff's injury. The very generality of the conception means both that it is not defined by reference to any particular situation in which a duty is found and that it informs all such particular situations. It therefore requires to be related to its instantiations through an exercise of judgment, the point of which is to exhibit what, in the view of the person making the judgment, the duty of care means in the circumstances of a particular case. Accordingly, the general conception of duty does not render superfluous this exercise of judgment but guides it, indicating that the judgment is to be directed toward the existence of a right and of negligence with respect to that right. In this way the exercise of judgment is an operation of practical reason that plays itself out within the ensemble of concepts that the law constructs for considering whether the defendant has done and the plaintiff has suffered the same injustice.

Lord Diplock's opinion is outstanding for providing an account by a great judge of how this process of judgment might be described. He does not regard the general conception of the duty as a "test" that is applied externally to the facts, like a touchstone to gold; that would "misuse as a universal"[93] what Lord Diplock regards instead as a useful guide to the relevant characteristics. Rather, because the process of judgment is supposed to bring together the general conception of duty and the determination of a particular duty, it operates simultaneously from both ends. On the one hand, it attends to the fact

___

[93] *Id.* at 1060.

situation at hand and to the history of judicial determinations in analogous fact situations. On the other hand, it elucidates the relevance of particular facts and similarities by reference to the general conception of duty that Lord Atkin articulated. As Lord Diplock says, the judge starts by identifying "the relevant characteristics common to the kinds of conduct and relationships between the parties which are involved in the case for decision and to the kinds of conduct and relationships which have been held in previous decisions of the courts to give rise to a duty of care."[94] Importantly, though, the judge must "know what he is looking for; and this involves his approaching his analysis with some general conception of conduct and relationships which ought to give rise to a duty of care."[95] The result is the fusion of general and particular in a judgment about whether the defendant in the case at hand breached a duty owed to the plaintiff.

Under the second notion of policy the scope for judgment need not involve, as it did in *Dorset Yacht*, a casuistic comparison of the characteristics that give or have given rise to a duty of care. It also can involve the elucidation through legal argument of the issues of law that pertain to the relationship of the parties as doer and sufferer of the same wrong, Among the legal issues that may require elaboration in any given case are the nature of the plaintiff's right (for example, under what circumstances, if at all, does the plaintiff have a right to security from psychiatric injury?),[96] the nature of correlative wrongdoing by the defendant (for example, is the distributor of a product under a duty of care with respect to its safety?),[97] and the relevance of the connection between the supposed duty of care and other juridical considerations affecting the parties. Thus, problems in determining the duty of care "may concern the need to preserve the coherence of other legal principles, or of a statutory scheme which governs certain conduct and relationships."[98] An example is the long-standing controversy, now exemplified in the varying treatments of

---

[94] *Id.* at 1058.

[95] *Id.* One can contrast Lord Dipock's view that casuistic analysis to proceeds under a general conception with that of Dawson J. in *Hill*, 188 CLR at 177:

> Reasoning by analogy from decided cases by processes of induction and deduction, informed by rather than divorced from policy considerations, is not, in my view, dependent for its validity on those cases sharing an underlying conceptual consistency. It is really only dependent on the fact that something more than reasonable foreseeability is required to establish a duty of care and that what is sufficient or necessary in one case is a guide to what is sufficient or necessary in another.

> However, it is hard to see how one case can serve as a guide to another unless there is implicit some common standpoint that informs the comparison between them.

[96] Weinrib, *supra* note 34. *See also supra* note 39.

[97] *Watson v. Buckley and Osborne, Garrett and Co. Ltd (Ogee Ltd.)*, [1940] 1 All ER 174.

[98] *Sullivan v. Moody*, 183 A.L.R. 404, 415 (2001).

economic loss arising out of a defect of quality, about the relationship between contract and the duty of care in negligence.[99] Even if the particular parties are not bound to each other by contract, the nature and limits of contractual obligation may nonetheless have the implications for the existence of a tort duty of care between them. For instance, the argument may be made in cases of defect in quality, that apart from contract one has no right to an object of a certain quality and that, therefore, no duty of care regarding quality arises in tort. Contemporary courts disagree as to the success of this argument,[100] but, whether successful or not, it is an argument that pertains to the relationship between the parties without invoking any independent policy. This is because the parties to a tort suit are related to each other as legal persons, that is, as parties whose legal relationships are expressive of the systematic coherence of the entire law of obligations. Accordingly, they do not interact juridically apart from the whole ensemble of intertwined legal concepts and principles that governs their participation in the law's systematic nature.[101]

The second notion of policy is merely a way of signaling the presence of a conception of the duty of care that becomes significant for particular cases

---

[99] *Murphy v. Brentwood District Council*, [1990] 2 All ER 908; *Winnipeg Condominium Corp. No. 36 v. Bird Construction*, 121 DLR (4th) 193 (1995); *Bryan v. Maloney*, 128 ALR 163 (1995).

[100] Contrast the *Murphy* and *Winnipeg Condominium* cases, *supra* note 99.

[101] The Supreme Court of Canada also held that "different types of policy considerations are involved at each of the two stages" of the two-stage test. *Cooper v. Hobart*, 206 DLR (4th) at 202 (2001). At the first stage policy goes to the definition of proximity in the circumstances of the case; it focuses on factors that arise out of the relationship between the parties. The Court describes this enquiry as follows, *id.* at 204:

> Defining the relationship may involve looking at expectations, representations, reliance, and the property or other interests involved. Essentially, these are factors that allow us to evaluate the closeness of the relationship between the plaintiff and the defendant and to determine whether it is just and fair to impose a duty of care upon the defendant.

Then at the second stage "the question remains whether there are residual policy considerations outside the relationship of the parties that may negative the imposition of a duty of care." *Id.* at 203.

This distinction between relational and extrarelational policy considerations is welcome, and one can expect, if the second stage recedes in significance (as suggested above in Section IV of this chapter), Canadian courts in the future will put greater effort into elucidating the relational aspect of policy. The Court, however, still has a confused conception of what the distinction really is. First, the Court seems to view both kinds of policy as involving a balancing of interests that legal reasoning embraces and yet conceals. *Cooper v. Hobart*, 206 DLR (4th) 193 (2001). Moreover, factors that are properly relational it views as extrarelational. For example, it regards the effect of recognizing a duty of car on other legal obligations as an extrarelational policy consideration. *Id.* at 206. Similarly, it regards as extrarelational the question of whether recognition of a duty of care would "create the spectre of unlimited liability to an unlimited class," *id.*, whereas, because the liability should be limited by the scope of the right to which the duty is correlative, this properly belongs to the relational analysis.

through the exercise of practical judgment. Such an exercise may involve the casuistic consideration and comparison of cases in the light of the conception of duty that they instantiate, or it may involve a process of legal argument that elucidates the right and the correlativity of the wrong and that coherently integrates the conception of duty with the other norms in play in the circumstances of the case. Recourse to practical judgment is concomitant to the inherent generality and abstractness of the legal concepts, including the duty of care, out of which the relationship between the parties is juridically constructed. Policy in this sense differs from the first notion of policy suggested earlier, which referred to independent goals outside the relationship and to the balancing of interests where these goals are in tension. The practical judgment involved in casuistic analysis and legal argument does not actualize goals extrinsic to the parties' relationship as doer and sufferer of a wrong but, rather, explicates the legal meaning of that relationship in its particular circumstances. Policy in this sense is not only consistent with but also required by the general conception of duty. For the very generality of that conception necessitates its being related to the particular case by an exercise of practical judgment. Through practical judgment the indeterminacy of the general conception of duty becomes determinate for the case at hand.

Thus, inasmuch as the general conception of duty is a constituent of the coherent legal relationship between the doer and the sufferer of the same wrong, it is only the first notion of policy but not the second that is inimical to it. Only the first notion of policy effaces the coherence of the parties' relationship in the name of external goals that favor (and may require balancing between) the interests of one party or the other. The second notion, by contrast, far from effacing that coherence, posits the exercise of practical judgment that renders it effective for a particular case.

Whence arises the mistaken idea that the duty issue, being (in Lord Denning's words) "at bottom a matter of public policy"[102] requires recourse to the first notion of policy? Perhaps the answer is that this idea is part of the *damnosa hereditas* of instrumentalist legal thinking. Confronted by legal concepts that are indeterminate, that is, that do not immediately dispose of the particular issue at hand but require a further operation of legal argument or casuistic reasoning, instrumentalists assume that two alternatives are available: either these concepts deductively produce legal certainty, or they are merely the rhetorical cover for the identification and balancing of external goals. Because no deductive framework is available, all that remains is reasoning in terms of external goals. Having realized that the legal material does not allow

---

[102] *Dorset Yacht v. Home Office*, [1969] 2 All ER 564, 567.

judges to be conceived as automata devoid of freedom, they assume that the only way to exercise this freedom is to choose and balance goals.[103]

This conclusion is mistaken for two related reasons. First, it poses a false choice between deduction and instrumentalism. Deduction is not the exclusive – or even a very important – mode of reasoning internal to the determination of liability. It may well be the case that no interesting legal question can be approached deductively, with the major premise being provided by an unambiguous statement of the law, the minor premise by an unambiguous recital of the facts, and an instant and unshakeable conclusion emerging from the subsumption of the latter under the former. But to think that the absence of deduction leads inexorably to the necessity for identifying and balancing independent policies is to assume that deduction is the only move internal to the elucidation of legal relationships. Ignored is the possibility of the kind of reasoning included under the second notion of policy, where the judge either compares the relevant characteristics of one case with other cases that instantiate the same general conception or elucidates the meaning of the conception in question in a way that coherently construes both the legal relationship between the parties and the whole ensemble of legal concepts.

Second, the instrumentalist conclusion moves too quickly from the indeterminacy of the general conception of duty to the external goals that are supposed to ground the decision in a particular case. The fact that the general conception of duty does not immediately determine particular cases merely indicates the existence of scope for practical judgment. It does not imply that the general conception is without meaning, a mere mirage that vanishes when one focuses on it from close in, leaving an empty space that can be filled up by whatever the judge thinks is a good idea. Rather, in leaving scope for practical judgment, the general conception indicates what the judgment must be a judgment about. What Lord Atkin himself postulated was "a general conception of relations giving rise to a duty of care."[104] Accordingly, the exercise of

---

[103] In Oliver W. Holmes, *Privilege, Malice and Intent*, 8 HARV. L. REV. 1 (1894), Holmes provides a classic example of this approach. In Holmes's view, adjudication involves the decisions about questions of policy, that is, legislative questions concerning relative advantages to the community of liability and no liability. These questions have to be addressed by comparing the gain from permitting the impugned act with the loss that the act inflicts. Judges shy away from acknowledging that this is the true ground of their decisions, because "the moment you leave the path of merely logical deduction, you lose the illusion of certainty which makes legal reasoning seem like mathematics. But certainty is only an illusion, nevertheless." *Id.* at 7. Accordingly, judges present their decisions not as grounded in legislative policy but as "hollow deductions from empty general propositions" or as unexplained postulates about what constitutes a wrong.

[104] *Donoghue v. Stevenson*, 1932 A.C. 562 (appeal taken from Scot) (emphasis added).

practical judgment through which this general conception is brought home to a particular case involves reasoning that is relational, not reasoning about goals that are independent of the relationship. Such relational reasoning is precisely what is encompassed in the second notion of policy. The first notion of policy, in contrast, cannot determine the meaning of the general conception of duty in a particular case, because it does not address itself to that conception. Instead, by inquiring into the independent goals that might be forwarded by decisions about liability, it offers an answer to a question that the law of negligence does not ask, while ignoring the question that it does ask.

VI. CONCLUSION

Lord Atkin's judgment in *Donoghue v. Stevenson* is one of the great monuments of the modern law of negligence. Sweeping aside the received idea that negligence law was comprised of a miscellany of particular duties, he suggested that there must be a general conception of duty based on the prospective injury to others from unreasonable risk-creation. This general conception implied coherence both among the particular duties and within the conception of duty itself. The argument in this chapter has been that this idea of coherence requires that the parties to a negligence action be understood as the doer and sufferer of a single wrong, and that the wrong must be seen as an integrated sequence in which prospect of the plaintiff's injury is a reason for considering the defendant's act negligent. The leading cases of Twentieth Century on the duty of care and on proximate cause developed this conception of a coherent civil wrong. By avoiding basing liability on one-sided justifications, this approach to the law of negligence was normatively coherent, consistent with the judicial role and judicial competence, and fair to both parties. In contrast, more recent cases, especially those that employ the two-stage test, are appealing to a notion of policy in which the promotion and balancing of external and independent goals is leading the law back to the disintegration of duty that Lord Atkin repudiated.

There is, however, another notion of policy that, avoiding reference to external and independent goals, elucidates the relational significance of the wrong through an exercise of practical judgment. This second notion of policy merely reflects the fact that the coherence of its underlying justifications is itself the supreme policy of the law of obligations.

CHAPTER SIX

MANAGING THE NEGLIGENCE CONCEPT: RESPECT FOR THE RULE OF LAW

James A. Henderson Jr.

ABSTRACT. This chapter evaluates the risks of open-ended judicial review of complex tort issues, and specifically design issues. Not confined to products liability design defect matters, this chapter examines other areas, including medical malpractice, governmental, and environmental designs that have been the subject of challenge by injured plaintiffs. It explores such themes as institutional competency, as well as the bona fides of traditional tort contemplations of enterprise liability, the prima facie case, and evidentiary requisites. The chapter concludes that courts have avoided open-ended design review in each of the major contexts in which the pressures to engage in such review are the greatest. In product design litigation, the primary means of controlling the negligence concept is the requirement, where adopted, that plaintiff prove both the technological feasibility of a safer alternative design and but-for causation. In medical malpractice litigation, where the safer-alternative-design approach is not available, courts rely on professional custom to supply specific standards that render negligence claims adjudicable. As for negligence claims against the government, where neither safer-alternative-design nor reliance-on-custom solutions are available, courts and legislatures have built on the traditional principle of sovereign immunity to allow courts to impose tort liability on governmental actors while avoiding open-ended review of complex institutional designs. In each context, courts have adopted an approach unavailable in the others by which to contain the negligence concept and keep it with its proper bounds.

I. INTRODUCTION

A lot can happen in thirty years. Just about that long ago, I published an article entitled *Expanding the Negligence Concept: Retreat from the Rule of Law*,[1] that described an expansionary trend in fault-based liability and expressed concern that it was taking courts beyond the proper bounds of their institutional competence. Framed and written in the mid-1970s and published in 1976,

---

[1] James A. Henderson Jr., *Expanding the Negligence Concept: Retreat from the Rule of Law*, 51 IND. L.J. 467 (1976) (hereinafter *Expanding Negligence*).

James A. Henderson Jr., Frank B. Ingersoll Professor of Law, Cornell University School of Law.

the earlier article has been referred to by appellate courts and legal scholars.[2] And I have used it from time to time in my own work.[3] This chapter returns to those earlier assessments and tests their current accuracy in light of the nearly three decades that have passed since their publication. Although the basic analysis has held up quite well, adjustments in its specific applications are necessary. I welcome this opportunity to consider once again how courts are managing the negligence concept and where our tort system may be heading.

II. THE EARLIER ARTICLE AND ITS AFTERMATH

A. What the Article Said

In 1975 United States tort law was on the move. The Supreme Court of California had, a few years earlier, expanded the negligence-based liability of occupiers of land.[4] The court discarded the traditional entrant categories of trespasser, licensee, and invitee in favor of an open-ended reasonable-care-under-the-circumstances standard, and both legal scholars and appellate courts enthusiastically embraced the new approach.[5] The California high court in the same year also had expanded the negligence concept by allowing, for the first time, bystander-plaintiffs to recover for mental upset from witnessing injuries inflicted negligently on close family members.[6] Sensitive to the need for practical constraints on their new approach to negligence, the California high court identified limiting factors.[7] But clearly the court envisioned that lower courts would develop an expanded, fact-sensitive negligence approach by which to accomplish individualized justice in every case.[8]

---

[2] *See*, for example, *State of Louisiana ex. rel. Guste v. M/V Testabank*, 752 F.2d 1019 (5th Cir. 1985); Ragnone v. Portland School Dist. No. 13, 633 P.2d 1287 (Or. 1981); Kenneth S. Abraham, *The Trouble with Negligence*, 54 VAND. L. REV. 1187 (2001); Phillip G. Peters, *The Role of the Jury in Modern Malpractice Law*, 87 IOWA L. REV. 909 (2002); Gary T. Schwartz, *The Beginning and the Possible End of the Rise of American Tort Law*, 26 GA. L. REV. 601 (1992).

[3] *See*, for example, James A. Henderson, Jr. & Aaron D. Twerski, *Doctrinal Collapse in Products Liability: The Empty Shell of Failure to Warn*, 65 N.Y.U.L. REV. 265 (1990); James A. Henderson, Jr., *Process Norms in Products Litigation: Liability for Allergic Reactions*, 51 U. PITT. L. REV. 761 (1990).

[4] *Rowland v. Christian*, 443 P.2d 561 (Cal. 1968).

[5] *See* Expanding Negligence, *supra* note 1, at n. 163.

[6] *Dillon v. Legg*, 441 P.2d 912 (Cal. 1968).

[7] *Id.* at 740. The court identifies three relevant factors, suggesting that there others will emerge over time.

[8] *Id.* at 741 ("In future cases courts will draw lines of demarcation on facts more subtle than the compelling ones alleged in the complaint before us.")

During this same period, from the late 1960s to the mid-1970s, American courts were overturning traditional immunities barring the negligence-based liabilities of governmental actors to third persons[9] and the liabilities of family members to one another.[10] It also appeared that tort recovery for pure economic loss was becoming easier to accomplish.[11] And in the field of products liability, courts had begun routinely to review the adequacy of manufacturers' conscious design choices, employing a reasonableness standard.[12] Prior to these developments in the early 1970s, courts had avoided product design review by relying on several relatively formal no-duty rules,[13] leaving manufacturers free to make product design choices without significant judicial oversight.

In *Expanding Negligence*, having described these expansionary developments, I opined that if they continued they would present courts on a regular basis with problems that did not lend themselves to being resolved by the traditional adjudicative process. Once courts jettisoned traditional rule structures, the article argued, the problems left to solve in determining liability under the general reasonableness standard were sufficiently many-centered – borrowing from Lon Fuller the term "polycentric" – to defy adjudication.[14] Their many-centeredness resided in the fact that most of the factual circumstances relevant to their sensible resolution were interconnected so that a change or shift in one circumstance required all or most of the others to be reconsidered. In cases that traditionally lend themselves to being adjudicated, applicable legal rules break down polycentric problems into discrete issues for decision, arranging them in linear sequences so that each may be considered and resolved before moving on to the next. Only by "depolycentrizing" the problems to be solved in court does applicable law assure litigants the opportunity to participate by presenting factual proofs and by arguing that the law applicable to the facts logically requires (not simply permits) a single right result favorable to their side.

The article suggested that, under a significantly expanded negligence concept, so much discretion would be given to triers of fact applying general reasonableness standards that tort litigants on both sides would be transformed

---

[9] See *Expanding Negligence, supra* note 1, and text accompanying note 133.

[10] *Id.*, at text accompanying n. 119.

[11] See *id.* at 502–03.

[12] See *id.* at nn. 55–60 and accompanying text. I had chronicled these developments several years earlier in James A. Henderson Jr., *Judicial Review of Manufacturers' Conscious Design Choices: The Limits of Adjudication*, 73 COLUM. L. REV. 1531 (1973).

[13] See *Expanding Negligence, supra* note 1, nn. 52–54 and accompanying text.

[14] See *id.* at text accompanying n. 23.

into supplicants, begging judges and juries to sympathize intuitively with their conflicting visions of justice and to decide liability issues accordingly. Although such a system of discretionary justice would benefit tort plaintiffs overall, strictly speaking this new regime also would deny individual plaintiffs their opportunities to insist on recoveries as a matter of right just as surely as it would deny defendants their rights, in turn, to insist on favorable outcomes. The result, the argument continued, would constitute a general retreat from the rule of law. If the retreat continued on the same path it seemed headed in the mid-1970s, some form of strict liability, which I assumed would be more adjudicable because it would be less discretionary, would take the place of negligence. The article concluded:

> From the process perspective, the only workable systems of tort liability may be those based upon one form or another of strict liability. Negligence, it may turn out, was an essentially unmanageable and therefore self-destructive method of getting us from one system of strict liability to another. In any event, this much seems certain: unless sufficient formality is preserved, and in some instances reintroduced, in the rules governing liability, our common law negligence system will not survive to the end of this century.[15]

B. What Has Happened Since Then

Obviously, our system of negligence-based liability has survived in reasonably good health into the twenty-first century. What explains the fact that the concerns I expressed thirty years ago have not come to pass? One possibility is that linking the continued expansion of negligence with pending disaster was wrong – that a significantly expanded negligence regime has been realized without any noticeable loss of judicial integrity. Another possibility is that courts and legislatures have managed to turn back from the precipice and have restored sufficient rule structures to avoid the lawlessness that concerned me thirty years ago. On this latter view, a contraction must have followed the earlier expansion, sufficient to put things back in balance. Or perhaps a combination of these explanations is accurate. That is, perhaps things never were quite so bad as I thought them to be, and at the same time the negligence system has changed course since the mid-1970s, correcting itself sufficiently to assure its survival in good health. I tend to believe the combination of factors hypothesis: (1) I was wrong to some extent about what is and is not important in connection with maintaining the integrity of the negligence system; and (2) tort doctrine has changed for the better in significant ways.

[15] *Id.* at 527.

Regarding how things have changed, Ted Eisenberg and I coauthored an article in 1990 that purported to demonstrate empirically that a "quiet revolution" in products liability law took place in the 1980s whereby American courts significantly changed direction from predominantly favoring plaintiffs to predominantly favoring defendants.[16] Admittedly, it would be a considerable leap to conclude from that finding concerning products liability trends that American courts have averted the across-the-board lawlessness in all areas of tort about which I had expressed concern in the mid-1970s. Indeed, the 1976 article did not frame the central issue in terms of plaintiffs versus defendants, although the expansionary trends in the 1960s and 1970s benefited tort plaintiffs on the whole. But there is more than the 1990 empirical piece to the story of what happened between 1976 and now. Professor Gary Schwartz, a highly respected torts scholar, published an important article in 1992 in which he described changes in judge-made tort law during the 1980s and early 1990s that arrested the tendencies toward lawlessness I had described fifteen years earlier.[17] He referred therein to negligence doctrine as having undergone a "process of stabilization and mild retrenchment."[18] After recognizing the expansionary trends in the 1960s and 1970s about which I had written, Professor Schwartz described an across-the-board shift toward the middle ground in United States negligence law that led him to conclude that "[m]ost of modern tort can hence be expected to persevere."[19]

For the purposes of this chapter, it is important to understand that Gary Schwartz's analysis relied on trend reversals and doctrinal stabilization in most of the same areas that I had described as dramatically expanding in the 1960s and 1970s. These areas included recovery for mental upset on the part of bystanders who observe physical injuries to others,[20] duties owed by possessors to entrants of land,[21] liabilities of manufacturers for harm caused by product defects,[22] tort recovery for pure economic loss,[23] legal standards applicable to harm caused by medical care,[24] and circumvention of traditional governmental immunities.[25] Gary's comprehensive analysis included other

---

[16] See James A. Henderson Jr. & Theodore Eisenberg, *The Quiet Revolution in Products Liability: An Empirical Study of Legal Change*, 37 U.C.L.A.L. Rev. 479 (1990).

[17] See Gary T. Schwartz, *supra* n. 2.

[18] Id. at 604.

[19] Id. at 701.

[20] Id. at 657–58.

[21] Id. at 659–60.

[22] Id. at 653–56.

[23] Gary T. Schwartz, *supra* note 2, at 658–59.

[24] Id. at 663–64.

[25] Id. at 674–75.

examples of the stabilization of tort doctrine, and it also recognized a few areas in which tort law had actually expanded in the 1980s.[26] It is fair to summarize his thorough study as demonstrating, by means of traditional legal analysis of relevant case law, that by the early 1990s U.S. negligence law had stopped, and in some areas reversed, the expansionary trends I had described in 1976.

Characteristic of Professor Schwatrz's searching and inquisitive mind, his 1992 article did something I had not attempted – it considered the factors that may have caused the doctrinal shifts we had identified. Among the possible causes Gary included agenda-completion,[27] altered composition of the judiciary,[28] doubts about the administrability of earlier expansions,[29] and concerns over increasing litigation and liability costs.[30] Of particular interest in the present context is the fact that Gary did not include in his list of possible explanations the factor on which my 1976 article had focused: increases in the relative polycentricity, and hence unadjudicability, of the tort problems being given to courts to solve. The closest his analysis came to that explanation is the administrability factor;[31] but clearly his concern was not with the polycentricity of negligence claims under the general standard of reasonableness but, rather, with their factual complexity.[32]

It remains briefly to recount what has happened in the decade-plus since Gary's essay. Quite simply, the process of stabilization and mild retrenchment that he identified has continued apace. In all of the tort law areas I had described in 1976, United States courts have refused to continue in the directions in which they appeared to be headed. For example, in the area of bystanders' emotional upset, a number of jurisdictions have rejected California's expanded factors approach, retaining, instead, the traditional impact and zone-of-danger requirements for bystander recovery.[33] And a number of others states, including California, have imposed formal requirements that greatly reduce the open-endedness of litigating the

---

[26] *Id.* at 649–52.

[27] *Id.* at 684.

[28] *Id.* at 684–87.

[29] Gary T. Schwartz, *supra* note 2, at 687–89.

[30] *Id.* at 689.

[31] *Id.* at 688–89.

[32] *Id.* at 688, and text accompanying n. 452. Polycentricity and complexity are closely related, but strictly speaking they are not the same thing. Polycentricity adds the dimension of conceptual interconnectedness. A problem can be complex without necessarily being polycentric. In this chapter, the adjective "complex" is sometimes used to refer to polycentric design problems.

[33] *See*, for example, *Consolidated Rail Corp. v. Gottshall*, 512 U.S. 532 (1994); *Slaton v. Vansickle*, 872 P.2d 929 (Okla. 1994); *Gary v. INOVA Health Care Servs.*, 514 S.E.2d 355 (Va. 1999).

relevant issues.[34] The same pattern holds true regarding the legal duties owed to entrants on land. A substantial majority of jurisdictions have rejected *Rowland v. Christian*[35] and continue to distinguish between, and treat quite differently, entrants who come onto another's land without permission and entrants who come on with permission.[36]

Further, in the other areas of tort law that the 1976 article identified as problematic, American courts since the early 1990s have curtailed expansionary tendencies. For example, regarding negligence-based recovery for pure economic loss, the special exception I noted earlier for fishermen's rights to recover for environmental damage to natural habitats has remained exactly that – an unusual (and uniquely manageable, it turns out) exception carved out of the general rule of no recovery in tort for pure economic loss.[37] Other exceptions, which might more clearly threaten to undermine the general rule of not allowing recovery for economic loss, have fared less well, often at the hands of courts that express concerns over the administrative difficulties presented by a more open-ended approach.[38]

C. A Retrospective Critique of the 1976 Analysis

The strength of the earlier analysis in *Expanding Negligence* lay in its articulation of the limits of adjudication and its explanation of how significant expansions of the negligence concept threaten to exceed those limits. The

---

[34] *See Thing v. LaChusa*, 771 P.2d 814 (Calif. 1989). *See also Fernandez v. Walgreen Hastings Co.*, 868 P.2d 774 (N.M. 1998); *Marchetti v. Parsons*, 638 A.2d 1047 (R.I. 1994).

[35] *Supra* note 4.

[36] *See generally* James A. Henderson Jr. et al., THE TORTS PROCESS 228 (6th ed. 2003). *See*, for example, *Alexander v. Medical Associates Clinic*, 646 N.W.2d 74 (Iowa 2002) (discussion of recent trend rejecting *Rowland*); *Mallet v. Pickens*, 522 S.E.2d 436 (W. Va. 1999).

[37] *See, generally*, Comment, *Recovery for Economic Losses by the Commercial Fishing Industry: Rules, Exceptions and Rationales*, 4 U. BALT. J. ENVTL. L. 86, 93 (1994) ("The exception to the . . . bar to recovery for economic losses for commercial fishermen injured by the pollution of ocean waters is well recognized."). The reason why the exception is relatively manageable is that, once the courts conclude that fishermen have the functional equivalent of a property interest in uncaught fish, the claims for destruction of the fish can be handled as would other, more routine property damage cases.

[38] Several decisions, reached after the 1976 article, threatened to open up claims for pure economic loss to open-ended, reasonableness-based analysis. *See*, for example, *People Express Airlines, Inc. v. Consolidated Rail Corp.*, 495 A.2d 107 (N.J. 1985). But courts since then have generally rejected such open-endedness. *See*, for example, 522 *Madison Ave. Gourmet Foods, Inc. v. Finlandia Center, Inc.*, 96 N.Y.2d 280, 290–92 (2001) ("Plaintiffs' reliance on *People Express* . . . is misplaced. . . . [L]imiting the scope of defendants' duty to those who have, as a result of these events, suffered personal injury or property damage – as historically courts have done – affords a principled basis for reasonably apportioning liability.")

article got that part right and, as the next section will demonstrate, the analysis remains as valid today as it was thirty years ago. As for weaknesses, I do not count among them any error in predicting that the negligence system would collapse and be replaced with strict liability. The article made no such prediction. Rather, it stated that "*unless sufficient formality is preserved, and in some instances reintroduced,* . . . our common law negligence system will not survive . . ."[39] Based on this "unless" language, it would be easy now to point to the doctrinal reversals described earlier and to insist that the negligence system has survived precisely, or at least in large part, because sufficient formality has been preserved and restored. But my earlier analysis was deficient in several respects and I want to set things right.

The first error in the earlier analysis resided in the stridency with which it advanced its thesis. I was so certain that I had identified an institutional concern of the first magnitude that I overstated the immediacy of the accompanying threat to judicial integrity. When I wrote the article in 1975, the twenty-five years remaining until the millennium seemed a very long time, and the threat to judicial integrity seemed very great. With the help of hindsight it would have been more sensible to avoid placing what now appears to have been a fairly short time frame on the analysis. My earlier sense of urgency reveals itself in other ways in the article, including my reactions to the substantial body of legal scholarship in the mid-1970s that enthusiastically supported the same expansionary trends that I deplored.[40] The harshness of my criticisms served no useful purpose other than to demonstrate my own immaturity. Were it possible to go back and do it over, I would be more circumspect in reacting to scholarship with which I happen to disagree, however strongly.

Another shortcoming in the 1976 article worth noting was the underlying assumption that, if the negligence concept continued to expand in the direction of lawlessness, the only solution would be some form or other of broad-based strict enterprise liability.[41] In the last thirty years I have had the opportunity to consider enterprise liability more carefully,[42] and I am now quite convinced that broad-based strict liability is an idea whose time will

---

[39] *See supra* note 15 and accompanying quoted text.

[40] *See Expanding Negligence supra* note 1, at 522–24.

[41] I employed the phrase "one form or another of strict liability." *See* quoted text accompanying note 15, *supra*. I imagined a no-fault system imposed by statute along the lines of worker compensation.

[42] *See*, for example, James A. Henderson Jr., *Echoes of Enterprise Liability in Product Design and Marketing Litigation*, 87 CORNELL L. REV. 958 (2002); James A. Henderson Jr., *Why Negligence Dominates Tort*, 50 U.C.L.A.L. REV. 377 (2002).

never come. Limited applications are possible and are in place today.[43] But a broad enterprise liability system is not realizable.[44] Rather than rehearse my reasons for this conclusion in this chapter, I invite the reader to accept as a premise for this discussion that broad-based enterprise liability is unrealizable, and to consider the implications of that premise for the future of tort. The most obvious implication is that the negligence concept is here to stay as the core principle of the American tort system. Clearly, this observation further highlights the naivete of my referring earlier to a twenty-five-year time frame for possibly replacing the negligence system. A paridigmatic change as fundamental as the abandonment of negligence would probably be required to take the form of the abolishment of tort altogether, accomplished at the federal level.[45] The theoretical and practical impediments to such a radical change are awesome to contemplate.[46]

Thus, if one assumes for the sake of argument that the negligence concept will remain as the foundation of American tort law, and one further assumes that judges understand that negligence law must provide sufficient guidance to allow them to avoid unadjudicable claims, it is hardly surprising that recent decades reveal courts containing and reversing the earlier expansionary trends I described in 1976. The truly astounding eventuality would be now to discover a continuation of the expansionary trends of the 1970s to the point that judges were powerless to resolve any claims as a matter of law and every negligence-based tort claim required application of the jury's intuition. Thus, I was mistaken to have adopted essentially a "shape up or ship out" attitude toward negligence law, because there was no place else for our tort system to go. Once one understands that courts must continue to rely on the negligence concept, it follows that judges must make reasonable efforts to manage that concept in order to maintain its integrity.

---

[43] See *Why Negligence Dominates Tort, id.* at 400–402.

[44] *Id.* at 393–400, 405 ("Broad-based strict liability will never be implemented because . . . it cannot be implemented.")

[45] Given that strict enterprise liability is unworkable (*see* note 43, *supra*, and accompanying text), some sort of no-fault accident compensation system along the lines of the New Zealand system would be the only remaining possibility. *See generally* JAMES A. HENDERSON JR. & AARON D. TWERSKI, TORTS: CASES AND MATERIALS 695–705 (2003).

[46] Even so time-honored an alternative to tort as worker compensation was successfully challenged as unconstitutional when first introduced. Thus, the New York Court of Appeals set aside that state's statute in *Ives v. South Buffalo Ry.*, 94 N.E. 431 (N.Y. 1911). A subsequent amendment of the New York Constitution, authorizing worker compensation, led to a more narrowly worded statute that was upheld in *New York Central R.R. v. White*, 243 U.S. 188 (1917). For more recent analyses of the difficulties facing tort reformers under state constitutions, *see generally* Symposium, 32 Rut. L.J. 897 *et seq.* (2001). For a discussion of the relevant cases, *see id.* at 939–952. *See also* Symposium, 31 SETON HALL L. REV. 563, 625–759 (2001).

Another analytical shortcoming in the earlier article, about which more
will be revealed in the next section, was its failure to distinguish adequately
between the more important and the less important expansions of the negligence concept, measured by their potential for undermining the integrity of
the judicial process. This deficiency derived from my analytical framework
for classifying the doctrinal expansions that had taken place up until then.
The article grouped the expansionary developments into three descriptive
categories: those that required courts to assess complex technology;[47] those
that required courts to define special relationships;[48] and those that required
courts to place practical limits on liability.[49] With the benefit of hindsight,
grouping the cases this way makes sense only superficially. After working for
three decades in the products liability vineyards, I better understand what was
happening in the 1970s, and would now group the decisions differently and
more simply. It turns out that asking courts to review complex technology, *per
se*, has less to do with exceeding the limits of adjudication than I had earlier
believed;[50] and the same is true with asking courts to define special relationships, and pressuring courts to place practical limits on liability. Each and all
of these tasks present courts with management difficulties of the general sort
I had described, but not necessarily of a level of seriousness that threatens the
downfall of the negligence system. Instead, regardless of the doctrinal context, the limits of adjudication are most sorely tested when courts undertake
to review institutionally implemented, polycentric design decisions under a
general reasonableness standard. And although all forms of judicial review of
complex designs threaten to some extent to exceed the limits of adjudication,
as the analysis that follows will make clear, only those that require courts to
consider designs independently, or "as a whole," seriously threaten the rule
of law.

It follows that my earlier analysis rested on an inadequate conceptual framework. The then-recent expansions in California of the liabilities of occupiers
of land and of actors who cause bystanders to suffer emotional upset did not,
it turns out, seriously threaten the survival of the negligence system. At most,
those expansions of the negligence concept were symptomatic of a lack of

---

[47] See *Expanding Negligence supra* note 1, at 484–501.
[48] *Id.* at 501–514.
[49] *Id.* at 514–521.
[50] More important is the availability to the court, however technologically complex the underlying problem, of methods by which the many-centeredness of the design issue may be
reduced. Thus, as will be explained in the next section of the text, the defectiveness of product designs under a reasonableness standard is rendered manageable by the requirement
that the plaintiff establish a reasonable alternative design.

judicial sensitivity to institutional limits that would have become life threatening to our tort system only to the extent that they carried over to those areas that truly mattered – areas in which judges were being pressured to determine the reasonableness of institutionally implemented designs on an "all factors considered" basis. Several of the doctrinal areas that I considered in the earlier article involved just such a potential for self-destruction: products liability,[51] environmental torts,[52] professional negligence,[53] and tort actions against governmental agencies.[54] But I assigned these examples to conceptual categories that somewhat obscured, rather than revealed, the structural features they share in common.[55] The next section of this chapter examines why these areas are especially threatening to judicial integrity and how courts have been managing the negligence concept in order to preserve the rule of law.

III. HOW COURTS MANAGE THE NEGLIGENCE CONCEPT IN THE
CONTEXTS THAT MATTER MOST: JUDICIAL REVIEW OF COMPLEX,
INSTITUTIONALLY IMPLEMENTED DESIGNS

A. Why Negligence-Based Review of Complex Designs
Threatens Judicial Integrity

The complex designs to which this discussion refers include, but are not limited to, product designs. Products liability is the subject on which I have focused over the past several decades and is the originating source of many of the observations that follow. But the following analysis applies generally to judicial review of all manner of complex designs including designs of products, services, contractual agreements, donative arrangements, business entities, personal relationships, social organizations, or governmental agencies, to name just a few.[56] My thesis is that for courts to attempt to review the

---

[51] *See* note 12 *supra*, and accompanying text.
[52] *See Expanding Negligence supra*, note 1, at 495–501.
[53] *Id.* at 491–495.
[54] *Id.* at 505–510.
[55] *See* notes 46–48, *supra*, and accompanying text. The closest I came to identifying judicial review of complex designs as the central concern was when I observed: "[These problems] might usefully be referred to as 'planning problems,' or 'design problems.'" *See Expanding Negligence, supra* note 1, at 476 n. 24. But that observation was clearly referring to the family vacation hypothetical (*id.* at 472–73) that preceded it, and I did not carry design through as a unifying theme.
[56] My upcoming research agenda includes a longer essay on the broader subject of how courts avoid reviewing complex designs in these other areas, whether or not they involve claims sounding in tort.

reasonableness of designs "as a whole" in any of these contexts exceeds the limits of adjudication and seriously threatens the institutional integrity of the judicial system. In the negligence cases of interest in this chapter, the plaintiff must show that the unreasonableness of a particular design – the negligence implicit in choosing an unreasonable design – has caused the plaintiff to suffer personal injury or property damage.[57] But the reader should understand that the analysis has much broader applications. In virtually every area of civil justice in our legal system, whether or not they involve tort claims to recover for physical harm, the rules of decision are formulated so as to avoid the necessity of courts determining the reasonableness of complex designs.

As noted earlier, the common characteristic of many complex designs that renders the issue of their overall reasonableness unadjudicable is their many-centeredness, or polycentricity. All social arrangements share this characteristic, and therein lies the universality of the analysis of tort law in this chapter. Essentially, the many-centeredness of design problems inheres in the fact that all of the various elements that comprise the design are related to one another as are the strands of a complex web, so that disturbing or changing one strand simultaneously rearranges all the other strands. For example, in connection with the design of a house, all of the constituent elements – the footprint, the walls, the roof, the various living spaces, and the like – are related to one another interdependently. To judge whether a given house design is reasonable calls for an intuitional assessment of how all of the elements relate to one another.

Moreover, to expand the size and change the position of, say, the kitchen in a house in order to improve functionality has implications for most of the other elements in the house design. In the end, enlarging and moving the kitchen may improve the functionality of a house design and thus be quite reasonable. But to decide whether such a significant change is reasonable within the broader context of the house as a whole one must, at least implicitly, redesign much, or all, of the rest of the house. A decision regarding the kitchen, based as it is on an implicit redesign of the house, can be made by a skillful designer exercising creative discretion. But in the absence of a specific criterion that substitutes for overall reasonableness – for example, whether the change makes the house larger or safer regardless of the effects of the change on other aspects of the house taken as a whole – it cannot effectively be accomplished by means of adjudication.

---

[57] The RESTATEMENT (THIRD) OF TORTS: LIABILITY FOR PHYSICAL HARM (BASIC PRINCIPLES) (TENTATIVE DRAFT No. 2) (March 25, 2002), dealing with the negligence concept, is limited to physical harms to persons and property.

Adjudication cannot solve polycentric design problems because it assures litigants the opportunity to argue, by means of linear chains of logic, toward a single right result.[58] The result, or solution, argued for by the litigants must not merely be *allowed* by the applicable law, but in a real sense it must be *required* by it. Unless the legal rules applicable to solving complex design problems succeed in breaking the problems down into constitutive components so that the litigants may address the components in a logical sequence, resolving each before moving on to the next, the litigants are effectively denied their day in court. In the absence of rule structures that depolycentrize complex design problems, those affected may be given an opportunity to appear in court to argue that their preferred version of the design is, or is not, reasonable. But the discretion granted to the tribunal to decide either way – in the absence of an adequate rule structure the court must exercise the same discretion as did the house redesigner in our earlier example – will deny the litigants an opportunity to respectfully insist on a favorable outcome as a matter of right. The lack of sufficiently specific rules of decision will, instead, place the litigants in the position of supplicants, entreating the tribunal to look favorably on their particular versions of what is reasonable under all relevant circumstances. Once again, the point here is not that complex design problems defy rational solution. General criteria for judging designs are available; some designs are clearly better than others, and some are very much better. Instead, the point is that, without adequate rule structures, courts cannot hope to solve such problems rationally via adjudication.

Is the question of the reasonableness of a complex design rendered adjudicable when the plaintiff focuses not on the entire design but on a narrower constituent component? As reflected in the house design example, the answer depends on the extent to which the component can be considered in isolation from the larger design of which it is part. And that, in turn, depends on the extent to which a change in the constituent element necessarily implicates changes in all, or many, of the other elements in the design. Many-centeredness is a matter of degree, and depends on the extent of the interconnectedness of the component focused on by plaintiff – in the house example, the kitchen – with the other components in the design, and the interconnectedness of those other elements with each other. As indicated earlier, focusing on a single criterion such as increasing size or safety does not significantly decrease the many-centeredness of the problem of redesign, so long as the increase is tied to "reasonableness as a whole." Returning to the example involving the redesign of a house, by focusing merely on changing the location (and not the size)

---

[58] *See Expanding Negligence, supra* note 1, at 469, n. 3, and accompanying text.

of the kitchen and proposing only moderate, marginal change, the plaintiff may avoid the necessity of considering some elements of the house design – rethinking the upstairs bedrooms, for example, may not be necessary. But separating and isolating the issue of the kitchen's location may not be possible even to that extent, because the location of the kitchen may affect the location of the stairs, which affects the arrangement of the upstairs bedrooms, and so on.

What if the redesign problem brought to court by the plaintiff focuses on the position of the oven in the kitchen? Such a narrowing of focus may avoid the necessity of considering the entire house design, but clearly it implicates the entire design of the kitchen. And the same "design within a design" problem arises even when the plaintiff focuses on a particular constituent component of the kitchen, such as whether the oven, itself, is unreasonably dangerous. The oven design, rather than the house design, becomes the arena in which a polycentric problem must be solved.[59] As one narrows one's focus by descending through the concentric circles, the practical significance of the decision to the overall house design may to a substantial extent be reduced; but certainly its many-centeredness is not necessarily eliminated and may remain significant enough to frustrate attempts to adjudicate solutions under a general reasonableness rubric.

This chapter explores these insights as they apply to specific examples drawn from several legal contexts, including products liability. It is important to appreciate that the judicial branch our legal system must reduce the many-centeredness of the design problems it confronts by providing rule structures that either incorporate specific standards by which to judge complex designs without addressing the open-ended reasonableness question, or by breaking up the interconnectedness of the constituent elements of those designs so that the reasonableness of a constituent element may be considered and resolved in relative isolation from the other elements. The discussion that follows will consider how this occurs in specific contexts. But this much is clear: the general negligence standard of "reasonable safety under the circumstances" is inadequate as a guide in adjudicating the acceptability of complex, polycentric designs. Because the general reasonableness standard by itself neither provides specific design standards nor breaks design problems into discrete elements, its application by courts effectively denies litigants the opportunity to rely on logical chains of argument that support favorable outcomes as a matter of right. This denial, in effect, turns them

---

[59] *See generally* James A. Henderson Jr., *Judicial Review of Manufacturers' Conscious Design Choices: The Limits of Adjudication*, 73 COLUM. L. REV. 1531 (1973).

into supplicants, begging for favors from the tribunals before whom they appear.

B. Courts Are Under Pressure to Review the Reasonableness of Complex Designs Because the Stakes for the Institutional Players on Both Sides Are Very High

Institutional actors play important roles on both the plaintiffs' and the defendants' sides in the cases of primary interest here. On the plaintiffs' side, most of these tort claims are managed by attorneys who specialize in representing injured victims. As repeat players who customarily share information and trial strategies, plaintiffs' lawyers have an institutional interest in achieving favorable outcomes. Moreover, a significant percentage of negligence claims in our tort system, including most of the claims of interest here, are brought against institutional defendants.[60] Not all tort claims against institutional defendants require judicial review of complex designs. Many of these claims rest on vicarious liability principles provided by master-servant law.[61] These claims do not implicate the reasonableness of institutional defendants' complex designs because the employees who cause harm are engaged in conduct that, while generally authorized and enabled by the employer, negligently deviate from the level of care explicitly or implicitly called for by the institutional design. For example, when the employee of a commercial product supplier operates a delivery truck negligently and harms the plaintiff, the design of the defendant company's delivery system is not ordinarily implicated because the individual driver's fault may be determined independently of the reasonableness of the delivery system. Of course, the driver's negligence must be adjudicated, and that task requires a judgment of the reasonableness of the care taken by the driver. However, as explained in my 1976 article, triers of fact are able to intuit appropriate solutions when judging the reasonableness of individual conduct with which they can empathize.[62]

In contrast to claims based on an institutional defendant's vicarious liability for an individual employee's negligence at the operations level, many of the tort claims brought against institutional defendants involve negligence at the planning, rather than at the operations, level. In those cases, the

[60] *See generally* Marika F. X. Litras, et al., Tort Trials and Verdicts in Large Counties, (1996) *Bulletin*, Bureau of Justice Statistics 3, table 3 (August 2000) (nonindividuals, such as governments, businesses and hospitals, comprise 76 percent of defendants in tort cases, other than automobile tort trials, brought by individual plaintiffs).

[61] *See generally* James A. Henderson Jr. et al., The Torts Process 135–144 (6th ed. 2003).

[62] *See Expanding Negligence, supra* note 1, at 478–79.

operations-level employees may perform exactly as they were intended to and may themselves be free from fault, but they nevertheless cause the plaintiff to suffer harm. Returning to the delivery truck example, suppose that the driver was driving non-negligently and the plaintiff ran into the truck allegedly because it and all the other trucks in the defendant's substantial delivery fleet were painted dark brown and had an unusual configuration of signaling lights in order to promote the delivery company's logo. The plaintiff's claim is that the trucks were not adequately visible, and that this caused the collision. In such a case the plaintiff's quarrel is with alleged deficiencies in the design of the defendant's commercial delivery system rather than with the behavior of the driver of the particular truck. These are the sorts of negligence claims that threaten to engage courts in the essentially unadjudicable process of reviewing the reasonableness of complex designs.[63] These are the sorts of claims with which this chapter is primarily concerned.

Negligence claims aimed at institutionally implemented designs are far more attractive to plaintiffs' lawyers than are negligence claims aimed at individual actors, particularly when the individual actor's negligence exposes the institution to vicarious liability based on respondeat superior. In the context of institutional design, an outcome favoring an individual plaintiff can potentially affect not merely several, or dozens, of similarly situated accident victims. Indeed, depending on at what level in the institutional hierarchy the design decisions giving rise to these claims are made, a favorable ruling for one victim may implicitly entitle thousands, or tens of thousands, of would-be claimants to relief. It is not lost on the plaintiffs' lawyer who wins such an institutional design claim that there will be many more claims, and clients, to follow. Nor are the implications lost on other institutional defendants similarly situated. To continue with the earlier delivery truck example, if a plaintiff were somehow to succeed with an ambitious claim directed at the highest level of institutional decision making – a claim that a business corporation's threshold decision to maintain an enormous fleet of potentially harmful delivery trucks was, in and of itself, unreasonable and therefore negligent[64] – the

---

[63] Whether the trucks in the delivery fleet were adequately visible in the context of all the relevant considerations would, if judged under a general standard of reasonable safety, threaten to exceed the limits of adjudication.

[64] Rather than expose institutional actors to liability based on their alleged negligence, courts otherwise disposed toward liability might find the concept of strict liability for abnormally dangerous activities more attractive. *See generally* James A. Henderson, Jr., *supra*, note 61 at 417–434. Perhaps the practical implications of such an expansion of liability helps explain why courts have not recognized it. *See* James A. Henderson Jr., *Why Negligence Dominates Tort*, 50 U.C.L.A.L. Rev. 377, 383–386 (2002).

economic implications for the plaintiffs' bar and the myriad other companies engaged in similar delivery activities would be truly monumental.

Given the potentially high stakes involved in advancing tort claims asserting the unreasonableness of institutional designs, the plaintiffs' bar could be expected to recognize their own interests as repeat players and press such claims eagerly and often. Moreover, procedural developments in recent years have enhanced the economic benefits that plaintiffs' lawyers stand to gain from pursuing such design-based claims. When the tort system affords so many potential victims the opportunity for recovery, class actions and other claims-aggregation techniques may allow specialist law firms to achieve economies of scale in reaping significant financial rewards for pressing complex design claims.[65] Taking these considerations into account, it is hardly surprising that U.S. courts are under constant pressure to exceed the limits of their institutional competence by undertaking to determine the reasonableness of complex institutional designs.[66]

C. The Best Example of Successful Judicial Management of the Negligence Concept: How Courts Have Avoided Open-Ended Design Review in Products Liability Litigation

Several factors support the conclusion that products liability provides the best example of how American courts have successfully managed the negligence concept. For one, product designs are exactly the sorts of many-centered, institutionally implemented designs that defy judicial review under a general standard of reasonableness care under all the circumstances.[67] For another, the pressures on courts to engage in such review are especially great. Once a mass-produced product or product category is determined to be defective in design, by implication all similar designs or categories are defective. Hundreds of thousands of accident victims may seek the assistance of the plaintiffs' bar. Moreover, courts and commentators from the beginnings of our products liability system have promised that product sellers would be strictly liable for

---

[65] *See generally* David G. Owen, et al., 2 Madden & Owen on Products Liability Ch. 26 (3rd ed. 2000). *Cf.* James A. Henderson Jr. & Aaron D. Twerski, *Asbestos Litigation Gone Mad: Recovery for Increased Risk, Mental Anguish, and Medical Monitoring*, 53 S. C. L. Rev. 815, 848–849 (2002). For a recent analysis of the various class and nonclass techniques of collective representation, *see* Howard M. Erickson, *Beyond the Class Action: Lawyer Loyalty and Client Non-Class Collective Representation*, 2003 U. Chi. Legal F. 519 (2003).

[66] *Cf.* Section III, discussing recent attempts to invoke public nuisance law to attack complex systems of products distribution.

[67] *See* James A. Henderson Jr., *supra*, note 12.

harm caused by all manners of product defects, including design defects.[68] Although most observers understand that product designs are actually being judged on the basis of negligence principles,[69] many courts continue to pay lip service to the strict liability principle, invoking rhetoric that only adds to the pressures on courts to provide remedies to injured plaintiffs.[70] The following description and analysis of how American courts have managed to resist those pressures will inform the discussion in the next section of how courts have managed the negligence concept in other significant tort liability contexts.

The beginnings of our modern products liability system in the 1950s and early 1960s did not involve judicial review of complex product designs. All of the early products liability litigation involved either manufacturing defects or noncomplex, self-defeating designs that did not call for judgments regarding reasonable product safety.[71] By the mid-1960s, American courts routinely imposed strict tort liability for harm caused by manufacturing defects without the necessity of reviewing the reasonableness of product designs because manufacturing defects constitute physical departures from intended designs.[72] In parallel fashion to the first version of the delivery truck hypothetical, in which the institutional employer is vicariously liable for harm caused by the negligence of the driver quite independently of the reasonableness of the design of the employer's delivery system, so the manufacturer of a mechanically defective product is strictly liable for harm caused by the defect independently of the reasonableness of the product design. So long as courts confined their liability decisions to manufacturing defects in the 1950s and 1960s, problems did not arise regarding judicial review of product designs.

Two circumstances combined to place pressures on courts to review the reasonableness of complex product designs. First, the drafters of § 402A of the Restatement (Second) of Torts, promulgating the rule of strict liability for

---

[68] See RESTATEMENT (SECOND) OF TORTS § 402A (1965).

[69] See RESTATEMENT (THIRD) OF TORTS: PRODUCTS LIABILITY § 2, cmt. d (1998); Sheila L. Birnbaum, *Unmasking the Test for Defect: From Negligence to Warranty to Strict Liability to Negligence*, 33 VAND. L. REV. 593 (1980).

[70] See generally DAVID G. OWEN, *supra* note 64, at vol. 3, p. 252 ("[C]ourts continued to claim that they were still applying liability that was 'strict,' but it became increasingly clear as time went on that the standards actually applied were truly based on fault.")

[71] See, for example, *Henningsen v. Bloomfield Motors, Inc.*, 161 A.2d 69 (N.J. 1960); *Greenman v. Yuba Power Products, Inc.*, 377 P.2d 897 (Cal. 1962); *Vandermark v. Ford Motor Co.*, 391 P.2d 168 (Cal. 1964).

[72] See RESTATEMENT (THIRD) OF TORTS: PRODUCTS LIABILITY § 2(a) (1998).

product defects in 1965, purported to apply that rule to all types of defects, including defects in design.[73] And second, all of the early design cases, in which plaintiffs' success gave credence to the universality of strict liability, happened to fall into a special subset of product design cases that did not require judicial review of the reasonableness of the designs alleged to be defective.[74] In these cases, today commonly said to involve "product malfunction," an inference of design defect may be drawn from the fact that the product that harmed the plaintiff did not adequately perform its manifestly intended function.[75] As with manufacturing defects, judicial review of the reasonableness of the manufacturer's product design is unnecessary in cases involving product malfunction because the court has available a built-in standard – here, the intended function – with which to determine the product design's defectiveness.[76]

Thus, early in the development of American products liability law, courts were able to maintain a fairly robust system of strict liability for product defects, including design defects of the product malfunction variety, without undertaking the independent review of the reasonableness of manufacturers' complex product designs. The problem, of course, was that the highly influential strict liability provision in § 402A, together with most scholarly commentators in the 1960s and early 1970s, advocated application of the strict liability rule to all types of product defects, including design defects other than those that caused product malfunction. For a time, up until the mid-1970s, courts managed to rely on a combination of single-factor, no-duty rules, such as the patent danger rule,[77] the bystander rule,[78] and the intended purpose doctrine,[79] to avoid judicial review of complex product designs under a general reasonableness standard. As the inherent illogic of these no-duty rules became increasingly transparent, the rules collapsed, leaving courts seemingly with no escape from attempting to fulfill the strict liability mandate

---

[73] *See* note 68 *supra* and accompanying text.

[74] *See* James A. Henderson Jr., *supra* note 58 at 1550–1551.

[75] *See* RESTATEMENT (THIRD) OF TORTS: PRODUCTS LIABILITY § 3, cmt. *b* (1998).

[76] *See* James A. Henderson Jr. & Aaron D. Twerski, *Achieving Consensus on Defective Product Design*, 83 CORNELL L. REV. 867, 873 (1998) (such a built-in standard represents an "implicit, internal safety standard" for judging design defectiveness).

[77] *See*, for example, *Campo v. Scofield*, 95 N.E.2d 802 (N.Y. 1950); *Bolin v. Triumph Corp.*, 305 N.E.2d 769 (N.Y. 1973).

[78] *See*, for example, *Hahn v. Ford Motor Co.*, 126 N.W.2d 350 (Iowa 1964); *Rodriquez v. Shell's City, Inc.*, 141 So. 2d 590 (Fla. Ct. App. 1962).

[79] *See*, for example, *Evans v. General Motors Corp.*, 359 F.2d 822 (7th Cir. 1966); *Winnett v. Winnett*, 310 N.E.2d 1 (Ill. 1974).

by accomplishing the institutionally difficult task of adjudicating the reasonableness of complex product designs.[80]

From the standpoint of preserving judicial integrity, one way to have
avoided the necessity of reviewing defendants' complex product designs
would have been to adopt industry custom as the standard for design defectiveness. Had courts been able and willing to follow this path, custom would
have supplied specific standards by which a significant percentage of product
design claims would have been rendered adjudicable. In many product design
cases, however, custom was not available.[81]

And even when design custom was available for comparative purposes,
courts often did not trust the integrity of the markets in which the customs
arose.[82] Thus, under the pressures created by their oft-repeated promises of
strict liability, American courts were compelled to undertake the independent
review of the acceptability of defendants' product designs.

A combination of circumstances have allowed courts to escape from the
product design review dilemma in which they found themselves in the early to
mid-1970s. First, courts have adopted essentially a fault-based test for defective design, notwithstanding § 402A's strict liability rhetoric, limiting their
reasonableness inquiry to situations in which safer alternative designs were
technically feasible at the time of original distribution.[83] Thus, instead of
approaching product designs categorically "of a whole," courts have focused
on more manageable marginal comparisons between the defendant's design

---

[80] Arguably the most influential decisions in the abandonment of these doctrines were: *Pike
v. Frank G. Hough Co.*, 467 P.2d 229 (Cal. 1970) (patent danger rule); *Elmore v. American
Motors*, 451 P.2d 84 (Cal. 1969) (bystander rule); *Larsen v. General Motors Corp.*, 391 F.2d 495
(8th Cir. 1968) (intended purpose rule).

[81] Competitive product markets encourage innovation and the development of "better mouse-
traps." In many product design cases, a majority of manufacturers may have addressed a
design problem in the same way, but plaintiffs are able to point to some firms who have
adopted a safer design alternative and argue that the defendant's design was inadequate for
having failed to follow the safer course. Indeed, the best-known American decision adopting the rule that industry custom does not set the legal standard, *The T. J. Hooper*, 60 F.2d
737, 740 (2d Cir.), *cert. denied* 287 U.S. 662 (1932), may not have involved "industry custom" in the strict sense of the phrase. ("[T]here was no custom at all as to receiving sets;
some had them, some did not; the most that can be urged is that they had not yet become
general.")

[82] *See* RESTATEMENT THIRD OF TORTS: PRODUCTS LIABILITY § 2, cmt. d (1998) ("while such
evidence [of common industry practice] is admissible, it is not necessarily dispositive.").
See also The T. J. Hooper, supra, note 81 at 740: "A whole calling may have unduly lagged in
the adoption of new and [technologically] available devices. It may never set its own tests,
however persuasive be its usages."

[83] *See* RESTATEMENT, *supra* note 82, § 2(b), cmts. d, f.

and proposed safer alternatives.[84] And they have insisted on fairly rigorous demonstrations by plaintiffs of both the technological feasibility of suggested alternative designs and the extent to which the safer alternative designs would have reduced or prevented plaintiffs' harm.[85] In these ways, American courts have converted the potentially unadjudicable question of the overall reasonableness of the safety levels presented by complex product designs into the marginal and more adjudicable question of whether a reasonable manufacturer would have adopted the plaintiff's suggested safer alternative design instead of the defendant's actual design. As already indicated, courts do not always admit that they are implementing negligence concepts, continuing to talk "strict liability;" but the analysis is unmistakably rooted in risk-utility analysis. Thus, a products liability plaintiff typically focuses on an element of the defendant's design that is relatively isolable from the other design elements and argues that a cost-effective modification of that element would have prevented the plaintiff's harm. In response, the defendant manufacturer typically insists that the plaintiff's suggested modification has serious implications for the product design taken as a whole.[86] The requirement that the plaintiff prove both technological feasibility of the alternative and but-for causation renders review of such product design claims adjudicable.[87]

Before developing the significance of the safer-alternative-design requirement further, I should point out that the 1976 *Expanding Torts* article underestimated its importance. That analysis took its cue from the fact that by the early 1970s courts had dispensed with the no-duty rules and had begun to review the reasonableness of defendants' product designs. That was enough, it seemed to me, to suggest that serious problems lay ahead.[88] To some extent, of

---

[84] For a discussion of how courts apply this "safer alternative" approach in connection with negligence claims in nonproducts contexts, *see* Mark F. Grady, *Untaken Precautions*, 18 J. Legal Stud. 139 (1989).

[85] *See*, for example, *Troja v. Black & Decker Manuf. Co.*, 488 A.2d 516, 520 (1985) ("[Plaintiff's expert] was unable to furnish a design demonstrating the actual placement of such a [safety] system, or to explain how it could be integrated in the saw without interfering with the [saw's] function..."). *See generally* James A. Henderson Jr. & Aaron D. Twerski, *Intuition and Technology in Product Design Litigation: An Essay on Proximate Causation*, 88 Geo. L.J. 659, 667 (2000) ("[The interplay] between design defect and but-for proximate causation is of enormous importance to maintaining the integrity of product design litigation.").

[86] *See*, for example, *Barker v. Lull Engineering Co.*, 573 P.2d 443, 230 (Cal. 1978) (defendant argued that plaintiff's suggested design modifications would have turned its high-lift loader into a crane). *Cf.* the earlier discussion of changing the size and location of a kitchen in the design of a house, at Section III. A.

[87] *See generally* James A. Henderson Jr., *supra* note 85.

[88] *See Expanding Negligence*, *supra* note 1, at 490, nn. 62, 65, 66.

course, product design litigation over the past thirty years has been difficult. Design litigation continues to be controversial and problematic, even today.[89] But I had not yet engaged fully in what has proven to be a thirty-year exploration of American products liability law; and I underestimated the extent to which the reasonable alternative design requirement could and would rescue courts from exceeding the limits of their competence.

To appreciate the importance of requiring plaintiffs in complex design cases to prove both a technologically feasible alternative and but-for causation, one need only consider what has happened in connection with products liability claims based on failure to warn. By all but eliminating the requirements that render design claims adjudicable, courts have transformed failure-to-warn into an entirely rhetorical, essentially lawless tort. Thus, in connection with warnings claims, courts do not rigorously require the plaintiff to establish the technological feasibility of a cognitively effective alternative warning or but-for causation.[90] And many jurisdictions do not require the plaintiff even to specify what the defendant should have provided by way of a more adequate warning.[91] Courts might have approached failure-to-warn litigation in a manner more analogous to how they have approached design litigation, requiring plaintiffs to prove the feasibility and the cognitive effectiveness of a specific alternative warning and the extent to which, and how, a more adequate warning would have prevented the particular plaintiff's harm.[92] By and large, however, courts have not followed this path. For reasons that probably reside in the lack of hard technology regarding how warnings function to reduce risks, together with implicit assumptions that better warnings cost nothing and explicit assumptions that better warnings would have been heeded,[93]

---

[89] Much of the current controversy centers on the reasonable-alternative-design requirement in § 2(b) of the RESTATEMENT (THIRD) OF TORTS: PRODUCTS LIABILITY (1998). See, for example, Patrick Lavelle, *Crashing Into Proof of a Reasonable Alternative Design: The Fallacy of the Restatement (Third) of Torts: Products Liability*, 38 DUQ. L. REV. 1059 (2000); Victor E. Schwartz, *The Restatement, Third, Tort: Products Liability: A Model of Fairness and Balance*, 10 KAN. J. L. & POL'Y 41 (2000).

[90] See James A. Henderson Jr., *supra* note 85, at 681–683.

[91] See, for example, *Ayers v. Johnson & Johnson Baby Products Co.*, 797 P.2d 527, 532 (1990), *aff'd* 818 P.2d 1337 (1991). The PRODUCTS LIABILITY RESTATEMENT § 2(c) does not explicitly require that the plaintiff show an "alternative" warning because, unlike the defective design context, it must accommodate instances where no warning has been given.

[92] See James A. Henderson Jr. & Aaron D. Twerski, *Doctrinal Collapse in Products Liability: The Empty Shell of Failure to Warn*, 65 N.Y.U.L. REV. 265, 323–325 (1990) ("[J]udges should require *both* sides to support their arguments regarding obviousness, sufficiency, and causation with testimony from qualified experts who give more than conclusory opinions...").

[93] See generally James A. Henderson Jr. & Aaron D. Twerski, PRODUCTS LIABILITY: PROBLEMS AND PROCESS 328 (5th ed. 2004) ("Some judges (and commentators) succumb to the

courts treat failure-to-warn claims much more leniently than design claims. Most warnings claims to reach the trier of fact on little more than plaintiffs' rhetorical assertions.[94]

It follows that the only issue of fact relating to the issue of defect in connection with a typical failure-to-warn claim is whether or not the risks that caused the plaintiff's harm were sufficiently obvious or generally known to eliminate the need for a warning, or the need for a better warning than the defendant gave the plaintiff.[95] Once the judge sends that issue to the jury and the jury finds that the risks were not obvious or generally known, in most cases the further question of the defendants' liability for failure to provide an adequate warning is for the jury to decide on the basis of little more than the jurors' intuitions. Elsewhere I have both described and lamented the lawlessness of the manner in which our courts are responding to claims of failure to warn, and will not rehearse the details here.[96] If warnings-based claims were available to plaintiffs in the sorts of complex product design cases of interest in this chapter – claims that have broad-reaching economic implications for the institutional players on both sides – the lawlessness of failure-to-warn litigation would threaten to overwhelm our products liability system. This has not occurred for the simple reason that the generic risks typically associated with the design cases of interest here are sufficiently obvious and generally well known to place them beyond the reach of failure-to-warn claims.[97]

Given that the obviousness of the risks in these cases bars recovery for failure to warn, it is understandable that plaintiffs seek recovery based on allegations

temptation to assume that . . . warnings are, so to speak, 'free.'"). And many courts recognize a "heeding presumption" that warnings, if given, would have prevailed plaintiff's harm. *See*, for example, *Pavlik v. Lane Limited/Tobacco Exporters International*, 135 F.3d 876, 883 (3rd Cir. 1998) (predicting that Pennsylvania would adopt a heeding presumption in failure to warn cases); *Coward v. Owens-Corning Fiberglass Corp.*, 729 A.2d 614 (Pa. Super. Ct. 1999) (apply heeding presumption in an asbestos warning claim).

[94] *See* James A. Henderson Jr., *supra* note 92, at 326 ("In most cases, the elements of the warnings cause of action require plaintiffs to do little more than to mouth empty phrases.")

[95] *Id.* at 280. ("Perhaps more than any other aspect of warnings doctrine, this traditional rule [that warnings need not be given about obvious risks] should help the courts cull unworthy failure-to-warn claims from the worthy.")

[96] *See* James A. Henderson Jr., *supra* note 92.

[97] For example, clearly the plaintiff's bar would benefit greatly from establishing that alcoholic beverages are defective because of their propensity to harm alcoholics. Design claims based on reasonable alternative designs are implausible because, by definition, beverages that do not contain alcohol are not "alcoholic beverages." So plaintiffs have, understandably, attacked alcohol distributors on the basis of failure to warn. In *McGuire v. Joseph E. Seagrams & Sons, Inc.*, 814 S.W.2d 385 (Tex. 1991), the court denied such claims as a matter of law because the inherent risks of alcohol to alcoholics are generally known and understood.

of defective design. In contrast to their duties to warn about hidden product risks, manufacturers owe duties to adopt reasonable designs even if the relevant risks are obvious and generally known, or fully warned against.[98] But if obviousness does not bar claims for defective designs, courts traditionally require plaintiffs to prove the availability to the defendant of a safer alternative design. Thus, given the enormous rewards to be reaped from persuading courts to abandon the rigor inherent in requiring plaintiffs to prove both the availability of technologically feasible design alternatives and but-for causation, it is hardly surprising plaintiffs' lawyers are pressuring courts to do just that. Toward this end, plaintiffs urge courts to replace the current approach to product design liability with other approaches that eliminate the need to prove that a technologically feasible alternative design was available at time of sale that would have prevented the plaintiff's harm. Success in these efforts would, from the plaintiff's perspective, combine the best of both worlds: neither the obviousness of the relevant risks nor the plaintiff's inability to show how the design could have been made safer would bar recovery. From the perspective of the plaintiffs' bar, this would truly be "the perfect tort."[99]

The first of these approaches – the consumer expectations test for design defect – requires only that the plaintiff prove that the defendant's product caused the plaintiff's harm and then gives to the jury the question of whether, in their discretion, the product design is more dangerous than reasonable consumers have a right to expect.[100] In the version of the consumer expectations test especially favored by the plaintiffs' bar, the plaintiff is not required to prove the availability of a safer alternative design or to make a separate showing that the defect was a but-for cause of her harm.[101] Suffice it to say that, under this essentially lawless approach, virtually every design claim would reach the jury because only the jury is presumably in a position to tell the court, based on their unreviewable intuitions, whether a given product design does or does not disappoint consumer expectations. Expert witnesses are not required because, in effect, the jurors are their own best source of intuitional expertise regarding how much safety consumers should be able to expect from product designs.[102]

---

[98] See RESTATEMENT (THIRD) OF TORTS: PRODUCTS LIABILITY § 2(b), cmt. f (1998) (obviousness of the relevant risks is relevant to the issue of defective design, but does not bar recovery). See also id. cmt. l.

[99] See James A. Henderson Jr., supra n. 85, at 679 n. 101 ("Thus, the consumer expectations test presents the perfect plaintiff's tort.").

[100] See generally, DAVID G. OWEN supra note 65, at § 8.3.

[101] See James A. Henderson Jr., supra note 85.

[102] For a recent proposal that experts in cognitive psychology should play a much more significant role under a reinvigorated version of the consumer expectations test, see Douglas Kysar, The Expectations of Consumers, 103 COLUM. L. REV. 1791 (2003).

In pressuring courts to adopt this embarrassingly unprincipled approach to product design liability, plaintiffs' lawyers insist that requiring technologically rigorous proof of a safer alternative design places arbitrary and costly burdens on claimants that they should not be required to bear. In truth, as has been explained, the safer alternative design requirement is the only fair and rational means, in the absence of specific design standards derived from legitimate internal or external sources,[103] of allowing product design claims to be adjudicated. Happily, from the standpoint of maintaining the integrity of the judicial process, a strong majority of American commentators,[104] courts,[105] and legislatures[106] have rejected the lawless version of the consumer expectations test promoted by the plaintiffs' bar, instead requiring proof of a safer alternative design. The Restatement (Third) of Torts: Products Liability reflects this majority view and rejects the consumer expectations test for defective design.[107]

The other approach to product design litigation urged by the plaintiffs' bar as a means of eliminating the requirement of proving a safer alternative design is product category liability. Under that proposed approach, courts could condemn as defective entire product categories – for example, alcoholic beverages or motorcycles – based on findings that the aggregate risks they present outweigh the aggregate social benefits they provide.[108] Proof of safer alternatives would not be necessary. By definition, once a product category is condemned as unreasonably dangerous, all design variations within the designated product category bring liability on their commercial sellers. Such an approach would ask courts to reach essentially legislative judgments regarding the social acceptability of broad product categories and would clearly exceed the limits of adjudication. Although it is easy to understand why plaintiffs' lawyers urge

---

[103] For a discussion of these internal and external explicit design standards, including safety statutes and regulations, *see generally* James A. Henderson, Jr., *supra* note 76, at 872–876.

[104] *See*, for example, *Peck v. Bridgeport Machine, Inc.*, 237 F.3d 614 (6th Cir. 2001) (applying Michigan law); *Vine v. Beloit Corp.*, 631 So. 2d 1003 (Ala. 1994); *Wright v. Brooke Group, Ltd.*, 652 N.W.2d 159 (Iowa 2002).

[105] *See generally* Sheila L. Birnbaum, *Unmasking the Test for Design Defect: From Negligence [to Warranty] to Strict Liability to Negligence*, 33 Vand. L. Rev. 593 (1980); W. Page Keeton, *Products Liability – Design Hazards and the Meaning of Defect*, 10 Cumb. L. Rev. 293 (1979); William Powers Jr., *A Modest Proposal to Abandon Strict Products Liability*, 1991 U. Ill. L. Rev. 639 (1991); Gary T. Schwartz, *Forward: Understanding Products Liability*, 67 Cal. L. Rev. 435 (1979); John W. Wade, *On Product "Design Defects" and Their Actionability*, 33 Vand. L. Rev. 551 (1980).

[106] Legislatures in Louisiana, Mississippi, New Jersey, Ohio, and Texas have enacted statutes requiring proof of reasonable alternative designs.

[107] *See* Restatement, Third, of Torts: Products Liability, § 2(b), cmt. g (1998) ("[c]onsumer expectations do not constitute an independent standard for judging the defectiveness of product designs.")

[108] *See id.*, at cmts. d, e.

courts to adopt product category liability, it is also easy to understand why the overwhelming majority of American courts and legislatures firmly reject it.[109] Once again, the Restatement (Third) of Torts: Products Liability reflects this clear majority view, and the issue appears to be settled.[110]

Briefly to summarize how the American products liability system imposes liability for defective product designs without engaging courts in "reasonableness under the circumstances" review of complex product designs, the centrally important element is the requirement that plaintiffs prove the availability to the manufacturer of a technologically feasible, safer alternative. Ill-conceived designs that cause products to malfunction do not require such proof because a built-in standard – intended function – is available by which to judge defectiveness. However, with regard to designs that perform as they manifestly were intended, the requirement of a safer alternative, combined with but-for causation, supports marginal comparisons between the product as it was actually designed and the product as it should have been designed. The marginality of this approach is what renders design claims adjudicable. Courts and legislatures have rightly rejected other approaches to product design liability, including the consumer expectations test and product category liability, that would eliminate the safer alternative design requirement and substitute the jury's intuitions as the measure of design defectiveness. These open-ended approaches would deliver the design-based portion of our products liability system to the same fate that has befallen the portion devoted to failure-to-warn, where lawlessness reigns supreme.

To these major doctrinal elements that help to maintain the adjudicability of product design defect claims may be added several others. One such development in recent years has been increasing judicial reliance on federal preemption. To an extent that surprises some observers who have followed preemption jurisprudence over the years, our courts seem increasingly willing to defer to federal administrative programs that address a wide variety of product safety concerns, including the reasonableness of manufacturers' product design and marketing decisions.[111] The Supreme Court has taken the lead in extending preemption in design litigation, to an extent that dismays some members of that Court.[112] Even when Congress appears eager to achieve product design safety objectives as rapidly as possible, a majority

---

[109] *See generally* James A. Henderson Jr. & Aaron D. Twerski, *Closing the American products Liability Frontier: Rejection of Liability Without Defect,* 66 N.Y.U.L. Rev. 1263 (1991).

[110] *See supra* note 108.

[111] *See generally* James A. Henderson, Jr. & Aaron D. Twerski, Products Liability: Problems and Process (5th ed. 2004).

[112] *See,* for example, *Geier v. American Honda Motor Co., Inc.,* 529 U.S. 861, 886–907 (2000).

of the Court insists that state law must not impose liability on manufacturers for failing to achieve those objectives sooner than federal law requires.[113] Although this increasing judicial deference to federal regulatory law puzzles and upsets some observers,[114] it is perfectly understandable from the perspective adopted in this article. Because federal administrative agencies do not rely on adjudication in setting safety standards, they are able to address highly complex design problems without compromising their institutional integrity. And once Congress assigns such problems to administrative agencies that are institutionally suited to solving them, the Supreme Court is sorely tempted to insist that courts applying state law not interfere with such solutions. Although the Court has indicated that it will not extend preemption beyond reasonable limits,[115] in general one may expect that doctrine to play a significant role in helping courts to avoid having to review complex product designs.

Another development in recent years that has helped to preserve the integrity of the adjudicative process in product design litigation is the Supreme Court's interpretation of the Federal Rules of Evidence to preclude reliance by litigants in federal courts on spurious, nonrigorous expert testimony.[116] The Court has made it clear that the new evidentiary regime applies not only to theoretical expert testimony at the outer edges of scientific knowledge but also to the type of applied-science, engineering testimony that plays a central role in product design litigation.[117] Given the importance of proof of technological feasibility to the viability of the safer-alternative approach to defective design, these evidentiary developments regarding expert testimony are helping federal courts hearing design claims to maintain judicial integrity. To the extent that state courts have followed the Supreme Court's lead in *Daubert v.*

---

[113] *Id.*

[114] *See*, for example, Mary J. Davis, *Unmasking the Presumption in Favor of Preemption*, 53 S.C.L. REV. 967, 1008–1012 (2002) (characterizing *Geier* as a "seismic shift" in the Court's preemption analysis that improperly drifts away from any meaningful assessment of Congressional intent); Susan Reaker-Jordan, *A Study in Judicial Sleight of Hand: Did Geier v. American Honda Motor Co. Eradicate the Presumption Against Preemption?*, 17 BYU J. PUB. L. 1 (2002) (criticizing the Court for muddying up its preemption jurisprudence and for enabling the preemption doctrine to more easily trump state law). *See also The Supreme Court 1999 Term: Leading Cases, Federal Preemption of State Law*, 114 HARV. L. REV. 339 (2000) (reading *Geier* as "signal[ing]" the Court's subtle drift away from the presumption against preemption in favor of a more functional federal law preference rule").

[115] *See*, for example, *Sprietsma v. Mercury Marine*, 537 U.S. 51 (2002) (Court refused to give preemptive effect to the decision of the Secretary of Transportation not to regulate the design of propeller guards).

[116] *See Daubert v. Merrell Dow Pharmaceuticals, Inc.*, 509 U.S. 579 (1993).

[117] *See Kumho Tire Co., Ltd. v. Carmichael*, 119 S.Ct. 1167 (1999).

Merrell Dow Pharmaceuticals, Inc.,[118] the concerns expressed in this chapter have been further ameliorated.

D. How Courts Have Avoided Complex Design Review
in Other Areas of Tort

1. *How Courts Have Avoided Reasonableness-Based Review*
of Complex Medical Procedures

In contrast to products liability litigation, where liability rests entirely on the reasonableness of the end-product delivered to consumer,[119] in the medical context liability rests not only on the end-product – the medical treatment provided to the patient – but also on medical providers' preliminary decisions leading to that treatment. Thus, medical professionals provide two basic components of care: they determine whether a patient requires a particular course of treatment, and they determine how that treatment should be delivered. The first aspect includes a broad range of decisions, from diagnosis to referral, typically reached by the primary medical provider from whom the patient first seeks help. The second component involves decisions regarding how the recommended course of treatment should be administered, often made by a specialist to whom the patient has been referred. Both the "whether" and the "how" components of medical care provision reflect complex, interconnected trade-offs of risks and benefits that would defy judicial review under a general reasonableness standard. Thus, when courts undertake to review the reasonableness of these care components they are reviewing the underlying designs of the procedures to no less extent than in the context of judicial review of product designs, with the same potential threats to judicial integrity.

As the 1976 article observed, courts traditionally have avoided a reasonableness-based review of the designs of medical services by regarding the procedures established by the medical profession as presumptively reasonable – that is, by accepting established custom in the medical profession as legally controlling.[120] In contrast to the products liability context, courts have traditionally felt they could trust the medical profession to set their own standards. And by relying on medical custom they have been able to apply specific standards that significantly reduce the many-centeredness of the issues

---

[118] *See*, for example, *Clement v. Griffin*, 634 So. 2d 412 (La. 1994).

[119] Although evidence of inadequate presale product testing is relevant to the issue of defective design, liability follows only if the product, itself, is defective at time of sale. *See* RESTATEMENT (THIRD) OF TORTS: PRODUCTS LIABILITY § 1 (1998).

[120] *See Expanding Negligence, supra* note 1, at 492 n. 68.

brought before them. However, as legal commentators have observed in the past three decades, judicial deference to medical custom has declined significantly.[121] Today, courts appear to be quite willing to judge for themselves whether medical professionals have exercised reasonable care under all the circumstances. Obviously these developments reflect an erosion in judicial confidence in the medical profession's trustworthiness in setting their own standards of care. But how does this new regime of more extensive judicial review accommodate the process concerns expressed in this analysis?

In answering this question, it is important to understand that this recent expansion in judicial review of medical procedures has occurred only with respect to the "whether" component, not the "how." That is, courts are willing to review the reasonableness of medical providers' diagnostic and referral decisions regarding whether their patients require certain types of treatment and care, and who should provide them.[122] But courts continue to defer to professional custom regarding how the various medical procedures – appendectomies, heart by-passes, and the like – should be performed.[123] Let us begin our analysis of these developments by examining more closely the continued judicial reliance on medical custom regarding how standard procedures should be designed. Why have courts not adopted the safer-alternative design approach from products liability and undertaken to review the reasonableness of the designs of customary medical procedures? The major reason for the continued judicial reliance on medical custom in this connection is that the alternative-design approach that works fairly well in products liability litigation would not be nearly as effective in the context of judging the designs of standard medical procedures. In the field of product design, where

---

[121] See generally Phillip G. Peters Jr., The Quiet Demise of Deference to Custom: Malpractice Law at the Millennium, 57 WASH. & LEE L. REV. 163 (2000).

[122] See, for example, Barbella v. Touro Infirmary, 596 So. 2d 845, 848 (La. Ct.App. 1992) (conformity to medical custom not a defense to claim of failure to diagnose cancer); Doctors Memorial Hospital, Inc. v. Evans, 543 So. 2d 809, 812 (Fla. Ct. App. 1989) (evidence of medical custom is relevant but not controlling in case involving alleged failure to inform patient of risks of diagnostic x-ray). The Washington Supreme Court decision in Helling v. Carey, 519 P.2d 98 (Wash. 1974), often credited with being the first decision to reject medical customs as controlling, involving the question of whether a certain diagnostic test should have been administered.

[123] Although courts often state that custom is not controlling, evidence of conformance invariably supports judgment as a matter of law for the defendant provider. See, for example, Chiero v. Chicago Osteopathic Hospital, 392 N.E.2d 203 (Ind. Ct. App. 1979). Indeed, I could not find decisions in which plaintiffs claimed that the designs of the medical treatments, themselves, were unreasonably dangerous and should have been modified marginally. For example, Chiero, supra, involved a claim that provider negligence could be inferred from the fact of a negative outcome from prostate surgery. No claim was made that the procedure, itself, was badly designed.

competitive markets are constantly seeking and developing "better mouse-traps" through product innovation, plaintiffs are able to draw upon industry innovations and "cutting edge" experts for support and inspiration when framing their proofs and arguments regarding marginally safer alternative designs. In product design litigation, in effect, courts and litigants tailor-make hypothetical alternative designs with which to judge the reasonableness of defendant manufacturers' product designs.[124]

By contrast, the medical profession traditionally relies on standard treatment procedures that are approved by the medical community.[125] Several different procedures for treating a particular medical problem may be available to the medical provider. But the design of each such procedure will have been approved by a subset of the medical community and may be said to be "standard." Thus, in the medical context, it would be much more problematic for plaintiffs to provide rigorous proof of tailor-made, nonstandard methods of providing medical care.[126] With presumably trustworthy professional custom readily available for all of the standard medical procedures, it is understandable why courts would continue to rely on custom regarding the "how" element in medical malpractice litigation. Of course, when two or more standard procedures are available with which to address the plaintiff's presenting condition, an alternative-design approach to professional liability is feasible.[127] But that is properly considered part of the "whether" component, to which attention will now turn.

---

[124] *See*, for example, *Dawson v. Chrysler Corp.*, 630 F.2d 950 (3d Cir. 1980) (examining alternative, competing industry designs to sustain the jury's determination that the design of the product in question was defective).

[125] *See* James A. Henderson Jr. & John A. Siliciano, *Universal Health Care and the Continued Reliance on Custom in Determining Medical Malpractice*, 79 CORNELL L. REV. 1382, 1384 (1994).

[126] *See* Tim Cram et al., *Ascertaining Customary Care in Malpractice Cases: Asking Those Who Know*, 37 WAKE FOREST L. REV. 699, 710, 717–18, 720 (2002) (noting the difficulties for expert witnesses to testify on the acceptability of any given practice and the difficulties for jurors to understand the testimony of "dueling experts" in a highly complex medical field).

[127] This occurs when courts have abandoned the traditional "locality" rule, allowing plaintiffs to reach juries on the ground that an alternative medical procedure, safer than the one that the plaintiff, was available to the defendant provider and used by providers in other localities. *See*, for example, *Abrogast v. Mid-Ohio Valley Medical Corp.*, No. 31314, 2003 WL 22470963, at *4–5 (W. Va. Oct. 31, 2003) (abolishing the locality rule in medical malpractice cases and finding the physician liable where he did not follow national standards); *Sheely v. Memorial Hosp.*, 710 A.2d 161, 166–67 (R.I. 1998) (holding that a "similar locality" analysis is no longer applicable in view of the present-day realities of the medical profession).

By contrast to the continued judicial reliance on custom in connection with the "how" component of medical care provision, courts have increasingly engaged in robust, reasonableness-based review of the "whether" component.[128] Not surprisingly, this review has proceeded on the same safer-alternative-design basis as is utilized in products liability design litigation.[129] Traditionally, courts deferred to medical custom even in connection with this "whether" component.[130] Given the availability of the alternative-design approach, this traditional deferral to custom was not dictated so much by limits-of-adjudication considerations as by substantive considerations, including an assumption that medical professionals always serve the best interests of their patients. Given that every individual patient presents a unique set of conditions and idiosyncrasies to his or her medical care provider, and given that the possibilities regarding diagnosis and referral vary significantly across patients, judicial review of the provider's conduct on a safer-alternative-design basis was not only feasible but, at least with the help of hindsight regarding the erosion of judicial confidence in the medical community, inevitable. Armed with medical experts, the plaintiff argues that a reasonable medical provider would have ordered different tests, made a different decision regarding referral and treatment.[131] With respect to each of these subparts of the "whether" component of medical care, the procedures implicated by the alternative choices – the methods of diagnostic testing, for example – may be, and probably are, standard in the sense that courts will defer to custom regarding their interconnected design details. But the defendant medical provider's overall treatment design regarding which set of choices and decisions were appropriate for a particular patient-plaintiff can, and will, be reviewed by courts relying on essentially the same safer-alternative-design approach as courts employ in products liability litigation.[132]

To summarize the comparison between medical malpractice litigation and products liability litigation: traditional judicial responses in the medical context resembled the responses that occurred early in the development of products liability. Individual medical providers were liable when they deviated from prescribed customary designs of medical procedures, in much the same manner as manufacturers were (and are) liable for manufacturing defects

---

[128] *See* authorities cited.
[129] For example, in *Barbella, supra* note 122, the plaintiff claimed that the defendant provider should have responded differently to X-rays indicating nodules on plaintiff's lungs.
[130] *See* note 121, *supra*, and accompanying text.
[131] *See* note 122, *supra*, and accompanying text.
[132] *See* notes 84, 85, *supra*, and accompanying text.

when product units deviate from their intended designs.[133] Moreover, courts traditionally delegated responsibility for designing medical procedures to the profession, in a manner similar to judicial delegation to the market in the early phases of development of product design liability.[134] In the products context, courts eventually developed the safer-alternative-design approach that allows them independently to monitor the reasonableness of product designs without exceeding the limits of adjudication.[135] In the medical context, a mixed approach has emerged in the three decades since my earlier article. In connection with what I have referred to as the "how" component of medical care provision, where a safer-alternative-design approach is not feasible and where medical custom is both available and trustworthy, courts continue to defer to custom in determining medical provider liability based on the designs of standard medical procedures.[136] But in connection with the "whether" component of medical care provision, where an alternative-design approach is feasible and where custom is not readily available, courts review medical treatment designs in a manner similar to their review of product designs. In both the medical and products contexts, courts avoid judging the reasonableness of complex designs, but they accomplish that necessary objective in different ways.

2. How Courts Have Avoided Reasonableness-Based Review of Complex Governmental Designs

The designs of interest here are not those imposed by governmental regulators on nongovernmental actors such as product manufacturers or medical care providers, but are rather the designs adopted by the regulators for guiding their own governmental activities. Typically, a governmental agency provides public services – police and fire protection, maintenance of streets and highways, and the like – that create risks of harm to others. When those risks materialize, the victim seeks to recover in tort against the governmental agency that caused injury. Frequently such a tort claim aims, explicitly or implicitly,

---

[133] *Compare*, for example, Tenn. Code Ann. § 29–26–115 *with* Restatement (Third) of Torts: Products Liability § 2(a) (1998).

[134] *See generally* W. Page Keeton et al., Prosser and Keeton on Torts § 32, at 189; Phillip G. Peters Jr., *supra* note 121, at 164–170.

[135] *See* notes 83–86 *supra*, and accompanying text. *See generally* James A. Henderson Jr. & Aaron D. Twerski, *Achieving Consensus on Defective Product Design*, 83 Cornell L. Rev. 867, 884–85 (1998).

[136] *See*, for example, *Robinson v. LeCorps*, 83 S.W.3d 718 (Tenn. 2002) (deferring to custom); *but see* Phillip G. Peters, Jr., *supra* note 121.

at the design adopted by the relevant governmental agency for the delivery of the services that caused harm, in much the same way that tort claims against nongovernmental institutions may implicate complex designs. And typically such governmentally implemented designs are sufficiently complex that courts would exceed the limits of adjudication were they to attempt to review the reasonableness of such designs on an "all factors considered" basis.

As might be expected, based on the preceding discussions of products and medical design liability, courts have avoided such reasonableness-based review in the governmental context. But rather than attempt to implement an alternative-design approach or defer to custom, courts have relied on the traditional rules governing sovereign immunity to avoid complex design review.[137] Courts and legislatures impose liability on governmental defendants when lower-level operatives act negligently under general standards of reasonableness,[138] or depart from the designs to which they are expected to conform,[139] causing harm to others. But courts and legislatures refuse to allow judicial review of the reasonableness of the governmental designs, themselves, on the ground that to impose design-based liability would violate the traditional norm that the sovereign, as such, can do not wrong.[140]

Might courts have chosen to review governmental designs on the basis of safer alternatives, as in products liability, or might they have deferred to custom, as in areas of medical malpractice? Of course, even if these approaches were viable, courts might nevertheless invoke sovereign immunity based on substantive considerations independent of concerns over the institutional limits of judicial process.[141] But the analysis in this chapter suggests that the refusal by courts and legislatures to allow judicial design review in this context also reflects concern over the proper limits of adjudication. It will lend support to this thesis to consider whether either the safer-alternative-design or the deference-to-custom approaches would be viable in this context.

---

[137] *See Expanding Negligence, supra* note 1, at nn. 129–131 and accompanying text.

[138] *See,* for example, *Brantley v. Dep't of Human Res.,* 523 S.E.2d 571 (Ga. 1999) (finding that foster parents' negligent supervision of their two-year-old foster child was not within the discretionary function exception of the GEORGIA TORT CLAIMS ACT).

[139] *See,* for example, *Scott v. Country of Los Angeles,* 32 Cal. Rptr. 2d 643 (Cal. Ct. App. 1994) (finding that the Department of Social Services' noncompliance with state regulations mandating monthly visits to foster homes was a failure to fulfill a ministerial duty, not a discretionary act).

[140] *See Expanding Negligence, supra* note 1, at note 137.

[141] *See generally* James R. Levine, *The Federal Tort Claims Act: A Proposal for Institutional Reform,* 100 COLUM. L. REV. 1538 (2000) (arguing that the discretionary function exception protects the separation of powers and the public fisc); Note, *Governmental Tort Liability,* 111 HARV. L. REV. 2009 (1998) (identifying federalism and the promotion of vigorous decision making as rationales supporting immunity).

The safer-alternative-design approach would not be viable in design-based tort actions against governmental defendants because, in contrast to actions based on allegations of defective product design, the technological feasibility of alternative governmental designs would almost never be in issue. Thus, in connection with a claim that the defendant governmental agency could have designed its operations so as to avoid injury to the plaintiff, a safer alternative design would always have been technologically feasible. In this respect, design claims against governmental agencies would be functionally similar to failure to warn claims against product manufacturers, where litigation has fallen into shambles because the requirement of technological feasibility is unavailable as a screen by means of which to sort out claims. But unlike product warning claims, where the obviousness of risks allows courts to some extent to screen claims, in the governmental design liability context the relevant risks are generated, as with claims based on product design, by the allegedly unreasonable deployment of tangible assets. Thus, liability would be appropriate when governmental designs are unreasonable even when the relevant risks are obvious.[142] It follows that tort actions based on unreasonable governmental designs, when compared with products liability claims, would present a "worst of both worlds" combination of circumstances from the standpoint of maintaining judicial integrity. Like product design claims and unlike product warnings claims, they would involve physical arrangements of tangible assets, and thus the relative obviousness of the risks would not be a bar to recovery. But unlike product design claims and like failure-to-warn claims, technological feasibility would not provide an effective screen with which to sort out plaintiffs' claims.

The unique problems that governmental design claims would present to courts may be understood by considering how such claims would be litigated. If governmental design litigation were allowed, the issues would be entirely budgetary in nature, raising essentially policy questions without, as just explained, any reference to technological feasibility. For example, were the injured victim of a violent mugging allowed to sue the city for failing to respond quickly enough to her emergency telephone call for police protection, whether greater protection was technologically feasible would not be in issue.[143] Instead, assuming that the police personnel involved conformed

---

[142] The modern rule is that obviousness of the risks is a relevant factor, but does not control, in determining the defectiveness of product designs. *See generally* RESTATEMENT (THIRD) OF TORTS: PRODUCTS LIABILITY § 2 cmt. d (1998).

[143] The plaintiff in most cases would be asking for a greater number of personnel available to be deployed more quickly in responding to such calls, not for new technology by which to make such responses.

to prescribed agency procedures,[144] the question to be decided in most cases would be entirely one of budgetary priorities. Should greater resources be allocated to police protection rather than to schools, or public sanitation? Within the police department, should more resources be spent on responding to emergency calls or on traffic control? How high can, or should, taxes be raised? None of these questions will typically involve the technological feasibility of allocating municipal resources differently. And without the effective screening provided by the technological dimension, such many-centered policy questions would be so numerous and so interconnected that adjudicating consistent, rational outcomes would not be possible.

Moreover, judicial deference to custom, which works to an important, albeit limited, extent in the medical services context, would not provide courts with a feasible option in the governmental liability context because no relevant customs would be available on which courts might rely. For custom to develop in ways that provide normative standards for resolving tort claims, the actors whose conduct might form the basis of custom must face essentially the same factual circumstances and share essentially the same values.[145] These conditions are presumably present in products markets and, to a more limited extent, in medical communities.[146] However, in connection with governmental deployments of resources, neither necessary condition for the development of custom is satisfied. For example, the plaintiff in our mugging case might point to neighboring municipalities that provide greater police protection to their citizens in emergency situations. But the decisions by other cities to provide greater protection are not legitimately relevant to the mugging victim's claim because they may reflect different sets of priorities by different groups of citizens, or simply the availability of larger tax bases reflecting higher property values. On reflection, virtually every municipality in the state would be uniquely different from all the others in these regards.

---

[144] When personnel fail to conform to prescribed agency procedures, liability is often imposed upon the governmental agency. *See*, for example, *Berkovitz v. United States*, 486 U.S. 531 (1988) (when personnel fail to act in accord with a mandatory agency directive, governmental immunity is not available.) *See also Roland v. New York*, 638 N.Y.S.2d 500 (N.Y. App. Div. 1996) (rejecting government's claim of immunity after finding that child abuse hotline personnel made a routing error).

[145] *See* James A. Henderson Jr., *supra* note 125 at 1384.

[146] In most cases, the relevant markets and communities are national in scope, and the relevant physical sciences, embodied in Sir Isaac Newton's laws and human physiology, are the same everywhere. In the medical context, to some extent different treatment procedures develop, reflecting different budgetary considerations and risk preferences. But each of these alternative procedures, to constitute an alternative to which plaintiffs may point in litigation of the "whether" issue, must be accepted by a significant subset of the medical community.

In connection with medical malpractice and products liability litigation, by contrast, the medical procedures and product designs adopted in one city, or state, are legitimately transferable to other jurisdictions because the relevant technology and underlying value structure and assumed to be more or less constant across such political boundaries.[147]

It follows that, to the extent that the process concerns identified in this analysis help to explain why courts and legislatures have refused to allow judicial review of complex governmental designs, the rules governing such refusals are quite predictable. When lower-level governmental operatives harm plaintiffs by failing to conform to existing design structures for the delivery of governmental services, these failures do not require review of the reasonableness of the designs, themselves, and therefore courts are willing to expose governmental employers to tort liability.[148] The legal principles governing sovereign immunity deem such conduct to be "administrative," or "ministerial," and governmental immunity does not bar plaintiffs' tort recovery.[149] In effect, such instances are functional equivalents of manufacturing defects; just as product units deviate from designs, so do health care providers' deviate from customary medical norms.[150] By contrast, when the conduct of the lower-level operatives conforms to the applicable governmental design structures, tort claims based on those activities call into question the designs themselves.[151] In such cases, the safer-alternative-design approach employed in product design litigation and, to a limited extent, in medical malpractice litigation is not available. Thus, to avoid judicial review of governmental designs, the principle of sovereign immunity intervenes to bar recovery. Courts deem the higher-level, resource-allocative decisions involved in designing the governmental units "discretionary," and hold that such decisions constitute sovereign acts that are beyond the reach of tort.[152]

---

[147] That was the traditional assumption, in any event. In the medical context, the traditional locality rule gave a parochial flavor to the value side of the equation. But that rule has given way to a national standard. *See* Phillip G. Peters, *supra* note 131, at 166 n. 15. For an argument that budgetary variations and constraints in the emerging world of HMOs may, over time, destroy the conditions necessary for the formation of medical custom, *see* James A. Henderson, Jr., *supra* note 125.

[148] *See* text accompanying note 61, *supra*.

[149] *See* notes 139, 140, *supra*.

[150] *See* notes 71, 72, *supra*, and accompanying text.

[151] *See* note 63, *supra*, and accompanying text.

[152] *See*, for example, *United States v. Gaubert*, 499 U.S. 315 (1991) (holding that the discretionary function exception of the Federal Tort Claims Act covered actions involving an element of judgment or choice, including decisions made at the operational or management level of a bank). *See also City of Lancaster v. Chambers*, 883 S.W.2d 650 (Tex. 1994) (holding that a police officer, by engaging in a high speed chase, is acting in a discretionary, not ministerial,

3. How Courts Have Refused to Review the Reasonableness of Complex Environmental Designs

Including this topic serves two purposes. First, because the 1976 *Expanding Negligence* article considered environmental litigation at some length, revisiting the subject in this chapter provides additional follow-up on what has transpired since that piece was published. And, second, recent judicial applications of public nuisance concepts in products liability litigation appear to threaten the integrity of the judicial process in exactly the ways that this article describes. The earlier article described how nuisance law historically departs from the rules governing trespass to land, replacing formal boundary-crossing concepts with a general reasonableness analysis.[153] The article also identified then-recent developments that appeared to ask courts to solve complex environmental problems on the basis of reasonableness under all the circumstances, thereby threatening to exceed the proper limits of adjudication.[154] Since then, consistent with the analysis in this article, the threats to judicial integrity described in the earlier article have not materialized. American courts have, by and large, refused to accept invitations to use nuisance law to exceed their institutional limits.[155]

Fairly recently, however, a few courts have suggested they might be willing to apply the common law of public nuisance in a manner that would, if the approach gained traction, seriously undermine the integrity of a significant branch of our products liability system.[156] The tort claims in these cases have no connection with interests in land or harm to the natural environment. Instead, they attempt to extend the public nuisance concept to allow aggregations of products liability claimants to recover pure economic losses from aggregations of product distributors in connection with product categories that are alleged to be inherently dangerous and antisocial.[157] One of the

---

manner); *Jackson v. Dep't of Human Res.*, 497 S.E.2d 58 (Ga. Ct. App. 1998) (holding the agency was entitled to immunity after finding that foster child placement is a discretionary act because it requires the caseworker to weigh alternatives and take a variety of factors into account).

[153] See *Expanding Negligence, supra* note 1, at 495–97.

[154] *Id.* at 497–98.

[155] See, for example, *City of Philadelphia v. Beretta U.S.A. Corp.*, 277 F.3d 415 (3d Cir. 2002) (applying Pennsylvania law); *Camden County Bd. of Chosen Freeholders v. Beretta U.S.A. Corp.*, 273 F.3d 536 (3d Cir. 2001) (applying New Jersey law); *Ganim v. Smith & Wesson Corp.*, 258 Conn. 313 (2001).

[156] See generally Donald G. Gifford, *Public Nuisance as a Mass Products Liability Tort*, 71 U. Cin. L. Rev. 741 (2003).

[157] These categories include tobacco products, lead paint, and firearms. *Id.* at 764. See, for example, *Whitehouse v. Lead Indus. Ass'n*, No. 99-5226, 2002 R. I. Super. LEXIS 90 at *6

most prominent of these cases involved an action by the City of Cincinnati against major manufacturers and distributors of firearms for economic losses allegedly sustained over a period of years because of the sale of small hand-guns in that part of Ohio.[158] The city sought to have the trial court review the overall reasonableness of the defendants' product distribution networks and declare the design and maintenance of that network to be a public nuisance for which the city could recover the substantial costs incurred in dealing with handgun-related activities, criminal and otherwise.[159] The trial court dismissed the complaint for failure to state a claim. However, the Supreme Court of Ohio reversed and sent the case back for evidentiary hearings.[160] Clearly the claims in that case ask Ohio courts to exceed the limits of their institutional capacities. Consistent with this analysis, the majority of courts before whom such claims have been brought have ruled against plaintiffs as a matter of law.[161]

Today, as the foregoing analysis makes clear, no general trend toward law-lessness appears to be in the offing. Rather, decisions such as *City of Cincinnati v. Barretta U.S.A.* are aberrations that will almost surely be corrected in due course, leaving our negligence system on a sensible middle course. It will be noted that these cases have come up on the pleadings, and the appellate courts have remanded to determine whether proof will be available to support the allegations. Although it is not clear whether the requisite proof will eventually be forthcoming, if plaintiffs such as the City of Cincinnati were to prevail on their claims and recovery of economic losses caused by product distribution networks were to gain widespread acceptance, such developments would not only vastly enrich the plaintiffs' bar but also undermine the integrity of our products liability system.[162] For this reason, actions of the sort brought by

---

(R.I. Super. Ct. July 3, 2002); *City of Cincinnati v. Beretta U.S.A.*, 768 N.E.2d 1136 (Ohio 2002); *White v. Smith & Wesson*, 97 F. Supp. 2d 816 (N.D. Ohio 2000) (applying Ohio law); *City of Gary v. Smith & Wesson Corp.*, 2003 WL 23010035 (Ind. 2003); *Young v. Bryco Arms*, 765 N.E.2d (Ill. App. Ct. 2001); *City of Boston v. Smith & Wesson Corp.*, No. 1999-02590, 2000 Mass. Super. LEXIS 352 (July 13, 2000) ("[t]o be sure, the legal theory is unique in the Commonwealth but...that is not reason to dismiss at this stage of the proceedings.").

[158] *See City of Cincinnati*, *supra* note 158, 768 N.E.2d at 1140. *Cf.* the hypothetical considered earlier involving the maintenance of a fleet of dangerous delivery trucks. *See* note 62, *supra*, and accompanying text.

[159] *See id.* at 1145.

[160] *Id.* at 1151.

[161] *See* note 156, *supra*.

[162] *See* Donald G. Gifford, *supra* note 156, at 837:

Courts should not replace the substantial bodies of mature doctrinal and policy analysis available to guide them in products liability actions with a vaguely defined tort that is being used in ways utterly foreign to its historical context. To do so would indeed allow public nuisance to become "a monster that would devour in one gulp the entire law of tort."

the City of Cincinnati against the firearms industry should not, and I predict will not, succeed. I am comforted in this regard to note that the plaintiffs in several of these cases voluntarily withdrew their claims after remand to the trial court.[163] These threats to judicial integrity, too, will pass. But even if these claims do not have a bright future, they are reminders of how very powerful and relentless are the pressures on courts to exceed their proper bounds.[164]

IV. CONCLUSION

Thirty years ago, I described a trend toward expanding the negligence concept in ways that seemed to threaten the integrity of the judicial process. In a number of doctrinal areas, courts were jettisoning traditional rule structures in favor of deciding negligence claims on a "reasonableness under all the circumstances" basis. If that trend continued, I suggested, the end result would so far exceed the limits of judicial competence that the negligence system would need to be replaced with some version or other of strict enterprise liability. Over the decades since that article, it has become clear that my worst fears were unfounded. American courts contained, and in some important respects reversed, the expansionary tendencies over which I had lamented. In 1990, I offered empirical support for these trend-reversals and, two years later, Gary Schwartz confirmed them in a comprehensive analysis of the relevant case law. Rather than try to claim that our courts must have shared my concerns at some primordial level of judicial intuition, this chapter has reexamined my earlier article and, in some respects, found it wanting.

For one thing, broad-based enterprise liability no longer appears to be a possible replacement for negligence-based tort liability. Thus, the negligence concept will continue to serve as the centerpiece of tort for the foreseeable future. For another, some of the expansions of the negligence concept evident in the 1970s were clearly more threatening to judicial integrity than were others. For example, expanding bystander plaintiffs' opportunities to recover

---

[163] The Ohio Court of Common Pleas for Hamilton County granted the City of Cincinnati's motion to dismiss without prejudice in Case No. A9902369, on May 14, 2003. The claim in the *City of Boston* case, *supra* note 157, was dismissed with prejudice by the Superior Court for Suffolk County in Civil Action No. 99-02590-C on March 27, 2001.

[164] The government recoupment actions and corresponding private individual products liability complaints brought against cigarette manufacturers in the 1990s provide a prime example. This fury of litigation ultimately induced the tobacco industry to adopt the "Master Settlement Agreement," whereby they were obligated to forty-six states to the tune of $206 billion. *See McClendon v. Ga. Dep't of Cmty Health*, 261 F.3d 1252 (11th Cir. 2001) (outlining the terms of the Master Settlement Agreement. For a broader discussion of the Master Settlement Agreement and related claims against tobacco manufacturers, *see* Donald G. Gifford, *supra* note 156.

for mental upset, as dramatic as it seemed at the time, turns out to have been relatively insignificant. It is reassuring that the same court that started that particular trend has subsequently reintroduced appropriate rule structures.[165] But bystander litigation would never have threatened the negligence system with self-destruction in any event. More significant were indications thirty years ago that our courts might begin to review the reasonableness of complex, institutionally implemented designs on an open-ended, "all factors considered" basis. The earlier article referred to appellate decisions pointing in that direction, including examples from the areas of litigation upon which this article focuses. But the conceptual outline in that article tended to obscure, rather than illuminate, the structural elements shared by those examples.

This chapter corrects these analytical shortcomings. Consistent with the earlier analysis, the central problem relates to judicial review of complex designs. Adjudication is incapable of addressing the adequacy of complex, polycentric designs under an open-ended negligence standard. I have described herein techniques by which courts have avoided open-ended design review in each of the major contexts in which the pressures to engage in such review are the greatest. In product design litigation, the primary means of containing the negligence concept is the requirement that plaintiffs prove both the technological feasibility of a safer alternative design and but-for causation. In medical malpractice litigation, in the contexts in which the safer-alternative-design approach is not available, courts rely on professional custom to supply specific standards that render negligence claims adjudicable. And in connection with negligence claims against the government, where neither safer-alternative-design or reliance-on-custom solutions are available, courts and legislatures have built on the traditional principle of sovereign immunity to allow courts to impose tort liability on governmental actors while avoiding open-ended review of complex institutional designs. In each context, courts have adopted an approach unavailable in the others by which to contain the negligence concept and keep it with its proper bounds.

Recent developments in products liability litigation, in which a few courts appear willing to apply the concept of public nuisance to systems of distribution for controversial products such as handguns, demonstrate how relentless are the pressures on judges to exceed the proper bounds of their institutional competence. Thirty years ago, I would have found such developments disturbing. Today, I am confident that our tort system's commitment to containing negligence litigation is sufficiently great that it will take such aberrations in

---

[165] *See* note 34, *supra*, and accompanying text.

stride, making sure that they do not take hold in a manner that would undermine the integrity of the judicial process. Most judges understand that they must not give in to pressures to second-guess the overall reasonableness of complex designs arrived at by other decision-making processes institutionally more suited to the task, whether such designs eminate from regulated product markets, the medical profession, or political entities that deliver governmental services. The methods of judicial containment described in this chapter are embedded so deeply in our tort system, and resonate so strongly with one another and with other areas of our broader system of civil justice, that one may reasonably conclude that the negligence system has arrived at a stable equilibrium. Retreat from the rule of law, if it every really existed, has given way to respect for the rule of law. From the standpoint of adjudicability, the future of our tort system seems secure.

CHAPTER SEVEN

REBUILDING THE CITADEL: PRIVITY, CAUSATION, AND FREEDOM OF CONTRACT

Richard A. Epstein

ABSTRACT. One of the fundamental choices that the law must make in dealing with physical and financial harm is whether to deal with these through the legal commands of the tort law or through the business arrangements of private contracts. The modern direction on this question has tended to displace contractual arrangements, which frequently impose sharp restrictions on the recovery of consequential damages, with tort rules that allow an injured plaintiff to recover the full measure of compensation for physical injury while allowing contractual limitations to control the recovery for financial loss. One theme of this chapter is that the structure of the arrangements in the two cases are sufficiently similar to undercut that distinction in ways that allow contract rules to govern in both settings. A second theme is to examine the decline of the privity rules, which traditionally allowed a purchaser to sue only his or her immediate vendor for various forms of harm. The original justification of privity was an effort to force distant parties, for example, manufacturer and consumer when there is an intervening retailer, to get into privity with each other. But the actual history is otherwise in that the principle of freedom of contract was largely rejected at the same time that the privity limitation was overcome: contracting was not possible even for parties in privity. Ironically, however, the privity limitation continues to play a role in a number of important contexts, environmental and financial losses, where unlimited liability is thought to be potentially ruinous. This chapter defends both those limitations and the contractual efforts to restrict recovery for consequential losses.

I. INTRODUCTION AND OVERVIEW

In this chapter I propose to examine again the relationship between three concepts that hover about the common law: privity, causation, and freedom of contract. The connections here are many and varied, and it is not possible to touch upon them all. In the second section to this chapter, I shall discuss the different senses of privity as it developed in contract and tort law, the former in relation to doctrines of third-party beneficiary

Richard A. Epstein, James Parker Hall Professor of Law, University of Chicago School of Law.

liability and the latter in connection with ideas of causation. Section III will examine the relationship between privity and third-party beneficiary actions, in light of the general rules that limit consequential damages by agreement. The fourth section treats the role of privity in the law of tort. Section V locates and evaluates the contract/tort divide generally, and the fifth section applies that distinction to the particular area of products liability with special reference to the difference between property damages and economic loss. The sixth section then examines the role of privity in connection with alleged cases of fraudulent misrepresentation. A brief conclusion follows.

The overall thesis of this chapter is that the recent denunciations of the privity limitation fail to see its use as a way to allow parties to organize their own affairs when they are in privity, and to force them to enter into key contracts when they are not. The traditional view often attacked manufacturers for seeking to keep themselves aloof from their purchasers, only to refuse to allow them the benefit of any contract when they did create direct relations. The doctrinal issues afoot in this area are many and technical, but we should not blind ourselves to the central debate that is going on in these cases. Whether we deal with physical damages or financial loss, to what extent does, and should, the common law displace the joint expressed intentions of the parties? The modern answer is routinely yes, for structurally the central proposition of the Restatement (Third) of Torts is not its many detailed rules, the definition of defects, and the intricacies of proof. Rather, it is the simple declaration that private agreements cannot displace tort law unless the Restatement explicitly allows it. Restatement (Third) of Torts: Product Liability § 18 flatly states: "Disclaimers and limitations of remedies by product sellers or other distributors, waivers by product purchasers, and other similar contractual exculpations, oral or written, do not bar or reduce otherwise valid products liability claims against sellers or other distributors of new products for harm to persons."

The explanation for this sweeping prohibition is found in comment *a* thereto: "It is presumed that the ordinary product user or consumer lacks sufficient information and bargaining power to execute a fair contractual limitation of rights to recover." The presumption is a legal fiction and the stated reasons offered treat sophisticated consumers and competitive markets as distant illusions. What is really needed here is not a detailed explanation of this justificatory structure but instead a public choice lecture as to how lawyers on both sides of these cases have generated for themselves a steady source of nonwaivable income. Clearly the right answer to the issue raised in § 18 is no. What follows is a partial explanation why.

II. TWO SENSES OF PRIVITY

A. Generally

The concept of privity has often been pronounced dead, but continues to survive in many contexts that deal with economic or financial, as opposed to, physical injury. Drawn from the law of contract, and of ancient origin,[1] this term originally stood for the proposition that a valid agreement only created rights and duties between the parties to it. As such, it represented an implicit limitation of judicial origin on the idea of freedom of contract: if two individuals agreed, and went through all the formalities required in any regular contract, nonetheless they could not provide the right of any third-party beneficiary to sue under the agreement. The promisor could discharge the obligation by payment to the third party. The promisee could sue for specific performance to that party, or damages for himself, which might be turned over to the third party. But the third party could not have any action of his own to enforce a benefit that promisor and promisee alike intended to be his.

This privity limitation is, of course, critical in cases where two parties seek by agreement to impose liabilities on a third, without his consent. That principle remains to this day the pillar of civilization, for one need only pause for a second to imagine the horrific consequences if A could be required to pay money to B and C solely because the latter two have agreed on that outcome. The legal incentives created by these two different applications of privity are wide enough apart to require no detailed explanation of the difference. But because the difference is so great that we must pause to ask why the common and Roman-law traditions both gave the same response to two rules that are so diametrically opposed. One possibility might be found in an ancient, if inarticulate, conviction that the principles of natural reason prohibited the creation of any obligation (which to the Romans mean the full relationship, not just the burden) between strangers. On the basis of this view, the action for the third-party beneficiary would be rejected for the (weak) functional reason of creating an ironclad rule that prevented a third party from having obligations imposed on it by an agreement between strangers. A more likely functional explanation is that it was rejected by judges who were uncertain of the way in which the new rights would develop once the basic cause of action were recognized. But no matter what the explanation, the privity principle, justified or not, represented some limitation on the ideal of freedom of contract.

---

[1] See for a clear articulation of the notion, GAIUS, INSTITUTES OF GAIUS 3–103 (William M. Gordon & O. F. Robinson, trans.) (1988).

The second sense of privity, as it developed in tort, is a recognizable variant of this basic doctrine. Yet far from being anticontractual, this variation purports to implement the principle that the stranger to a contract is not bound by its terms. In its classical formulation, the privity limitation holds that any undertaking by A under contract with B cannot create a duty to compensate C who has been injured by breach of that contract.[2] The individuals who fill these three distinct roles could be wide and varied. A could act as a repairman who makes a promise to fix B's broken wagon. A breach of that promise would not under the privity doctrine allow an action by C who was injured when the defective wagon broke down, no matter whether the action was framed in contract or tort.[3] Similar invocations of privity would allow the presence of a retailer to insulate the manufacturer of a product from a suit by an ultimate consumer, or a manufacturer of a chattel from a suit by an injured worker in the employ its purchaser. In this guise, the privity rule does not count as a limitation on freedom of contract because typically neither A nor B wish to bear the costs of any additional obligations to an injured C, for if they did so, then they could announce their joint intention, at least today when the conceptual objections to third-party beneficiary contracts have vanished. Indeed, in many cases the restrictions on third-party liability are built into the original arrangement, as with clauses that explicitly disclaim the possibility of a third-party suit.[4] Viewed in this context, the privity limitation of tort requires the plaintiff to proceed through a chain of contracts, and thus can be stopped anywhere along the way by a disclaimer of liability, which the principle of freedom of contract allows.

The objection to this tort use of the privity doctrine stems from a different quarter, namely, that it does violence to any coherent theory of causation that traces the consequences of A's given action through at least some actions of one independent third party, B, until it works harm on C.[5] The standard test that asks whether the third person has engaged in some deliberate action that breaks the chain of causation has to be answered in the negative if one could properly describe B as a person who is a "mere conduit" through whom the product flowed instead of a party who added his own labor to transform

---

[2] For discussion, *see* DAVID G. OWEN, M. STUART MADDEN, MARY J. DAVIS, 1 MADDEN & OWEN ON PRODUCTS LIABILITY (3D) § 2.2 (2000), noting the separation of manufacturer from customer by the interposition of retailers in a mass-production society.

[3] *See Winterbottom v. Wright*, 152 Eng. Rep. 402 (Ex. 1842). For a discussion of its evolution, *see* RICHARD A. EPSTEIN, MODERN PRODUCTS LIABILITY LAW 8–24 (1980).

[4] For an example of such a clause, *see*, for example, *Stacy v. Aetna Casualty & Surety Co.*, 484 F.2d 289, 293 (5th Cir. 1973).

[5] *See*, for example, William L. Prosser, *The Assault Upon the Citadel (Strict Liability to the Consumer)*, 69 Yale L. J. 1099 (1960).

the product into something different from what it was when it left the hands of the defendant. On this reading of the situation, C's argument is that he should not be bound by any limitation on liability that is contained in the A–B contract that purports to displace the tort rule that holds all persons liable for the harms caused to strangers, whether we adopt a strict liability or a negligence rule.

If this sketch is correct, then the doctrine of privity seems to be oddly out of place in both contexts in which it is used. It is for this reason that most writers who have addressed the subject take an overtly celebratory attitude toward its demise in both contexts. Indeed the use of the word "citadel" in the title is intended to reflect the strong literary tradition in favor of overrunning the privity limitation. The expression originates with the famous remark of Judge Cardozo in 1931: "The assault on the citadel of privity is proceeding in these days apace."[6] That same title – indeed that same sentence – was taken over by Dean William L. Prosser in his classic 1960 article, which both begins and ends with that sentence, first in quotations and then not.[7] The overwhelming sense of both authors is that the privity limitation is an obstacle to be overcome, not a legal doctrine to be explored. Elsewhere, Prosser called it a "fishbone in the throat of the law,"[8] which of course settles the matter.

In my view, the situation is far more complex. It is useful therefore to consider both the contractual and tortious uses of the doctrine in turn.

III. THIRD-PARTY BENEFICIARIES AND PRIVITY

There are strong, widely accepted, arguments to recognize rights of action in third-party beneficiaries. Why prevent two people from doing what they want to do? In many cases, of course, there is no reason to worry about the precarious legal status of the third-party beneficiary: the high level of contractual performance and the natural alliance between the promisee and the third-party beneficiary make unlikely any slip between the creation of the promise and its routine discharge by performance. There is of course the possibility that the original parties might wish to modify their agreement, and the question will then arise as to whether vesting rights in the third party will block a revision of an agreement by the only two persons who have had any input in it.[9] But here the appropriate response is to allow the

---

[6] *Ultramares Corp. v. Touche*, 174 N.E.2d 441, 445 (N.Y. 1931).

[7] Prosser, *supra* note 5, at 1099, 1148.

[8] William L. Prosser, et al., Handbook of the Law of Torts 681 (5th ed. 1985).

[9] Restatement (Second) of Contracts §§ 133–147 (1981), announcing the classification of creditor, donee and incidental beneficiaries. The difference between the first two classes

original parties to write in an exception that allows for contract modification, and, perhaps, to create some default rule that permits this modification to take place either before discharge of that obligation, or perhaps before the third-party beneficiary acts with knowledge of or reliance on that promise. Even with that limitation, however, the third-party beneficiary action remains useful because it allows the third party to sue after the death of the promisee (as in cases of life insurance policies) when the substitution of the executor or administrator (who should not normally have that right to modify) could interfere with the testamentary scheme of the of the original promisee.

Yet there are clear implicit limitations that should inform the use of this third-party-beneficiary argument. In the standard cases where the doctrine is used, its sole effect is to take a fixed and limited obligation that is owing to one party and allows a second person to sue for that action without the benefit of an assignment from the original promisee. One consequence of this side constraint is that the expected cost of performance does not increase in virtue of the creation of this new right of action, whereas the expected frequency of breach should be reduced because of the cheaper methods of enforce that this system of obligations entails. Once this condition is removed, however, there are good reasons not to extend the right of action in the absence of a very clear and powerful manifestation that the promisor has assumed this new liability. The anticipated risks are too great relevant to the price paid for the goods or services in question. The point here is not simply one of third-party beneficiary law. It is one about the general limitations on damages for breach of contract. Here the central insight is that any damage remedy that is afforded *ex post* must be consistent with the economic coherence of the transaction *ex ante*. The usual modern rendition of the rule in *Hadley v. Baxendale*,[10] which applies a test of reasonable foreseeability, even if narrowly construed, is not fully faithful to that tradition, for it allows the expected loss to be so great that the contract does not maximize the mutual gains to the parties in the *ex ante* position. Rather, the better test, which received more support in the nineteenth century, was that the loss in question was one that had to be assumed by the defendant.[11] In some cases this leads to expectation damages, as when the defendant sells the goods promised to the plaintiff to a third party and pockets the profits: it takes no great leap of imagination to require him to

involve the timing of vesting. The third classification are people who are for various reasons not entitled to sue at all. *Id.* at § 147.

[10] 156 Eng. Rep. 145 (Exch. 1854). For my views on the central ambiguity in the case, *see* Richard A. Epstein, *Beyond Foreseeability: Consequential Damages in the Law of Contract*, 18 J. Legal Stud. 105 (1989).

[11] *British Columbia & V. I. Spar, Lumber, & Saw-Mill Co. v. Nettleship*, 3 L.R.-C.P 499 (1868).

turn over that gain to the innocent party so that the price movements benefit the buyer, as was contemplated under the original agreement.

That same cautionary note applies with renewed force when third-party beneficiaries enter. One possibility is that the both the promisee and the third-party beneficiaries will have rights of action. In some cases, the number of third-party beneficiaries could be more than one, and each of these could claim an independent right of action that is not lost because some other third-party beneficiary has recovered. To prevent this form of piling on, the appropriate test for third-party beneficiary liability requires much more than foresight or even certain knowledge that such losses could result. It demands an unambiguous expression of an intention to be bound to the full extent of the losses in question. The best line of decisions by which to illustrate this point in connection is that represented by the old Cardozo decisions *Glanzer v. Shepard*[12] and *Moch v. Rensselaer Water Co.*[13]

In the former, the defendant, a public weigher, short-weighed some beans. One copy of its certificate was given to the seller of the beans and a second to the buyer, whose identity was evidently known under the circumstances. The buyer relied on the certificate in accordance with the standard practice of the trade, and was allowed an action against the weigher on the ground that his use of the information was the "end and aim of the transaction." As cautious a decision as this one is, it represents a small extension of liability beyond that allowable if the privity limitation were strictly observed. It seems clear in the first instance that the most appropriate single action is a suit by the buyer against the seller for breach of contract: the quantity delivered was less than the quantity promised.

At that point, the next question is whether the seller in turn could have recouped its loss from the public weigher. That action seems odd in the extreme. The whole affair arose because of the weigher's mistake, but is not as though he was responsible for the destruction or loss of any of the beans. If the weight had been correctly announced if the first instance, the seller would have only received from the buyer the same lesser amount that he kept after refunding the overcharge to the buyer. It would be odd for the public weigher to be required to pay money to the seller so that he could emerge from the affair better off than he would have done if the correct weight had been assigned the first time. The usual rules of restitution try to put each party in the position that it would have enjoyed if the initial mistake had never

---

[12] 233 N.Y. 236, 135 N.E. 275 (1922).
[13] 159 N.E. 896 (N.Y. 1928).

been made. Because there was no loss or destruction of any goods along the way, it follows that the right answer leaves the seller bearing the cost of the overcharge. Any contract between the public weigher and the owner of the beans certainly would have left the loss on the owner once the weight loss was discovered.

It follows therefore that this action against the public weigher would not have been allowed at the instance of the buyer if the seller were still in a position to make good on any contractual obligation on matters of quantity. But in this case the seller cannot answer for its loss because it has become insolvent. The case therefore involved the modest extension of the traditional rules of liability by making the public weigher a guarantor of his own accuracy in a ministerial type of situation to a buyer who was innocent of any loss and who was supposed to take no additional steps to verify quantity before accepting the beans. In principle, a full contractual stipulation that said that the buyer took the beans at his own risk should be accepted, for that provision could easily induce him to pay an additional premium to the public weigher, or to engage in some test of his own to avoid the risk. But even if *Glanzer* is wrong, the infrequency of the loss and the upper bound on the risk in question make it possible for this loss to satisfy the usual business condition that we should be able to find in the fee collected a sufficient sum to cover the premium for the loss in question.

That condition was clearly not satisfied in the subsequent decision in *Moch v. Rensselaer Water Co.*, in which the defendant had entered into a contract whereby it agreed to supply pressure for the operation of the city's water mains. The pressure failed when a fire arose, and the house next door burned in consequence of the failure to put out the flames. Actions were brought to recover under the statute, in tort and in contract, and writing for the court, Cardozo rightly rejected all three. The question to be asked again is whether the defendant when it undertook this obligation had received a premium that was sufficient to cover the loss in question, and as Professor Charles Gregory pointed out in pithy fashion over fifty years ago, Cardozo thought the $42.50 that the defendant received from the City to operate the hydrants did not cover insurance for a loss this large.[14] The better institutional arrangement was to allow all parties to secure first-party fire insurance to cover the loss. But even that system requires a clear denial of all actions, whether in tort or contract, for otherwise, the exposure of the defendant for

---

[14] Charles O. Gregory, *Gratuitous Undertakings and the Duty of Care*, 1 DePaul L. Rev. 30, 59–60 (1951).

its actions will be to actions brought by the insurers as subrogees on whatever theory of liability, be it in tort or in contract.

The fear was expressed by Cardozo in a wide range of cases in which he sought to limit the scope of voluntary undertakings. His fear was this: "every one making a promise having the quality of a contract will be under a duty to the promisee by virtue of the promise, but under another duty, apart from contract, to an indefinite number of potential beneficiaries when performance has begun. The assumption of one relation will mean the involuntary assumption of a series of new relations, inescapably hooked together."[15] His most famous rendition of the basic point echoed latter on in *Ultramares v. Touche*, where he cautioned against exposing a defendant "to a liability in an indeterminate amount for an indeterminate time to an indeterminate class."[16] Once again the potential liability is not in proportion to the fees charged for services, so that the denial of liability is a way to force the plaintiff to enter into direct relations with the accountant if it desires any guarantee of the loans that it made to the audited party.[17] In each of these situations, we have come a long way from the simple case where third-party beneficiary actions eliminate the need for an assignment of the right to collect a simple debt. *Moch* is not a case in which the defendant set the plaintiff's property on fire, so as to attract the uncompromising common law rule that holds the defendant strictly liable for harm even if the defendant is "utterly undone" by twenty other actions of the same sort.[18]

It is for this reason that the misfeasance/nonfeasance line looms so large in Cardozo's thought. By taking this line, Cardozo simply means to say that the defendant could not be held liable because it did not do the act which caused the harm, that is, did not set the fire that resulted in the destruction of the property. Accordingly, the case would be quite different if the defendant made a conscious decision to burn down the plaintiff's house in order to save his own, in which case we deal not with the liability for the nonperformance of services, but with the quite distinct question of whether private or public necessity is a defense against and ordinary tort suit for harm caused. But for our purposes, it seems quite clear that third-party beneficiary liability is not an appropriate vehicle to expand tort liability, either for physical injury as in *Moch*, or financial loss, as is *Ultramares*.

---

[15] *See Moch v. Rensselaer Water Co.*, 159 N.E. 896, 898–899 (N.Y. 1928).

[16] *See Ultramares Corp. v. Touche*, 255 N.Y. 170, 174 N.E. 441, 444 (1931).

[17] *See* Victor P. Goldberg, *Accountable Accountants: Is Third-Party Liability Necessary*, 17 J. Legal Stud. 295 (1988).

[18] *Beaulieu v Finglam*, Y. B. 2 Hen. 4, fol 18, pl. 6 (1401) (Thirning, C. J.)

IV. PRIVITY IN TORT

It seems clear that contractual doctrines have only a limited role to play in the expansion of liability for harms that are caused to remote parties. Yet these arguments do not explain without more what should be done in those cases where the traditional concepts of causation indicate that some liability could attach to the defendant for the dangerous conditions so created. In order to deal with these cases, it is necessary to offer some integration of the law of tort and contract: indeed, one reason why the privity limitation in the tort context may well make sense is that, like the third-party beneficiary arrangements, it actually works in aid of the principle of freedom of contract. In order, however, to see whether, and if so how, this might be the case, it is necessary to revisit one of the most difficult questions in legal theory, which is to determine the interaction between tort and contract generally. In this regard, the situation of three parties in two or more sequential contracts (manufacturer-distributor-consumer; manufacturer-employer-employee) occupies a unique position in the legal universe. In one sense, the parties at the two ends of these transactions look like strangers because there is no contract that links them together. But, and here the argument ultimately proves more powerful, the sequence of contracts, made in reference to each other, means that the parties should be treated just as though they were in privity to each other.

The argument in favor of the privity limitation in tort is that it paves the way for the reduction of the stress on the causation rules by altering C's status from stranger to contracting party. To be sure, transaction costs are often so high, as in bystander cases, that it becomes difficult to convert a mixture of contract (between A and B) and tort (A and/or B versus C) into a single comprehensive contractual regime. It is one thing to use default rules to supplement the terms of an agreement that has in fact been formed. But it is quite another to use default terms to form a contract between parties who are in all respects strangers to each other. But the strongest criticism of modern law is not that it refuses to invent contract between strangers, but the converse: it refuses to allow strangers to become trading partners with each other. In some settings the gains from transacting are large enough to encourage A and/or B to seek out C and to create an arrangement. Here, in principle it should be possible to use the now-regnant rule of third-party beneficiaries defensively, so that C agrees with B that he will not bring a direct action for personal injuries or financial losses against A. Of course, the contractual outcome need not be that extreme but could limit that action to certain forms of occasions and impose only certain limitations on the level of recovery for the action that is still allowed. In practice, there is nothing that should prevent

C from entering into a contract with B that defines C's relationship with A: if the third-party beneficiary rule does not work (because of the mutual and reciprocal obligations that are sought between A and C), then so be it. Let B become the agent of either A or C, so that they can be in direct privity with each other.

At this point, the source of uneasiness with the modern rejection of the privity limitation in tort contexts becomes clear. In classical analysis, the elimination of the privity barrier should allow ordinary contracts to govern the relationship between the two end parties. In general those principles rest on the norm of freedom of contract. But under the modern law, the collapse of the privity limitation did not lead to a rise of freedom of contract by treating remote parties on a footing of contractual parties. Rather, it allowed a strong if misguided legal tradition that rejected freedom of contract between certain parties for some kinds of losses to extend to situations of liability where there was no privity at all. If the initial repudiation of contractual freedom between parties in privity was a mistake, then the relaxation of the privity doctrine compounded that error and helped lead to the formation of a set of mandatory legal rules that are not in the *ex ante* interest of either of the parties to the transaction. In order to sort out these relationships it is necessary to say something about the relationship of tort and contract generally.

Treated as a matter of first principle, the distinction between contract and tort liability should be much sharper than it is in modern law. The law of torts has as its chief office the regulation of conduct between strangers and neighbors. In the first case, one deals with actions done by one person that may hurt some other unidentified person either near or far, and the question is what set of rules should be invoked to insure at the very least that every person will take into account the harms that they inflict these other people. In dealing with this issue there is wide agreement that deliberate harms are covered by the tort system subject to a limited set of justifications and excuses, for example, self-defense or defense of property, which we need not deal with here.

There is, alas, a much deeper division of sentiment on the question of what legal standard, and what set of defenses is applicable on the case of accidental harm, which may or may not be attributable to negligence. The root difficulty of course is that as a first approximation parties engaged in "unilateral" accidents (that is those with "passive plaintiffs") will take the same level of care under both a system of negligence and strict liability. Under either liability, the optimal strategy for the defendant is to take only those cost-effective precautions, while allowing some fraction of accidents to occur because they are not, as the expression goes, worth preventing. There looks therefore to be no divergence between private and social cost so that both rules can, in the usual optimistic language of the economist, count as efficient. At this point the inquiry shifts to second-order concerns such as the administrative costs and reliability of the different systems. Within this system one clear tendency in the decided cases has been to gravitate to a strict liability system in those cases where the causal contribution of the injured party is likely to be small, which typically involves those cases of injuries to real property, which after all cannot be moved into harm's way. Yet even here the closeness of the question has led to some odd distinctions, such as the historical insistence, now abandoned, that a strict liability rule govern the harms caused by blasting,[19] but not by concussion.[20] That rule with time gave away to a uniform rule of strict liability in both cases.[21] In most cases, however, as with falling planes or debris, the simple rule, you dropped on my property, cuts through the fog of multiple factors found fashionable in cases of ultrahazardous or unreasonably-dangerous activities, to give a clear outcome to the decided cases.[22] In these passive plaintiff cases, the strict liability rule tends to dominate because no one worries about the possible forms of latent misbehavior that the random landowner has when exposed to a plane crash. The strict liability rule places the loss on a defendant in possession of the dangerous instrumentality at the time of the loss. Even though the law itself looks to the pattern of causation to determine liability, it is very clear that this causation rule, derived out of an intuitive sense of fairness, in virtually all cases satisfies any economic test of placing the liability on the party in the best position to avoid causing the harm in question, which is why the strict liability rule that has proved so controversial in products cases (where the defendant is always out of possession) finds a natural home for various forms of abnormally-dangerous activities.

Now it is also a fair question as to whether the rules of tort do an adequate job in regulating the relationships between strangers and neighbors. In connection with the chance interactions between strangers, they generally do because they parties do not have any particular reason to engage in cooperative activities with each other. But neighbors fall into a different category because their necessary closeness means that they do have the opportunity to enter into fruitful negotiations that could result in a deviation from the simple common-law norm. In fact, the law of nuisance contains a rich number

---

[19] *Hay v. Cohoes*, 2 N.Y. 159, 51 Am. Dec. 279 (1848).
[20] *Booth v. Rome*, W. & O.T.R. Co., 140 N.Y. 267, 35 N.E. 592 (1893).
[21] *Spano v. Perini*, 250 N.E.2d 31 (N.Y. 1969).
[22] *See* RESTATEMENT (SECOND) OF TORTS § 520A (1977).

of rules that work in both directions.[23] Some of these remove liability from
certain nontrespasstory invasions, that is, in connection with low-level nui-
sances that are subject to the live-and-let-live rule. In other cases, as with
lateral support, the rules in question often make actionable noninvasive conduct for the mutual benefit of neighbors. It is a sign of the astuteness of the
common-law categories that few parties contract away ever from these rules.
But it is commonplace, both in covenants between neighbors and more critically, in planned unit developments that start with a single owner, to find the
massive infusion of new duties about décor and aesthetics that work *ex ante*
to the advantage of all. This set of developments shows, I think, the strength
of the maxim that contract should dominate tort because it allows parties to
adjust on the strength of the local knowledge of factors – income, physical
characteristics, technology – that tort law cannot take into account to create
new legal structures worth more to their owners than their holdings under
the original common-law rule.

V. THE TORT/CONTRACT DIVIDE

This approach to nuisance law is capable of generalization to other situations
where contracts might displace the background norms of tort law. If contracts
can refashion planned-unit developments, then they ought to work well for
the sale of goods, the provision of services, or the transfer of information.
One central question therefore inquires as to the legal response to physical
injury to person or property, or financial losses that arise out of consensual
arrangements. Why shouldn't tort law simply operate as default norms capable of displacement by the same techniques used in cases of planned-unit
developments: contracts and public notice? The usual line between tort and
contract states that tort duties are those that bind the world and are therefore
imposed on persons irrespective of consent.[24] The contract rules in contrast
are duties that look to performance of some specific obligation assumed by
consent. The clear implication is that the narrower contractual relationship
permits the creation of rights and obligations that are far more extensive
and articulated than the general "keep off" command applicable in ordinary stranger cases. In many of these contract settings, the "care" obligations

---

[23] For discussion, *see* Richard A. Epstein, *Nuisance Law: Corrective Justice and its Utilitarian
Constraints*, 8 J. Legal Stud. 49 (1979).

[24] *See* OLIVER WENDELL HOLMES, THE COMMON LAW 77 (1881): "The liabilities incurred by
way of contract are more or less expressly fixed by the agreement of the parties concerned,
but those arising from tort are independent of any previous consent of the wrong-doer to
bear the loss occasioned by his act."

require someone to figure out how to take care of some one else, for example, nurse and nurture, and not simply take care to avoid any interactions with them, which is what the negligence standard, if appropriate at all, requires in the typical stranger case.

These specific relationships will doubtless share some common characteristics, as standard-form transactions are easier to execute for similar engagements undertaken in volume. But many classes of cases may have distinctive features that are known to the parties, as a form of Hayekian local knowledge, but not to either judges or regulators. To deal with the first situation, it is important to develop a set of off-the-rack terms to which persons can resort in the event of a dispute when they have left their own engagements incomplete. To deal with the second, it is necessary to devise ways in which individuals can contract away from the default solution when circumstances require. Ideally, we should like the default terms to approximate the efficient solution, that is, maximize the surplus for both parties. But the greater the ease in moving away from the default solution, the less critical it is to get it exactly right.

In dealing with this contract solution, it is critical to remember that as a first approximation the validity of a contract depends on the circumstances of its formation and not the subject matter of its terms. That position certainly applies with great force when we put aside those specialized contracts among producers that count as contracts in restraint of trade and concentrate on the ordinary sales, leases, and service contracts that take place in relatively competitive settings.[25] To someone who follows the Hobbesian injunction that the justice of the contract terms is measured by the "appetite" of the parties, there is no distinction between contract stipulations that deal with products that do not perform up to specifications and those which explode on ordinary use. In each case we can assign to the loss in question a probability of occurrence and an anticipated severity. That expected loss (risk multiplied by severity) is something both sides have to take into account in allocating the loss and in setting the price under which goods are transferred and services rendered. In both cases one has to worry about whether the ordinary conditions of voluntariness are satisfied, which requires some consideration of the problems of fraud, misrepresentation, incompetence, and the like. But if this theory is correct, then in any relationship between the immediate parties, it should make no difference whether the loss in question counts as economic from disappointed expectations, or physical, from harm that results from the

---

[25] For discussion, see Richard A. Epstein, The History and Economic Structure of the Law Merchant, 5 Chicago J. of Int'l Law 1 (2004).

product's breakdown or malfunction. So long as the contract is formed in a proper fashion, and so long as there are no systematic externalities to third parties as in the restraint of trade case, then the usual conditions for advancing social welfare apply. The contract improves the welfare of the parties to it; and their increased wealth increases the opportunities of all third persons. What could be nicer?

VI. PRODUCTS LIABILITY: ECONOMIC LOSS VERSUS PROPERTY DAMAGE

One reason why the privity limitation is so important, however, is that the above-referenced model has no traction whatsoever under the modern law of products liability. Here the view that the content of contractual obligations should be determined by the parties is displaced by some essentialist view of the subject. The most powerful illustration of this confusion is found in the well-known case of *Seely v. White Motors*,[26] in which the spirited and influential debate between Justice Peters and Justice Traynor led both judges to commit different variations of the same error of substituting their own and flawed judgment for that of the parties. The simple facts of the case place the question of fundamental principle in stark relief. The plaintiff was the purchaser of a truck who sued the dealer with whom he was in privity to recover both the purchase price and his lost profits attributable to an uncorrectable bouncing defect in the vehicle. Three years prior to this decision, Traynor had persuaded a unanimous California Court to adopt strict liability for defective products in cases of physical injury even in the absence of privity.[27] In order to achieve that result he ran roughshod over any contractual defenses that the manufacturer might have raised. He did so by sticking physical injury cases into the tort box so that liability was imposed irrespective of consent. Both the privity defense and freedom of contract were dismissed, without argument, in a single sentence:

> Although in these cases strict liability has usually been based on a the theory of an express or implied warranty running from the manufacturer to the plaintiff, the abandonment of the requirement of a contract between them, the recognition that the liability is not assumed by agreement but imposed by law, and the refusal to permit the manufacturer to define the scope of its own responsibility for defective products make clear that the liability is not one governed by the law of contract warranties but by the law of strict liability in tort.[28]

---

[26] 403 P. 2d 145 (Cal. 1965). For general discussion, *see* 2 MADDEN & OWEN ON PRODUCTS LIABILITY, *supra* note 2 at § 17.13.
[27] *Greenman v. Yuba Power Products, Inc.*, 377 P. 2d 897 (Cal. 1962) (internal citations omitted).
[28] *Id.* at 701.

The prospect that contracts could bring remote parties into agreement was dismissed as irrelevant.

In *Seely*, however, Traynor took exactly the opposite tack with respect to financial and business losses that arose out of the sale of a truck. In terms that were equally conclusory, he insisted that financial losses and physical injuries were governed by different principles, and wrote: "[The manufacturer] can be appropriately held liable for physical injuries caused by defects by requiring his goods to match a standard defined in terms of conditions that create unreasonable risks of harm. He cannot be held for the level of performance of his products in the consumer's business unless he agrees that the product was designed to meet the consumer's demands."[29] Apart from the term "appropriately," there is no explanation as to why. Justice Peters strenuously disagreed with the effort to draw this distinction, and insisted in equally conclusory terms that the financial losses should be governed by the same rules that applied to physical injuries, for the perceived imbalances that led to the imposition of tort liability in physical injury cases operated with full force in the context of physical injury, writing: "What is important is not the nature of the damage but the relative roles played by the parties to the purchase contract and the nature of the transaction."[30]

Both judges were wrong, albeit for different reasons. The key element of the Peters position is that it makes explicit what *Henningsen v. Bloomfield Motors*[31] had decided at such great length, which is to say, that in dealing with defective products, the rules of tort, tied to the commission of harm, were allowed to trump the rules of contract. The doctrine of implied warranty, like the doctrine of strict liability, was not an effort to identify the default terms that could be displaced by agreement. It was a prohibition against the use of terms created by the parties to the transaction. In the classical legal tradition, it is consent that dominates over harm, contract over tort. In the modern products liability tradition, the reverse is true. Yet here there has to be some explanation for the displacement of agreements, which is most hard to do in the case of contracts between merchants (as many purchases of trucks surely are). We let the buyer settle on choice of vehicle, price, financing terms, and vehicle and business insurance, at the very least. The mercantile tradition in general has a strong pro–freedom-of-contract orientation. Why not allow the buyer discretion over the financial losses arising out of the vehicle, where there are evident trade-offs between the initial cost of the product and the warranty

[29] *Seely, supra* note 26, 403 P. 2d at 151.
[30] *Id.* at 153.
[31] 161 A.2d 69 (N.J. 1960).

coverage that the dealer or manufacturer supplies? The only justification for the Peters position is a view that buyers of vehicles have a selective competence that lets them make some business decisions well but not all. But if one asks the question, what defect in the process of contract formation infects the decision on what vehicle to buy but not what warranty to obtain, his opinion falls dead silent, and I am aware of nothing in the *Seely* line of cases that cures this gap in the argument. If incompetence or imperfect information infects one part of the transaction, then it infects them all. Why not shut down the voluntary automobile market altogether?

The Traynor argument fares no better. Apart from his standard of "appropriateness" he is unable to answer the Peters argument that there lies no meaningful difference between the capacity to deal with matters of physical injury relative to those of financial loss. Peters drew the wrong inference that the contract was invalid on both counts. Traynor avoids that unpalatable blanket conclusion only by fashioning an untenable distinction between financial losses and physical injuries that allows him to save his decision in *Greenman* without extending it into new areas.

To see why the Traynor distinction is wholly untenable, ask what is it about the two sorts of loss that makes the financial loss amenable to warranty limitations and the physical injury not. It cannot be the magnitude of the losses, for nothing is more common than huge consequential damages that flow from the breach of some business covenant. It is hard to deny that these losses are caused by the breach when their very name suggests the opposite. Yet there is no doubt that virtually every contract that deals with this issue imposes extensive limitations on the potential scope of recovery for this class of losses. I sell you defective film which fails to take a priceless picture at the top of Mount Everest. Yet the entire purpose of most warranty provisions is to remove the coverage for these losses, even as the manufacturer or dealer typically accepts a strict liability with respect to the far more limited obligation to repair or replacement of products damaged in ordinary use – which is the standard form of the contract obligation, as Traynor himself well knew.[32] The general view on this subject, however, uniformly takes the position that "less is worse" with respect to warranties. In writing on the subject, Prosser notes that the reason to switch to strict liability in torts is that "reputable makers" of products supply their warranties "on a large scale, but that almost all such

---

[32] See his concurrence in *Escola v. Coca-Cola Bottling Co.*, 150 P. 2d 436 (Cal. 1944), citing George Bogert and Eli Fink, *Business Practices Regarding Warranties In The Sale Of Goods*, 25 Ill. L. Rev. 400 (1930–1931). For a more modern explanation, *see* George Priest, *A Theory of Consumer Product Warranty*, 90 Yale L. J. 1297 (1980–1981).

warranties limit the remedy to replacement, repair, or return of the purchase price to make good the original bargain, and do not extend to compensation for injuries to the person of the buyer, or to his other property."[33]

Even so, the description of the limitation needs some explanation before it is converted into a condemnation. And it is hard to generate that condemnation when the object of attack is the uniform practice of reputable sellers, including their transactions with reputable and sophisticated buyers. It is a dangerous assumption that standard practices only prove that everyone misunderstands the nature of their own business transactions. Accordingly, the next question that Prosser should have asked himself, but did not, was why reputable parties always stop short of what the strict products liability theory requires? It cannot be because they are shady characters; nor is it remotely plausible that no one by hunch, chance or intuition would offer the expanded warranty protection if it in fact conferred a competitive advantage on its rivals. The result cannot be explained simply by assuming that dominant sellers exploited their superior market position, for then there is no explanation as to why these sellers did not exclude any and all liability for their products, or why small parties did not gain a competitive edge by offering better warranties. Note that such competition can and did take place with warranties on repair or replacement. The 20,000-mile warranty for parts and labor on engines was displaced by the 50,000 warranty, and so on down the line. We see competition altering terms in response to price and quality considerations in the areas where it is allowed to operate. Why then assume that it does not operate with physical or consequential damages as well? What is lacking in the orthodox literature is any functional explanation as to how this middle position is consistently reached.

Such an explanation can be supplied, but ironically only if we assume the kind of rational contracting behavior that is rejected under both the Traynor and Peters analysis. The point of the restrictions with respect to financial loss is twofold.

First, it lowers the variance in outcomes, so as to reduce the element of cross subsidies that exist as between different buyers of the same product. The seller of a good is not an insurance company that can divide risks by adopting an underwriting policy that screens out teenage male drivers from middle-aged female drivers. Rather, to the extent that it operates in mass production markets, it has to pick a single set of terms for all consumers. The right set of terms does not mirror the loss experience of various users, for then the more careful users will be driven away from the product if they

---

[33] Prosser, *supra* note 5, at 1119, *citing* Bogert & Fink, *supra* note 32.

know that their price contains a front-end load to pay for the anticipated loss of other buyers who pose higher risk of loss.[34] It is precisely because these losses are not only foreseen but known that sellers rightly exclude coverage for losses that did not arise out of the normal and proper use of the product in question. And, for the same, reason, manufacturers and retailers will not pool the losses associated with the residential and commercial users of product, given the systematic differences in their intensity of use.

Second, the knowledge of incomplete loss coverage has the desirable effect of inducing downstream users to take precautions against these losses, which, by virtue of being close to the scene of action, they are in a better position to do than either the retailer or manufacturer. Here the difference between the passive plaintiff in the ultra-hazardous activity and the product cases is most salient. The point of these warranty limitations is not to maximize the amount of coverage that is available after the occurrence of the breach. It is to minimize the associated losses that come from the manufacture and use of the particular product, in order to maximize the expected gain from the sale transaction.

It is also worth asking why the usual contract solution does not involve a total exemption from all liability of the retailer or manufacturer. That solution should be commonplace if the purpose of these transactions were simple exploitation of buyers: after all if there is no efficiency rationale for the contractual restrictions, why should the product seller use its enormous bargaining power advantage to wipe out all forms of liability. But the actual practice is not consistent with this diabolic account of market behavior. Product sellers typically stand ready to repair or replace goods in question when warranty coverage still applies. Even that limited warranty imposes real discipline on the seller who provides it. Let profit from the typical sale be 5 percent, and the original refund wipes out all the gains from twenty sales, and probably a good deal more when the loss of good will and the cost of executing those refunds is taken into account. The use of this warranty, limited though it be, carries with it a strong message that the implicit rate of product failure is low. The maker of an inferior product cannot mimic the warranties offered by better suppliers because he does not have the financial wherewithal to answer for the higher rate of claims at the same price. Hence a separating equilibrium emerges in which the sellers of lesser products cannot offer identical terms of those who sell good products, at least at the same price. Thus, the use of the limited warranty on consequential damages for financial loss is ubiquitous

---

[34] *See* Richard A. Epstein, *Products Liability as an Insurance Market*, 14 J. Legal Stud. 645 (1985).

for a good reason. It maximizes value, by minimizing loss, associated with the use contract products.

Now what are the insurance dynamics associated with running a system of insurance for physical losses that are sold with products? Answer: the same. The first issue in all these cases must deal with the variance associated with product use. That point was fully recognized by Judge Sanborn, in *Huset v. J. I. Case & Co*,[35] where he noted that the same product as it worked its way through extensive distribution channels for use by the intelligent and the ignorant, the skillful and the incompetent.[36] One way to stop the problem of cross subsidy is simply to eliminate all products liability at all (which I think that firms should be allowed to do by contract). But that approach carries with it the same danger that is found in the elimination of all warranties in cases of consequential financial loss from the use of defective products. It may not provide buyers with sufficient assurance of product quality. Hence the shift to warranties of repair or replacement that are, however, confined to cases of products that cause damage in normal and proper use – a limitation on strict liability that Justice Traynor sensibly incorporated into his concurrence in *Escola*.[37] These are imposed to respond to the cross subsidies between different classes of users in face of the original seller's inability to separate buyers into risk classes like insurers. Unfortunately, the strong anticontractual bias that dominates the area has eroded this requirement until today various forms of "foreseeable" misuse do not to bar, or in many cases, even diminish, recovery by the product user.[38]

The legal rule itself creates adaptive responses by manufacturers that are harmful to consumer welfare. It is of course possible to design products that might protect persons under these circumstances, by building in limitations on how particular products can be used or by restricting the range of products that are offered to sale. But here again there are powerful costs associated with these strategies that are often overlooked in the urge to maximize *ex post* compensation. For example, in *Barker v. Lull Engineering Co.*,[39] the question

---

[35] 120 F. 865 (8th Cir. 1903).

[36] *Id.* at 867.

[37] *Escola, supra* note 32, 150 P. 2d at 444: "The manufacturer's liability should, of course, be defined in terms of the safety of the product in normal and proper use, and should not extend to injuries that cannot be traced to the product as it reached the market." He makes no effort show how these limitations comport with the extensive rationales that he gives for strict product liability. For discussion, *see* Epstein, *supra* note 3, at 37–48.

[38] *See* Restatement (Third) of Torts: Products Liability § 17 (1998).

[39] 573 P. 2d 443 (Cal. 1978).

was whether a certain loader was defective in design because it could not be stabilized for use on rugged terrain. Justice Tobriner adopted a free-standing cost-benefit analysis to determine whether the product was safe not only for its intended use but also for its foreseeable (mis)use, and then sent the case back for a second trial after the first jury had sensibly found that the loader was neither dangerously nor defectively built. The tip-off in this case that the fault lay with the downstream owner is that the regular operator of the loader refused to report to work that day because he knew that the equipment could not be operated safely on uneven terrain. The substitution of an inexperienced actor, wholly beyond the manufacturer's control, doubtless increased the risk of accident. But once additional safety features are added to this loader, then the products liability law provides the disservice of preventing market segmentation in the downstream market. In a sensible environment, less expensive equipment will be trotted out for safer jobs on level terrain. Expensive equipment will be reserved for riskier operations on uneven terrain. The ideal market would have both sorts of equipment and allow the site operators to decide which equipment will be used.

In my view, market forces should be sufficient to assure that this is done without any special boost from the state. But even if this is wrong, the superior regulatory instrument for ensuring proper behavior relies on some mix of direct safety regulations, worker's compensation laws, and worker prerogatives (often guaranteed by union contracts, for example).[40] Wholly without regard to these institutional alternatives, the usual mantra behind extensive products liability law is that the manufacturer is in a position to "design out" defects from the product, but that is simply wrong when multiple products are needed to discharge the full range of tasks and assignments. Here only downstream selection can make the right choice of product, and the effect of imposing design defect liability in a case like *Barker* is to drive the lower-priced but suitable product from the market. It is yet another case of illicit cross subsidy. The efficient project manager will have to pay additional costs to buy or rent unwanted equipment so that the inefficient project manager will not use simple equipment in places where it is inappropriate. The shift from normal and proper use to foreseeable use thus disrupts the downstream market for no discernible social gain.

The point of this small exercise is to show that the loss allocation issues that arise out of physical injury and consequential damages are, on all relevant insurance dimensions, identical. If so, then there is no theory that supports

---

[40] *See*, for example, the contracts in *Gyerman v. United States Lines Co.*, 498 P. 2d 1043, 1052 (Cal. 1972), and *NLRB v City Disposal Systems, Inc.*, 465 U.S. 822 (1984).

the Traynor position that different legal regimes are appropriate for these two areas. Nor is there support for Peters's proposition that the uniform regime should consist wholly of judge-made rules that either ignore or underestimate the importance of downstream control for loss prevention in both classes of case. The switch from tort to contract in the absence of bargaining imperfections or negative externalities produces systematic social losses.

But it may be said in response, that the cases in question are those that deal with contracts between merchants and not those that deal with ordinary consumers who do not possess the same level of sophistication. To that riposte here there are several clear answers. In the first place, there is nothing in the received law that seeks to differentiate among the various classes of users, based on their ostensible level of bargaining power. Union workers, for example, have the protection of collective bargaining agreements, which defenders of extended products liability typically regard as a safeguard against contractual disadvantage. But the judicial decisions make no effort to cut back on the scope of potential liability in light of this argued independent source of protection against contractual exploitation. Nor is it ironic for a determined foe of the entire structure of collective bargaining in the United States and elsewhere to make this point. I do not believe that consumers are powerless to deal with manufacturers and retailers on matters of safety any more than they are helpless to deal with them on matters of price. The refusal to deal is a powerful threat that any seller who cares to remain in business has to take into account. But my point rather is this: those who think that workers and consumers are powerless to protect themselves against various kinds of risk are never satisfied with any single device to overcome that claimed gap. They will first demand the union protection, which does many other things, and then disregard what they treat as an additional layer of protection to invalidate any sensible restrictions that might be found in contracts of sale.

This first point then leads to a second. Do we see any variation in the terms of contractual warranties as a function of the apparent strength and sophistication of the bargaining parties? Here in a competitive industry the standard prediction is that these forms of discrimination across users cannot survive. Buyers will flock to the better alternatives. And that is pretty much what is observed today. The strongest protection for the ignorant consumer does not lie in the law. It lies in asking a knowledgeable friend to help with a purchase, or insisting that the dealer provide you with a nondiscrimination guarantee: did you offer me the same product on the same terms that you offered to a sophisticated buyer of the product in question? This ability to free ride, in ways that make the skillful folks feel good about themselves, is a powerful antidote to the charges of consumer, or worker, ignorance. Once again, there is no reason to prefer the tort to the contract solution, especially when the solutions crafted by the judges show little awareness of the relevant variables that influence the optimal contractual design.

One common characteristic of a distinction without traction is that it gives rise to a set of borderline cases that themselves defy ordinary good sense. Just that problem arises in the effort to police the line between disappointed contractual expectations and physical damage. The test cases on this issue all resolve around the question of which, if any, kinds of property damage are covered by the "economic loss" exception to the general products liability rule. In this regard, the dominant line of decision appears to be that tort actions are not allowed for the damage or destruction of the property that is subject to the contract of sale, but is allowed with respect to "other property" that is damaged or destroyed. For example, in *East River Steamship Corp. v. Transamerica Delaval, Inc.*,[41] the Supreme Court conducted an exhaustive review of the issue under admiralty law, and then solemnly refused to allow a tort action against the manufacturer of turbine engines that malfunctioned after they were installed into oil-transporting supertankers. But the Court shifted ground in *Saratoga Fishing Co. v. J. M. Martinac & Co.*,[42] when it treated the loss of "extra equipment (a skiff, a fishing net, spare parts) added by the initial user after the first sale and then resold as part of the ship" as "other property" for which an action in tort was appropriate. Here there is the obvious difference that the new property was not part of the original package, but it hardly takes any ingenuity for the parties to anticipate that these additions will be made in the ordinary course of business. The original contract could have dealt with losses to both present and future property, much in the same way that loan agreements can specify whether a security interest attaches to after-acquired property. Whether we speak of loans or losses, the same parties are involved in the negotiation regarding both sorts of property, the original goods and the add-ons. If both merchants have commercial competence with respect to the initial sale, it is hard to see what novel form of market failure justifies the need for tort intervention in the aftermarket. Nor does it matter in these cases whether the original property was retained or resold by the initial purchaser. It is commonplace in all these commercial arrangements to provide for the transfer of insurance or the purchase of new insurance to cover the risks in question. Here, as noted earlier, all the parties in the chain of contracts are linked to each other by contract, so that there is no reason to invoke the tort analogy to cover the basic situation.

[41]   476 U.S. 858 (1986).
[42]   520 U.S. 875 (1997).

Other cases again responsibly seek to police the dynamics of an unprincipled line.[43] The subject, moreover, has not generated any enlightenment in
the Third Restatement, which follows the majority position by limiting the
coverage of the Restatement to "harms to persons or property,"[44] which is
thereafter defined in § 21 to include only "the plaintiff's property other than
the defective product itself." The analysis of the issue is not advanced one
whit, for the Third Restatement rests itself with the observation that cases of
" 'pure economic loss' are more appropriately assigned to contract law and
the remedies set forth in Articles 2 and 2A of the Uniform Commercial Code.
When the UCC governs a claim, its provisions regarding such issues as statutes
of limitation, privity, notice of claim, and disclaimer ordinarily govern the
litigation."[45] The principles can apply across the board.

VII. PRIVITY IN MISREPRESENTATION CASES

In order to understand the role of privity in tort law generally, it is necessary
to explore its relationship not only to the cases of physical damages and
consequential losses that arise out of the use of defective products. Another
class of related cases involves the question of whether physical damage or
financial loss could come out of various forms of misrepresentation. Thus,
if a defendant motions to the plaintiff that it is safe to walk in a particular
direction, that action will lead to potential loss for consequential damages
if the defendant knows that the plaintiff is sure to be injured if he follows
those instructions. The misrepresentation cases in physical injury settings
are frequently folded into the defective product cases. But the same is not
necessarily true when we deal with other kinds of financial losses that are
rightly attributable to misrepresentations or other forms of conduct that do
not involve the supply of defective goods.

---

[43] See 2-J Corporation v. Tice, 126 F.3d 539, 544 (3d Cir. 1997), in which the court, in predicting
Pennsylvania law, held that the economic-loss doctrine did not prevent the plaintiff from
recovering for the goods that were damaged when defendant's warehouse collapsed: "If the
fishing equipment foreseeably added to the ship by the initial user in *Saratoga Fishing* did
not become a part of the 'product itself,' it necessarily follows that the inventory foreseeably
stored by the initial user in the warehouse here did not become part of the warehouse
itself." And so it is. But the parties can surely contract over these issues if allowed to do so.
   With 2-J Corporation, contrast *Seal-Land Service, Inc. v. General Electric Co.*, 134 F.3d 149
(3rd Cir. 1998), in which defective replacement GE engine rods installed in a GE engine were
treated as part of the "integrated" original product, since purchasers of the original product
were "aware" of the need for routine replacements.

[44] RESTATEMENT (THIRD) OF TORTS: PRODUCTS LIABILITY § 1 (1998).

[45] RESTATEMENT (THIRD) OF TORTS: PRODUCTS LIABILITY § 21 (c) & cmt. a.

This cautious attitude toward misrepresentation has been already noted in connection with *Ultramares*.[46] The cases that come after that decision have often been uneasy about the hard line that it took against the negligence liability of accountants to third parties, even though they recognize that open liability could lead to the elimination of auditor's services altogether if the risk becomes so large that no client is willing to cover that cost *ex ante*. But even here the decisions tend to show a certain commendable caution in the area. *Hedley, Byrne & Co. Ltd. v. Heller & Partners Ltd.*,[47] a famous and impassioned decision of Lord Devlin, attacked with great elegance the distinction between physical injury and financial loss and announced that the principle of negligence should apply with equal force to both areas. But the general disquisition completed, Devlin then meekly announced that no liability was appropriate in the particular case because the contract under which the information was provided contained an exemption clause against the potential liability, especially in gratuitous transactions,[48] where the want of consideration is a sensible signal that the recipient has assumed the risk of error, negligent or not. The U.S. cases follow the same general hostility to freedom of contract but then carry over to the financial loss cases the same "end and purpose" of the transaction language that proved so critical in the more limited context of *Glanzer*.[49]

The area is filled with pitfalls, which are illustrated by the recent run of cases that address the question of whether a tobacco company can be liable for its alleged fraud not only to the smokers who bought their products but also to the health plans that insured these smokers. The decision of *Laborers Local 17 Health and Benefit Fund v. Philip Morris, Inc.*[50] is one of the many that flatly reject the potential liability of tobacco companies.[51] In these cases,

---

[46] *See* note 16, *supra*.

[47] 1964 App. Cas. 465, 516–517 [H.L. 1963].

[48] *Id.*

[49] *Supra*, note 12. *See Walpert, Smullian & Blumenthal, P. A. v. Katz*, 762 A.2d 582, 597 (Md. 2000), which sets out the three lines of authority had grown up in the area:

> First [a] significant number follow the *Ultramares* formulation, under which a third party will be denied relief for an auditor's negligence in the absence of a relationship with the auditor that constitutes privity or that is equivalent to privity. The majority of jurisdictions, however, following the RESTATEMENT approach: liability is imposed on suppliers of commercial information to third parties who are actually foreseen as the users of the information for a particular purpose. The third view, followed by a few jurisdictions, allows third parties to recover for auditor negligence when their reliance on the audit report was reasonably foreseeable by the auditor.

> *Id.* (internal citations omitted).

[50] 191 F.3d 229 (2nd Cir. 1999).

[51] For a more recent rundown on the total, *see Service Employees International Union Health and Welfare Fund v. Philip Morris, Inc.*, 249 F.3d 1068, 1072 n.2 (D.C. Cir. 2001), noting that *Laborer's Local 17* represents the law in at least seven circuits.

the plaintiff's basic argument is that the tobacco companies worked a double deception in their advertisement campaigns. First, they led smokers to believe that cigarettes were far safer than they otherwise were, and thus induced them to purchase cigarettes that contributed to their various illnesses. The second claim is that the deception reached the health plans, which were also deceived and thus did not take prompt steps to start campaigns that would have induced covered workers and their families to reduce the level of tobacco consumption.

In dealing with these cases, there is no privity between the cigarette companies and the individual smokers, given that the tobacco was sold to them by third parties. Another privity layer separates the tobacco companies from the health plans that supply these individuals coverage. But in analyzing the potential liability to the health plans, the court in *Laborer's Local 17* treated the representations to the individual smokers as though the advertisements and the representations therein created a direct relationship with them, and assumed that if the elements of ordinary fraud could be proved, then these causes of action would lie. That assumption gives rise to a big "if" because of the potent defenses that are available to the tobacco companies under standard law. Here the critical element for these purposes is the level of reliance that is placed on any statement, express or implied, that tobacco products are healthy. It is possible (and here I speak as a former consultant to Philip Morris who did not work on the health-plan cases), that the defense against direct liability to smokers rests on the ability to show assumption of risk of dangerous conditions in two ways: First, the huge amount of public and common knowledge that cigarettes (a.k.a. "coffin nails") were dangerous for smoking long predated the Surgeon General's warnings. Second, the constant reminders that smokers receive in every day life about the risks in smoking from family, friends, physicians, the media, and companies that sell programs that allow people to quit smoking. In most cases, the one-two combination of this objective and subjective evidence makes it painfully clear that the hazards in question were known both generally and in the particular case. My own brief autobiographical contribution to this story was our successful family effort to make my father (a radiologist, no less) quit smoking back in the early 1950s when I was about eight years old. We knew exactly what was at stake. The Restatement (Second) followed this line of thought when it held that tobacco companies could be liable for contaminants in tobacco, but not for the dangerous properties inherent in the substance itself.[52] In effect the legal

---

[52] RESTATEMENT (SECOND) OF TORTS § 402A cmt i. "Good tobacco is not unreasonably dangerous because the effects of smoking may be harmful; but tobacco containing something like marijuana may be unreasonably dangerous." The generic nature of the claim explains

system created a conclusive assumption of risk defense that obviated the need for a particularized proof of no liability in each individual case. Amen.

For these purposes, however, we can assume that these objections have been overcome by one legal maneuver. The question then is what should be done for the health plans that claim additional costs for treating smoke-related ailments. One course is to ignore the doctrine of fraud altogether and to rely on contractual arguments of subrogation, which essentially allow the health plans to stand in the shoes of the original smokers as their subrogees. But the general rule here is that subrogees take subject to defenses available against their subrogors, so that these actions for the medical piece of the overall tort claim will do no better than the smoker's original claim, so that it will fail if the claim of the original smoker fails as well. The basic point here is not a tobacco-specific rule but one that lines up with the general principle that all assignees take subject to equities, that is defenses, that are available to the promisor if the action were brought by the assignor-promisee. This doctrine in turn is just an application of the more general principle that no contract between two persons can impose unwanted obligations on the third, discussed at the opening of this chapter.

The point of the fraud claim therefore is to allow a direct action, and the question that was put in *Laborers Local 17* is whether that claim could survive either under common law principles or under RICO, which incorporates in its operative provisions the traditional common-law limitations on proximate cause, which were important in determining whether the plaintiff had standing to sue.[53] In dealing with this issue, *Laborers Local 17* took the now standard (but wholly misguided) approach that treats the doctrine of proximate cause as though it is a necessary limitation on the philosophical account of causation that allows the cause of any individual act to stretch back

---

why individual smokers were not allowed to make claims that they were ignorant of what everyone else knew. Thus, cmt. i for that reason ties in the idea of "unreasonably dangerous" (on which the basic provision of § 402A rests) to the ordinary consumer. "The article sold must be dangerous to an extent beyond that which would be contemplated by the ordinary consumer who purchases it, with the ordinary knowledge common to the community as to its characteristics." *Id.*

[53] The operative provision of RICO (the Racketeering Influenced and Corrupt Organizations Act) reads:

Any person injured in his business or property by reason of a violation of section 1962 of this chapter may sue therefore in any appropriate United States district court and shall recover threefold the damages he sustains and the cost of the suit, including a reasonable attorney's fee.

18 U.S.C. § 1964(c) (1994). *See also Holmes v. Securities Investor Protection Corp.*, 503 U.S. 258, 268 (1992), in which the Supreme Court held that for a plaintiff to maintain an action under RICO required "a showing that the defendant's violation not only was a 'but for' cause of his injury, but was the proximate cause as well."

to the dawn of time. So heroic a notion means that each of billions of events is a cause of the billions of consequences, both good and bad, that are the stuff of everyday life. No one in ordinary talk begins at the dawn of civilization and works their way forward to the present. Rather, in a much more sensible fashion, they start with the harm and look back to the nearest event that could be regarded as its cause, which is why the term "proximate cause" continues to have resonance to this very day. The difficulties in this matter arise when the immediate act has been constrained in some fashion by some earlier act, so that it is possible in principle at least to argue that smokers were addicted to tobacco or otherwise compelled to smoke. But beyond this it is hard to think of how much further down the chain one would want to go beyond the companies that issued the advertisements to the smokers, assuming that addiction overruns the defense of assumption of risk, a point that need not be argued here.

Within this framework, the claim of the health plans can be put in a positive way. Suppose that the tobacco companies had come to the health plans *en masse* and had said to them, do not worry about the adverse effects of tobacco. We want to create a market for our product and will therefore offer to compensate you for additional costs that you incur by insuring individuals who use our products. Assume further that the tobacco companies knew that their statements were false and they hoped to induce reliance of the health plans to increase their own direct sales to consumers. This case does not look any different in its particulars from the great case of *Pasley v. Freeman*,[54] where the gist of the complaint was that the deception of the defendant led the plaintiff to lend money to a third person who, to the defendant's knowledge, was not a credit-worthy individual. There seems to be no problem with the remoteness of damages if this claim were correct.

One reason we know this to be the case is that the proximate cause limitation in these indirect suits is often stated as a requirement of standing. But it is a mistake to collapse notions of standing into the principle of proximate causation. Quite the opposite, there would be no need for a distinct doctrine of standing at all if the doctrine of proximate cause cut out all the claims that are covered under standing rules. But here, as I have argued elsewhere, the doctrine of standing is needed precisely because the usual limitation of proximate cause does not cut off the claims at issue.[55] Thus, suppose that a defendant pollutes waters in a public river, which results in the loss of a catch

---

[54] 100 Eng. Rep. 450 (K.B. 1789).

[55] For an extensive development of this theme, *see* Richard A. Epstein, *Standing and Spending – The Role of Legal and Equitable Principles*, 4 Chap. L. Rev. 1 (2001). For a shorter account, *see* Richard A. Epstein, *Standing in Law & Equity: A Defense of Citizen and Taxpayer Suits*, 6 GREEN BAG 2d 17 (2002).

to fishermen in the area. These individuals have standing, but what about the claims of the packinghouses that lose business in consequence of the failed catch? Generally these remote complainants are denied recovery, but it cannot be on the standard restrictive grounds that points to some deliberate third-party act or natural event that severs causal connection.[56] There is a continuous and uniform flow in these cases. But standing is invoked because once the inner circle of plaintiffs is allowed to sue, the social costs of additional suits seem hardly justified. Powerful deterrence is already in place; a direct system of fines can be added to the mix, so that the remote claims are cut out by rules that resemble the privity limitations. That notion is evident in the tobacco cases and other RICO suits, which is why standing and privity come so close together in this context. The whole point of standing is that some limitation on second-tier suits is thought desirable when the proximate causation doctrine (with which they are easily conflated) does not bar recovery.

But now let us back off and ask how the actual pattern of behavior differed in these health-plan cases. There was no specific request made by any tobacco company to any health plan to assume the loss in question. The sources of information about the generic risks of tobacco are widespread in light of the endless rounds of exposés of its dangers in ordinary conditions. The health plans had the opportunity to adjust their premiums to take into account the characteristics of the insured population, including their propensity to use tobacco and the harms that it causes. If the health plans had come to the tobacco companies and had asked for an express warranty to cover these particular costs, we know without further inquiry what the indignant response would have been: how much are you prepared to pay for such an extravagant level of protection? And it would quickly become clear that no warranty provision at all would make economic sense from the *ex ante* position. The fraud case becomes an elaborate effort after the fact to get something for nothing, which is why these claims have fared so poorly in the courts.

The actual pattern of argument here assumes of course that the false misrepresentations are actionable by smokers, but not by health plans, on the ground that the former should be treated as "direct" and the latter as "indirect." But the real logic lies in the answer to this question: if we got all the relevant parties, manufacturers, distributors, retailers, consumers, employers, and health plans in a single room, what is the likelihood that any comprehensive contract among them would have held the tobacco companies liable for the potential losses of the health plans? The answer is none. The tobacco companies would

---

[56] For the lineup of decisions, *see Pruitt v. Allied Chemical Corp.*, 523 F. Supp. 975 (E.D. Va. 1981).

have said "make your own inquiries into the safety of tobacco, but you neither have nor will have warranties, express or implied, from us." The absence of privity means that we have to rely on sequential contracts. Here there is little question that no manufacturer would assume huge tort liabilities for its products in any direct contract with distributors or retailers. These parties in turn would have disclaimed all liability from consumers, both by agreement and public notice, with reference to, interalia, if the background rules of tort, such as those found in comment i of Section 402A. The deals between the consumers and the employers could be a bit more complex, because the latter might classify its employees according to whether they smoke, and if so, charge differential premiums for the work in question. At this point the health plans could have recovered some of the additional costs of smoking, but there is no way they could climb back to the contractual claims to hold the manufacturer responsible for these risks.

The court in *Laborers Local 17* did not go the contractual route, but it did stress at length the complications that would be required to make the chain of causation go this extra link. In so doing it made arguments congenial to standing but not to proximate cause, properly understood. The health costs of any population are hard to determine in general, and figuring out which costs are attributable to smoking and which to other factors is not an easy task even under the best of circumstances. Why therefore allow the action when the allocations are sure to be wrong, especially as the overall level of risk is something that can be taken into account in setting the premiums payable by the health plans and the employees? The point here is that we do not need the action at the second level because we have the action at the first, which is why *Laborers Local 17* and similar cases refer to the ability of individual smokers to maintain their own tort actions. That observation is surely correct under the current system, which allows smokers to sue, but in a world with full contractual respect, the direct action by smokers would be barred by a full barrage of contractual limitations on liability. In this regard, the use of the privity doctrine represents a standing-like compromise that allows direct users to escape contractual limitations that are still respected in the much more difficult cases that arise when remote parties seek to bring the action. The privity limitation still lives, at least after a fashion.

The position taken in *Laborers Local 17* often proves fragile because the case does not represent an effort to show the dominance of contractual conceptions over tortious ones. It takes therefore only a little ingenuity for a determined judge to overcome these limitations – a description that surely applies to Judge Guido Calabresi. In *Desiano v. Warner-Lambert Co.*,[57] (in

---

[57] 326 F.3d 339, 349–50 (2d Cir. 2003).

which I worked on the ill-fated defense of Warner-Lambert), the plaintiff class consisted of a group of health benefit plans (HBPs) that had paid for their members to purchase Rezulin, which had been approved by the FDA for the treatment of Type II (adult onset) Diabetes. The drug, which had gone through an arduous and controversial FDA approval process, remained on the market from February 1997 to March 2000, when it was withdrawn from the market after reports of a series of deaths from liver complications. The complaint alleged that the FDA had approved the drug and kept it on the market as long as it did only because the defendant had lied to the FDA in the materials it submitted, both to obtain the initial approval and to keep it on the market. As a matter of general tort theory, parties who are injured under these circumstances normally have an action against the manufacturer based on the fraud in question, which would negate the force of any contractual limitations otherwise embodied in the sale.

In this case, however, the class action assumed a novel twist, for the HBPS sought to recover only for their costs in paying the prescriptions for those individuals who had taken it successfully. The HBPs demanded a refund under New Jersey's Consumer Fraud Act on the ground that the defendant's fraud had induced them to buy the "Defendants' product, rather than available cheaper alternatives, had they not been misled by Defendants' misrepresentations." The district court refused to allow the action on the authority of *Holmes* and *Laborer's Local 17* on the ground that the proper measure of recovery would turn on the effect of the drug on each patient for whom it was prescribed. Calabresi first noted that the requirements for proximate causation could be broader under New Jersey law than they were under RICO, and that *Holmes* and *Laborers Local 17* were distinguishable:

> Defendants argue, however, that "if Rezulin had been effective in all diabetic patients without any side effects, plaintiffs would have no basis for a claim." But it is easy to see how Defendants' reasoning is flawed. Consider, for example, a hypothetical in which a defendant drug company markets a "new," much more expensive drug claiming it is a great advancement (safer, more effective, etc. than metformin – the standard diabetes drug) when in fact the company is simply replicating the metformin formula and putting a new label on it. In other words, the only difference between metformin and the "new" drug is the new name and the higher prescription price (paid almost entirely by the insurance company). In that case, the "new drug" would be exactly as safe and effective as metformin, and thus there could be no injury to any of the insurance company's insured. Nevertheless, the insurance companies would be able to claim – precisely as they do here – that the defendants engaged in a scheme to defraud it, and that the company suffered direct economic losses as a result.

This counterexample shows the soundness of the rule in *Laborer's Local 17*, not its defect. The point here is not that a claim of this sort is a practical impossibility in light of comprehensive review of drug products by ordinary physicians, hospitals, and the FDA. Rather, it is because there would be no need whatsoever to override the privity limitation in a case of this sort. If indeed the products are identical, then the individual buyers clearly have a right to recover the excess paid for the product in question, for by assumption there is no offset against the increased purchase price for superior performance that the drug provided in the individual case. That recovery, however, need not remain with the individual purchaser if the insurance companies had paid for the excess. They could recover that sum from the individuals after they (the consumers) had recovered from Warner-Lambert. Alternatively, the HBPs could rely on their subrogation clause to initiate a quasi-class action to recover that excess. That new action would save in transaction costs. It would be of course subject to the general rule that subrogees take subject to defenses available against the subrogors. But in this case, there is no such defense in light of the clear swindle that was supposed in the hypothetical. The subrogation rules work so well that there is simply no reason to plumb the depths of the privity limitation or the associated standing rules in this connection.

That argument, however, wholly unravels in light of the evident difference in chemical compound and operative mechanism. Here, it is a sad truth of medical advances that potent drugs that do wonders for some patients can harm or maim others whose internal body chemistry proves vulnerable to the treatment. It is therefore commonplace to indicate that many treatments (e.g., Lipitor) should be taken only with various liver function and blood tests on a six-month cycle. But for some people the use of the high-risk drugs yields a high rate of return, and the aggregate decision of the FDA to remove any product from the market should not be seen as an unalloyed good if the residual set of choices leaves some portion of drug users worse off than they were before.

These basic truths play havoc with the effort to allow the HBPs to sue for their refund. The first point is that many of their patients were left better off with Rezulin than they were without it, so that it is no longer possible to posit the simple overcharge in Judge Calabresi's hypothetical. Let the overcharge be $1,000 for a given patient, and the net benefits of the Rezulin relative to metformin could exceed that total by many fold. Is it possible in any direct action by these customers that they would pay a premium for their drugs in order to obtain a refund in the cases that its use proved successful? In any event, the baseline for an alternative was not the return to metformin, for the removal of Rezulin from the market was brought on by the introduction of Avadia or Actos, both drugs that operated in a fashion similar to Rezulin. Here it is an open question whether these two drugs so dominated Rezulin so as to justify a restriction in consumer choice: even if these drugs had lower toxicities, they could have had lower rates of success for some customers, so that new warnings or labels, not recalls, become appropriate. But no matter how one slices the case, the individual customer who prospered from Rezulin should not receive a refund. Nor should the HBP that paid for the drug and may well have benefitted from the increased health of its patient population. The logic of the privity limitation from *Holmes* and *Laborer's Local 17* carries over with full force to the instant situation. Where the direct action is barred for good and sufficient reasons, then the indirect action, with its own set of complexities, should not be allowed either. There is no chance at all that Warner-Lambert would have agreed to a refund in these circumstances if it had been in privity with the HBPs. And there is no reason to introduce a new action for remote plaintiffs that results in massive over-deterrence. Even if one is suspicious of freedom of contract in these cases, a mix of regulatory actions and suits by injured parties is sufficient onto the day.

VIII. CONCLUSION

The question of privity and the associated issue of standing are complex doctrines that continue to have a place in the modern world just as they did in the nineteenth century. In principle, the ideal way to allocate losses among multiple parties is through a single simultaneous contract or through a set of sequential contracts. If that procedure is allowed to run its course, the usual solution will show a strong restriction on consequential damages, whether in the form of physical injuries or financial losses, of the original seller to both immediate and remote parties. The doctrine of freedom of contract has as one of its chief benefits the ability to make clear these limits on consequential damages, which in turn increase the ability to bring needed but risky products to the market as quickly as possible. The privity limitation prevents the remote users of the product from doing an end run around these contractual limitations, so that the basic controls against consequential damages are fully respected.

Modern decisional law adopts a schizophrenic attitude toward freedom of contract. Where it is allowed, as with economic losses, the usual efficient pattern of disclaimers applies. But where freedom of contract is rejected, the law still has to face the question of what to put in its place. The doctrine of full tort damages looks sustainable in cases of physician malpractice injuries, but much less so in cases of financial loss, so in those contexts the privity limitation serves as a crude compromise that cuts out the remote claims while allowing those of more immediate parties. The pattern here is halting and uncertain, and the analysis undertaken here could be extended to other contexts. But the basic point remains clear. The old concerns with massive liabilities are still not eliminated, and the privity limitation becomes the tool that, for all its limitations, is used to knock out broad classes of claims that should never see the light of day.

CHAPTER EIGHT

CONTROLLING THE FUTURE OF THE COMMON LAW BY RESTATEMENT

Jane Stapleton

ABSTRACT. This chapter considers, from the perspective of future users, an intriguing aspect of the architecture that the Reporters of the American Law Institute[1] have chosen for the current Draft Restatement (Third) of Torts: Liability for Physical Harm.[2] In restating legal principles currently applied in the United States, the ALI also must preserve the constitutionally vital phenomenon of judicial lawmaking by which the common law will continue to develop in the future. It is faced with stark political choices. The first concerns how welcoming a restatement text is to, say, the future expansion of liability beyond the current case law precedents. The second concerns what is the appropriate future balance of lawmaking power among trial judge, jury, and appellate court. These choices are the "ghosts at the feast" of restatement. This chapter argues that the otherwise puzzling, polarized treatment of the duty of care within the architecture of the Draft Restatement reflects choices made by the Reporters as to how much future common law development there should be and what is the most appropriate institutional location for it to take place. A consideration of those choices highlights a deep fracture in United States tort law between the loud rhetoric in support of jury decision making and the many, typically covert, maneuvers made to prevent issues from reaching the jury.

I. MAKING THE COMMON LAW: A VITAL CONSTITUTIONAL "SECRET" OF COMMON-LAW LEGAL SYSTEMS

Within the constitutional arrangements of any common-law jurisdiction, courts have a crucial lawmaking function that necessarily achieves results

---

[1] Hereafter "ALI" or "Institute."

[2] The parts relevant here being: THE RESTATEMENT (THIRD) OF TORTS: LIABILITY FOR PHYSICAL HARM: BASIC PRINCIPLES (Tentative Draft No. 2, March 25, 2002) (hereafter "TD No. 2"); THE RESTATEMENT (THIRD) OF TORTS: LIABILITY FOR PHYSICAL HARM: BASIC PRINCIPLES (Tentative Draft No. 3, April 7, 2003) (hereafter "TD No. 3"); THE RESTATEMENT (THIRD) OF TORTS: LIABILITY FOR PHYSICAL HARM: BASIC PRINCIPLES (Tentative Draft No. 4, April 1, 2004) (hereafter "TD No. 4").

Jane Stapleton, Ernest E. Smith Professor, School of Law, University of Texas; Professor, Australian National University. I would like to thank Richard W. Wright and John C. P. Goldberg for their characteristically generous help with references.

that also could have been achieved by the legislature. Walter Bagehot famously stated that "the efficient secret of the English Constitution may be described as the close union . . . of the executive and legislative powers" in the Cabinet.[3] Yet even more widely, throughout the common-law world, there is an equally vital "secret" of constitutional arrangements: the close union of the judicial and legislative powers in the courts. Our common-law legal systems embrace a form of the separation of powers doctrine that accommodates this substantial lawmaking capacity. Since the advent of legal realism in the United States, this role of the courts in constructing the common law has not been a mystery: realism "let daylight in on magic."[4]

That courts make law is nowhere more obvious than tort law in common law systems, especially in that most open-textured and therefore voracious tort: negligence. Those very few remaining critics of "the conscious making of new law by radical judicial destruction of the old"[5] have a problem in explaining why it is that the most admired common-law tort judgments are those characterized by realism and creativity such as that in *MacPherson v. Buick Motors.*[6] If we envisage the common law as a great sculptured garden which is being built up by usually incremental contributions from generations of cases, *MacPherson* shows that, for the garden to represent justice better, sometimes an accretion such as the privity fallacy must be lopped off. We only need to consider the uproar that would follow if courts were to reverse *MacPherson* and reinstate the privity fallacy to appreciate the radical extent of the legal entitlement that *MacPherson* created by judicial activism and the depth of approval that this redistributive act has evoked.

Yet, although the lawmaking role of courts in relation to the common law is openly accepted in the United States, it does not operate by the same arrangements we see in other common-law systems. Within the nation of the United States there is a multiplicity of tort-law jurisdictions and, therefore, a diverse range of persuasive precedents by which a court may be influenced. Within any one state jurisdiction, lower courts are subjected to weaker control by appellate courts, thanks in great part to the reverence paid to that institutional buffer or "black-box," the jury. The result is that, in the United States, courts enjoy greater freedom from the shackles of precedent, and therefore greater freedom to make law than that enjoyed by courts in other common

---

[3] WALTER BAGEHOT, THE ENGLISH CONSTITUTION 65 (1963).

[4] Contrast the view of Bagehot on the constitutional role of the monarchy: "Its mystery is its life. We must not let daylight in on magic" *Id.* at 100.

[5] *See*, for example, Dyson Heydon, *Judicial Activism and the Death of the Rule of Law*, 47 Quadrant 9, 17 (2003).

[6] *MacPherson v. Buick Motor Co.*, 217 N.Y. 382, 111 N.E. 1050 (1916).

law systems.[7] Any restatement project must confront and resolve questions of how to preserve yet adequately confine such freedom to make law.

At present the American Law Institute is restating United States tort law for a third time. In this project, the Institute must necessarily look in past cases for common-denominator standards and rules that can be set down and deployed by United States courts in the future, while weeding out flawed cases in order to protect future generations from the trap, in Gordley's apt phrase, of "deferring to a fossilized error."[8] But the Institute must do more than this. It also must nurture the legislative dynamic of the common law by preserving the freedom of future courts to expand or, a considerably more difficult and unpopular task,[9] constrain principle as circumstances demand, and do so at the pace and to the extent constitutional convention allows.

Finally, the Institute must devise techniques that encourage that legislative power to be allocated to the institutional player judged the appropriate one in the circumstances. For example, once the Institute identifies and distills a common standard, it may have a choice of allocating to trial judge or to jury the power to apply the standard. Conversely, the Institute must choose how to constrain the usurpation of power by the trial judge or jury. It follows that any analysis of a restatement text would be incomplete without an investigation into how it resolved such choices concerning institutional competition between judge and jury, and the techniques by which the Institute reflected them in the text of this Restatement.

In contrast to the United States, in the common-law systems of the United Kingdom, Canada, Australia, and New Zealand, doctrinal development is formally unified. This is so because in each nation there is only one final court of appeal on all issues of tort law. So although in the United States there may be fifty-one final pronouncements on a point of tort law, in, say, the United Kingdom there will only be one. In such countries, therefore, projects to identify and restate common denominator principles across many intra-national jurisdictions are unnecessary. A second feature of non–United States common-law systems is that in practice common-law legislative creativity is channeled to the final court because puisne courts adhere quite rigidly to precedent. Puisne judges are not elected but, rather, are seen as aspiring

---

[7] ROBERT S. SUMMERS & P. S. ATIYAH, FORM AND SUBSTANCE IN ANGLO-AMERICAN LAW (1987).

[8] James Gordley, *The Rule Against Recovery in Negligence for Pure Economic Loss: An Historical Accident?, in* PURE ECONOMIC LOSS IN EUROPE 56 (Mauro Bussani & Vernon Valentine Palmer, eds.)(2003).

[9] Jane Stapleton, *In Restraint of Tort, in* 2 THE FRONTIERS OF LIABILITY 83 (Peter Birks, ed.)(1994).

junior members of an elite class in whose hands the integrity of the rule of law and separation of powers are safe. Rogue trial judges off on a frolic of their own, say, to abandon privity, simply do not exist and so it is unnecessary to inject into any formal restatement of legal principle overt or covert control over such trial judge waywardness. In addition and in contrast to continental courts laboring under the formal supremacy of a private law code, final courts of appeal in non–United States common-law systems are noticeably more candid in their reasoning. The power of such an ultimate court of appeal to make law is accepted openly but tempered by the convention that this will usually proceed by a cautious and incremental[10] approach that addresses squarely the socioeconomic implications raised by the individual dispute. Discipline over trial courts is reinforced by the willingness of appellate courts to shoulder a considerable volume of interlocutory work, so that, for example, there are a large number of appellate decisions concerning whether a defendant owed a duty of care to a plaintiff, made on appeal from the trial court's decision on a striking out application.[11]

Finally, in these non-U.S. systems, juries are not only rare,[12] but even where juries do operate, their decisions do not attract the social reverence that jury decision making seems to do in the United States. A Scottish, Canadian, or Australian jury decision that reflected, say, an abandonment of privity would be swiftly and uncontroversially quashed by the higher court. So, again, it would not be necessary to include within any restatement overt or covert control over such jury waywardness. In short, in non-U.S. common-law systems principle and practice confirm that it is within the single national court of final appeal that common law legislation originates. Across the United States, tort law operates as a multiplicity of free-market systems within which trial judges and juries are less restrained, but in the United Kingdom tort law operates as a single command system.

---

[10]   The cricketing analogy is popular in the United Kingdom: "while engaged on the process of developing the law a judge is best advised to take his runs in singles rather than in fours," Lord Steyn, *Perspectives of Corrective and Distributive Justice in Tort Law: The John Maurice Kelly Memorial Lecture* at 17 (Faculty of Law University College Dublin, 2002). On the general point, *see* Mauro Bussani & Vernon Valentine Palmer, *The Liability Regimes of Europe – Their Facades and Interiors*, in PURE ECONOMIC LOSS IN EUROPE 124–5 (Mauro Bussani & Vernon Valentine Palmer, eds.)(2003).

[11]   The practice is discussed in *Barrett v. London Borough of Enfield*, [1999] 3 W.L.R. 628. *Donoghue v. Stevenson*, [1932] A.C. 562 is a famous historical example.

[12]   Although we must remember that "for most of its history, the jury was the crucial institution of English law. It was juries who set the standards and so determined how the law worked. In such a system there is little scope for judges to develop the law": Lord Rodger of Earlsferry, *What are Appeal Courts For?*, 10 OTAGO L. REV. 517, 518 (2004).

II. PURE THEORY AND RESTATEMENTS

A threshold question is of what help, if any, to the Reporters might high tort theory be in identifying the architecture within which the standards of the Restatement should sit? When a legislature enacts a law, the basis of that law in compromise and trade-off is well understood and accepted. No one expects the content of the statute to reflect a pure, autonomous and noninstrumental moral practice[13] nor that it should ruthlessly pursue a sole wealth maximization goal. One might, therefore, expect that in analysing the proper role of lawmaking by courts, commentators on United States tort law might be similarly accepting of the diversity of concerns that may legitimately be taken into account by tort judges when crafting the law of torts, and be contemptuous of claims that "tort law," if correctly defined, extends only to those rules that a certain pure theoretical construct would allow.

Yet, of course, much torts commentary in North America continues along the well-worn tracks of idealized theories. When those responsible for these intellectual constructs choose to address actual case law, they seek to rationalize it in a process akin to reverse engineering. But once we suspect that this approach can be used to justify either or both of two past decisions that conflict, this process fails to convince as an interpretative strategy and will be found of little use to counsel and to courts seeking a predictive legal tool. For example, no version of wealth maximization has been found, from which can be deduced the patterns we see in relation to the recovery of pure economic loss in tort law.[14] No version of corrective justice can accommodate within it a compelling explanation of the deeply entrenched uncontroversial phenomena of vicarious liability or the corporate veil. Nor can that theory seem to accommodate the phenomenon of a judge or a jury failing to see a relevant distinction between the conduct of a defendant who did not prevent a toddler picking up the defendant's loaded gun from the defendant's lap, and the conduct of a different defendant who gave his own loaded gun to a toddler.

Moreover, like many other "pure" theories of law, recent corrective justice scholarship fails to expound a convincing rationale of the core characteristic of the common law system, namely, the dynamic evolution of legal entitlements based as they are on shifts in what are perceived as acceptable forms of distributive justice: the redistributive nature of *MacPherson* is again a good example. Similarly, because such high theory is typically culturally blind, it

---

[13] ERNEST J. WEINRIB, THE IDEA OF PRIVATE LAW (1995).

[14] Jane Stapleton, *Comparative Economic Loss: Lessons from Case Law Focussed "Middle Theory,"* 50 UCLA L. REV. 531 (2002) (hereinafter *Comparative Economic Loss*).

also fails to address the phenomenon throughout the common-law world that there are major differences in the ambit of tort entitlements. For example, in the United States, a fraudster is typically not liable for coincidental consequences of his deceit, whereas in the United Kingdom he can be.[15] The same point applies more widely: in the civil code country of Germany, a parent may be vicariously liable for the tortious conduct of an underage child, whereas that doctrine does not reach parent-child relationships in the common law of North America or the Commonwealth. High theory is especially silent on the shifting balance that must be pragmatically struck between the relative powers of jury, trial judge and appellate court. Finally, because the contours of private law doctrine track local contemporary trade-offs made between "conflicting values and policies,"[16] those contours will naturally shift over time, and between locations and cultures. Indeed, in this light the concern with the corrective justice standard of justification of private law is itself revealed as no more than a Western cultural artifact, and indeed an artifact that ignores the phenomenon of societies elsewhere that happily base core sociolegal relations on group standing and group responsibility.

High theorists may defend their elegant exercise as merely one of characterisation, i.e., that within the law of tort as we see it, there is an "autonomous and nonpolitical"[17] closed core that can be rationalized and justified by an ideal theory, say Kantian right, plus a penumbra generated by a more open range of concerns. If so, the focus on determining what falls within that pure core, that carrot puree of high theory,[18] ignores fundamental questions about the substance of private law, such as what are the underpinnings for society's insistence on (1) legally enforceable obligations of affirmative action; or (2) forms of group responsibility such as vicarious liability?[19] Further to this, what makes the recoverability of coincidental losses from a fraudster acceptable in one culture at a given time and yet not in another? Why is a Bavarian parent vicariously liable for its child but not a Texan parent for his? Why in the United Kingdom is it accepted that a defendant can be liable for innocently defaming a public person with a statement that did no damage because no

---

[15] *Compare* Movitz v. First Nat. Bank of Chicago, 148 F.3d 760, 763 (7th Cir. 1998) *and* Smith New Court Securities Ltd. v. Scrimgeour Vickers Ltd., [1997] A.C. 254.

[16] Ewan McKendrick, *Traditional Concepts and Contemporary Values*, 1 EUR. REV. OF PRIVATE L. 94, 109 (2002).

[17] WEINRIB, *supra* note 13.

[18] *Comparative Economic Loss*, *supra* note 14 at 574.

[19] Lord Steyn, *supra* note 10 at 8. Lord Steyn thinks it may be that vicarious liability "ultimately rests on grounds of distributive justice" Note also Lord Steyn's appreciation that fairness intuitions may shift according to whether the defendant is an individual or the National Health Service. *Id.* at 6.

one believed it? Why in some cultures does a clan have standing to sue for damages but not in Scotland? In any case, by what objective yardstick should lawyers not treat these questions as at the core of tort law?

Such a corrective justice lens also ignores what the most eminent judges tell us: that in cases determined by the court of final appeal reasons of distributive justice may well be "decisive" and that more generally "tort is not underpinned by a single overarching rationale. It is a mosaic of interwoven principles of corrective and distributive justice."[20] In short, when we look to restate the actual lawmaking performed by courts, theory is of little use in identifying sufficiently clear standards let alone the appropriate overarching architecture.

III. THE POLITICS OF A RESTATEMENT PROJECT

Some determinations are unequivocally about facts: such as who shot the gun. But in many contexts an issue can be packaged in different ways. For example, suppose the security measures taken by a building owner do not prevent a vandal breaking in and deliberately starting a fire that spreads to the neighbouring property with disastrous consequences. In the generally jury-free United Kingdom system, whether the issue in the suit brought by the neighbor against the building owner is described as one of duty (a "question of law"), of breach (a "question of fact"), or of scope of liability for consequences (a "question of fact") will not be as controversial as in the United States. Indeed, it is not uncommon in the United Kingdom for it to be somewhat unclear which determinations are being put forward by a judge as precedent-generating general propositions of law and which are intended to be "limited to the facts of the case."[21] Even in the final court, the House of Lords, it is not unknown for one Law Lord to analyze the case in terms of duty, another in terms of breach and yet a third Law Lord to use scope as the analytical vehicle of exposition of the judgment.[22]

In contrast, in U.S. jurisdictions if the issue in dispute in such a case is described as a question of fact, be it concerning breach or scope, this reflects a strong normative choice that the issue will be one for the jury. From that choice flow important consequences: the decision will be unelaborated; it

---

[20] Lord Steyn, *supra* note 10, at 7–8.
[21] FRANCIS TRINDADE AND PETER CANE, THE LAW OF TORTS IN AUSTRALIA 461–62 (3rd ed.) (1999). *See* discussion of *Qualcast (Wolverhampton) Ltd. v. Haynes*, [1959] A.C. 743, infra at note 77 and accompanying text.
[22] *See*, for example, *Smith v. Littlewoods Organisation Ltd.*, [1987] 1 All E.R. 710 (the vandal case). *See also Dorset Yacht Co. Ltd. v. Home Office*, [1969] 2 Q.B. 412 (concerning damage caused by escapees from lawful custody).

will be heavily protected from appellate review; and it will not provide any precedent in the future. The choice of the institutional site of decision making is a highly political one, as Dean Powers, one of the Reporters, has made clear: "Reasonable people will disagree whether we are better served by giving juries or judges more or less normative work to do . . . that is largely a political judgment, not a legal one."[23]

Recent lurid confirmation of this is provided by the noisy reception given to the Restatement (Third) of Torts: Products Liability,[24] with its crystallisation of a rule mandating that plaintiffs bring proof of a reasonable alternative design in most defective design claims before a trial judge is authorized by the Restatement to pass the case to the jury. It has been alleged that this provision[25] constituted a blatant reorientation of legal principle crudely motivated by a biased determination to prevent cases getting to the jury. For example, Frank J. Vandall has argued that the Restatement (Third) of Torts: Products Liability "is a wish list from manufacturing America,"[26] a "political statement . . . [that] is not a restatement of the law and does not rest on an evaluation of cases and policies."[27] He asserts that its Reporters "began with a clean sheet of paper (favoring manufacturers)"[28] and produced a law reform measure that "does not accurately reflect the practice of courts today"[29] but instead puts "five hundred years of tort cases . . . into the paper shredder."[30] He concludes that "the ALI's mission is no longer to restate the law, but rather to issue pro-manufacturer political documents."[31]

It is in this fevered aftermath of the Products Liability Restatement that the Reporters of the Restatement (Third) of Torts: Liability for Physical Harm must face the political questions of how welcoming their text should be to the future expansion of liability and where the future balance of lawmaking power among trial judge, jury, and appellate court should be drawn. It cannot be doubted that some brake and guidance mechanisms must be available to

---

[23] William Powers Jr., *Judge and Jury in the Texas Supreme Court*, 75 TEX. L. REV. 1699, 1715 (1997).

[24] RESTATEMENT (THIRD) OF TORTS: PRODUCTS LIABILITY (1998) (herinafter sometimes PRODUCTS LIABILITY RESTATEMENT).

[25] *Id.* at § 2(b).

[26] Frank J. Vandall, *Constructing a Roof Before the Foundation is Prepared: The Restatement (Third) of Torts: Products Liability Section 2 (b) Design Defect*, 30 U. MICH. J. L. REFORM 261 (1997).

[27] *Id.* at 279.

[28] *Id.* at 269.

[29] *Id.* at 262.

[30] *Id.* at 265.

[31] *Id.* at 279.

courts within private law.[32] We know that control of liability is possible under either duty or scope, and that the orthodox position is that "duty is a question of law for the court . . . while scope of liability . . . is treated as a question of fact for the fact finder."[33] Formally, this division of labor tracks the nature of the issue in dispute. For example, the Reporters state that when liability depends on factors applicable to categories of actors or patterns of conduct, the appropriate rubric is duty, and that no-duty rules are appropriate only when a court can promulgate a relatively clear, categorical, bright-line rule of law applicable to a general class of cases.[34] In contrast, the Reporters state, when liability depends on factors specific to an individual case, the appropriate rubric is scope of liability.[35] Nevertheless, it has been well appreciated since *Palsgraf v. Long Island Railroad*[36] that, in a specific case, reasonable minds can differ as to how the issue in dispute should be formulated and therefore in which location it is better dealt with.[37]

One factor influencing that choice is the ability of the decision maker to effect brakes on liability growth. Of course, courts can throw out an individual case on the basis that no reasonable jury could find breach or no reasonable jury could find that the consequence fell within the perimeter rule governing the appropriate scope of liability.[38] But for those keen to formalize brake and guidance mechanisms on the future rate of growth of liability, the preferred location for the resolution of many disputes will be the duty of care rubric. Here an appellate court can elaborate firm no-duty rules of wide precedential influence and so it is here that a brake on liability can best be applied. For example, characterizing the issue in the vandal dispute as one of whether a duty is owed allocates it, as a matter of law, to the trial judge and ultimately to the appellate court where there is the opportunity to legislate a firm no-duty principle.

The dilemma for the Reporters is that, although a braking mechanism is clearly needed, their room to maneuver is limited. Simply empowering courts with broad grounds for deploying the no-duty mechanism may attract the criticism that this is too crude a device, too sweeping an usurpation of traditional jury power. A more nuanced control is possible if the court is

---

[32] Jane Stapleton, *In Restraint of Tort, in* 2 THE FRONTIERS OF LIABILITY 83 (Peter Birks, ed) (1994).

[33] TD No. 3 § 29 cmt. f.

[34] TD No. 4 § 7 cmt. a. *See also* TD No. 3 § 29 cmt. f.

[35] TD No. 4, § 7 cmt. a.

[36] *Palsgraf v. Long Island R.R. Co.*, 248 N.Y. 339, 162 N.E. 99 (1928).

[37] TD No. 3 § 29 cmt. f.

[38] The Reporters rightly decry the misleading practice of some courts of packaging this result in terms of no-duty: TD No. 2, § 7 cmt. i; TD No.4 § 38 cmt. c; TD No. 4 § 41 cmt. d and Reporters' Note thereto; TD No. 4 § 41 Reporters' Note to cmt. l.

permitted to cite more of the factual context as qualifying the extent of its negative finding on duty, but it too attracts this criticism.

Throughout the Draft Restatement, the Reporters are sensitive to the dilemma that future courts face. On the one hand, they urge any court prepared to embark on such particularized duties to acknowledge that this "constitutes an incursion on the role of the jury as fact finder and as the repository of commonsense normative wisdom in individual cases . . . [and] is a different endeavor from determining the legal rules that apply to classes of cases."[39]

On the other hand, the Reporters seem to signal that, in the future, at least outside the misfeasance area, appropriate judicial tools for restraining the growth of liability, may well require the acceptance of duty line-drawing that is far more fact-specific than hitherto has been seen as legitimate. The following discussion examines how the Reporters may have used the very orientation of the Restatement's architecture to strengthen the potential restraint that can be exercised over future liability.[40]

IV. DUTY: CHOOSING TO FACILITATE OR RESTRAIN FUTURE LIABILITY

A. Generally

Duty is not disintegrating. It is a unitary concept or device, although, importantly, in application to a diversity of fact situations it results in pockets, or islands, of liability in a sea of freedom from liability. On both sides of the Atlantic Ocean, courts agree that a defendant owes a general duty of reasonable care to not physically injure another by the defendant's affirmative careless act. In the United States, this is the realm for the saying that a duty is "owed to the whole world." So, for example, a driver owes a duty of care to the stranger he carelessly runs over; the manufacturer owes a duty of care to the user of the product; and so on. In the past, most attention was focused on the continent of liability produced by such direct misfeasance cases. But other large islands also were well charted, such as those duties on parties in status relationships that the law regarded as special, such as parent-child. In other words, outside this traditional core of the "running-down" type of case, duties have been recognized but usually only where some prior special relationship is said to exist. Recently, we have been sailing farther afield as plaintiffs argue for a myriad of instances of new duties. Should someone who leaves his car

---

[39] TD No. 4 § 38 cmt. c.

[40] In particular, see TD No. 4 § 7 cmt. a; TD No. 3 § 29 cmt. f; TD No. 4 § 38 cmt. c and Reporters' Notes thereto.

with the keys in the ignition owe a duty to a stranger who is run over by the thief who stole the defendant's car?

On their face, duty cases would seem to fall on a continuum where the normative analogy with the running down case becomes weaker as other concerns militate against recognition of a duty of care. So, what is immediately striking to the foreign common lawyer in the Draft of the Restatement (Third) as it stood on April 1, 2004 is that the discussion of duty is dramatically split between two poles: a duty-to-the-whole-world rule in § 7; and a no-duty rule in § 37. The respective sections provide:

> Section 7: *Duty*
> (a) An actor ordinarily has a duty to exercise reasonable care when the actor's conduct creates a risk of physical harm.
> (b) A court may determine that an actor has no duty or has a duty other than the ordinary duty of reasonable care. Determinations of no duty and modifications of the duty of reasonable care are exceptional. They are based on special problems of principle or policy that warrant denying liability, or modifying the ordinary duty of care, in a particular class of case.[41]

> Section 37: *No Duty of Care With Respect to Risks Not Created by Actor* Subject to Sections 39–45, an actor whose conduct has not created a risk of physical harm to another has no duty of care to the other.[42]

Here, then, are two opposite bright line rules, albeit with escape hatches included. Instead of a linear treatment of duty cases, the treatment is polarized. One section is a general duty section. One is a general no-duty section. Does the juxtaposition of these bright lines track a relevant phenomenon in the cases? Even if this were so, why would U.S. law have rejected the simple linear approach to duty that operates in jury free common-law systems? To shed light on these two questions, we should first look at the pattern of outcomes in United States law and see if these neatly fit the polarization set down in § 7 and § 37.

B. The § 7 Versus § 37 Distinction Cannot Be that of Misfeasance versus Nonfeasance

As we have seen, on both sides of the Atlantic it is well-settled that, except for rarely applicable reasons,[43] a person owes a duty to use reasonable care not

---

[41] At the time of going to press the current test was in TD No. 4 at 167.

[42] *Id.* at 2.

[43] This is the idea behind the Draft's § 7(b), namely, that in rare situations there may be acute policy reasons for refusing a duty such as those giving rise to the rule that in virtually all

directly to cause by his own affirmative act physical injury to another even when that person is a total stranger. I owe a duty not to drive my car carelessly into a stranger. In relation to such "negligent acts directly causing physical injury" (which I will call "misfeasance") cases, there is simply a consensus that a duty is owed. Within these limits, then, it is true to say that a duty is owed to the whole world. Direct misfeasance cases clearly fall squarely within the terms of the Draft Restatement's § 7(a).

Of course, the notion of "directly" here is something of a loose term. The principle applies just as uniformly to cases where the innocuous innocent behaviour of another intervenes. For example, the manufacturer of a defective product owes a duty of care to those who may be injured when the product is used normally by others, as when an unborn child, the classic bystander, is injured by the pharmaceutical its mother takes. In fact, the manufacturer also owes a well-settled duty in relation to those injured by foreseeable misuse of the product by intervenors, although, of course, the facts may well not satisfy some other prerequisite to a finding of ultimate liability.

It is worth pausing to consider why there is such a strong consensus that a duty is owed in misfeasance cases. One reason is that it avoids the law appearing to draw distasteful distinctions between individuals. If, in a misfeasance case, the court/jury are not going to impose liability on the defendant, the option of packaging this no-liability result in terms of no-duty, as Justice Cardozo controversially did in *Palsgraf v. Long Island R.R. Co.*,[44] sends a systemic and distasteful message that, although a defendant may owe a duty not to break a certain person's leg, there are circumstances in which that defendant in his actions does not have to take care to avoid breaking some other citizen's leg. This callous message unacceptably appears to rank different classes of citizens in relation to their entitlements to protection from having their legs broken by the defendant. This is avoided by packaging the no-liability result in terms, not of the victim, but in terms of the characterization of the injury: each citizen owes to every other citizen a duty of care to act as a reasonable person where there is a foreseeable risk that his positive act might cause physical injury to someone or something, but the scope of that obligation extends to only a limited number of the infinite physical consequences of the tortious conduct. This reformulation attractively shifts the doctrinal focus from distinguishing between victims to distinguishing between consequences. Where the injury

cases no duty is owed by social hosts who supply alcohol to a guest who then drunkenly injures plaintiff. E.g., Reeder v. Daniel, 61 S.W.3d 359 (Tex. 2001). On such reasons, *see* § 7 cmt. a, the current text of which is in TD No. 4 at 167–8. These no-duty results are flagged in § 7(b). *See also* note 63.

[44] *Palsgraf, supra* note 36, 248 N.Y. at 339.

suffered is not a physical trauma such as a broken leg but is, for example, pure economic loss or a mental injury, we may not have such a strong objection to ranking the entitlements to protection according to the classification of the victim. In these latter situations, no-duty distinctions between classes of citizens seem much more acceptable. For example, victims suffering from psychological injury may be distinguished merely on the basis of family relationship, and so on.

So far so good. Direct misfeasance cases clearly fall within the terms of § 7. But what is the distinction the Reporters intend to draw between § 7 cases and § 37 cases? It is well known that the line between duty situations and situations in which no duty is recognized is not a line drawn according to whether the negligence consisted of a careless act (misfeasance) or a careless omission (nonfeasance). Often careless omissions give rise to a duty without any controversy at all. Sometimes such an area of settled duty may simply be reformulated so as to appear as a case of a negligent act. For example, suppose a pharmaceutical manufacturer omits to provide an adequate warning with its drug. This might look like an omission but it can be reformulated as an omission "embedded" in an act. The act of "supplying a drug," by itself not a careless act, is transformed by the embedded negligent omission into a careless act: the careless act of "supplying a drug with an inadequate warning." The "embedded omission" case therefore qualifies as coming within the settled area of a duty being owed for direct misfeasance. Direct misfeasance (with an embedded omission) cases clearly fall squarely within the terms of the Draft's § 7(a).[45] So settled are such duties that, whatever the Reporters intended to be the distinction between § 7 and § 37, it would not have been the distinction between misfeasance and embedded nonfeasance.

C. The § 7/§ 37 Distinction Cannot Be that of Settled Duties/Novel Cases

Even where it may seem awkward to use this technique by which the infecting effect of an "embedded" careless omission transforms the wider positive conduct of the defendant into a careless act, the imposition of a duty may still be well settled. Many such settled instances of liability for careless omissions concern contexts where: the defendant is in a status ("special") relationship such as having lawful custody of, or being *in loco parentis* to, the victim (e.g., mother fails to feed her child) or third party perpetrator (e.g., mother fails to control her child who injures another); or where the defendant had previously, non-negligently, undertaken to act in the sense of representing to others

---

[45] TD No. 4 § 37 Reporters' Note to cmt. c.

that he would act (e.g., lifeguard undertakes to attempt rescue if necessary; brake repairer undertakes to repair brakes).

One way such cases might have been handled was by the same reformulation we used for the pharmaceutical manufacturer widening the formulation to the defendant's entire course of conduct: the conduct of "being a parent," by itself not a careless act, is transformed by the embedded omission to feed the child into positive careless conduct, namely the careless act of "parenting without providing adequate food." This admittedly awkward device might then allow such classic cases of liability to be seen as direct misfeasance cases and therefore as falling neatly under § 7.

It is here that we get our first glimpse that the Draft Restatement's architecture will not follow some obvious pattern. For, despite acknowledging the "entire course of conduct" device,[46] the Reporters have not chosen to locate such settled duty instances of careless omissions (embedded in a prior status or undertaking) under § 7 but as exceptions to the no-duty bright line rule in § 37. This tells us that, whatever the Reporters intended by the distinction between § 7 cases and others, it was not to collect into § 7 all the uncontroversial cases in which a duty is imposed.

D. Is the § 7/§ 37 Distinction Driven by the "Enabling Tort" Concept of Professor Rabin?

Outside these settled duty cases of direct misfeasance, status relationships and undertakings, duties are sometimes, episodically, recognized though their general formulation is problematic. What in the context of the case triggers the duty? Suppose a traveler is confronted with a baby drowning in a puddle but does nothing, even though such a rescue would be effortless and is what every reasonable person would do. Failure to turn the baby over is a but-for cause of the death. But the causal relevance of an omission, being simply too easily established, cannot be sufficient to generate a duty. After all, but for the failure of every Dallas citizen to stop Oswald, Kennedy would not have died. So the law holds that, *in the absence of any other factor of relevance in the context*, there is no liability on the stranger for failing to rescue the baby-in-the-puddle, a result the law packages as there being no duty in the circumstances: no-duty-to-rescue-a-stranger.

Yet we know that duties are sometimes recognized outside cases of direct misfeasance, status relationships, and undertakings. In other words, sometimes (and episodically) courts do hold a defendant liable for facilitating harm

---

[46] *Id.*

to a person who is a total stranger to the defendant, that is, someone with whom the defendant has no prior status-based or other special relationship. An example of such an episodic duty might be a keys-in-the-ignition case: some courts might well allow a jury to impose liability where a defendant leaves the keys in the ignition of his new sports car outside a beer hall in a lawless part of town for a week whereupon it is then stolen by a drunk from the bar who runs over the plaintiff.[47] Where is the line between the puddle case and its no-duty result, and the keys case where there can be a duty even to a stranger? Relative to the puddle case, what more needs to be identified from the context of the case to qualify for the imposition of a duty to a stranger? Where in the § 7/§ 37 architecture do these cases fall and why?

Remember that the dilemma the Reporters face is fourfold. First, they must determine and reduce to a formulaic standard what are the factors in the surrounding context of cases such as the keys-in-the-ignition case that distinguish those cases from the puddle case and thereby prevent the no-duty-to-rescue-a-stranger principle applying. Next they must accommodate such past duty-not-to-facilitate cases that rely on "context," in a way that preserves the no-duty-to-rescue-a-stranger principle for the future. Third, the Restatement text must permit novel duty-not-to-facilitate arguments to be brought in the future. Finally, that text must subject these future expansionary arguments to whatever systemic constraints are regarded as immanent within the current case law and legal principle more generally. Only then will a trial judge be equipped with the standards needed adequately to determine summary judgment and directed verdict applications.

At this point it should be stressed that some "episodic" duties that arise in contexts other than status or undertaking are well settled and uncontroversial, such as where the defendant negligently entrusted his vehicle to a grossly intoxicated person who then ran over the plaintiff. These situations when a duty is imposed on a defendant where his action merely indirectly facilitated a third party, perhaps a stranger, injuring the plaintiff, perhaps also a stranger, confirm that such *duties can be acceptable in the absence of a status relationship or undertaking*. A further crucial feature in such cases rests on other aspects of the context being seized on as being normatively relevant. Entrusting one's car to someone, even a stranger, is not a negligent act by itself; indeed, in certain circumstances, it may well be commendable. But, just as the inadequate warning on the pharmaceutical product transforms the otherwise innocent supply of a product into a careless act, the wider social

---

[47] For U.K. decisions, *see, generally*, John G. Fleming, *Injury Caused by Stolen Motor Vehicles*, 110 L. Q. REV. 187 (1994).

context in which the car is entrusted, such as the intoxication of the person entrusted, may transform that act of entrustment into one where it is judged that liability should be imposed. Of course, for this to occur, the law must find and explain why a duty had existed.

In a landmark article in the area,[48] Professor Rabin has distinguished the no-duty-to-rescue-cases, such as the puddle example, from others he calls "enabling torts" where the defendant has enhanced the risk to the plaintiff by facilitating the process by which a third party injures him. Rabin distinguishes three types of situations: cases in which the defendant's conduct created a new peril to the plaintiff (e.g., carelessly speeding in a car); cases in which, although the defendant's conduct did not create a new peril, he enhanced the risk that the plaintiff would be injured by another instrumentality (e.g., the keys-in-the-ignition case); and cases in which the defendant's conduct neither created a new peril nor enhanced the risk to the plaintiff (e.g., the baby-in-the-puddle-case). Might the architecture of the Restatement be based on this three-fold distinction? Might § 7's duty-to-the-whole-world be intended for cases where the defendant's conduct created a new peril to the plaintiff? Similarly, might §§ 39–45 duties be intended for cases where, through relationship, undertaking or otherwise the defendant, although he has not created a new peril, has "enhanced the risk" to the plaintiff by "enabling" injury to be inflicted on him? This then leaves § 37 to lay out the residual no-duty-to-rescue-a-stranger rule where the defendant neither created a new peril nor enhanced the risk to the plaintiff.

It is certainly true that the Reporters could not intend us to give § 7 and § 37 a face-value reading: that § 7 imposes a duty where there was risk creation; and § 37 declaring that there is no duty where there was no risk creation. This cannot be the correct reading of the sections for two reasons. First, the Reporters acknowledge that "when an actor's conduct is a factual cause of physical harm, the actor's conduct necessarily 'created a risk of harm.'"[49] If we took § 7 at face value, that it covered all cases where the defendant's alleged breach created a risk of the harm that befell the plaintiff, this would mean that there would be no need to carve out the exceptional duty provisions in §§ 39–45. This is because for a §§ 39–45 case to have any hope of success, the defendant's conduct would have to have been a cause of the injury and, as the Reporters acknowledge, this would mean every §§ 39–45 case would involve risk creation. Each would therefore simply have qualified as a creation-of-risk case under § 7.

---

[48] Robert L. Rabin, *Enabling Torts*, 49 DePaul L. Rev. 435 (1999).
[49] TD No. 4 § 7 cmt. a.

The second reason why a face-value reading of the distinction could not have been intended also lies in the Reporters' statement that whenever the defendant's carelessness was a cause of the plaintiff's physical injury, that carelessness would have created a risk.[50] This in turn would mean that a duty would *always* be owed in such circumstances because § 7 states a duty is always owed when the defendant's carelessness "creates a risk," subject to only the very rare exceptions contemplated by § 7(b). But to impose a duty whenever the defendant's carelessness was a cause of the plaintiff's injury is clearly not what the Reporters could have intended because, as we have seen, they rightly record that, even though an unreasonable failure to rescue may be a cause of the plaintiff's injury, there is no duty on a stranger to rescue in a puddle situation.

Now that we see that the Reporters could not intend § 7 and § 37 to be read on their face meanings, i.e., that § 7 imposes a duty where there was risk creation and § 37 declares that there is no duty where there was no risk creation, this opens the possibility that the Reporters were indeed intending the tripartite distinction Professor Rabin described. That this is a more plausible reading of § 7 and § 37 is suggested by comment b to § 37: "This section states ... that there is no duty of care when another is at risk for reasons other than the conduct of the actor, even though the actor is in a position to help."[51] This suggests that the Reporters intended the distinction between § 7 and § 37 to be *whether the actor's conduct created a new, special, separate, independent peril to the plaintiff.* If it did, it would be a § 7 case. If it did not, it would be a § 37 case. Under such a scheme, direct misfeasance such as speeding and direct misfeasance (with an embedded omission) such as supplying defective pharmaceuticals,[52] both fall simply into § 7(a). Such conduct interferes with the world and so it is easy to formulate it as having created a new peril the plaintiff faced.

There is, however, a striking problem with this scheme under which the § 7/§ 37 distinction tracks the distinction between cases in which the defendant created a new peril to the plaintiff and those in which he did not: it does not establish an internally coherent analytical scheme. The reasons why this is so emerge from a consideration of the cases that fall into the intermediate Rabin class of cases in which, although the defendant has not created a new peril, he has "enhanced" the risk to the plaintiff. The coherence of Rabin's tripartite scheme idea depends on the idea of "risk enhancement" being analytically distinct from the creation-of-peril cases the Reporters intend to

---

[50] *Id.*
[51] TD No. 4 § 37 cmt. b (emphasis added).
[52] TD No. 4 § 37 illus. 2.

be captured by § 7, and it also being distinct from and the no-peril-creation plus no-risk-enhancement cases that they intend to trigger the no duty rule in § 37. Regrettably, neither distinction holds. Both dissolve in the light of the law's normative focus on what would have happened had the alleged breach not occurred: what we might call the "baseline" perspective.

E. The Proactive Limitation to the Rabin-Based Distinction

Professor Rabin limits his "enabling" classification in a striking way:

> "Enabling" has a proactive connotation...that distinguishes this type of responsibility from failures generally to intervene on behalf of an endangered person...in the enabling situations that I have been discussing, defendant has affirmatively enhanced the risk of harm, and as a consequence, no special relationship is required to establish responsibility.... These [are] situations, in which a seemingly isolated careless act enhances the risk that a malevolent or consciously indifferent intervenor will seriously injure an innocent third party...[53]

A preliminary problem with the Rabin distinction is that Rabin's class only seems to include cases where the defendant has by a proactive, affirmative act facilitated the process by which a third party has injured a stranger. He gives the failure-to-remove-keys-from-the-ignition case as an example. His choice at first seems awkward because it requires us to find a way to treat *failing* to remove the keys from the car as an *act*. But of course, we can do this: we simply adopt the omission-embedded-in-an-act approach we used in the pharmaceutical failure-to-warn case, so that we can formulate the proactive, affirmative act that facilitated the third party as "being in control of an instrumentality which is inadequately secured against misuse by a third party." But, just as Rabin uses this device to see the keys-left-in-the-ignition case as one of proactive affirmative conduct, so we can do this reconstruction in all cases of negligent conduct embedded in a context: we can always use something positive in the context to envelope the negligent conduct, so that even if that conduct is an embedded omission, we can formulate it as embedded in the context of wider positive conduct. If we wanted to, we could even reconstruct the allegation about the failure to rescue the baby in the puddle as the stranger "acting as a citizen in an unreasonable way"!

The point is this: it does not matter if the conduct is a negligent omission so long as the context provides the appropriate normative envelope. What

---

[53] *Id.* at 442 (emphasis added).

this means is that, whatever is doing the work to set the boundary between the no-duty-to-rescue cases and the episodic duty for negligent facilitation cases, it is not any differential based on whether the defendant's conduct was an act or an omission. That boundary is being set by what we select from the context as normatively relevant.

Suppose a defendant is lawfully sitting on a park bench with his picnic utensils set out on the bench next to him. He consciously fails to prevent a toddler-stranger picking up one of his sharp fruit knives with which the toddler then injures herself. There is a normative argument for a duty being owed in such circumstances. That argument does not seem to be defeated by, or indeed in any way turn on, whether we characterize the defendant's conduct as an isolated piece of conduct of "failing-to-prevent," or in more positive, misfeasance terms. Rather, it seems fundamentally the same as the duty argument in a case where a knife owner advertently and positively places his knife on a public bench in a park frequented by children: namely, "being in control of an instrumentality which is inadequately secured against misuse by a third party." Ditto the keys-left-in-the-ignition cases.

F. Enhancing a Risk Cannot Distinguish the Entrustment Case from the Puddle Case because Baselines Cannot Be Ignored

A more fundamental problem with this limited Rabin class is that merely "enhancing the risk of harm" cannot be used to distinguish our episodic duty cases, such as the vehicle entrustment case, from the failure-to-rescue-a-stranger cases, such as the puddle example. In both, the defendant enhances the risk of injury to the plaintiff relative to the baseline the law must necessarily use as its normative frame of reference: where would the plaintiff have been had the defendant not committed the breach that is alleged? As we have seen, the Reporters acknowledge that "when an actor's conduct is a factual cause of physical harm, the actor's conduct necessarily 'created a risk of harm.' "[54] So, for example, in the puddle case in which a person fails to act as any reasonable person would and roll a drowning toddler out of a deep puddle, that omission is a but-for cause of the child's death, as but-for the omission the child would have lived. The failure created a risk of that outcome, relative to the hypothetical world with which the law compares the impact of the defendant's alleged negligence. This makes clear that the boundary between the no-duty-to-rescue cases and the duty found in the episodic facilitation cases, such as entrustment of one's car to a drunk person, cannot be captured by a

[54] TD No. 4 § 7 cmt. a.

formulation based on whether or not the defendant "enhanced" or "created" a risk.

Let me emphasize this last point. In the real world, the plaintiff will have been crafty enough to formulate any alleged negligence in such a way that it is a but-for factor leading to the injury: but for the stranger's failure to roll the baby out of the puddle, in other words, if the stranger had rolled the baby out of the water, the child would not have died. It is, therefore, the plaintiff's formulation of what action the defendant should have taken that constructs the hypothetical world and therein the normative baseline against which it will follow that the defendant's conduct created the risk of and was a cause of the outcome. In short, it is misleading to say that it is because the defendant had created a risk that a duty is imposed as there are many situations in which, as in the puddle case, the plaintiff can assert that the defendant's conduct created a risk of and was a cause of the death relative to what should have happened, yet no duty is recognized by the law.

G. Enhancing a Risk Cannot Be Distinguished from Creating a New Peril because Baselines Cannot Be Ignored

A second fundamental problem with Professor Rabin's class of intermediate conduct that merely "enhances the risk of harm" is that it cannot be used to distinguish our episodic duty cases, such as the vehicle entrustment case, from the creation of a new peril cases in § 7. Yet the Reporters' architecture relies on this distinction. By locating them as exceptions to § 37, the Reporters treat cases, such as a safety inspector who fails to detect a faulty gas valve[55] as cases where the defendant's conduct did not create a new, special, separate, independent peril to the plaintiff. Of course, this is adequate to describe in a loose way the many status or undertaking scenarios that may be recognized as duty situations such as: failure to assist a customer who has suffered a severe asthma attack, fallen or fainted;[56] failure to assist a friend found unconscious due to carbon-monoxide poisoning;[57] and failure to fulfil undertaking to assist an emergency landing of a plane on fire.[58] But, with respect, it is not a differentiation that can generate the § 7/§ 37 distinction. It is a distinction that, on examination, dissolves.

Take the following case, in which the plaintiff was "at risk for reasons other than the conduct of the" defendant,[59] and which the Reporters classify as a

---

[55] TD No. 4 § 37 illus. 1.
[56] TD No. 4 § 41 illus. 1, 3, 4.
[57] TD No. 4 § 43 illus. 1.
[58] TD No. 4 § 44 illus. 1.
[59] TD No. 4 § 37 cmt. b.

§ 37 case, albeit one that qualifies as an exception to the no-duty rule in that section:[60]

> Ahmed's neighbor, Meena, agreed to make daily visits to Ahmed's house to care for Ahmed's cat and dog while he was out of town. Meena forgot to do so. Meena owes a duty of reasonable care to Ahmed because he relied on Meena to attend to his pets. Meena is subject to liability for harm caused by her negligent failure to visit Ahmed's home and attend to his pets.

We can assume that, absent Meena's undertaking, Ahmed would have secured care for his animals and they would probably not have been injured. In fact, however, Ahmed changed his position in reliance on Meena's undertaking and did not secure other care for his animals. In this context, it is plausible to say that it is Meena who has created a new peril for Ahmed constituted by Meena giving an undertaking in reliance on which Ahmed changed his position. The line between § 7 and § 37 dissolves, because the case may plausibly fall directly into § 7(a).

Many more omission cases are susceptible to the same construction: where the defendant's later negligent omission to do X can be seen as crystallizing a separate peril that he had earlier created by generating within the context of prior status or undertaking, expectations that the defendant would do X, even though such a status or undertaking had been innocently assumed by the defendant. It is of no analytical value to describe such cases as ones where Ahmed's pets are "at risk for reasons other than the conduct of [Meena]." On its face, the case plausibly fits squarely within § 7, with no need to resort to the exceptions to § 37, yet it is the latter location that the Reporters chose for status and undertaking cases. By allocating these cases to § 37 and its exceptions, the Reporters have created a schema that is not administratively workable and has no analytical force or justification. Whenever a plaintiff, in reliance on the status or undertaking of the defendant, changed his position by no longer taking measures to avoid an external risk (e.g., the measures Ahmed would have taken to arrange care for his pets), the defendant has created the new peril which will be crystallised by the defendants' later failure to protect the plaintiff from the external risk.

The Draft itself illustrates these points, for the Reporters' Notes place *within* § 7 at least one scenario involving a failure to rescue occurring within a relationship innocently assumed: where a landowner, having invited another onto the land to consult about strip-mining operations, enticed the invitee to jump into a pond on the property. The Reporters state that the landowner, if he knew that his invitee was drowning, "would have a duty of reasonable

---

[60] TD No. 4 § 43 illus. 3.

care, under § 7, so long as the landowner was a cause of the invitee's decision to go into the pond."[61] To what extent does the allocation of the case to § 7 depend on the nature of the enticement? Can enticement consist of the passive encouragement of providing a diving board? In any case, who gets to define what is the peril here? It might well be defined as the external physical peril of drowning: in which case the Draft should allocate the case to § 37 and its exceptions because the invitee was at peril "for reasons other than the conduct of the" landowner. If the peril can be defined as that constituted by the landowner giving, perhaps silently, reassurance in relation to that physical peril, the case should be allocated to § 7.

The foregoing discussion addressed possible analytical bases on which the polarization of duty in the Draft Restatement may be based but found none to be sound. We are left wondering why the Reporters chose the awkward polarized arrangement. Why are settled duties such as those in status, undertaking, and some negligent entrustment cases hived off as exceptions to a no-duty rule when that arrangement is neither workable nor coherent?

H. Is a More Linear Arrangement Feasible?

Before we move to the nonanalytical motivation behind the duty polarization in the Draft Restatement, we should note, for completeness, that a "linear" arrangement of the case law would have been possible. Every torts textbook in non-U.S. common-law systems, in effect, adopts a linear exposition of duty, starting with the most settled areas of duty recognition and ending with the most controversial, an exposition that locates the duty/no-duty line neither on the shifting misfeasance/nonfeasance boundary nor on any similarly ambiguous distinction between creation-of-risk and no-creation-of-risk, or creation-of-new-peril and no-creation-of-new-peril. In non-U.S. systems debate, both in and out of the courtroom, about the appropriate position of that line focuses explicitly on the full range of legal concerns in favor of, and countervailing to, recognition of a duty that the final court of appeal has used to decide cases in the relatively recent past.[62]

Deploying that non-U.S. approach on the materials in the Draft Restatement, a common lawyer from a non-U.S. system might well arrange them, linearly, along the following lines: a first section, [1.1], would recognize a duty in cases of direct misfeasance, or direct misfeasance with an embedded omission. The following subsections, [1.2.1] and [1.2.2], would contain the

---

[61] TD No. 4 § 37, Reporters' Note to cmt. b. *Compare* Yania v. Bigan, 155 A.2d 343 (Pa. 1955).
[62] Many of these concerns are listed and discussed in Jane Stapleton, *Duty of Care Factors: A Selection from the Judicial Menus, in* THE LAW OF OBLIGATIONS: ESSAYS IN HONOUR OF JOHN FLEMING 59 (Peter Cane & Jane Stapleton eds.)(1998) (hereinafter *Duty of Care*).

uncontroversial areas of duty imposed on careless conduct embedded in an innocent prior status. A final sub-section, [1.2.3], would list, albeit in highly fact-specific criteria, those less-settled, "frontier" situations in which a duty might be owed to a stranger for careless conduct embedded in some other type of innocent prior context. For example, a template might be:

[1]   A duty is usually owed where:
　　[1.1]   defendant's own misfeasance directly caused physical injury to the plaintiff; or
　　[1.2]   defendant's negligence caused physical injury to the plaintiff where
　　　　[1.2.1]   defendant had lawful custody or was *in loco parentis* of a third-party perpetrator; or
　　　　[1.2.2]   defendant had lawful custody or was *in loco parentis* of the victim; or
　　　　[1.2.3]   the case falls into one of the scattered instances in which a defendant has been held liable for facilitating harm to a stranger, that is, someone with whom the defendant has no prior status-based special relationship.
[2]   [2.1]   Unless the case falls into [1], no duty is owed.
　　[2.2]   Even if the case falls into [1], no duty may be owed for policy reasons.[63]

Based on cases discussed in the Draft Restatement the list in subsection [1.2.3] might be:

[1.2.3]

a. mental heath care giver: the defendant is a mental health worker whose patient is the ultimate victim or is a third-party perpetrator of injury to the plaintiff.[64]
b. commercial premises: the victim's presence on the defendant's premises is a result of the defendant's active encouragement prompted by the defendant's pursuit of profit.[65]
c. control etc of instrumentality of property: defendant's negligent act or omission in relation to (1) the control of property that defendant owns;

---

[63]   *See* note 43.
[64]   *See* TD No. 4 § 42 cmt. g, illus. 1, which is loosely based on *Tarasoff v. Regents of Univ. of Cal.*, 551 P. 2d 334, 342 (Cal. 1976).
[65]   E.g., failure of municipal golf club to protect golfers from lightning (note here there is no third party perpetrator); failure of bouncer to protect patron from attack by other patron; failure of common carrier to assist a customer who has suffered a severe asthma attack, has fallen or fainted, or has been innocently stranded by the defendant.

(2) the control of property of which defendant has possession; (3) providing the finances necessary for perpetrator to have access to property or other instrumentality, permits another force to interact with that property or instrumentality in a way that poses a high foreseeable risk of harm to that other or a third party.[66]

d. commercial supply of such property or instrumentality.[67]

e. prior undertaking: defendant undertakes, explicitly or implicitly, to the plaintiff to conduct himself in a certain way, in reliance on which the plaintiff changes his position relative to where the plaintiff would have been had that undertaking not been received, and this change-of-position is a but-for factor in the plaintiff suffering injury when defendant fails to complete the undertaking.[68]

f. legal management of affairs: defendant has legal management of the affairs of a third party and undertakes to that third party that defendant will conduct himself in such a way that will allow the plaintiff to benefit from the assets of the third party.[69]

g. choice to rescue: defendant, otherwise under no duty to the plaintiff, chooses to act affirmatively to protect the plaintiff from a risk.[70]

---

[66] E.g., the defendant's ownership/occupancy of house/premises/campus; the defendant's possession of gun, explosives, etc. (e.g., left unsecured in place accessible to the public used by stranger to attack another stranger); the defendant's possession of motor vehicle (this is where the negligent entrustment and keys-in-ignition cases neatly fall); a great-aunt drives her semiblind nephew to a shooting range and pays for the hire of a gun without informing the range of his visual impairment. Note that the "other force" includes more than just another human force but extends to include, for example, lightning or an animal.

[67] E.g., a machine that is foreseeably dangerous (because, for example, of the foreseeable risk that an employer will remove a safety device); renting a car to a person without checking identification; commercial supply of liquor to a visibly drunk driver.

[68] E.g., foster parents seek and are given affirmative undertaking from fostering agency concerning a foster child's character and in reliance on the accuracy of that affirmative assurance the parents accept the child into their home, and the foster child then assaults their own child, when the foster placement would not have made without the receipt of the explicit assurance. *Compare Randi W. v. Muroc Joint Unified Sch. Dist.*, 929 P. 2d 582 (Cal. 1997) *with W L-6 v. Essex County Council & Anor*, [1998] EWCA Civ. 614.

[69] E.g., defendant is the lawyer of a third party and undertakes to draft a fresh will to benefit the plaintiff but through defendant's negligent delay this is not signed before the third party dies. Note that here there is no requirement for the duty that the plaintiff has changed his position in response to/relied on the undertaking of defendant.

[70] E.g., D sees a stranger-child playing with some discarded razor blades. D removes the blades from the child and puts them in his pocket. D thereafter decides he does not want to be part of a nanny-state so he lets the child remove the blades from his pocket. Child then injures herself with the blade; defendant starts to rescue an unconscious baby on a deserted road. Note that here there is no requirement for the duty that the plaintiff has changed his position in response to (or has relied on) the undertaking of defendant.

h. defendant had control of the physical instrument (e.g., his car) by which the defendant knows the victim has already been innocently injured. In these cases, the defendant comes under a duty of care to use reasonable care to assist an already injured victim.[71]

i. defendant knows he had, but has innocently lost, control of the physical instrument by which another has not yet but may well injure a third party or himself (e.g., the duty to report, once discovered, the theft of a loaded gun from a reasonably secured place by a child).[72]

I. Why Did the Reporters Adopt this Awkward Polarized Arrangement of the Duty Issue?

So our intriguing question remains: Why then did the Reporters adopt their awkward and inelegant analytical architecture? It might be suggested that the way tort law has long been taught in U.S. law schools is based on a polarization between the duty-to-the-whole-world idea and the no-duty-to-rescue-a-stranger idea, and that the Reporters have merely adopted that polarization. In my view, given how fresh a look these Reporters were prepared to take to other issues in the Restatement, such as the admirable separation of causal issues from scope issues, a simple mechanical acceptance of law school habits is unlikely to be the principal explanation. After all, any such habits are likely to be based on more than chance. What motive could lead the Reporters to accept the polarization of duty?

To the eyes of a foreign common lawyer, there is a deep fracture in United States tort law that divides the loud rhetoric of the importance, almost sanctity, of jury decision making and the typically covert, often frenetic, maneuvers that are made by U.S. courts and advocated by tort academics to prevent issues reaching the jury. It is not surprising that fundamental structures of United States tort doctrine reflect this fracture, nor should it be surprising that it is most nakedly exposed in cases where courts seek to restrain liability in negligence. The polarization of duty in United States tort law is a simply a very fine illustration of this schizophrenic attitude to jury decision making.

V. THE "NO-DUTY" TECHNIQUE FOR RESTRAINING LIABILITY IN JURY-FREE SYSTEMS

We have seen that, on both sides of the Atlantic, it is well settled that a person owes a duty to use reasonable care not directly to cause by his own affirmative

---

[71] *See* TD No. 4 § 40.

[72] *Id.*

act physical injury to another. For example, a product manufacturer owes a duty of care to the person who eventually uses the product. If a court is to deny liability here, it must be under another analytical rubric. Take the facts of a modern case, *Caterpillar, Inc. v. Shears*,[73] where the plaintiff was injured at work by a front-end loader supplied by the defendant to his employer. It had been supplied with a rollover protective structure (ROPS), which would have prevented the injury. The employer had removed this to allow the loader to be used in a confined space. The loader was later moved for use in a warehouse, whereupon the ROPS should have been reattached but the employer failed to do this. The plaintiff sued the product manufacturer alleging the misfeasance of supplying an unreasonably dangerous product design.

Suppose a court wanted to refuse liability in a fact situation such as the misfeasance case of *Shears*. In England and Wales, this no-liability could easily be presented by the court, the fact finder, in a way that did not prejudice the longstanding principle that in misfeasance-causing-physical-harm cases a person owes an unqualified duty to the whole world. The English court could formulate a no liability finding: in terms of no breach, on the basis that it was not reasonable to require the manufacturer of a multipurpose product to design it in a way (i.e., with a ROPS that could not be removed) that makes it impossible to use for one of its intended uses (i.e., in a confined space). Or the English court could find no liability in terms of scope, on the basis that, given the intervening carelessness of the employer, the consequence fell outside the perimeter of the appropriate scope of liability for the consequences of the tortious conduct by the manufacturer.

In jury-free systems, such as that in the jurisdiction of England and Wales, a smooth refusal of liability is also possible in cases falling outside the misfeasance-causing-physical-harm class. In these areas, the need to control liability is acute because so much passive conduct can plausibly be made the subject of a negligence allegation. An English judge wanting to refuse liability in such a nontraditional case again typically has a choice of how, analytically, he or she packages that result, though here that choice includes a finding of no duty: no duty; duty but no breach; duty and breach but outside the appropriate scope of liability and so on. Most now agree that systematic restraint on the growth of future liability is critically needed in cases falling outside the misfeasance-causing-physical-harm class and that, to achieve this, the language of duty is needed. Certainly, the keener a court is to send a systemic message about the reasons against liability, the more likely the court is to use

---

[73] *Caterpillar, Inc. v. Shears*, 911 S.W.2d 379 (Tex. 1995) discussed in William Powers Jr., *supra* n. 23.

the "no-duty" formulation because it allows the court to enunciate general concerns of the law, arising from the facts, on which the law takes a particular view: for example, that liability should not be indeterminate; or that the law should not positively encourage abortion.[74]

The clearer and more compelling the countervailing concern spelt out by the court, the more effective is this technique for restraining liability in the future because the doctrine of precedent requires later lower courts to give weight to that concern. Over time it then becomes possible for practitioners to set down the lists of concerns courts have cited, both those favouring the imposition of a duty of care and those countervailing to the recognition of a duty of care. When a novel situation arises, its complex facts may trigger a number of such concerns, some pro-duty and others countervailing to duty. In such a case, the astute lawyer will be able to anticipate the balance a court will strike between these concerns and advise his or her client accordingly.

Two features of jury-free systems such as England and Wales are important to stress. First, the courts have never accepted that any one factual feature of a case can trigger such an extreme concern of the law that it is regarded, without more, as justifying a factually specified no-duty rule. No-duty *results* occur and occur often: no-duty *rules* do not exist.[75] Nonetheless, the techniques for restraining liability work effectively. Second, courts that use the no-duty approach in such cases will probably want to combine it with a nuanced possibility that a duty may be recognized given the presence of certain facts. In a jury-free system, there is no brake inhibiting the courts from using an approach that combines a no-duty response with the possibility of fact-specific exceptions.

No rhetoric about or reverence for jury decisionmaking inhibits such an approach. Take the previous examples of the unsecured premises or car being used by a third-party wrongdoer who thereby injures a victim. Here an English court might hold that: in general, a building owner does not owe a duty to control a vandal; and a car owner does not owe a duty to remove keys from the ignition. The court would, however, be mindful that to accomplish this control of liability while also incorporating the nuance required for justice, it should combine the no-duty technique with the possibility that a duty might

---

[74] A concern that sometimes, on the facts, weighs in favor of the recognition of a duty (as in *Emeh v. Kensington A.H.A.*, [1985] Q.B. 1012, 1021, and sometimes, on the facts, militates against such a recognition (as in *Winnipeg Child and Family Services v. G*, 152 DLR (4th) 193, 3 SCR 925 (1997). *See generally Duty of Care, supra*, note 62 at 62, 73 & 86.

[75] Although in a few rare cases the status of the defendant has given rise to an *immunity* such as the immunity of a barrister for in-court performance, an immunity now widely under attack; *see Arthur J. S. Hall & Co. v. Simons*, UKHL 38, 3 WLR 543 (2000).

be owed in certain special circumstances. Special circumstances might be constituted, for example, by the specific factual feature that: this landowner knew that the vandal had threatened to firebomb the building; or the car owner left the car outside a beer hall in a lawless part of town for a week. As there is no institutional competition between the English court and a jury, there is no objection to the infusion into the duty issue of fact-sensitive distinctions. An associated technique used to restrain liability in such jury-free systems should be noted at this point. Appellate courts vigilantly police the duty/breach distinction in order to preserve the freedom of trial judges to deny liability on the basis that there has been no breach. As early as 1944, Justice du Parcq warned that:

> There is danger, particularly in these days when few cases are tried by juries, of exalting to the status of propositions of law what really are particular applications to special facts of propositions of ordinary good sense.[76]

If a court does not make it clear that its analysis of factual features of a case merely goes to that court's decision on breach, a later court may misinterpret those comments as a statement of a factually-specified duty, and that later court may feel constrained to uphold liability even though on the facts the trial judge would have refused liability.

Exactly this situation presented itself to the House of Lords in *Qualcast (Wolverhampton) Ltd. v. Haynes*,[77] where the trial judge felt compelled to find the defendant liable even though he personally was of the view that there was no breach on the facts. He read the judgments of earlier courts as laying down, as a proposition of law, that an employer not only had a duty of reasonable care to his employee, but that he owed a factually specified duty,[78] namely a duty to warn his employee to wear spats, even though on the facts the trial judge did not think the duty of care should require this and that liability should not be imposed. Lord Somervell noted:

> when negligence cases were tried with juries the judge would direct them as to the law ... there was not, and could not be, complete uniformity of standard. One jury would attribute to the reasonable man a greater degree of prescience than would another. The jury's decision did not become part of our law citable

---

[76] *Easson v. London & North Eastern Railway Co.*, [1944] K.B. 421, 426 (du Parcq L. J.).

[77] [1959] A.C. 743.

[78] An equal but opposite danger of inflexibility arises where a court rejects liability on the basis of there being "no duty to do X" "in the circumstances" but does not give sufficient emphasis to the many factual circumstances that might, in later cases, justify the imposition of a duty: *see*, e.g., statements that a commercial host owed no duty to its customer in *Cole v. South Tweed Heads Rugby League Football Club Ltd.*, [2004] HCA 29.

as a precedent... now that negligence cases are mostly tried without juries, the distinction between the functions of judge and jury is blurred. A judge naturally gives reasons for the conclusion formally arrived at by a jury without reasons... if the reasons given by a judge for arriving at the conclusion previously reached by a jury are to be treated as "law" and citable, the precedent system will die from a surfeit of authorities.[79]

Lord Denning added:

In the present case the only proposition of law that was relevant was the well-known proposition... that it is the duty of a master to take reasonable care for the safety of his workmen. No question arose on that proposition. The question that did arise was this: what did reasonable care demand of the employers in this particular case? This is not a question of law at all but a question of fact. To solve it the tribunal of fact be it judge or jury can take into account any proposition of good sense which is relevant in the circumstances, but it must beware not to treat it as a proposition of law.[80]

VI. THE "NO-DUTY RULE" TECHNIQUE FOR RESTRAINING LIABILITY IN THE UNITED STATES

In stark contrast to their virtual absence in the rest of the common law world,[81] no-duty *rules* have been relatively popular historically in the United States. Statements of such rules, applied unless the court accepted that special circumstances were present, have included not merely the iconic no-duty-to-rescue rule but also: a no-duty rule to protect against third-party wrongdoing;[82] a no-duty rule to warn of risks created by others; a no-duty rule on a parent to control its child;[83] a no-duty rule on a social host to those injured by a guest;[84] a rule that there was no general duty of care on a landowner to trespassers or licensees with regard to the condition of the land, and no duty to warn invitees of obvious risks;[85] and a no-duty rule on a railway company to warn of the "obvious" risk when a train stopped at a crossing.[86]

To many common lawyers outside the United States, the operation of these no-duty rules looks very peculiar given that they are not invariable bright-line

---

[79] *Qualcast (Wolverhampton) Ltd. v. Haynes*, [1959] A.C. 743, 757–8 (Lord Somervell of Harrow).

[80] *Id.* at 759 (Lord Denning).

[81] *But see supra* n. 75.

[82] *A. H. v. Rockingham Publ'g Co.*, 495 S.E.2d 482 (Va. 1998).

[83] *Cooper v. Meyer*, 365 N.E.2d 201 (Ill. Ct. App. 1977).

[84] *Ferreira V. Strack*, 652 A.2d 965 (R.I. 1995).

[85] *See* DAN B. DOBBS, THE LAW OF TORTS 592, 597, 604 (2001).

[86] *Dunn v. Baltimore & Ohio Railroad Co.*, 127 Ill.2d 350, 537 N.E.2d 738 (Ill. 1989).

rules but are starting points that can be relaxed in suitable circumstances. Why does United States law bother to crystallize a no-duty response to certain fact patterns but then subject that response to amelioration by a consideration of other factual features? What function is performed by this preliminary but not final prejudgment of a case? Crudely put, the answer is that the technique of a no-duty rule is the most effective way U.S. courts can control the incidence of liability, because the no-duty rule keeps the issue from the jury. In the tort of negligence, duty is a matter of law for the court[87] and what constitutes a special relationship or other special factual features allowing for relaxation of a no-duty rule also is a matter of law for the court and not the jury.[88] By being able to rely on a no-duty prejudgment of the facts of a case, a court can reserve to itself the normative evaluation of the specific factual matrix, yet appear to do so legitimately under the guise of dealing only with issues of law. The court is able to claim wide power to decide when, if at all, a jury is allowed to decide whether the negligent defendant is to be liable to his or her victim.

U.S. courts often have used this technique to sidestep the rhetoric of the sanctity of jury decisionmaking in areas outside the misfeasance-causing-physical-harm sphere. Take the claims in the vandal or car thief cases: a U.S. court that wants to reject such claims and do so on a principle that does not simply apply to the individual case but can prevail in later cases even when the jury would have imposed liability, must use a no-duty rule. Again, just as is the case with the English court, to accomplish control with the nuance required for justice, the U.S. court will want to frame that no-duty rule with fact-sensitive exceptions. Even though such an approach risks the appearance of usurping the role of the jury, many U.S. courts today deploy the approach of a no-duty rule subject to fact-specific exceptions in order to confine liability.[89]

A phenomenon that highlights how deep the fracture is in the U.S. system between pro-jury rhetoric and judicial determination to prevent some issues from getting to the jury is that this use of factually particularized duties to confine liability is deployed even in misfeasance cases.[90] Remember *Caterpillar,*

---

[87] TD No. 2 cmt. b.

[88] TD No. 4 § 41 cmt. e.

[89] Sometimes by manipulatively denying the foreseeability required for duty "when a reasonable jury might have found otherwise": TD No. 4 § 38 Reporters' Note to cmt. c.

[90] Mark Gergen states that this is happening "in a growing number of cases, [where] judges take the evaluation of conduct that would seem to fall within this general duty away from the jury, sometimes by announcing a particularized no-duty rule, and sometimes by an *ad hoc* no-duty decision." Mark P. Gergen, *The Jury's Role in Deciding Normative Issues in the American Common Law*, 68 FORDHAM L. REV. 407, 430 (1999).

Inc. v. Shears,[91] the case about the user of a front-end loader who sued the manufacturer? There the Texas Supreme Court wanted to prevent the imposition of liability. Because the litigation was a misfeasance case, the Court was confronted by the duty-to-the-whole-world principle. Nevertheless, the Court chose to abandon that principle and whittle down the manufacturer's duty in fact-specific terms: namely, the manufacturer had no duty to design a multipurpose machine in a way that makes it impossible to use in one of the settings in which the manufacturer had wanted it to be usable. In other words, this desire to lay down systemic rules to keep swathes of cases from juries can be so strong that U.S. courts are willing to lay down no-duty rules even in the area where the fundamental rhetoric of United States tort law says that a duty is owed to the whole world when physical injury was caused by the careless act of the defendant.

Nor is *Shears* at all an exceptional case. Another notorious example of a no-duty rule in a misfeasance context is provided by the "stopped-train rule,"[92] which some U.S. jurisdictions applied, and some continue to apply, when a vehicle hits a train halted on a crossing. When the plaintiff vehicle driver collides with the stopped train, the railway company is engaged in a course of positive conduct. The duty-to-the-whole-world rhetoric of U.S. tort law would suggest that, because this course of conduct foreseeably threatened the injury it eventually caused, it attracted a duty of care. This duty rhetoric in turn militates in favor of allowing the case to go to the jury, which, so another piece of rhetoric goes, is the "repository of commonsense normative wisdom in individual cases."[93] But, under the label, the "stopped-train/no-duty" rule, U.S. jurisdictions have declared that the railway owes no duty, unless certain factual circumstances exist.

The stopped-train no-duty rule offends both of these rhetorical sacred cows: the duty-to-the-whole-world rhetoric in misfeasance cases; and the sanctity of jury evaluation of the factual context of the individual case. The rule is calculated to ensure that judges, not juries, assess the wisdom of imposing liability in the individual stopped train case. This is because the no-duty rule prevents the case getting to the jury unless the facts justify a departure from the no-duty rule, and it is for the courts to decide if such facts do exist. United States courts impose this rule because of their fear of jury decision making: that without the rule there is the danger that a rogue pro-plaintiff jury might

---

[91]   911 S.W.2d 379 (Tex. 1995).
[92]   On which, *see,* e.g., *Malcome v. Toledo, Peoria & Western Railway Corp.*, 349 Ill. App. 3d 1005; 811 N.E.2d 1199 (Ill. Ct. App. 2004).
[93]   TD No. 4 § 38 cmt. c.

determine that, for example where a train with a bulky profile was stopped at an unobstructed clearly lit crossing on a flat plain where there was no other traffic, the railway should nevertheless be liable to a plaintiff who failed to see the train in time to avoid a collision and resultant injury. The no-duty rule prevents the jury ever getting its hands on such a case.

In the end, then, it seems that the architecture of the Draft Restatement is not as baffling as may first appear to the foreign common lawyer. In fact, it neatly tracks the pattern in U.S. cases, although like those cases it is, understandably, somewhat coy about the reasons for the polarization between the duty rule in § 7 and the no-duty rule in § 37. The major concern that shapes U.S. tort law here, and its Restatement, is fear of the future expansion of duties of care in relation to physical injury. This fear is fueled by a suppressed mistrust of jury decision making. To keep the scope of the tort of negligence firmly under the sober surveillance of the courts and as much out of the hands of the jury as possible, U.S. courts use a strategy of no-duty rules, ameliorated by fact-sensitive exceptions, that can be applied by trial judges in motions for summary judgments and directed verdicts, and can be used in turn by appellate courts to reign in trial judges.

On this interpretation of the Reporters' intentions, the tactics of the Draft's architecture become clear. The Restatement will subject cases of direct misfeasance or direct misfeasance (with an embedded omission) to a bright-line duty-to-the-whole-world rule in § 7. But the Restatement will subject all cases outside these settled areas to a bright-line no-duty rule in § 37, to which only certain highly circumscribed, factually delineated exceptions (§ § 39–45) are permitted, with permission to be decided by the court, not the jury. If the court decides a case does not fall into such an exception, the trial court will then have authoritative Restatement grounds to prevent the case getting to the jury and an appeal court has grounds to reverse a trial judge who permits a radical new duty argument in a fresh context to get to the jury.

Of course, these tactics offend the Reporters' account of the dogma said to govern the division of normative power between the U.S. court and jury: that no-duty rulings by a court are appropriate only when it can promulgate relatively clear, categorical, bright-line rules of law applicable to a general class of cases;[94] and that when liability depends on the normative evaluation of factors specific to an individual case, the appropriate rubric is scope of

---

[94] TD No. 4 § 7 cmt. a. *See also* TD No. 3 § 29 cmt. f; Gergen, *supra* n. 90: "a duty determination [should] take the form of either a general standard or of a categorical rule that applies beyond the immediate case" (*id.* at 431–2), and "for a judge to dispose of a negligence claim by finding no duty, he must state a rule or a standard that applies beyond the immediate case and that contains no factual or moral element that is open to doubt." (*Id.* at 432).

liability and the decision is that of the jury.[95] But this simply reflects a deeper schizophrenia in United States tort law toward the extent of power that juries should wield.

VII. CONCLUSION

A central feature of the constitutional arrangements of a common law system is that courts make law. At which point in the system, jury or appellate court, that lawmaking occurs, and how radical the legal change can be, are matters that are governed by conventions that are in turn formed by the operation of many different political forces over time and between places. In restating legal principles currently applied in U.S. courts, the ALI must preserve this constitutionally vital phenomenon and resolve the stark political choices they pose. A close reading of parts of the Draft Restatement suggests ways in which its Reporters seem to have responded to these choices, the "ghosts at the feast" of restatement. Specifically, there is a deep fracture in U.S. tort law that divides the loud rhetoric of the importance of jury decision making and the typically covert maneuvers that are made to prevent issues reaching the jury. It is not surprising that fundamental structures of U.S. tort doctrine reflect this fracture, nor should it be surprising that it has heavily influenced the duty architecture adopted by the Reporters of the Draft Restatement (Third) of Torts: Liability for Physical Harm.

[95] TD No. 4, § 7 cmt. a.

CHAPTER NINE

INFORMATION SHIELDS IN TORT LAW

David G. Owen

ABSTRACT. Responsibility theory suggests that the more correct information a person has about a dangerous thing or situation, the more likely it is that the person will make informed choices about how to confront such risks, and the more likely such choices will be cost-effective and rational. The premises for these conclusions include: (1) at an individual level, that people are rational beings, and that more and better information about risk permits people to make informed decisions; (2) at a social level, that people strive to make just, socially-beneficial choices when they can do so without undue harm to themselves; and (3) at a political level, that the more personal decision making that can be left to individuals, the less that government interferes with personal choice.

This chapter inquires into the extent to which tort law does and should impose responsibility on actors for harm to persons who possess full risk information, either because the risk was obvious or the victim was warned about it. Put otherwise, when a person chooses to engage a risk about which he or she has full information and is injured as a result, should that person bear responsibility for the harmful result?

The chapter proceeds to develop a model Liability Shield program that would shield manufacturers from liability if they provide consumers with full information of product hazards. Although such a program is attractive in abstract responsibility theory, it is seen to rest perilously upon twin pillars wrought of little more than fantasy: human rationality, an ideal that is undermined by real-world frailties of human cognition and behavior; and institutional responsibility, undermined by real-world obstacles to fair and efficient behavior by manufacturers and safety agencies.

The chapter thus concludes that developed tort law has correctly shifted consideration of a victim's possession of full risk information from the wooden construct of judicial no-duty rulings to an analysis of victim fault within flexible systems of comparative fault.

I. INTRODUCTION

Moral and legal responsibility for a person's choices that result in accidental harm are grounded to a large extent upon the amount and quality of risk

David G. Owen, Carolina Distinguished Professor of Law, University of South Carolina.

information available to both the actor and the victim. The more correct information a potential victim has about a dangerous thing or situation, the more likely it is that the person will make informed choices about how to engage the risks that he or she confronts. And the more informed a person's choices about risk engagement, the more likely it is that those choices will be cost-effective and otherwise rational. Or so theory might suggest.

The premises of these conclusions are familiar: At an individual level, people are rational beings; rational beings desire to make cost-effective decisions; more and better information about risk permits people to ascertain the cost-effectiveness of a contemplated action and, hence, to make informed decisions on whether and how to engage a risk. At a social level, people strive to make just, socially-beneficial choices that maximize net benefits to other persons as well as themselves when they can do so without undue harm to themselves. And, at a political level, the more personal decisions are left to individuals, the less government interferes with personal choice, the better. Or so theory might suggest.

The broad topic examined in this chapter is the proper relationship between risk information and duty in tort law. More particularly, the chapter inquires into the extent to which tort law does and should impose responsibility on actors for harm to persons who constructively possess full and complete risk information, either because the risk was obvious, widely known, or the victim was warned about it. If the above assumptions about risk information and responsibility are correct, fully-informed people who make risky choices that result in harm to themselves should bear responsibility for that harm. Put otherwise, when a person is injured as a result of choosing to engage a risk about which he or she has full information, the person normally should be responsible, morally and legally, for the harmful result. Again, theory might so suggest.

But what if an actor who creates a risk knows that a substantial number of persons, despite their knowledge of the danger, will nevertheless encounter the danger and be injured by it? And what if the actor has available a simple means for reducing or eliminating the hazard? The problem then becomes how the availability of risk information by a victim does and should affect the tort responsibility of an actor for accidental harm to the victim in situations in which the actor has available, but fails to employ, reasonable means to avoid the harm. The issue then reduces to how the law should resolve the resulting clash between individual responsibility and actor responsibility for harm.

A central aspect of the inquiry here is to explore whether this responsibility clash is better resolved by no-duty rules or by factual determinations of victim fault. One of the recurring doctrinal battles of tort law in the twentieth century concerned the responsibility of actors for dangers that are obvious, generally known, or warned about – notably the duties of (1) landowners and occupiers for injuries to persons entering the land; and (2) manufacturers for injuries to users of their products. For focus, the inquiry is limited here to the latter topic: the duty of manufacturers to design away dangers that are obvious or for which warnings have been provided.[1]

This chapter first reviews the rise and fall of the patent danger rule in products liability law, a doctrine that holds product users responsible for injuries from a product's obvious dangers of design. Although the case for shielding actors from responsibility for harm from the obvious dangers they create is not implausible,[2] conventional wisdom holds that the patent danger rule was given its last rites, and properly put to rest, deep in the last century. But the personal responsibility principles underlying the patent danger doctrine persist, and the doctrine still walks the land, albeit feebly, cloaked in the guise of the consumer expectations test for product defectiveness.

The chapter next examines the relationship between the duty to warn and the duty of safe design. This inquiry necessarily involves an examination of a mysterious sentence in comment j to § 402A of the Restatement (Second) of Torts that appears to shield manufacturers from their duty of safe design if they have warned consumers of a danger, a doctrine that closely mirrors the patent danger rule. Despite the heroic attempt of the Restatement (Third) of Torts: Products Liability[3] to bury the notion that warnings trump design, the new Restatement served ironically to revivify the warned-of danger rule.

Finally, the chapter tests the appropriateness of these doctrinal developments, by sketching out an Information Liability Shield program that would reverse these developments by shielding manufacturers from liability, for claims of unsafe design as well as inadequate warning, if they provide consumers with full and fair information about product hazards. Although such an approach appears sound in the abstract, it is actually rife with real-world problems: (1) difficulties in ascertaining the "fullness" of information; (2) adjudicatory problems in determining causation and scope of risk; (3) the transfer of accident costs from actors to third-party bystanders; (4) human cognitive and behavioral deficiencies that generate inadvertent behavior; and (5) the problem of agency bloating.

---

[1] This limitation excludes examination of how the doctrine of assumption of risk might affect liability in constructive knowledge cases.

[2] See RICHARD A. EPSTEIN, SIMPLE RULES FOR A COMPLEX WORLD 230–31 (1995).

[3] Hereinafter sometimes referred to as the PRODUCTS LIABILITY RESTATEMENT.

The chapter thus concludes that modern products liability law appears to have moved correctly in abandoning wooden no-duty constructs based on a victim's possession of full risk information in exchange for considering that information in assessing victim fault within flexible systems of comparative fault.

II. THE RISE AND FALL OF THE PATENT DANGER RULE

A. In General

Dangers may be divided into two categories: obvious (or patent) dangers, on the one hand, and hidden (or latent) dangers, on the other. Many products contain "open and obvious" dangers, dangers plainly appearing on a product's face that are manifest to buyers and to users. For example, the hazards to human limbs from electric fans, power lawn mowers, and punch presses not equipped with guards are quite obvious for all to see. By contrast, other kinds of products contain sharp, moving, toxic, or other kinds of hazards concealed from users, such as a sharp mechanism hidden beneath the armrest of an adjustable lawn chair or the toxic nature of a household cleaning solvent lethal to young children. This latter form of danger, the latent type, is the more pernicious, because people confronting dangers of this type have no opportunity to address the hazard with caution, or to avoid it altogether, so as to avoid the risk of harm.

Although products with obvious dangers are normally safer than products with hidden dangers, products containing no dangers of either type are even safer. Although the obviousness of a product's dangers suggests that there is no need to *warn* consumers of the hazard by other means, because the patent danger itself alerts users to the need to be cautious, the interesting question that remains is whether a manufacturer should be responsible for injuries that could have been prevented by simple and inexpensive design changes. This issue generated one of the most intriguing sagas in prod ·cts liability law – the rise and fall of the patent danger rule.[4]

B. The Rise of the Patent Danger Rule

Before the 1970s, victims of accidents from obvious design dangers in products were broadly barred from recovery under the patent danger doctrine.

---

[4] Earlier versions of Part II of this chapter appear in 1 DAVID G. OWEN, M. STUART MADDEN, & MARY J. DAVIS, MADDEN & OWEN ON PRODUCTS LIABILITY (3D) §§ 10.1 and 10.2 (2000) and DAVID G. OWEN, PRODUCTS LIABILITY LAW § 10.2 (2005) © Thomson-West.

The classic case so holding was *Campo v. Scofield*,[5] decided by the New York Court of Appeals in 1950. The plaintiff, working on his son's farm, was dumping a crate of onions into an "onion topping" machine when his hands were caught and injured in its revolving steel rollers. He sued the manufacturers of the machine for negligently failing to equip it with a guard or stopping device. The trial court denied the defendants' motion to dismiss, the Appellate Division reversed, and the Court of Appeals affirmed, ruling that the plaintiff's failure to allege that the danger was latent or unknown was fatal to the complaint. Writing for a unanimous court, Judge Fuld reasoned that a manufacturer satisfies the law's demands if it "does everything necessary to make the machine function properly for the purpose for which it is designed, if the machine is without any latent defect, and if its functioning creates no danger or peril that is not known to the user..."[6]

A manufacturer simply has no duty to protect people against "a patent peril or from a source manifestly dangerous." Otherwise, reasoned the court, the manufacturer of an axe, buzz saw, or airplane with an exposed propeller would be subject to liability to a user cut by the blade or propeller. "In such cases, the manufacturer has the right to expect that such persons will do everything necessary to avoid such contact, for the very nature of the article gives notice and warning of the consequences to be expected, of the injuries to be suffered. In other words, the manufacturer is under no duty to render a machine or other article 'more' safe – as long as the danger to be avoided is obvious and patent to all."[7]

Campo was by no means the first case so holding,[8] but it anchored the patent danger doctrine like a rock. Its simple statement of individual responsibility for self-protection struck a responsive chord throughout the nation, and, following *Campo*, many courts adopted the doctrine, or reaffirmed it if they had relied on it before.[9] In the 1950s and early 1960s, the *Campo* obvious danger rule was one of the most firmly-entrenched doctrines in all of products liability law. Professor Fleming James, ever critical of rules that limited recovery for injured persons,[10] derided the absolutist no-duty nature of the rule as

---

[5] 95 N.E.2d 802 (N.Y. 1950).

[6] *Id.* at 804.

[7] *Id.*

[8] Earlier cases had also barred recovery in cases of obvious dangers. *See, e.g., Stevens v. Allis-Chalmers Mfg. Co.*, 100 P.2d 723 (Kan. 1940); *Yaun v. Allis-Chalmers Mfg. Co.*, 34 N.W.2d 853 (Wis. 1948).

[9] *See, e.g., Stevens v. Durbin-Durco, Inc.*, 377 S.W.2d 343 (Mo. 1964); *Parker v. Heasler Plumbing & Heating Co.*, 388 P.2d 516 (Wyo. 1964); *Tyson v. Long Mfg. Co.*, 107 S.E.2d 170 (N.C. 1959).

[10] *See generally* VIRGINIA E. NOLAN & EDMUND URSIN, UNDERSTANDING ENTERPRISE LIABILITY (1995); Priest, *The Invention of Enterprise Liability: A Critical History of the Intellectual Foundations of Modern Tort Law*, 14 J. LEG. STUD. 461 (1985).

"a vestigial carryover from pre-*MacPherson* days when deceit was needed for recovery."[11] Yet, even two decades after *Campo*, the Maryland Court of Appeals opted to align itself with other vestigial jurisdictions in adhering to the rule.[12]

Most design danger claims before the 1970s involved hidden or "latent" dangers,[13] and courts at the time showed little tolerance for claims involving design dangers that were obvious. For example, in *Bartkewich v. Billenger*,[14] decided in 1968, the hand of a glass-breaking machine operator was crushed when he reached into the machine to free a piece of glass that was jamming, and he thought damaging, the machine. Addressing the operator's design claim against the manufacturer for failing to provide guards or strategically located cut-off switches, the court held that the manufacturer had no such duty: "If he thought the machine was being damaged, what did he think would happen to his hand?"[15]

C. The Fall of the Patent Danger Rule

But not all courts were unsympathetic to the plight of workers and others injured by obvious product dangers, and as the consumer protectionist perspective of Restatement (Second) of Torts § 402A spread across America in the late 1960s, judicial attitudes toward the patent danger rule began to change as well. Some courts, persuaded by the safety, representational, and risk-spreading rationales thought to support the new strict tort doctrine, began to ignore defendants' pleas to apply the patent danger doctrine.[16] And, by 1970, courts had begun expressly to reject the obvious danger rule as outmoded and improper.

One such case explicitly rejecting the patent danger rule, *Pike v. Frank G. Hough Co.*,[17] involved a design claim against the manufacturer of a large earth-moving machine (a "paydozer") that backed over a worker. The paydozer had a large engine box in the rear that created a large blind spot behind the machine,

---

[11] Fleming James Jr., *Products Liability (pt. 1)*, 34 Tex. L. Rev. 44, 52 (1955). *See also* 2 F. Harper & F. James, The Law of Torts § 28.5, at 1544 (1956).

[12] *See Blankenship v. Morrison Machine Co.*, 257 A.2d 430, 433 (Md. 1969). More recently, compare *Halliday v. Sturm, Ruger & Co.*, 792 A.2d 1145 (Md. 2002) (barring recovery in gunshot case based on consumer expectations).

[13] *See Luque v. McLean*, 501 P.2d 1163, 1168 (Cal. 1972) ("the great majority of reported decisions dealing with products liability have involved defects classifiable as latent.").

[14] 247 A.2d 603 (Pa. 1968).

[15] *Id.* at 605.

[16] *See, e.g., Wright v. Massey-Harris, Inc.*, 215 N.E.2d 465 (Ill. App. Ct. 1966).

[17] 467 P.2d 229, 235 (Cal. 1970).

and it was not equipped with rearview mirrors. Contending that the danger of being struck by the paydozer was obvious, the manufacturer claimed that it had no duty to install safety devices to protect against such a patent peril. Rejecting this defense, the California Supreme Court relied on the analysis of the patent danger doctrine, and the criticism of *Campo v. Scofield*,[18] by Professor Fleming James[19] in his tort law treatise, in which he observed that "the bottom does not logically drop out of a negligence case against the maker when it is shown that the purchaser knew of the dangerous condition. Thus, if the product is a carrot-topping machine with exposed moving parts,[20] or an electric clothes wringer dangerous to the limbs of the operator, and if it would be feasible for the maker of the product to install a guard or a safety release, it should be a question for the jury whether reasonable care demanded such a precaution, though its absence is obvious."[21] Reversing the nonsuit of the plaintiff, the *Pike* court concluded that "the obviousness of peril is relevant to the manufacturer's defenses, not to the issue of duty."[22]

Other courts at the time also were beginning to reject the patent danger doctrine as contrary to the policies of the day. In *Palmer v. Massey-Ferguson, Inc.*,[23] for example, a farmer sued the manufacturer of a hay baler for injuries he suffered to his hand when it was caught in the mechanism of the machine. Observing that the patent danger rule conflicted with the trend toward expanding manufacturer responsibility, the court reasoned that "a rule which excludes the manufacturer from liability if the defect in the design of his product is patent but applies the duty if such a defect is latent is somewhat anomalous. The manufacturer of the obviously defective product ought not to escape because the product was obviously a bad one. The law, we think, ought to discourage misdesign rather than encouraging it in its obvious form."[24]

---

[18] 95 N.E.2d 802 (N.Y. 1950).

[19] Before publication in his treatise with Professor Harper, Fleming James first included his discussion of the obvious danger doctrine in Fleming James, Jr., *Products Liability* (pt. 1), 34 TEX. L. REV. 44, 51–54 (1955).

[20] Citing *Campo*, although the product in *Campo* in fact was an onion-topping machine.

[21] 2 F. HARPER & F. JAMES, THE LAW OF TORTS § 28.5, at 1542–1543 (1956). *Pike* quoted some of the HARPER AND JAMES materials quoted above, together with some other excerpts. *Pike* also relied on similar conclusions by Dix Noel, in *Manufacturer's Negligence of Design or Directions for Use of a Product*, 71 YALE L.J. 816, 838 (1962). *See Pike*, 467 P.2d at 235.

[22] *Pike*, 467 P.2d at 234.

[23] 476 P.2d 713 (Wash. Ct. App. 1970).

[24] *Id.* at 718–19. The fallacy here, of course, is that it is the *danger* that is obvious, not the "defect." Indeed, the ultimate legal question in cases involving obvious product dangers is whether the obviousness of the danger renders the product excessively dangerous, or, in other words, "defective."

Once the 1970s were under way, the expansionary principles of modern products liability law took hold quickly, and courts increasingly began to reevaluate the role that the obviousness of a danger should play in the determination of design defectiveness. For example, in *Luque v. McLean*,[25] the California Supreme Court in 1972 reexamined the applicability of the patent danger doctrine to design claims brought under § 402A in a case in which the plaintiff was injured when he slipped on wet grass and his hand slid through an unguarded area in the front of a power lawn mower he was using. Relying on language in *Greenman v. Yuba Power Products, Inc.*[26] suggesting that a plaintiff must establish that he was not aware of the product's defective condition,[27] the trial court so instructed the jury, which returned a verdict for the defendant. Reversing for error in this instruction, the California court repudiated the patent danger rule in strict products liability.[28] As the decade of the 1970s progressed, more and more courts rejected the patent danger doctrine in design defect cases, holding that the obviousness of a danger is merely one factor in assessing the negligence of a defendant, the defectiveness of a product's design, or the appropriateness of a plaintiff's conduct, rather than an absolute bar to liability.[29]

The landmark decision repudiating the obvious danger doctrine was decided in New York, in 1976, by the same court that in 1950 had provided the doctrine's bedrock decision of *Campo v. Scofield*. In *Micallef v. Miehle Co.*,[30] the New York Court of Appeals reconsidered its renowned *Campo* patent danger rule. The plaintiff, who operated a huge photo-offset printing press, some 150 feet in length, discovered a foreign object on the printing plate, which was rotating at high speed. He proceeded to try to remove or "chase the hickie on the run," as was the custom in the industry, in order to avoid stopping the machine, which took at least three hours to restart, by lightly touching the revolving plate with an eight-inch-wide piece of plastic. While so doing, the plastic and the plaintiff's hand were drawn together into the

---

[25] 501 P.2d 1163 (Cal. 1972).

[26] 377 P.2d 897 (Cal. 1963).

[27] "To establish the manufacturer's liability it was sufficient that plaintiff proved that he was injured while using the Shopsmith in a way it was intended to be used as a result of a defect in design and manufacture *of which plaintiff was not aware* that made the Shopsmith unsafe for its intended use." *Id.* at 901 (emphasis added).

[28] As *Luque* pointed out, the California Supreme Court had repudiated the obvious danger rule in the *negligent* design context in *Pike v. Frank G. Hough Co.*, 467 P.2d 229 (Cal. 1970).

[29] *See, e.g., Byrns v. Riddell, Inc.*, 550 P.2d 1065 (Ariz. 1976); *Micallef v. Miehle Co.*, 348 N.E.2d 571 (N.Y. 1976); *Stenberg v. Beatrice Foods Co.*, 576 P.2d 725 (Mont. 1978); *Auburn Machine Works Co. v. Jones*, 366 So.2d 1167 (Fla. 1979).

[30] 348 N.E.2d 571 (N.Y. 1976).

machine. The plaintiff's expert engineer testified that the machine should have been equipped with guards, which were available and would not have impeded hickie chasing, to prevent a user's hands from entering the machine. The defendant countered that the absence of guards was an open and obvious condition that it had no duty to correct. Judgment on a jury verdict for the plaintiff was reversed by the Appellate Division, relying in part on *Campo*'s patent danger doctrine, and the plaintiff appealed.

Reversing the Appellate Division, the Court of Appeals began: "The time has come to depart from the patent danger rule enunciated in *Campo v. Scofield...*".[31] In support of its decision to overrule *Campo*, the court noted the "sustained attack" on that opinion, stemming from "the belief that, in our highly complex and technological society, we fall victim to the manufacturer who holds himself out as an expert in his field." Furthermore, the court pointed to charges that the patent danger rule was little more than an assumption of risk defense as a matter of law; that it was anomalous for requiring manufacturers to develop reasonably safe products but then immunizing them from obvious dangers no matter how unreasonable; and that its rigidity produced harsh results for consumers who could not always recognize and appreciate obvious hazards. Accordingly, the court held that a manufacturer must design its products with reasonable care to avoid unreasonable risks of harm to persons who might be exposed to a foreseeable danger, dependent on "a balancing of the likelihood of harm, and the gravity of harm if it happens, against the burden of the precaution which would be effective to avoid the harm."[32] Thus, although the obviousness of a product danger might reduce the likelihood of accidents, and so factor into the calculus of risk, and although a danger's obviousness might affect the issues of contributory negligence and assumption of risk, "the patent-danger doctrine should not, in and of itself, prevent a plaintiff from establishing his case."[33]

Once the *Campo* patent danger doctrine was repudiated in its own home state, the rule proceeded to collapse around the nation. One court after another, usually for claims in both negligence and strict liability in tort, abandoned the rule's absolute no-duty power and reduced the obviousness of danger to mere "factor" status in the cost-benefit evaluation of the safety of a product's design.[34] Some states continued the obvious danger rule into the

---

[31] *Id.* at 573.
[32] *Micallef*, 348 N.E.2d at 576–77.
[33] *Id.* at 578.
[34] Also repudiating the open and obvious hazard doctrine, *see, e.g., Stenberg v. Beatrice Foods Co.*, 576 P.2d 725 (Mont. 1978); *Auburn Machine Works Co., Inc. v. Jones*, 366 So.2d

1980s,[35] and a few lingering offshoots of the doctrine still showed signs of life in five or six states even into the 1990s.[36] Perhaps the doctrine's last real stronghold was the state of Georgia,[37] and the Supreme Court of that state finally surrendered in 1998.[38]

Despite the formal collapse of the patent danger doctrine in recent decades, it is important to note that the obviousness of a product's risk still serves as a total bar to liability in some jurisdictions in special situations[39] and in other

---

1167, 1170 (Fla. 1979):

> The patent danger doctrine encourages manufacturers to be outrageous in their design, to eliminate safety devices, and to make hazards obvious. For example, if the cage which is placed on an electric fan as a safety device were left off and someone put his hand in the fan, under this doctrine there would be no duty on the manufacturer as a matter of law.

See also *Holm v. Sponco Mfg., Inc.,* 324 N.W.2d 207 (Minn. 1982); *Owens v. Allis-Chalmers Corp.,* 326 N.W.2d 372 (Mich. 1982) (restricting patent danger rule to cases involving simple tools and products); *Morrison v. Kubota Tractor Corp.,* 891 S.W.2d 422 (Mo. Ct. App. 1994) (absence of rollover protection system on tractor); *Seymour v. Brunswick Corp.,* 655 So. 2d 892 (Miss. 1995); *LeBlanc v. American Honda Motor Co.,* 688 A.2d 556 (N.H. 1997); *Perkins v. Wilkinson Sword, Inc.,* 700 N.E.2d 1247 (Ohio 1998); *Hernandez v. Tokai Corp.,* 2 S.W.3d 251 (Tex. 1999).

[35] See, e.g., *Estrada v. Schmutz Mfg. Co.,* 734 F.2d 1218, 1220 (7th Cir. 1984) (Posner, J.) (Ind. law) (factory worker's hand caught while brushing ink on rollers: if you "go to the zoo and put your hand through the lion's cage, and the lion bites your hand off,... you do not have an action against the zoo"); *Miller v. Dvornik,* 501 N.E.2d 160 (Ill. Ct. App. 1986); *Hedgepeth v. Fruehauf Corp.,* 634 F. Supp 93 (S. D. Miss. 1986); *Coast Catamaran Corp. v. Mann,* 321 S.E.2d 353 (Ga. Ct. App. 1984).

[36] Such as a no-duty rule with respect to simple product designs, which may still exist in both Illinois and Michigan. See, e.g., *Scoby v. Vulcan-Hart Corp.,* 569 N.E.2d 1147 (Ill. Ct. App. 1991); *Mallard v. Hoffinger Indus.,* 564 N.W.2d 74 (Mich. Ct. App. 1997) (no duty to design away risk of injury from diving headfirst into above-ground swimming pool). *See also Kearney v. Philip Morris, Inc.,* 916 F. Supp. 61 (D. Mass. 1996) (R. Keeton, J.) (suggesting that Massachusetts might endorse a similar approach).

In Indiana, although the patent danger doctrine does not apply to that state's statutory strict liability actions, it still applies to common law negligent design claims. See, e.g., *Miller v. Todd,* 551 N.E.2d 1139 (Ind. 1990); *Welch v. Scripto-Tokai Corp.,* 651 N.E.2d 810 (Ind. Ct. App. 1995) (pajamas of child playing with disposable butane lighter caught fire; no duty to warn of or make lighter child-resistant to obvious risk from flame; open and obvious doctrine precluded negligence claim, and statutory consumer contemplations test precluded strict liability claim).

[37] See, e.g., *Vax v. Albany Lawn & Garden Center,* 433 S.E.2d 364, 366 (Ga. Ct. App. 1993) (riding mower not equipped with smooth-start clutch or dead-man's control; "the fact that the defect was not latent but open and obvious constitutes an absolute legal defense," the court observing: "Despite criticism of the 'open and obvious' rule, it remains the law in this state."). See also *Ream Tool Co. v. Newton,* 433 S.E.2d 67 (Ga. Ct. App. 1993).

[38] *Ogletree v. Navistar Int'l Transp. Corp.,* 500 S.E.2d 570, 571–72 (Ga. 1998) ("The overwhelming majority of jurisdictions have held that the open and obvious nature of the danger does not preclude liability for design defects.").

[39] Remaining offshoots of the patent danger rule for obvious design dangers still appear to exist in several states, as noted earlier.

states under the guise of the consumer expectations test[40] or a misreading of Restatement (Second) of Torts § 402A's comment j, as discussed later. That said, the rise and fall of the patent danger rule in design defect cases during the last half of the twentieth century is one of the most fascinating tales of products liability law. Having now been discredited as an absolute limitation on a manufacturer's duties of design by courts across the land,[41] the status of the patent danger doctrine as an independent no-duty rule in design defect cases may be stated simply: the rule essentially is dead.[42]

III. PRODUCT WARNINGS AND THE DUTY OF SAFE DESIGN

A. Generally

Closely related to the issue of how the obviousness of a hazard should affect the duty of safe design is the question of how a warning of a danger should affect a manufacturer's design obligations. This question involves a curious puzzle that lies at the heart of § 402A of the Restatement (Second) of Torts, the fountainhead of modern products liability law. The puzzle is this: § 402A, crafted by Dean William Prosser, generated the expansive, plaintiff-friendly doctrine of strict liability in tort for the sale of products that may be defective in any of three very different ways – in manufacturing, warnings, or design.[43] Yet a sentence in one comment to § 402A, comment j, can be read quite literally to mean that by providing a warning a manufacturer avoids its duty of safe design. If this be true, as a number of courts have held, then § 402A is

---

[40] *See, e.g., Ahrens v. Ford Motor Co.*, 340 F.3d 1142 (10th Cir. 2003) (Okla. law) (2003) (absence of seatbelt on tractor from which decedent was thrown); *Halliday v. Sturm, Ruger & Co.*, 792 A.2d 1145 (Md. 2002) (gunshot case); *Dickerson v. Cushman, Inc.*, 909 F. Supp. 1467 (M. D. Ala. 1995); *Griebler v. Doughboy Recreational, Inc.*, 466 N.W.2d 897 (Wis. 1991).

[41] Perhaps the last academic holdout for the patent danger rule is Richard Epstein, whose purist arguments for the doctrine appear half-hearted, unrealistic, and anachronistic. *See* RICHARD A. EPSTEIN, SIMPLE RULES FOR A COMPLEX WORLD 230–31 (1995).

[42] This is the clear position of the PRODUCTS LIABILITY RESTATEMENT:

> Subsection (b) does not recognize the obviousness of a design-related risk as precluding a finding of defectiveness. The fact that a danger is open and obvious is relevant to the issue of defectiveness, but does not necessarily preclude a plaintiff from establishing that a reasonable alternative design should have been adopted that would have reduced or prevented injury to the plaintiff.

RESTATEMENT (THIRD) OF TORTS: PRODUCTS LIABILITY § 2 cmt. d. *See also* Reporters' Note to *id.* ("A strong majority of courts have rejected the 'open and obvious' or 'patent danger' rule as an absolute defense to a claim of design defect. The obviousness of the danger is one factor among many to consider as to whether a product design meets risk-utility norms.").

[43] This section draws from David G. Owen, *The Puzzle of Comment j*, 55 HASTINGS L.J. 1377 (2004); DAVID G. OWEN, PRODUCTS LIABILITY LAW § 6.2 (2005).

a much weaker doctrine than generally is believed. The paradox is this: Dean Prosser, in a single sentence of a single comment to a single section of the Restatement, may have stripped the doctrine of strict products liability in tort of much of its intrinsic power.

In attempting to ascertain the proper relationship between a manufacturer's duty to warn and its duty of safe design, most courts and commentators have side-stepped the problem by simply ignoring the enigmatic sentence of comment j. And the commentators who have studied the comment most closely, including the Reporters for the Restatement (Third) of Torts: Products Liability, have interpreted it as meaning that a manufacturer's warnings somehow cancel out its duty of safe design.[44] But this interpretation is wrong. In fact, the riddle of comment j has a key that really is quite simple, that is discoverable from examining the history of § 402A within the context of the times, and that is consistent with the way products liability law in fact has evolved for the last half century. Until now, the curious comment j sentence has remained a riddle wrapped in a mystery inside an enigma.[45] No more.

B. The Distinctness of the Product Defect Concepts

In products liability litigation, both the Second and Third Restatements of Torts base liability on the concept of product defect. Section 402A of the Second Restatement provides liability for selling a product in a "defective condition unreasonably dangerous"[46] and § 1 of the Third Restatement provides liability for selling "a defective product." Notwithstanding this common grounding, the two Restatements treat the defect concept entirely differently. When Dean Prosser crafted § 402A of the Second Restatement in the late 1950s and early 1960s, products liability law was in its infancy.[47] At this very early stage in the development of this branch of law, the defect concept was only roughly understood and conceived of quite naively as a unitary concept: products were either too dangerous (defective) or safe enough (nondefective).[48]

---

[44] *See, e.g.*, RESTATEMENT (THIRD) OF TORTS: PRODUCTS LIABILITY § 2 cmt. l; James A. Henderson Jr. and Aaron D. Twerski, *The Politics of the Products Liability Restatement*, 26 HOFSTRA L. REV. 667, 689 (1998); Howard Latin, *"Good" Warnings, Bad Products, and Cognitive Limitations*, 41 UCLA L. REV. 1193, 1294–95 (1994); George L. Priest, *Strict Products Liability: The Original Intent*, 10 CARDOZO L. REV. 2301, 2303 (1989).

[45] Comment j in the early 2000s may be less inscrutable than was Russia in the late 1930s, but Winston Churchill's inimitable characterization nevertheless seems apt.

[46] RESTATEMENT (SECOND) TORTS § 402A.

[47] *See* 1 MADDEN & OWEN ON PRODUCTS LIABILITY (3D ED.) §§ 5.2, 5.3 (2005).

[48] *See id.* §§ 5.3 and 5.5.

As courts in the 1960s and 1970s applied the principles of § 402A to an ever-widening array of products in an ever-broader range of contexts, the disparities among the various forms of product dangers increasingly revealed themselves. Over time, courts and commentators came to understand the fundamental distinctions between the three very different forms of product defect: (1) manufacturing flaws – unintended physical irregularities that occur during the production process; (2) design inadequacies – hazards lurking in a product's engineering or scientific conception that may reasonably be avoided by a different design or formula; and (3) insufficient warnings of danger and instructions on safe use – the absence of information needed by users to avoid product hazards. In the decades since § 402A first roughly sketched a general doctrine of strict products liability in tort, the need to accord separate treatment to the liability issues distinctive to each of these very different defect contexts has become a well-accepted axiom. Today, the independent existence of each of these three separate types of defect is a fundamental premise of American products liability law.[49]

C. The Puzzle of Comment j

That the three types of defect beget distinct and largely independent obligations would seem to be so obvious as to be beyond dispute. From time to time, however, this fundamental principle of products liability law escapes an unwary court. Typically, the source of this confusion is an ambiguous sentence in comment j to § 402A of the Second Restatement, which a number of decisions have construed as meaning that a manufacturer who warns of danger eludes the duty of safe design – that warnings trump design.

Comment j basically sets forth, in a largely noncontroversial manner, a product seller's duty to warn of foreseeable hazards.[50] However, the comment

---

[49] *See* Products Liability Restatement § 1 Reporters' Note to cmt. a, and § 2 cmt. a. Early in the development of modern products liability theory, some theorists conceived of the duty to warn as a subcategory of the duty to design. For remnants of this conceptualization, *see, e.g., Chellman v. Saab-Scania AB*, 637 A.2d 148, 150–51 (N.H. 1993) ("[t]he duty to warn is part of the general duty to design, manufacture and sell products that are reasonably safe"); John W. Wade, *On the Effect in Products Liability of Knowledge Unavailable Prior to Marketing*, 58 N.Y.U. L. Rev. 734, 740 (1983) ("although 'failure to warn' is usually treated as a separate basis for finding a product actionable, 'failure to warn' cases may be properly viewed as 'defective design' cases").

[50] Comment j to § 402A provides in full:

    j. Directions or warning. In order to prevent the product from being unreasonably dangerous, the seller may be required to give directions or warning, on the container, as to its use. The seller may reasonably assume that those with common allergies, as for example to eggs or strawberries, will be aware of them, and he is not required to warn against them. Where,

concludes with the following "unfortunate language:"[51]

> Where warning is given, the seller may reasonably assume that it will be read and heeded; and a product bearing such a warning, which is safe for use if it is followed, is not in [a] defective condition, nor is it unreasonably dangerous.

This language is indeed "unfortunate," because its ambiguity permits it to be interpreted in any number of significantly different ways. For example, it may be read as meaning that *any* warning, no matter how inadequate, satisfies the *informational* obligations addressed in comment j; or that a warning *if adequate* satisfies those obligations; or that *any* warning, no matter how inadequate, satisfies *every* duty of whatever type owed by the seller to the user; or that an *adequate* warning will satisfy every duty of whatever type owed by the seller to the user. The proper interpretation of this sentence, as explained later, is really none of these,[52] but instead the much narrower proposition that the only obligation of sellers of inherently dangerous products like food, alcohol, tobacco, and drugs, in addition to the duty to supply them free of impurities, is to warn consumers of the unavoidable, latent

---

however, the product contains an ingredient to which a substantial number of the population are allergic, and the ingredient is one whose danger is not generally known, or if known is one which the consumer would reasonably not expect to find in the product, the seller is required to give warning against it, if he has knowledge, or by the application of reasonable, developed human skill and foresight should have knowledge, of the presence of the ingredient and the danger. Likewise in the case of poisonous drugs, or those unduly dangerous for other reasons, warning as to use may be required.

But a seller is not required to warn with respect to products, or ingredients in them, which are only dangerous, or potentially so, when consumed in excessive quantity, or over a long period of time, when the danger, or potentiality of danger, is generally known and recognized. Again the dangers of alcoholic beverages are an example, as are also those of foods containing such substances as saturated fats, which may over a period of time have a deleterious effect upon the human heart.

Where warning is given, the seller may reasonably assume that it will be read and heeded; and a product bearing such a warning, which is safe for use if it is followed, is not in defective condition, nor is it unreasonably dangerous.

[51] This is the characterization by the Reporters for the Third Restatement. *See* PRODUCTS LIABILITY RESTATEMENT § 2 Reporters' Note to cmt. j.

[52] Most courts avoid this interpretive problem simply by ignoring it, which makes good sense. After all, this problem resides in a single sentence of a single comment to a single Restatement section that has now been superseded. Of the interpretations offered here, the best is the second: that a manufacturer satisfies its duty to provide safety information to purchasers and users – and only this duty – by providing them with warnings and instructions adequately explaining the risk and how to avoid it. Such an interpretation may be largely tautological, but it is the only interpretation that makes sense today. Yet, even this interpretation falsely assumes that comment j applies to the effect of warnings on the general duty to design any type of product, whereas comments i, j, and k in fact apply only to products possessing inherent, unavoidable dangers that cannot be designed away.

dangers such products foreseeably may contain. Understanding why this narrow interpretation is correct requires deconstructing comment j by reading it in the context of other comments, examining the "legislative history" of those comments, considering the relevant policies, and reviewing related products liability developments over time.

1. *Deconstructing Comment j*

Reading comment j in context

In attempting to unravel the inscrutable meaning of this clause of comment j, one needs to read it in context by considering the comments that precede and follow it (comments i and k) and the narrow subject all three comments in fact address. In examining this context, it must be remembered that the Restatement Reporter, Dean William Prosser, researched and drafted comment j in the late 1950s and early 1960 to accompany a narrow draft of § 402A of the Second Restatement limited to defective *food* and related products – such as drugs, alcoholic beverages, and tobacco – several years before a *general* doctrine of strict liability in tort applicable to *all* products was even being considered.[53]

A close reading of comments i, j, and k to the Restatement (Second) of Torts § 402A, together with their "legislative history," reveals that these comments were directed exclusively to a narrow set of issues pertinent to a limited class of products, to wit, the liability (and limits of liability) of sellers of certain types of products – food, drugs, whiskey, cigarettes, and similar products that contain unavoidable dangers. Although the titles to comments i ("*Unreasonably dangerous*") and j ("*Directions or warning*") unfortunately suggest that they might have general application to *all* products, these comments, together with comment k ("*Unavoidably unsafe products*"), in fact are limited to a single narrow topic: the responsibility of sellers of products such as food, alcoholic beverages, tobacco, and drugs containing inherent product dangers that cannot be designed away.

The premise of each of these three comments is that strict liability under § 402A does not apply unless a manufacturer has a reasonable way to eliminate a product's hazards. Based on this premise, the main point of these particular comments is that the only duties of manufacturers of food, whiskey, cigarettes, drugs, and similar products containing inherent dangers is to warn

---

[53] In commentary on early drafts of § 402A, Dean Prosser stated that no case authority supported extending strict liability beyond the narrow food-type class of products.

consumers of hidden dangers. The comments thus explain that this limited
class of products, accompanied by proper warnings, are not in a "defective
condition unreasonably dangerous" with respect to the unavoidable dangers
inherent in products of this type.

Comment i

Comment i explains why the ALI added the phrase "defective condition" to
modify the "(unreasonably) dangerous" phrase used in an earlier, preliminary
draft of § 402A. The "defective condition" language was added (at the urging
of the ALI Council) to make clear that the new "strict" liability in tort would
not give rise to design liability for selling products like food, whiskey, and
cigarettes that contain inherent dangers that cannot be eliminated.[54] Comment i thus makes the single point that the strict liability principle of § 402A
is inappropriate for some products that are widely known to be inherently
dangerous such that consumers who choose to use such products are deemed
to accept those inherent risks.[55]

Comment j

Comment j, first attached to the 1961 draft of § 402A that applied only to food
and similar products, also discusses and applies only to dangerous foods,
alcoholic beverages, and drugs – products that by their nature cannot be
rendered safe except by warnings. This comment makes three points: first,
continuing the reasoning of comment i, that sellers of food, tobacco, alcohol,
drugs, and similar products widely known to be inherently dangerous are
not generally subject to strict liability for such dangers because consumers
understand that products of these types necessarily include such risks; but,
second, that sellers of such products *do* have a duty to warn consumers of any
latent risks of which consumers generally are unaware; and, third, because
there simply is no way *other than by warning* that sellers of *such* products can
minimize their inherent risks, that the only reasonable duty for manufacturers
of these such inherently hazardous products is to warn consumers of any
hidden dangers.[56]

   The premise here is that sellers of *inherently hazardous products* may trust
that users, properly informed of any hidden dangers, will read and heed any

---

[54] *See* AMERICAN LAW INSTITUTE PROCEEDINGS 87–89 (1961).
[55] "Many products cannot possibly be made entirely safe ... " RESTATEMENT (SECOND) TORTS
   § 402A cmt. i.
[56] Putting aside, of course, the duties to produce a product without manufacturing defects and
   not to misrepresent a product's safety.

(adequate) warnings and take responsibility for such inherent risks.[57] Thus, properly interpreted, comment j's concluding sentence actually means:

> Where [adequate] warning [of any hidden dangers] is given, the seller [of inherently dangerous products like food, drugs, alcoholic beverages, and cigarettes] may reasonably assume that [the warning] will be read and heeded [because there is nothing else the manufacturer can do to avoid the danger]; and [such] a product bearing such a warning, which is safe for use if it is followed, is not in [a] defective condition, nor is it unreasonably dangerous.

So seen, comment j actually addresses only the narrow issue of a seller's duties with respect to food, tobacco, drugs, alcoholic beverages, and similar products containing inherent and unavoidable risks that cannot be designed away.[58] Conversely, comment j does *not* address how warnings may affect the duty of safe design for *other* types of products whose dangers *can* reasonably be designed away.[59]

Comment k

Reiterating the overarching theme of all three comments – that a limited class of inherently and unavoidably dangerous products should be exempt from any design obligations under the strict liability rule of § 402A – comment k explains how, in particular, the principles of comments i and j apply to prescription drugs. In the context of this special type of unavoidably dangerous product, comment k makes the dual points that a seller does have a duty to provide proper warnings but that it is not otherwise liable for any inherent risks that cannot be designed away.[60]

In sum, a careful reading of comments i, j, and k makes clear that they are addressed *only* to the narrow unavoidable danger issue with respect

---

[57] Indeed, manufacturers must trust in the good sense of users of such products, for there is nothing else to be done.

[58] This interpretation of comment j is further supported by its direction that any required warnings be placed on the product's "container," surely the best place to warn of inherent dangers in food, drugs, whiskey, and cigarettes, but nonsensical when applied to the vast array of durable products that come without containers – tools, clothing, power mowers, automobiles, vacuum cleaners, and punch presses – for which the law requires that warnings against significant hidden dangers be located in the most appropriate place.

[59] Dangers that can reasonably be designed out of products are by definition neither "inherent" nor "unavoidable."

[60] Comment k provides in pertinent part that "some products ... , in the present state of human knowledge, are quite incapable of being made safe for their intended and ordinary use [and the] seller of such products [particularly drugs], again with the qualification that they are properly prepared and marketed, and proper warning is given, where the situation calls for it, is not to be held to strict liability for unfortunate consequences [from] a known but apparently reasonable risk."

to inherently dangerous products such as foods, cigarettes, whiskey, and drugs.[61] Everything in the comments points to their limited applicability, and nothing[62] suggests they were intended to limit a seller's duty to design its products safely if there is a reasonable way to do so.[63]

Comment j's "legislative history"

The above contextual interpretation of comment j is confirmed by an examination of the evolution of § 402A drafts from 1958 through 1964, together with the contemporaneous scholarship of Dean Prosser and several key Restatement Advisers. Preceded by at least a couple of committee drafts,[64] § 402A was presented to the full American Law Institute three times, beginning with Tentative Draft No. 6 in 1961. In this draft, § 402A imposed strict liability in tort upon sellers of "food in a defective condition unreasonably dangerous to consumers." In three small paragraphs, a single comment f (entitled "*Unreasonably dangerous*") contained the entire discussion of the issues that in the final, published version eventually spanned three comments: i, j, and k. Although the § 402A black letter spoke only in terms of "food," comment c defined that word to embrace "all products intended for internal human consumption," including beverages, candy, chewing gum, chewing tobacco, snuff, unground coffee beans, and drugs. The next year, 1962, in order to embrace these nonfood items more comfortably, the black letter of § 402A was expanded in Tentative Draft No. 7 to cover, in addition to food, "other products for intimate bodily use." In this draft, the discussions in comment

---

[61] The only examples in comments i–k are, in order: sugar (diabetes), castor oil (used by Mussolini for torture), whiskey (drunkenness), tobacco (cancer), butter (cholesterol and heart attacks), eggs (allergies), strawberries (allergies), alcohol (drunkenness), fatty foods (heart attacks), Pasteur rabies vaccine (allergic reactions), and other drugs and vaccines (side effects).

[62] Except possibly for the unfortunate generality of their titles, left over from early tentative drafts of § 402A that applied only to food, and then food, drug, and bodily-use products. Once *Greenman v. Yuba Power Prods., Inc.*, 377 P.2d 897 (Cal. 1963), was decided, Dean Prosser promptly expanded the black letter of § 402A from food and products for "intimate bodily use" to all products. In his haste to revise the draft in this manner, as discussed later, Prosser neglected to adapt most of the comments to their now much broader scope, leaving most of them in the form in which they had originally been drafted with a much more limited type of product in mind. Had he had more time, he likely would have added a major heading over comments i, j, and k, entitled "Unavoidably Unsafe Products," and then changed the title of comment k to "Prescription drugs."

[63] It has been said, in sum, that the comments simply recognize that you cannot put a safety device on a stick of butter.

[64] *See* Preliminary Draft No. 6, for review by the Advisory Committee (Jan. 3, 1958), *and* Council Draft No. 8 (Nov. 1, 1960). These early versions contained no direct reference to the unavoidable danger issues eventually addressed in comments i, j, and k.

f of the previous draft (Tent. Draft No. 6) were expanded upon and divided into comments i, j, and k. In early 1964, several months after Justice Traynor's landmark ruling in *Greenman v. Yuba Power Products, Inc.*,[65] the black letter of § 402A was expanded again, in Tentative Draft No. 10, to broaden the applicability of strict liability in tort to the sale of *all* products in a "defective condition unreasonably dangerous to the user or consumer." In this final draft,[66] which Dean Prosser hurriedly rewrote to accommodate *Greenman*,[67] comments i, j, and k (all three of which sprang from the comment f that had been written to accompany the "food" black-letter draft of 1961)[68] remained essentially unchanged.[69]

The contemporaneous scholarship of Dean Prosser and key ALI Advisers also suggests that comment j was intended only to address the narrow unavoidable danger issue in foods, drugs, cigarettes, whiskey, and the like. In his only three products liability articles published after § 402A was published in 1965,[70] and in the next edition of his hornbook,[71] Dean Prosser examined

---

[65] 377 P.2d 897 (Cal. 1963).

[66] TENTATIVE DRAFT No. 10 was approved by the ALI in 1964 and promulgated in final, published form the next year.

[67] Once *Greenman* was rendered in 1963, Dean Prosser had to scramble to convert § 402A from its prior, narrow coverage to all products. Apart from his many other duties as TORTS RESTATEMENT Reporter, dean, and professor, he had to prepare TENTATIVE DRAFT No. 10 for circulation, first, to the Advisers, then to the Council, and finally to the whole ALI membership in time for the May 1964 annual meeting.

[68] And which he had fleshed out in the 1962 DRAFT to accommodate other products for intimate bodily use.

[69] Apart from the addition of a butter example to comment i, and corrections of technical errors throughout, the comments in TENT. DRAFTS 7 and 10 are substantially the same.

There is only sparse discussion of the comment j issue in the RESTATEMENT debates, but nothing there suggests that Dean Prosser or anyone else contemplated that limiting a seller's responsibility to a duty to warn extended beyond the inherently dangerous food-type products then being considered; certainly there is no intimation that this limited duty might apply to manufacturers of durable goods whose dangers may reasonably be designed away. In discussing a manufacturer's duty to warn, Dean Prosser noted: "It is not correct to say that [the manufacturer] can always avoid liability by giving reasonable notice." A.L.I. Proceedings 68 (1961). Although the meaning of this sentence is somewhat unclear in its context, Dean Prosser's general remarks do make clear that the last sentence of then comment f (now comment j) only addressed the kinds of inherent, unavoidable risks dealt with in the food and drug examples covered by then comment f (now comments i, j, and k).

[70] William Prosser, *Products Liability in Perspective*, 5 GONZ. L. REV. 157, 164 et seq. (1970); William Prosser, *The Fall of the Citadel (Strict Liability to the Consumer)*, 50 MINN. L. REV. 791, 807 et seq. (1966); William Prosser, *Strict Liability to the Consumer in California*, 18 HASTINGS L.J. 9 et seq. (1966).

[71] WILLIAM PROSSER, HANDBOOK OF THE LAW OF TORTS § 99, at 660 (4th ed. 1971) (beginning, "The second, and more important, question concerns [whether 402A should apply to] products that in the present state of human skill and knowledge are unavoidably dangerous, and cannot be made safe.").

the unavoidable danger issue, using the same examples and reasoning as he had used in comments i, j, and k. The only salient difference of his treatment of these issues in his scholarship[72] (distinguished from the comments) is that he reverted in his scholarship to lumping the inherent danger issues all together, under a single "unavoidable danger" umbrella, as he had originally done in comment f of Tentative Draft No. 6.[73] This suggests that Prosser, the Reporter for § 402A, intended the narrow, contextual interpretation of comment j discussed earlier.

Although it appears that Dean Prosser never directly addressed the availability of design defect claims under § 402A for failing to adopt a reasonable alternative design, his writings indicate that he believed § 402A properly applied to such cases without regard to whether the danger was obvious or a warning had been given.[74] This conclusion is confirmed by his observation that § 402A's applicability to design defect cases was, with respect to

---

[72] In his last, and least formal article, Dean Prosser explained in fairness terms the rationale for imposing only a duty to warn (and keep pure) on sellers of food, drugs, and other useful products containing dangers that cannot be avoided: "You cannot impose strict liability upon a man who sells what appears to be a perfectly reputable product and is actually extremely beneficial to the human race; you cannot make him strictly liable because once in a while something goes wrong with it in a way which he cannot prevent." William Prosser, *Products Liability in Perspective*, 5 Gonz. L. Rev. 157, 166 (1970).

[73] In all three articles and the hornbook, Prosser states that the question whether § 402A should apply to unavoidably dangerous products is one of the two or three most important issues on the proper reach of strict liability, and he organizes this discussion (that the final draft of § 402A had splintered into comments i, j, and k) under the general heading, "Type of Product" (in the articles) and "Unsafe Products" (in the hornbook).

[74] In the only edition of his hornbook after § 402A was published in 1965, Dean Prosser addressed the meaning of § 402A's key phrase, "defective condition unreasonably dangerous," noting that it applies to design defects as well as manufacturing defects. William Prosser, Law of Torts § 99, at 659 (4th ed. 1971). For this proposition, Prosser cites a safety device case, *Pike v. Frank G. Hough Co.*, 467 P.2d 229 (Cal. 1970). *Pike* explains why strict liability applies to design defects as well as warnings defects, and it explicitly repudiated the "patent danger rule" ("the obviousness of peril is relevant to the manufacturer's defenses, not to the issue of duty," 467 P.2d at 234) and with it the defendant's argument there that the manufacturer had no duty to design away dangers which were known to the user. The court quoted long passages from Harper and James on Torts, and Dix Noel, *Manufacturer's Negligence of Design or Directions for Use of a Product*, 71 Yale L.J. 816, 838 (1962) (the latter of which concluded, "Under the modern rule, even though the absence of a particular safety precaution is obvious, there ordinarily would be a question for the jury as to whether or not a failure to install the device creates an unreasonable risk."). *Pike* also relies substantially on *Garcia v. Halsett*, 82 Cal. Rptr. 420 (Ct. App. 1970), which permitted a design defect claim under strict liability in tort for injuries that the defendant should have prevented by equipping the machine with an electrical interlock (a "micro switch") that would have automatically cut off the electricity to the machine. Prosser in this manner endorsed the applicability of § 402A to design dangers which manufacturers reasonably can avoid.

manufacturers, essentially coincident with negligence law[75] which, even prior to § 402A, allowed recovery against manufacturers for negligently omitting feasible safety devices.[76]

The scholarship of at least four key ALI Advisers, Professor James, Deans Keeton and Wade, and Justice Traynor,[77] confirms that the duty of safe design is largely independent of the duty to warn. A decade before § 402A, Professor James wrote, "the risk that warning will not be heeded, and the danger likely to ensue if it is not, may be so great as to call for some safety device or even for abandonment of the process or the product if its utility is outweighed by the danger. Surely an automobile manufacturer would be negligent in marketing cars without brakes, even if that fact were known to all the world."[78] Dean Keeton's scholarship reveals that products liability scholars at the time were concerned principally with whether strict liability should be applied to manufacturing defects and, much more controversially, to inherently dangerous products such as food, drugs, cosmetics, whiskey, and tobacco.[79] As for more common kinds of durable products, Dean Keeton rejected the view that a manufacturer's duty of safe design somehow vanishes if the danger is obvious or the user otherwise (as by a warning) is aware of the danger.[80]

---

[75] "Since proper design is a matter of reasonable fitness, the strict liability [under § 402A] adds little or nothing to the negligence on the part of the manufacturer...." PROSSER ON TORTS § 99, at 659 n. 72 (4th ed. 1971).

[76] *See* PROSSER ON TORTS § 96, at 645 ("There is no doubt whatever that the manufacturer is under a duty to use reasonable care to design a product that is reasonably safe for its intended use, and for other uses which are foreseeably probable.") Among the cases cited by Prosser in this excerpt is *McCormack v. Hankscraft Co.,* 154 N.W.2d 488 (Minn. 1967), which involved a hot-water vaporizer that a young child tipped over by mistake, causing the extremely hot water to scald the child when the unattached lid fell off. Because the plastic top easily could have been threaded to permit it to be screwed onto the top of the hot-water reservoir jar, which would have prevented the injury, the court allowed design claims against the manufacturer in both negligence and strict liability in tort under § 402A.

[77] Professor Fleming James Jr. (HARPER AND JAMES ON TORTS) of Yale, Dean W. Page Keeton of the University of Texas, and Dean John W. Wade of Vanderbilt University were prominent tort law scholars of the day. Chief Justice Roger J. Traynor authored the principal judicial authority for § 402A, *Greenman v. Yuba Power Prods., Inc.,* 377 P.2d 897 (Cal. 1963), theoretically grounded in his concurring opinion in *Escola v. Coca-Cola Bottling Co.,* 150 P.2d 436, 439 (Cal. 1944).

[78] Fleming James Jr., *Products Liability,* 34 TEX. L. REV. 44, 58 (1955).

[79] *See* W. Page Keeton, *Products Liability – Liability Without Fault and the Requirement of a Defect,* 41 TEX. L. REV. 855 (1963); George L. Priest, *Strict Products Liability: The Original Intent,* 10 CARDOZO L. REV. 2301, 2303 (1989); John W. Wade, *Strict Tort Liability of Manufacturers,* 19 Sw. L.J. 5, 22 (1965).

[80] "[T]he proposition that the user's knowledge of a particular hazard involved in the use of a product should necessarily preclude recovery by him if victimized by that hazard is rejected..." W. Page Keeton, *Products Liability – Inadequacy of Information,* 48 TEX. L. REV.

Dean Wade was more explicit, explaining that "a warning will not always be sufficient."[81] Chief Justice Traynor, an ALI Adviser for § 402A as well as the author of *Greenman*, addressed this issue head-on in an article published the year § 402A was published. Observing that the last sentence of comment j was directed at inherently dangerous products such as poison and cigarettes, products with dangers that cannot be designed away,[82] he specifically noted that comment j in no way insulates manufacturers who provide warnings from liability for the other two types of product defects – manufacturing defects and defects in design. That is, manufacturers cannot use warnings to shift responsibility to consumers injured by one of these other, independent types of defects.[83]

It is evident that the comments to § 402A were not provided as a complete products liability "code" but in fact addressed only certain limited aspects of the new doctrine of strict products liability in tort. Outside of the narrow context of unavoidably dangerous products, the comments simply do not

---

398, 401 (1970) (also rejecting an economic argument "that a consumer and others who are injured through the use of a product do not have any right to be secure from harm from dangerous products apart from a right to be informed or apart from safety legislation.") (emphasis omitted).

[81] John W. Wade, *On the Nature of Strict Tort Liability for Products*, 44 MISS. L.J. 825, 842 (1973). Dean Wade provided some examples: "An electrical appliance with uninsulated wires would not be made duly safe by attaching a warning to look out for the danger of electric shock." *Id.* n. 56. "A rotary lawn mower, for example, which had no housing to protect a user from the whirling blade would not be treated as duly safe, despite the obvious character of the danger." *Id.* at 843. He also notes the similarity of issues in cases in which a danger is *warned* about and where it is *obvious*. *Id.*

[82] *See* Roger J. Traynor, *The Ways and Meanings of Defective Products and Strict Liability*, 32 TENN. L. REV. 363, 367–73 (1965) (examining the cases on food, drugs, tobacco, and similar products). "Some dangers are generic to the goods, so that people regard the goods as fit for ordinary use even with such qualities. The manufacturer would not be liable, under the RESTATEMENT test, for harm caused by generic dangers." *Id.* at 370 (referring to comment i). *See also id.* at 367 (§ 402A "would impose no strict liability for what are classified as 'unavoidably unsafe products'") (citing comment k); *id.* at 372 (warnings "cannot be used, however, to mask a disclaimer of responsibility that would shift the risk to the consumer.") (referring to comment j).

[83] *See id.* at 372:
> What is the effect of warning or notice? The Restatement provides: "Where warning is given, the seller may reasonably assume that it will be read and heeded; and a product bearing such a warning which is safe for use if the warning is heeded, is not in a defective condition...." [*citing* cmt. j.]
> Example: poison. A warning or notice cannot be used, however, to mask a disclaimer of responsibility that would shift the risk to the consumer. Thus, a notice by a manufacturer of soft drinks listing the possible foreign substances that might be contained in a bottle of its beverage, or a notice by an automobile manufacturer listing possible difficulties that might be encountered by the user of the car, would not preclude liability.

directly address the broader issue of the relationship between the general duties of warnings and safe design. As seen above, however, contemporaneous scholarship of Dean Prosser and his key ALI Advisers quite firmly suggests that comments i, j, and k were intended to address only the narrow issue of the limited manner in which the new strict liability section applied to unavoidably dangerous products whose inherent risks cannot be designed away. Their scholarship suggests, and the comments to § 402A imply, that the new strict liability doctrine in fact requires manufacturers to physically remove substantial dangers – even if they are warned about, obvious, or generally known – if there is a reasonable way to do so.[84]

2. Policy

It makes good sense to interpret comment j narrowly, as limiting the duties of sellers of inherently dangerous products (such as drugs, cigarettes, and alcoholic beverages) to providing products that are uncontaminated and possess adequate warnings of hidden dangers. Because there is no way (other than by providing warnings) that manufacturers of such products can minimize the inherent dangers of such products without also destroying their utility, there is no good reason in the logic of either corrective justice or economic efficiency to force manufacturers to insure consumers against risks of harm they have chosen to accept by purchasing or using products with inherent risks of which they are fully aware. But if a product contains substantial risks that *can* reasonably be designed away, then a manufacturer that does not do so should be faulted, in both fairness and economics, for failing to respect the rights of consumers to reasonable product safety. These fundamental precepts, explored elsewhere in greater depth,[85] support the logic and fairness of keeping the manufacturer's duty of safe design largely independent of the duty to warn. To hold that warnings immunize manufacturers from the duty of safe design (or the duty of safe manufacture) would unreasonably

[84] Scholarship on the origins of § 402A concludes that the Reporter, the Advisers, and the ALI were focused at the time on the narrow issue of liability for injuries from products containing inherent unavoidable dangers, *not* on the general duty of manufacturers of ordinary products to design them safely. *See* Gary T. Schwartz, *Considering the Proper Federal Role in American Tort Law*, 38 Ariz. L. Rev. 917, 947 and *id.* n. 185 (1996) ("402A is obtuse [in] dealing with design issues only indirectly and by implication" and noting the section's "failure to focus on design issues"). *See also* George L. Priest, *Strict Products Liability: The Original Intent*, 10 Cardozo L. Rev. 2301 (1989).

[85] *See* David G. Owen, *The Moral Foundations of Products Liability Law: Toward First Principles*, 68 Notre Dame L. Rev. 427 (1993).

and regressively subordinate the interests of consumers to the interests of manufacturers.[86]

A rule that fulfilling *one* of several independent tort law duties fulfills them *all* is quite preposterous. Surely a driver has a duty of reasonable care to give warning, by tooting the horn, to all pedestrians endangered by the car's approach, even if they are at fault for being in the roadway. But a driver also has duties to maintain a proper lookout, to operate the car soberly and with reasonable skill, to obey traffic signals, and not to speed. It would be absurd to interpret an ambiguous traffic rule in a manner that would relieve a driver of all responsibilities to pedestrians so long as the driver, though violating all the other duties, tooted the horn. Applying this principle to the products liability situation here at issue, it makes no sense to relieve a manufacturer of all its other duties – notably its duties to design and manufacture its products safely – simply because it places a warning on its products. Such a rule would senselessly allow a manufacturer of household fans to substitute a warning on the base of the fan for the fan's protective cage; it would allow a manufacturer of power mowers to attach a warning on the engine and then remove the protective housing around the blade; and it would permit a manufacturer of industrial machinery a simple but completely unsatisfactory means to avoid its basic duty to equip dangerous industrial products with simple guards and electric interlocks when such safety devices are reasonably demanded in the circumstances to avoid substantial harm.

---

[86] *See generally* Howard A. Latin, *"Good" Warnings, Bad Products, and Cognitive Limitations,* 41 UCLA L. Rev. 1193, 1294–95 (1994) (thoroughly critiquing interpretation of comment j to mean that warnings trump manufacturer's duty of safe design):

> [T]he comment j presumption is unrealistic from a behavioral perspective, inefficient from an accident-prevention perspective, and inequitable from a normative perspective. ... Good product warnings may be useful, indeed necessary, in many accident-prevention settings but their value is inherently limited and they consequently should not be treated as legally acceptable alternatives to safer product designs. ...

Id. See also James A. Henderson Jr. and Aaron D. Twerski, *A Proposed Revision of Section 402A of the Restatement (Second) of Torts,* 77 Cornell L. Rev. 1512, 1538 (1992) ("Product warnings cannot bear the full burden of ensuring that products will be used safely. If a sensible design alternative can significantly reduce risk, the law will demand that the manufacturer design out the risk rather than merely warn against it.").

The issue was debated by Professors Jerry J. Phillips and Richard C. Ausness. *See* Jerry J. Phillips, *Products Liability: Beyond Warnings,* 26 N. Ky. L. Rev. 595, 602 (1999) ("It seems too late ... to return to an unbridled doctrine of laissez faire or caveat emptor, in the modern-day of complex products, advertising blandishments, and clearly foreseeable human frailty."). *Compare* Richard C. Ausness, *When Warnings Alone Won't Do: A Reply to Professor Phillips,* 26 N. Ky. L. Rev. 627, 646 (1999) (Professor Phillips "rightly criticizes" comment j, but the Third Restatement's approach in comment l to § 2 goes too far the other way). *See also* Kenneth Ian Weissman, *A "Comment J" Parry to Howard Latin's "Good" Warnings, Bad Products, and Cognitive Limitations,* 70 St. John's L. Rev. 629 (1996).

3. The Evolving Products Liability Jurisprudence

Comment j, as previously discussed, addresses the narrow issue of how § 402A allocates responsibility for harm caused by unavoidable dangers inherent in a narrow class of products whose dangers cannot reasonably be designed away. But even in the unlikely event that comment j was intended to make warnings a *general* shield against the duty of safe design, such an approach contrasts starkly with developments in products liability law over the past half century. When Dean Prosser researched and initially drafted comment j in 1959 and 1960, products liability law was still dominated by many strictures from the early 1900s. Liability was rarely imposed for a manufacturer's conscious design choices; the patent danger doctrine still reigned supreme in limiting a manufacturer's design responsibility to only latent dangers; consumer expectations were the only gauge of strict products liability (in warranty and, later, under § 402A). Furthermore, consumer carelessness in any degree, even in the face of an egregious and unnecessary design danger, served to bar recovery altogether; and the intended use doctrine barred liability for most forms of consumer misuse ("abnormal use"), including the failure to follow a seller's instructions, on the ground that it superseded the manufacturer's responsibility. Yet, soon after § 402A (with its comments, including comment j) was published in 1965, the law took several sharp turns the other way. By the 1970s, courts began with a gusto to apply judicial oversight to manufacturer design choices; the patent danger doctrine began a precipitous decline into virtual extinction; the risk-utility standard began to swallow up the consumer expectation test for evaluating the safety of a product's design; the total bar for user carelessness was rapidly giving way to damages apportionment based on comparative fault; and the scope of a manufacturer's responsibility for product safety was widening broadly from intended uses to all foreseeable uses.

In the twenty-first century, the most sensible way to interpret comment j's ambiguous last sentence is in the manner it was intended – that it applies only to the narrow category of inherently dangerous products with unavoidable dangers like food, drugs, alcoholic beverages, and tobacco. If for some reason a court feels impelled to interpret this sentence more broadly, as applicable to *all* types of products, then the sentence should be interpreted as meaning nothing more than that a manufacturer may fulfill its informational obligations to consumers by providing adequate warnings and instructions.[87] According

---

[87] *See, e.g., Moulton v. Rival Co.*, 116 F.3d 22, 28 (1st Cir. 1997) (Maine law) (cmt. j restricted to cases involving only duty to warn); *Evridge v. American Honda Motor Co.*, 685 S.W.2d 632,

any greater import to comment j, as meaning that a warning cancels the
fundamental duty of manufacturers of ordinary products to take reasonable
steps to design away serious hazards, would elevate consumer responsibility
for accidents to the archaic position it has not occupied for almost half a
century,[88] and it would revive a host of discredited doctrines that long ago
were properly put to rest.[89]

4. Present Status of Comment j

With the exception of a handful of misguided decisions that have misin-
terpreted comment j as negating the general duty of safe design,[90] a great
majority of courts, some explicitly rejecting comment j on this point,[91] hold

---

636 (Tenn. 1985). *See also Uptain v. Huntington Lab, Inc.*, 723 P.2d 1322, 1331, 1332–33 (Colo.
1986) (Quinn, C.J., dissenting). *Cf. Delaney v. Deere & Co.*, 999 P.2d 930, 941–42 (Kan. 2000).
In *Delaney*, ironically, the *defendant* proposed this interpretation but it was rejected by the
court.

[88] Imposing absolute responsibility on consumers ignores real-world limitations on human
cognition. *See* Howard A. Latin, *"Good" Warnings, Bad Products, and Cognitive Limitations*,
41 UCLA L. Rev. 1193, 1206 (1994) (cognitive theory shows that warnings should only be used
to supplement reasonable designs, not to substitute therefor, because people are unable "to
read, understand, remember, and follow innumerable product warnings to protect themselves from all product-related risks they may confront."). *See also* Aaron D. Twerski et al.,
The Use and Abuse of Warnings in Products Liability: Design Defect Comes of Age, 61 Cornell
L. Rev. 495, 506 (1976); Products Liability Restatement § 2 Reporters' Note to cmt. l.

[89] Defense lawyers, who are quite happy to try to revive the old defendant-protective rules,
argue that comment j should be interpreted to mean that a manufacturer that provides a
warning should be relieved of its duty of safe design. *See, e.g.,* Stephen G. Morrison, *Warning
v. Design in Products Litigation: Third Time's Not Always a Charm*, 10 Kan. J. L. & Pub. Pol'y
86 (2000); Victor E. Schwartz, *See No Evil, Hear No Evil: When Clear and Adequate Warnings
Do Not Prevent the Imposition of Product Liability*, 68 U. Cin. L. Rev. 47 (1999). Yet even
Mr. Schwartz is reluctant to endorse this extreme position. *See* 68 U. Cin. L. Rev. at 59–
60 (recognizing the Restatement (Third)'s "legitimate concern" that people may not in
fact read and heed all warnings, and noting the possibility that "courts could 'over-read'
Comment j . . . to mean that a manufacturer who warns about a risk is not liable" – giving
example of power lawnmower, which carries warning to stay away from unguarded blade,
as situation in which warning would not protect manufacturer from duty to add guard).

[90] Interpreting comment j to mean that a warning eliminates the manufacturer's duty to
provide a safe design, *see, e.g., Curcio v. Caterpillar, Inc.*, 543 S.E.2d 264 (S.C. Ct. App. 2001),
rev'd on other grounds, 585 S.E.2d 272 (S.C. 2003); *Ferguson v. F. R. Winkler GMBH & Co.*, 79
F.3d 1221 (D.C. Cir. 1996); *Freas v. Prater Constr. Corp.*, 573 N.E.2d 27 (Ohio 1991); *Simpson v.
Standard Container Co.*, 527 A.2d 1337 (Md. Ct. Spec. App. 1987). *Cf. Dugan v. Sears, Roebuck
& Co.*, 447 N.E.2d 1055 (Ill. App. Ct. 1983) (jury issue on whether user's ignoring warning
was sole proximate cause, based largely upon its foreseeability).

[91] Until recently, most courts have basically ignored the offending language of comment j as
saying anything serious about the relationship between warnings and design. The Third
Restatement's explicit rejection of this aspect of the Second Restatement's comment j,

that the separate forms of defect give rise to separate obligations that may independently support a products liability claim.[92] Thus, except in certain limited contexts,[93] it is abundantly clear that a manufacturer is subject to liability for a product's *manufacturing* defects, no matter how clear the product's warnings or how perfect its design;[94] for *warning* defects, no matter how perfect the product's manufacture or how impeccable its design;[95] and for

---

however, has focused courts and lawyers specifically on this point. For examples of recent cases explicitly rejecting the warnings-trump-design interpretation of comment j, *see, e.g., Delaney v. Deere & Co.,* 999 P.2d 930, 942 (Kan. 2000) ("just because there is a warning on a piece of equipment does not prevent the equipment from being dangerous"); *Uniroyal Goodrich Tire Co. v. Martinez,* 977 S.W.2d 328, 335–37 (Tex. 1998); *Rogers v. Ingersoll-Rand Co.,* 144 F.3d 841, 844 (D.C. Cir. 1998). *See also Leaf v. Goodyear Tire & Rubber Co.,* 590 N.W.2d 525, 529 (Iowa 1999) (dictum critical of cmt. j).

[92] Even critics of the Third Restatement's rejection of the warnings-trump-design approach acknowledge that the Third Restatement position is widely embraced by the courts. *See, e.g.,* Richard C. Ausness, *When Warnings Alone Won't Do: A Reply to Professor Phillips,* 26 N. Ky. L. Rev. 627, 638 (1999).

[93] As with pharmaceutical drugs containing unavoidable dangers, where warnings normally are the only way to eliminate the risk. *See* Restatement (Second) Torts § 402A cmt. k.

[94] *See, e.g., Falada v. Trinity Indus. Inc.,* 642 N.W.2d 247, 251 (Iowa 2002) ("defective design and defective workmanship are separate concepts"); *Chapman v. Maytag Corp.,* 297 F.3d 682 (7th Cir. 2002) (Ind. law) (" 'adequate warnings will not render a product with a manufacturing defect nondefective,' regardless of whether compliance with the warning would have rendered the product safe"); *Glover v. BIC Corp.,* 987 F.2d 1410, 1416 (9th Cir. 1993) (Or. law) (same).

[95] *See, e.g., Lewis v. Sea Ray Boats, Inc.,* 65 P.3d 245 (Nev. 2003) (" 'Strict liability may be imposed even though the product is faultlessly made if it was unreasonably dangerous to place the product in the hands of the user without suitable and adequate warning concerning safe and proper use.' "); *Stahl v. Novartis Pharms. Corp.,* 283 F.3d 254 (5th Cir. 2002) (La. law) ("Even if a product is not defectively designed or constructed, a manufacturer may still have a duty to warn consumers about any characteristic of the product that unreasonably may cause damage."); *Wilkinson v. Duff,* 575 S.E.2d 335 (W. Va. 2002) ("A failure to warn cause of action covers situations when a product may be safe as designed and manufactured, but which becomes defective because of the failure to warn of dangers which may be present when the product is used in a particular manner."); *Wabash Metal Prods., Inc. v. AT Plastics Corp.,* 575 S.E.2d 683 (Ga. Ct. App. 2002) ("A duty to warn can arise even if a product is not defective."); *Hennegan v. Cooper/T. Smith Stevedoring Co., Inc.,* 837 So.2d 96 (La. Ct. App. 2002) ("The lack of an adequate warning renders a product defective and unreasonably dangerous even if there is no manufacturing or design defect in the product."); *Wheeler v. HO Sports,* 232 F.3d 754 (10th Cir. 2000) (Okla. law) (although no evidence that flotation vest was not properly manufactured or designed, jury could find that manufacturer should have warned that vest would not keep wearer afloat); *Wilson v. U.S. Elevator Corp.,* 972 P.2d 235, 237 (Ariz. Ct. App. 1998) (" 'A product faultlessly made may be deemed defective if it is unreasonably dangerous to place the product in the hands of a user without a suitable warning.' "); *Richter v. Limax Int'l, Inc.,* 45 F.3d 1464 (10th Cir. 1995) (Kan. law) (failure to warn of risk of stress fractures to ankles from repetitive use of exercise trampoline; "even if a product does not have a design defect, failure to warn of a foreseeable danger arising from the product's normal use makes the product defective."); *Deines v. Vermeer Mfg. Co.,* 755 F.

design defects, no matter the precision of its manufacture or the abundance of its warnings.[96] This latter point is the most significant, because of the lingering, perverse effects of comment j's long tentacles in a number of jurisdictions.[97]

"Decisively" repudiating the "primitive" interpretation of comment j that would accord warnings the power to override a manufacturer's design

Supp. 350, 353 (D. Kan. 1990) ("A product may be perfectly manufactured and meet every requirement for its designed utility and still be rendered unreasonably dangerous through failure to warn of its dangerous characteristics."). *See also Emery v. Federated Foods, Inc.,* 863 P.2d 426 (Mont. 1993) (no warning of risk to young children from ingesting marshmallows); *Ayers v. Johnson & Johnson Baby Prods. Co.,* 818 P.2d 1337 (Wash. 1991) (no warning that baby could be paralyzed from ingesting "Baby Oil").

[96] *See, e.g., Delaney v. Deere & Co.,* 999 P.2d 930, 942 (Kan. 2000) ("just because there is a warning on a piece of equipment does not prevent the equipment from being dangerous"); *White v. ABCO Eng'g Corp.,* 221 F.3d 293, 305–06 (2d Cir. 2000) (N.J. law) (notwithstanding clearly adequate warnings, conveyor manufacturer was subject to liability for failing to provide side guarding); *Lewis v. American Cyanamid Co.,* 715 A.2d 967, 977 (N.J. 1998); *Rogers v. Ingersoll-Rand Co.,* 144 F.3d 841, 844 (D.C. Cir. 1998); *Crow v. Manitex, Inc.,* 550 N.W.2d 175 (Iowa Ct. App. 1996) (manufacturer of improperly-used crane, contrary to adequate warnings and instructions that would have prevented accident if heeded, subject to liability for failing to design crane so as to prevent the accident); *Glittenberg v. Doughboy Recreational Indus.,* 491 N.W.2d 208, 216 (Mich. 1992) ("A warning is not a Band-Aid to cover a gaping wound, and a product is not safe simply because it carries a warning."); *Robinson v. G.G.C., Inc.,* 808 P.2d 522, 525 (Nev. 1991) ("a warning is not an adequate replacement when a safety device will eliminate the need for the warning"); *Evridge v. American Honda Motor Co.,* 685 S.W.2d 632, 636 (Tenn. 1985) (interpreting comment j to allow simultaneous warnings and design claims); *Uloth v. City Tank Corp.,* 384 N.E.2d 118 (Mass. 1978) ("If a slight change in design would prevent serious, perhaps fatal, injury, the designer may not avoid liability by simply warning of the possible injury. We think that in such a case the burden to prevent needless injury is best placed on the designer or manufacturer rather than on the individual user of a product."). For early recognition that a manufacturer has a duty of safe design independent of any warnings, *see, e.g.,* Fleming James, Jr., *Products Liability (pt. 1),* 34 TEX. L. REV. 44, 49, 58–59 (1955).

[97] *See* decisions cases cited earlier at notes 95 and 96. To the extent that comment j retains any beneficial vitality in the modern world, it is as a source of consumer protection on an entirely separate issue. Indeed, most courts addressing the last paragraph of comment j have applied it in a consumer-*friendly* way – ruling, in cases in which adequate warnings are not provided, that comment j supports the creation of a presumption in favor of consumers that, had the manufacturer provided an adequate warning, the plaintiff (or someone acting on his or her behalf) would have read and heeded it. This widely adopted "heeding presumption" is used to satisfy the consumer's burden of proof on cause in fact. *See, e.g., Coffman v. Keene Corp.,* 628 A.2d 710 (N.J. 1993). After *Coffman,* a manufacturer that had warned of a danger asked the New Jersey court to apply comment j in *its* favor to bar the plaintiff's design defect claim. The court would not allow this nonsense: "Allowing such a warning to defeat a design-defect claim ... would frustrate the imposition of liability when a product's design fails to take into account an injured party's objectively foreseeable misuse of the product." *Lewis v. American Cyanamid Co.,* 715 A.2d 967, 977 (N.J. 1998). On the heeding presumption, *see generally* DAVID G. OWEN, PRODUCTS LIABILITY LAW § 11.4 (2005).

responsibilities,[98] the Products Liability Restatement declares in no uncertain terms that the law does not permit a manufacturer to hide behind a warning in an attempt to insulate itself from its independent duty of safe design:

> In general, when a safer design can reasonably be implemented and risks can reasonably be designed out of a product, adoption of the safer design is required over a warning that leaves a significant residuum of such risks. . . . Warnings are not . . . a substitute for the provision of a reasonably safe design.[99]

The courts have quite colorfully expressed the same idea. For example, the Michigan Supreme Court has observed that "[a] warning is not a Band-Aid to cover a gaping wound, and a product is not safe simply because it carries a warning";[100] and, in the words of the United States Court of Appeals for the District of Columbia Circuit, "[i]t is thus not correct that a manufacturer may . . . merely slap a warning onto its dangerous product, and absolve itself of any obligation to do more."[101] More succinctly, warnings do not trump design.

D. The Proper Role of Warnings in Design Defect Determinations

Although the three forms of defect generate independent safety obligations, such that the satisfaction of one obligation does not *ipso facto* satisfy the others, fulfilling one duty sometimes *helps* to satisfy another. This overlap of safety responsibilities is clearest in the area of design and warnings. The safer a manufacturer *designs* its products, the fewer dangers there will be about which to *warn*. As seen earlier, however, the issue usually is posed the other way: How may a *warning* affect a manufacturer's duty of safe design?

---

[98] The RESTATEMENT Reporters frequently have castigated this interpretation of comment j. For example, after the completion of the THIRD RESTATEMENT, the Reporters commented on their treatment of this aspect of comment j: "The Products Restatement rejects this primitive notion decisively." James A. Henderson Jr. and Aaron D. Twerski, *The Politics of the Products Liability Restatement*, 26 HOFSTRA L. REV. 667, 689 (1998).

[99] PRODUCTS LIABILITY RESTATEMENT § 2 cmt. l. *See* Aaron D. Twerski, *In Defense of the Products Liability Restatement: Part I*, 8 KAN. J.L. & PUB. POL'Y 27, 29 (1998) ("[C]omment j took the position that a product whose dangers are warned against, is not defective. We took the position in section 2 comment l of the Restatement (Third) of Torts that one cannot warn one's way out of a defective design case. If there is a reasonable design which would make the product safer, the mere fact that one warned against it does not insulate the seller from liability. . . . We vehemently disagree with the Second Restatement."); James A. Henderson Jr. and Aaron D. Twerski, *The Politics of the Products Liability Restatement*, 26 HOFSTRA L. REV. 667, 689 (1998).

[100] *Glittenberg v. Doughboy Recreational Indus.*, 491 N.W.2d 208, 216 (Mich. 1992).

[101] *Rogers v. Ingersoll-Rand Co.*, 144 F.3d 841, 844 (D.C. Cir. 1998).

Although warnings will only rarely satisfy a manufacturer's duty of safe design, as previously discussed, warnings sometimes are the only practical way to reduce a risk, particularly in the case of pharmaceutical drugs and other chemical and inherently toxic products.[102]

For example, a furniture polish that is very harmful if swallowed by young children would clearly be defective if sold without adequate warnings of the danger.[103] Assuming there is no way to change the chemical formulation of the polish to reduce the risk without sacrificing its effectiveness, a manufacturer in a case like this who warns of such an unavoidable hazard also might be seen as having thereby satisfied any design obligations as well. In truth, however, such a manufacturer has no relevant duty of safe design in a case like this, because there is no duty to do the impossible, to design away an unavoidable risk. So, cases such as this are properly viewed as involving purely a duty to warn and not a duty to design away a danger inherent in the product.

Because warnings and instructions may in fact serve to reduce design hazards, at least to some extent, the provision of such information may have *some* bearing on design defectiveness. Just as the obviousness of a hazard reduces the likelihood of resulting harm,[104] so, too, do warnings and instructions.[105] Thus, because warnings reduce the risk of injury from design hazards, the presence of a warning is one factor – sometimes an important one – to be balanced in the calculus of considerations involved in a determination of design defectiveness. In balancing the risk factors relevant to design defectiveness, a trier of fact should consider among other factors whether the design hazard was obvious, warned about, or generally known.[106]

IV. HOW FULL INFORMATION *SHOULD* AFFECT DUTY

Whereas U.S. products liability law has concluded that design and warnings defectiveness issues are largely distinct, that the duty of safe design ordinarily

---

[102] This is particularly so in the case of many generic product risks, as discussed in comment j.
[103] See, e.g., Spruill v. Boyle-Midway, Inc., 308 F.2d 79 (4th Cir. 1962) (Va. law).
[104] See DAVID G. OWEN, PRODUCTS LIABILITY LAW § 10.2 (2005).
[105] See id at § 9.1.
[106] The THIRD RESTATEMENT makes this point in describing the "broad range of factors" that may be relevant to the defectiveness of a product's design, including "the magnitude and probability of the foreseeable risks of harm, the instructions and warnings accompanying the product, and the nature and strength of consumer expectations regarding the product ... " PRODUCTS LIABILITY RESTATEMENT § 2 cmt. f. See, e.g., Wright v. Brooke Group Ltd., 652 N.W.2d 159 (Iowa 2002) (adopting and applying PRODUCTS LIABILITY RESTATEMENT § 2 cmts. g and j on the role of consumer expectations in the RESTATEMENT's risk-utility analysis to a case involving cigarettes).

exists even if full risk information is available to consumers, this chapter has not yet answered the normative question of whether the law's trend is misconceived, whether an injured person's possession of full risk information *should* provide a manufacturer with a shield to the normal duty of safe design. Should the law create a set of full-information rules, erected on the premise that consumers should have the freedom and responsibility to make and conform their behavior to rational choices. The reasonableness of this question suggests that it might be helpful to sketch out a rough model of "information liability shield" principles to see how such a program might work, if it might provide a sensible set of rules of responsibility for accidents involving victims to whom full knowledge of the risk was available, and if such a system might practicably be implemented.

A. Information Liability Shields – An Ideal-World View

In an ideal world, a world in which rules and institutions can be designed to maximize personal freedom ("choice") and personal accountability (responsibility for the consequences of choices), and where governmental interference can be minimized, the law might well choose to shield actors from the duty to protect potential victims from accidental harm when the latter possess full information about the risks arising from the actor's conduct. In such a world, actors could fairly expect that potential victims fully informed on the risks to which they are exposed will take reasonable steps to protect themselves from harm and, because they make informed decisions of what dangers to encounter, potential victims should bear responsibility for such risk-incurring choices. Otherwise stated, persons injured by their own informed choices to engage risks should not be permitted to externalize resulting injury costs onto others: people choosing to encounter risk should have no right to eat their cake (take the benefits of risk) and have it (externalize its costs) too. Such a principle, protecting actors from liability in such cases, might be called an "information liability shield, or "information shield" for short.

In such an ideal world, an Information Liability Shield (ILS) program might operate something like this. First, the federal safety agencies would need to be enhanced considerably to give them "Warning Tsar" authority to approve and enhance warnings proposed by manufacturers, and to declare certain risks as "obvious" (that knife blades can cut human tissue) or generally known (that cigarettes can cause cancer). Once a product receives such certification, both its warnings and its design – whose dangers were certified as being fully telegraphed to consumers by a warning, the product's appearance, or general knowledge – would be immune from judicial challenge with respect to all risks certified as being warned of, obvious, or generally known. A liability shield in such cases would be logical because an ILS approval would be grounded on the fullness and fairness of the risk information available to consumers which would assure that they are well equipped to make rational decisions about when and how to engage a risk.

Only product warnings would need to be approved, not designs, because the market would move design safety toward optimality. This would be so because rational consumers, armed with full risk information, would tend to purchase products with the best benefit-cost ratios and to avoid products with adverse ratios. Under such a program, producers would have a strong incentive to offer full warnings in exchange for premarketing liability protection. Conversely, they would have a strong disincentive to bypass ILS certification and so risk judicial declarations, *ex post*, that their products' warnings or designs were inadequate, subjecting them to liability for resulting harm.

B. Real World Obstacles

In the real world, an Information Liability Shield program would confront a number of substantial obstacles. Among the problems are at least the following: (1) difficulties in determining whether the information available to consumers was full but not excessive – the "fullness" problem; (2) adjudicatory problems in determining causation and scope of risk – the "causation" problem; (3) the transfer of accident costs from actors to third-party bystanders – the "bystander" problem; (4) cognitive and behavioral deficiencies in product users – the "behavioral" problem; and (5) the growth of federal safety agencies – the "bloated agency" problem. It may be useful to sketch out briefly these real-world obstacles to a successful ILS program.

1. The "Fullness" Problem

First is the problem of assuring that the information proposed by a manufacturer is full and fair. Courts have had difficulty, to say the least, in rendering principled determinations of whether warnings are "adequate."[107] Logic and the law both teach the dangers of "information pollution," so that a "full" warning will be one that provides optimal, rather than maximum, information. And the science and psychology of cognition and behavior are in their infancy, rendering the very idea of an optimal warning nearly unintelligible

[107] *See generally* DAVID G. OWEN, PRODUCTS LIABILITY LAW § 9.3 (2005).

and undermining the ability of a regulatory agency to render principled determinations of when warnings properly should be classified as "full." Nor could an ILS agency possibly be expert on all risks associated with the universe of products for which certification is sought.

An inherent advantage to an ILS program that would tend to alleviate the fullness problem is that manufacturers themselves will have an incentive to make their risk disclosures as full and fair as possible in order to avoid liability for those risks. That is, the liability protection offered under an ILS program is limited to the risks disclosed, so that manufacturers (who *are* expert on their products' risks) should normally want to disclose as much information about as many risks as they possibly can discover. Thus, the liability shield incentive itself should inspire manufacturers to engage in optimal research into risk. And this same incentive should discourage manufacturer fraud, in hiding risks, because the shield protection will only operate if the risks are in fact disclosed. Indeed, an ILS program might well be plagued with the opposite problem – an effort by manufacturers to overwarn of every conceivable type of risk that might ever arise, raising anew the problem of warnings pollution.

2. The "Causation" Problem

Although the fullness and fairness of a warning would preempt judicial review of the adequacy of an approved warning or related design safety issues, courts still would need to address whether an accident victim's injuries were caused by, whether they fell within or outside of, the risks about which information was provided and certified. This is because a manufacturer whose product receives ILS certification is shielded from liability only for risks about which information was available to consumers, certified risks that were warned about, obvious, or generally known. For example, even if a commercial glue manufacturer receives ILS certification for warnings that its glue's fumes are "flammable," a court might need to decide whether "flammable" includes the risk that the invisible fumes might travel under a door to an adjacent room, become ignited by an appliance pilot light, and explode. This example suggests again that manufacturers might see the wisdom of warning of every possible risk, leading to a surfeit of warnings.

3. The "Bystander" Problem

Another problem with an ILS program is the third-party injury problem, where accident costs are transferred from manufacturers and users to third-party victims. For example, a disposable butane lighter manufacturer may obtain certification for a warning to "Keep Away from Children," yet the owner of a lighter with such a warning might leave it on a table within reach of a child who might use the lighter to start a fire that burns the child or another. Even if child-resistant starting mechanisms were feasible and cost effective, an ILS program would insulate the manufacturer from design defect liability for failing to include such safety devices in the lighter's design.

And what should be done about a worker walking by an unguarded machine who slips on a grease spot and falls into the machine? Or a worker crushed by a large crane, equipped with neither rear view mirrors nor outriggers, when it backs up or tips over? Or a pedestrian struck by a projectile shot by a power lawnmower not equipped with a protective guard? Assuming that each of these dangers could be cost-effectively designed away, the obviousness of these dangers to *users* is little consolation to these injured *bystanders*. Nor is it good social policy to allow manufacturers to transfer to bystanders accident costs that cost effectively can be removed.

One might argue that injured bystanders often have tort claims against the product user who often is the party most in control of risks at the time of accidents (and so most in need of tort incentives), and this sometimes is the case. But a tort claim by a child against a parent is usually an insufficient remedy, and giving incentives to a parent who left a butane lighter in the reach of his or her now-deceased child closes the proverbial barn door too late. As for a crane that backs over a worker at a construction site, the workers' compensation system inadequately covers accident costs, and the operator will likely have few assets. Other than market incentives, which in these situations probably are quite weak, the only way to reduce the incidence of excessive design hazards for bystanders would be by administrative regulation, by agencies such as the Consumer Product Safety Commission and the Occupational Safety and Health Administration.

4. *The "Behavioral" Problem*

To the extent that an ILS model rests on a premise that consumers provided with full risk information will act rationally to avoid harm, it rests on a premise that is false. In fact, no person is capable of perfectly harmonizing action with perfectly rational decision making. All humans sometimes act irrationally, and they are sometimes injured as a result. Psychologists and, more recently, legal and economic theorists, increasingly emphasize the cognitive limitations of human behavior.[108] Putting aside the frailty of the human

---

[108] Literature in the various subfields of law and behavioralism is rich and growing rapidly. Important early works include Howard A. Latin, *Problem-Solving Behavior and Theories of*

body, which may slip or collapse into an obvious danger, the human mind simply cannot process properly the myriad facts and problem-solving situations with which it is constantly barraged. If human choice and behavior thus is often actuated by factors other than rationality, a model of justice resting entirely on responsibility for rational choices might seem to be infirm.

Moreover, the liberal model of responsibility for choice ignores another desideratum: maximizing utility, the social pie. Utilitarians and economists both explain that the quality of conduct and rules may be judged by the extent to which they promote net utility, benefits over costs. The rationale is simple: the more that individual activity generates net benefits, the more goods there are to go around, the better for the group. Because the most convenient metric of net social welfare is economic efficiency, it usually is helpful to assess the quality of both actions and rules in terms of their efficiency, an approach that has the added benefit of requiring actors to accord equal value to the rights of others as their own.[109]

An Information Shield program would be efficient when consumers act rationally and their bodies respond to their will. It would be inefficient, however, when humans make mistakes, when people act carelessly, otherwise make bad choices, and when their bodies do not bend to their wills. That is, the ILS approach by hypothesis shields manufacturers from liability for failing to make cost-effective design improvements to their products which possess obvious or warned of dangers. This raises the issue of whether the law should seek to maximize individual freedom and responsibility through

---

Tort Liability, 73 CAL. L. REV. 677 (1985); Robert C. Ellikson, *Bringing Culture and Human Frailty to Rational Actors: A Critique of Classical Law and Economics*, 65 CHI.-KENT L. REV. 23 (1989); Howard A. Latin, *"Good" Warnings, Bad Products, and Cognitive Limitations*, 41 UCLA L. REV. 1193 (1994). More recently, *see, e.g.*, Jon D. Hanson & Douglas A. Kysar, *Taking Behavioralism Seriously: The Problem of Market Manipulation*, 74 N.Y.U.L. REV. 630 (1999); Jon D. Hanson & Douglas A. Kysar, *Taking Behavioralism Seriously: Some Evidence of Market Manipulation*, 112 HARV. L. REV. 1420 (1999); Cass R. Sunstein, *Hazardous Heuristics*, 70 U. CHI. L. REV. 751 (2003); Chris Guthrie, *Prospect Theory, Risk Preference, and the Law*, 97 NW. U. L. REV. 1115 (2003); Russell B. Korobkin & Thomas S. Ulen, *Law and Behavioral Science: Removing the Rationality Assumption from Law and Economics*, 88 CAL. L. REV. 1051 (2000); Christine Jolls *et al.*, *A Behavioral Approach to Law and Economics*, 50 STAN. L. REV. 1471 (1998); Cass Sunstein, *Behavioral Law and Economics: A Progress Report*, 1 AM. L. & ECON. REV. 115 (1999); Jeffrey J. Rachlinski, *The "New" Law and Psychology: A Reply to Critics, Skeptics, and Cautious Supporters*, 85 CORNELL L. REV. 739 (2000); Note, *The Elephant in the Room: Evolution, Behavioralism, and Counteradvertising in the Coming War Against Obesity*, 116 HARV. L. REV. 1161 (2003). Important early work on how humans make decisions was done by Daniel Kahneman and Amos Tversky. *See* JUDGMENT UNDER UNCERTAINTY: HEURISTICS AND BIASES (Daniel Kahneman, Paul Slovic, & Amos Tversky, eds.) (1982) (collecting key papers).

[109] *See* David G. Owen, *Philosophical Foundations of Fault in Tort Law*, in PHILOSOPHICAL FOUNDATIONS OF TORT LAW (David G. Owen, ed.) (1995).

an Information Shield program despite its tendency toward inefficiency and disutility. Put otherwise, the question might be viewed as whether the law should shield manufacturers who design products which are safe only for their *proper* uses,[110] in order to maximize personal responsibility, or whether the law instead should require manufacturers to take all reasonable (optimal) care to design their products with leeway for people to make the most common types of mistakes, in order to maximize social utility. The answer to this question is not self-evident, for it depends on whether priority should be given to autonomy or utility, and on whether one prefers placing responsibility and risk incentives on (corporate) actors or potential (human) victims.

5. *The "Bloated Agency" Problem*

Finally, while a major goal of a Liability Shield program would be to reduce government intrusion by courts second-guessing conscious design choices of manufacturers and use choices by consumers, such a program contemplates a major increase in the size, intrusiveness, and cost of governmental product safety agencies. As discussed earlier, the perverse incentive on manufacturers operating under an ILS program to provide excessive information on risks would have to be fully addressed by agency safety communication experts, a discipline that would mushroom enormously under such a program. Moreover, because design safety oversight by courts would be substantially curtailed under an ILS program, safety agencies would need to enlarge their staffs with experts charged with determining how the full information promoted by an ILS program should be supplemented by design regulations, as in the disposable butane lighter example mentioned earlier. In short, *ex ante* safety regulation by federal safety agencies would need to be considerably enlarged to compensate for the diminished use of *ex post* judicial oversight. Hence, such a program, leaning heavily on a liberal model that seeks to minimize the role of government regulation of product safety matters, appears internally conflicted.

V. CONCLUSION

Over the last four decades, U.S. tort law has witnessed the rise and fall of two related doctrines developed to shield manufacturers from design liability in cases in which consumers possess full information about product risks that result in harm. The patent danger rule was the most formidable of the two,

---

[110] We might here define "proper" use as reasonable use in view of the product's apparent risks.

explicitly placing on potential victims all responsibility for accidental harm from open and obvious design hazards. But the rule did not last long, and in shifting the basis of design liability from consumer expectations to risk-utility, the courts in the late twentieth century converted the patency of danger from a no-duty rule to a mere factor in determinations of defectiveness and consumer responsibility.

The issue of how a warning should affect a manufacturer's design obligations is less developed in products liability jurisprudence, but it occasionally confounds the courts. Ever since Restatement (Second) of Torts § 402A was published in 1965, the puzzle of comment j has interfered with an understanding of how the duties of design and warning properly relate to one another. Comment j may be read to relieve manufacturers who provide warnings of their duty of safe design; but that is wrong. Design and warning defects are conceptually distinct and generate obligations that are largely independent. Interpreting comment j to make the duty of safe design contingent on a manufacturer's failure to warn is contrary to the original purposes of § 402A; contrary to a fair reading of comment j in context with the other comments; contrary to the intentions of § 402A's author, Dean Prosser, and the Restatement Advisers; and contrary to the developed jurisprudence of products liability law for forty years.

Although these doctrinal developments illustrate a trend that rejects the notion that manufacturers should be shielded from liability when consumers are fully informed on product risks, the soundness of these developments may be tested by designing a program that reverses these doctrines. Erected on a premise of consumer sovereignty and rationality, Congress might create an Information Shield program that would shield manufacturers from liability when consumers possess full information about product hazards. Such a program appears reasonable in the abstract because giving consumers more and better information about product risk provides them with an opportunity for greater self-determination while tending to optimize product safety by squeezing out inefficient risk. But any program of this type confronts a number of real-world problems that substantially undercut its value, including difficulties in ascertaining the "fullness" of information; judicial problems in determining causation and scope of risk; the transfer of accident costs from product users to third parties; cognitive and behavioral deficiencies in humans that undermine rational action and generate inadvertent behavior; and the problem of bloating the federal safety agencies.

These real-world problems with implementation of an Information Shield program suggest that responsibility in most situations where persons are injured despite being fully informed on risk is best resolved by flexible

principles of comparative fault, backed up by a robust doctrine of sole proximate cause, rather than on the basis of no-duty constructs that provide a
complete escape to manufacturers. Thus, U.S. products liability law appears
to have developed properly in addressing the fact of a victim's possession of full
risk information principally through the doctrines of comparative fault (and
proximate cause), secondarily in risk-utility terms of product defectiveness,
and only rarely through no-duty resolution by a court.

CHAPTER TEN

THE COMPLEXITY OF TORTS – THE CASE OF PUNITIVE DAMAGES

Guido Calabresi

ABSTRACT. Law, and particularly tort law, serves definable human goals. Often these goals are multidimensional, and too often, those who view tort law in a goal-oriented way move quickly to a single, simple goal – whether it be economic efficiency, furthering loss spreading or anything else – and, having examined tort doctrines and cases on that basis, are properly attacked for being reductionists. The thesis of this chapter is that the pursuit of one-dimensional goals in tort law is fraught with such risks.

Generally speaking, courts are unlikely to be reductionist. Judges derive law from many sources. The problem arises from the ever-increasing incursions by federal courts into the tort process, and is worsened when the incursion is by the Supreme Court. This chapter concentrates on punitive damages. Its thesis is that punitive damages in tort law can perform at least five very different functions, and that each is a sufficient reason for a state to seek to impose exemplary awards. These objectives may reveal or include a desire to: (1) enforce societal norms, through the use of private attorney's general; (2) employ "the multiplier," in the sense that the proper size of the deterrent assessed on those one would deter is not the harm to any one victim but rather that harm multiplied by all those victims whose harms are not likely to be charged to the injurer; (3) the "Tragic Choice" Function, such as in the *Pinto* case; (4) permit Recovery of Generally Nonrecoverable Compensatory Damages; and (5) permit Righting of Private Wrongs.

The Supreme Court's modern decisions regarding punitive damages fail to take into account the multiple functions these awards have performed. Tort law and its many parts have long been characterized by complexity of functions, goals, and methods of achieving these. That is true of notions like causation, duty, punitive damages, and *respondeat superior*, to name but a few. Without this complexity torts would be a very different subject. It is rare that single minded views can fully encompass and understand a slowly developed field of law like torts.

I. INTRODUCTION

I am a functionalist. That is, I believe law, and particularly tort law, does not exist in a vacuum or as a self-contained and self-concerned system. It is there

Guido Calabresi, Judge, United States Court of Appeals for the Second Circuit; Sterling Professor of Law Emeritus, and Professorial Lecturer, Yale Law School.

instead to serve quite specific and definable human goals. As such, I believe its doctrines, and how they are applied, can be evaluated – and criticized or confirmed – on the basis of how well they do their jobs and serve their functions. But to say this is very far from saying that these functions or goals are simple, let alone unidimensional. Too often, those who view tort law in a "goal oriented" way move quickly to a single, simple goal – whether it be economic efficiency, furthering loss spreading, or anything else – and, having examined tort doctrines and cases on that basis, are properly attacked for being reductionists.

This is no big deal when the reductionists are academics. After all, the job of academics is to propound half-baked ideas . . . and be ignored, at least for a time. It is this lack of responsibility for (and at most only indirect impact on) real-world decision making that gives academics their freedom, that allows them to tell the truth, that motivates them to seek justice (as they see it) although the heavens fall. Reductionism is much more dangerous when it infects courts (or, for that matter, legislatures). In the hands of decision makers, reductionism can too easily result in quick responses to single-minded views, and those responses, although well intentioned, can destroy the complex balance that our legal system (and especially the parts of it that are derived from the common law, and hence slowly-developed) has long struck between multiple goals.

My thesis is that this danger is particularly great at present. In this respect, I am not especially concerned with so-called legislative reforms. That statutory interventions in common-law fields can create havoc is nothing new; hence we have developed venerable (and suspect) notions like strict interpretation of statutes in derogation of the common law[1] and Edward Levi's expansive view of the role of courts in reading new statutes,[2] all designed to protect Blackstone's complex garden from conversion into rational seeming, but in the long run less satisfactory, topiary plantings. Nevertheless, I am not so worried about legislative incursions because the give and take of the political process, and of the various interest groups at play in it, makes the victory of a single-minded, reductionist reform unlikely. The political process has many flaws in torts (especially its lack of responsiveness to the needs of victims, as against repeat players, including victims' lawyers).[3] But undue, and simplistic,

---

[1] See, e.g., State v. Heck, 112 N.M. 513, 515, 817 P.2d 247, 249 (1991); Bonner v. Minco, Inc., 159 Ariz. 246, 256, 766 P.2d 598, 608 (1988); Friehe v. State Bd. of Educational Lands & Funds, 199 Neb. 504, 506, 259 N.W.2d 925, 926 (1977).

[2] See EDWARD LEVI, AN INTRODUCTION TO LEGAL REASONING 32 (1949).

[3] See, e.g., Guido Calabresi and Jeffrey O. Cooper, New Directions in Tort Law, 30 VAL. U. L. REV. 859, 863 (1996) (discussing the control repeat players exercise over tort reform).

rationality isn't usually one of them. My concern focuses elsewhere – in the courts, and particularly in the federal courts.

Generally speaking, courts are unlikely to be reductionist. The way we make law – deriving it from many sources, and case by case – tends to protect us from it. We are less likely to cite an article or theory, to rely on what is sometimes called scientific policy making, than on the usually imprecise words that are the core of the precedents that guide us. Requirements like causation can – as I have written[4] – be converted into focused functional ones. But they carry much other luggage that contains what John Stuart Mill, in criticizing Jeremy Bentham, rather grandiosely called "the unanalyzed experience of the human race."[5] Why, then, am I concerned?

The problem arises from the recent, and ever-increasing, incursions by federal courts into the tort process. This incursion is bad enough when done by lower federal courts whose judges are rarely picked for their knowledge or sense of common-law methods or of fields like torts, and who, therefore, can be led to view unidimensionally and simplistically the state tort doctrines they purport to apply. It is worse when the incursion is by the Supreme Court of the United States, both because it is even less qualified in common-law matters and because it is more likely to state its opinions in ways that make corrections of reductionistic results extremely difficult.

When lower federal courts misunderstand (as they not infrequently do) the complexity of New York's notions of duty, and confuse the question of whether court or jury, in that state, is empowered to establish or negate the existence and level of duty, with the quite different question of who in New York usually decides whether there is or is not a breach of duty, the result may be wrong in any given case, but it does little permanent damage to New York tort law. The New York courts, guided by its distinguished and torts-knowledgeable Court of Appeals, can keep things from going too far astray. And anyway, as I have elsewhere written, the answer to mistakes of this sort is readily available in frequent certification of state law questions by lower federal courts to the state's highest court.[6]

When lower federal courts treat requirements of causation, and especially of proximate cause, as if they meant the same thing under widely different

---

[4] *See* Guido Calabresi, *Concerning Cause and the Law of Torts*, 43 U. Chi. L. Rev. 69 (1975) (distinguishing different notions of "cause" and "causation" in tort law, and suggesting that causation requirements can be used effectively to achieve policy goals).

[5] John Stuart Mill, *Essay on Bentham*, in The Philosophy of John Stuart Mill: Ethical, Political, and Religious (Marshall Cohen, ed.) (1961).

[6] *See* Guido Calabresi, *Federal and State Courts: Restoring a Workable Balance*, 78 N.Y.U. L. Rev. 1293 (2003).

federal statutes and under "the common law" – as if causation embodied a single and uniform set of rules in the different states – the mistake is more serious.[7] But even there, the systemic effects of the error are limited. The purposes of a federal statute may be undermined if a federal court fails to focus adequately on congressional intent with respect to that statute and assumes instead that all invocations of some causal connection are meant to be the same. But the more dangerous effect that such reductionist views of causation have – as when they are subsequently applied by the federal courts to state law causation requirements – is again curable by the (dare I say it?), in this area more sophisticated, state courts.

The problem gets much more serious when the incursions are made by the U.S. Supreme Court, for then errors of unidimensionality are far harder to cure. And so, though I would love to spend much more time on how and when courts of my ilk misunderstand the complex purposes, and hence the equally complex doctrines, of tort law, I will in this chapter focus on the Supreme Court's errors and missed opportunities. There are many that could be discussed. Preemption and the confusion between minimum and maximum standards, and the wonderful mess that surrounds the treatment of "purely" emotional damages, are but two examples. In this piece, however, I will concentrate on a third – punitive damages.

My thesis is this: (a) punitive damages in tort law can perform at least five very different functions; (b) each function, if it were the sole object of such extracompensatory damages, would have rules and limits that make no sense if one examines punitive damages through the prism of a different function; (c) by concentrating essentially on one – albeit an important – role of such damages, the Supreme Court has, effectively and thoughtlessly, made it much more difficult for the states to further, through tort law, some of the other functions that extracompensatory damages can serve.[8] In saying this, let me be clear, I am not especially interested in criticizing the High Court. Nor do I wish to downplay the importance of the function of punitive damages which that Court deemed – not incorrectly, I think – to be in need of regulation. I am rather trying to make a broader point: that the common law of torts is

---

[7] See, e.g., Laborers Local 17 Health and Benefit Fund v. Philip Morris, Inc., 191 F.3d 229, 242–43 (2d Cir. 1999) (construing the Racketeer Influenced and Corrupt Organizations Act (RICO) to incorporate the traditional "proximate cause" requirements of the common law).

[8] See State Farm Mut. Auto. Ins. Co. v. Campbell, 538 U.S. 408 (2003). This is not the first time that the Supreme Court has looked at punitive damages and their function too single-mindedly. See, e.g., City of Newport v. Fact Concerts, Inc., 453 U.S. 247 (1981). I followed and then criticized Justice Blackmun's opinion in that case in Ciraolo v. City of New York, 216 F.3d 236, 242 (2d Cir. 2000) (Calabresi, J., concurring).

complex, is messy in its mixture of goals. And that control and rationalization of it is dangerous precisely because such rationalization may interfere with perfectly plausible aims of that law, aims that once removed from torts must then be served in other, often less effective, ways.

II. FIVE FUNCTIONS OF PUNITIVE DAMAGES — AND THEIR ATTRIBUTES

Let me list five (and there may well be more) functions that assessing damages beyond those needed to compensate a particular plaintiff can serve, functions that is, that a state may, although it need not, wish to have as part of its tort law.

A. To Enforce Societal Norms Through the Use of Private Attorney's General

This is akin to the award of treble damages in RICO or antitrust cases and is often focused on behavior that is criminal or semicriminal. In principle, such punitive damages could be awarded regardless of the existence or size of the compensable damages sought by the plaintiff, so long as the plaintiff has sufficient interest in the outcome to make him or her a good private attorney-general. In this sense a plaintiff who gets nominal damages or an injunction may do very well.[9]

Noncompensatory damages of this sort obviously require serious wrongdoing on the part of the defendant and, if they are to be effective, such semicriminal "enforcement" penalties must be assessed with a view to the defendant's capacity to pay. And precluding their insurability is perfectly rational, although not necessarily essential. They are, in this sense, a form of "tort fine."[10] Similarly, they can properly be based on the totality of the defendant's wrongdoing and not just the wrong to the particular private attorney-general who blew the whistle.

---

[9] And indeed, in some situations, a plaintiff need not even receive nominal damages in order to collect significant punitive damages. *See, e.g., Cush-Crawford v. Adchem Corp.*, 271 F.3d 352, 359 (2d Cir. 2001) (holding that when discrimination has been established in contravention of Title VII, "punitive damages may be awarded within the limits of the statutory caps," even if the plaintiff does not receive an award of compensatory or nominal damages).

[10] For a discussion of the differences between "fine" systems and traditional "damage" systems (at least, in the products liability context), *see* Alan Schwartz, *Proposals for Products Liability Reform: A Theoretical Synthesis*, 97 YALE L. J. 353 (1988). For an earlier discussion of these differences, one that notes their relationship to the wealth of the wrongdoer, *see* GUIDO CALABRESI, THE COSTS OF ACCIDENTS 119–28, 270 n. 5 (1970).

Because their object is akin to criminal law deterrence, and the penalties are apt to be severe, many of the protections of criminal law – like prohibitions on double jeopardy, *ex post facto* application, and perhaps rights to adequate counsel – properly, and perhaps even constitutionally, should be required.[11] Conversely, the total size of the penalty, like most criminal sentences, should be in the very broad discretion of the sovereign state that seeks to impose the sanction. If "three strikes, you're out, and for life" laws as applied to petty crimes get by constitutionally, much leeway should be given to states to calibrate the size of this sort of "punies." Moreover, whether behavior outside the state can be taken into account in determining the size of the penalty (as against wrongdoing within the state, but to others than the whistle-blowing plaintiff, which is clearly relevant to this form of noncompensatory damages) depends on the degree to which we wish to allow State A, in its criminal laws, to calibrate its sentences at least in part based on crimes committed in State B.

Finally, to serve this function there is no reason why the whole of the punitive damages assessed should accrue to the whistle-blowing plaintiff. All that is needed is a sum sufficient to give the private A.G. an adequate incentive to step in and aid in law enforcement. That may be a significant amount but it need be nowhere the full amount that defendant should pay. The rest can properly be assigned to a variety of people and purposes that I need not here consider.

B. The Multiplier

With this function of extracompensatory damages we can profitably compare another one – discussed, not surprisingly, by Dick Posner and me in court opinions,[12] and analyzed well and at some length by scholars such as Sharkey,[13] Polinsky and Shavell,[14] and Hylton,[15] among others. This basis for awarding damages beyond the hurt of a particular plaintiff derives from the insight,

---

[11] *Cf., Restrepo v. McElroy*, 369 F.3d 627, 635 n.16 (2d Cir. 2004) (discussing the punitive elements of deportation, and suggesting that those punitive elements require additional due process protections in deportation proceedings).

[12] *See Ciraolo, supra* note 8, 216 F.3d at 243–44 (Calabresi, J., concurring); *Federal Deposit Ins. Corp. v. W.R. Grace. & Co.*, 877 F.2d 614, 623 (7th Cir. 1989) (Posner, J.).

[13] *See* Catherine M. Sharkey, *Punitive Damages as Societal Damages*, 113 Yale L. J.347 (2003).

[14] *See* A. Mitchell Polinsky and Steven Shavell, *Punitive Damages: An Economic Analysis*, 111 Harv. L. Rev. 870 (1998).

[15] *See* Keith N. Hylton, *Punitive Damages and the Economic Theory of Penalties*, 87 Geo. L. J.421, 456 (1998).

first noted in criminal law by Becker,[16] that the proper size of the deterrent assessed on those one would deter is not the harm to any individual victim. It is rather that harm multiplied by all those victims whose harms, though real, are not otherwise likely to be charged to the injurer. These include all the costs the defendant is, in theory, liable for in the relevant jurisdiction, which, however, are not likely to result in successful suits. These are, *inter alia*, the suits wrongly lost by plaintiffs minus any suits wrongly won, plus all the valid suits simply not brought – all the times, Becker wrote, that the perpetrator was likely not to be caught.

Although Becker mentioned the need for a multiplier in criminal law, its significance is potentially as great or greater in torts. But if this reason for extracompensatory damages is what a state wishes to serve, then the nature, limits, and characteristic of those damages will be very different from those served by a private attorneys-general rationale. Let me go down the list quickly.

First, there is no reason whatever to require a high degree of wrongfulness or indeed any wrongfulness at all – to justify use of a multiplier. Whatever the reason – fault or nonfault based – that a state properly has for assessing damages on a defendant in order to give that defendant a correct incentive to chose wisely between safety costs and accident costs, also justify use of a multiplier. They do so, that is, whenever the state has reason to believe that some of the costs properly due to the defendant's activity would otherwise escape consideration. The point is to charge the proper cost avoider/decision maker all that is relevant to the decision he or she must make. And wrongfulness – let alone wanton and willfulness or criminality – has nothing necessarily to do with it.

If, however, the object is internalization of costs, in a transaction cost heavy world, then there is no reason whatever to prohibit insurance coverage of the multiplied damages – quite the contrary. And as the point is to induce the defendant to make correct decisions based on a more accurate cost/benefit assessment, there is no apparent basis for looking at the defendant's wealth in deciding the size of the multiplier. Moreover, as no semi criminal law objectives are at play, there is no reason to impose procedural safeguards like prohibition of double jeopardy on the assessment of a multiplier. Computation of damages, already assessed in the past, and of those likely to be charged in the future, in order to avoid "double counting," is an essential part of determining the multiplier. It is needed in order to make the total "cost" to be considered as nearly correct as possible. But the ways in which such "double counting" is to be avoided sound in civil law procedural safeguards, not criminal ones.

---

[16] *See* Gary Becker, *Crime and Punishment: An Economic Approach*, 76 POL. ECON. 169 (1968).

Again, in stark contrast with the first function discussed, the existence of compensatory damages to someone, and most likely the plaintiff, is essential to this basis. It forms the item to be multiplied. Without it one hardly knows how to start. Moreover, the size of the multiplier depends on the existence and size of other, uncompensated, legally compensable damages. In this sense a relational assessment is essential. Because the multiplier is based on the size of otherwise unaccounted for damages, however, that relationship cannot be grounded in any preconceived "appropriate" figure. What is too large or too small a multiplier is exceedingly case specific and has nothing whatever to do with the wrongfulness of defendant's acts.[17]

Perhaps most important of all, there is no justification in this rationale for extracompensatory damages to give much of the "multiplied" damages to the particular plaintiff who has sued for compensation.[18] That plaintiff should be made whole, and that means also awarding an amount to cover the costs/risks of raising the multiplier issue. But the bulk of the multiplier – once its function of leading the defendants to do a proper cost/benefit analysis is achieved – should in the ordinary course go to those whose damages would otherwise be uncovered. If these are not findable, then the damages should perhaps go to activities that, if subsidized, would reduce the relevant costs to the unfindable victims.[19] Can one imagine two more different – yet each plausible – reasons for extracompensatory damages than those described in (a) and (b), above? The answer, in fact, is yes!

C. The "Tragic Choice" Function

If the two previous reasons for what we, perhaps improperly, call "punitive damages" have been frequent players in the literature, the next basis has not.

---

[17] The point is nicely illustrated by Polinsky and Shavell, *supra* n. 14, who correctly argue that no multiplier should apply to a tort such as the enormous oil spillage of the Exxon Valdez, as such an event, while certainly outrageous, is highly unlikely to go undetected and unpunished in other instances.

[18] Hence the recent suggestion that such damages be allocated to the state, and not the plaintiff in any particular case. *See* Sharkey, *supra* n. 13.

[19] For example, imagine that the smoke emitted by a factory hurts the air quality of a community. This makes it more costly for residents to launder clothes, as the polluted air dirties clothes faster than would clean air. Distributing the "multiplier" type punitive damages of this harm to those adversely affected would be extremely expensive, even if feasible. In such a circumstance, one might contemplate using the extracompensatory damages to subsidize the construction of local laundromats. By increasing the supply of laundry services (and as a consequence, reducing the price of those services to residents), such a properly calibrated subsidy would offset the cost-increasing effects of the factory's air pollution.

It can be discerned, however, in the celebrated *Pinto* case[20] and is part and parcel of those subterfuges that are an inevitable element of law in tragic situations.[21] In the *Pinto* case, Ford sought to defend itself against charges that it had improperly placed the gas tank in a place where the gas could, after a crash, explode. In doing so it claimed that a cost/benefit analysis of different gas tank placements had been done correctly.[22] The cost of putting the tank in a safer place was too high, it argued, in relation to the number of lives that would be saved by doing so. As a result, Ford seemed to be saying, what it had done could not be faulted. The jury, nonetheless, not only found liability but assessed huge punitive damages.

Why, after all, doesn't the Learned Hand test for negligence[23] presume just such a cost/benefit test? And didn't the great Cardozo say about the same thing in *Adams v. Bullock*,[24] a case in which no negligence was found after a youngster was electrocuted as a result of climbing a post bearing electric wires that were "needed" to run trolleys? What was wrong with what Ford did?

It is possible that the jury believed that Ford only took into account those lost lives that led to lawsuits, and, having determined that taking all lives lost into consideration would lead to negligence under a Learned Hand standard, applied a multiplier, as described earlier. But that seems unlikely to explain the jury's apparent anger. More plausibly, the jury was deeply offended by the fact that Ford had justified burning up little babies by proffering cold statistics about the cost of placing gas tanks elsewhere. Yet that is precisely what the Learned Hand test would seem to ask Ford to do.

The problem is that although we know at some level that not every safety measure is worth paying for and that some accidents – however horrible – are "worth having," yet we are committed to the ideal that life is a pearl beyond price. And we are determined, as a society, to hold to both contradictory views. Thus, shortly after I wrote an article provocatively titled *The Decision for Accidents*,[25] the *New York Times* thundered in an editorial that when safety

---

[20] *See Grimshaw v. Ford Motor Company,* 174 Cal. Rptr. 348 (Cal. Ct. App. 1981) (hereafter "the *Pinto* case").

[21] For a discussion of these choices, *see* GUIDO CALABRESI & PHILIP BOBBITT, TRAGIC CHOICES (1978).

[22] Obviously, and for any number of reasons, this was not Ford's primary line of defense in that case. For a discussion of how this cost/benefit analysis eventually came to dominate the parties' litigation strategies in the Pinto case, *see* Gary T. Schwartz, *The Myth of the Ford Pinto Case*, 43 RUTGERS L. REV.1013, 1020–22 (1991).

[23] *See United States v. Carroll Towing Co.,* 159 F.2d 169 (2d Cir. 1947).

[24] 227 N.Y. 208, 125 N.E. 93 (1919).

[25] *See* Guido Calabresi, *The Decision for Accidents: An Approach to Nonfault Allocation of Costs,* 78 HARV. L. REV. 713 (1965).

is at stake, no amount of expenditure is too much.[26] I was tempted to write them welcoming the fact that thereafter all their delivery trucks would, I supposed, drive no faster than five miles an hour. I did not do so, of course, because I realized that the *Times* was saying something important, and in a way true, when it denied the acceptability of safety/cost tradeoffs, just as I was when I asserted their inevitability.

I have, of course, written much on this both in Tragic Choices[27] and in talking about the Gift of the Evil Deity in Ideals, Beliefs, Attitudes, and The Law.[28] I have not, however, noted the relation of this paradox to punitive damages. It is a relationship that I think deserves underscoring.

We want Ford to make a cost/benefit analysis, and, through that analysis, to choose the cheaper way. But – especially in cases as gruesome as the *Pinto* one – we certainly don't want to have that analysis thrown in our face. We cannot accept the blatant statement that burning babies is not only something that, tragically, will occur from time to time, but that Ford was somehow right in choosing to bring it about, and therefore should not pay damages. What, then, is the answer?

At least in cases like *Pinto*, our seeming adherence to a fault standard described in cost/benefit terms is a false one. We may not, ultimately, object to where Ford put its gas tanks enough to forbid Ford's doing so. We may not even think it wrong for Ford to decide on the tank's placement through a cost/benefit analysis. But we will not let Ford defend against liability to those killed or injured by citing that cost benefit analysis. The cost to us, of being blatantly told what, even if inevitable, is unacceptable, is simply too high. Despite, then, the supposed applicability of a fault standard to such situations, we require, in these extreme cases, that the defendant pay damages, regardless of Learned Handisms, and shut up! And we enforce this subterfuge – this actuality of strict liability despite the nominal dominance of cost/benefit determined fault – by assessing punitive damages on any defendant foolish enough not to appreciate our self-contradictory but not irrational rules.

And this is exactly the point. The assessment of punitive damages – and huge ones – in a *Pinto*-like situation may be unwise, may be devious, may even in a sense be unfair. But it is not irrational. It is a way of achieving societal ends that is no more irrational than much else we do; like spending millions to save fools who choose to cross the Atlantic in a rowboat, or risking innumerable

---

[26] *See New Attitudes on Auto Safety,* N.Y. Times, May 1, 1966, at 21.
[27] *See* Calabresi & Bobbitt, *supra* n. 21.
[28] *See* Guido Calabresi, Ideals, Beliefs, Attitudes, and the Law 1–3 (1985).

lives to save an unfortunate hostage. And, whether it is reasonable or not, whether it is the best way to hold in balance conflicting needs and ideals or not, it is a way of doing so. As such, it is an explanation for punitive damages that is totally different from the first two I gave.

Lack of time and energy keep me from going down the line and examining, as to this rationale, as I did as to the two earlier ones, each of several crucial "questions" frequently asked with respect to the assessment of extracompensatory damages. I will not, in other words, examine under this rationale: (1) whether wanton and willful wrongdoing – or even faulty behavior – is a prerequisite; (2) whether the size of the damages should take defendant's capacity to pay into account; (3) whether there must be significant compensatory damages to the plaintiff before "punies" can be assessed; (4) whether the defendant should be allowed to insure against such punitive damages; (5) whether only the damage and wrong to the particular plaintiffs can be considered in determining the size of the punitive damages or whether harms to others in the same jurisdiction or even outside of it can be taken into account; (6) whether the plaintiff should receive any, some, most, or all of the extracompensatory damages assessed; and (7) whether criminal law-like procedures and rules should apply – perhaps by constitutional requirement – to the determination of such damages. You can, if you wish, easily enough do so yourself. I need only point out that the answer to the questions that apply to this basis for punitive damages bear little relation to the appropriate answers if the grounds for extracompensatory damages are either (a) encouragement of private attorneys general, or (b) the multiplier.

D. Recovery of Generally Nonrecoverable Compensatory Damages

It is equally so with respect to a fourth possible basis for seemingly extracompensatory damages. In his brilliant and innovative – if ultimately unidimensional – article on punitive damages, Tom Colby points out that historically, in England, punitive damages were used to award the equivalent of compensation in certain situations in which the law seemed to preclude ordinary compensatory damages.[29] Punitive damages served as a means to expand the capacity of the law to give what was needed to make a victim whole, in the face of rules that would forbid such compensation. With the expansion of the scope of liability and hence of the availability of ordinary

---

[29] See Thomas B. Colby, *Beyond the Multiple Punishment Problem: Punitive Damages as Punishment for Individual, Private Wrongs*, 87 MINN. L. REV. 583 (2003).

compensatory damages, Colby says in passing, this reason for punitive damages dissolved.[30]

I am convinced by Colby's historical analysis. I do not, however, agree with him that this old rationale for punitive damages no longer has significance. On the contrary, I believe that, on occasion, it is still the most plausible basis for their assessment.

Despite the broad expansion of liability there remain many areas in which compensatory damages are unavailable or are inadequate. Mentioning just a few different ones will suffice to make my point. Compensatory damages for purely emotional or psychic harm that does not derive from physical injury remain problematical. How to compensate those who perform significant, but unpaid, services is a question that has not yet been adequately resolved. How to compensate injured parties for the cost of the legal representation they incurred in seeking compensation perdures as one of the knottiest issues in tort law. And it is made no easier by the desire of those who believe themselves injured to pool, or coinsure, with others similarly situated so that those who ultimately win pay the legal charges of those who lose.

There are very good reasons for some, and plausible explanations for all, of the areas in which tort law limits the availability of what would be needed to make a victim whole. Just thinking even a moment about the three examples – out of many possible ones – that I have mentioned should make that clear. But it is also clear, with respect to each of these areas, that there exist circumstances in which – even though states might believe that the normal restrictions ought not to apply – full compensation is nevertheless unavailable. Sometimes in such circumstances the restrictions can be lifted directly;[31] at other times the easiest way of "compensating" is – now, as it once was in England – through the giving of compensation, under the guise of awarding punitive damages.[32]

The nature and limits of such punitive assessments – the seven questions I previously posed – will obviously depend on the reasons why fully

---

[30] *Id.* at 628.

[31] For examples of state statutes directly addressing one of these restrictions on full compensation, *see* WASH. REV. CODE ANN. § 4.84.250 (1988) (Washington) (providing attorney's fees to the prevailing party in any tort action where the requested damages are less than $10,000); O.C.G.A. § 13-6-11 (1982 & Supp. 1991) (Georgia) (providing for attorney's fees in all tort suits where "the defendant has acted in bad faith, has been stubbornly litigious, or has caused the plaintiff unnecessary trouble and expense"). And for an argument that federal courts can use Rule 11 of the Federal Rules of Civil Procedure to accomplish similar fee-shifting goals in many tort cases, *see Hays v. Sony Corp. of America*, 847 F.2d 412, 418–19 (7th Cir. 1988) (Posner, J.).

[32] *See, e.g.,* Colby, *supra* note 29, at 246–47 (summarizing early American cases sympathizing with, and at times accepting, this English rationale for punitive damages).

compensatory damages are generally not available in a particular context and why they are deemed to be desirable in the special circumstances at hand. As a result, even if I wished to do so, I could not go down the list effectively with respect to this rationale for "punitive" damages. It is, yet again, enough to say that, when the rationale for such damages is this last one, what constitutes proper "punitive" damages and what are proper limits on those damages, is completely different from when the rationale for the damages is one of the three previously discussed.

E. Righting Private Wrongs

The final reason for punitive damages that I will discuss here – there are likely to be others, but I have not yet thought of them – is the centerpiece of Colby's important article. Whereas this grounding had – to my knowledge – not previously been clearly explicated in the literature, it is also, I think, the one that most readily explains the Supreme Court's decision in *State Farm*.[33] Let me redefine this rationale in my own terms.

America is a rights-based society. This is nothing new; the first thing that worthy band of Puritans who landed in New England in the seventeenth century did was to start suing each other to enforce their rights to this, that, and the other thing.[34] This rights-based attitude goes beyond a belief in mere compensation, it finds expression in the not very salubrious desire to make others "pay" for the wrongs they have done us, no less than in the great charters of rights that protect us from state ordained infringements. It helps explain, although in my view not justify, the fact that we are one very few wealthy industrialized societies that retains the death penalty. It also can be seen in the almost unique devotion we have long had to punitive damages.

When someone has injured us in a particularly grievous and wrongful way, this attitude gives rise to the demand for more than compensation, it cries out for punishment of the wrongdoer in order to make us, the victim, feel fully whole, and to "bring closure" (a phrase often used in the capital punishment context) to the injured and to the injured's family. This rationale for punitive damages is explored at length by Colby,[35] and so I will not explain it further here. It is important, however, to emphasize that it is this basis that is most

---

[33] *See State Farm Mut. Auto. Ins. Co. v. Campbell*, 538 U.S. 408 (2003).

[34] *See, e.g.,* Claire Priest, *The Nature of Litigation in Early New England*, 111 YALE L. J. 1881 (2002).

[35] *See* Colby, *supra* note 29, at 213–43.

consonant with Justice Kennedy's opinion for the Supreme Court in *State Farm*.

Although the High Court did not cite Colby, it is not surprising that this reason should dominate its opinion. As I said earlier, the Supreme Court is not particularly concerned with tort law or with its complex goals. Nor is it, in the bulk of its business, a common-law court. It concerns itself mainly with infringement of rights, as set out in the Constitution and, to a degree that it surely finds wearying, with those very death penalty cases in which a recurring theme is the asserted "rights" of those whose loved ones have been killed. That its intuitive focus when dealing with the proper limits on, and justifications for, punitive damages should be this rationale seems, therefore, almost inevitable.

The result is a Supreme Court opinion that is completely understandable, one might even say admirable, if this were, in fact, the only basis for punitive damages. It is, instead, dangerous, and almost silly, if one accepts the possibility that the common law of any given state may have had some or all of the other rationales "in mind" when it developed its own rules and limits on punitive damages. One need only go down the list of the seven attributes of such damages, apply them to the Colby-Supreme Court rationale, and then contrast how they play out with respect to the other possible bases for non-compensatory damages. One need only do that and, I believe, the foolishness of the Supreme Court's constitutional ukase becomes obvious. What may well be right from a unidimensional and reductionist view of a torts problem, what is the basis of a very helpful and deep analysis by a scholar like Colby, what may even be correctly seen – as Colby asserts – as the historical origin of punitive damages in America, becomes dangerously wrong when applied across the board as a matter of constitutional necessity by a torts-ignorant Court to a multidimensional and complex set of problems!

III. WHAT IS TO BE DONE?

There are two ways of reacting when a court (or a legislature, for that matter) imposes a unidimensional "reform" on a complex, multipurposed set of rules. I will very briefly explore them here, still using the example of punitive damages. First, one can, by a change in terminology, try to do an end run around the requirements of the reform. One can, in other words, change the name that one gives to the noncompensatory damages one wishes to award so that they are no longer covered and limited by the "reform." For that reform, in its terms, applied only to punitive damages, as described in the Supreme

Court's decision.[36] To the extent that the new names properly represent functions and rationales for extracompensatory damages different from those the Supreme Court was thinking of when it imposed its rule and limits, this device may succeed and thereby save to the states the ability to further these other functions through the torts system. Second, one can try to achieve the functions that were previously served by extracompensatory damage awards through other – nontort – devices. Each may work, but each has its costs.

A. A Change in Nomenclature

Long ago, Jerome Frank wrote that Estate and Gift Tax Law would work far better if, instead of one word, "Gift," we had at least three words: "Gift," "Geft," and "Gaft" to describe different types of transfers for less than ordinary full consideration.[37] Each "word" could then be attached to a different set of rules and requirements. The same could well be said of extracompensatory damages. We could call them – more elegantly than I will do now – by names that describe their rationales and functions: (a) Rewards to Whistle Blowers; (b) Socially Compensatory Damages; (c) Ideal Preservation Damages; (d) Exceptionally Awardable Compensatory Damages; and (e) Punitive Damages (thereby seeking to limit the scope of the Supreme Court's holding to this last category). One could then define rules, limits, and attributes for each category.

The advantages of doing this, in the light of the Supreme Court's decision, are obvious. The disadvantages are only slightly less so. One attribute of punitive damages, as they grew up in the common law, was precisely that they fulfilled many different – and, at times, contradictory – functions, or at least functions that were in tension with each other, and did so at the same time. That is frequently the case in complex common-law fields such as torts, and is, more than an analysis of punitive damages, the point of this chapter. Although there is much to be said for examinations and rationalizations of, often fuzzy and at times no longer useful, common-law rules by scholars given to scientific policy making, in the end a society may, instead, be better served by the retention of multipurposed, somewhat inconsistent concepts. For such concepts (a) allow a society to do more than one thing at once, (b) retain values that even the most careful of rationalizations will miss, and (c) permit goals to be served – such as the "Tragic Choice" function – which, if

---

[36] *See State Farm, supra* note 33 at 426.
[37] *See Commissioner v. Beck's Estate*, 129 F.2d 243, 246 (2d Cir. 1942) (Frank, J.).

done openly, may destroy their very purpose. In the hands of juries, especially, which give results and not reasons, and which (as I have said before[38]) are meant to reflect the unspoken and sometimes unspeakable values of a society, such forms of rules, laws, and results may well be the most effective way to achieve society's multifaceted aims.[39]

If we require, in order to preserve some of these functions, that each be spelled out and given a separate name, we lose something. Whether it is a little or a lot will depend on the particular area. And it is not for me, today, if ever, to do a cost/benefit analysis of the separation and renaming of what we have been calling punitive damages. That the Constitution should *require* that we do so, however, seems to me highly dubious. The Supreme Court's opinion in *State Farm*, regardless of its possible merits in dealing with the fifth goal, is of no use whatever on this point.

Let me once again be absolutely clear: I have no objection at all to sorting out and naming individual functions served by a complex common-law or statutory legal concept or doctrine. It is one of the prime objects of scholarly work, and it helps us all to update and rationalize the law. Looking into dark places is exactly what the academy is paid to do. Without it we would retain rules and concepts that reflect timeworn values or continuing effects of past explorations. Indeed, I have spent a good deal of my time as a scholar trying to do just that. And I continue to do it now, from time to time, even from the bench – though when I do, it is usually in opinions "concurring separately" in my own holdings. All that is more than useful; it is essential to the good health of a dynamic, functional legal system. It is, however, very different from the reductionist adoption by a court or a legislature of a single function out of a complex doctrine, with the resulting requirement that the area be rationalized, then and there, if it is to continue to adhere to its goals.

---

[38] *See* CALABRESI & BOBBITT, *supra* note 21, at 57–62.

[39] One example is euthanasia – despite the existence of laws clearly banning the practice, jury acquittals in prosecutions of physicians and family members participating in assisted suicides have been frequent. *See id.* at 57; *see also* Stephen L. Pepper, *Counseling at the Limits of the Law: An Exercise in the Jurisprudence and Ethics of Lawyering,* 104 YALE L. J. 1545, 1551 (1995) (collecting instances of what Pepper terms "jury nullification" in euthanasia prosecutions). For a related example of courts shifting the institutional responsibility for tragic decision making (in this case, away from courts and legislatures and towards physicians), *see Washington v. Glucksberg,* 521 U.S. 702, 737–38 (1997) (denying the existence of a constitutional right to assisted suicide, while simultaneously emphasizing that "[t]here is no dispute that dying patients in Washington and New York can obtain palliative care, *even when doing so would hasten their deaths.*") (emphasis added).

B. Other Ways to Serve the Functions

The second likely response to the selection from a multidimensional concept of one function to the exclusion of others, is to find other ways to serve the "abandoned" functions. This can be done within the same area of law by making appropriate modifications to it. It also can be done by expanding other areas of law. Let me sketch out how this might happen with respect to the sets of functions downplayed in the Supreme Court's approach to punitive damages. In doing this, I do not mean to be exhaustive or even to pick the most effective alternatives. I simply want to show that other ways of achieving "the law's" goals exist (as they almost always do), that such ways have their own merits and demerits, and that one should hesitate before mandating that the several states, which had come up with a multiheaded approach, adopt such alternatives in order to further their goals.

Very quickly, then: (A) the Private Attorney General function could probably be served, at least in part, by the adoption of approaches – not unrelated to, if somewhat the reverse of, those in the civil law – such as permitting a civil plaintiff to require that a criminal action be brought together with, or at least at the same time as, the civil suit. (B) the Multiplier's job could perhaps be done by expanding the availability of class actions. (C) the Ideal Preservation goal could be accomplished by an express abandonment of the fault requirement and the adoption of straightforward strict liability in the appropriate areas. (D) the Exceptionally Awarded Compensation needs could be met by expanding the right to compensation in those circumstances in which the rules barring such compensation have seemed wrong. Obviously, the means used would vary from area to area. Thus, as to emotional damages, one could try to define areas where such damages might be appropriate – at least if subject to judicial control.[40] And as to compensation for those doing unremunerated jobs, tables relating that job to compensated ones could be developed. Finally, as to (E) the Righting of Private Wrongs goal could be advanced by the award of lawyer's fees, or by any number of other devices, including (heaven forfend) expansion of pain and suffering damages or national legal aid insurance, could be used.

I am not for a moment urging any of these. The problems with each of them are obvious. My point is simply that awarding punitive damages, or even

---

[40] See, e.g., Nelson v. Metro-North Commuter R.R., 235 F.3d 101, 107–111 (2d Cir. 2000) (discussing situations in which the Federal Employers' Liability Act might permit damages, regulated by courts, for emotional harms).

expanding other tort remedies, are not the only ways to achieve the goals that
were previously part of the complex punitive damage notion. There are always
other ways. If deterrence is diminished in torts, the loss can be remedied – to
some extent – by greater use of regulation and criminal law. If compensation
is hampered as a result of some tort reforms, its place can – in part or even
more fully – be taken by expansions in health insurance or in Social Security.
And so on and so forth. All of these have their advantages and their costs.
And so it is with punitive damages.

That alternatives are available, however, cannot, without more, justify the
replacement of a multidimensional doctrine with a single minded one. As
I hope to have made clear, alternatives are always available in the law. And
the choice of whether to employ them or not is a paradigmatic function of
lawmaking, which, at least as to torts, is generally meant to be local. It follows
that the Supreme Court's action, which comes close to imposing the use of
such alternatives, is highly problematical. This is especially so as the move to
alternatives entails not only the rationalization of the field that I described
and criticized in an earlier section of this chapter, but also the additional
disadvantages and costs that the particular alternative adopted brings with it.
As such, the burden should be on those who wish to impose the abandonment
of a complex, common-law concept's multidimensionality to explain why that
should be done. When a constitutional court is the moving force, moreover,
meeting that burden also requires an explanation of what specifically in the
Constitution (or in its broad concepts of fundamental fairness) makes the
abandonment mandatory.

IV. CONCLUSION

Punitive damages have been the apparent focus of this chapter. And yet that
is not the real object of my concerns. Indeed, I think I have scarcely scratched
the surface of what would be needed to treat adequately the fascinating topic
of extracompensatory damages. My concerns, instead, relate more directly to
the subject matter of this book: the proper understanding of torts. So let me
end with that question directly in mind. Tort law and its many parts have
long been characterized by complexity of functions, goals, and methods of
achieving these. That is true of notions like causation, duty, punitive damages,
and *respondeat superior* to name but a few. This complexity is reflected also in
torts' reliance on courts, juries, legislatures, and even administrative agencies
as occasional sources (and enforcers) of law. The complexity has come about
haphazardly, over time, and in significant part through the common-law
development of the field. It shows up in the use of words that only imperfectly

translate into concepts that some (like me, when I do economic analysis of the field) seek to have them mean.

All this is not in itself either good or bad...but it is the field. It is one of its prime characteristics. And without this complexity torts would be a very different subject. When we contemplate the future of tort law, we must keep this fact in mind. As scholars, we are, and often should be, given to single minded analyses of doctrines and of concepts. That is a job we do very well. We look at torts, or at one of its doctrines, with a fierce light, derived perhaps from a neighboring social science such as economics, or now, once again frequently, from philosophy. And we see things in that doctrine that are important and that others have missed. All that is to the good.

Occasionally also, as a result of our looking into dark places with our fierce light, parts of the field are changed and rationalized. And that, too, is just fine. But let us not fool ourselves. It is rare that such single minded views can fully encompass and understand a slowly developed field of law like torts. If Mill could chide as great a figure as Bentham for approaching all ideas as a stranger and, out of hand, rejecting those that did not fit his system as "vague generalities,"[41] we should recognize how much the same criticism must apply to us who cannot hold a candle to old Jeremy! In all this we should be especially humble when we act not as academics, that is, as propounders of ideas, but rather as reformers, judges, or other makers of law. For it is there that the quick application of reductionist, if clear-headed, views becomes most dangerous. Not that any damage we might do cannot be repaired. The law – as I said – can always find alternatives. But it does so at a price.

Fortunately – despite the various recent examples of reductionism's dominance that one could cite, and the particular instance (that of punitive damages) that I have discussed – torts retains its maddeningly enthralling complexity of functions and of ways of achieving them. Perhaps some day we will be convinced that it should be replaced by a more rational and better (a quite different notion) system. But that is nowhere near at hand. And for that reason its future as a wonderful subject to teach, to criticize, to try to correct and make – in small or large parts – more coherent, more functional, and more just, remains assured!

[41] See MILL, *supra* note 5.

CHAPTER ELEVEN

THE FUTURE OF PROPORTIONAL LIABILITY: THE LESSONS OF TOXIC SUBSTANCES CAUSATION

Michael D. Green

ABSTRACT. The reform of contributory negligence into a scheme of apportioning liability based on comparative fault is among the most significant developments in tort law during the Twentieth Century. Its significance goes beyond the rejection of the common law's "all or nothing" attitude about liability and has extended to modification of many other aspects of tort law that developed because of the entrenchment of contributory negligence.

At about the same time as courts and legislatures adopted comparative fault, the advent of large toxic substances case congregations emerged – asbestos, Agent Orange, DES, silicone gel breast implants, and tobacco are among the most notable of such. Many of these cases present difficult problems of causation because the connection between exposure to the agent and disease is only dimly understood. The best scientific evidence is provided by epidemiology, which is group-based and statistical in nature.

The confluence of comparative fault principles and probabilistic evidence of causation raises the question of whether liability should be imposed proportionally based on the probability of causation in toxic substances cases. Many scholars have argued for rejection of the customary "more likely than not" standard for the burden of proof and for adoption of a proportional liability rule. This chapter critically assesses those proposals by looking carefully at the precision and fallibility of the epidemiological evidence on which the scholars' proposals rely. After concluding that proportional liability would not provide the deterrence benefits claimed for it, this chapter considers the implications of its analysis for employing proportional liability in other areas of tort law.

I. INTRODUCTION

Modern tort law has, in several respects, become more receptive to carving up and apportioning liability. Commenting on this trend, Judge Calabresi

Michael D. Green, Bess and Walter Williams Distinguished Chair in Law, Wake Forest University. This chapter has benefitted from an ongoing exchange with Sander Greenland, an epidemiologist at UCLA, and discussions with Joe Sanders of the University of Houston. Greenland would not want to be associated with the errors he is convinced I've made in this chapter, despite his valuable counsel. I am grateful to Andy Klein for helpful comments on an earlier draft of this chapter and to participants in a colloquium at the University of North Carolina Department of Public Health for their insightful comments.

characterized it as the most important development in tort law since the advent of liability insurance.[1] The most prominent manifestation of this receptivity to apportionment is comparative responsibility and comparative contribution. No longer is liability all or nothing between plaintiff and defendant, and comparative contribution recognizes that liability can, in a refined manner, be divided among multiple defendants.[2]

Apportioning liability among parties who are found liable for the plaintiff's harm on the basis of a normative judgment about relative culpability or responsibility is different from employing probabilistic assessments of the existence of an element of a *prima facie* case to determine the liability of a party and the damages for which the party is liable. The preponderance of the evidence standard employs a 50 percent threshold for determining when a party will be subject to liability. Yet, here as well, we might employ proportional assessments reflecting probabilities to impose liability for an appropriate percentage of the harm, especially when the probability is less than the 50-percent threshold.

The most attractive context in which to relax the preponderance threshold is when defendants have acted tortiously, and there are deficiencies in the available evidence on another element of the case. When defendants bear responsibility for the gap in evidence, the case is especially strong. So long as we don't suspect plaintiff is concealing evidence or failing diligently to pursue reasonably available evidence, there is a strong claim for ameliorating the outcome dictated by the preponderance standard and the burden of proof. Two such areas in which courts have accepted the idea of proportional liability based on probabilities come readily to mind.[3] First, when a physician's negligence in diagnosing or treating a disease diminishes the patient's likelihood of successful treatment, courts have permitted recovery for the lost opportunity when the probability is less than 50 percent.[4] Professor Joe King's

---

[1] *See* Guido Calabresi & Jeffrey O. Cooper, *New Directions in Tort Law*, 30 VAL. U.L. REV. 859, 868 (1996); *see also* Robert L. Rabin, Chapter 2 to this volume (identifying comparative fault as one of the five most significant developments in twentieth-century tort law).

[2] As Prosser described the earlier attitude, "[t]he common law courts always have been entirely unwilling to make or permit any such division [of damages]." WILLIAM L. PROSSER, THE LAW OF TORTS § 67, at 434 (4th ed. 1971). Great Britain underwent a similar transformation in apportioning tort liability. *See* W. V. H. ROGERS, WINFIELD & JOLOWICZ ON TORT 233–35 (15th ed. 1998).

[3] A recent paper reports that as far back as the seventeenth century, discomfort with non-apportionment of liability was evidenced by such scholars as Hugo Grotius. *See* HUGO GROTIUS, DeIURE BELLI AC PACIS (W. Whewell ed. 1853), cited in Francesco Parisi & Vincy Fon, *Comparative Causation*, __ AM. L. & ECON. REV. __ (2005) (forthcoming).

[4] *See, e.g., Alberts v. Schultz*, 975 P.2d 1279 (N.M. 1999). *See generally* David A. Fischer, *Tort Recovery for Loss of a Chance*, 36 WAKE FOREST L. REV. 605, 611–14 (2001).

article providing a model of liability based on the probability that defendant's tortious conduct caused the harm, along with a reconceptualization of the harm caused by the defendant, was quite influential in this development.[5] For the most part, courts have followed Professor King's suggestion that the harm be reconceptualized as a lost opportunity for cure rather than by adopting proportional liability for the adverse outcome. But let us make no mistake that the plaintiff is recovering for the physical harm discounted by the probability that the physician's negligence caused the plaintiff's harm.[6]

An inability to identify the manufacturer of the drug that caused a plaintiff's disease produced market-share liability, another proportional-based liability scheme that also addresses gaps in the evidence on causation.[7] The California Supreme Court's recognition of market-share liability in *Sindell v. Abbott Laboratories*[8] prompted a number of scholars to examine the case for expanding proportional liability beyond the market-share context.[9]

The case for apportioning liability on a broader scale is alluringly attractive and straightforward. Evidence is never perfect; uncertainty always exists. Why not recognize the uncertainty entailed in any attempt to reconstruct history, particularly with the difficulties of the necessarily counterfactual inquiry required by causation? Shouldn't law frankly acknowledge the probabilistic nature of factual assessments such as causation and adjust the extent of liability accordingly? Such recognition, the argument goes, would, through more accurate outcomes, provide more fine-tuned deterrence

---

[5] *See* Joseph H. King Jr., *Causation, Valuation, and Chance in Personal Injury Torts Involving Preexisting Conditions and Future Consequences*, 90 YALE L.J. 1353 (1981).

[6] *See, e.g., Alberts v. Schultz*, 975 P.2d 1279 (N.M. 1999) (recognizing the harm as the probabilistic lost chance of successful treatment, but requiring that the plaintiff also suffer a physical injury as a condition for recovering for the lost chance).

   There is a difference between compensation for a "lost opportunity," which presumably would be available to all who suffer a diminution in the chance for a cure, and compensation for the probability that the defendant caused the harm, which would be limited to those who suffered the outcome to be avoided. If the recovery were for the latter, it should be for somewhat more, as the probability that the plaintiff was harmed is greater than the lost-opportunity percentage. Thus, if plaintiff's chance of cure is reduced from 50 percent to 25 percent, the value of the lost opportunity is 25 percent of the value of the harm. But the probability that such an individual who suffers the harm was harmed by the defendant's negligence is 33 percent. That is because we know that a harmed individual is not among the lucky 25 percent who, despite delayed treatment, are cured. The probability that the delay in treatment caused the plaintiff's harm is found by taking the 25 percent who are harmed due to the delay as the numerator and the 75 percent who are harmed as the denominator. *See* ARIEL PORAT & ALEX STERN, TORT LIABILITY UNDER UNCERTAINTY 124 (2001).

[7] For a stirring defense of market-share liability, *see* Saul Levmore, *Probabilistic Recoveries, Restitution, and Recurring Wrongs*, 19 J. LEGAL STUD. 691, 698 (1990).

[8] 607 P.2d 924 (Cal. 1980).

[9] *See supra* text accompanying notes 17–46.

incentives.[10] The argument is also made that proportional liability would contribute to corrective justice.[11] And, just as modified comparative fault entails the inequity of a "cliff" that treats virtually-similarly-situated parties distressingly differently, doesn't the preponderance of the evidence standard treat cases that are trivially different in the probability of causation like night and day?

Section II canvasses the case that scholars have made for adopting a rule of proportional liability based on the probability of causation. Tort scholars of a variety of schools display a remarkable consistency in favor of jettisoning the preponderance standard and adopting some form of proportional liability.[12] The idea behind probabilistic-share liability theories such as market share and lost opportunity could have been expanded to encompass this proportional liability rule. The transition to proportionate liability based on the probabilistic risk that a defendant contributed is significant but no greater than other transitions that have led to other landmark developments.[13] Are we on the threshold of moving more generally toward apportioning liability on a proportional or probabilistic basis?

In this chapter, I examine proportional liability for toxic-substances harms, a particularly attractive context for this reform. Very often, the statistically-based scientific evidence permits only a probabilistic assessment of causation of less than 50 percent, and the absence of better evidence must be laid at the foot of science's limits rather than plaintiffs.

A related problem is also addressed in Section II. When a plaintiff employs statistically-based studies to prove causation, what threshold increase of risk, in light of the existing preponderance standard, is required for the plaintiff to satisfy her burden of production? The Ninth Circuit in its consideration of *Daubert* on remand held that greater than a doubling of the incidence of disease among those exposed was necessary.[14] Yet when other evidence

---

[10] *See, e.g.,* John Makdisi, *Proportional Liability: A Comprehensive Rule to Apportion Tort Damages Based on Probability,* 67 N.C.L. REV. 1063, 1066 (1989). Saul Levmore explores the accuracy-enhancing (or error-minimizing) effects of a probabilistic rule in Levmore, *supra* note 7.

[11] *See id.; see also* text accompanying notes 28–30, 42–46 *infra.*

[12] For a list of commentators who have advocated some form of proportional liability in a variety of contexts, *see* Makdisi, *supra* note 10, at 1064 n. 3. Richard Wright, although not an enthusiastic advocate, has acquiesced in market-share, lost-opportunity, and risk-enhancement proportional schemes. *See infra* notes 37–41 and accompanying text.

[13] Indeed, Professor Makdisi has taken just such a position, relying on the market-share cases to argue for proportionate liability generally and especially in toxic substances cases. *See also infra* text accompanying note 17.

[14] *Daubert v. Merrell Dow Pharms., Inc.,* 43 F.3d 1311 (9th Cir. 1995). For an explanation of the relationship between a doubling of disease and the preponderance standard, *see* text accompanying notes 53–59 *infra.*

supplements statistical evidence, the argument goes, plaintiffs may be able to demonstrate that the probability of causation is actually greater than 50 percent. The current Restatement (Third) of Torts endorses that position in its treatment of the burden of proof on causation in toxic substances cases.[15] Both the proportional liability and less-than-doubling advocates have in common reliance on scientific evidence that provides evidence by which the probability of causation can be determined.

Section III proceeds to explain the statistically-based evidence that is employed to prove causation. These studies would be the basis for the probabilistic assessments. A variety of scientific study methods exist to investigate causation when the outcome is a disease rather than a traumatic event, the most salient of which is epidemiology. The explanation of observational epidemiologic studies and their frailties leads to Section IV, which takes issue with the scholars who advocate proportional liability, at least in the toxic substance arena. Section IV also more cautiously and qualifiedly supports the courts, like the Ninth Circuit in *Daubert*, that have insisted on a threshold for increased incidence in disease for a plaintiff to satisfy her burden of proof under the traditional preponderance standard. The reason for this support, however, is distinctly different from the reasoning of the courts' adopting it. In the end, the resistance exhibited by courts to the scholarly entreaties to adopt a proportional liability scheme, at least in the toxic substances mileau, strikes me as appropriate given the quality of evidence on which probabilistic assessments would be made.[16] There may be some cases in which courts

---

[15] *See* RESTATEMENT (THIRD) OF TORTS: LIABILITY FOR PHYSICAL HARM § 28 cmt. c (Tentative Draft No. 3, 2003).

[16] Richard Stewart briefly raised the concern I explore, concluding that the issue of whether to adopt a proportional liability scheme is "a close one." "In most cases, available scientific knowledge and evidence could not determine even the approximate extent of additional risk over background contributed by the defendant." Richard Stewart, *The Role of the Courts in Risk Management*, 16 ENVTL. L. REP. (ENVTL. L. INST.) 10,208 (1986). Donald Elliott raised the same issue a year earlier. *See* E. Donald Elliott, *Why Courts? Comment on Robinson*, 14 J. LEGAL STUD. 799, 802 (1985). Yet by the conclusion of his commentary on Glen Robinson's proposal that increased risk be compensated by damages reflecting the probability that the risk would mature into disease, Elliott was agreeable to adopting such a scheme, albeit one placed in an administrative scheme rather than the courts. Elliott did qualify his support, insisting on a *de minimis* exception, and his primary focus was the greater accuracy and efficiency of administrative proceedings as opposed to the tort system. Peter Schuck sketched out a critique of the "public law" proposals of David Rosenberg, *see infra* text accompanying notes 27–28 and 31–32, similar to the one fleshed out in this chapter in his book about the Agent Orange litigation. *See* PETER H. SCHUCK, AGENT ORANGE ON TRIAL 271–72 (1987).

      David Fischer expressed dubiety about the scholarly consensus in favor of proportional liability in an article on a related topic. *See* David A. Fischer, *Proportional Liability: Statistical Evidence and the Probability Paradox*, 46 VAND. L. REV. 1201 (1993). His concern was that the precaution incentives provided by a proportional liability scheme depend on the number of

should accept statistical evidence that reveals less than a doubling, but those instances are sufficiently infrequent that I doubt they are worth the candle.

In the conclusion, I attempt to tease out some reflections on the lessons of toxic substances for the future of proportional liability.

II. PROBABILISTIC APPORTIONMENT OF LIABILITY IN TOXIC SUBSTANCES LITIGATION

A remarkable number of academic writers with striking consensus have endorsed the idea of proportional liability based on the probability of causation.[17] The earliest of these, Glen Robinson[18] and Richard Delgado,[19] spurred by *Sindell*, advocated apportioning damages proportionately to the probability of causation when evidence does not permit determination of the individual plaintiffs harmed with a high degree of certainty.[20] The primary focus

other potential causes of harm that exist, and the greater the other potential causes, the less a potential injurer would be expected to invest to avoid harm. Thus, although three polluters who each may cause the same harm to Greenacre would each have an incentive equal to the harm to Greenacre to avoid harm if acting alone – each would have only one third of that incentive if all three are acting simultaneously. Whether Professor Fischer is right, his concerns are not peculiar to a proportionate liability scheme, as he recognizes. They exist as well even with a preponderance standard and full damages. The concerns raised by Stewart, Elliott, Schuck, and Fischer have had no appreciable impact on the contrary scholarly consensus.

[17] Most commentators and courts that have addressed this subject have ignored the position of those who make up the frequentist school of statistics. The frequentists insist that there is no meaning to the use of a probability about a specific event. *See* Lee Loevinger, *On Logic and Sociology*, 32 JURIMETRICS J. 527, 530 (1990); *see also* Steve Gold, Note, *Causation in Toxic Torts: Burdens of Proof, Standard of Persuasion and Statistical Evidence*, 96 YALE L.J. 377, 382–92 (1986). Subjectivists, by contrast, comfortably employ probabilities to describe a subjective belief as to the likelihood that a discrete event occurred. *See* David H. Kaye, *Apples and Oranges: Confidence Coefficients and the Burden of Persuasion*, 73 CORNELL L. REV. 54, 54–62 (1987). The commentators advocating apportioning liability based on the probability of causation are adopting the subjectivist approach – one that, although lacking statistical rigor, has considerable practical utility.

[18] Glen O. Robinson, *Multiple Causation in Tort Law: Reflections on the DES Cases*, 68 VA. L. REV. 713 (1982).

[19] Richard Delgado, *Beyond Sindell: Relaxation of Cause-in-Fact Rules for Indeterminate Plaintiffs*, 70 CAL. L. REV. 881 (1982).

[20] Sam Estep, the first legal academician to confront the thorny issues posed by toxic substances for the tort system, advocated a compensation fund that would tax those responsible for the agent, radiation, based on their causal contribution to the total incidence of disease. *See* Samuel D. Estep, *Radiation Injuries and Statistics*, 59 MICH. L. REV. 259 (1960). Estep also adverted to the possibility of compensation for all victims based on the probability that the agent caused the victim's harm. However, Estep addressed these proposals to the specific case of radiation, about which much was known of its toxicity. Estep recognized the problem of accurately determining general causation as a condition for taxing and compensation under his scheme. *See id.* at 297.

of commentators such as Robinson and Delgado are plaintiffs who can show some probability, through statistical evidence, that their harm was caused tortiously, but the probability is below the 50-percent threshold required by the preponderance standard.

In the mid-1980s, the law and economics school of thought produced a spate of scholarship about apportioning liability based on the probability of causation.[21] Some also addressed the matter of apportioning liability among multiple tortfeasors, each of whom had contributed to causing the plaintiff's harm. In so doing, the economists employed the concept of the quantitative *risk* to which the plaintiff was exposed by the defendant's conduct from an *ex ante* perspective. Indeed, economists frequently use *ex ante* risk in addressing causal issues.

There is an important distinction between proportionate liability and apportioning liability among multiple tortfeasors.[22] They are related in that both rely on the quantitative risk contribution to the plaintiff's harm. However, for proportionate liability, the question is whether the risk created by an individual defendant was *a* cause of the plaintiff's harm. I use the word "a," of course, because causation contemplates a necessary but not a sufficient condition.[23] That is the instance in which probabilistic assessments are employed and damages adjusted to reflect the probability that a defendant's toxic agent was a cause of the harm. By contrast, when multiple defendants are each a cause of the plaintiff's harm (and of course the evidence for each of them may be of a probabilistic nature), the question arises how to apportion liability among them. The latter question has engaged much commentary, especially when a pure form of strict liability is employed,[24] eliminating fault as a basis

---

[21] The central idea was that a defendant should pay for the damages incurred discounted by the probability that the defendant caused the damages. The preponderance-of-the-evidence standard could result in too little deterrence when the probability of causation was less than 50 percent and excessive deterrence when the probability was in excess of 50 percent but less than 100 percent. *See* Steven Shavell, *Uncertainty Over Causation and the Determination of Civil Liability*, 28 J.L. & ECON. 587 (1985).

[22] Glen Robinson appears to address both without distinguishing them. *See* Glen O. Robinson, *Multiple Causation in Tort Law: Reflections on the DES Cases*, 68 VA. L. REV. 713, 751–54 (1982). Robinson's discussion of the Second Restatement's "substantial factor" requirement for causation reveals the considerable mischief of which it is capable. A necessary cause is a factual cause even if it is the straw added to a considerable load that breaks the proverbial camel's back. *See* RESTATEMENT (THIRD) OF TORTS: LIABILITY FOR PHYSICAL HARM § 36 (Tentative Draft No. 3, 2003).

[23] I put aside for the sake of simplicity causes of overdetermined outcomes, the classic "two-fires" situation. *See* RESTATEMENT (THIRD) OF TORTS: LIABILITY FOR PHYSICAL HARM § 27 (Tentative Draft No. 2, 2002).

[24] The "strict liability" contemplated by the economists is a quite abstract, disembodied form of absolute liability that has little relationship with the pockets of strict liability existing in the current torts landscape.

for apportioning liability.[25] It is particularly problematical when multiple risks exist that interact synergistically. I limit this chapter to consideration of proportional liability for defendants in their liability to plaintiffs. Although that consideration has implications for apportioning liability among defendants, it is limited to situations in which the probability that a defendant caused a plaintiff's disease is less than 50 percent. Apportionment among defendants is not so limited.[26]

David Rosenberg also was among the early advocates of proportional liability, and his article on the use of statistical evidence to prove causation in toxic substances cases has been quite influential and widely cited.[27] Yet Rosenberg did more than advocate acceptance of statistical evidence to prove causation. Rosenberg also sought to replace the preponderance standard with a probabilistic rule for apportionment of damages and to aggregate multiple victims' claims by means of class actions. Rosenberg, unlike the economists, grounded his case on corrective justice, in addition to asserting instrumentalist grounds.[28]

Christopher Schroeder has undertaken the most focused effort to assess the fit between corrective justice and proportional liability.[29] Schroeder argues

[25] Mario Rizzo and Frank Arnold were the first, but a number of others have subsequently addressed this matter. *See* Mario J. Rizzo & Frank S. Arnold, *Causal Apportionment in the Law of Torts: An Economic Theory*, 80 COLUM. L. REV. 1399 (1980); David Kaye & Mikel Aickin, *A Comment on Causal Apportionment*, 13 J. LEGAL STUD. 191 (1984); Mario J. Rizzo & Frank S. Arnold, *Causal Apportionment: Reply to the Critics*, 15 J. LEGAL STUD. 427 (1986); Robert N. Strassfeld, *Causal Comparisons*, 60 FORDHAM L. REV. 913 (1992).

[26] *See* Ariel Porat & Alex Stein, *Indeterminate Causation and Apportionment of Damages: An Essay on Holtby, Allen, and* Fairchild, 23 OXFORD J. LEGAL STUD. 667, 679–80 (2003) (making same distinction between proportional liability and apportionment of damages).

[27] David Rosenberg, *The Causal Connection in Mass Exposure Cases: A "Public Law" Vision of the Tort System*, 97 HARV. L. REV. 849 (1984).

[28] Rosenberg's ability to use corrective justice to support his position is, in my view, a consequence of the inherent ambiguity in the concept and its consequent "eye of the beholder" quality. *See* ARIEL PORAT & ALEX STERN, TORT LIABILITY UNDER UNCERTAINTY 106 (2001) (describing the conflicting views of three different corrective justice scholars on whether compensation for imposing risk on another is inconsistent with corrective justice, sometimes permitted by corrective justice, or required by corrective justice); Kenneth W. Simons, *Corrective Justice and Liability for Risk-Creation: A Comment*, 38 UCLA L. REV. 113, 125–26 (1990).

[29] *See* Christopher H. Schroeder, *Corrective Justice and Liability for Increasing Risks*, 37 UCLA L. REV. 439 (1990). Schroeder addresses liability for increased risk rather than the probability of causing harm. However, the compromising of a causal connection is, if anything, greater in the increased risk context that he addresses than *ex post* proportional liability. As Ernie Weinrib would put it, there is no "sufferer" to connect to the "doer" in the increased risk case. *See* Ernest J. Weinrib, *Causation and Wrongdoing*, 63 CHI.-KENT L. REV. 407, 448 (1983). Jules Coleman, I believe, would accept proportional liability, while denying that it could be justified as an aspect of corrective justice. Coleman recognizes the legitimacy of other schemes for addressing accidental losses being adopted and displacing corrective justice,

that a wrongful act is complete once it has been committed and whether it causes harm to another is a fortuity over which the actor has no control. From there, he concludes that imposing liability for increased risks – the proceeds of which will be used to pay those who ultimately suffer harm – is not only consistent with corrective justice but preferable to a cause-based system.[30] Professor Schroeder recognizes that administrative costs are an impediment to adopting an *ex ante* increased risk scheme. Nevertheless, he concludes that toxic substances cases would be amenable to his risk-based liability proposal.

Rosenberg's proportional-liability-with-class-action was given a boost in an article by Judge Weinstein that masqueraded as a judicial opinion. In *In re "Agent Orange" Products Liability Litigation*,[31] Judge Weinstein explained the statistical nature of epidemiologic proof and its inability to distinguish from among exposed individuals the ones whose disease was caused by exposure and ones whose disease was caused otherwise. Working through the mathematics of small increases in risk that would not support a probability greater than 50 percent, Judge Weinstein cited and endorsed Rosenberg's proposal for proportionate liability coupled with class actions. Yet that portion of his opinion had no operative significance, as the issue he was addressing was the fairness of the $180 million settlement on behalf of the class of Vietnam veterans exposed to Agent Orange, and the settlement was not justified on a basis for which the defendants' proportional liability was a relevant factor.

Although Rosenberg has been the most vigorous advocate for proportional liability on the basis of the probability of causation, he concurred with the law and economics school, which limited its focus to optimal deterrence.[32] All

a characterization he would likely apply to a proportional liability scheme. *See* JULES L. COLEMAN, RISKS AND WRONGS 397–406 (1992).

   David Fischer is the only commentator I have found who specifically addresses the fit between proportional liability and corrective justice and finds it wanting. *See* Fischer, *supra* note 16, at 1220–21 (finding that proportional liability undermines corrective justice by imposing liability when there is no basis for a belief defendant harmed plaintiff and because plaintiffs who are harmed by defendant are undercompensated). Given Professor Fischer's criteria, corrective justice cannot satisfy both of these in any proportional liability context in which the probability is below 50 percent.

[30] To be fair, there are times when Schroeder suggests that risk-based liability is consistent with corrective justice and others when he asserts that liability for creating risk better serves corrective justice norms.

[31] 597 F. Supp. 740, 835–36 (E.D.N.Y. 1984), *aff'd on other grounds*, 818 F.2d 145 (2d Cir. 1987).

[32] *See* Shavell, *supra* note 21. Landes and Posner initially were a bit less enthusiastic, expressing concern about the administrative costs entailed in adjudicating a larger number of cases with smaller damages, while still endorsing the concept of proportional damages. *See* William M. Landes & Richard A. Posner, *Causation in Tort Law: An Economic Approach*, 12 J. LEGAL

agreed on the desirability of apportioning liability based on the probability of causation.

Dan Farber also concurred with the earlier commentators' criticism of the preponderance threshold, endorsing the theoretical attractiveness of proportional liability.[33] On the grounds of providing compensation to the persons who were most likely the victims of a defendant's toxic substance, Farber argued the advantage of a "most-likely-victim" rule. That scheme would provide full compensation to those with the highest probability of having been harmed by defendant's agent, while denying recovery to those with the lowest probability. Defendants would be liable when their agents caused an increase in risk less than a doubling,[34] but the damages they paid would be provided to Farber's most likely victims. Farber, almost alone among those addressing proportional liability, dug into the source of evidence that would provide the probabilities on which damages would be apportioned and explained that several factors, such as dose and extent of exposure to background causes, could affect victims' individual probabilities of having been harmed by the defendant's substance.[35]

Farber's appreciation that individuals' probabilities of causation can – almost always do – vary depending on a variety of individual characteristics reveals a well-accepted dichotomy in toxic substances causation. "General

STUD. 109 (1983). Four years later, Landes & Posner embraced recovery for exposure to risk that would discount the damages recoverable for the disease by the probability that each person exposed to the risk would contract the disease. WILLIAM M. LANDES & RICHARD A. POSNER, THE ECONOMIC STRUCTURE OF TORT LAW 260–68 (1987). Landes and Posner prefer *ex ante* compensation for risk to *ex post* damages, discounted to reflect the probability of causation. They express the concern that when the probability is low the latter approach provides too little in damages to provide adequate incentives for enforcement and the inconsistency of such an approach with current tort doctrine. The first concern would seem even more profound for their risk-based approach, which would result in more claimants with less individually at stake. As to the second concern, recognition of exposure to risk as a legally-cognizable injury, may be more conceivable than *ex post* proportional liability, but it is still a far way from acceptance in American tort law. Posner and Landes's response to the inadequate incentive concern for risk-based recovery is class actions, but that device is equally available for *ex post* proportional recovery.

[33] *See* Daniel A. Farber, *Toxic Causation*, 71 MINN. L. REV. 1219 (1987).

[34] See *infra* text accompanying notes 53–58.

[35] For further explanation of why the increased risk found in a study may not be an accurate assessment of the increased risk for a different, exposed individual, *see* RESTATEMENT (THIRD) OF TORTS: LIABILITY FOR PHYSICAL HARM § 28 Rptrs' Note to cmt. c(4) (Tentative Draft No. 3, 2003). Farber also appreciated that the ability to make reliable estimates of increased risk when small increases in risks of widespread diseases are involved is critical. Increases in the 1 to 10 percent range were unlikely to be reliable, Farber recognized. Farber, *supra* note 33, at 1254–56. Yet Farber, like other commentators, accepted the idea that greater risks, yet ones that did not double the risk could be reliably identified.

causation" addresses the matter of whether an agent can cause the disease of interest in human beings. Sometimes that definition is further modified by the requirement that it cause the disease at dosages to which humans are ordinarily exposed. By contrast, "specific causation" confronts the question of whether a specific plaintiff's disease was caused by that plaintiff's exposure to the agent. An agent may cause disease, but not be the cause of a specific plaintiff's harm. Most commentators, such as Farber, focus on proof of specific causation when they address proportional liability for small risks. For those who do not address individual variation among plaintiffs, the increased proportion of disease in a group can be turned into an average probability of causation for each individual.[36]

At the same time, Richard Wright, a critic of the use of probabilistic evidence to prove causation, weighed in on this question. Because of his criticism of the use of general evidence to prove specific causation in his prior work,[37] I would have expected him to oppose proportional liability. His concern is preserving the formal distinction between statistical or other probabilistic proof of a general causal relation (general causation) and proof of the conditions necessary for that causal relation to have produced a specific plaintiff's harm. Wright is also motivated in his criticism of the use of *ex ante* risk for causation, often employed by economists, by his spirited defense of corrective justice rather than economic efficiency as the driving force in tort law.

Wright objects that general statistical evidence does not tell us what happened on the occasion of interest. Rather, he claims, it only provides a basis for causal predictions. He distinguishes *ex ante* statistical evidence, such as epidemiologic evidence, from *ex post* assessments of the probability that an agent caused the outcome in question. The latter is different, he claims, because it is based on particular evidence about whether all of the necessary conditions for the agent to cause the outcome are present for the plaintiff and particular evidence that rules out potential competing causes.[38] Yet,

---

[36] *See infra* note 56.

[37] Richard W. Wright, *Causation, Responsibility, Risk, Probability, Naked Statistics, and Proof: Pruning the Bramble Bush by Clarifying the Concepts*, 73 IOWA L. REV. 1001 (1988).

[38] I also find myself in disagreement with Wright's claim that *ex post* causal assessments are based solely on particularistic evidence: "*Ex post* causal probabilities, which are based solely on particularistic evidence, also are needed for causal explanation." Wright, *supra* note 37, at 1054. After the fact, we may use the *ex ante* statistically-increased risk along with other particularistic evidence (the asbestos-exposed lung cancer victim was not a smoker) to assess the probability of causation. Wright believes that only particularistic evidence is probative as to what happened on a given occasion. I wonder how Wright would respond to a case in which a high quality statistical study showed a very high risk – in excess of 90 percent – that someone exposed to an agent would contract the disease from which the plaintiff suffers

Wright's distinction collapses when all we have after a plaintiff develops disease is an epidemiologic study and no other evidence about the plaintiff's exposure to competing causes to differentiate the plaintiff from the study subjects.[39]

Despite Wright's formalist concern about preserving the distinction between probabilistic evidence of harm and evidence specific to what occurred to the plaintiff, he does not oppose probabilistic assessments of damages for lost opportunity and increased risk, so long as the harm is recognized as the lost opportunity or increased risk, rather than the physical harm.[40] Similarly, Wright, if a bit grudgingly, accepts the use of proportional recovery in toxic substances cases by conceptualizing the harm as exposure to risk.[41]

John Makdisi joined the earlier proportional advocates and proposed a broad rule of proportional liability (both for probabilities below and in excess of 50 percent) to reflect the probability of causation.[42] Makdisi justified this proposal primarily on grounds of accuracy and deterrence incentives, although he also found support in corrective justice concerns. At about the same time as Makdisi, Saul Levmore confronted the defendant "who is more than 0 percent but possibly never more than 50 percent likely to have caused an injury."[43] Levmore sympathized with the earlier commentators' concern with inadequate deterrence and suggested that, as an alternative to damages discounted by the probability of causation, restitutionary measures be employed when the probability was below the 50 percent threshold.[44] Dan Farber, commenting on Levmore's proposal over a decade ago, observed that "there is now widespread scholarly agreement that the preponderance rule should be discarded in favor of some form of probabilistic recovery."[45] Most recently, Ariel Porat and Alex Stern argue that both deterrence and corrective justice are served by permitting a cancer victim exposed to radiation that

---

and in which an eyewitness claims to have observed the plaintiff contract the disease from an alien bite. The point is that most would find the *ex ante* probabalistic evidence far more probative than the *ex post* particularistic evidence Wright advocates.

[39] *See infra* notes 60–64 and accompanying text.

[40] Yet proof of both of those different conceptions of harm – loss of a chance of a cure and an increased risk of harm – rely on the sort of statistically-based evidence that Wright criticizes, as he recognizes. Wright, *supra* note 37, at 1072.

[41] Wright, *supra* n. 37, at 1050 n. 273.

[42] Makdisi, *supra* note 10.

[43] Levmore, *supra* note 7, at 706.

[44] Levmore, *supra* note 7.

[45] Daniel A. Farber, *Recurring Misses*, 19 J. LEGAL STUD. 727 (1990). Heidi Feldman, while expressing comfort with using proportional liability, recognized that it could not be a solution to "strong" uncertainty about general causation. *See* Heidi Li Feldman, *Science and Uncertainty in Mass Exposure Litigation*, 74 TEX. L. REV. 1, 39–41 (1995).

increases the incidence of cancer by 25 percent to recover on a probabilistic basis.[46]

The model employed by virtually all commentators includes plaintiffs who have suffered disease allegedly as a result of exposure to a toxic substance.[47] These are recurring cases, in which the best form of evidence is statistical in nature and provides a probabilistic assessment of causation. Yet such evidence leaves considerable uncertainty in each individual case about whether the defendant's agent was the cause of a specific plaintiff's harm. Moreover, the focus of these commentators is cases in which the probability of individual causation is less than 50 percent. That threshold, given the preponderance of the evidence standard, is critical to a plaintiff meeting her burden of proof under current law. Many, although not all, of the commentators remain consistent with regard to proportionality and argue that even when the probability of causation is greater than 50 percent, damage awards should be adjusted to reflect that probability rather than awarding full damages.[48]

Most of these commentators assume, without discussion, that, despite the existence of uncertainty about who was the *ex post* cause, courts can determine the probability that a given defendant was a cause of the plaintiff's harm with reasonable accuracy.[49] The most notable exception is David Rosenberg

---

[46] Porat & Stein, *supra* note 6, at 125–28, 175–78, 193–94. Porat and Stein reiterate and elaborate on their proposal in Porat & Stein, *supra* note 26.

[47] E.g., Shavell, *supra* n. 21, at 606–7; Rosenberg, *supra* note 27; William M. Landes & Richard A. Posner, *Causation in Tort Law: An Economic Approach*, 12 J. LEGAL STUD. 109, 123–24 (1983); Schroeder, *supra* note 29. *See generally* Fischer, *supra* note 16, at 1218 (1993) ("Courts most likely will apply proportional liability in toxic tort cases, which are based largely on epidemiological evidence."). *But see* Makdisi, *supra* note 10 (advocating a comprehensive proportional liability scheme).

[48] Delgado's proposal, like many, focuses on plaintiffs who cannot prove, even with statistical evidence, their harm more likely than not was caused by defendant's wrongful conduct and advocates proportional liability. Unlike the others, Delgado does not argue for proportional liability on the other side of the preponderance coin; he contemplates that those who can prove that their injury more likely than not was caused by defendant can recover their full damages, although he acknowledges the fairness claim of such defendants that liability should be discounted in the latter situation as well. *See* Delgado, *supra* note 19, at 899 n. 91.

[49] *See* Shavell, *supra* note 9, at 590. Landes and Posner are less agnostic about the availability of good information, suggesting that the development of "sophisticated statistical analyses" will remedy the problem of an absence of "minimally reliable estimates of the actual probability," thereby permitting *ex ante* probabilistic recovery based on exposure to risk. WILLIAM M. LANDES & RICHARD A. POSNER, THE ECONOMIC STRUCTURE OF TORT LAW 268 (1987). Earlier, they asserted that even an increase of 10 percent in the incidence of cancer because of a nuclear reactor accident could be detected, "with near certainty from the law of large numbers." William M. Landes & Richard A. Posner, *Tort Law as a Regulatory Regime for Catastrophic Personal Injuries*, 13 J. LEGAL STUD. 417, 423 (1984). For reasons explained

who explicitly confronts the matter. Rosenberg states in a recent article that: "Epidemiological studies can predict (with increasing accuracy over time) the rate of cancer incidence in the exposed population attributable to the toxic substance in question."[50] In an earlier article, Rosenberg implied that science could provide reasonably accurate evidence about the increase in risk, suggesting that because most studies are performed by neutrals – university or public health researchers – disagreement about the probabilistic estimates are likely to be modest.[51]

An issue related to proportional liability has arisen in the current toxic substances legal climate: What is the minimum increased risk that an epidemiologic study must find for the plaintiff to meet her burden of proof?[52]

<hr>

infra, I think Landes and Posner are wrong unless we already are confident about the causal relationship between the agent and disease (general causation). Large numbers can reduce sampling error, but they do nothing for biases and confounding, two other serious sources of error. *See infra* text accompanying notes 91–115. Even when we are confident about general causation, measuring exposure for an environmental accident such as Three Mile Island poses a major obstacle to proportional liability.

[50] David Rosenberg, *Individual Justice and Collectivizing Risk-Based Claims in Mass-Exposure Cases*, 71 N.Y.U. L. REV. 210, 217–18 (1996). Porat & Stein similarly suggest the existence of reliable statistical data: "In cases involving industrial diseases, medical malpractice damages, or injuries sustained through exposure to hazardous substances, judges would be able to seek guidance in the growing body of scientific research. This body of research contains an impressive amount of statistical data upon which judges would be able to rely." Porat & Stein, *supra* note 26, at 689. Porat and Stein were addressing the question of apportioning liability among defendants based on the probability of causation, but their prior work advocated proportional liability in what they termed the "radiation case," in which the probability that defendant's agent caused plaintiff's harm is 25 percent. Indeed, one of the cases that they do discuss, *Allen v. British Rail Eng'g Ltd.*, [2001] ICR 942 (CA), was a case involving non-tortious contributions to the risk that, at the extreme, becomes the same as their radiation case.

[51] Rosenberg, *supra* note 17, at 897–98. A student note questioned Rosenberg's sanguinity about the existence of valid evidence about probability just two years after Rosenberg first made his case for proportional liability. *See* Gold, *supra* note 17, at 398 nn. 114–15. Even when investigator bias is removed, the matter Rosenberg addressed, other potential sources of error in epidemiologic studies raise the possibility for substantially different assessments of their implications. *See* Joint Discussion of Science, Technology and Law Panel and American Law Institute on Restatement of Torts, National Academy of Sciences 18–21 (Jan. 21, 2003), available at <http://www7.nationalacademies.org/stl/ALI_Transcript.pdf>. Moreover, university-employed investigators are often funded by industry or have other ties to industry. *See*, e.g., MICHAEL D. GREEN, BENDECTIN AND BIRTH DEFECTS 141–42 (1996).

[52] Although I cast the question as one arising from the burden of proof, many courts address the matter under the *Daubert* admissibility umbrella in deciding whether an expert's testimony is sufficiently reliable to be admitted. In a number of cases, the basis for the expert's opinion – epidemiology – is assessed for its sufficiency and that becomes the basis for whether the expert's testimony is admissible. *See*, e.g., *Vargas v. Lee*, 317 F.3d 498 (5th Cir. 2003) (concluding absence of scientific studies connecting trauma to fibromyalgia required ruling expert's contrary testimony inadmissible); *Newman v. Motorola, Inc.*, 218 F. Supp. 2d 769

This is a question different from adopting proportional liability because it accepts the existing preponderance standard and its all-or-nothing outcome, but similar because it also relies on the outcomes of epidemiologic studies. Explanation of this matter and the controversy over it requires a brief detour to a subject that is addressed in more detail later, the output of an epidemiologic study.[53] Epidemiologists who investigate disease causation measure the association between exposure to an agent and the incidence of disease with a concept called relative risk. They conduct their studies by measuring the incidence of disease in groups of individuals with different exposures to an agent of interest. The relative risk is the incidence of a given disease in a population exposed to the agent divided by the incidence of the disease in a population that has not been exposed. For a powerful agent such as cigarette smoking, researchers might find a relative risk around 12 for lung cancer among a group of pack-a-day smokers. That means the incidence of lung cancer in smokers is twelve times what it is among nonsmokers, and 11/12 of the lung cancer found in the exposed group can be attributed to smoking. By contrast, a relative risk of 1.0 means that there is no difference in the incidence of disease between those exposed and those who are not exposed.[54]

A relative risk of 2.0 is thus critical in terms of the preponderance of the evidence standard for specific causation.[55] If the relative risk is above 2.0, more instances of the disease in the exposed population can be attributed to the agent than to other causes. If we employ group-based data to infer the probability of causation for any exposed individual, a relative risk above 2.0 would satisfy the preponderance standard, while a relative risk of 2.0 or less would not.[56] Thus, a number of courts, led by the Ninth Circuit in the remand

(D. Md. 2002) (absence of reliable evidence of connection between cellular phones and cancer fatal to admissibility of expert's testimony); *Daniels v. Lyondell-Citgo Refining Co.*, 99 S.W.3d 722 (Tex. Ct. App. 2003) (reviewing three epidemiologic studies on which plaintiffs' experts relied for their opinion and concluding that none was sufficient to support a finding of causation); *see also Exxon Corp. v. Makofski*, 116 S.W.3d 176 (Tex. Ct. App. 2003) (examining scientific studies and evidence relied on by experts in determining the sufficiency of the evidence on causation).

[53] There are a number of qualifications that I omit from this discussion for the sake of clarity and brevity. Those matters are addressed in Section III.

[54] The relative risk reflects the mean increase in disease incidence for all exposed individuals but gives no indication of the variance in risk among those individuals.

[55] *See, e.g., In Re: Silicone Gel Breasts Implants Products Liability Litigation*, 318 F. Supp. 2d 879 (C.D. Cal. 2004) (concluding that California law requires a relative risk in excess of 2.0 but rejecting defendant's claim that this requirement bears on general causation; instead it bears only on specific causation). *But see infra* text accompanying notes 70–72.

[56] The Attributable Proportion (or Percentage) of Risk ("APR") reflects the average probability of causation for each member of the exposed group. It can be calculated by the following

of *Daubert v. Merrell Dow Pharmaceuticals, Inc.*,[57] and the Texas Supreme Court in another Bendectin case,[58] have insisted that plaintiffs' epidemiologic evidence find a relative risk greater than 2.0 in order to meet their burden of proof. Despite the logic of courts like the Ninth Circuit in *Daubert*, there is considerable controversy over this matter and approximately half of the courts to address the matter have declined to insist on a threshold risk of 2.0.[59] There are three reasons that support the courts who decline to insist on a threshold doubling of the risk to meet the burden of proof: (1) the average risk reflected in a study may not accurately reflect the risk for any exposed individual; (2) an increase in risk is relevant and therefore admissible, even if insufficient; and (3) a risk less than 2.0 may reflect a more-likely-than-not acceleration of the onset of disease in cases in which exposed individuals would have contracted the disease at some later time without exposure.

As Dan Farber explained in his most-likely-victim article,[60] we can distinguish among exposed individuals based on a variety of factors that affect the probability of agent causation for that individual.[61] Those factors would,

---

formula: $I_e - I_u/I_e$, where I_e is the incidence of disease in the exposed population and I_u is the incidence of disease in the unexposed population. *See* Michael D. Green et al., *Reference Guide on Epidemiology*, in Federal Judicial Center, Reference Manual on Scientific Evidence 333 (2d ed. 2000).

   Ariel Porat and Alex Stein have recently made a point that the increase in risk produced by the defendant's tortious conduct over the background risk that exists is not the same as the probability that the defendant's conduct caused the harm. Porat & Stein, *supra* note 26, at 683–87. Thus, if there is a background incidence of disease of 5 percent per year and a defendant's toxic agent increases the incidence to 10 percent a year, the probability the defendant caused an individual's disease is not 5 percent, the difference between the increased incidence and the background incidence. Instead, the probability is 50 percent, because the 5 percent who contract the disease (the numerator) are one half of the 10 percent, which is the population (denominator) of persons who suffer the disease. The APR reflects Porat & Stein's observation on the lack of equivalence between the *ex ante* increased risk and the probability of causation.

[57] *Daubert v. Merrell Dow Pharms., Inc.*, 43 F.3d 1311, 1320 (9th Cir.) (requiring that plaintiff demonstrate a relative risk of two), *cert. denied*, 516 U.S. 869 (1995).

[58] *Merrell Dow Pharms., Inc. v. Havner*, 953 S.W.2d 706, 718 (Tex. 1997) ("The use of scientifically reliable epidemiological studies and the requirement of more than a doubling of the risk strikes a balance between the needs of our legal system and the limits of science.").

[59] In a paper published in 2001, Carruth and Goldstein report on twenty-nine opinions addressing whether a relative risk of 2.0 is required to prove causation. They found the cases split almost evenly in answering that question. Russellyn S. Carruth & Bernard D. Goldstein, *Relative Risk Greater Than Two in Proof of Causation in Toxic Tort Litigation*, 41 Jurimetrics J. 195 (2001). A somewhat more recent list of the cases is contained in Restatement (Third) of Torts: Liability for Physical Harm § 28 Rptrs' Note to cmt. c(4) (Tentative Draft No. 3, 2003).

[60] *See* Farber, *supra* note 33.

[61] See *supra* note 35, and accompanying text.

in some cases, provide a basis for adjusting for an exposed individual the average probability of causation from an epidemiologic study. That adjustment, based on factors distinguishing a plaintiff from the subjects in a study, could produce an estimate of the probability for that individual as more likely than not, even though the relative risk in the study does not exceed 2.0.[62]

Adjusting for individual variations is the best reason to explain the courts that, contrary to *Daubert* and *Havner*, have not insisted on a relative risk in excess of 2.0 as a threshold for proof of specific causation. Indeed, on a purely logical basis, a study with a relative risk of 2.0 or less should provide admissible evidence under the relevancy standard, even if it is not sufficient.[63] However, courts have, in the implementation of *Daubert*, collapsed admissibility and sufficiency, permitting an expert to testify only when there is sufficient scientific evidentiary support for the expert's opinion to satisfy the sufficiency standard.[64]

The Third Restatement of Torts weighs in on the side of relative risks less than 2.0. It observes that employing a threshold relative risk of 2.0 is "usually inappropriate," and, depending on the availability of evidence particular to the specific plaintiff, advocates permitting the jury to decide whether to draw an inference of negligence.[65] The Restatement is backed by a considerable body of scholarship addressing this question. Professor Lucinda Finley, in an article critical of the courts' use of *Daubert* screening in toxic substances cases, castigated use of a relative risk threshold of 2.0 as "seriously scientifically and legally misguided."[66] Finley's main objection is that such evidence is

---

[62] That adjustment can only be performed to the extent that factors that affect the risk of the disease are known. Thus, for example, approximately two thirds of all birth defects are due to unknown causes. *See* Robert L. Brent, *The Complexities of Solving the Problem of Human Malformations,* 13 CLINICS IN PERINATOLOGY 491, 493 (1986) (citing various estimates of the proportion of birth defects due to unknown causes). A differential diagnosis cannot be effectively performed when a substantial proportion of the background causes of the disease are unknown.

[63] *See Pick v. Am. Med. Sys., Inc.,* 958 F. Supp. 1151, 1160 (E.D. La. 1997) (stating that a relative risk of 2.0 implies a 50 percent probability of specific causation, but acknowledging that a study with a lower relative risk is admissible, if not sufficient to support a verdict on causation).

[64] *See, e.g.,* Lucinda M. Finley, *Guarding the Gate to the Courthouse: How Trial Judges Are Using Their Evidentiary Screening Role to Remake Tort Causation Rules,* 49 DEPAUL L. REV. 335, 347 (1999) ("A review of post-*Daubert* cases reveals that many judges have resolved this apparent epistemological conundrum by making what are plainly legal rulings about the type and nature of scientific evidence plaintiffs must produce to even attempt to prove causation.").

[65] RESTATEMENT (THIRD) OF TORTS: LIABILITY FOR PHYSICAL HARM § 28 cmt. c (4) (Tentative Draft No. 3, 2003). The author is one of the Co-Reporters for this RESTATEMENT.

[66] Finley, *supra* note 64, at 348. Professor Jean Eggen subsequently endorsed Professor Finley's critique. Jean Macchiaroli Eggen, *Clinical Medical Evidence of Causation in Toxic Tort Cases: Into the Crucible of Daubert,* 38 HOUS. L. REV. 369, 378–79 (2001). Her main complaint was the

admissible and, if supplemented with other toxicological evidence, including animal toxicology, *in vitro* studies, chemical structure analysis, case reports, and biological mechanism evidence might be sufficient to permit a jury to find specific causation. Professor Margaret Berger, a prominent scholarly voice in the area of toxic substances causation, has joined Professor Finley in criticizing the use of a threshold relative risk for specific causation.[67] Professor Tom McGarity joins Professor Finley in advocating the use of studies that find a relative risk of 2.0 or less, on the ground that the decision about acceptable levels of proof is one of policy rather than of science.[68]

Recent work by several epidemiologists has strengthened the case against the use of a 2.0 threshold for specific causation.[69] A 2.0 relative risk threshold relies on an often unappreciated assumption that the agent caused disease in a person who, otherwise, would never contract the disease.[70] An alternative possibility is that the agent accelerates the onset of disease that would otherwise have occurred in those individuals, albeit at a later time.[71] If an

collapsing of the admissibility and the sufficiency decision in excluding expert testimony based on a relative risk less than 2.0. Presumably, Professor Eggen also means to adopt Finley's argument that other evidence, especially differential diagnosis testimony which she advocates, along with general causation evidence from an epidemiology study should be sufficient to satisfy the requirement of specific causation. *See also* Christopher B. Mueller, *Daubert Asks the Right Questions: Now Appellate Courts Should Help Find the Right Answers*, 33 Seton Hall L. Rev. 987, 999 (2003).

[67] *See* Margaret A. Berger, *Upsetting the Balance Between Adverse Interests: The Impact of the Supreme Court's Trilogy on Expert Testimony in Toxic Tort Litigation*, 64 Law & Contemp. Probs. 289, 304–6 (Spring/Summer 2001). Professor Berger concurs with Finley's observation that the relative risk only expresses an average for the exposed group and might be refined based on the individual characteristics of a specific plaintiff. She also makes a more sophisticated argument about two assumptions on which measurement of relative risk rests. *See infra* text accompanying notes 68–72.

[68] Thomas O. McGarity, *Proposal for Linking Culpability and Causation to Ensure Corporate Accountability*, 26 Wm. & Mary L. & Pol'y Rev. 1, 28–29 (2001).

[69] In addition to the explanation in the text, the relative risk cannot be relied on to provide the probability of causation when there is an interaction (i.e., the combined incidence of disease in those exposed to some other risk factor and to the agent is other than additive). The appropriate probability is a matter complicated by a lack of understanding about the underlying biology. *See* Restatement (Third) of Torts: Liability for Physical Harm § 28 Rptrs' Note to cmt. c(5) (Tentative Draft No. 3, 2003); Louis A. Cox Jr., *Probability of Causation and the Attributable Risk*, 4 Risk Analysis 221 (1984).

[70] This is true of diseases, like cancer, that can occur at different times. Other outcomes, such as birth defects, that only occur at a given time are not subject to acceleration and the qualification discussed later. *See* Sander Greenland, *Relation of Probability of Causation to Relative Risk and Doubling Dose: A Methodologic Error That Has Become a Social Problem*, 89 Am. J. Pub. Health 1166, 1166 (1999).

[71] *See* Sander Greenland & James M. Robins, *Conceptual Problems in the Definition and Interpretation of Attributable Fractions*, 128 Am. J. Epidemiology 1185 (1988); Sander Greenland & James M. Robins, *Epidemiology, Justice, and the Probability of Causation*, 40 Jurimetrics

agent accelerates the onset of disease, rather than causing it in persons who would never otherwise have suffered from it, the excess incidence of disease in a group study will understate the proportion of persons whose disease was accelerated by the agent.[72] Thus, a plaintiff might prove that even though the relative risk was less than 2.0, the agent more likely than not resulted in his contracting the disease a period of time earlier than he would have otherwise contracted it.[73]

Those who advocate the sufficiency of relative risks less than 2.0 thus differ from the proportional liability advocates. They accept the traditional preponderance approach to proving causation and imposing liability. What they share with the proportionate liability advocates is reliance on small increases in the relative risk as an accurate measure of the increased risk posed by an agent. The courts that have accepted the idea that a relative risk of less than 2.0 can be sufficient may be taking a small step toward proportional liability, although I'm dubious about that assessment.

In summary, a substantial number of scholars have made normative arguments for changing or modifying the law on the burden of proof and causation based on group studies when those studies reveal only a small or modest increase in risk. The most radical of these reformers advocate a scheme of proportional liability based on a probability obtained from group

---

321 (2000). Acceptance of acceleration as the harm also would require an adjustment in the damages for which a defendant would be liable.

[72] Greenland and Robins explain that ordinarily we assume that all of those exposed to an agent who develop disease include the background cases of disease that would have occurred in the absence of exposure. Thus, if we find twelve persons out of one hundred thousand exposed to benzene for twenty years develop leukemia in a given year and the incidence of leukemia among those not exposed is ten per one hundred thousand, we assume that of the twelve exposed cases of leukemia, ten would have occurred without exposure. However, if benzene merely accelerates the time at which one contracts leukemia by one year, all twelve of the exposed cases are the result of benzene exposure accelerating contraction of leukemia. *See* Sander Greenland & James M. Robins, *Epidemiology, Justice, and the Probability of Causation*, 40 JURIMETRICS 321, 326–27 (2000); *see also* Ofer Shpilberg et al., *The Next Stage: Molecular Epidemiology*, 50 J. CLINICAL EPIDEMIOLOGY 633, 637 (1997) ("A 1.5-fold relative risk may be composed of a 5-fold risk in 10% of the population, and a 1.1-fold risk in the remaining 90%, or a 2-fold risk in 25% and a 1.1-fold for 75%, or a 1.5-fold risk for the entire population.").

[73] In some instances, evidence may exist that permits determining which of these models is most likely. Understanding the genetic role in disease may enable identification of individuals for whom the development of the disease is only a matter of time and trigger. In the absence of better evidence, my intuition is that a reasonable default is nonacceleration. That is a matter with which others might disagree. Regardless of which assumption is more plausible as a default, however, the question of a threshold relative risk for general causation remains the same. Error in an epidemiologic study is independent of the biological mechanism actually at work.

studies. More modest proposals retain the current all-or-nothing character of liability awards but would permit those same small or modest increases in risk to suffice under certain circumstances as sufficient proof of specific causation.

III. THE LIMITS OF OBSERVATIONAL EPIDEMIOLOGY

Determining causal relationships between agents and disease is not easy. Indeed, it is not even easy to understand why we encounter such difficulty. Recall that agent-disease causation has two components. The first is general causation, the capacity of an agent to cause a given disease in the human population. By contrast, specific causation is about whether an agent has caused a given individual's disease, as when a lung cancer victim claims that smoking cigarettes caused the lung cancer. General causation is antecedent to specific causation – if an agent doesn't cause disease in the human species, we need not address specific causation. Moreover, the evidence about general causation often provides at least the starting point for making a judgment about specific causation.

A number of commentators[74] have attributed the difficulty in determining general causation to the long latency period between exposure and disease.[75] As Landes and Posner put it, "the longer the delay between the accident and the injury, the harder it is to exclude the other causal factors."[76] Landes and Posner have fingered the primary culprit: the existence of competing causes

---

[74] See W. PAGE KEETON ET AL., PRODUCTS LIABILITY AND SAFETY 921 (2d ed. 1989); Jean Macchiaroli Eggen, *Clinical Medical Evidence of Causation in Toxic Tort Cases: Into the Crucible of Daubert*, 38 HOUS. L. REV. 369, 372 (2001) ("Specific causation is often oppressively problematic in toxic tort cases, where latency periods and generic categories of disease make causal identification difficult."); Andrew R. Klein, *A Model for Enhanced Risk Recovery in Tort*, 56 WASH. & LEE L. REV. 1173, 1174 (1999); Thomas O. McGarity, *Proposal for Linking Culpability and Causation to Ensure Corporate Accountability for Toxic Risks*, 26 WM. & MARY ENVTL. L. & POL'Y REV. 1, 28–29 (2001) ("specific causation has frequently proven to be an insuperable barrier in toxic torts cases because of the long latency periods that often exist between the exposure to a toxic substance and the onset of disease"); Glen O. Robinson, *Probabilistic Causation and Compensation for Tortious Risk*, 14 J. LEGAL STUD. 779, 784 (1985) ("Assuming the risk victim is not hermetically sealed following exposure to a particular risk, a plausible (if not scientifically precise) generalization is that the complexity of assigning causal responsibility is proportional to the elapsed time between the exposure and its causal determination.").

[75] Joe Sanders bears as much responsibility for the analysis of the role of latency periods that follows as I do. As has been the case for many years, our conversations have contributed enormously to my understanding of the issues involved in this area of law.

[76] William M. Landes & Richard A. Posner, *Tort Law as a Regulatory Regime for Catastrophic Personal Injuries*, 13 J. LEGAL STUD. 417, 418 (1984).

that may instead be responsible for the plaintiff's disease. More precisely, both the existence of competing causes and the relative proportion of the disease for which the competing causes are responsible is the nub of the problem. To put the point somewhat differently, powerful toxic agents can be readily identified. The latency period plays only a modest and confined role in the toxic-causation problem.[77]

Thus, vaginal adenocarcinoma doesn't develop until a generation after a mother takes DES during pregnancy and exposes the fetus to the drug. Yet in the late 1960s, physicians identified DES as the cause of a cluster of cases that arose, because there simply are no other competing causes of vaginal adenocarcinoma in young women.[78] Similarly, with Thalidomide, once investigators identified the drug as the common agent associated with the massive increase in limb-reduction birth defects, the culprit was found.[79] By contrast, despite a relatively short latency period of six to nine months – the same as Thalidomide – investigators had a difficult time determining whether Bendectin was a cause of birth defects. After substantial investigation, we still cannot rule out the possibility that Bendectin causes some quite small increase in birth defects, although researchers have given up (and funding has dried up because of its removal from the market). It was no easier to ascertain the existence of a causal relationship between silicon gel breast implants and connective tissue disease for women whose disease developed shortly after their implants than for those whose disease occurred decades later.[80] These examples reveal that it is not the length of the latency period that is critical, but the

---

[77] Donald Elliott also expressed doubt about the role of the latency period as creating difficulties in determining causation. Elliott, *supra* n. 16, at 801. He points alternatively to the absence of records regarding exposure as the culprit. Yet evidence of exposure is correlated with and related to latency periods; the evidence surely deteriorates with the passage of time. Elliott also observed that the passage of time actually improves our ability to determine causation because scientific evidence improves with time. That is true, but the critical question is whether shorter latency periods would make easier the scientific inquiry that provides the evidence.

[78] *See* Herbst, Ulfeldor & Prokanzer, *Adenocarcinoma of the Vagina*, 284 NEW ENG. J. MED. 878 (1971).

[79] *See* PHILIP J. HILTS, PROTECTING AMERICA'S HEALTH: THE FDA, BUSINESS, AND ONE HUNDRED YEARS OF REGULATION 154–55 (2003).

[80] A qualification on the statement in the text is required. Long latency periods (if not appreciated) can complicate investigation into a suspected toxic agent if the researcher doesn't design the study to account for the latency period. Precisely that problem biased an effort to examine the safety of insulation workers in naval shipyards published in 1945 that concluded that "asbestos covering of naval vessels is a relatively safe operation," because the authors failed to wait sufficient time for asbestotic disease to develop. Fleisher et al., *A Health Survey of Pipe-Covering Operations in Constructing Naval Vessels*, 28 J. INDUS. HYGIENE 9 (1945), quoted in *Borel v. Fibreboard Paper Prods.*, 493 F.2d 1076, 1084 (5th Cir. 1973).

existence of competing causes and the proportion of disease that they cause. Powerful agents, because they cause a large proportion of disease, are readily identified, while those that cause small increases are much more difficult to identify, regardless of the latency period.

Indeed, unless we have a pretty good understanding of the biological mechanism through which the disease develops, we don't even know what the latency period is when searching for causal agents. The young women who presented with vaginal adenocarcinoma might have had a latency period of twenty-one days or twenty-one years. Anything in their history could have been responsible, at least in theory.

The "at least in theory" is an important qualification. It highlights the role that understanding of biological mechanism plays in determining causation. Some day, with advances in molecular biology, toxicology, identification of biomarkers and genetics, we may have an understanding of the development of disease that rivals our understanding of the mechanism by which bones break in an accident.[81] With more modest understanding of the disease process, we may be able to pin down the latency period, for example by determining that environmentally caused cancers are not an acute disease but require a substantial latency period from initial exposure to clinically identifiable disease. Biological understanding thus assists in identifying potential causes and ruling out other suspected causes. That screening ability is not a function of the latency period but instead depends on the quality of biological mechanism understanding.

Thus, the power of the agent and understanding of biological mechanism emerge as the key determinants in the difficulty of determining general causation. To be fair, a lengthy latency period does complicate identifying general causation, as one cannot find an effect if it doesn't develop for many years after exposure.[82] And long latency periods can complicate the ability of researchers to determine exposure and measure dosage with precision, especially for occupational exposures.

For specific causation, once again the power of the agent plays an important role. If the agent is the only cause of the disease, as is the case with DES and vaginal adenocarcinoma or as is nearly the case with asbestos and mesothelioma, we can readily make individual causal judgments. But these are not the cases with which the proportional-liability advocates are concerned. Rather, they are concerned with situations in which the agent causes a quite modest

---

[81] See Christiana P. Callahan, Note, *Molecular Epidemiology: Future Proof of Toxic Tort Causation*, 8 ENVTL. LAW. 147 (2001).

[82] See note 79 *supra*.

increase in the incidence of the disease. Here our knowledge of competing causes and ability to determine whether they may have played a causal role is the critical determinant. If the other causes of the harm are known and can be ruled out, as is the case when a previously healthy automobile passenger involved in a car crash emerges with a broken arm, then a causal judgment can readily be made. And here we see the role that biological mechanism plays when we know that the latency period is short: potential competing causes must occur within the relevant time window or they can be ruled out. Knowledge of the latency period is important here, but its length is not.[83]

Let us consider Landes and Posner's example of lost hair following shortly after a radiation accident. They assert that this provides an easy case of causation, absent an alternative explanation. The difficulty is that the hair loss could be the result of a wide variety of environmental exposures or genetic factors at any point during the individual's life, despite the short latency period for hair loss due to radiation. We can make a causal assessment as readily as Landes and Posner suggest only because we know the mechanism by which most other potential causes of hair loss operate excludes sudden hair loss and that the competing short-term causes of hair loss – chemotherapy or scalping – can be ruled out by percipient observation. Here, again, it is mechanism (and the ability to rule out competing causes because of observation) that enables an uncomplicated causal judgment. When knowledge of mechanism provides the time frame from exposure to outcome, potential competing causes are more readily identified and ruled in or out.

In summary, toxic substance causation is most likely to be difficult when there are alternative causes of much of the disease, and the agent in question is only a potential cause of a small proportion of the disease. The extent of understanding about the biological mechanism involved also bears on how easily we can make causal assessments.[84]

The proportionalists' interest is with precisely these agent-disease relationships. These are the small increases in risk for which they propose reform. To explore the difficulties with these proposals requires some consideration of how epidemiologists work and the limitations of the studies they produce.[85]

---

[83] Evidence relevant to specific causation may deteriorate because of longer latency periods. Thus, an individual's exposure to the agent and its dose may be more difficult to determine decades after exposure, as may evidence of exposure to other potential causes of the disease.

[84] The frequency with which the disease in question occurs also affects the difficulty of determining causation, as small numbers are more subject to random error.

[85] There is an abundance of thorough descriptive treatments of epidemiology in the legal literature, and I do not repeat them fully here. See, e.g., 2 DAVID L. FAIGMAN ET AL., MODERN SCIENTIFIC EVIDENCE 300–53 (1997); Green, supra note 56, at 352; Gerald W.

Modern epidemiological methodology involves the selection of two (or more) groups for comparison. One study design consists of an exposed and a control group. Another type of study compares a group with a disease of interest and a group without the disease.[86] The first type, a cohort study, compares the incidence of disease in the two groups and produces a relative risk that, as explained earlier, reflects the ratio of the incidence of disease in the exposed group to the incidence in the control group. The second study type, a case-control study, compares the incidence of exposure to the agent among those with the disease to the incidence of exposure among those without the disease and produces an odds ratio that is, when the incidence of disease is small, quite similar to the relative risk.[87]

In some epidemiology studies, researchers examine groups who have already suffered disease and been exposed, often relying on historical records, such as medical records. These studies employ retrospective designs. By contrast, prospective studies follow participants in a study for a period of time and during that time ascertain exposure and disease. Each of these specific study designs is differentially susceptible to the potential errors explained below, but I do not differentiate between these different study designs in the discussion.

The first and most important step in understanding the limits of epidemiology is appreciating that it does not entail experiments, in which conditions are controlled and study subjects randomized. Epidemiologists who look for the causes of disease are limited to observations of people who have been or will be exposed to the agent of interest in the course of events. These observational studies are different from experiments such as clinical trials in which the participants are randomized into different groups with some receiving a treatment (a predetermined "dose") and another group a placebo. Epidemiology is employed to determine whether suspected agents cause disease, while clinical trials are employed when there is some reason to believe that the agent or intervention will reduce the risk of disease or, in some other way, improve health.[88]

Boston, *A Mass-Exposure Model of Toxic Causation: The Content of Scientific Proof and the Regulatory Experience*, 18 COLUM. J. ENVTL. L. 181 (1993). Rather, I limit myself to a stylized account of epidemiology sufficient to explain the position contained in this chapter.

[86] There are other study designs but they have little application to investigating toxic agents. See Green, *supra* note 56, at 343–45.

[87] See Green, *supra* note 56, at 350.

[88] Even better than randomized, placebo-controlled human clinical trials are *in vivo* animal trials in which not only is the exposure to the agent controlled but all other conditions in the life of the animals are also kept constant. That is a distinct advantage of animal toxicology, but extrapolating the results of those high-dose studies to a different species at lower doses

The second point to appreciate is that an association found in an observational study does not necessarily reflect a causal relationship. It may, but there are three sources of error that might produce a spurious association. Biases – methodological problems that can produce error – a spurious association – is one such concern.[89] A second impediment to accuracy – confounding – occurs when a relationship between exposure to an agent and a disease is found but is not caused by the agent. Rather, a confounding factor – one differentially associated with exposure to the agent – is the causal agent.[90] Finally, the third major source of error is random chance. Observed differences between two groups may be the result of the same type of random outcomes that produce ten heads in a row of a fair coin toss. The risk of random error is especially large when the disease is rare and exposure uncommon. Each of these three problems can cause errors in two different directions: some will tend to exaggerate the true relationship that exists between the agent and disease (whether protective, noncausal, or causal); others, however, will tend to understate any relationship that exists.[91] I proceed to explain each of these sources of error and how they can affect the outcome of an epidemiologic study.

One difficulty epidemiologists confront in conducting observational studies is gathering accurate data. Inaccurate or incomplete data contribute a number of the many types of bias – errors in a study that may lead to skewed outcomes – that epidemiologists have catalogued.[92] I highlight here the most salient for studies seeking the cause of chronic diseases like cancer, neurological impairment, or birth defects that populate the toxic substances cases that courts confront. Critical to any such study is determining the existence

---

poses substantial difficulties. Most neutral observers prefer good quality epidemiology to comparable animal toxicology for determining causation for humans.

[89] "Bias" is defined as "any systematic error in the design, conduct, analysis, or interpretation of a study that tends to produce an incorrect assessment of the nature of the association between an exposure or risk factor and the occurrence of disease." Manning Feinleib, *Biases and Weak Associations*, 16 PREVENTIVE MED. 150, 150 (1987).

[90] Thus, an association between coffee drinking and lung cancer might be because of confounding, as coffee drinkers are more likely to be cigarette smokers than those that do not drink coffee.

[91] To generalize, bias (or other sources of error) may produce an association that: (1) incorrectly suggests a causal relationship exists when there is no causal relationship; (2) incorrectly suggests a causal relationship exists where the agent serves a preventive function; (3) correctly suggests a causal relation but overstates or understates its strength; and (4) correctly suggest an association and a reasonably accurate measure of its strength. Similarly, a study may find a protective association, that is, an association less than 1.0 that would have similar characteristics to those above, save that the association suggests a protective causal effect.

[92] Dozens of biases are catalogued in David L. Sackett, *Bias in Analytic Research*, 32 J. CHRON. DIS. 51 (1979).

of exposure and the biologically-relevant dose[93] as well as the existence of the disease of interest in the population being studied. There are numerous pitfalls for researchers – some can be avoided or minimized if identified – but some are an unavoidable consequence of limited knowledge and resources.

Accurately determining the dose of those in the exposed group is most difficult with retrospective studies – studies that examine exposure and disease that have already occurred. Prospective studies, by contrast, follow study participants and can measure exposure during the study. Unfortunately, prospective studies tend not to be the study design of choice for the types of suspected toxic substances – asbestos, breast implants, and drugs – that are the major source of toxic substance litigation. Irving Selikoff's pathbreaking work identifying the risks of disease among those who worked with asbestos products such as insulation employed retrospective studies.[94]

Thus, the dose of asbestos fibers to which an insulation or ship worker was exposed depends on the concentration of fibers at various times and the duration of those exposures.[95] Occupational exposures can be difficult to measure accurately, as is also the case with exposure to hazardous chemicals or waste. Efforts to identify the effects of Agent Orange on those who served in the Vietnam War were plagued by inadequate records that permitted only primitive estimates of exposure.[96] Prescription drug exposures are easier to measure accurately, especially in a prospective study, but can pose problems in retrospective studies, which require reliance on subjects' memories or historical records that sometimes do not exist or are incomplete.[97] Case-control

---

[93] Paracelsus is credited with the dictum that "the dose makes the poison." More fullsomely and especially relevant to drugs, he wrote: "All substances are poisons; there is none which is not a poison. The right dose differentiates a poison from a remedy." Michael A Gallo, *History and Scope of Toxicology*, in CASARETT AND DOULL'S TOXICOLOGY: THE BASIC SCIENCE OF POISONS 1, 4 (Curtis D. Klaassen ed.)(5th ed. 1996).

[94] *See* I. J. Selikoff, J. Churg & E. C. Hammon, *Asbestos Exposure and Neoplasia*, 188 JAMA 22 (1964); I. J. Selikoff, J. Churg & E. C. Hammond, *The Occurrence of Asbestosis in Insulation Workers in the United States*, 122 ANNALS N.Y. ACAD. SCI. 139 (1965).

[95] The ideal measure of exposure requires understanding of the mechanism by which the agent operates. *See infra* nn. 99–100 and accompanying text.

[96] *See, e.g.,* Howard Frumkin, *Agent Orange and Cancer: An Overview for Clinicians*, 53 CA-CANCER J. CLIN. 245, 246 (2003) ("One of the challenges in assessing the health effects of Agent Orange exposure is quantifying the exposures. There is little precise information for any individual veteran, about how much exposure he or she sustained, or even to what herbicides.").

[97] Thus, a study of the effect of spermicides on spontaneous abortions and birth defects relied on computerized pharmacy records and classified a woman as exposed if she had filled a prescription for a spermicide within twenty months of delivery or abortion. *See* H. Jick et al., *Vaginal Spermicides and Congenital Disorders*, 246 JAMA 1329 (1981).

studies, which are particularly helpful when the disease of interest is rare, confront recall bias, the tendency for those who have suffered calamitous events to search their minds for the cause, thereby better recalling the agents to which they have been exposed compared to others who did not suffer the same outcome.[98] "Wish bias" reflects the tendency of patients to misreport exposure to agents where there is disapprobation for voluntary exposures. Thus, lung cancer patients tend to overreport occupational exposures that were involuntary and underreport voluntary smoking.[99] Indeed, ascertaining exposure through self-reporting always entails the problems of memory and willingness to report accurately.

Complicating exposure measurement is the determination of the appropriate dose to measure. Depending on the biology of the disease, the total dose (intensity integrated over time), early doses, or peak doses may be the most important, while in other cases the length of the exposure is more critical than the magnitude at any point in time.[100] Thus, in determining the role of oral contraceptives in causing breast cancer, one measure of exposure might be the total dose of oral contraceptives.[101] However, if the mechanism by which breast cancer is caused is the suppression of ovulation, the appropriate dose is the number of months of use of oral contraceptives. If the biology, however, is that the mechanism by which cancer occurs is change to breast tissue prior to first childbirth, the dose from initial use until first childbirth becomes the appropriate one. Informed and thoughtful causal mechanism hypotheses can assist in minimizing error in specifying the appropriate exposure measure, but this remains a serious impediment to accuracy in epidemiological work.

---

[98] See Martha M. Werler, *Reporting Accuracy Among Mothers of Malformed and Nonmalformed Infants*, 129 AM. J. EPIDEM. 415 (1989) (finding recall bias among mothers exposed to several agents during pregnancy based on whether they bore a malformed child); *see also* Manning Feinleib, *Biases and Weak Associations*, 16 PREVENTIVE MED. 150, 156 (1987).

[99] See Ernest L. Wynder, *Guidelines to the Epidemiology of Weak Associations*, 16 PREVENTIVE MED. 211, 211–12 (1987).

[100] Thus, in some cases *when* the exposure occurs may be more important than the total lifetime dose. Given the latency period for most environmentally caused cancers, the most recent exposures play little or no role in causing the disease. KENNETH J. ROTHMAN & SANDER GREENLAND, MODERN EPIDEMIOLOGY 82–84 (2d ed. 1998). The most relevant exposures are older ones about which information is usually less available. Similarly, for an exogenous agent to cause a birth defect requires that the fetus be exposed to the agent when the organ is developing, rather than after the first trimester when the embryo has become fully formed. J. KLINE ET AL., CONCEPTION TO BIRTH: EPIDEMIOLOGY OF PRENATAL DEVELOPMENT 28–30 (1989).

[101] L. A. Brinton et al., *Oral Contraceptives and Breast Cancer Risk Among Younger Women*, 87 J. NAT'L CANCER INST. 827 (1995).

Errors in exposure measurement and classification will skew any association found in the study. Some errors, when they are equally applicable to those with the disease and those without it – nondifferential misclassification – will result in understating the true association.[102] However, when the errors in exposure measurement are differential, as is the case when recall bias results in the case cohorts better remembering their exposure, such as drug-taking, work history, or exposure to other potential toxic agents, than the control cohorts, differential misclassification occurs, which will tend to exaggerate the true association.[103]

Ascertaining disease status is another potential source of error and begins with the definition of the disease. If the disease is one that requires judgment to diagnose, such as chronic bronchitis or angina, investigators who are diagnosing participants in a study may be biased in their assessments based on exposure, unless those investigators are blinded to exposure status. Diagnosing some diseases, such as Alzheimer's, in those who are living, depends on certain signs or symptoms – surrogates for the disease, which cannot be definitively diagnosed until death, when invasive tests can be conducted. When researchers have to depend on historical death or medical records, errors may occur for a variety of reasons.[104] One of the impediments to identifying asbestos as a cause of mesothelioma is that the disease was frequently misdiagnosed because of its unfamiliarity and similarity to other diseases.[105] Employing a consistent definition of disease is impossible when relying on medical or death records prepared by different individuals operating without coordination.[106] As with exposure error, diagnostic error can skew the results of a study in either direction; nondifferential bias based on exposure – that is, making the same errors in diagnosis for those exposed and those who were not – will tend to understate any real relative risk.[107]

---

[102] Steven S. Coughlin, *Recall Bias in Epidemiologic Studies*, 43 J. CLIN. EPIDEMIOL. 87 (1990).

[103] *Id.*

[104] Another pitfall in disease ascertainment is precision in the definition of the disease. There are two major types of acute leukemia, lymphocytic and myelogenous. Conducting a study of whether an exogenous agent causes acute leukemia requires a hypothesis about whether the two leukemias are caused by the same agents or different ones for purposes of defining the disease of interest. However, error in specifying both leukemias when only one is caused by the agent investigated will tend to skew the true association downward, rather than exaggerate it. Researchers aware of problems like this can stratify their groups into those with each kind of leukemia and analyze the data separately.

[105] W. T. McCaughey, *Neoplastic Asbestos-Induced Disease*, 53 MT. SINAI J. MED. 416, 417 (1986).

[106] Manning Feinleib, *Biases and Weak Associations*, 16 PREVENTIVE MED. 150, 152 (1987).

[107] It also will tend to understate any protective effect, but for reasons explained below errors of that sort do not have similar costs for the legal system.

Differential misclassification will exaggerate the true association.[108] A relevant example, here, is asbestos. After researchers identified its three primary effects – asbestosis, lung cancer, and mesothelioma – the search began for other diseases that it might cause. Those exposed to asbestos were examined more frequently than the general population because of their asbestos exposure. This then creates a risk that diseases among those who are asbestos exposed will be more frequently diagnosed than for others who work in similar occupations but without exposure to asbestos. This creates differential misclassifications that overstate the difference in disease incidence between exposed and unexposed groups, thereby producing an inflated association.[109]

Another potential source of error – selection bias – exists when the control group and exposed group differ, other than in their exposure to the agent under investigation. Observational studies, unlike clinical studies, do not have an established control group, and an investigator must select an appropriate one. Sometimes, the general population is selected, because disease rates are well documented. But the general population may differ from an exposed group of, say, military personnel, because the military is younger than the general population and, even independent of age, healthier.[110] Similarly, a study of heart disease in middle-aged pipe smokers with a control group of nonsmokers of the same age would erroneously find a greater association between pipe smoking and heart disease because the exposed group is predominantly males who are, because of their gender, subject to a higher risk of heart disease than the general population.

Confounding is another potential source of error that occurs because of differences between the control group and the exposed group.[111] Confounding, if not identified and controlled for, can skew the outcome of a study or even produce a spurious relationship. The agent-disease relationship, then, is not real; rather, the relationship is between some factor other than the agent and the disease, but that other factor is differentially associated with the agent under study. Thus, a study of the connection between alcohol abuse and

---

[108] There are "many opportunities for differential misclassification." DAVID A. SAVITZ, INTERPRETING EPIDEMIOLOGIC EVIDENCE: STRATEGIES FOR STUDY DESIGN AND ANALYSIS 218 (2003).

[109] A potential bias as obvious as this one would be anticipated by a researcher, and corrective measures employed. The difficulty is with potential biases that researchers do not anticipate when designing and conducting their studies.

[110] The "healthy worker" phenomenon is well known in the epidemiologic industry. *See* Manning Feinleib, *Biases and Weak Associations*, 16 PREVENTIVE MED. 150, 160 (1987).

[111] For an assessment that confounding is far more prevalent than one might expect, *see* David A. Freedman, *From Association to Causation: Some Remarks on the History of Statistics*, 14 STAT. SCI. 243 (1999).

pancreatic cancer found a relative risk of 1.4. However, when the investigators adjusted for confounding because alcoholics are more likely to smoke and smoking is a cause of pancreatic cancer, the authors estimated that all of the excess cancer was due to smoking rather than alcohol.[112] In other words, the relative risk of 1.4 did not reflect a true causal relationship. Similar problems exist for scientists studying the connection between coffee and cancer, because cigarette smoking is also differentially associated with coffee drinking.[113] If potential confounders can be identified in advance and measured, statistical methods exist to adjust for their effect.[114] Unknown, unidentified, and unmeasurable confounders cannot be adjusted for and can bias outcomes in either direction.[115] Confounding is of greatest concern in studies that find relatively small relative risks, as it is unlikely to produce large errors in the magnitude of the true association.[116]

The third source of error is random error, which occurs whenever a sample of a larger universe is measured. Epidemiologists employ samples of the larger population, and random error is most problematical when the frequency of disease and the number of persons exposed are very small.[117]

The possibility of random error creates uncertainty about whether the results of a given study reflect the true case or is the product of the same type of randomness that produces ten heads in ten flips of a fair coin. We

---

[112] W. Ye et al., *Alcohol Abuse and the Risk of Pancreatic Cancer*, 51 GUT 236 (2002).

[113] Thus, a study of coffee drinking and cancer found relative risks of 1.08, 1.05 and 1.24 for three coffee-drinking groups (each of different doses). *See* I. Stensvold & B. K. Jacobsen, *Coffee and Cancer: A Prospective Study of 43,000 Norweigian Men and Women*, 5 CANCER CAUSES CONTROL 401 (1994). However, adjusting for confounding, including smoking, produced relative risks of 1.04, .96, and .99, which in all likelihood, means that there is no causal connection between coffee drinking and cancer. The difficulty with that conclusion, however, is that coffee may cause some specific kind of cancers and by investigating all cancers, the effect was masked by the large number of cancers that are not affected by coffee drinking. Failure to identify the outcome properly can produce erroneous conclusions. For a case study that concluded that bias is more likely to produce spurious weak associations than confounding, *see* Steven D. Stellman, *Confounding*, 16 PREVENTIVE MED. 165 (1987).

[114] Good measures of nondichotomous confounding factors are required to assure that confounding is adequately controlled. Thus, to account for smoking as a confounder requires consideration of the amount of smoking by study participants. *See* American Health Foundation, *Conference Report on Weak Associations in Epidemiology and Their Interpretation*, 11 PREVENTIVE MED. 464, 471 (1982).

[115] As one prominent epidemiologist explains, "Regardless of how thorough and careful that evaluation [of confounders] may be, uncontrolled confounding remains a candidate hypothesis to explain an observed association or lack of association." Savitz, *supra* note 107, at 160.

[116] *See* Savitz, *supra* note 107, at 144; J. J. Schlesselman, *Assessing Effects of Confounding Variables*. 108 AM. J. EPIDEM. 3 (1978).

[117] The discussion of random error draws on Green, *supra* note 56, at 355–63; Savitz, *supra* note 107, at 243–59.

know that can happen, and we can even determine the probability it will occur in any given test. But if we are conducting a test to determine whether the coin toss is fair or not and get ten straight heads, we don't know if the explanation for the result is an unfair coin toss or sampling error. Similarly, when an epidemiologic study finds a difference in the incidence of disease between an exposed group and an unexposed group, that result might reflect a causal relationship or it might reflect random error. More accurately, some degree of random error affects the outcome, but its extent cannot be known.

As with bias and confounding, random error produces both erroneously higher and lower measures of an association than truly exist. A small association of 1.2 found in a study might understate a true relative risk of 1.5 because of sampling error. Random error might affect a study in the opposite direction, producing an association of .9 despite a true relative risk of 1.2. The likelihood that random error will operate in either direction is equal. Just as the probability is greater that random error will produce seven heads out of ten rather than ten out ten, random error will produce smaller errors more frequently than larger ones. The probability of random error can be reduced (but not eliminated) by increasing the number of subjects in the study; we'd have more confidence that the outcome was not the result of random error if we flipped a coin one hundred times and it resulted in ninety heads than if ten flips produced nine heads. It is worth emphasizing that although random error can be reduced with larger numbers, the other two sources of error, bias and confounding, are unaffected by the size of the sample.[118]

Statistical methods exist to evaluate the likelihood that a result of a study[119] would occur if the true case were that there is no difference between the exposed and unexposed populations, that is, no effect.[120] More sophisticated statistical methods (confidence intervals) exist to enable an evaluation of the range of outcomes that random error may have produced for a given

---

[118] The Fifth Circuit failed to appreciate the independence of bias and confounding on the one hand with random error on the other in *Brock v. Merrell Dow Pharms., Inc.*, 874 F.2d 307, 311–12 (5th Cir. 1989). The court identified the problem of recall bias among women who bear children with birth defects and concluded that to prevent erroneous conclusions about causation, a plaintiff would be required to provide statistically significant epidemiology in order to satisfy the plaintiff's burden of production. Statistical significance testing addresses sampling error only and does nothing to identify or correct errors due to biases or confounding. *See* Michael D. Green, *Expert Witnesses and Sufficiency of Evidence in Toxic Substances Litigation: The Legacy of* Agent Orange *and* Bendectin *Litigation*, 86 Nw. U.L. Rev. 643, 667 (1992).

[119] To be accurate, the likelihood is of the test result or a more extreme result, that is, in the case of a positive association an association of that magnitude or a greater one. I omit this qualification in later discussion of the meaning of this measure.

[120] This is not the same as the probability that an association reflects a truly causal relationship.

study outcome.[121] Those methods are complicated and do not require additional explanation here to appreciate that random error is always present in an unknown but probabilistically-predictable magnitude and that random error is greatest with both small numbers of individuals in a study and a low incidence of disease.

In the end, the best that statistical methods can provide is a tool for an educated researcher to assess the extent to which random error plausibly affected the outcome of the study. Researchers can never know whether the outcome they obtained was biased in one direction or the other and, especially when the result is close to null (i.e., an association of 1.0), whether a positive or negative association is real or an artifact of sampling error.

To summarize, there are many sources of error in an observational study. Many can be avoided or minimized with a rigorous study design that is carefully conducted. Studying larger numbers of subjects reduces random error, but it can never be eliminated. Finally, errors are most likely to have a significant impact when a study finds a small effect.

Epidemiologists are aware of the potential for error; they know that an association is not the same as a causal relationship. Before an inference of causation is drawn from a study (or studies), an assessment of both the likelihood of error and other evidence bearing on causation is examined to determine whether a study's outcome justifies a causal assessment. Sir Austin Bradford Hill catalogued the relevant considerations in an article published in 1965, and they are commonly referred to as the "Hill criteria."[122]

[121] Narrow confidence intervals indicate more robust findings that are likely less influenced by random error than studies with broader confidence intervals.

[122] One formulation of these criteria is:
1. Is the temporal relationship correct? Does the "effect" follow the "cause"?
2. Is there evidence from true experiments in humans?
3. Is the association a strong one?
4. Is the association consistent from study to study?
5. Is there a dose-response gradient?
6. Is the association specific?
7. Does the association make biological sense?
8. Is there an appropriate analogy to other known causal relationships?

See Austin Bradford Hill, *The Environment and Disease: Association or Causation?*, 58 PROC. ROY. SOC. MED. 295 (1965). Another popular form of these guidelines is contained in ADVISORY COMMITTEE TO THE SURGEON GENERAL OF THE PUBLIC HEALTH SERVICE, SMOKING AND HEALTH (USPHS pub. no. 1103, 1964).

For discussion of these criteria and their respective strengths in informing a causal inference, *see* 2 DAVID L. FAIGMAN ET AL., MODERN SCIENTIFIC EVIDENCE § 28–2.2.3 (1997); LEON GORDIS, EPIDEMIOLOGY 176–81 (1996); DAVID E. LILIENFELD & PAUL D. STOLLEY, FOUNDATIONS OF EPIDEMIOLOGY 263–66 (3d ed. 1994); Douglas L. Weed, *Epidemiologic Evidence and Causal Inference*, 14 HEMATOLOGY/ONCOLOGY CLINICS N. Am. 797 (2000). For a definition of and critical inquiry into what is meant by the seventh criterion, biologic

The Hill criteria are employed when a study finds a positive association to assess whether the association is causal or spurious.[123] Judgments about causation necessarily assess the likelihood that any of the sources of error identified above produced the association rather than a true causal relationship. Sometimes the possibility of a bias or uncontrolled confounding factor can be identified, although without a high degree of certainty. Hypothesized specific biases or confounders permit assessment of the direction in which they would skew the association, but a refined assessment of the magnitude by which any bias or confounding would affect the association is almost never possible. The same is true with sampling error. Thus, even if the process of evaluating the outcome of a study to determine if it reflects a true causal relationship is reasonably accurate, there would still be considerable uncertainty about the strength of the causal effect.

Epidemiologists are quite aware of the limits of observational studies and skeptical about studies finding weak results. An article in the widely respected journal *Science* highlights the limits of epidemiology in identifying small increases in risks.[124] Focusing on public misperceptions about risks based on media reports of the outcome of studies, the article chronicles the impediments to finding causal relationships with observational studies that have been catalogued previously. Those sources of error are illustrated in a variety of studies finding small effects that were later determined to be incorrect. Several prominent epidemiologists express concerns that epidemiology's lens is just not sensitive enough to detect small relative risks. Ken Rothman, an influential epidemiologist and the co-author of one of the leading epidemiology texts, capsulizes the situation: "We're pushing the edge of what can be done with epidemiology."[125] A number of others suggest that only relative risks above the range of 2.5 to 3.0 can reasonably be relied on for drawing causal inferences.[126]

---

plausibility, *see* Douglas L. Weed & Stephen D. Hursting, *Biologic Plausibility in Causal Inference: Current Methods and Practice*, 147 AM. J. EPIDEM. 415 (1998) (examining use of this criterion in contemporary epidemiologic research and distinguishing between a plausible hypothesis and one supported by evidence based on molecular biology and molecular epidemiology research).

[123] Error can produce an association that incorrectly suggests that the agent has a protective effect. Such results are usually of little interest in epidemiologic research, as studies are generally conducted because an agent is suspected of causing disease. Although scientists use the null hypothesis as a convention for designing and analyzing a study, rarely are agents studied in which the researchers believe the agent to be noncausal.

[124] Gary Taubes, *Epidemiology Faces its Limits*, 269 SCI. 164 (1995).

[125] *Id.*

[126] *Id.*; *see also* Samuel Shapiro, *Meta-analysis/Shmeta Analysis*, 140 AM. J. EPIDEM. 771, 772 (1994) (contending that meta-analysis can only minimize sampling error, leaving bias and confounding – "[r]elative risks of low magnitude (say, less than 2) are virtually beyond the

IV. THE CASE AGAINST PROPORTIONAL LIABILITY

So where does this discussion leave us with regard to proportional liability? My view is that employing a threshold increase of risk when epidemiology is the predominant source of evidence about causation would appropriately cabin the limits of that discipline. Any threshold employed will be arbitrary in the sense that values somewhat smaller or larger might equally well be justified. I would venture that a threshold relative risk of 2.0 is reasonable in light of the limitations of epidemiology, the concurring views of a number of epidemiologists,[127] and the traditional preponderance of the evidence standard. This threshold, I would emphasize, is about proof of general causation, not specific causation.[128]

The reasons that support a threshold also affect the debate, described above, about the admissibility and sufficiency of studies finding a relative risk of less than 2.0 for specific causation. Although those who advocate permitting use of such studies, along with other evidence specific to the plaintiff, to meet the preponderance standard have a good argument, it misses the difficulty of establishing general causation with studies finding relative risks less than 2.0. In that respect, the RR < 2.0 proponents are crawling out on the same limb as the proportional liability advocates.

Before proceeding with the reasons for a threshold, I would like to clarify that I am not advocating a requirement that a plaintiff must prove causation with an epidemiologic study finding a minimum relative risk of

---

resolving power of the epidemiologic microscope"); N. E. Breslow & N. E. Day, *Statistical Methods in Cancer Research, in* THE ANALYSIS OF CASE-CONTROL STUDIES 36 (IARC Pub. No. 32, Lyon, France 1980) ("[r]elative risks of less than 2.0 may readily reflect some unperceived bias or confounding factor"). Federica P. Perera, *Environment and Cancer: Who Are Susceptible?*, 278 SCI. 1068, 1072 (1997) ("In epidemiology, it has been difficult to detect relative risks of 1.5 or even 2.0."); David A. Freedman & Philip B. Stark, *The Swine Flu Vaccine and Guillain-barré Syndrome: A Case Study in Relative Risk and Specific Causation*, 64 LAW & CONTEMP. PROBS. 49, 60 (2001) ("If the relative risk is near 2.0, problems of bias and confounding in the underlying epidemiologic studies may be serious, perhaps intractable."); Lena Williams, *Stalking the Elusive Healthy Diet; In Scientific Studies, Seeking the Truth in a Vast Gray Area*, N.Y TIMES, Oct. 11, 1995 at C1 (Harvard epidemiologist characterizing epidemiology as "a crude and inexact science").

Biological plausibility is an important criterion for making causal inferences, especially when the increased risk is small. *See, e.g.,* Dmitri Trichopoules, Letter, 269 SCI. 1326(1995). Generally, if there is a good biological-mechanism explanation for a causal relationship, epidemiologists are more willing to judge an association causal. The difficulty is that biological explanations are easy to construct and difficult to judge when the legal system is the one called upon to make the latter assessment.

[127] *See supra* notes 123–25 and accompanying text.

[128] One important implication of this attribution to general causation is that general causation might be established at higher doses than those to which the plaintiff was exposed. *See infra* text accompanying note 144.

2.0. Epidemiology is expensive, can take a long time to conduct, and sometimes, because of the rarity of the disease or the infrequency of exposure,
simply is not capable of determining much of anything.[129] In other instances,
the agent is so powerful that epidemiology is not required in order to determine that a causal relationship exists. Thalidomide is one prominent example.
When epidemiology is absent, examination of the available evidence to determine whether causation exists is more attractive than the alternative, which
is to turn all plaintiffs away for failure to meet their burden of proof.[130] Likewise, the existence of an epidemiology study with a weak association should
not prevent a plaintiff from seeking to show, with other evidence, that an
agent is the cause of her disease. So long as the plaintiff has adequate other
evidence to demonstrate causation, a study finding a weak association should
not prevent that effort. But in these cases the inquiry would be about whether
causation was established by a preponderance of the evidence, not whether
there was a 25 percent probability of causation by a preponderance of the
evidence.

Agents with weak causal effects no doubt exist.[131] I don't know of any
reason to believe they are more or less likely than agents with more powerful

---

[129] This appears to be the situation in the Parlodel litigation. The issue is the role of Parlodel,
a drug prescribed to suppress postpartum lactation, in causing strokes. Because strokes
in the period after pregnancy occur so infrequently (around five per one hundred thousand pregnancies), researchers who conducted an epidemiologic study concluded that they
could not draw any statistically-meaningful conclusions, save that Parlodel did not have
an extraordinarily powerful effect. *See* Kenneth J. Rothman, *An Epidemiologic Evaluation of
the Possible Relation Between Bromocriptine, Puerperal Seizures and Strokes* (Epidemiology
Resources, Inc. Sept. 30, 1988) (discussed in Dunn v. Sandoz Pharms. Corp., 275 F. Supp.
2d 672, 679–80 (M.D.N.C. 2003)). Another example is the prescription drug overdose in
Zuchowicz v. United States, 140 F.3d 381 (2d Cir. 1998). Not only was the overdose unusual
but the plaintiff's disease was a rare one. Animal toxicology evidence would have been quite
persuasive in that case; the court's opinion makes no mention of any such evidence, however.
See also Westberry v. Gislaved Gummi AB, 178 F.3d 257 (4th Cir. 1999) (acute response tested
with dechallenge, rechallenge tests of plaintiff).

[130] *See* Joseph Sanders, *The Merits of the Paternalistic Justification for Restrictions on the Admis-
sibilty of Expert Evidence*, 33 SETON HALL L. REV. 881, 938–39 (2003) ("There is also some
available evidence that courts have been sensitive to the quality of the available evidence
when making admissibility decisions. As better evidence becomes available, courts may
not let experts base opinions on less reliable evidence that would be admissible in another
context").

[131] Indeed, what distinguishes "strong" from "weak" agents is not some inherent quality of the
agent. Rather, its strength is a function of the frequency of occurrence of the other factors that
are required to concur with the agent to cause disease. It is also a function of the frequency
of other causal sets sufficient to cause the disease. *See* Kenneth J. Rothman & Charles Poole,
A Strengthening Program for Weak Associations, 17 INT'L J. EPIDEM. 955, 955–56 (Supp.
1988).

effects.[132] These weak-effect agents are, however, quite difficult for scientists to identify accurately with current investigational methods.

Why employ a bright-line rule when we will screen out a number of true toxic agents? Wouldn't a system that seeks a more refined assessment of the validity of each case – based on informed scientific judgments in light of the Hill criteria, which considers nonepidemiologic evidence – do a better job than a rigid rule? Furthermore, as Part III explained, errors can skew the results of a study in both a positive and negative direction. Thus, might the errors in each direction cancel out, at least from a global perspective? And shouldn't we ease the burden of proof on causation when defendants have tortiously exposed others to these risks?

There are several reasons for my negative response to these inquiries. First, at least in some cases the question of negligence (or strict liability) is not independent of the causal issue. These cases, then, do not involve an already-identified tortfeasor for whom only causation is in question. Second, there is an asymmetry to the way in which a proportional liability scheme would operate. It would have legal consequences for false positive findings of causation but none for the complementary error of incorrectly finding an agent has a protective effect. Even more seriously, the lack of precision in the magnitude of even truly weak causal effects would produce more asymmetry in a proportional liability scheme. Third, the methodology for inferring causation from an association is, because of its vagueness, subjective and judgmental. I am not confident about the legal system's capacity accurately to resolve these scientific judgment calls. Finally, I doubt that any net incremental liability appropriately imposed on defendants based on an informed judgment, proportional liability scheme would have much utility in furthering deterrence goals. In the end, employing a threshold relative risk of 2.0 for general causation would save transaction costs, although not appreciably affecting the deterrence signal provided by tort law. Tort law, like epidemiology, is not capable of imposing liability that is finely calibrated to provide optimal deterrence.

A. The Assumption of Independence of Tortious Conduct and Causation

As I observed at the outset, proportional liability is particularly attractive when the defendant has acted tortiously. Indeed, a variety of legal rules rely

---

[132] One of the Hill criteria considers the strength of the association. That criterion does not mean that weak associations exist less frequently, only that weak associations are less likely to be causal because of the sources of error explained in Section III. Confounding, thus, is most likely to be a problem with small relative risks. Random error will more frequently produce smaller errors than it will larger ones.

on the culpability of a defendant to deal more harshly with those defendants on other, independent issues in the case.[133] Proportional liability advocates make the assumption that the defendants in toxic substances cases have acted culpably, whether or not causation can be established.

That assumption is true in some cases, but in others the issues of culpability and cause are not independent. Consider the Bendectin and the silicone gel breast implant cases. The predominant claim in both of those cases was that the manufacturers should have warned of the dangers of birth defects or connective tissue disease, respectively, or not marketed the product at all. However, if Bendectin was not a teratogen and silicone gel breast implants do not cause connective tissue disease, none of the manufacturers acted tortiously in these respects. Codependence of breach and causation will not always be the case;[134] indeed it was almost certainly not in Bendectin and perhaps not in breast implants because of misconduct in research or marketing or both. Nevertheless, we should be cautious about assuming that proportional liability will always be employed against those defendants who have acted culpably, independently of the causal issue.

B. The Asymmetry of Proportional Liability

Even on fine-tuning terms, the errors that produce mis-estimates of an association are troubling because they will tend to produce excess liability.[135] To illustrate, let us assume an agent that has no causal role with respect to a

---

[133] See Summers v. Tice 199 P.2d 1 (Cal. 1948) (alternative liability); Sindell v. Abbott Labs., 607 P.2d 924 (Cal. 1980) (market-share liability); RESTATEMENT (SECOND) OF TORTS § 433B(2) (1965) (burden of proof on defendants to apportion plaintiff's harm causally among themselves); RESTATEMENT (THIRD) OF TORTS: LIABILITY FOR PHYSICAL HARM (BASIC PRINCIPLES) § 28 cmt. b (Tent. Draft No. 2 2002) ("In tort cases in which the defendant's tortious conduct is clear, many courts are lenient about the plaintiff's proof of causation. . . . ").

[134] See, e.g., Zuchowicz v. United States, 140 F.3d 381 (2d Cir. 1998) (defendants negligently provided 100 percent overdose of drug to plaintiff's decedent); Trach v. Fellin, 2003 WL 282804 (Pa. Super. Ct. 2003) (pharmacy provided incorrect drug in filling prescription). Judge Calabresi in Zuchowicz relied on the defendant's negligence in providing an overdose and that such negligence at least increases the risk of harm to the plaintiff to suggest that the burden of proof be shifted to the defendant on causation. That suggestion seems at least overstated. Defendant's negligence *must* increase the risk of future harm to be negligent; thus, if we take Zuchowicz seriously it would always shift the burden of proof on causation to a defendant who acted negligently.

[135] "[R]elative risk point estimates derived from nonexperimental studies are, by their nature, crude and imprecise. Given the small amounts of bias that it takes to distort such estimates, their expression to more than one decimal place is pseudoprecision." Samuel Shapiro, *Bias in the Evaluation of Low-Magnitude Associations: An Empirical Perspective*, 151 AM. J. EPIDEM. 939, 945 (2000).

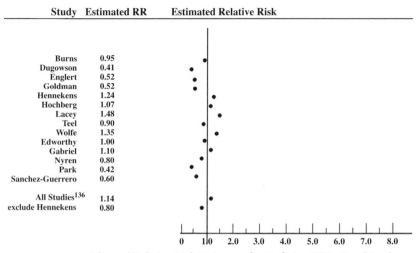

Study	Estimated RR	Estimated Relative Risk
Burns	0.95	
Dugowson	0.41	
Englert	0.52	
Goldman	0.52	
Hennekens	1.24	
Hochberg	1.07	
Lacey	1.48	
Teel	0.90	
Wolfe	1.35	
Edworthy	1.00	
Gabriel	1.10	
Nyren	0.80	
Park	0.42	
Sanchez-Guerrero	0.60	
All Studies[136]	1.14	
exclude Hennekens	0.80	

FIGURE 11.1. Adjusted Relative Risk Estimates for Definite CTDs Combined

specified disease. Some number of errors would occur in studies that examine its toxicity, with smaller ones occurring more frequently than larger ones. I also assume that errors in either direction occur with the same frequency and that the magnitude of those errors in either direction is the same.[136] An example of the sort of scattershot, yet spurious, outcomes that one might find if multiple studies were conducted is revealed in Figures 11.1 and 11.2. These figures are adapted from the Report prepared by the court-appointed experts in the silicone gel breast implant litigation and reflect all epidemiology studies that were located on the connection between silicone gel breast implants and connective tissue disease (Figure 11.1) and rheumatoid arthritis (Figure 11.2).[137]

---

[136] Whether this assumption is correct would require knowing whether biases and confounding errors tend in one direction or the other. It would also require understanding the magnitude of the impact on the association (more to the point, the attributable percentage of risk or protection) of each such error. Thus, for example, when errors are made in disease classification, do they have an equivalent impact on the association when the errors involve differential under and over-counting those with disease. No epidemiologist with whom I have spoken claims any idea about the overall direction of all potential errors.

    Positive and negative errors in the relative risk can not occur with the same magnitude, as the scale for a protective association has a magnitude of 1.0 (from 0.0 to 1.0), while the scale for a positive causal association is infinite. However, the scale for attributable percentage of risk or its complement, the prevented fraction, has the same 100 percent scale. Thus, each increment of relative risk below 1.0 means a greater percentage are protected than the corresponding number are harmed by the same incremental increase in the relative risk above 1.0.

[137] I have simplified the inclusion criteria employed by the experts; the precise criteria are contained in the Report at III-10 to 11. *See* Barbara A. Diamond, et al., SILICONE BREAST

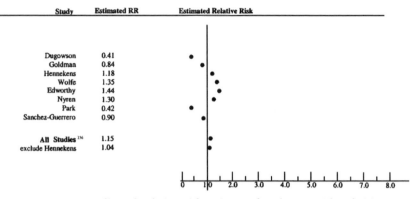

FIGURE 11.2. Adjusted Relative Risk Estimates for Rheumatoid Arthritis

One can see from these figures that the outcomes cluster around the null effect, but deviate small amounts in either direction. If the outcomes reflect small errors instead of real effects – as one might suspect from looking at the overall dispersal of results – errors that overstate and find a positive association will always result in excess damages being imposed in a proportional liability regime.[138] Yet that excess liability will not be cancelled by errors that occur in the opposite direction. Defendants are not provided a credit for protective associations – indeed they are not involved in lawsuits when the evidence suggests a protective effect.[139]

This asymmetry in imposing excess liability is not limited to agents having no causal role. It occurs whenever the magnitude of the error in a study is greater than the true increase in risk. Once again, assume an agent has a true causal effect and an accurate relative risk of 1.11. Proportional liability would result in damages of 10 percent of full damages. Now, let us suppose that an

---

IMPLANTS IN RELATION TO CONNECTIVE TISSUE DISEASE AND IMMUNOLOGIC DYSFUNC-
TION: A REPORT BY A NATIONAL SCIENCE PANEL TO THE HONORABLE SAM C. POINTER
JR., COORDINATING JUDGE FOR THE FEDERAL BREAST IMPLANT MULTI-DISTRICT
LITIGATION (undated), available at <http://www.fjc.gov/BREIMLIT/SCIENCE/report.
htm>. See also Esther C. Janowsky et al., Meta-Analysis of the Relation Between Silicone
Breast Implants and the Risk of Connective-Tissue Diseases, 342 N. ENG. J. MED. 781 (2004).

[138] So long as the erroneous association is greater than 1.0. That is, an exaggerated association
that still remains below 1.0 will not result in liability improperly being imposed.

[139] See, e.g., Jun Zheng, The Puzzling Association Between Smoking and Hypertension During
Pregnancy, 181 AM. J. OBSTET. GYNECOL. 1407 (1999) (finding that smoking during pregnancy had a substantial protective effect against hypertension and preeclampsia, a condition
in pregnancy characterized by high blood pressure and fluid retention that leads to swelling);
Hilary Klonorr-Cohen, Sharon Edelstein & David Savitz, Cigarette Smoking and Preeclampsia, 81 OBSTET. & GYNECOL. 541 (1993) (similar findings for preeclampsia).

error produces a relative risk exaggerated to 1.41. Proportional liability would impose liability for 29 percent of full damages or 19 percent in erroneous damages. By contrast, an error in the opposite direction can, at most, result in a 10 percent underassessment of damages.

Although less severe, a similar problem exists for the RR < 2.0 advocates. Errors that overstate the association when there is none *may* be the basis for damages being incorrectly imposed on the defendant. But complementary errors in the opposite direction – that is, finding a protective effect when there is none – do not result in a compensating entry in the damages balance sheet on behalf of defendants. I'd expect this asymmetry to be most pronounced with small relative risks right above and below 1.0, the former of which are the target of the RR < 2.0 advocates. Of course, even with a threshold relative risk of 2.0 for general causation, instances in which the error in a study was greater than the increased risk would produce excess liability, although this should occur far less frequently. Even when it does, because the magnitude of error is substantial, both epidemiologists and the legal system should have a better chance of recognizing that error.

Thus, the courts that have insisted on a threshold relative risk of 2.0 may be right but for the wrong reason.[140] The justification for a threshold relative risk is with regard to general causation not because of specific causation, the ground relied on by courts that require it. If we were otherwise persuaded that the agent is capable of causing the disease in question, there are a number of reasons why, even under the preponderance standard, a plaintiff might successfully establish specific causation despite studies that find less than a doubling of risk.[141] The Third Restatement, which sides with the RR < 2 advocates, recognizes that general causation remains a matter of concern and is reflected (if in understated fashion) in its qualification that "[s]o long as there is adequate evidence of general causation," imposing a threshold relative risk requirement for proof of specific causation is inappropriate.[142]

An important implication of this focus on a threshold for general causation is that if good evidence of general causation exists, specific causation should be based on the available evidence bearing on the probability of causation for that individual.[143] Thus, consider a study finding that exposure to an agent

---

[140] *See supra* note 59.

[141] *See supra* notes 63–64.

[142] Restatement (Third) of Torts: Liability for Physical Harm § 28 cmt. c (4) (Tentative Draft No. 3, 2003).

[143] Thus, Samuel Shapiro, an epidemiologist, who had previously expressed doubts about the validity of small relative risks (those below 2.0), *see* Shapiro, *supra* note 125, at 772, later acknowledged that lower relative risks might well be interpreted as causal if studies found

at a specified dose has a relative risk of five, and an inference of causation is appropriate. When a plaintiff who has been exposed to only a fraction of the dose in the study sues, we should make our best estimate of whether the plaintiff's disease was caused by the agent regardless of any epidemiology for doses at the level to which the plaintiff was exposed and the relative risk determined in any such study.[144]

C. Variance in Judgments About Whether an Inference of Causation is Appropriate

As Section III explained, epidemiologists recognize the risk of error in the outcome of observational studies. The Hill criteria are employed to assess whether a positive association reflects a true causal relationship or a spurious one. This entails consideration of the likelihood of methodological errors previously discussed and estimation of the direction and the magnitude of any such errors as well as consideration of evidence extrinsic to the study, such as other epidemiologic and toxicologic (animal) studies. Biologic

---

greater risks at higher doses. *See* Samuel Shapiro, *Is There Is or Is There Ain't No Baby: Dr. Shapiro Replies to Drs. Pettiti and Greenland*, 140 AM J. EPIDEM. 788, 790 (1994).

[144] *See Tompkin v. Philip Morris USA, Inc.*, 2004 WL 614514 (6th Cir. 2004) (defense expert testified that smoker's relative risk for lung cancer was 1.59 based on modest history of smoking and that a minimum relative risk of 2.0 is required before even an association exists). The defense expert was wrong about when an association exists, but he might have meant that associations below 2.0 are too unreliable to be the basis for a causal inference. Yet, precisely here, where we know very well that higher doses of smoking are a cause of lung cancer, we might well give legal effect to the 1.56 relative risk.

These extrapolations of risk from higher doses are complicated by uncertainty about the shape of the dose-response curve and whether there is a threshold of exposure required to cause disease at all. The current thinking is that the shape and threshold for the dose-response curve is different for different agents and diseases and the biological mechanisms involved. *See* Edward J. Calabrese & Linda A. Baldwin, *The Hormetic Dose-Response Model Is More Common than the Threshold Model in Toxicology*, 71 TOXICOLOGICAL SCI. 246 (2003) (arguing that a hormetic response (beneficial effect at lower doses with toxic effects only occurring at higher doses) occurs more frequently than thresholds); Marvin Goldman, *Cancer Risk of Low-Level Exposure*, 271 SCI.1821 (1996) (discussing research that suggests cancer does not follow a linear dose-response curve and that a zero-threshold assumption might no longer be supported by the evidence, at least in some cases); Bruce N. Ames, Renae Magaw & Lois Swirsky Gold, *Ranking Possible Carcinogenic Hazards*, 236 SCI. 271 (1987) (arguing that animal toxicology studies that support no threshold cannot be extrapolated to humans); COMMITTEE ON THE INSTITUTIONAL MEANS FOR ASSESSMENT OF RISKS TO PUBLIC HEALTH, NATIONAL RESEARCH COUNCIL, RISK ASSESSMENT IN THE FEDERAL GOVERNMENT: MANAGING THE PROCESS 25 (1983) (identifying five alternative models for dose-response relationships but recognizing that different ones will be more appropriate based on the underlying biologic mechanism by which disease develops).

mechanism evidence can be particularly helpful when it exists, as it does for traumatic injury – we know pretty well the way in which the forces generated in an automobile collision break bones. Other studies conducted with independent study designs are not likely to be subject to the same biases. No doubt some situations exist in which the basis for an inference of causation is quite persuasive despite a weak association. In a greater number, the propriety of the inference will not be so clear, but we would have some confidence in the ability of a jury of epidemiologists to reach reasonably accurate determinations.[145]

I am not nearly as confident that the legal system can make accurate assessments of general causation or the magnitude of the effect based on weak associations. Most significant is the nature of the determination – the Hill criteria are unweighted factors;[146] no algorithm or empirical method exists for employing them. Judgment is required as to the appropriate weight for each of the factors based on the characteristics of the specific study and causal relationship being examined.[147] Even reasonable scientists can (and do) reach different conclusions about whether an inference of causation is appropriate.[148]

As Section III explained, there are many reasons why a study's relative risk will deviate from the true relative risk. Even if we were confident that the study reflected a true causal relationship, experts engaged in adjusting a study's true increase in risk based on their assessment of the errors identified in Part III,

---

[145] That assessment, however, must be qualified by the system in which scientists operate. They are free to, and often do, conclude that the evidence doesn't support a causal inference but instead requires further study. In the legal system, such a judgment results in a verdict against the party with the burden of proof.

[146] An exception is the first factor, requiring that the effect occur after the causal agent. That is a necessary but not sufficient condition for a causal inference.

[147] See, e.g., Kenneth J. Rothman, Causation and Causal Inference, in DAVID SCHOTTENFELD & JOSEPH F. FRAUMENI, CANCER EPIDEMIOLOGY AND PREVENTION 21 (1982) ("No rule exists, however, to weigh the extent to which the evidence conforms to these criteria, nor is there any formal method by which one criterion can be weighted relative to the other. Ultimately, causal inference is an informal, rather than a rigorous, judgment."); American Health Foundation, Conference Report on Weak Associations in Epidemiology and Their Interpretation, 11 PREVENTIVE MED. 464, 465 (1982) ("When weak associations are observed, there will always remain areas of doubt requiring the application of judgment and experience before final conclusions can be drawn.").

[148] A meeting arranged by the Science, Technology and Law Program of the National Academy of Sciences on January 21, 2002, about the Third Restatement of Tort's treatment of toxic causation emphasized the lack of rigor in application of the Hill criteria. A transcript of that meeting is available at <http://www7.nationalacademies.org/stl/ALL_Transcript.pdf>. See also Douglas Weed, Epidemiologic Evidence and Causal Inference, 14 HEMATOLOGY/ONCOLOGY CLINICS N. AM. 797 (2000).

their magnitude, and direction would, I expect, often yield widely varying estimates, given the extent of judgment entailed.

When the legal system addresses these questions, several impediments to accurate assessments exist. The experts who appear in court have been culled to find the ones most supportive of the side that calls them. Parties are free to canvass the available experts to find ones whose judgments are most favorable to their position.[149] Because of the judgmental process required for causal assessments, experts are more likely to be affected by their own biases and worldviews, resulting in a wider range of opinion than would exist when more rigorous methods exist. The adversarial system also produces pressure on testifying experts to state their opinions more strongly, to eliminate or understate qualifications, and otherwise to express stronger opinions on behalf of the party retaining the expert than the expert might express in a professional forum.[150] Moreover, because parties are often limited in the number of experts they are permitted to call on any issue, the jury often fails to appreciate when one expert is testifying contrary to mainstream scientific thought.[151]

The enhanced role of the judge in reviewing expert witness testimony as the result of *Daubert v. Merrell Dow Pharmaceutical, Inc.*[152] is a possible remedy for at least some of the concerns about the adversarially-induced excesses of expert testimony.[153] Judicial opinions that confront epidemiology today demonstrate a considerably more sophisticated understanding of epidemiologic methods generally than they did before the *Daubert* gatekeeping era dawned. Yet, asking judges to examine the reasoning of experts employing an uncontroversial method, albeit an unstructured one requiring informed judgment, is a considerably more demanding task. This is especially so in the arena of the strength of the biological mechanism evidence, which can

---

[149] *See* Samuel R. Gross, *Expert Evidence*, 1991 WIS. L. REV. 1113.

[150] *See* Sander Greenland, *The Need for Critical Appraisal of Expert Witnesses in Epidemiology and Statistics*, 39 WAKE FOREST L. REV. 291 (2004). The author, a prominent epidemiologist who has served as an expert witness, notes "the all-too-human tendency of experts to feel obligated (or to be manipulated) to frame the evidence favorably for their client." *See also* Sanders, *supra* note 129, at 916–22 (discussing different biases of expert witnesses, including those induced by the role that experts play in an adversary system); *cf.* Mike Redmayne, *Expert Evidence and Scientific Disagreement*, 30 U.C. (DAVIS) L. REV. 1027, 1071 & n. 180 (1997) (explaining influence of legal disputes on scientific experts' activities out of court).

[151] *See* Joseph Sanders, *From Science to Evidence: the Testimony on Causation in the Bendectin Cases* 46 STAN. L. REV. 1 (1993).

[152] 509 U.S. 579 (1993).

[153] That *Daubert* has made a difference – whether it has improved the accuracy of outcomes is a different matter – in federal courts is documented in a recent Rand Institute study. *See* LLOYD DIXON & BRIAN GILL, CHANGES IN THE STANDARDS FOR ADMITTING EXPERT EVIDENCE IN FEDERAL CIVIL CASES SINCE THE *DAUBERT* DECISION (2001).

vary from rank speculation to well supported by other scientific methods.[154] And unlike general empirical epidemiologic methods, this assessment almost always entails a specific biological question for which judges will have little in the way of an established methodology as guidance.

D. The Crudity of Tort Law

The final reason for doubting the benefit of proportional liability is the matter of its potential to enhance deterrence. As related in Section II, many of the proportional advocates argue that deterrence would be enhanced by adopting proportionate liability. We could, after all, have a weak agent that causes a great deal of harm because many are exposed to it. Even if, as seems more plausible, there is more modest exposure, defendants whose agents cause less than a doubling of disease would be free to continue selling their products without the deterrent incentives that tort law provides.

The law and economics literature is replete with suggestions for making marginal improvements in tort law to fine-tune the deterrence it provides. The idea is that if actors bear just the right amount of liability for the harm that they cause, we will reach an optimal balance between accident costs and prevention costs. In an influential article, the late Gary Schwartz canvassed the theoretical and empirical literature on the tort system's deterrence signal.[155] His conclusion, which has been quite influential among torts scholars, is that while tort law does have an impact on socially detrimental conduct, it falls substantially short of providing the optimal deterrence that economists sometimes assume, especially in their efforts to tweak the tort system to move it marginally closer to that goal.[156] The real world is far too messy, infected with error, and the tort system plagued by under- and overenforcement for

---

[154] *See* Transcript of Meeting, *supra* note 148. Even well-accepted understandings of biologic mechanisms can be incorrect. In the middle part of the Twentieth Century, the belief that chemicals did not cross the placental barrier resulted in ignoring the possibility of reproductive toxicity when a drug was provided to a pregnant woman. That understanding contributed to the Thalidomide calamity – Thalidomide never underwent any reproductive toxicity testing before it was marketed and promoted as a sedative for pregnant women. *See* Henning Sjöström & Robert Nilsson, Thalidomide and the Power of the Drug Companies (Harmondsworth: Penguin, 1972); The Insight Team of the Sunday Times, Suffer the Children: The Story of Thalidomide (London: Andre Deutsch, 1979). A more recent example of an apparently-erroneous understanding about the mechanism by which anemia affects cancer treatment is revealed in Denise Grady, *Anemia Drug May Impair Some Cancer Treatments*, NY Times, Oct. 17, 2003, at A22.

[155] Gary T. Schwartz, *Reality in the Economic Analysis of Tort Law: Does Tort Law Really Deter?*, 42 UCLA L. Rev. 377 (1994).

[156] *Id.* at 444.

tort law to provide a liability signal precisely calibrated to the costs of accidents worth avoiding.

Aside from whether fine-tuning is worthwhile, there is reason to believe that the current system does not systematically underdeter. The preponderance standard imposes excess liability on toxic substances defendants who are found liable because those defendants must pay damages for all victims exposed to their agent. Except in the case of signature agents, some of the disease is not the result of the defendant's agent. Whether there is any balance, however rough, between this excess liability and the liability that a preponderance rule incorrectly fails to impose is impossible to know. But that is true for manufacturers and other enterprises responsible for toxic substances. The same uncertainties involved in the determination of weak toxic agents along with the severe consequences of being wrong about whether an agent will cause less than a doubling of disease make it implausible that reliance on the preponderance standard to engage in socially inappropriate behavior with a toxic agent would be an attractive or rational strategy.[157]

V. CONCLUSION

The common-law principle that liability is unitary and cannot be divided or apportioned has long been abandoned. Contribution became widely accepted in the middle of the Twentieth Century, albeit on a pro rata basis. More fine-grained apportionment was accepted as comparative responsibility replaced contributory fault. Although finding less overwhelming support, both market-share liability and loss of opportunity have gained significant traction in tort law in the United States. All of these developments rely on carving up liability and apportioning it and, at least in the market-share realm, basing it on the probability of causation.

Despite a strong scholarly consensus, proportional liability has failed to establish a foothold in the courts.[158] Indeed, the courts' failure to adopt proportional liability has occurred without any serious engagement with the

---

[157] See David A. Fischer, *Proportional Liability: Statistical Evidence and the Probability Paradox*, 46 VAND. L. REV. 1201 (1993) (explaining that the proportional risk created by a defendant and hence the probability of causation is a function of how many other potential causes of the disease exist and that those can change over time).

[158] See DAVID A. FISCHER ET AL., PRODUCTS LIABILITY 443 (3d ed. 2002). The best evidence of this rejection is the alternative course that courts have taken when confronted with studies finding a relative risk below 2.0. The terms of the debate over that issue – whether such studies can ever be the basis for a plaintiff meeting her burden of proof on causation – reveals the courts' commitment to an all-or-nothing resolution of causation in these cases. See supra notes 55–72 and accompanying text. But see supra text accompanying note 31.

numerous scholarly entreaties on its behalf. Perhaps most curiously, courts have embraced one of the proposals by David Rosenberg – the acceptance of naked statistical evidence as proof of causation in toxic substances cases – while ignoring his proposal for proportional liability in the very same seminal article on this subject.[159]

What does the lack of engagement to date mean for the future of proportional liability? I would venture that there is good reason for the courts' unwillingness to adopt a proportional liability scheme in the toxics arena. Although courts have not articulated it, the devil is often in the details, and the proportional liability advocates have not attended to those details. At least in the toxic substances arena, the quality of the evidence on which proportional liability would rely just isn't up to the standard required of it. Epidemiology, limited as it is to observational methods, is too fraught with error to provide the fine-grained probabilistic data needed for a well-functioning proportional liability scheme.[160]

Increased risk as a compensable harm is another possibility for employing a proportional liability scheme and an alternative that some have championed to the *ex post* proportional recovery proposals discussed above in Part II.[161] Here, we should distinguish those agents and diseases for which there is good evidence of general causation from the weak associations addressed in this chapter. The relative risk of a toxic agent is determined by the number of competing causes and the proportion of disease that they cause. The risk that those exposed to that toxic agent will contract the disease is a different matter and determined by the prevalence of the other necessary factors that must concur with the agent to result in the disease. Thus, a toxic agent may have a

---

[159] The failure of courts to adopt a proportional liability of the form advocated by the legal academy could simply be a result of inertia. Perhaps we can at least attribute it to a certain conservatism borne of appreciation that what you see is considerably less than what you get. Proportional liability, at least based on epidemiology, just isn't ready for the Twenty-First Century.

[160] Outside the disease realm, there may be cases in which a sufficiently good understanding of the causal mechanism exists to satisfy concerns about general causation. Indeed, in many traumatic injury cases with uncertain specific causation, causal mechanisms are well enough understood to find general causation. Consider the classic case of the victim who falls down a negligently unlit staircase. See *Wolf v. Kaufman*, 237 N.Y.S. 550 (App. Div. 1929). We can be sure that the lack of light causes some increase in the number of falls (general causation). The difficulty with these cases is that we rarely have anything useful with regard to the relative incidence of the agent (lack of light) and other causes of staircase falls, such as clumsiness. See also Aaron Twerski & Anthony J. Sebok, *Liability Without Cause? Further Ruminations on Cause-in-Fact as Applied to Handgun Liability*, 32 CONN. L. REV. 1379 (2000) (addressing general and specific causation issues in litigation over negligent marketing of handguns).

[161] *See generally* Andrew R. Klein, *A Model for Enhanced Risk Recovery in Tort*, 56 WASH. & LEE L. REV. 1173 (1999).

substantial relative risk – one about which we are confident of causality – but only modestly increase the risk of disease in those exposed.[162] There are other considerations in whether to recognize increased risk as a compensable injury, but the concerns expressed in this chapter are not among them.[163] Whether to permit a plaintiff who suffers from one disease to recover for the probability that she will contact another disease in the future when that probability is less than 50 percent raises a similar issue. As with increased risk there may be good evidence about the general causal role between the exposure for which the defendant is responsible and the future disease – or there may not be. But that is an independent question from the magnitude of the probability of contracting the disease in the future.

There are some additional implications worth mentioning. If epidemiology isn't capable of supporting a proportional liability scheme for agent-disease causation, other appropriate applications of *ex post* proportional liability may be rare. In what other contexts will we have reliable information about the general probabilities involved? Market-share liability, at least in the case of products with generic risks for which there is a substantial market, may provide reasonably accurate data by which to apportion liability as was done with DES. But there haven't been many more appropriate invocations of market-share liability in the quarter century since it was born in *Sindell v. Abbott Laboratories*.[164] Surely not in the case of a plaintiff who falls down a landowner's unlit staircase.[165] I wonder about the quality of evidence employed even in medical malpractice lost-opportunity cases.[166] Perhaps there is reliable data in some of these cases,[167] but surely the incidence of failures or delays in treatment due to malpractice outpace the available

---

[162] Thus, smokers have a relative risk of somewhere around 20 for contracting lung cancer, a very substantial increased risk. But their lifetime probability of contracting lung cancer is only 20 percent. *See* Diane Prager et al., *Bronchogenic Carcinoma, in* II Textbook of Respiratory Medicine 1415, 1415 (John F. Murray et al., eds., 3d ed. 2000).

[163] Andy Klein, who has tentatively endorsed recognition of increased risk as a compensable harm, would condition recovery for such a claim to those who can show that their risk was doubled by the exposure. *See* Andrew R. Klein, *A Model for Enhanced Risk Recovery in Tort*, 56 Wash. & Lee L. Rev. 1173 (1999). Professor Klein bases this limitation on corrective justice and administrative feasibility grounds. This chapter suggests that such a limitation is also justified on deterrence grounds.

[164] 607 P.2d 924 (Cal. 1980). On the lack of other invocations of market share, *see* Restatement (Third) of Torts: Liability for Physical Harm § 28 cmt. o (Tentative Draft No. 2, 2002).

[165] *See, e.g., Wolf v. Kaufman*, 237 N.Y.S. 550 (N.Y. App. Div. 1929).

[166] Those cases rarely reveal the source of an expert's testimony about the probabilities involved.

[167] *See* Mark A. Hall et al., *Measuring Medical Practice Patterns: Sources of Evidence from Health Services Research*, 37 Wake Forest L. Rev. 779 (2002) (canvassing sources of data available for health services research).

information. Moreover, lost opportunity is not limited to the medical mal-practice context; it could be applied to a wide variety of activities in which an available, but omitted, precaution would have reduced the risk of harm suffered by another.[168] Thus, failures to warn or to employ other safety equipment could be characterized as lost opportunity cases, albeit ones in which I suspect there is very little statistical evidence about the probabilities. We should be cautious about employing legal rules to do more than the available data permits.

[168] *See* David A. Fischer, *Tort Recovery for Loss of a Chance*, 36 WAKE FOREST L. REV. 605 (2001).

TORTS IN A SHRINKING WORLD

CHAPTER TWELVE

CAUSATION IN PRODUCTS LIABILITY AND EXPOSURE TO TOXIC SUBSTANCES: A EUROPEAN VIEW

Federico Stella

ABSTRACT. European nations have yet to elaborate a developed body of decisional law, individually or collectively, in the subject matters of toxic torts and products liability. In the final decades of the twentieth century, European countries, and Italy particularly, were confronted with a surge of criminal litigation that placed in question whether the obstacles to proving individual causation have been overcome by the expedient of replacing the notion of *condicio sine qua non*, or but for causation, with the standard of risk elevation. Beginning in 2000, in Italy and elsewhere, courts took this different tack. There followed, however, an influential decision of the Italian Supreme Court that held that simple risk elevation would not suffice to prove individual causation in criminal prosecutions. Rather, the prosecution would be required to prove not only "but for" cause, but also sustain that burden beyond a reasonable doubt. The high bar established by the Italian court has been implemented in numerous holdings by inferior courts.

At the same time, in an increasing number of Italian universities, professors of civil liability systems have begun to teach the evidentiary and doctrinal approaches used by U.S. civil courts. The effect has been to make clear that toxic torts and products liability ought not be considered a part of criminal law, but instead should be discussed and litigated in civil trials, pursuant to the preponderance of the evidence standard. Should this development continue, the salutary effect of Italy's employment of U.S. tort model can only increase in the future, particularly in light of the Restatement (Third) of Torts to traditional causation standards.

I. THE HOMOGENIZATION OF THE ANGLO-AMERICAN AND EUROPEAN CONTINENTAL LEGAL SYSTEMS

I can only agree with the statement that in the era of globalization the differences, often meaningful, between the European and the Anglo-American legal concepts are getting increasingly blurred. This is to say, today any form of isolationism in developed countries such as those in Europe, or the

Federico Stella, Professor of Criminal Law, Universita' Cattolica of Milan.

403

United States, turns out to be completely out of date. It therefore becomes necessary to follow the same path of "universalization" aimed at in the past by ancient Roman law. For this approach to succeed, people who practice with legal concepts, both in Europe and in the United States, need to become aware of the differences between the two legal systems (common law and civil law), and the consequences that follow from those differences. Only through this awareness will the two legal systems overcome avoidable incongruities that are at odds with the process of homogenization of the several legal cultures.[1]

One of the most important targets of this new challenge is the interpretation of causation, particularly in products liability and liability for exposure to toxic substance cases. This chapter discusses the evolution of European tort cases treating such subjects, and concludes with some suggestions for changes to the ongoing process of the Restatement (Third) of Torts.

II. PRODUCTS LIABILITY

The enormous difference between Anglo-American and European decisional law is quite evident in the area of products liability. In European countries, sustaining the burden of proving causation in a criminal trial is extraordinarily difficult, as prosecutors must, as must their U.S. counterparts, prove all elements of the *prima facie* case beyond a reasonable doubt. This burden of proof constitutes a strong disincentive for European litigants to try cases involving injuries caused by defective products or by exposure to toxic substances as counts in a criminal complaint. At the same time, it is at least a partial reason why in the American legal system, products liability cases are brought in tort, either in the form of individual or class actions. The attractiveness of the "more likely than not" standard of civil litigation is coupled with other incentives, such as, upon certain showings, the shifting of the burden of proof, the availability, albeit limited, of market share liability, and the general adoption of the cost internalization premises of enterprise liability.[2] Within this relatively inviting legal environment, claimants enjoy more of a level playing field with corporate defendants, and are able to secure verdicts in circumstances that would be impossible in criminal trials.

---

[1] About the homogenization of the cultures and the existence of a "deep structure" of all systems of criminal law, *see* George P. Fletcher, Basic Concepts of Criminal Law 3 *et seq.* (1988).

[2] On the exemptions to the more likely than not standard *see* Fred O. Harris Jr., *Toxic Tort Litigation and the Causation Element: Is There Any Hope of Reconciliation?*, 40 Sw. L. J. 909, 964 (1986); *see also* Gerald W. Boston, M. Stuart Madden, The Law of Environmental and Toxic Torts (2d) 339 *et seq.* (1990); David Rosenberg, *The Causal Connection in Mass Exposure Cases: a "Public Law" Vision of the Tort System*, 97 Harv. L. Rev. 851 (1984).

Further to the uncertain future of application of criminal trial standards to products liability suits, in European countries,[3] in criminal trials the presumption of innocence and the "beyond any reasonable doubt" standards have been frequently undermined by the courts. Nevertheless, many national constitutions in Europe, including that of Italy, have reaffirmed the presumption of innocence standard.[4] In September 2002, the Italian Supreme Court[5] held that the "beyond any reasonable doubt" standard lies at the foundation of criminal trial, although the highest courts of other European countries remain silent on the same issue. Equally unsettling, even though the commentators unanimously believe that this standard represents a fundamental principle of civil trials,[6] in European civil law, the "more probable than not" standard has never been genuinely effective.

Increasingly, however, certain courts trying products liability cases have put aside the traditional model of criminal liability based on individual causation. As importantly, several courts have also dispatched with the concept of what is called *condicio sine qua non*, or "but for" causation. These criminal courts, particularly in Germany and Spain, have adopted the idea that the proof of general causation is sufficient to establish criminal liability. This judicial trend begun in 1971, when the Territorial Court of Aachen[7] in Germany rendered the famous decision about the birth defects arising from the use of the drug Contergan.[8] Scientists and academicians strongly

---

[3] WILLIAM BLACKSTONE, COMMENTARIES ON THE LAWS OF ENGLAND 352 (1796), quoted in *Coffin v. United States*, 156 U.S. 432 (1895) (espousing the maxim that it is better that ten guilty persons escape than one innocent suffer).

[4] *See, e.g.*, the Italian CONST. art. 27 co. 2 ("the accused is to be considered innocent until the final sentence of conviction"), which the commentators have concluded means that there is no burden of proof on the accused and the presumption *in dubio pro reo* stands in favor of him.

[5] Italian Supreme Court, United Sections, 11.9.2002, RIVISTA ITALIANA DI DIRITTO E PROCEDURA PENALE, 2002, 1133 *et seq.*

[6] MICHELE TARUFFO, LA PROVA DEI FATTI GIURIDICI 271 *et seq.* (Milano, 1982).

[7] Territorial Court (Landgerichte) of Aachen, 18.12.1970, JURISTENZEITUNG, 1971, 510 *et seq.*

[8] The drug in the United States was marketed under the label of Kevadon. In September 1960, Richardson-Merrell Co. petitioned the Food and Drug Administration to obtain the license for distribution. The FDA requested additional documentation because the first studies on the drug reported cases of birth defects and multiple neuritis in babies whose mothers took Kevadon during pregnancy. In November 1961, Contergan was withdrawn from the market in Germany and, subsequently, the producer asked the FDA to withdraw the petition. For a detailed account of the Thalidomide trial, *see* HENNING SJÖSTRÖM & ROBERT NILSSON, THALIDOMIDE AND THE POWER OF THE DRUG COMPANIES (Hammondsworth 1972); FEDERICO STELLA, LEGGI SCIENTIFICHE E SPIEGAZIONE CAUSALE NEL DIRITTO PENALE (2D) 22 *et seq.*, 175 *et seq.* (2000); FEDERICO STELLA, GIUSTIZIA E MODERNITÀ (3D) 227 *et seq.* (2003); MANFRED MAIWALD, KAUSALITÄT UND STRAFRECHT. STUDIEN ZUM VERHÄLTNIS VON NATURWISSENSCHAFT UND JURISPRUDENZ 91 *et seq.* (Göttingen, 1980); LOTHAR KUHLEN, FRAGEN EINER STRAFRECHTLICHEN PRODUKTHAFTUNG 3, 175, 190 *et seq* (Heidelberg, 1989).

disagreed as to its teratenogenic effects, particularly in evaluating the meaning of the statistical inferences arising from the relationship between birth defects and patient ingestion of the product. The German Court stated the principle of "general causation," by which it meant a standard that assessed the *capability* of the product to cause birth defects and damages to the central nervous system. The Court reasoned that proof of causation, in criminal trials, need not be "scientific," because the criminal Court may infer the general capability of the product in causing physical damages from its *intime conviction*, even in the absence of the scientific studies that would suffice to prove the two necessary showings in United States courts: (1) general causation; and (2) specific causation. Paradoxically, the Contergan case was dismissed before being examined on its merits, because of a particular rule of German criminal procedure that allows the dismissal of the case following recovery or payment of damages by the defendant.

The decision was criticized by German commentators, such as Armin Kaufmann,[9] who explained that because causation is connected with the idea of deterministic causal laws, which are universally recognized, general causation and statistical frequencies cannot be considered as adequate standards in order to establish criminal liability.[10] Nevertheless, this criticism was not heard and the approach of the Aachen Court was followed by the Court of Appeals of Frankfurt and by the German Supreme Court (Bundesgerichtshof) in two other notable cases, in 1990.[11]

In the first case, the issue was whether a particular form of lung cancer (adenoma) could be causally related to the use of a leather spray. Despite the lack of scientific knowledge of the possible negative effects of the substances used in the product, the German Supreme Court (Bundesgerichtshof) rendered a verdict for the state against the accused, stating that this knowledge within the scientific community was not necessary, since it had been shown that the raw materials used in the product were capable of causing toxic effects in consumers.[12]

---

[9] Armin Kaufmann, *Tatbestandmässigkeit und Verursachung im Conterganverfahren*, in JURISTENZEITUNG 569 *et seq* (1971).

[10] *See also* MANFRED MAIWALD, KAUSALITÄT UND STRAFRECHT, 91 *et seq.*

[11] German Supreme Court (Bundesgerichtshof), NEUE JURISTISCHE WOCHENSCHRIFT, 1990, 2560 *et seq.*; Territorial Court (Landgerichte) of Frankfurt, NEUE ZEITSCHRIF FÜR STRAFRECHT, 1990, 592 *et seq.*

[12] *See*, e.g., WINFRIED HASSEMER, PRODUKTVERANTWORTUNG IN MODERNEN STRAFRECHT 32 (Heidelberg 1996); Lothar Kuhlen, *Strafhaftung bei unterlassenem Rückruf gesund heit-gefährdender Produkte*, NEUE ZEITSCHRIFT FÜR STRAFRECHT 556 *et seq* (1990); FEDERICO STELLA, GIUSTIZIA E MODERNITÀ 227 *et seq.*

In the second case, the Frankfurt Court of Appeals faced an issue of whether wood preservatives generally used in the construction industry, could be considered the origin of health-related damages to the claimants. Notwithstanding the scientific uncertainty about general causation in this case, the Court of Appeals wrote that the scientific methods of proving cause and effect differ from methods used by the judges (both in criminal and in civil tort cases) and, therefore, even scientific uncertainty about general causation should not prevent judges from concluding that specific causation has been proven in a particular litigation.[13]

The principle derived from these German decisions is that the plaintiff may prove causation by a demonstration that the product or process was "capable" of causing injury to humans. It has subsequently been adopted by several other European Courts. For example, in the leading case on rapeseed oil,[14] the Spanish Supreme Court, after recognizing the lack of scientific proof of specific causation, affirmed that for a criminal conviction it is enough to prove general causation.

The academic world promptly reacted against these decisions. In Germany, Winfried Hassemer criticized the negation, by the German Supreme Court, of the maxim *in dubio pro reo* and that court's promotion of the idea that general causation is sufficient to establish specific causation. In the history of German criminal law, Hassemer argued, criminal liability had always been based on specific causation on the assumption that the defendant's conduct must be *condicio sine qua non* of the harm caused. Therefore, *condicio sine qua non*, or specific causation, cannot be put aside in favor of general causation, Hassemer wrote, because the latter represents a poor and potentially misleading standard to prove causation, and conclusions based upon a naked statistical showing of risk elevation result, in fact, in the judge "groping in the dark." Similar criticisms were formulated by Josè Paredes in Spain against a decision of the Spanish Supreme Court.[15]

These decisions in German and Spanish case law illustrate symptoms of a profound crisis in the administration of criminal justice in Europe, particularly when law courts in such civil law countries are applying, or purporting to apply, criminal law standards of causation to product defect or toxic exposure claims. As demonstrated earlier, the focal points of this crisis are: (a) the

---

[13] *See* Winfried Hassemer, Produktverantwortung im modernen Strafrecht, *supra*, note 12 at 34.

[14] TS 23 April 1992, A 6783, quoted in Enrique Gimbernat Ordeig, La omissiòn impropria en la dogmatica penàl alemana – una exposiciòn, Ensajos penales 257 *et seq.* (Madrid, 1999).

[15] Jose Paredes, Poder Judicial 103 *et seq.* (1995).

supremacy of *intime conviction,* used without any connection to the standard of "beyond any reasonable doubt"; (b) the potential violation of the constitutional principle (known in Europe as "principle of legality") that forbids the departure from the stringent *condicio sine qua non* standard and specific causation; and (c) the distortion of long-standing precepts governing the proof of causation, and the risk that some Courts, by accepting proof of general causation as sufficient, may be perceived to be tilting decisions in favor of the claimant.

This spiritual crisis of the European case law leads me to suggest, first, that the Restatement (Third) of Torts should introduce a provision stating that in tort cases there is a clear distinction between general and specific causation. Any such statement should recognize further that the plaintiff in a suit alleging personal injury or property damage because of use of, ingestion of, or exposure to a defective product, or a dangerously toxic product or process, must prove both general causation and specific causation.

III. LIABILITY FOR EXPOSURE TO TOXIC SUBSTANCES

As or more serious than the current tensions described above as to the proper standards of causation for products liability litigation is the situation in the toxic tort area. In Europe, and especially in Italy, a tremendous number of toxic exposure claims, brought as criminal complaints, have reached the courts in recent years. One outgrowth of this situation, burdensome to prosecutors and the courts alike, was the development of a new legal category, namely the "criminal class action," distinguishable from the American version because of the central role played by the prosecutor.

Unfortunately, the courts hearing such toxic exposure claims have too frequently rendered decisions against the accused based on an unauthorized and incorrect interpretation of the basic rules of the Italian legal system. Frequently, these cases have arisen because claimants alleging that their tumors and diseases arise from exposure to toxic substances did not find any relief in civil trials, because the courts did not apply the "preponderance of evidence" standard. Italian prosecutors, who have a constitutional duty to present the case in front of a judge, received so many criminal complaints by alleged victims that the prosecutors did not dismiss the cases and instead presented them in court. That numbers of claimants who have been able to prevail in criminal suits after failing in civil trials is surely counter-intuitive. The reason, though, that so many of the verdicts have not been in favor of the defendants is readily seen: it is because the "beyond any reasonable doubt" rule is not applied uniformly by the courts.

To take a step back: European and American courts substantially agree on the appropriate meaning of the term "cause" in both criminal and civil trials. In the European legal systems, as explained previously, this notion is identified by reference to the idea of *condicio sine qua non*, which corresponds to the notion of "but for" cause used in common-law countries. Both of these expressions imply specific causation, that is, a cause leading to a single person through the reconstruction of a causal chain[16] or by the implication that "given *A*, *B* necessarily follows."[17]

Both common-law and civil-law countries use the notion of general causation when referring to the general capability of a toxic substance, inferred from epidemiological studies and in vivo experiments, to cause harm in a population. However, as explained earlier, in criminal trials European courts often use the concept of general causation as a substitute for the *condicio sine qua non* standard, even though a specific provision in the Italian criminal code[18] expressly requires, in order to establish criminal liability, the presence of the element of the *condicio sine qua non*.

In recent years, however, the Italian courts have made telling changes in their approaches to causation. In 2002, the Italian Supreme Court[19] reaffirmed the past orthodoxy of the proof required to show causation in a criminal trial. It stated that the increased risk standard is inadequate to establish criminal liability because it's not part of the criminal law system, and that the prosecutor must, therefore, prove specific causation, or *condicio sine qua non*, beyond any reasonable doubt. In the same period, a trial court in Venice rendered a widely-noted decision in a criminal trial related to the petrochemical plant located in the Venice Lagoon. The accused were acquitted because the prosecutor failed to prove, beyond any reasonable doubt, specific causation and proof solely of the increased risk was insufficient.[20] In 2002 a criminal court in Milan reached a similar result in a case concerning the issue of asbestos exposure.[21]

This evolving trend in the Italian case law is concededly in its early stages, and, honestly, it is very hard to predict what may happen in the future. In

---

[16] *See* Troyen A. Brennan, *Causal Chains and Statistical Links: the Role of Scientific Uncertainty in Hazardous Substance Litigation*, 73 CORNELL L. REV., 469, 484 (1988).

[17] Richard W. Wright, *Causation, Responsibility, Risk, Probability, Naked Statistics and Proof: Pruning the Bramble Bush by Clarifying the Concepts*, 73 IOWA L. REV. 1001, 1051 (1985).

[18] *See* art. 40 c.p. "Nobody can be punished for a crime if the dangerous or harmful result from which the existence of that crime depends is not the consequence of his/her action or omission".

[19] *See* note 5, *supra*.

[20] Territorial Court (Tribunale) of Venezia 29.5.2002, CASSAZIONE PENALE 647 *et seq.* (2003).

[21] Territorial Court of Milano, sez. IX, 13.2.2003, quoted in FEDERICO STELLA, GIUSTIZIA E MODERNITA' at 66.

many European countries, there are no positive signals that the courts will recognize specific causation as the minimum standard to establish criminal liability in toxic tort cases.

It is against the above backdrop of the uncertain path European courts are taking regarding toxic exposure suits that I now share my personal belief that American case law should be the driving factor in the European legal systems. The recent decisions rendered in Italy clearly represent the translation, in our legal system, of American legal concepts. In this view, the decision of the Criminal Court of Venice in 2002 is paradigmatic. The Italian court recognized that in the American legal system there is unanimous consent about the impossibility of proving specific causation, beyond any reasonable doubt, in toxic tort cases. Therefore, the court suggested, it is preferable to present the case to civil courts that employ the less stringent standard of the preponderance of evidence.[22] In this way, the Italian court suggested the withdrawal of criminal trials by the prosecutors in toxic tort cases in favor of civil trials, and emphasized the distinction, developed in the United States, between the strong and the weak version of this standard.[23] According to the Italian Court in Venice, civil judges should adopt the weak version, i.e., the simple showing of a doubling of relative risk.

Italian case law is enormously influenced by the decisions of the American courts. It is likely that in the future this influence will increase, particularly if the American courts confirm the approach based on the doubling of the risk. Hopefully this will lead to toxic tort cases being resolved in front of civil, not criminal, courts.[24] My thoughts are intended to highlight the relevance of the evolution of the American case law for European countries and to state

---

[22] The sentence quoted the following United States opinions in *Raynor v. Merrell Pharms. Inc.*, 104 F.3d 1371 (D.C. Cir.1997) and *Cimino v. Raymark Industries, Inc.*, 151 F.3d. 297 (5th Cir. 1998).

[23] The court quoted *Merrell Dow Pharmaceuticals v. Havner*, 953 S.W.2d 706 (Tex. 1997): "general causation is whether a substance is capable of causing a particular injury or condition in the general population, while specific causation is whether a substance caused a particular individual's injury."

[24] *In re Agent Orange Prod. Liability Litigation*, 818 F.2d 145 (2nd Cir. 1987); *Thompson v. Southern Pacific Trans. Co.*, 809 F.2d 1167 (5th Cir. 1987); *Sterling v. Velsicol Chemical Corp.*, 855 F. 2d. 1188 (6th Cir. 1988); *In re TMJ*, 67 F. 3d 1103 (3rd Cir. 1995); *Barnes v. The American Tobacco Co.*, 161 F. 3d 127 (3rd Cir. 1988); *In re Fibreboard Corporation*, 893 F. 2d 706 (5th Cir. 1990); *Cimino v. Raymark Industries, Inc.*, 151 F.3d. 297 (5th Cir. 1998); *Ambrosini v. Labarraque*, 101 F. 3d 129 (D.C. Cir. 1996); *Earl v. Cryovac*, 115 Idaho 1087, 772 P.2d 725 (1989); *Miller v. National Cabinet*, 8 N.Y. 2d 277, 168 N.E. 2d 811, 204 N.Y.S. 2d 129 (1960); *Merrell Dow Pharmaceuticals v. Havner*, 953 S.W.2d 706 (Tex. 1997); *Bartley v. Euclid, Inc.*, 158 F.3d 261 (5th Cir. 1998); *Abuan v. General Electric Co.*, 3 F. 3d 329 (9th Cir. 1993); *Hall v.*

the importance of the distinction, to be adopted in the Restatements (Third) of Torts, between general and specific causation, with reference to the cases discussed above.[25]

IV. EPIDEMIOLOGY AND SPECIFIC CAUSATION

A fundamental issue raised by American courts' decisions concerns the role of epidemiological studies in the toxic tort area. It is commonly believed that epidemiological studies are characterized by the impossibility of proving that a certain individual is affected by a certain disease causally linked to the exposure to a specific toxic substance or to the consumption of a particular drug or agent. Epidemiological studies are conducted on a population called a "cohort," and they describe groups of people exposed to certain substances and compare these groups' health with the health of nonexposed control groups. The REFERENCE MANUAL ON SCIENTIFIC EVIDENCE points out that the data concerning statistical frequency, such as the incidence of harmful effects on the cohort, are not capable of identifying the specific cause of a certain disease or of a particular condition of the individual.[26] The overwhelming majority of the epidemiologists agree on this issue.

In Italy this argument is made by the epidemiologist Berrino. According to Berrino:

> [W]hen it is said that "such-and-such a percentage" of tumors is due to profes-sional [workplace] causes, the numerator of the proportion ("expected cases") does not derive from a census of cases proved to have been caused by exposure, but from the difference between the number of cases observed in those exposed and the number of cases that would have been expected in absence of exposure. Therefore, there is no way to distinguish, among the cases, who would not have become ill in the absence of exposure and who would have become ill in any case. To give an example, in the ten years of activity of the tumor registry in the Region of Lombardy, we know of the existence of over three thousand cases of lung cancer in the Province of Varese. About two thousand of these patients have had contacts, in the course of their professional activity, with one or more substances which provoke tumors in the respiratory organs. We know, beyond any reasonable doubt, that about a thousand of these cases would not have taken place in the absence of these specific occupational factors. But we do not know

Baxter Healthcare Corp., 947 F. Supp. 1387 (D. Or. 1996); *Cook v. United States*, 545 F. Supp. 306, 308 (N.D. Cal. 1982); *Grassis v. Johns Manville Corp.*, 591 A. 2d 671 (N.J. Super. 1991).

[25] See note 22, *supra.*
[26] See note 34, *supra.*

which ones. Naturally all the names are available to the judge. But what is he supposed to do? Draw lots?[27]

This approach is common to other Italian epidemiologists, including Carlo Bracci,[28] Giusti and Carnevale,[29] Gobbato and Larese,[30] Franchini and Mutti,[31] Buiatti and Kriebel,[32] Mazzella Di Bosco,[33] Gobbato, Larese, Negro and Gubian,[34] and Umani Ronchi.[35]

In common-law countries, the list of epidemiologists and occupational risk scholars is even longer. Worthy of mention are Kenneth J. Rothman and Sander Greenland, who state that there is currently no way to tell which exposures are responsible for a given case; we cannot measure the individual risks, and assigning the average value to everyone in the category reflects nothing more than our ignorance.[36] Scholars Armstrong, Tremblay, and Thériault state that since the cancers caused by exposure are not distinguishable pathologically or otherwise from those occurring "naturally," it is impossible to say with certainty whether an individual case was caused by the occupational exposure or not.[37] Similarly, Rodricks says that, with a few exceptions, cancer experts cannot determine with high confidence the specific cause of cancer in an individual. At best, they can understand the factors that contribute to the cancer rates observed in large populations.[38] According to Woodhead, Bender,

---

[27] Franco Berrino, *Candido Atteggiamento o Denuncia di Comportamenti Inadeguati*, LA MEDICINA DEL LAVORO 167 *et seq.* (1988).

[28] Carlo Bracci, *La Nuova Tabella delle Malattie Professionali: Il Problema dei Tumori*, ASSISTENZA SOCIALE, 19, 510 (1989).

[29] Giusto Giusti-Aldo Carnevale, *Possibile Azione Cancerogena del Cloruro di Vinile: Aspetti medico-legali*, AGGIORNAMENTO SCIENTIFICO IN TRAUMATOLOGIA FORENSE 275 (1995).

[30] Ferdinando Gobbato-Francesca Larese, *Approccio alla valutazione dei tumori professionali nel Friuli-Venezia Giulia*, ASSISTENZA SOCIALE, 23 (1998) quoted in MAURO BARNI, IL RAPPORTO DI CAUSALITÀ MATERIALE IN MEDICINA LEGALE 75 (Milan 1995).

[31] Innocente Franchini-Antonio Mutti, *Tumori Professionali e Patologia Degenerativa: Clinica, Epidemiologia o Epidemiologia Clinica?*, LA MEDICINA DEL LAVORO 419–20 (1988).

[32] Eva Buiatti-David Kriebel, *Almeno per la Denuncia di Malattia Professionale, Criteri Esistono*, LA MEDICINA DEL LAVORO 163 (1988).

[33] Michele Mazzella Di Bosco, *I Tumori Professionali Alla Luce di Alcuni Recenti Contributi*, RIVISTA DEGLI INFORTUNI E DELLE MALATTIE PROFESSIONALI 653 (1989).

[34] Ferdinando Gobbato-Francesca Larese-Corrado Negro-Francesca Gubian, *Contributo alla Diagnosi di Tumori Professionali*, 52° CONGRESSO NAZIONALE DELLA SOCIETÀ ITALIANA DI MEDICINA LEGALE 468 (1989).

[35] GIANCARLO UMANI RONCHI, LA TUTELA ASSICURATIVA DEGLI INFORTUNI SUL LAVORO E DELLE MALATTIE PROFESSIONALI 105 (Padua, 1990).

[36] KENNETH J. ROTHMAN – SANDER GREENLAND, CAUSATION AND CAUSAL INFERENCE 8 (1998).

[37] Ben Armstrong-Claude Tremblay-Gilles Thériault, *Compensating Bladder Cancer Victims Employed in Aluminium Reduction Plants*, J. OF OCCUP. MED. 771 (1988).

[38] JOSEPH V. RODRICKS, CALCULATED RISKS 116 (Cambridge 1992).

and Thériault, results from epidemiological studies provide data gathered from examining a population of individuals; however, they do not normally demonstrate causation, and are generally inapplicable to a single individual.[39] Similarly, Charlton states that the imputed causal association is at the group level, and does not indicate the cause of disease in individual subjects.[40]

In the United States, a striking number of tort law scholars agree with the approach followed by the epidemiogists cited here. Among them, Harris affirmed that statistical evidence emanating from epidemiological studies is by its very nature a population group study and not an individual study. This evidence does not necessarily shed light upon the cause of an individual's injury.[41] According to Troyan Brennan it is impossible to state that a given carcinogen caused any individual cancer, because scientists do not yet understand the molecular model of carcinogenesis. Epidemiology makes statements only about the group, not the individual.[42] In Applegate's opinion, the best that can be done to determine the carcinogenic potential of such substances is to describe their effects statistically, that is, to state quantitatively the level of risk they pose. Consequently, public officials cannot base regulatory controls on specific causation of actual harm, instead, they must regulate risk *per se*.[43] To Dore, the limitations on epidemiology's ability to prove specific causation stem from its general and statistical nature. Epidemiological studies are general in that they deal with sources of disease in groups of people rather than in particular individuals. They cannot answer the critical question of whether the defendant's conduct actually injured the claimant.[44]

Barr suggests that even an epidemiological study which demonstrates significant statistical association does not establish a causal relationship.[45] Green affirms that when there is a question of whether the agent is capable of causing the disease, because both epidemiology and toxicology study disease in groups, they are particularly well suited to addressing this question. However, Green continues, in a tort case there is also the specific causation question – was the plaintiff's disease caused by exposure to the defendant's

---

[39] Avril D. Woodhead, Michael A. Bender & Robin C. Leonard, Phenotypic Variation in Populations: Relevance to Risk Assessment 286 (1988).

[40] Bruce G. Charlton, *Attribution of Causation in Epidemiology: Chain or Mosaic?*, 49 J. Clin. Epidemiol. 105, 107 (1996).

[41] Fred O. Harris Jr., *Toxic Tort Litigation and the Causation Element*, quoted *supra*, note 2, 947.

[42] Troyen A. Brennan, *Causal Chains and Statistical* Links, quoted *supra*, note 16, 475, 512.

[43] John S. Applegate, *Worst Things First: Risk, Information and Regulatory Structure in Toxic Substances Control*, 9 Yale J. on Reg., 282 (1992).

[44] Michael Dore, *A Commentary on the Use of Epidemiological Evidence in Demonstrating Cause-in-fact*, 7 Harv. Envtl L. Rev., 429, 436 (1983).

[45] Craig A. Barr, *A Practical Guide to Proving and Disproving Causation in Radiation Exposure Cases: Hanford Nuclear Site and Radioactive Iodine*, 31 Gonz. L. Rev., 7, 16 (1996).

agent or was there another cause? This is because most diseases have multiple potential causes, and epidemiology provides virtually no information about specific causation.[46] According to Spyridon, to define a cause-and-effect relationship, the epidemiologist examines the general population and compares the incidence of the disease among those people exposed to a particular substance to those not exposed. Because an epidemiological study evaluates groups rather than individuals, it is usually not case-specific and, therefore, cannot conclusively establish causation in a toxic tort case.[47] Rosenberg is very firm in his statement:

> Epidemiologists can estimate the proportion of disease incidence attributable to the "excess risk" created by the toxic agent and the proportion attributable to the "background risk" – the cumulative risk attributable to all other factors. But given current limits on our knowledge of the etiology of insidious diseases, and given the generality of statistical data, it is impossible to pinpoint the actual source of the disease afflicting any specific member of the exposed population.[48]

Particular emphasis should be given to the opinion of Richard Wright, who highlights the opportunity of distinguishing between the *ex ante* and the *ex post* probability:

> Although *ex ante* causal probabilities are relevant – indeed necessary – for causal prediction of what will or might happen, they are irrelevant for causal explanation of what really happened. They are nonparticularized class-based probabilities that provide no information on which competing causal generalization actually was instantiated on the particular occasion.[49]

There are however, some epidemiologists who continue to argue that, in exceptional cases, epidemiology proves specific causation.[50] For example, when the expected events in the cohort study are numerically less than 1 (.1, .2, .3, etc.) and the observed cases are in larger numbers, for example, twenty or thirty (paradigmatic is the liver cancer – angiosarcoma due to exposure to vinyl chloride), it would be impossible to consider specific causation

---

[46] Michael D. Green, *Science is to Law as the Burden of Proof is to Significance Testing*, 37 JURIMETRICS, 205, 223 (1997).

[47] Gregg L. Spyridon, *Scientific Evidence vs. "Junk Science" – Proof of Medical Causation in Toxic Tort Litigation*, 61 MISS. L. J. 287, 294 (1991).

[48] David Rosenberg, *The Causal Connection in Mass Exposure Cases: a "Public Law" Vision of the Tort System* quoted *supra*, note 2, 849, 851.

[49] Richard W. Wright, *Causation, Responsibility, Risk*, quoted *supra*, note 17, 1001, 1052.

[50] Paolo Vineis, *L'interpretazione causale degli studi epidemiologici*, LA CAUSALITÀ TRA DIRITTO E MEDICINA, ATTI DEL CONVEGNO NAZIONALE DI MEDICINA LEGALE 47–51 (1991).

unproven, as the association with the exposure is so obvious that there is no room for dissent. This argument cannot be accepted for the following reason: the number of observed events is only a naked statistic and is not representative of cases in which the causal relation has been proven. In other words, when epidemiological researches show a relevant number of tumors or diseases (twenty or thirty), the real meaning of this circumstance is that in a high number of cases the exposure was a preceding factor of the disease. However, it is widely recognized that in the circumstances described, the existence of the causal connection can be asserted only on the basis of the maxim *post hoc, ergo propter hoc*, which was discredited in the scientific community because it generated what is usually referred to as the "fallacy of the false cause."[51]

In order to infer specific causation from the statistical number of observed events we need more than this. We need proof that each of the observed events of tumor or disease, following a universal, not merely statistical causal law, is a case of specific causation and is, therefore, linked to the exposure by a causal relationship and not by naked statistics. This consideration would represent an innovation in the Restatement (Third) of Torts, because, as far as I know, it is currently undeveloped in judicial decisions and in the comments of the scholars. Accordingly, at this point in research it is only possible to define a general principle, not subject to any exception. It is true that the epidemiological studies may help us assessing whether a certain substance is capable of causing a disease or a tumor, but they are always silent as to the requirement of specific causation.

V. GENERAL CAUSATION OF THE LOW DOSAGE LEVELS

The more relevant issue for industries nowadays is the exposure to low dosage levels of toxic substances. On the one hand, it is commonly said that the current occupational standards in the chemical industry are safe, after the renovation of the chemical plants which followed developing scientific knowledge. On the other hand, it can be said that no safety exists today because of the lack of evidence of a safe threshold, as demonstrated by linear extrapolations from high to low dosage levels.

The assumption that it is not possible to define a threshold below which a certain substance has no harmful effects is still expressed in some areas of the scientific community. In a criminal trial of a toxic exposure case in Venice,

---

[51] IRVING M. COPI-CARL COHEN, INTRODUCTION TO LOGIC (1964).

the prosecutor's experts openly acknowledged that there is no scientific evidence to prove general causation at low doses, but argued that the current occupational standards are unsafe and declared the lack of a threshold a "metaphysical dogma." These statements made by the prosecutor's experts reveal the fundamental relevance of several decisions of the U.S. Supreme Court, which has recognized the impossibility of using linear extrapolation from high to low dosages as a proof of the absence of a threshold. Several decisions of that Court on these topics turned out to be extremely important for the Italian Courts. In *N.R.D.C. v. EPA*[52] – a case regarding the effects of vinyl chloride – the Court repeated that emission levels should be calculated on the basis of the evaluation of experts as to the significance of the health risk. In other words, emission levels based on concrete scientific knowledge and not on mathematical calculations based on extrapolations from high to low doses. In the words of the Supreme Court: "There is no particular reason to think that the actual line of the incidence of harm is represented by a straight line."[53]

Statements made by the National Research Council (NRC) are also quoted in the *Venice* case. The NRC, established by Congress, is in charge of controlling the activity of another federal agency, the Evironmental Protection Agency. The NRC argued that historically the political choices of federal agencies were greatly influenced by the idea that *any* level of exposure to carcinogenic substances generates some degree of risk to public health. However, this view is inconsistent with the developing scientific knowledge related to biological mechanisms, which are responsible for the tumors deriving from the exposure to toxic substances. Concerning the extrapolations from animals to humans, the NRC states that their scientific foundations have not yet been strictly established. This is the reason why the "*default options*" express political evaluations and not convincing scientific evidence.[54] The opinion of Bruce Ames was very important in the criminal trial of *Venice*. Ames, a leading scientist, explained why the extrapolations from animals to humans

---

[52] *N.R.D.C. v. U.S. EPA*, 824 F. 2d 1146 (D. C. Cir. 1987).

[53] An analogous case, concerning benzene, was decided by the Supreme Court in *Indus. Union Dep't AFL-CIO v. American Petroleum Inst.*, 448 U.S. 607 (1980). In this decision the Supreme Court censured the reduction, carried out by the OSHA, of the permissible exposure limit for benzene from 10 ppm to 1 ppm. As Justice Stewart stated, the no-risk policy adopted by the agency is not "a proper substitute for the findings of significant risk of harm required" by the law. *See also Ciba-Geigy Corp. v. EPA*, 46 F.3d 1208 (D.C. Cir. 1995); *Appalachian Power Co. v. EPA*, 135 F.3d 791 (D.C. Cir. 1998); *Chlorine Chemistry Council v. EPA*, 206 F.3d 1286 (D.C. Cir. 2000).

[54] NRC, *Science and Judgement in Risk Assessment, supra* note at 58 *et seq.*

are controversial: "[T]here is increasing evidence that cell division caused by the high dose itself, rather than the chemical *per se,* is increasing the positivity rate."[55]

Additionally, the conclusions drawn by the recent European multicentric studies conducted by the International Agency for Research on Cancer (IARC) (the European agency of the World Health Organization [WHO][56]) were very useful to the Venetian judges. For example, no harmful effects have been shown below the threshold of 288 ppm during a period of ten-year exposure to vinyl chloride (VC). Another relevant contribution in the Venice trial was offered by Swenberg, who performed experimental studies concerning DNA adducts. Swenberg concluded that the current occupational standards are safe.[57]

To summarize, the trial Court of Venice, in order to establish the absence of general causation at low dosage levels, discussed the opinions of American courts, the statements of the NRC, Ames, Swenberg, and the conclusions of the multicentric study about vinyl chloride, many of which sources derived directly from United States litigation and scientific experiences. It seems clear therefore, that the issue of exposure to low doses will be hotly debated between the European judges and a reference to it in the Restatement (Third) of Torts would be extremely helpful to the European legal system.

VI. SPECIFIC CAUSATION, CAUSAL CHAINS, AND INSTANTIATION OF CAUSAL LAW

Now it is necessary to elaborate on the discussion surrounding specific causation. Following the strong version of the "more probable than not" rule, as Troyen Brennan explains, the proof of specific causation may be reached primarily by reconstructing the causal chains and connecting the exposure to the harm suffered.[58] However, this kind of proof is often impossible to reach with regard to carcinogenic substances. The future challenge for the scientific

---

[55] Bruce Ames-Lois Gold, *Environmental Pollution, Pesticides and the Prevention of Cancer: Misconceptions,* FASEB JOURNAL, 1041 (1997).

[56] ELIZABETH WARD, PAOLO BOFFETTA ET AL., UPDATE OF THE FOLLOW-UP OF MORTALITY AND CANCER INCIDENCE AMONG EUROPEAN WORKERS EMPLOYED IN THE VINYL CHLORIDE INDUSTRY, IARC, Iarc Internal Report 00/001 (Lyon, Sept. 2000).

[57] James A. Swenberg, Matthew S. Bogdanffy, Amy-Joan L. Ham, Sharon Holt, *Formation and Repair of DNA Adducts in Vinyl Chloride – and Vinyl Fluoride – Induced Carcinogenesis;* DNA CYCLIC ADDUCTS 29 *et seq* (B. Singer & H. Bartsch eds. (Lyon-IARC 1999).

[58] Troyen A. Brennan, *Causal Chains and Statistical Links,* quoted *supra* note 16 at 490.

community is to penetrate the structure of the carcinogenic substances and explain their mechanisms in producing harmful effects. This point is also made clear by those epidemiologists who argue that, even respecting the procedural criteria developed by Bradford Hill, epidemiological studies are not completely reliable even to prove general causation, because when a preceding flaw or bias is present, all the subsequent conclusions of the study are flawed by it. Because the replication of the results is not a sufficient standard to draw reliable inferences in epidemiological studies, epidemiologists continue to be engaged in the attempt to explain the mechanism of causation of harmful effects provoked by carcinogenic substances.

The Italian epidemiologist Lorenzo Simonato, who supervised the European multicentric study conducted by the IARC in the 1990s, had no hesitation in stating that one of the intended purposes of the study was to investigate the biological mechanism of VC, in order to match and to harmonize, to the extent possible, the epidemiological with the biological sections of the study. Eventually this objective was abandoned, because the actual scientific knowledge did not affirm the existence of a specific mechanism of action of VC.[59]

Naturally, and unfortunately this conclusion, formulated with specific reference to the mechanism of action of VC, is valid for other carcinogenic substances. Other respected Italian epidemiologists, such as Pietro Comba, a member of the ISS,[60] identify the "ideal" causal paradigm as the one used in microbiology. According to Comba, at the beginning of the history of epidemiology, scientists used to refer to the microbiological paradigm to explain the mechanism by which a microorganism causes a certain disease. The aim of their research was to verify that the microorganism was present in all the different forms of the disease. The microorganisms were isolated, put in a test tube or petri dish, cultivated and, when reinjected for laboratory experiments in animals, were able to reproduce the disease.

Comba says it was ludicrous when, for precautionary reasons, the IARC proposed that a "probable carcinogenic substance," be classified in the same category as a carcinogenic agent whose harmful effects are definitely ascertained. This recommendation raised an intense debate in the scientific community. On the one hand, some scientists argue that the aim of prevention imposes one to consider the association between the exposure to toxic substances and the disease only if it is possible to demonstrate the intermediate causal events linking the exposure to the harmful effects. This approach is

[59] Territorial Court (Tribunale) of Venezia 29.5.2002 (testimony of Simonato, 12.7.2000), quoted *supra*, n. 20.
[60] The ISS is the Italian Institute of Public Health.

commonly known as "the glass box" theory. On the other hand, others prefer the method of the "black box", which is to say, if there is no knowledge of the adverse effects of the agent, the agency reduces the exposure levels on the basis of the available epidemiological results. In other words, according to Comba, the scientists tend to favor the analysis of the mechanism of action of the substance rather than the analysis of general causation based on epidemiological data confirmed in the replication of the studies.[61]

We can only agree with the American civil courts which, adopting the strong version of the "more likely than not" standard, require the plaintiff to prove the causal chain linking the exposure to the disease, in order to demonstrate specific causation. This is, in my opinion, the main direction to follow to prove specific causation, and its relevance should be clearly stated in the Third Restatement.

An alternative approach to proving specific causation is to refer to a causal generalization instantiated in the specific occasion. For example, in *Barnes v. The American Tobacco Co.*,[62] the Court of Appeals for the Third Circuit decided a case concerning a plaintiff who was allegedly victimized by his addiction to cigarette smoking. The court concluded that specific causation may be proven only if it can be demonstrated that cigarette smoking always causes an addiction. The court endorsed the general principle that specific causation may be proven if the particular case can only be explained in terms of a universal law of this kind: "given *A*, *B* necessarily follows," or, in other words, in the case of instantiation of a causal law.

Wright[63] elaborated on this approach, noting that the borderline between general and specific causation is self-evident, writing that evidence that cigarette smoking may cause addiction makes reference only to general causation, whereas proof that cigarette smoking is always followed by addiction would allow us to prove specific causation.

In Italy, this approach has been followed by some decisions of the Supreme Court and by the project to reform the current Penal Code.[64] Nevertheless, in some decisions, the Italian Supreme Court has held that criminal trials do not require the reconstruction of the causal chains or demonstration of the instantiation of a causal law. In such holdings, the court has held that

---

[61] Territorial Court (Tribunale) of Venezia 29.5.2002, hearing of Comba, 1.7.1998, quoted *supra* note 20.

[62] *Barnes v. The American Tobacco Co.*, 161 F. 3d 127 (3rd Cir. 1988).

[63] Richard W. Wright, *Causation, Responsibility, Risk*, quoted *supra* note 17, at 1050 *et seq.*

[64] Commissione Ministeriale per la Riforma del Codice Penale, Progetto preliminare di riforma del Codice Penale, parte generale, *Relazione*, 12.9.2000. This Project is called "Progetto Grosso" from the name of its proponent.

reference to statistical laws, even those referring to a pattern of events with a medium to low frequency, would be enough to prove causation.[65] Such holdings only serve to emphasize how extremely important it is that the American civil courts reaffirm the concept that proof of specific causation can be based only on two fundamental elements, namely (1) the biological demonstration of the mechanism of action of the agent; or (2) the instantiation of a scientific universal law in the particular occasion. Only by moving toward this direction will the European criminal courts absorb the recommendations of the leading European commentators on causation, such as Armin Kaufmann,[66] Manfred Maiwald,[67] Winfried H. Hassemer,[68] Josè Paredes,[69] and this author.[70] This is the only way for the European criminal courts to affirm the principle that it is practically impossible to prove causation in criminal trials (that correspond to American toxic torts trials), because only the reconstruction of the causal chains (or the instantiation of a causal law in the particular occasion) may give proof of specific causation, beyond any reasonable scientific doubt.

VII. SPECIFIC CAUSATION AND ALTERNATIVE EXPLANATIONS

In the context set forth here, the issue of alternative explanations or of a plurality of causes is no longer relevant. It is obvious that there is no room for the intervention of alternative causes when either the causal chain is well established, or a causal law, linking exposure to disease, is available. To think differently would be a *fallacy*, as it would assume that the reconstruction of the causal chains or the instantiation of a causal law could not lead to proof of causation. Karl Popper illustrates the concept of causal explanation with the example of breaking a thread to which a weight has been attached. As he argues, "the fact that a load of 2 lbs. was put on a thread with a tensile strength of 1 lb. was the 'cause' of its breaking." The breaking is the instantiation of the underlying causal law, that is to say of a law which states that "whenever a weight of 2 lbs. is attached to a thread with a tensile strength of 1 lb. the thread breaks." In this example, alternative causation is clearly not an issue.[71]

---

[65] Italian Supreme Court, United Sections, 11.9.2002, quoted *supra* note 5.
[66] See *supra* note 9.
[67] See *supra* note 8.
[68] See *supra* note 12–13.
[69] See *supra* note 15.
[70] See *supra* note 8.
[71] KARL POPPER, THE LOGIC OF SCIENTIFIC DISCOVERY (London 1934).

The issue of alternative causation may be raised only when the considered antecedent can be defined as the potential cause, not excluding the intervention of other causes (but here, once again, we are in the area of general causation). This is the reason why the American civil courts analyze the issue of alternative causation under the general causation approach.[72] These considerations are extremely relevant in Europe because prosecutors often erroneously demand a decision against the accused on the basis of unproven causal hypotheses coupled with the lack of alternative explanations offered by the defense. All of these ideas – in my opinion – should be pointed out in the Third Restatement of Torts.

VIII. RELIABILITY OF THE SCIENTIFIC HYPOTHESES: THE *DAUBERT* REQUIREMENTS

The U.S. Supreme Court analyzed another fundamental issue in two recent and noteworthy tort cases.[73] The issue of the lack of certainty of science and of other technical or "specialized" disciplines reveals its importance mainly in toxic tort cases dealing with general causation. Scientific uncertainty is linked to the mutability of science and to the limits that science meets and is destined to meet.

For example, until twenty years ago, scientists held that the majority of tumors were due to environmental contamination. In 1981, Sir Richard Doll and Richard Peto published their encyclopedic analysis of the causes of tumors. Their conclusions were that industrial pollution was associated with about 4 percent of all tumors.[74] This estimate is fairly similar to the one made subsequently by the EPA, which calculated that only a percentage (ranking between 1 and 3 percent) of tumors could be linked to industrial pollution.[75] The history of epidemiology is rich in hypotheses of these kinds which are not confirmed by successive studies or are shown to be false. As a result, Dimitrios Trichopoulos, Head of the Department of Epidemiology of the Harvard School of Public Health, concluded that epidemiological studies will

---

[72] *Raynor v. Merrell Pharms., Inc.*, 104 F.3d 1371 (D.C. Cir. 1997). In *Raynor* the Court of Appeals for the District of Columbia dismissed the plaintiff's complaint because he failed to exclude any other alternative causes of the birth defects allegedly because of the use of Bendectin.

[73] *Daubert v. Merrell Dow Pharmaceutical, Inc.*, 509 U.S. 579 (1993); *Kuhmo Tire Co. v. Carmichael*, 526 U.S. 137 (1999).

[74] Richard Doll, Richard Peto, *The Causes of Cancer: Quantitative Estimates of Avoidable Risks of Cancer in the United States Today*, 66 J. NAT'L CANCER INST. 1191 *et seq.* (1981).

[75] This percentage is reported in Steven Gough, Michael Milloy, *EPA's Cancer Risk Guidelines: Guidance to Nowhere*, CATO POLICY ANALYSIS 263 (1996).

inevitably generate false positive and false negative results "with disturbing frequency."[76] Similarly, Kenneth Rothman states that "we are pushing the edge of what can be done with epidemiology."[77] Notable errors are present in the history of prestigious organizations such as the IARC (WHO). For example, until 1987, the agency strongly affirmed that VC causes tumors in the lungs, the brain and the lymphopoietic system.[78] Qualitatively superior epidemiological studies conducted after 1987 by the IARC reached the opposite conclusion: VC does not cause tumors to the lungs, the brain, and the lymphopoietic system.[79]

In such a situation, the reader himself will pose the following question: What can we say about holdings finding toxic tort liability decided on the basis of epidemiological hypotheses that were subsequently found to be false or not accepted by the whole scientific community?

Going beyond the limited area of toxic substances, the debate about the existence of a scientific method is another issue that came by force to the fore during the last century. The conclusion of the debate between epistemologists is that there are as many scientific methods as there are philosophical theories inflaming the debate: from Rudolf Carnap's and Carl Hempel's inductive approach,[80] to Karl Popper's "falsifiability" theory,[81] to Thomas Kuhn's paradigm of general acceptance in periods of "normal science,"[82] to the image of science as a competition between research programs proposed by Imre Lakatos,[83] to the problem of demarcation between science and nonscience

---

[76] See Gary Taubes, *Epidemiology Faces its Limits*, SCIENCE 164 *et seq.* (1995).

[77] The statement is reported in Gary Taubes, *Epidemiology Faces its Limits*, at *id.* In this situation, the call for "methodological caution" has become a "leitmotif" of the most authoritative researchers. For Richard Doll no epidemiological study should be considered accepted unless, with a 95 percent confidence interval, it indicates a threefold risk. Other researchers, as such Dimitrios Trichopoulos, prefer a fourfold risk as the lowest limit. For Robert Temple, director of the pharmacological evaluation service of the FDA, the rule to adopt is that a risk which has not increased by at least three or four times is a risk to forget about. But this "caution" is not enough. Epidemiological research is, in any case, exposed to the risk of being shown false on account of systematic errors, biases, and confounders.

[78] IARC, MONOGRAPHS ON THE EVALUATION OF THE CARCINOGENIC RISK OF CHEMICALS TO HUMANS 1979 (updated in 1987).

[79] LORENZO SIMONATO, MORTALITY AND CANCER INCIDENCE RESULTS OF THE EUROPEAN MULTI-CENTRIC COHORT STUDY OF WORKERS EMPLOYED IN THE VINYL CHLORIDE INDUSTRY 1 *et seq.* (Lyon-International Agency for Research on Cancer) (1989).

[80] *See* RUDOLF CARNAP, PHILOSOPHICAL FOUNDATIONS OF PHYSICS, 1–20 (1966); CARL HEMPEL, PHILOSOPHY OF NATURAL SCIENCE 17 *et seq.* (1966).

[81] KARL R. POPPER, CONJECTURES AND REFUTATIONS: THE GROWTH OF SCIENTIFIC KNOWLEDGE (London, 1963).

[82] THOMAS S. KUHN, THE STRUCTURE OF SCIENTIFIC REVOLUTIONS (1962).

[83] IMRE LAKATOS, FALSIFICATION AND THE METHODOLOGY OF SCIENTIFIC RESEARCH PROGRAMMES 130 (1970).

according to Larry Laudan.[84] At one extreme, Paul Feyerabend negates the existence of a scientific method and defiantly suggests that the governmental funds financing the philosophy of science be suspended.[85]

In the midst of this debate, the courts found themselves in a situation of *impasse*. Luckily, the decision in *Daubert v. Merrell Dow Pharmaceuticals, Inc.*[86] enabled the courts to overcome these difficulties. The Supreme Court, faced with the lack of certainty in science, argued that it is possible to derive a rule that might lie at the foundation, as Sheila Jasanoff says,[87] of the juridical construction of science and technology. This rule requires that the laws of science be provided with the highest degree of reliability, and the lowest degree of fallaciousness. In order to ensure the highest possible degree of reliability, the scientific hypotheses must be characterized by a high degree of confirmation, based on observation and experiments (Carl Hempel's practical certainty), or by corroboration after overcoming attempts of falsification (Karl Popper's approach). General acceptance by the scientific community can also "have a bearing on the inquiry."[88] The confirmation, the corroboration and the general acceptance by the scientific community remain inevitably provisional: the truthfulness or untruthfulness of a scientific hypothesis will always be an open issue. Nevertheless, the combination of the three requirements of scientific method explained in *Daubert* adequately assures the reliability of the provisional hypotheses, separating science from "junk science" and from those scientific hypotheses that are not adequately reliable (the "shaky but admissible evidence" in Justice Blackmun's words). In this way, the judge becomes the "gatekeeper"[89] of the scientific method.

---

[84] Larry Laudan, *The Demise of the Demarcation Problem*, in COHEN & LAUDAN, PHYSICS, PHILOSOPHY AND PSYCHOANALISIS 111 *et seq.* (1983).

[85] PAUL FEYERABEND, AGAINST METHOD. OUTLINE OF AN ANARCHISTIC THEORY OF KNOWLEDGE 23 *et seq.* (London, 1975).

[86] 509 U.S. 579 (1993).

[87] SHEILA JASANOFF, SCIENCE AT THE BAR: LAW, SCIENCE AND TECHNOLOGY IN AMERICA 19 *et seq.* (1995).

[88] "General acceptance can yet have a bearing on the inquiry" *Daubert v. Merrell Dow Pharmaceuticals Inc.*, 509 U.S. 579 (citing *Frye v. United States*, 293 F. 1013, 1014 (D.C. Cir. 1923)).

[89] "The trial judge must ensure that any and all scientific testimony or evidence admitted is not only relevant, but reliable.... The subject of an expert's testimony must be 'scientific' knowledge. We recognize ... in practice a gatekeeping role for the judge...." *Daubert v. Merrell Dow Pharmaceutical Inc.*, 509 U.S. 579 (footnotes omitted).

In *Kuhmo Tire Co.* the Court stated that *Daubert* gatekeeping obligation applies not only to 'scientific' testimony, but to all expert testimony.... It would prove difficult, if not impossible, for judges to administer evidentiary rules under which a gatekeeping obligation depended upon a distinction between 'scientific' knowledge and 'technical' or other 'specialized' knowledge. There is no clear line that divides the one from the others.... Neither is there a convincing need to make such distinctions."

Vesting this role, the court in Venice, referring to the epidemiological evaluations of the WHO in 1979 and 1987, held that because the considered epidemiological studies were not corroborated by subsequent research, they were, therefore, unreliable.[90] The court held it was unnecessary to wait for the outcomes of WHO studies conducted after 1987.

The *Daubert* opinion had a tremendous influence in the evaluation, by the courts, of the admissibility of expert testimony not only in the United States but also in Europe, where it spread its beneficial effects over Italian case law, particularly in criminal trials related to toxic torts. The trial court of Venice, in the decision referenced above, held that:

> [T]he reliability of our knowledge, however modifiable or falsifiable in the future by new, different, scientific developments, is determined by the degree of confirmation, the general or prevailing acceptance of the scientific community, and from the overcoming of the attempts of falsifiability. Whenever an area of scientific uncertainty should remain as to causal relationship, the problem should be solved applying the standard of beyond any reasonable doubt."[91]

This decision by the trial court of Venice represents the translation, by the civil-law countries, of the principles established in *Daubert*. We hope that the Third Restatement of Torts will include a reference to the *Daubert* case, so that it will represent, in the future, the benchmark for all European countries. I am aware of the fact that the rules about the reliability of scientific experts are part of the law of evidence, but I believe it is appropriate to embody this issue also in the regulation of causation in the Third Restatement.

IX. SUGGESTED CHANGES TO THE RESTATEMENT OF TORTS

In conclusion, when referring to causation, the Restatement (Third) of Torts should provide for: (a) advancement in the general part of the "but for" causes as a constant requirement of causation; (b) clarification of the provision following which the "but for" cause needs to be the final step of the instantiation of a causal law, sufficiently reliable following *Daubert*'s requirements, or of the reconstruction of the causal chains. The role of gatekeeper vested by the American judge in the evaluation of admissibility of expert testimony becomes an element of connection between the functions of the judge, on one side, and the jury, on the other; (c) in toxic tort cases, the concept of "substantial factor"

---

[90] Territorial Court (Tribunale) of Venezia, 29.05.2002, quoted *supra* note 20, at 279 et seq (translated by author).

[91] Territorial Court (Tribunale) of Venezia, 29.05.2002, quoted *supra* note 20, at 280 (translated by author).

causation should be abandoned because of its vagueness, in favor of the "but for" cause; (d) attribution of great emphasis, in the general part, to the distinction between general and specific causation and to the idea that evidence of general causation is not sufficient to prove specific causation.

These amendments, in my opinion, are necessary to accomplish the globalization process and the homogenization of European and American legal cultures.

CHAPTER THIRTEEN

COLLECTIVE RIGHTS AND COLLECTIVE ACTIONS: SAMPLES OF EUROPEAN AND LATIN AMERICAN CONTRIBUTIONS

Juan Carlos Henao

ABSTRACT. The goal of achieving remediation for violation of collective rights is well matured in civil law and common law nations. Modern collective rights identified in an increasing number of constitutions in civil law countries include, to name only two: (1) the right to a safe and healthy environment; and (2) the right to preservation of public space. It is seen readily that collective vindication of such rights has the potential to sound in the common law themes of private nuisance and public nuisance. These collective rights and their remediation have recently acquired great importance in Latin America, due most significantly to their increasing inclusion in national constitutions and civil codes. To a degree, the same phenomenon has visited Europe, both at the level of the law of individual nations and in their current examination by a European Union Commission.

This chapter is based upon the foregoing, together with the congruence of certain of these collective rights with rights protected in the modern law of torts as recognized in one or another form in many common law and civil code nations. Adverting with special focus to the constitutions and the civil codes of Colombia and France, one approaches the question of how the process might work with these questions, among others, in mind: What are the limits of the judge to put into practice these rights? What is the popular action and how does it work? What other participative mechanisms exist to vindicate collective rights? What are the types of claims being presented currently? How does the protection of collective rights affect the security of individual rights? Juxtaposing the law of France with that of Colombia, the chapter examines how, based on the Colombian definition and examples of collective rights, collective rights are being protected. In order to do this, the French litigation-administrative scheme is studied in respect to the defense of collective rights, and specific French cases similar to the Colombian popular action are described. The corpus of the chapter is devoted to the analysis of such diverse issues as separation of powers, democratic participation in the protection and preservation of public property, and the respective powers of the judge and the citizen.

Juan Carlos Henao, Permanent Professor in Universidad Externado de Colombia; Guest Professor in the Universities of Paris 3 (Iheal), Cergy-Pontoise and Montpellier 1; Lecturer in the Institut d'Etudes Politiques de Paris – Sciences Pol. This chapter is dedicated to Fernando Hinestrosa, on the celebration of his forty years as president of and fifty years as a professor at The Universidad Externado de Colombia.

I. INTRODUCTION

The general topic of this chapter, the vindication of collective rights in civil actions, has long been studied by the scholars of comparative law. Emilio Bonaudi's 1911 work[1] is quoted as the first modern contribution in this subject. Widely known experts such as Mauro Cappelletti have dedicated many pages of commentary to this subject,[2] as have numerous other commentators on comparative law.[3] The depth of the existing bibliography is such that it would be pretentious to try to exhaust it. It is therefore a topic to be approached by the scholar with a humility that is consistent with an awareness both of the multiple contributions of the academic community, and the placement of collective actions among the most important modern topics in the field of civil law.

Collective rights have been recognized since ancient times. In Roman law the popular action already existed, although in a different context[4] and "the history of medieval common law offers an important number of examples of litigation with the participation of diverse collectivities."[5] Nevertheless, the contemporary practical and social importance of collective rights has been the result of historical transformations beginning only from the twentieth century onward.

---

[1] EMILIO BONAUDI, LA TUTELA DEGLI INTERESSI COLLETIVI (Torino, Bocca 1911).

[2] *See, e.g., Essay, Appunti Sulla Tutela Giurisdizionale di Interessi Collettivi o Diffusi*, LE AZIONI A TUTELA DI INTERESSI COLLETTIVI, Atti del Convegno di Studio (Pavía, 11–12 giugno 1974); Pedova Cedam, *Governmental and Private Advocates for the Public Interest in Civil Litigation: A Comparative Study, in* I ACCES-TO JUSTICE: A WORLD SURVEY (M. Cappelletti and B. Garth, eds.) (1978); *La protection d'intérêts collectifs et de groupe dans le procès civil (Métamorphoses de la procédure civile)*, in 1975 REVUE RICD 571–97 (1975); *Formaciones sociales e intereses de grupo frente a la justicia civil* 31–32 BOLETÍN MEXICANO DE DERECHO COMPARADO, 1 *et seq.* (1978).

[3] *See, e.g., Accès à la justice et Etat Providence* (dir. M. Cappelletti), publications of Institut Universitaire Européen, Economica, Paris, 1984; *Strumenti per la tutela degli interessi diffusi della collettività*, Atti del Convegno nazionale (Bologna, 5 dicembre 1981), Maggioli Editore. Rimini, 1982; *Acces to Justice* (ed. Cappelletti, M.), Milano, Giuffrè. Alphenaandenrijn, Sijthoff y Noorddhoff, 1978–79 (4 vols.); *Rilevanza e tutela degli interessi diffusi: modi e forme di individuaziones e protezione degli interessi della colletività*, Atti del XXIII Convegno di Studi di Scienza dell'Amministraziones (Varenna-Villa Monastero, 22–24 settembre 1977), Giuffrè. Milano, 1976; LAS ACCIONES DE INTERÉS PÚBLICO. ARGENTINA, CHILE, COLOMBIA Y PERÚ No. 7 (F. González Morales, ed.) (Santiago de Chile, 1997).

[4] In this respect, Louis Boré in *La défense des intérêts collectifs par les associations devant les juridictions administratives et judiciaires*, 1997 L.G.D.J. 145 (Paris, 1997) establishes: "[the] popular action was not for the Romans what we conceive today as the open action to everyone in the interest of the law. It had a mixed character, brought [on] occasions under a private interest, but serving always to the public interest".

[5] Philippe Didier, *De la Répresentation en Droit Privé*, 2002 L.G.D.J. 264 (Paris, 2000) *quoting* S. YEAZELL, FROM MEDIEVAL GROUP LITIGATION TO THE MODERN CLASS ACTION 38 (1987).

A very significant revamping of existing social structure would be required before so-called new rights could be identified, and the means for their vindication implemented. Such progress would require departure from classical legal remedies that have focused upon redress for offences to individual rights, and appurtenant liberties, tied to the notion of subjective law, and the breaking of many extant legal constructs before the new rights could arise, such as the "subjective right" to defend the environment.

What is the impact today of the very old, and yet still emerging, subject of collective actions? The answer is framed in the two legal systems examined in this chapter: that of Colombia and that of France. Both countries are representative of the regions to which they belong. Regarding the Latin American experience generally, and that of Colombia particularly, Felipe González introduces the above-mentioned book on public interest actions on various nations in this way: "Colombia seems to be the more advanced in the development of legal mechanisms that allow the development of public interest actions."[6] The same conclusion is reached in recent publication by the Mexican theorist Ovalle Favela in connection with popular actions, for whom "the country where actions have developed in a wider and more systematic way is, with no doubt, Colombia."[7] It would be neither necessary nor appropriate to ignore outstanding developments in other countries of the region, such as Brazil, well explained by the author Pellegrini,[8] but this is not an obstacle to concluding that Colombia is a representative country in the area. Even more if, as will be seen, from the Political Constitution of 1991 and specially from Law 442 of 1998 on, a strong wave of case law is now available.

France's juridical tradition and its high status among civil code nations makes its legal system a logical focus of our inquiry. The fact that, to our knowledge, there exist no rules of the European Community or of its member countries, individually considered, that regulate popular actions as conceived

---

[6] LAS ACCIONES DE INTERÉS PÚBLICO, *supra* n. 3, at 32.

[7] Brazil's developing law regarding collective actions is described in Lecture, José Ovalle Favela, *Acciones Populares y Acciones para la Tutela de los Intereses Colectivos*, in VII *Seminario* INTERNAZIONALI SU FORMAZIONE E CARATTERI DEL SISTEMA GUIRIDICO LATINOAMERICANO E PROBLEMI DEL PROCESSO CIVILE (Instituto Italo-Latinoamericano and the Instituto Iberoamericano de Derecho Procesal, Rome, 2002), at <http://www.juridicas.unam.mx/publica/rev/boletin/cont/107/art/art6.htm#N*>.

[8] *See* Ada Pellegrini Vinover, *Acciones colectivas para la defensa del ambiente y de los consumidores (La ley brasilera núm. 7347 de 24 de julio de 1985)*, 3 REVISTA DE DERECHO PROCESAL 705 (1998); Spain, No. 3, 1998, pg. 705; A PROBLEMÁTICA DOS INTERESSES DIFUSOS IN LA TUTELA DOS INTERESSES DIFUSOS (Sao Paola, 1984); O NOVO PROCESSO DO CONSUMIDOR (Rio de Janeiro 1996).

in Latin America,[9] allows one to choose a country with strong legal tradition under an administrative law system characteristic of Europe. In fact, as it shall be seen, France, which as well as the rest of the European countries has implemented only limited mechanisms for the defense of only supraindividual rights, has in its legal system a series of actions that "underline the need to include the collective interests in the procedural system."[10] Additionally, even though in both countries theoretical bases for prosecuting collective rights have long existed, the judicial exercise of such rights is still in its incipiency.

In Colombia, the popular action/public interest action was introduced in a strange way in the civil codification of the nineteenth century. The term "strange" is used because said action was unknown to the French Civil Code, translated by Andrés Bello, and implanted in most of Latin America.[11] As explained by Dr. Fernando Hinestrosa, the President of Universidad Externado de Colombia: "When drafting the Chilean Civil Code, afterwards adopted by Nueva Granada, today's Colombia, from 1859 on, all of the different states of the Granadine Confederation, with one exception, adopted successively the Chilean Code. Later on, when changing in 1873 to a Central State, Colombia adopted its Code of the Republic section 1, Law 57, 1887." Hinestrosa continues: "Dn. Andrés Bello introduced to that legal system some significant variations. Among the mentioned variations, it is important to note:... the introduction of contingent damages (sections 2333 [and] 2359) and popular actions (sections 2334 [and] 2360)."[12]

Notwithstanding the early recognition of these concepts in Colombian law, only isolated cases of its implementation were seen by the end of the

---

[9] In this regard, *see* Pablo Gutierrez de Cabiedes e Hidalgo de Caviedes, *La tutela jurisdiccional de los intereses supraindividuales: colectivos y difusos*, ARANZADI EDITORIAL 212–14 (Navarra, 1999).

[10] Joaquín Salguero Estagnan, *La tutela jurisdiccional de los intereses colectivos a través de la legitimación de los grupos*, EDITORIAL DYKINSON 231 (Madrid, 1995).

[11] The "clue" to this phenomenon can be traced in Alejandro Guzmán Brito, *Historia de la codificación civil en Latinoamérica*, EDITORIAL JURÍDICA DE CHILE (Santiago, 2000); XIV ANDRÉS BELLO, OBRAS COMPLETAS: CÓDIGO CIVIL DE LA REPÚBLICA DE CHILE (Caracas, 1954); Luis Claro Solar, *Explicaciones de derecho civil chileno y comparado*, EDITORIAL JURÍDICA DE CHILE (1992); Vols. 1 and 2, Alejandro Guzmán Brito, Andrés Bello Codificador. *Historia de la fijación y codificación del derecho civil en Chile*, EDICIONES DE LA UNIVERSIDAD DE CHILE (Santiago, 1982); Joaquín Escriche, DICCIONARIO RAZONADO DE LEGISLACIÓN CIVIL, PENAL, COMERCIAL Y FORENSE (Paris, 1831); *Le Code Napoleon et le Code Civil du Chili*, XLIV CIRCULATION DU MODÈLE JURIDIQUE FRANÇAIS 141 *et seq.* (1993).

[12] Fernando Hinestrosa, *Devenir del derecho de daños, Roma e America. Diritto romano commune*, AMERICA LATINA: PRINCIPI E REGOLE COMUNI IN MATERIA DI RESPONSABILITÁ EXTRACONTRATTUALE' 22 (2000).

twentieth century.[13] Not until the enactment of Law 472 of 1998 did there develop a substantial body of decisions involving the defense of collective and group rights.[14]

In France, popular actions did not exist in the Napoleonic Civil Code. The apparent basis for this absense was section 3 of the Declaration of the Rights of Man and Citizen, according to which sovereignty was vested in the Nation, and the people were forbidden to exercise any authority that had no express delegation or empowerment from the nation's representatives. The apparent goal was to adopt more of a representative than a purely participative democracy. Support for this sentiment can be found as far back historically as the Middle Ages, in which period there are examples of the banning of associations, as associations might express interests opposed to those of the state. In fact, Law 14–17 of June 1791, called Chapelier Law, "...became the symbol of the abolition of corporations and, even more, of the prohibition of the right of association [,]"[15] which rights were only reinstated in July 1, 1901. With this concept in mind, it is easy to understand that the French scheme of judicial proceedings was based on impeding the exercise of popular actions.[16]

Nevertheless, the situation described here cannot allow one to suppose that the logic of collective rights does not inhere in the French system, or that historically there have not been possibilities for their prosecution. In fact, the most significant work by the Maximum Court of Administrative Law (*Conseil d'Etat*), the *Recours pour excès de pouvoir*, has long permitted, as we will see, an attack on the illegality of decisions where collective rights are involved. Furthermore, there is a new invitation to permit such challenges. It started with popular Law Rover of December 27, 1973, reformed by the laws of January 5, 1988 and January 18, 1992, that jointly constitute a general statute on actions available in justice to consumers' associations. These laws, together

---

[13] *See generally* GERMÁN OROZCO OCHOA, JURISPRUDENCIA DE LA CORTE SUPREMA DE JUSTICIA (DE 1887 A 1944) (1945) (reviewing decision of the Colombian Supreme Court of Justice, S.N.G., April 23, 1941).

[14] According to statistics published by the Public Defender in *Gacetilla de Acciones Populares y de Grupo*, year 1, # 1, at 96 (August, 2003), *Defensoría del Pueblo y Embajada Real de los Países Bajos*, Bogotá, D.C., one notes that "from issuance of Law 472, 1998 to May, 2002, there have been 1800 popular actions filed, among which there [have] already been a favorable decision in 320. The rest [have] been unfavorable or [have] not been decided yet. Among the favorable decisions, 133 have protected public security and public health, 115 have protected the access to the rendering of efficient public services, 114 relate to a healthy environment, 83 to the rights of consumers and users, etc. It must be taken into consideration that a decision may protect several different collective rights."

[15] Louis Boré, *supra* n. 3, at 151.

[16] *See*, in this respect, Jean-Claude Venezia, *Intérêt pour agir*, II REPERTOIRE DE CONTENTIEUX ADMINISTRATIF n° 67 (Dalloz, Paris, 1985); Michel Rousset, *Droit Administratif, id.* at 118; Jean-Michel Lemoyne de Forges, *Recours Pour Excès de Pouvoir (Conditions de Recevabité), id.* at 262; Georges Vedel y Pierre Delvolvé, 2 DROIT ADMINISTRATIF, P.U.F. 262 (Paris 1990).

with the Law dated July 26, 1993, known as the *Code de la Consommation*, for example, represent significant French legislative interest in the topic studied in this chapter. The fact that France belongs to the European Community elevates the importance of these issues, as the other member countries have different positions on the matter. The French view of the pertinence of this topic, from the standpoints of both comparative law as well as arguably more practical pursuits, has been stated in this way: "French liability law is, regarding its own capacities, below those offered, for example, in an Anglo Saxon legal system, that differentiates 'private' from 'public' nuisance actions,"[17] or with the observation that only the recognition of a general right to the environment, where individuals as well as associations could bring actions before tribunals, permits one to call the interests known as "collective." "A step toward this recognition has already been taken in the international and foreign arena."[18]

It can be seen that the present issues, presented by the law of Colombia and France, notwithstanding their historical difference, allows the understanding of why the topic chosen is of the highest importance in the future to both nations. It is true that the historical and ideological differences place difficulties in the analysis of the legal systems of both countries, as their approaches to the mentioned subjective rights, as already noted, has been very different. But such difficulty is only a further stimulus to the comparative law method.

Given the mentioned differences between the legal systems of Colombia and France it seems desirable to allocate separate sections to the discussion of the chosen topic under the rules of each country's legal system. In what follows, sacrificing originality on behalf of organization, I will start with a definition of the significance for each country of the subject under discussion. I will then review first the example of Colombia, because of the clarity of its legal system with respect to collective rights, at least at the level of applicable written rules. We will then turn to the example of the French legal system in order to reach some conclusions under comparative law.

II. THE CONCEPT OF COLLECTIVE RIGHTS IN BOTH LEGAL SYSTEMS

A. General Approach

The initial difficulty in approaching this subject is reflected in the fact that the notion of collective rights is of uncertain existence in French law, and certainly has different meaning under Colombian and French law. In addition

---

[17] JBooklet 1005, Contentieux – Problématique et Perspectives, 40 JURISCLASSEUR (1992).

[18] Marcel Sousse, *La notion de réparation de dommages en droit administratif français*, 1994 L.G.D.J.389 (Paris, 1994).

to this, one must take into consideration that in Spanish, the concept of collective rights has various definitions. It has been written, there is "a 'dance' of concepts, in which one uses the same word with very different meanings and different words with the same meaning."[19]

In Colombia, collective rights are clearly enunciated in section 88 of the National Constitution[20] and developed by section 4 of Law 472, 1998.[21] In particular, the Colombian Constitution as well as the statutory law have expressly defined fourteen "collective" rights. To this list, one must add other collective rights, considered as such by other national laws and international treaties, because Law 446 adopts an open formula.

Following the lines of written law, which does not define collective rights, case law has established that a: "collective interest is . . . an interest that belongs to all and each one of the members of a defined collectivity and takes form through its active participation before the administration of justice, demanding protection."[22] The Maximum Court in Administrative Law has had the

---

[19] Pablo Gutierrez de Cabiedes e Hidalgo de Caviedes, *La tutela jurisdiccional de los intereses supraindividuales: colectivos y difusos,* 1999 ARANZADI EDITORIAL 64 (Navarra, 1999).

[20] The referenced section referred to states: "Article 88. The law will regulate popular actions for the protection of collective rights and interests related to the public assets, space, public safety and health, administrative morality, the environment, free economic competition, and others of a similar nature. It will also regulate the actions arising out of harm caused to a large number of individuals, without barring appropriate individual action. In the same way, it will define cases of strict liability for damage caused to collective rights and interests."

[21] Section 4 of Law 472, 1998, states:

> *Collective rights and interests.* Collective rights and interests are, among others, those related to: a) the enjoyment of a sound environment, as it is established by the Constitution, the written law and other regulations; b) administrative morality; c) the existence of an ecological equilibrium and the rational management of natural resources in order to guarantee a sustainable development, its conservation restoration and substitution of the environment. The conservation of animal and vegetable species, the protection of areas of special ecological importance, of ecosystems in near-by frontier territory, as well as other interests of the community related with preservation and restoration of the environment; d) The enjoyment of the public space and the use and defense of assets of public use; e) the defense of public property or heritage; f) public safety and health; h) access to the infrastructure of public services that would guarantee public health; i) free economic competition; j) access to public services and to an efficient and timely rendering of such services; k) the prohibition of manufacturing, importation, possession and use of chemical, biological or nuclear weapons, as well as the introduction into the national territory of nuclear or toxic waste; l) the right to security and forecast of technically foreseeable disasters; m) the building of edifications and urban developments following the applicable legal laws in an organized way and providing to their inhabitants the benefits of a good quality of life; n) the rights of consumers and users. Equally are rights and collective interests those defined as such by the Constitution, ordinary written laws and international treaties executed by Colombia.
>
> Rights and interests enounced in this section will be defined and ruled by the applicable rules or any rule issued after the present law.

[22] Colombian Constitutional Court, open court, April 14, 1999, justice "ponente": Martha Victoria Sáchica de Moncaleano, plaintiff: Andrés de Zubiría Samper et al., consolidation of files numbers D-2176, D-2178 and D-2196.

opportunity to add that the said rights "intrinsically, must virtually engage all society in their exercise,"[23] because "they respond to the urgency of satisfying collective and social needs and are exercised by the members of human groups in an identical, uniform and shared way."[24] This concept implies that the notion of collective right goes together with the possibility that they can be exercised by any member of the community, not because the individual is the one direct and exclusive owner but because the interest belongs to and identifies the community of which the individual is a part. In this sense, the judicial defense of a collective right "does not suppose the existence of true and real dispute, because the objective is not to settle a controversy, but to make effective a collective right, stopping damage or the threat of damage, or requiring that things return to the state prior to the damage if this is possible."[25]

We can therefore state that in Colombia, collective rights are those defined by written law and their exercise engages society as a whole, as their direct defense before the judges is exercised via popular action pursuant to subjective law. Subjective law is another way of stating substantive law, while the opposite, adjective law, pertains to the procedures for its implementation.[26] Thus, according to substantive/subjective law, "any person in town" to repeat the wording of the Civil Code of the nineteenth century, uses the popular action to claim protection for the benefit of the community. Even though the right does not belong exclusively to the individual, he does have the right to protect it.

---

[23] Decision AP-021 (March 16, 2000).

[24] Decision AP-043 (June 1, 2000), Colombian Maximum Court in Administrative Law, Third Section, December 6th, 2001, Justice "ponente" Alier Hernández Enríquez, plaintiff: Nestor Gregory Díaz, file AP-221.

[25] Colombian Maximum Court in Administrative Law, Third Section, March 11th., 2003, justice "ponente": Hoyos Duque, plaintiff: General Controller of the Republic, file AP-11001031500020021011–01.

[26] Subjective rights are the possibility to require a performance, the content of the obligation of giving, doing or not doing something. See Fernando Hinestrosa, TRATADO DE LAS OBLIGACIONES. CONCEPT. STRUCTURE. VICISSITUDES 301 (2002): "... subjective rights imply a prerogative that each rule confers to someone in front of others, for the satisfaction of this person's interests, because it is in a situation that justifies such protection in the ethical and social patrons, and that allows one to expect with sufficient reasons, the respect and cooperation from others and request for these coactively if it were necessary, with preventive, restitutory and remedial pretentions, in accordance with the circumstances and one's free will."

See Norbert Foulquier, Les droits publics subjectifs des administrés, EMERGENCE D'UN CONCEPT EN DROIT ADMINISTRATIF FRANÇAIS DU XIX E AU XX E SIÈCLE 405 (Dalloz, Paris, 2003): "A citizen is the owner of a subjective public right when it meets the conditions that would allow him to be considered beneficiary of the power to demand – recognized by a general or particular rule, with a legitimate social objective, without being forced to use it –, a defined behaviour from the public persons – which constitute the object of its obligation –, to procure a certain moral or material advantage that the legal system has, expressly or implied, considered illegal."

In France, on the contrary, the concept of "*droit collectif*" does not exist in the same sense as the Colombian notion. As already mentioned, this is due in part to the fact that popular action is not expressly allowed. The intention is not to confuse the notion of right with that of legal standing to bring an action, as each legal system is free to choose whether collective rights are attached to the popular action. But we must note that the concept of collective right is not even found in the digests of France's general administrative law manuals,[27] nor in its administrative law in relation to public property,[28] nor in its constitutional law,[29] nor its law for challenging administrative action ("contentious administrative law"),[30] nor, finally, in the law governing state civil liability.[31] Perhaps, one can infer that the concept of public domain does exist, that public property belongs to this concept, and that its use may belong to all the inhabitants of the territory (river, land, and maritime public domain, among others).[32] However the subjective right that allows a party to bring action to protect this property is not vested in "any person in town," that is, in any *one* person in a town.

This conclusion is supported by the interesting doctrinal debate on the issue of whether the state is the owner of, or simply the guardian of, the mentioned public property. In this respect, in the nineteenth century "the majority of the scholars agreed on the idea of rejecting any intention of property in public domain. The state alone had the right of a guardian."[33] This way of thinking was abandoned, thanks to the important influence of the theory of *administrative property*, developed by Hauriou, according to which "property of the state as to public goods was vigorously refuted."[34] Various arguments supported

---

[27] To quote two examples: René Chapus, Droit Administratif Général, Editions Montchrestien, Paris, 2001; Jacques Moreau, Droit Administratif, P.U.F., Paris, 1989.

[28] E.g., Jean-Marie Auby y Pierre Bon, *Droit Administratif des Biens*. Domaine, travaux publics, expropriation pour cause d'utilité publique (3d ed) (Dalloz, Paris).

[29] E.g., Louis Favoreu and Loïc Philip, *Les Grandes Décisions du Conseil Constitutionnel* (8th ed.) (Dalloz, Paris, 1995).

[30] E.g., Jean-Marie Auby y Roland Drago, Traité des recours en matière administrative (Paris, 1992); René Chapus, Droit du contentieux administratif (9th ed.) (Paris, 2001).

[31] See Répertoire de la Responsabilité de la Puissance Publique, Encyclopédie Dalloz, (Dalloz, Paris, 1992).

[32] See Philippe Godfrin, Droit administratif des biens. Domaines, travaux, expropiations (5th ed.) 16 (Paris, 1997).

[33] Norbert Foulquier, Les droits publics subjectifs des administrés. Émergence d'un concept en droit administratif français du XIX e au XX e siècle 118 (Dalloz, Paris, 2003).

[34] See Jean-Marie Auby y Pierre Bon, Droit administratif des biens. Domaine, travaux publics, expropiation pour cause d'utilité publique (3ème ed.) 71 (Dalloz, Paris, 1995).

Hauriou's theory: "The anti-property theory advanced a presumption against the state or administration in any claim that it alone had rights ragarding the protection of domaine/property and its affectation. These concerns, inspired by memories of the *Ancien Régime*, have no support nowadays. – This theory impeded the state or administration from [claiming] the exclusive right to benefit from, or to protect, public land or property. If the Administration does not possess the right to 'abuse' *(abusus)*, it does have some of the prerogatives of the right of property (*usus, fructus*). – Only, the theory of property permits explanation of certain solutions. In the case of modifying the public domaine of assets pertaining to public property, the Administration is still with no doubt the owner under this new approach. How could one understand the existence of that right of property if the Administration was not owner before?"[35]

In the long battle fought for the recognition of public subjective rights of the citizens in French law,[36] the concept of collective rights combined with popular actions to indicate them had no support then, either in written law or in doctrine. In fact, as opposed to the experience in Colombia, the means of pursuing a collective or public action to declare written laws or administrative actions unlawful did not and does not exist.

This does not mean that the concept of *intérêt collectif* has been unknown to French law. Thus, thanks to the important role played by associations, the concept mentioned above became of high importance for the defense of rights beyond the orbit of the individual. A collective interest was defined then as "an interest held by an association or a union that acts to defend the interests for whose defense the group is constituted."[37] The concept of collective interest was subordinated to the purpose of the associations to the extent that if the documents creating the association did not so state, there was no collective interest. But, "collective" interests reflected in the by-laws or articles of incorporation represent one matter, and of a very different pedigree are the collective rights, supported in the Colombian definition, obligatorily connected with popular action and with rights belonging to "any one person in town."

Even though it is true that collective rights and associations *can* coincide, for example, when an association constituted for the defense of the environment

---

[35] *Id.*

[36] *See* the words of Professor Frank Moderne in the preface to the quoted book de Foulquier, *supra* note 26: "The idea, that the people could benefit from subjective rights opposable to the state, that is to the public power, and eventually bring action before a judge, seemed to the eyes of the majority of scholars (including all the schools) dangerous (. . .) and useless."

[37] Jean-Claude Venecia, *Intérêt pour agir*, II Répertoire de Contentieux Administratif No. 23 (1985).

contains such collective interest, one must note that "the principle of special-ity in corporations and associations" restrains French law from sharing the Colombian concept. The said principle "limits the action of associations (and all corporations different from the state) to the domain defined by the pur-pose of such entity, that is, to the collective interests that such persons defend. If those interests are not affected, the association has no legal capacity/is not empowered to act, either in general action or in non-general action."[38]

Therefore, as to whether one has standing to bring suit to challenge a state or administrative action, "case law and doctrine make a distinction between general and collective interest, in accordance with an organic criterion: the first one is defended by public entities and the second one by private entities or individuals. We consider that an association with the purpose of claiming, for public order, maintenance or assurance of public security must be declared illegal, since the purpose is so general that it would not be compatible with the principle of specialty of corporations and associations. It would then be a state inside the state. The Maximum Court of Appeal in Administrative Law judged an action brought by an association to "fight injustice under any possible form" to be noncognizable at law or equity because "due to the generality of the terms, the claimant does not justify an interest giving legitimacy to act and to claim for the annulment of the Secretary's act."[39] On the contrary, under Colombian law, as everybody is vested with the public interest and this does not permit the criticism that to permit such a challenge to an administrative action would create a "state" within a "state".

We will start then with the Colombian concept of collective rights, with-out meaning by this that there is no possible existence of such right in the French system. The intention is to find out how and to what extent these collective rights exist. The starting point is then one in which the notion of collective rights that will illustrate the comparison of both countries is the one considered under Colombian law, in the sense in which collective rights are defined by the law as such rights as are exercised by the society as whole, with the society benefitting from them in an indivisible way, and, that includes the notion of popular action that converts a collective right to a subjective right in favor of "any person." This starting point supposes that when one approaches French law, one will do it from the perspective of those rights that have been defined as "collective" in Colombia, to determine if there exists or not a protection of the same type in France. This is, because as previously noted, the absence of any direct reference to the popular action does not by definition preclude the conclusion that, there exist collective rights that may

[38] Louis Boré, *supra* note 4, at 204.
[39] *Id.* at 12.

be protected. In other words, the definition of collective rights in Colombia will be used in this comparative law study. Such use will be incomplete precisely because of the nonexistence of the popular action in France, but this does not impede our study of how such rights are defended in this country, the rights defended by means of the popular action in Colombia.

Before we start, we must mention the hierarchy or ranking that doctrine and case law have made of such rights. One sees that the "nature of rights protected by actions established in section 88 of the Colombian Constitution is of third generation[,] which is to say, twice or thrice removed from its constitutional or statutory origins."[40] This may be accepted on the assumption that each one of the above-mentioned rights in the Colombian legal rules belongs to the third generation. But what cannot be accepted, even if one follows the French doctrine according to which said rights exist but are indeed "proclamatory"[41] or hortatory, is that in Colombia these rights are only proclamatory because any person can request performance from others. In Colombia, political decision reflected in the Constitution and the actions of lawmakers has followed "the path that must lead to collective rights,"[42] expected and wanted by the French law professor Rousseau.

Let us then study the legal system of both countries.

B. Colombia

In Colombia, as we have noted, there are general written rules that refer to collective rights and popular action: Section 88 of the Political Constitution of 1991 and Law 472 of 1998, which regulated this section of the Political Constitution. The mentioned written rules make Colombia a privileged country in this respect. Colombia has legal mechanisms that go further than perhaps any other nation in protecting collective rights as well as providing for the enforcement of those rights. The notions of collective right and popular action are enshrined in the Colombian legal system.

At the same time there exists in Colombia, as in France, the action of nullification, by virtue of which "any person may request directly, or by means of a representative, the declaration of the illegality of administrative action"

---

[40] Essay, Daniel Suárez Hernández and Ruth Stella Correa Palacio, *Acciones populares y de grupo: Ley 472 de 1998*, XX Congreso Colombiano de Derecho Procesal, Instituto Colombiano de Derecho Procesal, at 534 (1999). In the same sense of the three categories of rights, *see* Corte Constitucional Colombiana, Decision T-008/92, Justice "ponente": Morón Díaz, plaintiff: Matilde Bohorquez, file T-399.

[41] Dominique Rousseau, *Les droits de l'homme de la troisième génération*, 1987 Revue Interdisciplinaire d'Etudes Juridiques (RIEJ) 19 *et seq.* (1987); *see* Norbert Foulquier, *supra* note 33 at 542 *et seq.*

[42] Dominique Rousseau, *id.* at 31.

(Section 84 of the Administrative Litigation Code). This Colombian action is inspired in the French *recours pour excès de pouvoir*, as it has been recognized by respected scholars.[43] Even though it is undeniable that such action may serve to protect collective rights, because it "is the normal means at disposal of the citizens against every unilateral act of the Administration with the objective of re-establishing... legality,"[44] the originality of the Colombian system by creating a specific action to protect the same permits one to devote particular attention to the Colombian mechanisms for the "nullification" action.

In order to study the way collective rights work presently in Colombia, we will first study the definition and purpose of popular action, followed by an illustration of the protected collective rights, and, finally, examine when collective rights prevail over individual rights.

1. *Definition and Purpose of Popular Action*

Popular actions are defined by the law as "procedural means for the protection of collective rights and interests" mentioned in Section 4 of Law 472. According to Section 12 of the same law, they can be used by "any individual, corporation or association" without statutory limitation in action[45] and "are used to avoid contingent or prospective damages, to stop the danger, threat, or existing injury or damage to collective rights and interests, or to return conditions to their previous state if possible" (Section 2).

In its passage through the Colombian Congress, this section suffered the deletion of an additional purpose for which popular action was conceived, which was "to obtain indemnification in the benefit of the state." The events were as follows: the President of the Republic opposed the proposed law, alleging that the proposed bill was unconstitutional. Therefore, both chambers of Congress would have to have insisted on the proposed law for the Constitutional Court to be obliged to study the objection and decide the issue. As only the Senate (High Chamber) and not the Chamber of Representatives (Lower Chamber) insisted in contesting, the sentence mentioned was deleted.[46] This legislative history is outlined to illustrate that the notion of collective right is

---

[43] *See* Jaime Orlando Santofimio, II DERECHO ADMINISTRATIVO. ACTO ADMINISTRATIVO, PROCEDIMIENTO, EFICACIA Y VALIDEZ (3d ed.) 532–38 (1998).

[44] Carlos Betancur Jaramillo, DERECHO PROCESAL ADMINISTRATIVO (4th ed.) 40 (1994).

[45] Colombian Constitutional Court, April 14, 1999, C-215: In this decision the High Court held there was no conformity with the Constitution for the wording of the written rule that stated that there would be five years of statutory limitation for action, in this event, the intention of its excercise were to "bring conditions back to their previous state."

[46] Colombian Constitutional Court, in open court, February 19, 1998, justice "ponente": Eduardo Cifuentes, file O.P. 021.

not conceived in favor of public property belonging to the state, but rather because this notion permits the right of enjoyment of collective rights belonging to the citizens, even though at a certain moment both categories – public property and collective rights – may coincide.

Therefore, taking into consideration the existing law and its contents, one can state that popular action has various objectives that depend on which hypothesis of the rule given in Section 12 of Law 472 is being used: to avoid damages, to make stop existing damages or to bring back or reestablish original conditions. Thus, "to avoid" is different from "to stop" and these two expressions are in turn different from "to reestablish," which demonstrates that there are three different hypotheses.

Even though law normally employs the word "to avoid" solely in relation with "contingent damages," one must construe that, bearing in mind that in this damage "there only exists a threat"[47] – Section 2359 of the Civil Code – , "to avoid" means the same as "to make the danger (or) the threat stop," but it does not mean the same as to make "the offense, injury or wrong stop." Neither does it mean the same as to "reestablish" the original conditions before the damage occurred.

When one is attempting to stop a threat, it is in a circumstance where there was no damage committed. In contrast, when one halting an injury or wrong, a damage has occurred and the intention is to stop its harmful ripple effects or reestablish the conditions modified by the damage. If one were placed in a continuum where the last stage will be marked by damage, a situation where you must reestablish the collective rights harmed, one would identify as the first step the stage of "to avoid," and as the middle step, the stage of "to stop." Therefore, you can state that popular action includes a preventive stage as well as a restitutory one.[48]

---

[47] Javier Tamayo Jaramillo, Las acciones populares y de grupo en la responsabilidad civil 57 (2001).

[48] *See* in this respect: Colombian Maximum Court in Administrative Lawon, Fifth Section, November 9, 2001, justice "ponente": Quiñonez Pinilla, file AP-194, plaintiff: Rodolfo Puentes Suárez et al. "In accordance with section 2 of Law 472, 1998, the popular action is used to i) avoid contingent damages, ii) stop the danger, threat, injury or damage to collective rights and iii) re-establish things to their previous state, if this is possible. As one can observe, the first two objectives of this procedural instrument have a preventive nature, since they look to impede the consummation of damages or to avoid the damage from being greater. The third objective of popular action is addressed to re-establish or bring conditions back to their previous state, not intending principally to compensate economically but as an instrument to re-establish the right that has been damaged. For these reasons, the objective of the action is not to punish an action but to protect the collective rights and interests from the threat or harm of the contingent damage"; Colombian Constitutional Court, April 14, 1999, justice "ponente": Martha Victoria Sáchica de Maldonado, cumulative files D-2176, D-2184

Let us give some examples of the different hypotheses.

The first hypothesis, of an essentially preventive nature, considers the situation when the harm to the collective has not yet occurred. The judge must verify that there is an imminent threat to a collective right, caused by the administrative action being contemplated. He must establish that the harmful action will certainly damage a collective right and he must take any relevant action to avoid the damage. This situation is common, for example, in some events where public property and administrative morality are at play. In this hypothesis, case law has stated that: "if public property is affected, the judge has preventive faculties and, consequently, he may adopt transitory or definitive measures, which can only be assessed in each particular case."[49] This was done in the above-mentioned decision, in which the popular demand questioned a public offering proceeding for the privatization of the local public services, which had been prepared by a consulting service. The Maximum Court of Administrative Law decided to issue an injunction forcing the mayor's office and the public enterprise to "suspend immediately the concession process, until the necessary measures to consider the balance sheets and figures that reflect the true financial circumstances of the concessionaire are taken, and, afterwards, to define the management scheme to make certain that it ensures the efficient rendering of the public services of water supply and sewage."

In such cases, the judge considers that the collective rights under consideration were *ad portas* of being injured and avoids this injury by taking measures that would step the threat. The damage is not produced, we repeat, because the collective rights are not injured; therefore we are in the preventive stage of this action.

In the second hypothesis considered by Law 472, you want "to stop" damage. The objective is to prevent or impede the damage or its aggravation, without excluding the restitution of that portion that has already suffered damage. By definition, in this case, the violation of the right must have already taken place. In this hypothesis, as we have previously said, there are two functions, one preventive and one restitutive. The first one is aimed at impeding the damage, and the second at restoring the collective right that has been injured, to the extent that this is possible.

D-2196: "Now, another essential characteristic of popular actions is their preventive nature, which means that the existence of harm or damage to rights and interests is not and can not be a condition to bring the action, as it is enough to face the threat or risk of damage production. This is due to the public objectives and intentions that inspire this concept.

[49] Colombian Maximum Court in Administrative Law, Fifth Section, August 24, 2001, justice "ponente": Quiñonez Pinilla, file AP-100, plaintiff: Procuraduría Provincial de Ibagué.

Such was the case in one decision in which, after establishing that non-potable water for human consumption was being supplied, and finding the violation of a collective right, the Maximum Court of Administrative Law ordered future weekly maintenance to the water filters and further required that the respondent keep Court informed every two months as to whether the water delivered was potable or not,[50] thus avoiding further injury. There is also a case in which after finding an injury to rights related to public property and public security, the construction of a football stadium, contracted for by a municipality, was suspended and the municipality was ordered to use the land and the portion already built for a different purpose.[51] Following a similar logic, it was decided to "suspend the performance of a contract to buy and sell liquors" agreed between a public entity and a private consortium, until the action to declare the contract null and void brought by the public entity could be decided. The reason given was that the said contract "constitutes a threat to public assets," because "the conditions set by the state to agree on this contract: the minimum amount to be acquired by the contractor and the installed capacity of the factory that is to be placed out of service, added to the economic conditions, price and compensation, will continue to cause damages to the public enterprise if it is permitted to perform the contract."[52]

In these cases, one must distinguish two situations: (a) damage caused to collective rights and (b) aggravation or worsening of damage. Frequently, the latter objective may be easily accomplished, as it refers to the preventive aspect of the popular action. Nevertheless, the first situation will not necessarily presuppose a remedy of restitution *in natura* or by pecuniary compensation of the portion of the damage that has already been caused to the collective right. This is so because it may well occur that it is not possible to order such remedies or measures. This is what happens in the above-mentioned examples of this hypothesis, in which collective rights cannot be reestablished, because it would require a distortion of the popular action into a class or group action,[53] which are alien in form and in objective to popular action; or what

---

[50] Colombian Maximum Court in Administrative Law, Third Section, December 6, 2001, justice "ponente": Hernández Enríquez, plaintiff: Nestor Gregory Díaz, file AP-221.

[51] Colombian Maximum Court in Administrative Law, Third Section, June 7, 2001, justice "ponente": Alier E. Hernández Enríquez, file AP-166, Plaintiff: Manuel Jesús Bravo et al.

[52] Colombian Maximum Court in Administrative Law, Third Section, October 31, 2002, justice "ponente": Hoyos Duque, plaintiff: Jesús Orlando Mejía, file: AP-520001233100020001059-01.

[53] Colombian Maximum Court in Administrative Law, Fifth Section, November 11, 2002, justice "ponente": Quiñonez Pinilla, file AP-737, Plaintiff: Henry Díaz Cubides: "Thus, if the citizens are affected by the injury to collective rights and interests, they may claim for damages but not by means of the popular action but by other procedural means, such as the group action."

happens in the case of the stadium or the liquor contract, where one must determine the damage caused by suspending construction of the stadium or by the suspension of the performance of the conditions of the liquor contract, as well as imputability and causation in law.

In the third hypothesis considered in Law 472, in connection with the restitutory function, one must try "to reestablish things to their previous state when this is possible." Even though the law as written does not mention what happens when it is not possible to reestablish things to their previous state, one must conclude that payment by pecuniary equivalent is also permitted.

In other words, the popular action may lead mainly and exclusively an economical indemnification of the injured collective right.[54] This concept coincides with Section 34 of Law 472, which states, when referring to the final decision, that it "may contain an injunction to do or to preclude from doing, to condemn to pay damages, when a collective right or interest has been injured, to the benefit of the non-guilty public entity on account of that collective right or interest and demand the performance of necessary actions to re-establish conditions to the state previous to the injury, when this is physically possible."[55]

The usual situation will be one in which the action of the tribunal pretends to return the injured collective right to its previous state. But it also may occur when the wrong is already done, the right is injured and, because there is no possibility to perform restitution *in natura*, only economic compensation is available, as would be the case if the judge enjoins performance of both obligations because he considers that this is needed in order to arrive at a complete indemnification of the damage caused. Even though there are no decisions, to our knowledge, in which the state has been required to indemnify a collective

---

[54] We agree with the conclusion on this point brought by Professor Tamayo Jaramillo at p. 170 of the quoted book: "In conclusion, we believe that the popular action is also perfectly possible, when it exclusively demands for indemnification of a collective damage already suffered."

[55] We consider it unfortunate that the request that the decision to pay damages will be done "in favor of the non-guilty public entity," because we think it confuses the control and administration that a public entity may have on a right that being collective belongs precisely to "everyone" and the judgment on the action or omission of that public entity. This has nothing to do with the need to repair the injured right. In the event that the guilty public entity is the same guardian of that collective right, a situation that may occur frequently, the judge must be creative to guarantee the indemnification of the damage in favor of another public entity, related with the collective right injured and with the express indication of the objective of indemnification, or in favor of the same entity. In this case, the exception of unconstitutionality should be applied, with the argument of the prevalence of the substantial right that implies that one cannot leave without indemnification a collective right that constitutionally and legally must be repaired.

right by granting a certain economic amount due to the impossibility of reestablishing *in natura*, case law has already established that such a *possibility* does exist.[56] This is seen in the illustration of this hypothesis of the popular action that can only be vindicated with a judicial order that the Administration must comply with or undertake some affirmative action or duty.

A decision dated November 9, 2001, is a good example of the working of Law 472, in its third hypothesis – "to re-establish conditions to their previous state" – in this event, the irrational killing of ten thousand wild animals (*Hydrochaeris hydrochaeris*, known popularly in Colombia as "chigüiro"). This was done, and their meat was exported, due to the existence of an exporting and environmental license, wrongly granted by the environmental authorities. In this case, the Court of Appeal in Administrative Law entered an injunction requiring that "the responsible entities put into practice the necessary measures to replace the sacrificed animal population, for which they must use sufficient funds to carry out programs to be developed for this purpose."[57] This would guarantee the return to the situation previous to the injury to the collective right. The same would happen when the state of deterioration of a colonial church was claimed to injure the cultural assets of the nation and its restoration is enjoined.[58]

Note that in these events, even though the state was required to pay to reestablish the animal species or to conserve the cultural assets, the state was not paying the pecuniary equivalent of the damage but rather compensating for it with the performance of the obligations enjoined. A similar logic is observed in decisions made in defense of the enjoyment of the public space, where, once it is established that a right has been violated, the judge enjoins the authorities "in the fifteen (15) days subsequent to the judgment, and in no event later than three (3) months, to take measures to re-establish the integrity of the public space."[59]

---

[56] Colombian Maximum Court in Administrative Law, Third Section, September 20, 2001, justice "ponente": Hernández Enríquez, plaintiff: María Consuelo Romero Millán et al., File AP-182: "In other terms, the law admits that popular action has a special indemnification character which, of course, is conceived in its finality, which is the protection and guarantee of collective interests: indemnification is created in order to repair the damage caused in direct way to the collective right and not to repair those damages caused indirectly to the individual rights of the members of an affected community."

[57] Colombian Maximum Court in Administrative Law, Fith Section, November 9, 2001, justice "ponente": Quiñonez Pinilla, plaintiff: Rodolfo Puentes et al, file AP-194.

[58] Colombian Maximum Court in Administrative Law, Third Section, September 20, 2001, File AP-125, plaintiff: Jaime Umaña Díaz, justice "ponente": María Helena Giraldo.

[59] Colombian Maximum Court in Administrative Law, First Section, November 8, 2002, justice "ponente": Quiñonez Pinilla, plaintiff: Ismael Forero Mongui, file AP-25000-23-24-000-2001-0495-01.

Along similar lines, it has been found that when the judge identifies
an excessive payment with public monies made by a ministerial office to
an individual in accordance with a settlement agreement, the payment is
unenforceable and without legal effect, by virtue of the popular action,
and the individual is enjoined to return with present value the monies
received.[60] In this type of event, compensation for collective damage caused
is guaranteed because this permits the return of conditions to the *status
quo ante*.

2. *Collective Rights Protected by Popular Action*

From the above-mentioned language used in Section 88 of the Colombian
Political Constitution and in Section 4 of Law 472, 1998, one can identify which
collective rights can be protected by popular action. As this is a generous and
exhaustive listing, each particular case that is analyzed by the judges will
involve, in the majority of the decisions taken, various collective rights.

Let us see some examples.

In relation with public health, after establishing that the water supplied to
its citizens by a municipality is not potable, the judge enjoins the mayor to
"perform a weekly maintenance of the filters of the Treatment Plant FIME
and verify every six months the sand graduation of all the filters in the plant in
order to optimize its operation." The mayor is also enjoined to render reports
that show that water is potable.[61] But this right is not only protected when
the water service is not being efficient, but when it is not provided at all, as
one must relate it with the access to a service infrastructure that guarantees
public health, as well as with the right to access to public services in general
and to their efficient and timely rendering. And so, if there is no sewage
system treatment, a mayor is enjoined to put into practice a mechanism for
this treatment[62] or a mayor is enjoined to "define the managerial scheme
that assures the efficient rendering of the public services of water supply and
sewage system for all the inhabitants" in a public service concession[63] or, even,
authorities are enjoined "to adopt an action plan with a schedule in order to
carry out studies and projects of the sewage system in the neighbourhood, to

---

[60] Colombian Maximum Court in Administrative Law, May 31, 2002, File AP-300, plaintiff:
Contraloría General de la República et al., justice "ponente": Ligia López Díaz.

[61] Colombian Maximum Court in Administrative Law, Third Section, December 6, 2001, justice
"ponente": Hernández Enríquez, file AP-221, plaintiff: Nestor Gregory Díaz.

[62] Colombian Maximum Court in Administrative Law, Fourth Section Section, August 24,
2001, justice "ponente": Quiñonez Pinilla, file AP-162, plaintiff: Defensoría del Pueblo.

[63] Colombian Maximum Court in Administrative Law, Fifth Section, September 14, 2001,
justice "ponente": Palacio Hincapié, file AP-100, plaintiff: Procurador Provincial de Ibagué.

be included in the current fiscal budget, no later than two months after the judgment."[64]

In relation to collective rights involving the defense of public property, the violations of which are very frequently associated with administrative morality, one can find precedent cases, refered to above, where some citizens are enjoined to return monies that the state had paid pursuant to a settlement agreement with them, based on the termination of a previous agreement with the state.[65] There is also the example of injunction "to immediately suspend the concession process of the defendant until measures are taken to consider balances and figures that reflect the financial reality of the enterprise"[66] or the example in which the performance of a liquor contract is suspended until a decision is taken on its legality and enforceability, which is being contested in another proceeding.[67]

With respect to administrative morality, popular action cannot be brought when the act or omission that allegedly violates or threatens to violate the collective right is not *per se* illegal.[68] This is so because it has been stated that "any action that does not respond to the interest of the collectivity and, specially, to the development of the intentions that guide the faculties of the authority that is acting is considered inmoral" and therefore if this predicate showing is not satisfied, the collective right is not protected.[69] This is the case, for example, when "the plaintiff did not allege or prove that in the contested action there existed a deceitful intention on the part of the managers to obtain unlawful benefits, in addition to which after the file evaluation there is no conduct considered manifestly dishonest, corrupt or unethical that implies violation of administrative morality"[70] or when an environmental license for

---

64 Colombian Maximum Court in Administrative Law, Fifth Section, January 31, 2003, justice "ponente": Arciniegas Andrade, file 18001-23-31-000-2000-0343-01, plaintiff: Sandra Milena Rivera.

65 Colombian Maximum Court in Administrative Law, May 31, 2002, Exp. AP-300, plaintiff: Contraloría General de la República et al., justice "ponente": Ligia López Díaz.

66 Colombian Maximum Court in Administrative Law, Fifth Section, August 24, 2001, justice "ponente": Quinonez Pinilla, file AP-100, plaintiff: Procurador Provincial de Ibagué.

67 Colombian Maximum Court in Administrative Law, Third Section, October 31, 2002, justice "ponente": Hoyos Duque, file AP-059-01, plaintiff: Jesús Orlando Mejía Yepez.

68 Colombian Maximum Court in Administrative Law, Third Section, February 16, 2001, justice "ponente": Hernández Enríquez, file AP-170, plaintiff: Epaminonda Moreno Parrado et al. See, in the same sense: Colombian Maximum Court in Administrative Law, First Section, April 30, 2003, justice "ponente": Arciniegas Andrade, file AP-00654-01, plaintiff: Melly Rocío Mojica Castro.

69 Colombian Maximum Court in Administrative Law, Third Section, October 31, 2002, justice "ponente": Hoyos Duque, file AP-059-01, plaintiff: Jesús Orlando Mejía Yepez.

70 Colombian Maximum Court in Administrative Law, First Section, April 24, 2003, justice "ponente": Arciniegas Andrade, file AP-8122-01, plaintiff: Fernando Alberto García Forero.

the exploitation of underground waters to extract petroleum meets the legal requirements.[71]

Regarding public security, there are several types of cases in which this collective right has been protected. In one case, the judge was requested to enjoin the recovery of a public space occupied by people displaced to a certain city by civil unrest in their former hometown. Because of this, the city had turned into a so-called "pot of street peddlers." But the judge denied the requested injunction because he considered that it was not legal to order the street peddlers to leave by force. Nevertheless, public security was protected by enjoining the public authorities to guarantee permanent police action in the area under consideration, to prevent delinquency and drug sales, as well as "to guarantee the residents of Comunas 1 and 3 of Villavicencio, the right to security and tranquility."[72] The subject right has also been protected by the administration being enjoined to put into practice "permanent police action to organize and control the traffic of people and vehicles," in a dangerous and crowded area.[73] In other circumstances, public security has been protected as the right to security and natural disaster prevention when technically foreseeable. This is the case when the administrative authority is enjoined "to adopt in a permanent plan to prevent the danger of overflow of the waters of the subject creek, to which the inhabitants and homes of neighbourhood El Bohío are exposed."[74]

Further to the already-mentioned examples regarding the right to Domicillary Public Services, yet another example of a judicial response to the violation of this right was a claim brought by the users of the phone service of a town because of the erroneous billing of said service, combined with the fact that there was no claim office, that in order to file a claim one was required to pay first, and that the tariffs were discriminatory. The judge proceded to grant the requested relief by enjoining the public service to "fix and apply the same

---

[71] Colombian Maximum Court in Administrative Law, Second Section, February 14, 2002, justice "ponente": Lemos Bustamante, file AP-25000232400020000000601-212, plaintiff: Rodolfo Puentes Suárez. *See*, in a similar sense, in respect to an environmental license: Third Section, November 15, 2001, "justice" ponente: Giraldo Gómez, plaintiff: Junta de Acción Comunal de la Arrobleda (Cauca), file AP-230.

[72] Colombian Maximum Court in Administrative Law, First Section, March 20, 2003, justice "ponente": Arciniegas Andrade, file AP-0059, plaintiff: Luis Gustavo Guzmán Neira et al.

[73] Colombian Maximum Court in Administrative Law, First Section, October 24, 2002, justice "ponente": Arciniegas Andrade, plaintiff: Lenis Francisco Saavedra y Sara Isabel Ríos, cumulative files 25000-23-26-000-2001-9404-01 and 01-547.

[74] Colombian Maximum Court in Administrative Law, First Section, January 31, 2003, justice "ponente": Arciniegas Andrade, plaintiff: Sandra Milena Rivera, file 18001-23-31-000-2000-0343-01. *See also* First Section, February 27, 2003, justice "ponente": Arciniegas Andrade, plaintiff: José del Carmén Espinoza, file AP-3448.

tariffs applied in another towns, to adjust, depurate and compensate the invoices as well as to install a claim office."[75]

As can be seen in the above-mentioned examples, which are just a few among the various existing decisions, Colombian judges protect directly and efficaciously various and broadly defined collective rights. This does not mean that judges ignore the historical, economical and social realities of the country. Colombian judges have had the opportunity to remark that "nobody is obliged to do the impossible,"[76] because as it happens in the system of civil liability, judges must analyze, weigh and measure in each particular case the appropriate limits to the obligations of the state.[77] In other words, the "relative character of the failure of service," so precious in this subject, is introduced in popular actions which are also actions in civil liability. The discussion will then be focused on which are the limits to "excuse," or not, the state in complying with respect to collective rights.

3. Individual Rights Against Collective Rights

It is necessary to appreciate the relationship between individual and collective rights. As one can observe from the above-mentioned examples, the defense of collective rights can imply that popular action can contest the enforceability of administrative unilateral and contractual actions. In this regard, the issue raised is the determination of whether the popular action and the rights defended by it, have or do not have the ability of nullifying rights of a different nature that might be affected by another action of the Administration.[78]

---

[75] Colombian Maximum Court in Administrative Law, Second Section, September 28, 2000, justice "ponente": Orjuela Góngora, plaintiff: Judith Correa Luque, File AP-117.

[76] Colombian Maximum Court in Administrative Law, First Section, March 20, 2003, justice "ponente": Arciniegas Andrade, file AP-0059, plaintiff: Luis Gustavo Guzmán Neira et al.

[77] As examples of rulings which address this subject, *see* Colombian Maximum Court in Administrative Law, First Section, February 27, 2003, justice "ponente": Arciniegas Andrade, plaintiff: José del Carmen Espinoza, file AP-3488; First Section, October 25, 2001, justice "ponente": Mendoza Martelo, plaintiff: Adalberto Castro Mendez, file AP-0303; First Section, October 24, 2002, justice "ponente": Arciniegas Andrade, plaintiff: Lenis Francisco Saavedra and Sara Isabel Ríos, cumulative files 25000-23-26-000-2001-9404-01 y 01-547.

[78] Let us remind you of Section 15 of Law 472, 1998 which states that "the administrative law jurisdiction will be in charge of the litigation raised when any party brings popular actions originating in *acts, actions or omissions of the public entities* and of the private entities and individuals that carry out administrative functions, in conformity with what was disposed in the applicable law on the subject" (italics added). Also with respect with applicability of the popular action in relation with an administrative contract, one must take into consideration the second paragraph of Section 40 of the same law, when it sates that, "for the purposes of this section and when the issue relates to overcharges and other irregularities arising in connection with contracts, the legal representative of the respective organ or contracting

The example of the football stadium is very useful in this respect: the contractual rights of the other party that was performing the contract are voided because of the injunction to suspend the performance of the contract. That is, by defending the collective rights you come to the suspension of the contract and all the actions that had been performed. The same happens in the above-mentioned case in which the environmental licenses are annulled, in the cases in which a settlement agreement is annulled, the tariffs of the telephone service are modified, and so on.

What position should we take in this respect?

In a very important essay by the magistrate of the Court of Appeal in Administrative Law, Alier E. Hernández Enríquez,[79] this problem is analyzed, and two principal possible theories are quoted.

The first theory, called negative theory, assumes the impossibility of nullifying administrative acts by popular action, taking into account that those actions are protected by a legal presumption that covers administrative action and because there exist other types of actions for declaring such administrative action null and void. The Colombian Court of Appeal in Administrative Law has applied this theory stating that, for example, one can not make null and void an environmental license that supposedly has violated a collective right, because that "administrative act is presumed legal until there is a judicial decision that suspends or declares the act null and void, and this decision must not be derived from the popular action and must be the result of a proceeding advanced by those who are entitled to do it."[80]

The same court has held that because it is true that "the concept of administrative morality is too broad and, therefore, it is involved in any contract of the Administration...this cannot be a basis for, in the case that there have been irregularities in the contract and its performance, converting the popular action into the adequate action to declare the illegality or caducity of a certain act, in replacement of pertinent ways established by the legal system."[81]

---

entity or party will be held jointly liable with any other author in the actions, up to the total recovery of what was paid in excess." The constitutionality of this section was ratified by decision C-088 of 2000 of the Constitutional Court.

[79] "La presunción de legalidad de los actos administrativos y de validez de los contratos estatales en las acciones populares," published in Review Responsabilidad Civil y del Estado by the Instituto Antioqueño de Responsabilidad Civil y del Estado, year 2002.

[80] Colombian Maximum Court in Administrative Law, Third Section, May 18, 2000, File AP-038. See, in the same sense: Second Section, March 23, 2000, File AP-025; Fourth Section, March 31, 2000, File AP-005.

[81] Colombian Maximum Court in Administrative Law, Second Section, Subsection A, July 5, 2001, Justice "ponente": Nicolás Pájaro Peñaranda, plaintiff: Sintrareginal, defendant: Registraduría Nacional del Estado Civil et al, file AP-068-01.

The second theory, or positive theory, supposes that the administrative actions or contracts lose validity as a result of the popular action, because this action is not considered subsidiary but autonomous and because its objective is the protection of collective rights, that have a superior and special nature. According to the Constitutional Court, those rights "refer to issues of such nature that their injury endangers or attacks valuable societal goods such as life, health, healthy environment, ecological equilibrium, security, public assets and administrative morality."[82] On the basis of this theoretical position, decisions have been entered such as the above-mentioned one in reference to the football stadium, the suspension of the concession process of an enterprise or a liquor contract, and so on, which clearly constitute a real interference with administrative contracts.[83] The same thing occurs in the case of unilateral administrative actions, where even though there is no formal nullification, these actions lose their validity because it is considered that, for example "when you issue administrative actions without the required care and without verifying compliance with legal requirements," the collective right has been injured.[84]

This consequence of the Colombian scheme is troubling because it creates a high level of legal insecurity. Thus, around every administrative action, contractual or not, there will be a permanent threat that will last only as long as the legal situation created lasts, because, as we may remember, popular action is not subject to statutory time limits. This is not a very desirable consequence for the certainty of individual legal situations and one must pay strict attention to avoid promoting a false populism.

The above-mentioned position, when taken to an extreme, can create major problems. As stated by Melleray, "in any legal system of any state exist, in variable proportions depending on the country and the time, rules of holistic inspiration and others of individualist inspiration. . . . We shall not be afraid to

---

[82] Colombian Constitutional Court, April 14 1999, File C-215.

[83] Colombian Maximum Court in Administrative Law, First Section, May 14, 2001, justice "ponente": Olga Inés Navarrete Barrero, plaintiff: Personero municipal de Sopó, file. AP-076, where the Court of Appeal, opposite to what had been stated by the judge in the first instance, admitted an action brought to contest the termination of a sales contract. The following was stated: "On the contrary, from the wording of the transcribed rules one can deduce that the collective right or interest can be violated by acts, actions or omissions of the public entity or of the private entity or individual in administrative functions, which means that in the final analysis only the judge can decide on the legality and enforceability of those acts, actions or omissions. The fact that the mentioned activity of the administration can also be judged or studied by other actions brought, does not imply that one should necessarily exercise those actions, if a collective right or interest is involved, a popular action is also applicable."

[84] Colombian Maximum Court in Administrative Law, Fifth Section, November 9, 2001, justice "ponente": Quiñonez Pinilla, AP-194, plaintiff: Rodolfo Puentes Suárez et al.

congratulate ourselves for this principle of pluralism. Thus, a society where the 'dominant public opinion' is moved by exclusively holistic values and where the more refined legal rules have the same vein, can only be totalitarian. In this respect, the [N]azi regime is the most horrible illustration and constitutes, as legal doctrine and technique, a denial of the principles of individualist inspiration, the most perfected holistic. On the other hand, a society where those who decide are moved by exclusively individualistic values could only take one, undoubtedly, to anarchy."[85]

One cannot forget that the same problem appeared in ancient law. Thus, Pericles, in creating a democratic tribunal where citizens could accuse any party and obtain a financial reward for bringing a successful popular action, brought about the institution of "sycophants." These were individuals that made a practice of bringing criminal accusations against their adversaries and received part of any penalty and eventually, of any confiscated goods in the event of condemnation. As it has well been written, "if that economical motivation led to the condemnation of the truly guilty people, nothing could be criticized in the system. But the real perversion came when professional denouncers would persecute rich citizens who had not committed any injury. The sycophants managed to obtain judgments against their victims by moving the resentment of popular juries against the rich."[86] It is said that the excesses were such that the resulting reaction in certain occasions was to eliminate democratic practices, even though as corrective measure the system contemplated penalties for those who desisted of bringing actions or for those who did not obtain at least one fifth of the votes of the jury.

The evolution of Colombian law towards resolution of this conundrum remains to be seen and there are no decisions, to my knowledge, that permit an explanation of how the loss of the rights of the individual in favor of collective rights are to be solved. It would be useful if Law 472 of 1998 were modified to include a section that could solve the inevitable tension between collective and individual rights, for example, by way of giving express guarantee to acquired rights and indemnifications to parties acting in good faith, who see their own individual situations altered.

But this aspect of the problem does not prevent one from recognizing that under Colombian law, collective damage is a damage of higher rank than individual damage. This is why even in situations in which paying or repairing for collective damage supposes voiding of individual rights, the

---

[85] Fabrice Melleray, *Essai sur la structure du contentieux administratif français. Pour un renouvellement de la classification des principales voies de droit ouvertes devant les juridictions à compétence générale*, Editorial L.G.D.J., Paris, 2001, p. 278.

[86] Louis Boré, *La défense des intérêts collectifs par les associations devant les juridictions administratives et judiciaires*, L.G.D.J., Paris, 1997, p. 136.

latter must give way before the former.[87] It must be emphasized that, even though this position may create legal uncertainty, we believe that there is no way to resolve it, given the explicit choices made by the authors of the Colombian Constitution and Law 472, respecting the hierarchy of rights. These choices mean that individual rights can only be enjoyed as long as they do not trespass on collective rights. The discussion of the source of the indemnification of individual rights that must give way to the popular action remains pending. In this context, case law has made a good start in indicating that "as regards administrative action (not a general action but an administrative action addressed to a particular subject), such are protected by legitimate confidence and presumption of legality, which can be broken, among other causes, when it is evident that the action occurred by illegal means."[88] One must pay attention and observe how the "causes" mentioned in the above-referenced decision will be managed, taking into account that any interpretation or construction must be restrictive in favor of the particular individual or entity that has been deprived of its right.

The administrative law judge must then weigh each situation, but one cannot accept that the uncertainty created by this element of the legal system would lead one to foreclose the possibility of popular action. Those fears also existed, and to a greater degree in connection with the *acción de tutela*, which undoubtedly has been one of the major legal achievements in Colombian history. Colombia is a legal social state and, as such, the legal conflicts that might occur because of any excess in the powers of the authorites are clearly regulated in the Constitution.

[87] We share integrally the statement by Luis Felipe Botero, who gives another important argument to support the position that we are here defending and that is contained in one of his multiple comments to the quoted book of professor Tamayo Jaramillo, at 178: "3. In connection with the possibility of contesting an administrative act, via popular action, may I add in defense of such possibility the following: section 69 of the Contentious Administrative Code contemplates as cause for annulling administrative acts, in its second paragraph, the following: 'when they are not conformed to the general or social interest or violate or threaten to violate it'. This rule, I think, matches, in a particular way, the conclusion we are defending in this paragraph as well as in previous lines. An act that 'threatens' (which according to Law 472 is equivalent to threat or contingent damage) 'public or social interest' (one can connect this terminology with collective rights or interests even though they may not necessarily coincide) is enough for it to be modified by the Administration; then, even more, it can be annulled by the judge responding to a popular action when a collective right or interest is violated. Even more, if to protect a subjective economic non-fundamental right one can nullify an administrative act (by using the action to declare null and void and to re-establish the respective right), there is more legal basis to do the same when faced with a violation of a collective right."

[88] Colombian Maximum Court in Administrative Law, Fifth Section, November 9, 2001, justice "ponente": Quiñonez Pinilla, file AP-194, plaintiff: Rodolfo Puentes Suárez et al.

One must remember one obvious issue that frequently is forgotten by those who state that judicial actions must be limited in order to avoid judicial excesses, advanced by "minor groups" who, lacking political support, use judges to obtain that which is unobtainable by way of political elections: "One must not forget that since Montesquieu we know that absolute power corrupts and that it is necessary that power stops power. Magistrates must not be afraid of using the power of law creation; in any event, Congress will always, if in disagreement with case law, vote for a new and opposite law to reform the previous one."[89]

This subject was recently restated by famous French precedent, *Perruche*. It refers to Law 2002-303, dated March 4, 2002, Section 1 of which established that "nobody may claim damages based on birth." This written law eliminated case law position, according to which damages were granted when derived from a child born with birth defects because of medical negligence consisting of not having informed a mother of the defect, that in turn impeded making decision to have a timely abortion.[90] Neither may one forget the concept of "Loi validant des actes administratifs" (law that gives validity to administratif action), according to which Congress may issue law that reimposes rules previously nullifed by Administrative judges.[91]

As a consequence of this principle, one can conclude that individual rights can only be enjoyed or used as long as they do not violate or threaten to violate collective rights, because collective damage is of a higher rank than individual damage. Another consequence is that if there are individual damages for which reparation is not requested by whomever is entitled to it, the possibility of remediating collective damage must be made available, even though this may affect the personal decisions of the person who suffers the damage to or loss of an individual right.[92] This logic has a justification that starts the moment when, as previously seen, collective rights are conceived as subjective rights in favour of "any person in town." With this concept, the nature of human being conceived in the classical rules of civil law is modified.

---

[89] Louis Boré, La Défense des Intérêts collectifs par les associations devant les juridictions administratives et judiciaires, L.G.D.J., Paris, 1997, p. 125.

[90] Supreme Court of Justice (Cour de cassation française), Civil Section, March 26, 1996, Perruche vs. Ponnoussany: Bull. Civ. 1, # 156.

[91] *See* Dominique Rousseau, Droit du Contentieux Constitutionnel, 6eme édition, Montchrestien, Paris, 2001, p. 256, and following pages.

[92] *See* in this sense my essay "La responsabilidad del Estado colombiano por daño ambiental", article pertaining to the book: Responsabilidad por Daños al Medio Ambiente, edited by Editorial de la Universidad Externado de Colombia, Bogotá D.C., 2000, pgs. 127–99.

C. France

Under French law, actions to defend collective rights are neither provided for in an express way, as they are under the Colombian law, nor have they been developed by specialized doctrine in the matter. Thus, for example, as far as it concerns damage to the environment, it has been established that "the general tendency of case law is rather restrictive."[93] Further, it has been stated that popular action is proscribed.[94] Even in a difficult subject such as the legal standing or capacity of associations to bring actions contesting the legality of town planning acts, the Maximum Court of Administrative Law has reminded citizens that one is not facing a popular action.[95] The words *action populaire* do not exist under the French legal system and the language *droit collectif*, as previously seen, has a different meaning to that construed under Colombian law.

Nevertheless, it would be premature to state that French law does not offer any possibility of a legal action to avoid, enjoin, or repair damages caused to collective goods or property, that is, to conclude that there is no way of defending collective rights. The fact that there are no rules for popular actions, does not allow one to infer that damages repaired via popular action under Colombian law are not redressable under French law. To take such

---

[93] Laurent Richer, Préjudice réparable, *in* Répertoire de la responsabilité de la puissance publique, Dalloz, Paris, 1987, N° 65.

[94] Benoît Buzon, Les féderations d'associations et l'intérêt à agir devant le juge administrative, commentaires à l'arrêt CE, 8 février 1999, Féderation des associations de protection de l'environemment et de la nature des côtes d'Armor, n° 176779, *in* Droit de l'environnement, Victoires Editions, Paris, March 1999, n° 66, p. 6: "In this subject, administrative judge continues to trace a difficult limit in respect to legal capacity of associations and groups to bring actions: proscription of popular action, strict evaluation of the terms of the articles of association in relation to the purpose of the association and, even, a certain softening of the conditions required to bring actions"; Jean Raymond, En matière de defense de l'environnement: la qualité pour agir des associations et le *recours pour excès de pouvoir*, Revue Juridique de l'environnement, 1991, I, p. 453: "It is admitted, after decision Ministère de l'agriculture c / dame Lamotte, that the *recours pour excés de pouvoir* is available for the administrative judge even without a previous written law which establishes it and has as consequence the assurance of the respect of legality, in conformity with the general principles of law. Nevertheless, the Maximum Court of Administrative Law has not accepted to make this action a popular action and has limited the required interest to bring actions".

[95] French Maximum Court of Administrative Law, July 26, 1985, Union régionale pour la défense de l'environnement, de la nature, de la vie et de la qualité de la vie en Franche-Comté, A.J.D.A. 1985.741, conclusions of Comissaire de Gouvernement M. Dandelot, R.J.E. 1985.473, note R. Hostiou, who was followed by the Maximum Court of Administrative Law when stating: "when, like in this particular case, the association has a regional purpose, in four departments, the interest to bring actions can not be admitted with the same scope, unless one wanted to privilege the association with the 'quasi-popular action.'"

position would be false insofar as it might lead to the implication that the absence of the possibility of popular action means lack of concern for collective rights.

To study the real extent of the lack of the popular action in France, it is necessary to follow the path of the general French legal system. Therefore, we will first focus below on the general study of the French scheme of administrative litigation, and then present some of the litigation hypotheticals. We will then consider the specific field of *Contraventions de Grande Voirie*, closely related to collective rights, and finally discuss the powers of judges. In this way we will be able to analyze if under the French administrative litigation scheme it is possible to bring the indemnification claims that arise under Colombian law regarding actions brought in favor of collective interests.

1. *General Presentation of the French Administrative Adversarial Scheme*

Regarding the French administrative adversarial ("contentious") system, one can state in general terms that an adversarial scheme "is objective when judges are asked the question of whether the action is in accordance with the group of rules imposed on the author of the action by the Constitution, written or case law.... The adversarial scheme is subjective when the question is to determine if a person will be recognized a subjective right, such as the payment of damages. Judges will, in this latter situation, verify conformity of an [administrative] act with legal rules, such as to searching and deciding whether an action has injured subjective rights in particular situations."[96] This general classification of the administrative jurisdiction over such causes of action comes from Waline and Duguit's theories that take into consideration the matter or issue raised to judges, and it differs from Laferriéres's thesis, according to which the adversarial administrative jurisdiction is classified in accordance with the powers of judges. Even though in doctrine Waline and Duguit's theories are more widely accepted, as mentioned earlier in the quote from Professors Auby and Drago, it is clear that both positions "meet together ... one must not forget the distinction between objective and subjective contentious schemes [,] and [thus] it is convenient to maintain Laferriére's classification."[97]

---

[96] Bruno Lasserre, Recours, Répertoire du Contentieux Administratif, Tomo II, L.G.D.J., Paris, 1985, n. 39–40.

[97] René Chapus, Droit du contentieux administratif, Montchrestien, 9th edition, Paris, 2001, p. 185.

The most important expression of the objective adversarial scheme is the *recours pour excès de pouvoir*. In this respect, one may say that "it was described by Dame Lamotte in 1950 'as the suitable claim to contest any administrative action, even though not previously defined as such by a direct written law, a claim with the purpose of securing the observance of legality, in accordance with the general legal principles.'"[98] The *recours pour excès de pouvoir* is an "action to claim for the nullification of an administrative decision, based on the violation of a rule of law. . . . There is no *recours pour excès de pouvoir* if the plaintiff claims for something other than the nullification."[99] This concept is strict to the extent that if the "action brought by the *recours pour excès de pouvoir* contains other claims for relief [i.e., such as for money damages], it must be rejected."[100]

However, the fact that indemnification claims are not permitted does not mean that the conditions created by the unlawful administrative action are not to be reestablished as a consequence of the nullification. On the contrary, the conditions created previously must be reestablished because the claim is precisely "to reestablish integrally the legal conditions that existed before the annulled act. Therefore, the administration may be obliged to make retrospective decisions with the purpose of obtaining a real *restitutio in integrum*."[101] Even though such *restitutio* does not entail the payment of pecuniary indemnifications, it may occur "that the nullification implies the recognition of a subjective right,"[102] with which the action commented upon maintains its original nature. Thus, in the not necessarily most frequent cases in which the subjective right is recognized, the administration has the obligation to reestablish the injured subjective right, not as a consequence of injunctions or judicial orders, but as a consequence of the nullification and its effects.

---

[98] *Id.* at 187.

[99] Jean-Marie Auby y Roland Drago, Traité des recours en matière administrative, Paris, 1992, Litec, n° 108.

[100] *Id.*

[101] *Id.* at n° 377.

[102] René Chapus, Droit du contentieux administratif, Montchrestien, 9ª edition, Paris, 2001, p. 664. It must be noted that when the author expresses the quoted sentence, he refers to No. 242 in his book, where he states: "D.- One confusion to avoid. Given the above-mentioned, a possible confusion must be avoided. To say that a recourse/action only entails lawfulness problems does not mean that from the judicial decision there may not derive subjective rights. For example, the public employee that has brought the *recours pour excès de pouvoir* to contest the decision which has declared him redundant, obtains nullification of the decision which has been declared null and void and has the right to go back to work as well as right to the reestablishment of his career."

In contrast, the *recours de pleine juridiction* is the most important French expression of the administrative contentious scheme. This action has been defined as that one "in which judges are invited to determine the existence, content and effects of subjective rights that individuals or legal entities claim against an administrative authority."[103] Characteristics of this action are: "it pertains to a subjective right; its purpose is mainly but not exclusively pecuniary; administrative judges have powers that go beyond nullification of the contested action, and it entails the possibility of condemning the Administration to pay an amount of money and even to modify the legal situation or the conditions that is or are under litigation."[104] This jurisdiction is also called *plein contentieux*, precisely because "judges have powers that allow them to go beyond the nullification of the contested act."[105]

Nonetheless, these distinctions between both actions is not absolute. This is why scholars mention the "new *recours pour excès de pouvoir*"[106] or the "new *recours de pleine juridiction.*"[107] In these two cases, one studies the intersection between both actions, that is, cases in which the *recours pour excès de pouvoir* is considered as *recours de plein contentieux*, and vice-versa. This practical situation shows that the traditional classification of the contentious scheme may be questioned when one ceases to focus exclusively on the objective or subjective character of the action brought or the powers of judges. That is, there is no real and substantive distinction if one refers to either the traditional characters of both actions or the powers of the judges in both actions. New classifications have been proposed recently. For example, there is a possible classification based on the dichotomy (holistic vs. individualistic) that allows one to distinguish actions in justice brought with either holistic or individualistic objectives. But this classification accepts that the *recours pour excès de pouvoir* has both purposes or potential results,[108] because "this action has been a recourse/action between two legal entities/individuals: a subjective action,"[109] which implies also an individualistic point of view.

---

[103] Jean-Marie Auby y Roland Drago, Traité des recours en matière administrative, Paris, 1992, Litec, n° 394.

[104] *Id.* at n° 402.

[105] René Chapus, Droit du contentieux administratif, Montchrestien, 9th edition, Paris, 2001, p. 208.

[106] *Id.* at 210.

[107] Jean-Marie Auby y Roland Drago, Traité des recours en matière administrative, Paris, 1992, Litec, n° 403.

[108] Fabrice Melleray, Essai sur la structure du contentieux administratif français. Pour un renouvellement de la classification des principales voies de droit ouvertes devant les juridictions à compétence générale, Edited by L.G.D.J., Paris, 2001, p. 16.

[109] Norbert Foulquier, Les droits publics subjectifs des administrés. Émergence d'un concept en droit administratif français du XIXe au XXe siècle, Dalloz, Paris, 2003, p. 163.

A way of evidencing the truth of these comments can be illustrated when an individual uses the *recours pour excès de pouvoir* to seek the nullification of administrative actions that have caused damages to him individually, without seeking compensation or payment of damages. This hypothesis is based on the traditional operation of civil liability in tort, that is, to claim for oneself. Then, one can see that it is not true that the objective contentious scheme does not contemplate the recognition of subjective rights, because the interest being defended and protected is an individual interest, even though the arguments used in arriving at a decision are strictly legal. This is so because when an individual administrative action injures a person, what the victim is looking for is precisely the reestablishment of the injured right.

Perhaps the best support for the above comments can be found in that part of the administrative adversarial scheme governing labor law, in which claims or challenges are brought via the *recours pour excès de pouvoir*, and in which "every public agent may contest legality of decisions addressed to that public agent (denial of a right, a promotion, a nomination, a disciplinary measure, etc.) with the only condition that the challenged decision must be unfavorable to him and the corresponding nullification must grant him an advantage."[110] It is clear that the advantage granted to the "victim" by the nullification of the administrative action must be recognized by the administration, to the extent that, as we will see below, to guarantee compliance the judge may issue *injunctions* and *astreintes*.

We also must bear in mind that the person injured by the administrative action may file the *recours pour excès de pouvoir* and afterward continue with the *recours de pleine juridiction*.[111] There, one may appreciate that the *recours pour excès de pouvoir* represents a hypothesis of the traditional operation of tort-type civil liability whenever the nullification of the administrative action produces or carries as consequence the reestablishment of an individual right

---

[110] Jean-Michel Lemoyne de Forges, Recours pour excès de pouvoir (conditions de recevabilité), Répertoire de Contentieux Administratif, Tomo II, Dalloz, Paris, 1985, n 121.

[111] Jean-Marie Auby y Roland Drago, Traité des recours en matière administrative, Paris, 1992, Litec, n° 439: "an important problem is that one in which there is interruption of statutory time limits by bringing a recours pour excès de pouvoir. The situation may appear as follows: a citizen suffers damages caused by an administrative decision (i.e., a public employee is made redundant); he attacks the said decision by bringing a *recours pour excès de pouvoir* and the decision is in his favor. With this nullifying decision, may the employee obtain payment of damages? If conditions to obtain reparation are met, there is no problem. Notwithstanding, in the majority of the cases, the statutory time limits have been reached and the question raised is whether one has additional statutory limits from the nullifying decision on. [...] Thus, the *recours pour excès de pouvoir* produces interruption of the statutory time limits. But, case law has restrictively interpreted the law in some cases..."

or liberty. This is so because by this reestablishment, individual property and public patrimony are safeguarded.

Even though one must pay attention to theoretical discussions, it is important recognizes that presently in France there are two general actions/recourses with specific and defined purposes, although there might be polemic differences between them. One might accept and agree with Melleray, that with the *recours pour excès de pouvoir* one also can obtain recognition of subjective rights. However, central to the themes developed in this chapter is the study of the administrative litigation hypothesises that appear in respect to supra-individualistic rights.

Before we proceed with the study of such hypotheses, one must remember that associations of individuals have played a fundamental role in the history of French legal defense of collective rights. After being first permitted in 1901, such associations have been the vehicles for the protection of rights that surpass the strictly individual sphere. Collective rights are primarily safeguarded by associations, which are an essential feature of the French legal system. This is so to the extent in which one can say that "50% of the French citizens are members of an association."[112] In this sense, membership in an association satisfies the rule "pas d'intérêt, pas d'action" – "without interest there is no action" – , which means that interest to bring actions requires a personal, direct and legitimate interest in the plaintiff, to the extent that "nul ne plaide par procureur" –"every person must litigate in its own interest." This essential rule must be understood in the context in which it arises: the interest to act is required in the *recours pour excès de pouvoir* as much as in the *plein contentieux* and associations play a fundamental role in safeguarding those rights that are not a claim in favor of an individual as plaintiff. With this in mind, it is guaranteed "to citizens a means to defend any interest they choose: it is enough to create an association (two persons are enough) with the mission to safeguard what is precious."[113] Consequently, it is useful to proceed with the study of the extent of each one of the relevant French legal actions, analyzing at the same time the inner role played by associations in defense of different categories of rights. Notwithstanding the essential role of associations, one must note, as we will see later, that a proceeding initiated by an association is not the only way of defending collective rights.

---

[112] Louis Boré, La défense des intérêts collectifs par les associations devant les juridictions administratives et judiciaires, L.G.D.J., Paris, 1997, p. 1.

[113] René Chapus, Droit du contentieux administratif, Montchrestien, 9th edition, Paris, 2001, p. 424.

2. *Presentation of the Main Litigation Hypotheses of "Collective Rights" in the French Administrative Adversarial System*

We may now proceed to study the concrete defense of collective rights under French law. One must find out if collective rights, as conceived in Colombia, are safeguarded in the French system by way of the existing actions and including those brought on the basis of associations. In order to choose the examples that will be described now, one must remember that the methodology is to study how those cases of protection and defense of collective rights analysed under the Colombian legal system, are, or are not, contemplated under the French legal system. For this, one must follow the *summa divisio* of French Contentious Administrative Law.

In respect to *recours pour excès de pouvoir*, we shall see two hypotheses in relation to the defense of collective rights. In the first place, an individual that brings action as member of a social category may claim for nullification of actions that threaten his own category of persons. This hypothesis is interesting because it seems similar to the approach to popular action, without partaking of its logic.[114] However, this hypothesis does admit that a citizen may claim in defense of group interests just because that citizen is part, conceptually, of the group, even though the group is not a legally recognized association or union.

In this event, one may state that the *recours pour excès de pouvoir* is useful to protect collective rights to the extent that the citizen may claim for nullification of the challenged actions. Thus, for example, in connection with public property, the category of "taxpayer"[115] has been long recognized as justifying an interest in bringing actions. Said criterion permitted, *verbigracia*, the claimants' standing in a lawsuit "seeking the nullification of an implicit decision by which Guidel's mayor refrained from ordering some corporations (parties in a contract) to refund the amounts of money allegedly paid by mistake by the commune," in the case of a contract previously annulled

---

[114] Michel Rousset, Droit Administratif. II. Le contentieux administrative, Presses Universitaires de Grenoble, 1994, p. 118: "One must distinguish personal interest which belongs to one single person and individual interest that may belong to a category made up by various individuals.... In practice, case law has established this notion; thus, in the beginning of the century case law admitted that the quality of user/consumer of a public service implies interest to contest a decision of service deletion: Maximum Court in Administrative Law, December 21, 1906, Syndicat des propriétaires et contribuables du quartier de la Croix de Seguey-Tivoli, GAJA 90 ... "

[115] French Maximum Court in Administrative Law, March 29, 1901, Casanova, Rec. p. 33, D 1902.3.33, S 1901.3.73, note M. Hauriou; June 25, 1920, Le Doussal et Métour, p. 639, D 1920.3.8.; February 13, 1930, Dufour, p. 176, DH 1930, p. 255; February 9, 1955, Soc. La Belle Baule, p. 77, 2 esp.; November 23, 1988, Dumont, p. 418, JCP 1988, IV, p. 412.

by the corresponding judge of the contract. In this case, the decision was not made null and void but because it was established that "Mme Courtet did not explain that part of the amounts paid by the commune to the corporations (parties in the contract) as a result of the school building work had been wired by mistake."[116] One must clarify then that if the occurrence of such a situation had been established – wiring monies by mistake – nullification would have taken place. It is evident that this is very close to popular action to the extent in which, if there had been nullification of the actions, the mayor would have had to recover the sums overpaid, and conditions of the public property would have been reestablished. The fact that such reimbursement may or may not be ordered by the judge is a problem of the powers granted him, in the same sense that the issue of the extent given to the injunctions has nothing to do with the substantive recognition of the corresponding right.

Let us take another example, quoted by Professor Chapus and in which the right of a frequent camper to enjoy the environment was injured: "A camper filed a lawsuit and claimed for the nullification of a municipal action in which camping was prohibited in a place where he had never camped before. Since he was a frequent camper, it was not impossible that he would have the idea to camp in said county one day: [thus although] his interest is not injured in a very evident way, however, the lawsuit is admitted."[117] The sphere of this logic is even larger because in addition to the "camper" category referenced in the above-mentioned example, judges have entertained suits, for example, from users or consumers of a service,[118] members of a profession,[119]

---

[116] French Maximum Court in Administrative Law, February 10, 1992, Mme Courtet, 1 / 4SSR 116582 B, M. de Bellescize, rapp., M. Le Chatelier, c. du g., Rec. p. 1210, D 1992, SC, p. 414, obs. P. Terneyre, DA 1992. n. 6, p. 1, concl. G. Le Chatelier.

[117] René Chapus, Droit du contentieux administratif (9th ed.) 437 (Paris, 2001). We refer to a decision dated February 14, 1958, Abisset, Rec. p. 98, concl. M. Long, AJ 1958, 2, p. 221, chron. J. Fournier et G. Braibant: decision that admits the action brought but rejects the contested matter.

[118] French Maximum Court in Administrative Law, December 21, 1906, Syndicat des propriétaires et contribuables du quartier de la Croix de Seguey-Tivoli, GAJA 90; December 19, 1979, Meyet, Rec. Cons. d'Etat, p. 475, D. 1980, Inf. Rap. 124, note by Delvolvé: administrative action related to service organization and functioning by which a decree ruling on certain tariffs of telecommunication is declared null and void; November 24, 1933, Zenard, Rec. Cons. d'Etat, p. 1100; December 13, 1939, Seguinaud, Rec. Cons. d'Etat, p. 588: traders in competition with a public industrial and commercial service.

[119] French Maximum Court in Administrative Law, November 4, 1971, Claude, Rec. Cons. D'Etat, p. 654: action brought by an architect to contest the rule that establishes conditions to be met in this profession; October 4, 1974, Dame David, Rec. Cons. d'Etat, p. 465, D. 1975, 369, note Auby, AJDA 1974, 546, note Drago: action brought by a judicial journalist to contest a written rule that limits publicity for debates; July 7, 1978, Essaka and Syndicat des avocats

parents,[120] foreign workers,[121] municipal inhabitants,[122] hotel businessmen,[123] and so on. Characterization made by French case law shows how, by the concept expressed in each of the above categories, that is, by the interest implied by the category, one refers to collective claims that in certain occasions are difficult to distinguish from group claims even though they are all clearly "supra-individual" claims.

One must also outline that case law has accepted that third parties in a contract may question the validity of certain clauses that, in what matters here, affect collective rights. Without breaking the principle of the relative effect of the contract, it has been urged that "the granting of a public service is not integrally a contract but a mixed act, that the clauses related with the organization and functioning of those public services are *réglementaires* (of general interest) and consequently the rights of users to the correct application of said clauses are not contractual rights born from a *stipulation pour autrui* (stipulation for another), but they traduce the right that any interested person may have in the application of those general rules."[124] As it has been well said by Professor Folliot-Lalliot, "since the door to a judge of the contract was closed, third parties have entered . . . by the window of the judge of *excès de pouvoir*,"[125] which is to say that by means of their category or status as "beneficiary" as much as by means of the category of taxpayer to show interest in the general clause (*clause réglementaire*). This is how, following a case-law tradition,[126]

de France, Rec. Cons. d'Etat, p. 297, Rev. dr. publ. 1979, p. 263, concl. Théry: the category of attorney-in-law allows one to contest a circular that may affect defense rights.

[120] French Maximum Court in Administrative Law, July 7, 1922, Grille: Rec. Cons. d'Etat, p. 336: action brought by parents to contest a municipal act related to the status of certain schools; December 12, 1953, Rolin, Bellanger, etc.: Rec. Cons. d'Etat, p. 546, Dr. soc. 1954, p. 241, concl. Mosset: action brought by parents to contest decree that regulates vaccinations.

[121] French Maximum Court in Administrative Law, January 13, 1975: Rec. Cons. d'Etat. p. 784, AJDA 1975, p. 258, note Jean-Marc André: the category of foreign worker allows one to attack circulars related to residence permit renewals.

[122] French Maximum Court in Administrative Law, February 6, 1931, Dame Doré, Rec. Cons. d'Etat, p. 156: case related to modification in highway classification; April 29, 1932, Cayez, S. 1932, 3, 96: case related to a decision that widens a cemetery; February 13, 1914, Hazera, Rec. Cons. d'Etat, p. 186: case of a municipal council decision, which defines municipal property.

[123] French Maximum Court in Administrative Law, May 28, 1971, Damasio, Rec. Cons. d'Etat, p. 391, concl. Théry, AJDA 1971, 406: the category of hotel businessmen allows one to attack an administrative act that changes school holidays, as "the schedules of the school year between holidays and work days is an issue of national interest, of interest to education".

[124] André de Laubadère, Franck Moderne and Pierre Delvolvé, Traité des contrats administratifs, L.G.D.J., Paris, 1983, vol. 1, p. 795.

[125] Laurence Folliot-Lalliot, *La responsabilité et les tiers au contrat administratif* (forthcoming).

[126] French Maximum Court in Administrative Law, December 21, 1906, Synd. de propiétaires et contribuables du quartier Croix-de-Séguey-Tivoli, D. 1907.3.41, concl. Romieu; S. 1907.3.33,

the Maximum Court of Administrative Law concluded in one decision that "the dispositions that Cayzeele has claimed to be annulled have a general character (*caractère réglementaire*); consequently, they may be brought to the judge of *excès de pouvoir*."[127] In that specific case, the claimant acted as the owner of a building apartment to whom the administrative contract imposed the obligation to buy containers to deposit waste disposals, as was requested of all the owners of buildings in town. Even though the Maximum Court of Administrative Law found the clause legal, one must note that as it was qualified as general. This permitted a third party to question it. This also might occur, for example, in the event in which the user of a highway obtains an annulment of rules in the document containing the public offering conditions attached to an administrative contract granting a public service, as it is considered illegal to include the expenses of highway patrols as an expense in the granting of the public service.[128]

This case law logic of allowing third parties in a contract to challenge them is reinforced by codified law. This is the case in the important subject of administrative contracts, in which the Code of Communes (L-316-5) allows a taxpayer to bring, with previous authorization from the administrative tribunal, the actions that correspond to those that a town or collectivity might, but is not willing to, bring, the town and that this collectivity is as long as the action is of interest to the town and has a possibility of success. Thus, for example, a taxpayer may start a process for reviewing an arguably extremely low price in the purchase contract of common township lands.[129] Responding to another claim, the Maximum Court of Administrative Law took into account that there were two different purchase contracts with different sale prices, the first one was from the commune to a semipublic corporation, and the second one – fifteen days after the first – from this corporation to another completely private one. The Court authorized the taxpayer to bring the action because

---

note Hauriou: In this case an association was allowed to request for a contractual party to operate a tramway line, and the petition was not successful because the Maximum Court of Administrative Law considered that the arguments of the *préfet* in the sense that such line was not included in the contract, and were not validly questioned.

[127] French Maximum Court in Administrative Law, July 10, 1996, Cayzeele, 138536, Mme. Touraine-Reverand, rapp., M. Sanson, c. du g., Rec. Cons. d'Etat, p. 274; AJDA 1996, p. 732, chron. Chauvaux et Girardot; CJEG 1996, p. 382, note Ph. Terneyre; RFDA 1997, p. 89, note P. Delvolvé.

[128] French Maximum Court in Administrative Law, October 30, 1996, Mme Wajs and M. Monnier, 136071, Mme. Brechtel, rapp., M. Combrexelle, c. du g., Rec. Cons. d'Etat, p. 387 CJEG 1997, p. 52 et RFDA 1997, p. 726 concl. Combrexelle; AJDA 1996, p. 973, chron. Cauvaux et Girardot; JCP 1997, II, p. 22777, note Peyrical.

[129] French Maximum Court in Administrative Law, July 22, 1992, Grapin, 134986, Mme. Laroque, rapp., M. Kessler, c. du g., Rec. Cons. d'Etat, p. 302.

there was sufficient communal interest in the process, and a probability of success. As one can observe, it is not directly a popular action in as much as in this French example the defense of public property is subject to certain conditions and to the authorization of the administrative tribunal. Without pertaining to the logic of Colombian law, as it is stated that although "the contract by which a town authorizes a corporation to build an elementary school is not one of those of which nullification can be requested by a third party," the taxpayer may judicially oblige the commune to start a process of nullification.[130] The two mentioned examples bring two different hypotheses, as in the first case, the taxpayer is authorized to act directly in the name of the commune to defend a collective right, meanwhile, in the second example the commune can be obliged to start the process in defense of such type of right. The difference is a matter of degree and not of substance, because in both the initiative of the defense of the collective right is, with certain requirements, with the taxpayer.

Second, an association or union may bring a claim for the defense of collective rights protected by their articles of association. Thus, in an interesting case in which the municipal council had requested that wolves be removed or killed, an association filed a lawsuit contesting the action, claiming it to be contrary to European Community environmental rules. The Court of Appeal of Marseille accepted the claim.[131] By the same token, when an urban project creates risks of imminent damages to the environment, nullification may be ordered.[132] In yet another dispute, an action was permitted in response to

---

[130] Administrative Court of Appeal of Paris, July 7, 1999, M. Secail, 96PA02322, Mme Adda, rapp., M. Lambert, c. du g.

[131] Administrative Court of Appeal of Marseille, December 28, 1998, 97MA00712, C, Commune de Roquebillière, M. Gonzales, rapp., M. Bocquet, c. du g.: "Considering that for the April 26, 1996 deliberation, the Roquebillière municipal council requested Alpes-Maritimes governor to capture Mercantour wolves and, in case governor did not answer the request, municipal council requested mayor to apply section L.2122-21-9° of the general code of territorial collectivities and request inhabitants of the county to eliminate wolves; considering that Administrative Tribunal of Nice nullified this decision because it implied the application of a decision which was not compatible with the convention related with European wild and natural life conservation, subscribed the 19th of September in Berne."

[132] Administrative Court of Appeal of Marseille, 1st Section, July 1, 1999, Société de réalisation foncières et industrielles de la Mediterranée, 96MA02405 C, M. Bidard de La Noe, rapp., M. Bénoit, c. du g.: "[...] as a result of the previous rules, quarries can not be authorized if they affect specifically the essential characteristics of the natural surroundings; considering that from the instruction it is clear that the place chosen to exploit the quarry under open skies is in a hill with trees, very green, classified as protected space; considering that the ecosystem of this zone presents, in relation with flora and fauna, a particular interest which would be damaged irreversibly by the above-mentioned exploitation; considering that studies on the environmental impact confirm the presence of multiple important bird species;

the French Secretary of state's authorization of bird hunting during a time forbidden by European Community norms.[133]

This French approach permitting the *recours pour excès de pouvoir*, should be highlighted because many of those claims that can be brought in Colombia by popular action, also may be studied in France under this action/recourse. Thus, associations may defend collective rights and use the preventive stage popular action conceived in Colombia. But this issue remains pending: What happens if the nullification of administrative action is obtained, already protecting to the collective right injured, and the judge adds other declarations and orders to his decision? For example, what would happen if during the operation of the administrative action that permitted wolf killing, various wolves had been killed? Could one bring a claim, *verbigracia*, asking the judge to order the administration to invest in the reproduction of this species to reduce the threat of its extinction? We shall come back to this point.

We shall now see which hypothesis may be presented in respect to the *recours de plein contentieux*. Recall that this claim is one in which associations seek payment of damages suffered as a direct consequence of the injury to rights the preservation of which is provided for in the purposes of the association as per its articles of association. Thus, an association may in its representative capacity pursue the nullification of administrative action, and simultaneously raise a claim for injuries sustained by the group, such as, for example, if temporary workers have been unlawfully employed during a strike.[134] One also

considering that it is not established whether the foreseen measures to limit risks related to the exploitation of the quarry are sufficient or not to reduce inconveniences to an acceptable level; considering that in consequence, having in mind the essential characteristics of this zone, the governor of Var incurred in a manifest error of appreciation when authorizing, by decision dated April 18, 1991, the exploitation of the quarry."

[133] French Maximum Court in Administrative Law, June 9, 2000, Association France Nature Environnement, 6 SS 211294 C, M. Chaubon, rapp., M. Lamy, C. du G. *See* in this same sense: May 21, 2000, Association France Nature Environnement, 6/4 SSR 210347 C, M. Lerche, rapp., M. Lamy, C. du G.

[134] French Maximum Court in Administrative Law, Ass., January 18, 1980, Synd. CFDT des P et T du Haut-Rhin, Rec. p. 30, AJ 1980, p. 88, chron. Y. Robineau et M – A Feffer, D. 1980, IR, p. 302, JCP 1980, n. 19450. In the same sense: Administrative Tribunal of Caen, October 17, 1972, Syndicat de la Défense contre la pollution atmosphérique autour de la zone portuaire de Caen vs. le Ministre de l'Industrie (J.C.P., 1973.17351, note P.A.-R.M.). This decision states: "Considering that the plaintiff union does not only pretend to defend particular interests of its members, it may bring action against the state for reparation of possible damages caused by the negligence of the service; considering that plaintiff claims a double damage: pecuniary and non-pecuniary; Considering that to claim for an indemnification of 50.000 French Francs, the union proves expenses incurred in a procedure before the Tribunal of Grande Instance of Caen; considering that in connection with this last issue, the damage claimed is not direct, nor present nor certain; [...] considering that under these

must consider unusual cases in the administrative contentious jurisdiction such as those in which associations for the defense of collective rights incur *motu proprio* in expenses for the conservation and reparation of such rights. In this respect, there have been claims for expenses in fish cultivation[135] or beach cleaning.[136] Such payment of damages should be sustained as long as the expenses are not those that the association incurs for its normal operation.[137] This approach is premised on the logic of the "occasional collaborator of public services." An association can also raise a claim for payment of fees paid to an expert engaged in the preparation of a claim to protect a group of neighbors from the excessive noise caused by a nearby establishment[138] or even for expenses required in the preparation of evidence of contamination in an oral proceeding involving such contamination.[139]

One may note from these decisions that the administrative court "construes a wide notion of the interest required as a condition to bring actions" and this may have as consequence a "multiplication of lawsuits filed by associations

conditions and taking into consideration the circumstances of this procedure, thorough evaluation of reparation to be payed to the union must be made, by granting one franc of indemnification." *See* in the opposite sense: decision dated March 30, 1981, Min. Transports, Min. Agriculture c/ Association pour la défense des sinistrés de la région morlaisienne, Rec., p 175: "... considering that an association has been created to defend the victims of the region; considering that if the association pretends to repair injury affections that would have been caused, it is not evidenced that the above-mentioned association justifies/evidences to have suffered damages known as injury affections produced by negligence of the service imputable to the state."

[135]   Pau, February 25, 1970, JCP 70, éd. G, II, 16532, note Despax.

[136]   Rennes, November 3, 1965: RTD com., 1967, 919, note Pontavice.

[137]   French Maximum Court in Administrative Law, October 26, 1984, Fédération des associations de pêche et de pisciculture de la Somme, 10SS 49134 C: "Considering that it is not evidenced that the plaintiff (federation) has proceeded to carry out exceptional planting destined to remedy the destruction of fish, due to pollution and that these represent additional expenses to those incurred the precedent year." *See* in this same sense: Administrative Court of Appeal of Lyon, April 25, 2002, Fédération départementale des associations agrées de pêche et de protection du milieu aquatique du Cantal, n 96LY02602, Droit de l'Environnement, 2002, n. 98, p. 111: "Considering that even though it has been established that the year previous to the accident various plantings of fish were performed in the said river, it was not established, nor alleged that such operations represented additional expenses to those normally incurred nor that they had an exceptional character destined to remedy the destruction of fish."

[138]   French Maximum Court in Administrative Law, sect., May 18, 1979, Association Urbanisme judaïque de Saint-Seurin, Rec., p 218: "Considering that the association ... claimed ... for an indemnification of 600 French francs to repair the damage related to the payment of technical services to measure the intensity of the noise coming from the store operation. (claim was rejected because there was no negligence of service)."

[139]   Administrative Court of Appeal of Lyon, Fédération du Pays-de-Dôme pour la pêche et la protection du milieu aquatique, no. 96LY01886, Droit de l'environnement, 2002, no. 98, p. 112.

that justify more or less specific interests."[140] However, there is no reason to criticize this, as we are dealing with a legal entity that as such has the right to obtain payment of damages. The fact that such an award of damages is granted to a legal entity instead of granted to its individual members does not change the situation as everything will depend on the extent to which case law construes rights of associations. Thus, as stated in another comment, "since there is a collective interest in the union, different from the interest of its individual members, the injury to such interest constitutes a damage that should be repaired."[141] What is important then in this hypothesis is that the plaintiff claims for himself, even though his final and real interest is to protect collective rights. In this French hypothesis that the collective right – as conceived by Colombian law – is what is injured is not compromised. Only the interest of the association is remediated, notwithstanding that, it represents a group and its articles of association include the defense of collective rights.

Strictly speaking, the same situation occurs when an individual brings action in the name of an inheritance, or a jointly-owned interest, or even in the name of a commercial corporation. In these cases, the beneficiary or recipient of any damages awarded is the community or the legal entity that represents the commercial corporation. In the cases described here, payment of damages is justified on more collective grounds that surpass the strictly individual interest, as the group interest is considered more important. This hypothesis is nevertheless interesting to the extent that payment or award of *pretium affectionis* or payment of expenses incurred in defending a collective right is granted to whom suffers such pain or incurs such expense. Thus, we are confronted by a claim for one's self that turns the action to the *plein contentieux*, even though in the end we are dealing with the defense of a collective right.

If the payment of damages to associations is illustrated by the previous examples, one must note that there are no cases in which associations claim for reparation of collective damages in favor of the community. Thus, in connection with the *plein contentieux*, the situation involves two hypotheses. In the first one, associations claim for themselves the reparation of damages affecting their own interests, as in the above-mentioned cases of *pretium affectionis* or expenses incurred to defend a collective right. The second hypothesis refers to an association claming in favor of direct reparation of a collective damage. This second type of claim is not, to date, provided for under French law.

---

[140] Note P.A.-R.M., J.C.P., 1973.17351.

[141] Rev. trim. droit sanitaire et social, January–March, 1973 at 313(case law notes by Louis Dubouis).

Let us illustrate the situation with an example: an association brings action for damages produced by water pollution that reduced business and caused a loss of biological richness. The action was accepted in connection with the first type of damage; the "damages consisting of 'loss of biological diversity' of the water" were considered "not legally reparable."[142] The same situation occurs in the cases mentioned when studying the defense of collective rights from the point of view of legality. For example, in the case of the association that obtained nullification of the administrative action that gave instructions to proceed with the killing of wolves, could the action brought for the damages caused by the killing of wolves before nullification be the *plein contentieux*? Could the same take place in the case of the association that obtains the compliance with European Community rules regarding allowable dates for the bird hunting season as a result of the violation of which rules the population of the related species of birds has been diminished?

It would seem that under the current interpretation of the French legal system, the response to this questions would be negative, and so it is in the case of *Saint Quentin*. It appears that, as "damages to ecology *stricto sensu* essentially have [a] collective character,"[143] the traditional administrative adversarial scheme in France is not prepared to consider or award damages for this type of claim. Therefore, we can demonstrate that this type of damages, as stated by Remond-Gouilloud: "cannot be assimilated by a traditional legal approach." This is why there is no indemnification for damages to the environment or the ecology even though the prevention of such harm falls within the purposes established in the articles of association of a legal entity.

Nevertheless, this traditional operation of the French administrative litigation scheme may be overcome even with the existent legal mechanisms.

---

[142] French Maximum Court in Administrative Law, July 12, 1969, Ville de Saint-Quentin et al., Rec., p. 383: An association of fishermen can not obtain compensation for a river's "biologic loss." The above-referenced decision states: "In respect to lawsuits numbers . . . filed by the Departmental Federations of Fish and Pisciculture Associations of Aine and Somme – Considering that due to a launching of Saint-Quentin sewage waters . . . the only damages that could eventually be repaired to the Federations would be those related to expenses of fish population in the river, excluding damages for loss or 'biological wealth' in said waters, for which there would be no right of compensation . . . Considering, *contrario sensu*, that the fishermen company 'Les Pêcheurs Hamois' justifies having lost, due to water contamination, an important number of members between 1964 and 1965 (indemnification of 5,000 Francs)." *See* in similar sense: February 1, 1967, Commune de Gaillagos, Estaing, Arcizans, Dessus et Bun, Rec., Table, p. 933: a county does not suffer pecuniary loss for damages to water fountains of a lake. Decision summary published states: "Damages caused to water fountains of a lake for fixing an electricity generating waterfall. Open lake: Neighbour counties have no property right on fish found there. Absence of reparation for loss of capital."

[143] Martíne Remond-Gouilloud, *Réparation du prejudice écologique*, 1060 JC Environnement (Editions Techniques – Juris – Classeurs) n 100 (1992).

In effect, one can conceive that the French judge enjoins the administration to repair injured collective rights. There are various arguments in favor of such a statement. In the first place, if one accepts the granting of payment for the individual damage that originated in the injury of a collective right, it should then be permitted that preceding (conceptually) the redress of this last (collective) right, the *recours pour excès de pouvoir* prevents that which will be indemnified by the *plein contentieux*. This would guarantee more protection of collective rights and less cost for the state.

Second, the openness of the Maximum Court of Administrative Law in relation to the interest to bringing actions that, even without following the logic of Colombian law, has permitted the widening of the category of persons that may attack administrative action – "taxpayer," "user," "third party in the contract," and so on. – allows many people to sue for the prevention of the injury of a collective right as much as for its reestablishment. Third, the logic under the *recours pour excès de pouvoir* and the *plein contentieux* are similar when the support of the decisions taken in the latter are based in the fault of the service. This means that if the state is held liable for fault of the service when there has existed individual damage caused by an illegal administrative act, one must arrive at the same conclusion of nullification as if the recourse chosen were the *recours pour excès de pouvoir*. In effect, "if in the subject administrative decision there is no *excès de pouvoir*, it is clear that there will be no indemnification because this could only be like this under fault-based liability."[144] *A contrario sensu*, in the event of an illegality, this should entail success in the *recours de illegality*. In the fourth place, if the French judge has mechanisms such the injunction, that permits him to order a governmental agency or agent to act on a certain way, this may guarantee not only the preservation of collective rights but their reestablishment where they have been injured.

Let us illustrate these statements with some examples. In one case in which indemnification was granted in favor of the owner of land next to a river for the diminution of value caused by the pollution of the river, the Maximum Court of Administrative Law, after concluding that "the pollution of the water . . . was partially caused by the municipal waste system that had insufficient capacity,"[145] ordered the district to pay the damage of loss of value of private property. It is clear that, for example, if there were an association created for the defense of the environment that had provisions in its associational

---

[144] Jacques Moreau, *Dommages causés par des décisions entachées d'excès de pouvoir*, Jurisclasseur-7 Administratif fasc. 720, n° 76 (1985).

[145] French Maximum Court in Administrative Law, October 15, 1976, District de Reims, 92792, M. Teissier du Cros, rapp., M. Labetoulle, Comm. du gouv., Rec., p. 420.

statement of purposes relating to water pollution, any claims for the solution of the problem caused by the insufficient capacity of the waste disposal system, the claim should be permitted to proceed, i.e., the offending administrative actions could be nullified.

Second, one must underline those events in which state liability is claimed for not taking the measures that would have prevented the damage, for example, because a corporation of pig breeding continues to dispose of waste into waters without respecting the conditions of the functioning permit and "pollutes the natural media, thereby damaging seriously the lake of Mr. Michallon,"[146] or, because the action of a governor that "without even intending to take any measures to remedy the infractions against the environment resulting from illegal waste" causes damage to a neighbor,[147] or, because a syndicate created for the protection of the environment of a zone obtains the nullification of an implicit administrative act reflected by the French administrator's refusal to respond to demands for action by the organization with the result that the judge found "moral damage" to the public and awarded nominal damages of one French France.[148] It is clear that if the administrative authority refuses to act when the sewage overflow was caused by an inadequate municipal sewage system, or when municipal water disposal did not conform to the established permitting system, or when it was demonstrated that the environment was being injured with unlawful pollution, or when the syndicate claims collective injury because of governmental inaction, these acts or omissions to act represent administrative acts subject to control by the judge of *excès de pouvoir*, who may nullify or void the governmental action.

Third, one can observe examples in which the same logic appears between public organizations, such as the event in which the town obtains indemnification from the state for not being able of obtaining compliance with an order given to a corporation to remove some buried barrels of pollutants, when in the absence of such action the town itself had to undertake the removal at its own expense.[149] If, instead, before undertaking the cleanup, the mayor of town used a *recours pour excès de pouvoir*, it might possibly have avoided the

---

[146] French Maximum Court in Administrative Law, July 11, 1986, Min. env. c/ Michallon, 61719, M. Girault, rapp., E. Guillaume, Comm. du gouv.

[147] Administrative Court of Appeal of Lyon, October 6, 1998, Roy, 94LY00217, M. Bonnet, rapp., M. Veslin, Comm. du gouv.

[148] Administrative Tribunal of Caen, October 17, 1972, Synd. de défense contre la pollution atmosphérique autour de la Zone Portuaire de Caen, M. Bluzat, rapp., M. Delbecque, Comm. du gouv., JCP 1973, II, 17351, note P.A.-R.M.

[149] Administrative Court of Appeal of Paris, January, 21, 1997, Cne. Saint-Chéron, 94PA00119, M. Mille, Comm. du gouv. Rec. tables, pg. 951.

necessity of the later expenses for which reimbursement was sought by means of the *recours du plein contentieux*.

These examples permit the conclusion that this much is considered acceptable for the French adversarial administrative scheme: if citizens, as individuals, as associations, or even if public entities, are free to bring an action before a judge to request protection of a collective right without having to ask for individual indemnification, the judge should take cognisance of the claim and evaluate it on its merits.

Having presented the way of conceiving litigation on collective rights in the French contentious administrative scheme, let us now illustrate a specific area of much interest to this chapter, that of indirect citizen procedures to protect collective rights.

3. *Contraventions de Grande Voirie: Indirect Citizen Procedures to Protect Collective Rights*

In order to complete this presentation of the French approach to the bringing of such claims, we must mention one specific area: the manner for raising claims arising from blocking access to or interfering with the use of highways and other public areas (*contraventions de grande voirie*, or CGV). The rules of this type of administrative litigation "do not pretend to impose penalties on offenders but to give protection to public domain, with no reference to classic notions of criminal liability and to guarantee the reparation of damages caused to public domain."[150] As stated by the noted author, Perrier, the areas of application of this regime are comparable to the protection of certain collective rights that are the subject of other procedures under Colombian law: "1. Degradation of a public domain installation . . . 2. Illegal occupancy (squatting) of a public domain . . . 3. Sand retrieval from a public domain . . . ; grass cutting in public lands . . . 4. dumping of rain water and sewage on railway tracks . . . of defective wine into a stream . . . or industrial waste in a river . . . or of petroleum products in a harbour . . . or hydrocarbons in a river . . . or sewage on seashore rocks,"[151] and so on. It is then evident that such CGV regime is conceived to protect public property: public space, the environment, cultural wealth,[152] and so on, and that is why one can say that, ". . . referring

---

[150] Jean-Claude Périer, *Voirie (Contraventions de grande voirie)*, II Répertoire de Contentieux Administratif n. 3 (Dalloz, Paris, 1985).

[151] *Id.* at nn. 42–45.

[152] An additional reference on the subject is Pierre-Laurent Frier, *Droit du patrimoine culturel*, 1997 PUF, Paris. At page 131, thereto, the author states:

Law allows the administration to bring civil action, claiming, specifically for damages. This rule originates in Law dated 31 March 1887. In that time, agreement of the owner was required

to its remedial element which permits obliging the infractor to pay a penalty, or its restitutive element that allows...reparation and restitution of the damage caused to public domain, the holistic objective of the CGV is undeniable."[153]

It is true that although legal standing/capacity to bring actions that look for protection of public domain is clearly determined by written law,[154] "no written rule allows an association to bring an action directly before the tribunal of CGV."[155] Nevertheless, "the obligation to bring actions prohibits the Administration from refusing, without legitimate grounds, the admission of lawsuits for CGV. Thus, when a governor is prevented from investigating a violator, specifically a public space squatter, a third party may petition for an investigation thereto. The governor may refrain from acting, but such refusal may not be justified on the basis of 'simple administrative convenience grounds.'"[156]

in order to modify any property to make it part of public domain. There was a special type of contract that could not be breached. These rules were maintained in Law of 1913. These rules allow the state, in the events in which the investigated citizen is not condemned criminally (for criminal law considerations) to obtain at least reparation for the injury to the monument. In practice this rule has not been used.

[153] Fabrice Melleray, *Essai sur la structure du contentieux administratif français. Pour un renouvellement de la classification des principales voies de droit ouvertes devant les juridictions à compétence générale*, 2001 L.G.D.J. 310 (Paris, 2001).

[154] Legal opinion of the *Commissaire de Gouvernement* M. Dumarais dated October 8, 1993, files n. 147604 147605: "Thus, you have judged that the authority expressly designated by Congress to file, before the jurisdiction, lawsuits in relation to high way contraventions (CGV), in which the legal capacity is given to the governor exclusively. Such is the sense of our decision dated December 14, 1981. Ministre des transports c/ Société VARIG, T. déc. 2891."

[155] Administrative Court of Appeal of Paris, Second Section, April 25, 1996. Association Te Kua O Te Henua Enana, 94PA01494 C, Mme Albanel, rapp., Mme Brin, c. du g. See in the same sense: Administrative Court of Appeal of Nantes, *Pleniére*, December 20, 1995, Port Autonome de Nantes Saint-Lazare, 94NT00709 A, Mme Lackmann, rapp., M. Cadenat, c. du g.: "Considering, on one hand, that the action for repairing injuries caused to the maritime public domaine may only be brought before the tribunal by the governor, according to rules established under section L 13 above-mentioned...."

[156] Amavi Kouévi, *L'obligation de poursuite en matière de contravention de grande voirie*, 2000 AJDA n. 5 at 395 (Paris, 2000). As an example, *see* the following decision: Administrative Court of Appeal of Nantes, Second Section, February 4, 1998, M. Robert Veau c/ Ministre de l'équipement, du logement, des transports et du tourisme, 97NT00437 B, Mme Tholliez, rapp., Mme Devillers, c. du g.:

Considering that the authorities in charge of the police function as well as of the conservation of the maritime public domain must, in accordance with the principles that rule public domain, watch over the normal use of beaches and use powers coming from the applicable laws, including the power of filing lawsuits before the judge of CGV to stop [squatters] and impede illegitimately created obstacles that oppose the public exercise of the right to use maritime public domain; considering that, even if the above-mentioned obligation finds limits in other general interests for which the above-mentioned authorities are responsible, specifically, those originated in public order needs, they could not be legally excused based on grounds of simple administrative convenience[.]

As one can observe, the fact that a third party may request an administrative authority to bring an action to repair a CGV demonstrates the feasibility of protecting collective rights under the French legal system by this route. Thanks to this mechanism of citizen participation, a citizen can contribute to the protection of property that belongs to public domain. Additionally, in this hypothesis, authorities have obligatory powers, as opposed to discretionary powers. Thus "refusal of an administrative authority to initiate investigations is an administrative decision that can be contested before the competent judge for deciding on *recours pour excès de pouvoir.*"[157] This possibility means that the administration that omits performance in its tasks of protecting public domain may be held liable for "systematic lack"[158] or for simple negligence of service.[159] By way of example, in the squatting case referenced above, the commune was enjoined to "take the required measures to make stop the irregular squatting of the public way, if necessary by bringing action before the ordinary jurisdiction" and the defendant was ordered to pay a symbolic amount of one French franc.

On the basis of the squatting case, it is now clear that any citizen may indirectly request and obtain protection for public property. One must note further that "the Tribunal may order the infractor (violator) to reestablish conditions back to their original state or reestablish squatted public property or pay for expenses incurred in repairing damages caused to such property," to the extent that "reparation must be enjoined even if it has not been specifically requested by plaintiff."[160] Thus, it is clear that France does indeed have a functioning mechanism for responding to claims of injuries to collective rights, which although different from a popular action since it is an indirect system, is capable of providing the same relief to petitioners.

Thus, we may illustrate two hypotheses of this chapter.

The first hypothesis addresses the case when one who has injured a collective right is enjoined to cease and desist from such conduct, and to reestablish such conditions as existed before the injury occurred. It is in this scenario that we get closer to the objective of the preventive popular action under

---

[157] Administrative Court of Appeal of Marseille, July 23, 1998, M. Paravisini, 97MA01853 C.

[158] Amavi Kouévi, L'obligation de poursuite en matière de contravention de grande voirie, AJDA, 2000, n. 5, p. 401.

[159] Administrative Court of Appeal of Marseille, July 23, 1998, M. Paravisini, 97MA01853 C: "Considering that when refraining illegally to take the required measures to make stop the squat of the public way, the mayor of Velone Orneto is guilty and is engaging the county's responsibility."

[160] Jean-Claude Périer, Voirie (Contraventions de grande voirie), Répertoire de Contentieux Administratif, Volume II, Dalloz, Paris, 1985, no. 121.

Colombian law as well as to reparation *in natura*,[161] both typical of collective damage reparation. Thus, for example, the owner of a ship unlawfully placed in maritime public space is enjoined to leave the place immediately;[162] one who places a chain which impedes walking in a rural path must remove it;[163] one who has built a wall on public space must demolish it;[164] a municipality is enjoined to "to stop within a month following the judgment, the dumping of sewage by the municipal sewage system of industrial residues in river Meuse," even though the residues may come from a particular industry;[165] a municipality is enjoined to stop the flooding by of rain and sewage waters on train tracks;[166] and so on.

The second hypothesis is illustrated by examples in which tribunals order the respondent to repair any economic damage or loss sustained by public goods or other property. In one case, the respondent was not only required to stop the injury to collective rights, which happened to be damage to the state telecommunications system,[167] but was also ordered to "pay France

---

[161] *See* in this sense, Martine Remond-Gouilloud: "Repairing *in natura*. In this field only 'restitution in integrum' is privileged, that is, to return conditions to an identical previous state, which seems to really delete ecological damages. In the end, the judgment, destined to avoid the repetition is turned into an obligation to perform (facere) (examples for works related with soundproofing, Lyon December 23, 1980: CPEN bruit, n. 118). Several written laws do establish specifically this type of reparation: thus, in accordance with garbage and waste / law dated 1975, 'the tribunal may enjoin, under penalty to re-establish the conditions of the damaged place to its original situation (section 24 9ᵉ L.); demolition of buildings and reestablishment of lands to the conditions they had before, are contemplated by the Urbanism Code (Sections L. 160-1, L. 480-4-2, L. 430.9); the written code of laws on forests and related matters states that trees must be re-planted whenever there has been an illegal cutting down of trees (Section L. 313-1, al. 3); and written laws on industries establish that any business man with companies which have had to pay damages, may be ordered to perform tasks to stop damages and pay penalties related thereto," *in* Réparation du préjudice écologique, JC Environnement, Editions Techniques – Juris – Classeurs, 1992, fasc. 1060, No. 37.

[162] French Maximum Court in Administrative Law, September 10, 1999, Voies navigables de France, 8/9 SSR 179628 B, Mme Belliard, rapp., M. Arrighi de Casanova, c. du g.; Administrative Court of Appeal of Paris, December 26, 1995, M. Krylischin, 95 PA01518 B, M. Spittz, rapp., M. Paitre, c. du g.

[163] French Maximum Court in Administrative Law, December 29, 1999, Commune de Breteau, c/ Mme Gérardin, 5/3 SSR 145760 C, M. Sansón, rapp., M. Chavaux, c. du g.

[164] Administrative Court of Appeal of Paris, First Section, July 23, 1991, Mme Foucque, 89 PA01591 B, Mme Jeangirard-Dufal, rapp., Mme Mesnard, c. du g.

[165] French Maximum Court in Administrative Law, March 22, 1961, Ville de Charleville, Rec. Lebon 1961, p. 204.

[166] French Maximum Court in Administrative Law, December 10, 1954, Commune de Champigny-sur-Yonne, Rec. Lebon 1954, p. 658.

[167] Administrative Court of Appeal of Paris, Second Section, July 22, 1993, Société Immobilière Meaux Jaurés, 92 PA00075 B, Mme Matilla-Maillo, rapp., Mme Moureix, c. du g.

Telecom the amount of 17.191 F to repair damages caused to a telephone booth.[168] In another example in which an inquiry was initiated to determine whether materials extracted from the bottom of a river were extracted without the required protection to the river bed and banks,[169] a judge would be empowered to enter an order requiring the violator to remediate the harm within a time certain, and should it disobey, to authorize that remediation of the nuisance be undertaken by a third party, with costs assessed against the violator.[170] An ordinary scenario for this type of claim could be one of damages to the environment, as was a case involving "sand extraction from the river Loire which affects the stableness of the river bank and allows tides to cause erosion on the river bottom[;]"[171] or the case of "damages . . . caused to the river Vorey public domain."[172] It is necessary, of course, to establish a cause and effect between the respondent's action and the harm suffered.[173]

4. Judicial Powers in the Protection of Rights

We now examine the powers of the judges to obtain performance and protection of rights claimed pursuant to the above-mentioned procedure, and analyze further the extent to which the subject rights are similar in both France and Colombia, including such considerations as the capacity of the judiciary to issue injunctions as widening the applicability of the actions.

---

[168] Administrative Court of Appeal of Nantes, Second Section, April 23, 1997, Entreprise Stalter, 95 NT00917 C, M. Margueron, rapp., Mme Devillers, c. du g.

[169] French Maximum Court in Administrative Law, February 3, 1978, Mariani ès qualités et société de terrassement et de mécanique dite Durance Agrégats, Rec. p. 48, AJDA 1978, p. 225.

[170] Administrative Court of Appeal of Nantes, 2ª Section, December 8, 1999, M. et Mme Luois Depalle, 97 NT01274 B, M. Margueron, rapp., M. Lalauze, c. du g.: "Considering from what has been previously seen, that M. Depalle must be convicted to re-establish the lands, if he has not yet done, to the existent conditions previous to the building of the house, located in the place called 'Kérion' in Arradon, on maritime public domain, in the term of three months, to be counted from the moment of the notice of the present decision, and the administration may, after the above-mentioned term, proceed to perform this action on account and risk of M. Depalle."

[171] French Maximum Court in Administrative Law, January 7, 1983, Société des sablières d'Ancenis, 6/2 SSR 30441, 35700 B, M. Cazin d'Honincthun, rapp., M. Robineau, c. du g.

[172] French Maximum Court in Administrative Law, Section, June 26, 1984, M. Maire, 6/2 SSR 32568 C, M. Van Ruymbeke, rapp., M. Dandelot, c. du g.

[173] Administrative Court of Appeal of Lyon, First Section, May 9, 1989, Secrétaire d'Etat à la mer c/Société Borg Shipping Ltd, 89 LY00244 A, M. JANNIN, rapp., M. JOUGUELET, c. du g.

The general rule is that "in principle, every defendant found liable by the judges has the obligation to comply with a decision made persuant to law."[174] Said principle is fundemental to any legal state, as it would be untenable for any state to allow decisions made by judges to remain without the power of enforcement. However, under the French legal system, because of the existence of the principle of the separation of powers, it has been traditionally considered that "citizens may not oblige public powers, naturally, to use public force against their own public powers." According to this same author, this is "explained by a constant rule, according to which ordinary private legal *executione judicii* may not be applied to public entities."[175] Nonetheless, this position has sustained recent and substantial modification, giving a new dimension to powers of judges, who, today, can employ injunctions and *astreintes*. The Law dated February 8, 1995, expressly authorized judges to enter injunctions,[176] which has allowed one scholar to state that "providing specifically for injunctions implies a modification that may be qualified as spectacular. There is no doubt that the Law of February 8, 1995 turned a page in history of Administrative-contentious fields."[177]

In respect to injunctions, it has been considered that, even though this law is an important step under French law, "as gravely injured as the principle of prohibiting judges to give orders to the administration can be considered, one can not state that said principle has been rejected."[178] In fact, various case law examples remind us that injunctions are still limited by the law.[179]

---

[174] Olivier Dugrip, Exécution des décisions de la juridiction administrative, Répertoire de Contentieux Administratif, Volume II, Dalloz, Paris, 1985, no. 13.

[175] Olivier Dugrip, Exécution des décisions de la juridiction administrative, Répertoire de Contentieux Administratif, Volume II, Dalloz, Paris, 1985, no. 3.

[176] Section 77 of Lay dated February 8, 1995 states: "When pronouncing judgment on the merits in a conflict which necessarily implies executory measures in a specific sense, the Maximum Court in Administrative Law, on the request of a party, gives orders for such measures to be applied and may add a penalty from a specific date."

[177] René Chapus, Droit du contentieux administratif, Montchrestien, 9th edition, Paris, 2001, p. 872.

[178] Id. at 867.

[179] French Maximum Court in Administrative Law, March 31, 1995, M. Hatterer-Four, 3 SS 116161 C, M. Gervasoni, rapp., M. Savoie, c. du g.: "Considering that except for the case established in section 77 of the above-mentioned Law dated February 8, 1995, which contains rules not applicable to the specific case, the Maximum Court of Administrative Law may not enjoin the administration; consequently, the request of M. HATTERER-FOUR for the Maximum Court of Administrative Law to enjoin the administration to take into consideration, for the pension payment calculation, services rendered after the age limitation which were deducted from his pension, may not, under [any] circumstance, be declared." See in the same sense: decision dated May 5, 1995, Commune d'Arques c/Mme Dupuis-Matton, 10/7 SSR 111720 B, M. Simon-Michel, rapp., M. Scanvic, c. du g.

Nevertheless, various doctrinal criticisms can be found concerning the rigidity of the French system in this matter.[180] One author has questioned "if the exclusive character of repairing damages by equivalent reparation or remuneration is not overcome and if one cannot conceive, consequently, judicial decisions with condemnations including obligations of public authorities to do or to refrain from doing."[181] The questioning of the traditional position by the new written law has permitted the reconsideration of classical theories such as "intangibility of public works," which provided that "it is better a wrongly built building than a destroyed building." This premise is already starting to change under case law.[182] That is why "abandoning this principle is a suggestion for the field of the environment, by the Commission of 'Public Actions and Ecology.'"[183]

In any event, because of the new law, judicial powers have been enhanced notably. Thus, by virtue of the power of injunctions, a state secretary may be ordered to override administrative decisions,[184] or to issue an administrative

---

[180] Michel Rousset, Droit Administratif. II. Le contentieux administrative, Presses Universitaires de Grenoble, 1994, p. 57: "In sum, we may ask if our administrative system is not lacking the means of the British judge: the possibility to *enjoin* the administration. A scholar wrote in the beginning of the century that this situation 'could not be justified' (G. Jese); there exists thus, some sort of taboo that today should be abandoned; one [cannot] admit that the state is submitted to the law if it has the possibility of not performing a judicial decision."

[181] Christine Cormier, Le préjudice en droit administratif français. Etude sur la responsabilité extra-contractuelle des personnes publiques, L.G.D.J., Paris, 2002, p. 415.

[182] See French Maximum Court in Administrative Law, January 29, 2003, Synd. Départamental de l'electricité et du gas des Alpes Maritimes et Commune de Clans, AJDA 2003, No. 15, p. 784. This decision states: "Considering that when the administrative judge is requested the judicial execution of a decision in which poorly built public works are involved, the judge must take into account the following considerations in determining whether to issue an injunction to demolish the works: 1) if it is possible to rebuild them correctly, that is to regularize the public works, 2) if the answer to 1) is negative, on the one hand, the inconveniences that the presence of the works implies for diverse public and private interests, and specifically for the affected landowner and, on the other hand, the consequences of such demolition for the general interest, and to determine, taking into account the above-indicated matters, whether the demolition does not imply an excessive injury to the general interest"; *see* in the same sense: Administrative Tribunal of Nantes, July 25, 1996, Derenne, JCP 1997, No. 1701: a municipality is obliged to suppress and move a camping area, which was installed without complying with the applicable urban rules, and it is not possible to use the principle of intangibility of public works.

[183] JC Environnement, Booklet 1005, Contentieux – Problématique et perspectives, Editions Techniques – Jurisclasseur, 1992, no. 42.

[184] *E.g.,* French Maximum Court in Administrative Law, March 20, 2000, Groupe d'information et de soutien des immigrés, 2/1 SSR 205266 A Mlle Verot, rapp., M. Martin Laprade, C. du G.: "the Labor and Solidarity Secretary of state and the Budget Secretary of state are required to repeal administrative act dated March 17, 1997, which established the amount of contribution to be paid to the International Migration Office for the medical examination performed on foreigners that request a permit to stay, which must be done in a fifteen-day period from the present decision on."

decision.[185] By the same token, orders may be given to issue a provisional residence permit;[186] to recover public space illegally squatted;[187] to repair a public channel for navigation by water in order to permit normal use of private property;[188] and so on. If the plaintiff has requested in his lawsuit an *astreinte*, the judge may grant it, and the remedy may represent considerable amounts of money.[189]

One must not forget to mention the important subject of the *référés administratifs*, which, in accordance with the new legislation on injunctions, has been implemented recently by Law 2000-597, dated June 30, 2000. Without devoting time to explanation of the various hypothesises that exist or the differences amongst them,[190] simply bear in mind that collective rights may also be protected by means of these "urgency" procedures in which, in accordance with the law, the judge of *référés* acts by provisory measures (Section 2), a notably simple procedure, as with the *référé d'urgence*, to "enjoin the suspension of the execution of the administrative decision, or of certain of its effects, when

---

[185] *E.g.*, French Maximum Court in Administrative Law, June 16, 2000, Syndicat national CGT du Ministère des Affaires Etrangères, 10/9 SSR 204962 B, M. Gounin, rapp., Mme Daussun, C. du G.: "Considering that the execution of the present judgment implies necessarily that the government issues the application decrees, established by section 79 and 80 of Law dated January 11, 1984, needed for the titrating of those agents that are not titulars, holders of an office in the ministry of cooperation and who have the possibility of being named in a category A group; considering that it is proper to enjoin this measure."

[186] French Maximum Court in Administrative Law, June 19, 2000, Préfet du Val d'Oise c/M. Laaji, 10 SS 214365 C, Mme Dayan, rapp., Mme Mitjavile, C. du G.: "Considering that the decision which nullifies the administrative act which denied a residence permit, violating the respect to private and familiar life consecrated in section 8 of the European Convention for the safeguard of rights of man and fundamental liberties, implies at least, under the condition that the *factum* and legal circumstances for the granting of a residence permit, the granting of a temporary permit indicating the above-mentioned "private and familiar" life consecrated by section 12 bis of *ordenanza* dated November 2, 1945 [.]"

[187] Administrative Court of Appeal of Marseille, First Section, June 23, 1998, M. Paravisini, 97MA01853 C, M. Moussaron, rapp., M. Bocquet, c. du g.: "Considering that the execution of the present decision implies that the municipality Velone Orneto takes the required measures to make stop the squatting of the public road in parcel No. 713, specifically bringing action before the competent ordinary jurisdiction."

[188] Administrative Tribunal of Limoges, December 7, 1995, Consorts Descat et Calary de Lamazière c/Département de la Corrèze, RFDA 1996, p. 348.

[189] Administrative Court of Appeal of Paris, 4th Section, October 22, 1998, SA Borie SAE et autres, 96PA03378 C, Mme ADDA, rapp., M. LAMBERT, c. du g.: "Decision...Section 2: A penalty is established against the Régie Immobiliére de la Ville de Paris if it does not justify the payment, in the term of three months following the notice date of the present decision, of the sums related in the whereas of the present decision, to guarantee the execution of the decisions of the Administrative Tribunal of Paris dated June 25, 1991 and March 30, 1996. The amount of such penalty is 10,000 Francs per day."

[190] *See* in this sense: René Chapus, Droit du contentieux administratif, Montchrestien, 9ª ed, Paris, 2001, pgs. 1201–1318.

urgency justifies it and there is a state that may create a serious doubt of the legality of the decision (Section 5)."

Such "urgency" is established "when the questioned administrative decision damages a public interest, [and] the situation of the claimant or the interests being defended, [is being damaged] in a gross and immediate way,"[191] such as when, for example, authorization given by a county to broaden some beaches is suspended as being in violation of law, placing flora and fauna in risk.[192] One must note that only four months – which could have been even more prompt if the specific case had required it – elapsed between the issuance of the challenged authorization and the issuance of injunction of the Tribunal suspending the administrative act.

The petitioner must demonstrate urgency of the need for suspension of the administrative act, as well as the serious doubts as to its legality, for it may occur that prior to the authorization given to a corporation to use a municipal waste place, for example, neither urgency nor illegality are established by the mere allegation of the supposed risk.[193]

However, the scope of injunctions in connection with protecting collective rights, that also may be conceived by way of the *référés administratifs*, is yet to be defined in the case law. As far as we know, there exist no injunctions issued by French judges giving orders to the administration to put in place specific programs protecting pertaining to collective rights and, even less, to indemnify economic collective rights which have been injured. As Professor Guettier recites, the Maximum Court of Administrative Law has been reluctant to apply the new powers – created by written law and not by case law – because "traditionally there is the principle of separation between jurisdictional administration and active administration to justify the limitation of the powers of the judge." Consequently, "it would seem that final reliance must be placed upon the Government, which 'decides on the administration' (Const., 4 Oct. 1958, Section 20) and the Prime Minister who leads it, to call attention to the need to enforce judicial decisions, and thus respect the rule of law. But then, everything depends on the good will of the administration. Can we be happy? It does not look like it."[194] One must therefore wait on the

---

[191] French Maximum Court in Administrative Law, January 19, 2001, Confédération nationale des radios libres, 228815, M. Arrighi de Casanova, rapp., M. Touvet, C. du G., AJ 2001, p. 150, chron. M. Guyomar and P. Collin, D 2001, IR, p. 597.

[192] French Maximum Court in Administrative Law, December 30, 2002, Commune de Six-Fours-les-Plages, 245621, Mme Vialettes, rapp., M Guyomar, C. du G.

[193] French Maximum Court in Administrative Law, December 30, 2002, Association Sauvegarde du patrimoine et du cadre de vie de Solerieux c/ Département de la Drôme, 242324, M Chaubon, rapp., M Lamy, C. du G.

[194] Christope Guettier, *Injonction et astreinte*, 1997 JURISCLASSEUR-ADMINISTRATIFF fasc. 1114, No. 3 (Paris, 1997).

development of the administrative jurisdiction on this important issue, more specifically, in connection with what will be understood to be the required executory measures for judicial decisions, with which the future of injunctions will be marked.

III. CONCLUSION

The following propositions follow from this discussion:

(1) The absence of the popular action in a legal system does not mean that there are no means for bringing such actions. The explicit adoption of the popular action is a political choice that implies more citizen participation in the destiny of collective rights. In the systems with popular action the relations between the person and the public property representing the collective right are more close than in those systems where this action doesn't exist. But this does not imply that in those countries where this action is not established, collective property protection belongs only to the state. It is true that the existence of the popular action grants more citizen participation in the evolution of the protection of public property, so one can state that this type of property is more judicially protected under the Colombian legal system than under the French legal system. Nevertheless, one cannot infer that a legal system that does not allow for popular action impedes all ways of citizen participation.

(2) Colombian law expresses a category of right "for any one person in town" to bring action in order to protect a generous number of collective rights, because there is an express rule, written in the Constitution and in the law, as it corresponds to the written legal system to which it belongs. In France, to the contrary, the approach to the popular action scheme to defend collective rights is by way of exception, and depends, in great measure, on the case law advances and on the scope that the judge may want to give to his own powers. In this sense, Colombia represents a leading participative position in defense of the above-mentioned rights.

(3) The scope of the effective protection of collective rights varies in each system: there is more protection in those systems that recognize popular actions explicitly because if this action does not exist, one can only see its preventive stage as limited by the scope of the *recours pour excès de pouvoir*. The absence of the popular action in France has implied that the state has the direct monopoly on requesting the reestablishment of the situation prior to the damage or harm, or the payment of collective damages to public property. Neither individuals nor associations have been allowed to stretch the limits of the defense of public property allowed to them, and their challenges are limited to considerations of legality. But this practice comes more from a historical habit of not requesting payment for collective damages from the

state than from actual legal norms. In the future, much will depend on the scope given to the new powers of issuing injunctions recently received by the administrative judges in France, in relation to "orders to act" or injunctions that may be given to the administration.

(4) The existence of two different actions under Colombian law – action for nullification and popular action – has the effect of avoiding the necessity of collective rights having to be protected by means of the nullification action – *recours pour excès de pouvoir* – as it occurs presently in France. In addition, the wide powers of injunction given to the Colombian judge in the popular action do not require interpretative efforts either for the scope of the nullification action or for the judicial powers, as it does in France.

(5) The Colombian legal system differs from the French system in that it grants a subjective right to any individual or entity to defend collective rights. Bearing this in mind, we can bypass the discussion on the "proclamatory" character of such rights, and one can incorporate them into a system of complete protection of rights, as it may exist for rights of other generations. In France, the situation is different and this gives rise to the discussion of the nature of collective rights, even though in reference to social rights, it has been stated that "there are no specific means for obliging the state to perform a positive action to ensure a social right."[195]

(6) The presence of the popular action in a legal system creates the risk that the enjoyment of an individual right, such as the right of contract, will be subordinated to the pursuit of collective rights. This is a risk implied in the choice of which rights to enforce or favor, made by each legal system. For this reason, one can state that if the protection of individual rights is more precarious under the Colombian legal system, it is because of the possibility of invalidating individual rights by means of popular action.

(7) Popular actions in Colombia apply, in a different way, the democratic principle of the separation of the three powers and allow one in certain circumstances to speak of the "judge-administrator." This characteristic may perplex a French legal expert who may well consider that judges substitute for the administration, and in addition, that the normal interplay of powers in a democracy is overriden. One may infer that, at least in a first stage, there will not be in France the wide variety of cases to be found in Colombia in which the judge enjoins the administration to include certain accounts in the

---

[195] Essay, Maire Luce Pavia and Dominique Rousseau, *La protection des droits sociaux fondamentaux dans l'ordre juridique de la France*, in LA PROTECTION DES DROITS SOCIAUX FONDAMENTAUX DANS LES ETATS MEMBRES DE L'UNION EUROÉENNE 359 (Athens, Brussels, and Baden, 2000).

budget; to build public service devices; to repair national historic patrimony buildings; and so on, which is to say, cases in which the administrative adversarial system intrudes substantially into the tasks of the coordinate branches of national or local government. Nevertheless, one may consider that, as the Colombian judge acts by virtue of powers granted by legal rules issued by its democratically-elected national legislature, there is no genuine risk of damage to the overall ideal of separation of powers. Indeed, the sturdiness of ongoing respect among the judiciary, the legislative, and the executive branches is actually reinforced under the principle of harmonious collaboration.

INDEX